MOTOCOURSE

THE WORLD'S LEADING GRAND PRIX ANNUAL

HAZLETON PUBLISHING

CONTENTS

ACKNOWLEDGEMENTS

The Editor of *Motocourse* wishes to thank the following for their assistance in compiling the 1989-90 edition:
E.J., Carlo Canzano, Anne-Marie Gerber (FIM), Charlie Henneken, Hans van Loozenoord, Ian MacKay, Toni Merendino, Dennis Noyes, Serge Rosset, Paolo Scalera, Garry Taylor, Mike Trimby and Gunther Wiesinger.

Photographs published in *Motocourse 1989-90* have been contributed by:
Chief Photographer: Malcolm Bryan; Peter Clifford, Colorsport, Kel Edge, John Flory, David Goldman, Patrick Gosling/Zooom Photographic, Henk Keulemans, John McKenzie, Phil Masters, Alexander Savel, Jad Sherif/International Press Agency and Two Plus Two/Andy Gibb.

Motocourse is published by Hazleton Publishing, 3 Richmond Hill, Richmond, Surrey TW10 6RE.
Typeset by First Impression Graphics Ltd, Richmond, Surrey.
Colour Reproduction by Adroit Photo Litho Ltd, Birmingham.
Printed in Spain by Graficas Estella SA, Estella.

ISBN: 0-905138-63-5

DISTRIBUTORS

UK & OTHER MARKETS
Osprey Publishing Limited
59 Grosvenor Street
London W1X 9DA

NORTH AMERICA
Motorbooks International
PO Box 2
729 Prospect Ave
Osceola
Wisconsin 54020, USA

Paul Oxman Publishing
17165 Newhope
Unit M
Fountain Valley
CA 92708, USA

AUSTRALIA
Technical Book & Magazine Co. Pty
289-299 Swanston Street
Melbourne
Victoria 3000

Universal Motor Publications
c/o Automoto Motoring Bookshop
152-154 Clarence Street
Sydney 2000
New South Wales

NEW ZEALAND
David Bateman Ltd
PO Box 65062
Mairangi Bay
Auckland 10

PUBLISHER
Richard Poulter

EDITOR
Peter Clifford

EXECUTIVE PUBLISHER
Elizabeth Le Breton

ART EDITOR
Steve Small

PRODUCTION MANAGER
George Greenfield

PRODUCTION CONTROLLER
Peter Lovering

PRODUCTION ASSISTANT
Deirdre Fenney

ADVERTISING CO-ORDINATOR
Blanche Symes

SECRETARY
Gayle Bengston

RESULTS AND STATISTICS
Kay Edge

CHIEF PHOTOGRAPHER
Malcolm Bryan

The dust-jacket illustration by Malcolm Bryan depicts 1989 World Champion Eddie Lawson on his 500 cc Rothmans Honda in the final Grand Prix of the season in Brazil.

Malcolm Bryan's photograph on the title page features 1989 World Sidecar Champions Steve Webster and Tony Hewitt in the Swedish TT at Anderstorp. The machines of Rolf Biland and Alain Michel follow.

Below: **The prize they were all fighting for. Eddie Lawson carried the World Champion's number on his bike in 1989 and will do so again in 1990.**
Photo: Malcolm Bryan

NGK
COPPER CORE
SPARK PLUGS
In tune
with today's
engines
NGK Spark Plugs (UK) Limited,
7/8 Garrick Industrial Centre,
Hendon, LONDON NW9 6AQ.
Telephone: 01-202 2151/4.
Number One
in the
500cc World
Championship
1989 World Champion Eddie Lawson
Sparked by NGK.

FOREWORD
by EDDIE LAWSON

‘ Many people have asked me if trying to win a World Championship gets any easier, or if this is the hardest World Championship I have ever been involved in.

To me they are all hard. They are hardest when you don’t win them and I have been involved in a few of those.

This year I obviously set out to win the World Championship. I had the right people around me and I knew it was possible. Things were hardest at the Australian Grand Prix, but I never thought winning was impossible.

I have to thank Erv and the rest of the team for believing that it could be done and putting everything into it. As with all championships it was a team effort, and they deserved to win. ’

Eddie Lawson

Malcolm Bryan

ONE OF THE FEW TIMES YOU'LL SEE IT STANDING STILL.

Be quick or you'll miss it. Because once the FZR1000 gets on the road, it's difficult to catch.

This 'pure sports' motorcycle has a 20-valve, twin overhead camshaft engine. A perfectly-balanced aluminium Deltabox frame with a light alloy triangulated swinging arm. An Ultimate Powervalve Exhaust System (EXUP). A fresh air intake system. A high-precision disc braking system. And microprocessor-controlled ignition.

So while you may already know that Yamaha builds the most advanced technology into its motorcycles, you won't know the thrill of the FZR1000 until you get into gear.

See it at your local Yamaha dealer. But hurry. It rarely stands still for long.

FZR1000

YAMAH
YAMAHA
YAMAHA MOTOR EUROPE N.V.

EDITOR'S INTRODUCTION

HUMBLE PIE

Malcolm Bryan

A certain honesty is forced on the editor of *Motocourse* by the nature of its production. The book is written Grand Prix by Grand Prix, shortly after the events, but will only be read at the end of the year when what at the time may have been pure conjecture has been shown to be fact or fiction.

Before the season started I thought that Eddie Lawson stood every chance of winning the World Championship. The strongest opposition, I suspected, would come from Wayne Gardner who, in two previous seasons, had demonstrated the willingness to push his machine further and harder than Lawson yet stay on it. In my mind Gardner was favourite.

The opening races indicated that other riders would have a large say in the determination of the championship. It might well be a battle between Rainey and Schwantz too, and Lawson looked the least likely of the four to take the title.

I thought then that Lawson had made a mistake switching to Honda, had bitten off more than he could chew. I felt he would become dispirited with the Honda's wayward antics, fighting a machine so different from the Yamaha he had ridden since he first started Grand Prix racing.

The early Grand Prix reports reflect my feelings at the time, and when Lawson had some hard words to say to Rainey after the Austrian Grand Prix I thought it was a sign that the World Champion was taking defeat badly. Lawson demonstrated that writing him off before it was numerically impossible to win the championship was a mistake. He and his team did as much work on the Honda as they could: they made it as manageable as was possible, given the basic engine and frame layout, and then he just rode it harder and harder until he started beating Rainey consistently.

I cannot say I am happy to be proved wrong – who is? – but it did make for one of the most incredible Grand Prix seasons I have been privileged to witness. So many great races...the wheel-to-wheel Schwantz/Rainey duel at Suzuka, Gardner's personal triumph in Australia, Rainey's last-lap move at Hockenheim, the sparkling genius of Schwantz and Lawson's intense dedication to his own cause.

Eddie Lawson made the Honda a better bike than it should have been, and when he could no longer mould its characteristics he adapted his own riding. It was, honestly, a stunning achievement.

The Brazilian Grand Prix rostrum. The championship is over. To the victor the spoils...and to Rainey?...So close...look... but don't touch.

MOTOCOURSE
Marlboro
WORLD CHAMPIONSHIP TEAM

MOTOCOURSE
Marlboro
WORLD CHAMPIONSHIP TEAM
1990

IN 198
RIDERS
SHO
THEIR I

World 500cc Grand Prix Champion.
Eddie Lawson.

World 250cc Grand Prix Champion.
Sito Pons.

World TT Formula One Champion.
Carl Fogarty.

After cracking six world championships,

RIDE WITH STYLE

FOR SAFETY'S SAKE, ALWAYS WEAR PROTECTIVE AND BRIGHT CLOTHING. ALWAYS CONCENTRATE AND BRAKE IN PLENTY OF TIME. BE AWARE OF OTHER ROAD USERS AND NEVER RIDE AFTER DRINKING ALCOHOL.

9, OUR
REALLY
WED
BOTTLE.

F.I.M. World Endurance Champion.
Alex Vieira.

World 500cc Moto Cross Champion.
Dave Thorpe.

World 250cc Moto Cross Champion.
Jean Michel Bayle.

we've never had more to celebrate.

HONDA

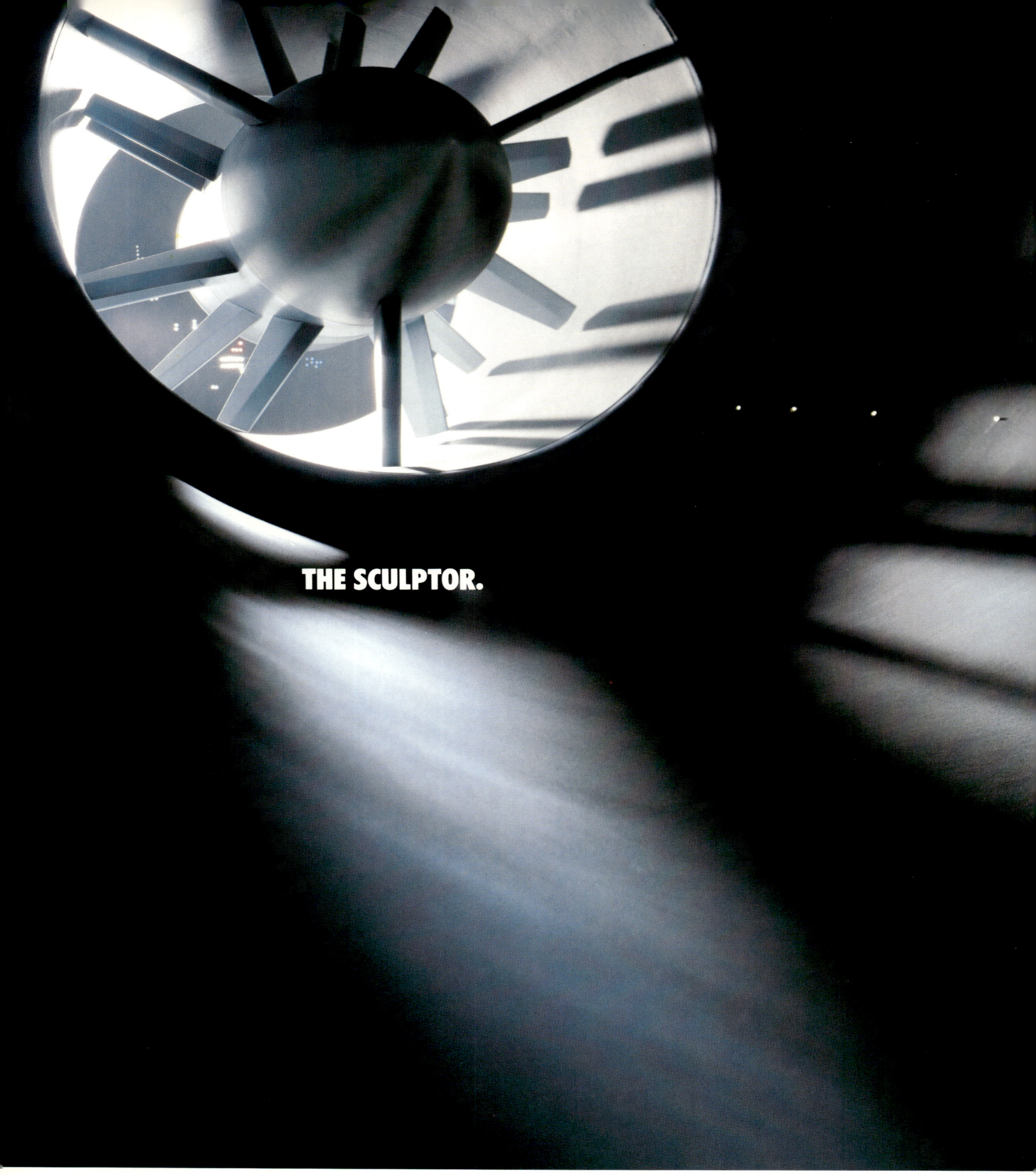

Cast your eyes upon BMW's latest creation. As a critic from 'Motorcyclist USA' observed:

"It is a rare combination of usable technology, a distillation of what is possible, blended with a shrewd knowledge of what is truly needed."

Praise indeed. Fashioned by the natural artistry of the wind, the K1 is the world's most aerodynamic motorcycle. Its highly advanced design cuts through the air and shields the rider from the rigours of nature.

The bike's streamlined body also flows majestically on the test track.

From a standing start, it helps the 16 valve machine reach the 100 kph mark in a mere 3.9 seconds.

Although the 1000cc engine is capable of such a flying performance, the aerodynamics keep both wheels firmly on the ground.

Monitoring all four cylinders is BMW's computerised management system. Known as Motronic, it unceasingly 're-tunes' the engine 300 times every second.

Naturally a bike with such advanced engine design requires the sort of braking technology to match.

THE K1 COSTS £7,295. BMW FIRST TO INTRODUCE ABS FOR MOTORCYCLES, AVAILABLE AS AN OPTION ON K1 AND ALL K100 MODELS, COSTING £625. PRICES, CORRECT AT TIME OF GOING TO PRESS, INCLUDE CAR TAX AND VAT. ALL CURRENT BMW MODELS CAN RUN ON LEADED OR UNLEADE

Sure enough, between the front Marzocchi forks are twin fully floating Brembo discs.

Each disc is spirally perforated to cut down weight and increase cooling.

Each calliper has four pistons for more powerful, more balanced braking.

For those who don't want to stop at that, there is ABS.

A highly innovative safety system for two wheels, that was once only available for four.

To improve handling, the K1 has been blessed with BMW's much praised Paralever suspension system.

A unique secondary torque arm that runs parallel to the swinging arm, counteracting the ups and downs which befall many a shaft driven machine.

Not only does it iron out every crease and wrinkle in the road, it also provides better traction.

Over once more to 'Motorcyclist USA':

"The K1 represents a technological milestone."

A piece of sculpture it may be.
A museum piece never.

THE ULTIMATE RIDING MACHINE

FUEL. FOR FURTHER DETAILS AND THE NAME OF YOUR LOCAL DEALER PLEASE WRITE TO: BMW INFORMATION SERVICE, PO BOX 46, HOUNSLOW, MIDDLESEX, OR TELEPHONE 01-897 6665. (LITERATURE REQUESTS ONLY.) FOR TAX FREE SALES: 56 PARK LANE, LONDON W1. TELEPHONE 01-629 9277.

TETRARCHY – SCHWANTZ & RAINEY GRADUATE TO JOIN RULERS LAWSON & GARDNER

By Peter Clifford

David Goldman

Malcolm Bryan

Top: **The thoughtful face of Wayne Rainey. It is not that he is a particularly earnest person; he is cheerful and light-hearted in conversation but racing is a serious business. Rainey will give any reasonable question due consideration and an intelligent answer. He takes the trouble to remember people: politeness is part of his personality, as well as his professionalism.**

Schwantz *(above)* **is, superficially at least, the most easy-going of the four men who dominate the 500 class and a natural to succeed Mamola as the people's hero. All riders need to concentrate when there's a problem with the machine, and being tense on race day is only to be expected, but normally Kevin is very friendly and approachable.**

With the success of Wayne Rainey and Kevin Schwantz this year the racing world is a better place. The pair contributed a great deal to the Grand Prix scene, not only in terms of talent but also as personalities. Rainey is no Mamola-style extrovert, but he is friendly, honest and forthcoming, as well as incredibly fast. And Schwantz gets the crowds standing and shouting with his vividly dramatic riding style, while his easy-going openness enhances paddock life.

The fact that the pair are great rivals comes from their history in American racing. While they don't rush to park next to each other in the paddock they don't avoid each other either and, on occasion, will play a round of golf together.

It was easy enough to see that Schwantz preferred to see Lawson win the championship. The two spent time together away from the race track and, as far as Kevin was concerned, Eddie Lawson was the established champion – and if anyone was going to beat him it would be Schwantz, not Rainey. It's probably easier for Schwantz to accept that Lawson can hang on to the championship by dint of his greater experience than to see Rainey, whom Kevin obviously considers as a contemporary, become World Champion.

Kevin Schwantz never let that rule the way he rode his races, however. The Texan was always out to win, from Japan to Brazil. When he finished he almost always did so in front. He finished second to Rainey in America and second to Lawson in France but beat both men in straight races in Japan, Austria, Yugoslavia, Britain, Czechoslovakia and Brazil.

But after non-finishes in Spain and Germany, Schwantz's only chance of the title was to go out for the win every time. After the Dutch Grand Prix, though, any possibility of being champion had virtually disappeared so winning each race

Good-natured rivalry off the track, hard men in battle. Here Rainey squeezes Schwantz in Brazil, trying to keep his championship hopes alive.

Malcolm Bryan

was his single aim.

Rainey had a very different job to do and it did not make him look anything like as exciting. But when both men were on an equal footing, in Japan and America, there was little to choose between them. In fact, at Suzuka, it was Rainey who looked the more dramatic, if anything. He was obviously right on form after a winter of concentrated training and testing, and when the season started he hit the ground running. He took the Lucky Strike Yamaha over the edge at almost every corner – and held it there. Schwantz and Rainey passed the lead between them: there was no one else in the race.

The Australian round was a perfect example of just how narrow the dividing line is between hitting the headlines and hitting the tarmac. Almost everyone falls off at some time or another on a tyre that is not warm enough – it is a fairly common occurrence in practice – but this time Schwantz did it on the first lap of the race. Rainey raced Gardner, Sarron and Magee all the way to the finish but Wayne Gardner was at his most inspired and won the day.

Wayne Rainey won at Laguna Seca in a very different manner from the way he had raced with Schwantz at Suzuka. It was a very different sort of race. The Californian was fast, superbly accurate and very controlled, and did not really have to race his Texan opponent since the Rainey–Yamaha–Dunlop combination was simply working better.

One thing that both riders maintained throughout the season was that their successes were not theirs alone. Rainey would analyse the relationship between his riding, the winter development of the machine and tyres, the time needed during practice to get the machine combination at its best for each track, plus the support of his team. The combination could be likened to a simplified NASA space project, with Rainey the astronaut, supremely skilled but supported by a well-developed system of technology and personnel. Schwantz was more the artist who, given a palette of incandescent colour, might create a masterpiece. Unfortunately on three occasions he attacked the canvas with too much gusto and racing allowed him no chance to paint over his mistakes. Three times the colours ran and, while the winning masterpieces can be cherished, the championship system rewards consistency; and six non-finishes leaves the championship a long way out of reach.

With the current scoring system a single failure of any sort is too many. If a rider falls or retires while leading the first race of the season he loses 20 points to the eventual winner. If he then beats that rider consistently in ensuing races he gains only three points a race over him, so that it will only be after the eighth race of the

Malcolm Bryan

The Austrian Grand Prix *(below right)* was just one of the occasions when Eddie Lawson had a great deal of trouble trying to stay ahead of Rainey and Schwantz. The Texan on the Suzuki could hold a line that neither the Honda nor the Yamaha could follow, while Rainey looked to have the better of Lawson until his new 16-in. front tyre gave trouble.

The most spectacular photographs are usually of Schwantz – but Rainey *(right)* can get the power on just as hard when it's necessary. This is Phillip Island. Early in the year Wayne was sliding the rear with gusto, and when he got in front of Lawson on the last lap at Hockenheim he held the advantage with a huge power slide. In subsequent races a more reserved style seemed appropriate, to retain his championship lead.

Below right: Schwantz slams the Pepsi Suzuki on its side: the two have developed together. Many who saw the way the Suzuki turned and held a tight line reckoned it the best machine in the class; others said the superiority was down to the rider and the way that he dominated the machine.

season that he takes a single point lead in the championship.

That situation will give both Suzuki and Schwantz a good deal to think about over the winter. But as Kenny Roberts pointed out, 'It is a lot easier to stop crashing than it is to try and go a second or two quicker at every track.'

If Wayne Rainey had not made his single race mistake of the year in Sweden he would have been champion. Having taken a commanding championship lead, by pushing the Yamaha over the edge yet keeping the Dunlop rubber on the road, he then modified his attack: he declined to race Schwantz or, if it meant pushing his luck, Lawson. His points lead was obviously defendable, and as many times as he finished behind Lawson he finished in front of him.

The first three races saw Wayne finish in front of Eddie: no contest. Lawson had the upper hand in Spain, but Rainey dealt what looked at the time like a decisive blow when he dived inside him on the last lap at Hockenheim. It was a championship-winning move – he saw the opening and took it. A tyre construction problem held Rainey back in Austria and he finished third to Lawson's second. Those positions were reversed in Yugoslavia, as Lawson ran off the track.

In Holland Rainey was winning again, but he won in Belgium only to have the points taken away by the FIM. It would be too easy to point to that as the sole reason for Wayne Rainey losing the championship. It would be wrong to say that he went to pieces after that happened. On the other hand, the effect should not be under-rated. The FIM decision only cost Rainey five-and-a-half points – but it turned a lead that could be easily defended into a relatively tenuous advantage. It took away that winning move at Hockenheim, practically if not psychologically.

Just as Rainey's points gap started to dwindle, so the team's machinery advantage was diminishing as well. The Honda was still no dream to ride, but Lawson was now proving that it was at least usable. The Lucky Strike team had done all their work before the season started. Warren Willing said that, watching Rainey at those tests, he knew he was fit to win the championship. 'He did hundreds of laps and I never saw him do one that wasn't at Grand Prix pace, sliding out of every corner.'

Wayne and his wife, Shea, had temporarily moved out of their comfortable home in Los Angeles to take a flat in Modesto so that he could train every day during the winter at Kenny Roberts's farm, riding dirt track and motocross to make sure that he started the season with his riding as sharp as possible. For the first time he had done weight training as well, to make sure he had the strength to dominate the motor cycle.

Rainey had so much obvious confidence in both himself and the machine at the start of the year. He and the bike were fit to be champions. But the bike did not appear to get any better, and when the Honda proved faster and the Michelins, at times at least, superior, that confidence was less apparent.

Kenny Roberts explained that the team simply did not have the manpower to do mid-season development. Yamaha could not send them new parts every week, like Honda did, because Yamaha had a smaller race department and would have had to make the parts for five or six riders.

While Lawson was testing at Donington for the British Grand Prix, Rainey was in Japan at the Suzuka Eight Hour. Even with that commitment, Schwantz had a day's testing at Donington. Honda also did pre-race testing at Le Mans, Anderstorp and Brno. Even if the team did not have any new parts to test it was obvious that they had such a large number of wheel, brake, tyre, frame and suspension combinations that the possibilities were rarely exhausted in normal practice.

You can hardly accuse the Roberts team of laziness – they make as much if not more effort than anyone in the paddock – and Kenny refused to point the finger at the budget, but they have always appeared to be a little short of cash. At Donington, Sweden and Brno, Rainey did not look to be on the best Yamaha. Part of the fascination of road racing is that it is virtually impossible to separate man from machine – but Mackenzie's Marlboro Yamaha looked superior at Donington and Christian Sarron's Gauloises Blondes machine had the beating of the Lucky Strike bike at Anderstorp and Brno.

When Rainey was winning he gave full credit to the team, the mechanics, the bike, the tyres. When things started to look a little shaky he just talked in terms of not having the bike as well sorted as was necessary. By Czechoslovakia the frustration proved too much and he pointed the finger at the Dunlops.

Brno was a bad weekend for the Lucky Strike team, but might they have pointed the finger at Wayne for the previous weekend's mistake? Recriminations are pointless and the team had been unusually free of them. Rainey is normally guarded when things go wrong but, with the championship taking a walk to the other end of the pit lane, he let his feelings show.

Roberts signed Dunlop because being the only major 500 team using them would give them the advantage of singular attention. At times this has worked for them, at times against; the balance is hard to judge.

Rainey's part in the operation has been almost faultless. He resisted the temptation to race with Schwantz when it wasn't necessary, and refused to rise to Lawson's jibes – but he did fall off in Sweden. Was that solely Wayne's fault – or was the team partly to blame for giving confusing pit signals? And, if so, had they not learned a lesson from the Japanese Grand Prix? But blaming the Lucky Strike team would be grossly unfair, because they were the only team who put in the sort of winter effort that enabled Rainey to start the season with such an advantage.

On the face of it the situation in the Pepsi Suzuki team would seem a great deal more straightforward. The Suzuki stopped three times and an equal number of blanks on the score card were down to the rider: both are due to the youthfulness of the components. The Suzuki engine needs more development time and Schwantz more experience. An error of judgement can cause an accident and you could nail the Australian fall to that cause. Spain and Belgium can hardly be attributed to simple errors of judgement, because Schwantz puts in too many error-free miles on the machine. He is not prone to running off the track or falling in practice or races. Both these falls occurred at the end of races, which could point to a loss of concentration.

Loss of concentration can be linked to lack of physical training. Schwantz was hampered in his winter preparations by a knee operation to remove the pinning from his 1988 Spa crash repair. To clear up the concentration problem and to sort out the engine reliability require effort from the man and the company. Both have the ability to win the championship and, if both put in the effort, they must be favourites for the 1990 season.

SHOEI
3
LUCKY STRIKE

Arai
34
SUZUKI
MICHELIN

No matter how closely you look, you won't get a bike that looks closer to a racer than the Kawasaki ZXR750.

Based on our ZXR-7 works machine, the ZXR750 is a potent machine on track or road.

But there is one small difference between the ZXR-7 and the ZXR750. About £82,000.

Raced by Team Green, the ZXR750 has seen success on the Isle of Man and finished well in the Le Mans endurance race.

All we ask is that you don't let your heart rule your head. Wear proper clothing, don't exceed the limits of your skills or our machine

Kawasaki Motors (UK) Ltd can make n

Kawasaki

TOP 10 RIDERS OF 1989

1. EDDIE LAWSON
2. WAYNE RAINEY
3. SITO PONS
4. KEVIN SCHWANTZ
5. LUCA CADALORA
6. CHRISTIAN SARRON
7. REINHOLD ROTH
8. ALEX CRIVILLE
9. JOHN KOCINSKI
10. KEVIN MAGEE

1

EDDIE LAWSON

Malcolm Bryan

The soubriquet 'Steady Eddie' that Lawson has lived with ever since he first rode the Marlboro Yamaha was not something that pleased him. It half suited him – the half that was as reliable as a rock, not the half that was meteorically fast.

At first he did live in Freddie Spencer's shadow a little, though he fought to get out of that position. The fact that he was so smooth suggested, to some, that he was uninspired. Winning three World Championships is hardly uninspiring but because he so rarely allowed the Yamaha to get out of shape people congratulated him warmly on his success rather than screamed ecstatically at his achievements.

Lawson's ice-cold analysis of what was required to win the World Championship each season made him ride in a conservative fashion, going for points rather than glory. He and the Yamaha developed side by side. It became a very different bike from the violently powered, ill-handling machines that Kenny Roberts had ridden in the early 1980s. The Yamaha that Lawson rode for six years was a most useful tool and Eddie became a craftsman.

There remained the question of whether Lawson could ride a bike that was less well behaved than the Yamaha – but 1989 has erased any doubts. The NSR was not a nice motor cycle to ride. It may have been marginally more useful than the 1988 version which gave Gardner so many nightmares, but it was hardly the sound machine that Lawson had been used to as the number one factory Yamaha rider.

Lawson tried to make the Honda work like his old Yamaha, but failed. Erv Kanemoto convinced him not only that it could not be done but also that, if they pursued that line of attack, they would merely take away what good points the Honda did possess. Lawson changed tack. He and Kanemoto got Honda to do what they could with the bike without completely redesigning it.

By progressively stiffening the frame they made its handling more predictable and controllable, even if they could not make it turn and steer as well as Lawson would have liked. And what the bike could not do, Lawson did. That the Honda was fast was about the best thing that could be said about it. It was not that the bike was turned into a winner in the second half of the season; the bike was no longer bad enough to stop Lawson winning on it.

Winning on the Honda made Lawson ride harder than he ever had before. No longer did he look infinitely accurate and unhurried. In his seventh season he looked to be trying harder than ever. He was more often out of shape and off-line. It made him look almost hairy. When he had to stick his neck out to get the points back from Rainey he was ready – and no longer steady.

2

WAYNE RAINEY

Malcolm Bryan

Wayne Rainey was the surprise of 1988. He was consistently fast, though let down on occasion by his equipment. A year later he was even faster and came so close to winning the World Championship.

He might have studied the way that Eddie Lawson had won three World Championships and, after establishing an early points-lead, formed a Lawson-style strategy. He won when he could but took no risks, accepting second or third if prudent. Surely what worked for Lawson could be used effectively against him? But Lawson stopped playing by those rules, and pushed harder and harder. When Rainey responded he was unlucky: a momentary loss of concentration plus two races when his tyres were no match for the competition were a rotten way to finish the season.

Personally Rainey has everything needed to win the World Championship. He puts in the effort, he has the skill – but Lawson has often said you need a certain amount of luck to take the title. If there was a single thing that Rainey lacked, that was it.

It is not surprising that Wayne Rainey is a good friend of Sito Pons: they share the same total professionalism.

3

SITO PONS

Malcolm Bryan

The rough edges in Pons's 1988 World Championship-winning season were eradicated during the winter. This year his performance was absolutely faultless: it was not just that he didn't fall off, he never put a wheel out of place. And, more than the fact that his lines were perfect, his race tactics always produced the right results.

Even when he might have continued his march to the championship with a second or third place he won races. He won five of the first eight races and thus established an almost unassailable championship lead. Only then did he ride in a slightly more reserved manner, taking two seconds and a third.

Yet he took the title with a win at the British Grand Prix – and still summoned the enthusiasm to win again in Sweden the following weekend. As Roth put it, the sooner Pons moved to the 500 class the better, because no one could imagine winning the 250 championship while he remained.

Whether or not Pons's talent translates to the 500 class is beside the point. His organisational, management and promotional skills created his team. His development ability produced a bike that was better than the other Hondas and he rode it better than anyone else. His victory was complete.

Niall Mackenzie *(below)* **had some fine rides on the Marlboro Yamaha. Mid-season was spoilt by the Hockenheim crash and a long period of recuperation from the resulting knee injury. The highlight of his year, obviously, was leading the British Grand Prix at Donington. That brought the crowd to its feet.**

Luca Cadalora *(above)* **was the Marlboro Yamaha team's star this season, with two tremendous Grand Prix victories in Spain and Brazil. A threat at every race, with his aggressive and inspirational style, the Italian always pushed the bike right to the limit.**

The talent of 19-year-old Alex Criville *(right)* **stands out in any crowd. He did not start the year as favourite, lining up against much more experienced opposition. But the Marlboro Cobas team provided excellent backing and Criville blossomed. There seems no limit to what the Spaniard might achieve in the future.**

Photos: Malcolm Bryan

69
FM
Marlboro
28
Marlboro
61

4

KEVIN SCHWANTZ

Malcolm Bryan

Without Schwantz the 500 championship would have been like a game of chess between Lawson and Rainey – a very fast game, tense and absorbing, but inspirational only to the *cognoscenti*. The Suzuki rider gave it a dimension that anyone could appreciate: crudely exciting to any observer, but deeply, incredibly skilled when studied more exactly.

The fact that he made three mistakes endeared him all the more, giving him that touch of imperfection which allowed many to feel some empathy. No one watching could ride a motor cycle like he does, but we all make mistakes.

Kevin won more races than anyone else, and he did so more convincingly. Words cannot describe his brilliance on a motor cycle – and if his brilliance was flawed, then just give him time.

But there can be no mistakes in 1990 if he is to be World Champion. Will the need to ride an error-free season take the edge off the excitement? It should not, for it is the Schwantz style that thrills, not the touch of fallibility that produces a fall.

5

LUCA CADALORA

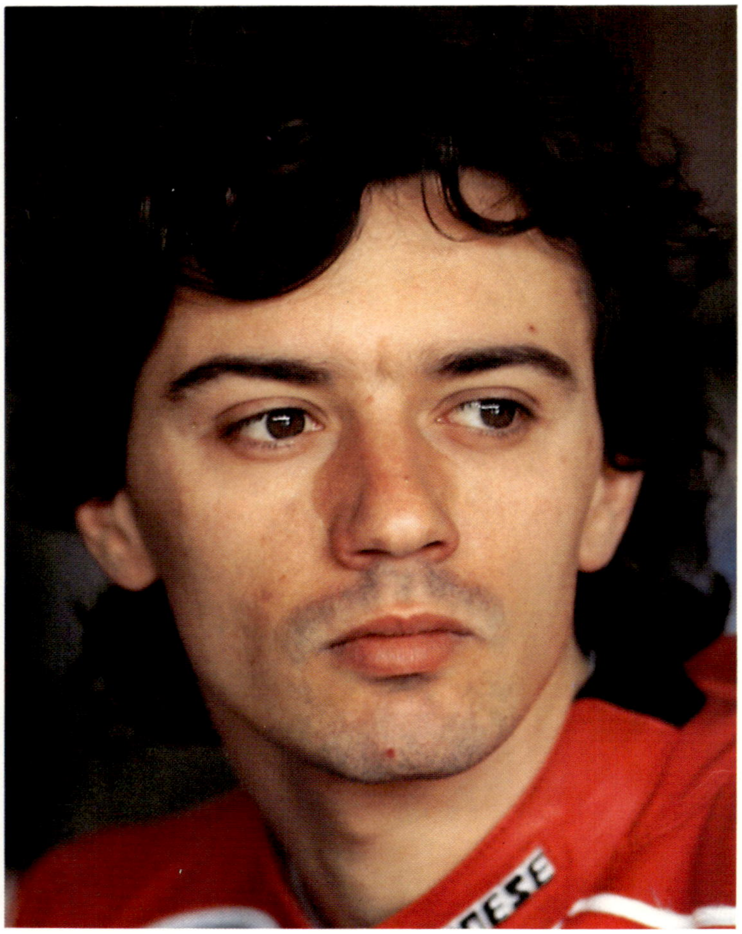

Malcolm Bryan

This Italian is greatly respected by many of the best riders in the sport, including Eddie Lawson. He rode his 250 Yamaha harder than anyone else during the season. He only won two Grands Prix, but then the Yamaha was not a machine that could win every weekend.

Occasionally Cadalora pushed the Yamaha too hard and crashed, but perhaps his greater failing was making bad starts. A disastrous start led to his first-lap crash in Italy, and slow starts cost him many more points during the season.

To a certain extent Cadalora coped with the fact that the Honda was a better machine, but when the Yamaha broke down while he was fighting to stay with the leaders, in both Austria and Holland, any chance he had to challenge Pons for the championship was destroyed.

Given the chance to ride a 500 he was immediately impressive, yet he decided that he wanted to go after the 250 championship again before moving to the bigger class.

6

CHRISTIAN SARRON

Malcolm Bryan

The lone European who could regularly run with the American triumvirate, Christian Sarron is still improving with every season, even though he talks of retiring. He was prepared to go only so far in pursuit of points this year – and it was a successful tactic, because he made no mistakes.

Overstepping the limit has always been Sarron's problem in the past, but this year he never pushed his luck. His best chance of a Grand Prix win came in Sweden, but he refused to get involved in the Lawson/Rainey championship battle and so stayed behind them. He also hung on behind Rainey in Czechoslovakia, to keep his fellow-Yamaha rider's title hopes alive.

Christian does not look a serious contender for the World Championship in 1990, because he cannot ride a 500 as hard as the Americans do, when the tyres are past their best. He could well be a Grand Prix winner, though, in what he says will be his last season. The Frenchman is one of the most humorous, best-liked riders in the sport, and any success of his will please a great many people.

7

REINHOLD ROTH

Malcolm Bryan

The German gets faster as he gets older – and to be beaten by Sito Pons is no disgrace. He made a slow start to the season, which gave the Spaniard an advantage that he never relinquished but, as Roth later admitted, his nasty accident at the end of the 1987 season which had slowed him throughout '88 was still affecting him at the start of this year. Having realised that, he successfully put it behind him.

Reinhold also changed the way he viewed practice. Previously he'd considered his place on the grid as relatively unimportant, thinking that it had little relationship to race speed. After the Austrian Grand Prix he vowed that he would revise his thinking and went for as good a grid position as was practicably possible. And from that point he appeared much more consistently on the rostrum.

It is difficult to predict how much quicker Roth can get. If he could maintain the pace that he was attaining at the end of the '89 season throughout the coming year he would be a hard man to beat. He makes use of his experience, and the lessons that Pons has taught him will certainly not be lost on this very likeable rider.

8

ALEX CRIVILLE

Malcolm Bryan

To win the 125 cc World Championship on a new machine with a small team ranged against the mighty Derbi factory was a major achievement – and Criville also got the better of the well-supported Honda men, simply by out-riding everyone in the class.

As the youngest-ever World Champion, the Spaniard obviously has a great future. Given the right backing he could well make a very rapid move to success in the 250 class and continue that learning curve into the 500 category. His is the sort of natural talent that knows no bounds and will only be limited if he does not gain the right sort of experience while he is still at this most rapid stage of his development.

Though Alex has relatively few Grands Prix behind him he is very cool under pressure, and became more so as the season progressed. The way he won the final round in Czechoslovakia was masterful, taking the lead as it became obvious that it was more risky to remain in the tumult of the pack. He is the latest example of the strength and depth of riding talent available from Spain.

9

JOHN KOCINSKI

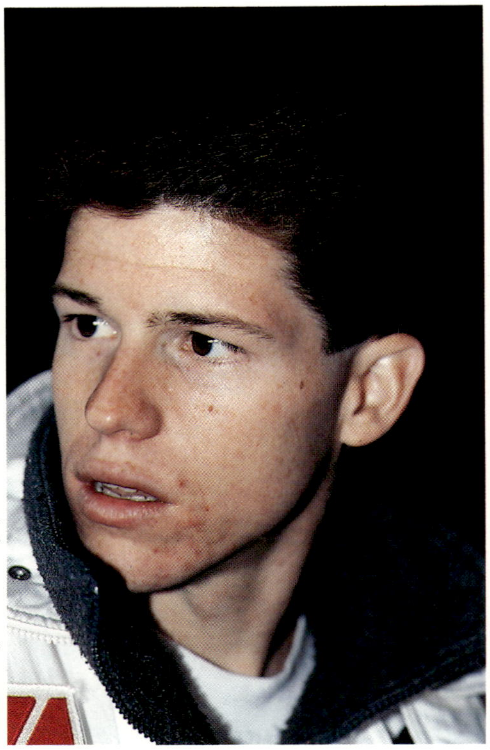
Patrick Gosling/Zooom Photographic

Two wins out of two rides on the 250 Yamaha and a superb performance in his single outing on a 500 mean that the diminutive young man from Arkansas has to be considered one of the best riders in the world. Judging him against the rest when he only competed in three races is unfair – and yet his blatant talent means that he cannot possibly be left out.

The way Kocinski rode the 500 in the wet at Spa was a revelation. To display such control when completely unused to the amount of power available in very difficult conditions suggests that there is little that he cannot achieve.

He makes his own rather accurate analysis of the situation when he suggests that he would have been competitive on a 250 every weekend, had he done a full Grand Prix season. On a 500 he felt he was riding more on instinct and reaction, and to be reliably consistent needed more time so that every move became second nature.

Time is all that he needs. If Yamaha can provide him with a reasonable machine he would start as favourite to be 1990 250 cc World Champion. Given a 500 he would have a reasonable chance of finishing in the top three, as consistency would surely not be slow in coming.

10

KEVIN MAGEE

Malcolm Bryan

Fully fit for the whole season Magee would have been a great help to Wayne Rainey in his quest for the championship. We still have to see the best of the Australian, however, as his riding through the middle of the season was affected by his Laguna Seca injuries, particularly his damaged knee.

More than that, his results were also restricted on occasion by the inconsistency of his tyres. His riding has improved greatly in a year; he can now ride fast almost anywhere, and for the entire race distance. The one track he still hates is Spa, as he considers it too dangerous.

Though Kevin has benefited from the backing of a very good team he is very much his own man, not a Roberts clone. Like Rainey he has said that he wants to ride on Michelins in 1990 but, as long as his team changes tyres, he wants to stay with them. The team provides the environment he needs to succeed and another year of improvement should see him a regular Grand Prix winner.

WAYNE GARDNER

Nothing could be more personally fulfilling than Wayne's electrifying victory at his own Grand Prix. The satisfaction not only of winning at Phillip Island but of being the single greatest influence in making Grand Prix racing a major sport as far as Australians are concerned should have lasted a long time. Unfortunately a week was all it took for Gardner's season to go from peak to trough. His broken leg took some time to mend and his riding did not return to its pre-accident level. However, a winter of recuperation and testing could put the Australian right back at the top again.

JACQUES CORNU

A vital part of the Grand Prix scene, Cornu contributes more than just his great skill, for he is extremely popular as a happy-go-lucky joker. The Swiss ace talks of racing for at least two more seasons, and every year he gets faster and more consistent. In the past he has had some nasty accidents, and also spent time off racing thanks to a car crash. This year he only fell once, and could be relied upon to be competitive every weekend.

Photos: Malcolm Bryan

PIER FRANCESCO CHILI

Pirelli tyre engineer Peter Ingley commented that this Italian rider is 'better than he thinks he is'. Chili could lap as fast as the Americans but could not quite bring himself to race them. Winning races depends so much on a rider's belief in his own superiority; lacking that makes it impossible to commit oneself to a passing move in the certain knowledge that the other man must brake first.

If Chili can capture that confidence, and continue the development of the skill that was so apparent throughout the season, then he should be able to take over from Sarron as the lone European challenging the Americans.

JEAN-PHILIPPE RUGGIA

Much improved from 1988, the Frenchman started the season as a genuine challenger for the championship. The Yamaha was not fast enough in Germany and Austria, which took care of that possibility – and then Ruggia made the mistake of getting too close to Cadalora on the first lap at Assen.

If Ruggia made the same kind of improvement for the coming season as he did this year then he would be a championship favourite. Instead he has taken the step into the 500 class. His style would appear to suit the 250 in that he uses the maximum angle of lean, and that does not necessarily translate to the 500. Yet he is still in the process of learning rapidly and perhaps stands more chance of adapting than those who have ridden 250s for many seasons. He could even make the transition more readily than Pons.

of very high
temperatures
on Duckhams
QXR
DUCKHAMS
QXR
HIGH PERFORMANCE
ENGINE PROTECTION

TECHNICAL FEATURE

THE RADIANT GLOW OF SUCCESS:

AP Lockheed

THE STATE OF THE DISC BRAKE

By Peter Clifford with Ray Bailey of AP Lockheed

The discs on the front of the Pepsi Suzuki were glowing as Kevin Schwantz went after pole position at Donington Park. No one captured it on film and, because of the shrouds that cover the discs, it could only have been seen from the other side of the wheel. Nevertheless, the discs reached a high enough temperature to glow red.

Carbon discs won a single Grand Prix in 1988, eight in 1989. At one time or another they were used by all the top riders but that, according to Ray Bailey, the project engineer of AP Lockheed, does not mean that he is satisfied with the situation. 'We are working towards the point where they are a "fit and forget" item, like our iron discs.'

The advantages of carbon discs are so clear that there is little doubt they will eventually become standard fittings on all 500 cc Grand Prix bikes. At the moment temperature variations cause such changes in performance that rain or specific circuits lead some riders to go back to the old faithful iron discs on occasion.

Development will sort out these problems and the research is worthwhile. A single carbon disc weighs 900 g – half the weight of the larger diameter iron disc that it replaces. That amount of weight reduction from any part of the machine would be worthwhile, but this is all the greater because the mass is unsprung and rotating. Getting rid of this weight helps both the suspension and the steering as well as the acceleration. With the two discs there is a saving of almost 2 kg, which is considerable.

The other advantage of the carbon disc is that it does not fade with hard use: the pads do not wear out. In fact, the pads will last two Grands Prix and are made from a very similar material to the discs. 'At the start of the year the disc and pad material were the same,' explained Bailey. 'Then we started to use some slightly different pad material, that you might describe as being a slightly softer compound. That is not an accurate description, but the pads do wear in quicker. They still last two races.'

The discs themselves stand up well considering that the material is very similar, and while

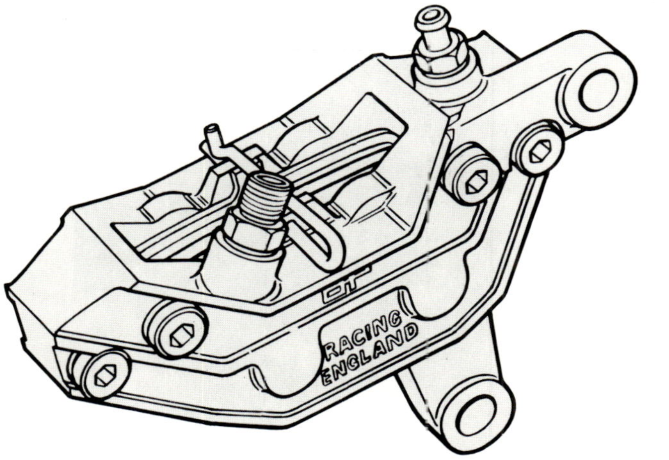

Left: **A carbon disc glowing during a dynamometer test at AP Lockheed's racing division at Leamington Spa. This is actually a Formula One car disc and caliper, thicker than the motor cycle version.**

Right: **The cast caliper is a cheaper alternative to the machined version and was used on various occasions by the teams.**

Bottom: **The carbon discs fitted to the Lucky Strike Yamaha, with and without the shrouds that keep up the temperature.**

keeping track of discs that are swapped from wheel to wheel and used on some occasions and not others is difficult, Bailey believes that the discs are good for about eight races.

Because wear is slow, the matching of discs to pads is important. Both acquire matching shallow grooves and using one worn pad with a different worn disc would cause problems. 'At first we suggested that pads were kept with discs, but when wheels are swapped so often that is not practical. The new softer pads wear in quickly enough so that new pads can be utilised with used discs.'

The carbon discs take time to come up to working temperature and, ideally, should be working at about 500°F (260°C). Each disc has temperature paint daubed on its peripheral edge so that the temperature it has achieved can be seen when it returns to the pits. 'The paints we use turn at 370, 430 and 620°F (188, 221 and 327°C). The paint works on a time base, so that it takes a few laps at temperature before the paint records it by changing. We would like to have one that works at about 500°F (260°C) but the only one that is available, which turns at 560°F (293° C) has something in it that oxidises the disc. The manufacturers cannot tell us why it does that.'

The carbon discs cannot stand oxidisation, which effectively delaminates the material, causes it to puff up at the edge like a wafer of flaky pastry, and would eventually cause the disc to start falling apart. 'Too high a temperature also causes the disc to oxidise and we began to see that in practice at Donington, where the discs must have been running at around 700° (371°C). It is always hard to say why one circuit causes higher temperatures than another, but it must be the three hard stops at Donington. At the end of the main straight there is a very high-energy stop, then a short burst of acceleration down to the Melbourne hairpin, which is another hard stop downhill, then another short straight to another hairpin. The discs were running hotter at Donington than anywhere else and that is why the teams took the shrouds off for the race.'

The fact that carbon disc performance is so sensitive to temperature variation is the main point of development. The power and structural reliability are there, and the discs are free from fade, but the variation in feel that the rider gets is what requires most attention.

'There are various things that the rider is feeling,' explains Bailey. 'Sometimes there is a juddering when the disc is used from cool. That is because the disc starts to get hot in one area and grips in that patch before the whole disc warms and works evenly. The rider just has to use the disc harder, and then that goes away. There have been occasions when riders have reported a pulsing back through the lever, and that is down to a manufacturing problem which we have to put right. It is unfortunate that this occurred with a batch of discs mid-season, when things were very close in the championship, and that made the riders feel a little uneasy.'

Brakes are naturally a very sensitive issue for riders. It is easy to see why Lockheed equipment is so universally respected among the top teams, though, for Ray Bailey makes no attempt to gloss over problems.

'Gardner's crash during practice at Laguna Seca was down to the temperature relationship. He was trying to warm up the disc and said that when the wheel locked he let go of the lever. As the temperature rises the lever pressure required falls. He would have been squeezing hard to get the disc to work from cold, and as the temperature came up he lowered his lever pressure, but he was expecting the reduction in pressure to work like an iron disc. Even with one finger on, the carbon disc was still working enough to keep the wheel locked.

'Wayne said at the time that he would never use carbon discs again and I can understand that reaction – but he has gone back to them since.'

The fact that the friction, and therefore the braking force, increases with temperature means that as the rider brakes into the corner the braking force gets greater as the disc warms. He must ease off the lever pressure more as he leans into the corner so that he does not have too much braking load on the front tyre as it has to cope with cornering force. Just holding a constant lever pressure would see the braking force rise as the temperature of the disc rises.

This was the reason given by Wayne Rainey for going back to the iron discs at Anderstorp and Brno. It was not something that proved a problem for Schwantz. 'Both run the same equipment,' said Bailey. 'There is a very slight difference in the mounting systems but I don't think that explains it. Why it is a problem for Wayne and not Kevin I don't know; it could be as little as the position of the handlebar lever.'

The temperature reaction is something that Lockheed and the company that produce the disc material aim to modify. Bailey would rather not divulge the name of the company making the material, and the manufacturing process that makes the carbon blank is definitely secret. 'It all goes on behind closed doors. I know very little about it,' says Bailey. 'It takes about five months to grow a blank for a motor cycle disc, six months for the thicker Formula One car disc.'

The manufacturing process may be secret, but a close inspection of the disc and pad material reveals something of its make-up. The starting point is obviously carbon filaments, just as it is for carbon fibre cloth and many varieties of carbon composites. Going from the appearance of the material, bunches of the filaments are then woven into cloth. The weave had an equal amount of material running in both directions; the cross-angle was 90 degrees in the pad material but looked to vary slightly in the disc.

The really secret part is the process of binding layer after layer of the weave into a solid blank, because this is not a composite material, it is pure carbon. There is no glue or resin, because they would not stand the temperature. One can imagine that the layers are pressed together at an elevated temperature, probably in a vacuum, and over a period of time cross-linking occurs between the carbon strands so that a certain percentage of the carbon-to-carbon bonding that gives the filaments such incredible tensile strength is broken and carbon-to-carbon bonds are formed between one filament and another.

The blanks are milled, ground and lapped flat. Bailey commented that the material destroys tungsten-tipped tools at a high rate. When you

Malcolm Bryan

John McKenzie

Malcolm Bryan

Far right: **The basic parts: carbon disc on aluminium carrier, machined aluminium caliper and cast aluminium master cylinder.**

Right: **The Gauloises Blondes team started the year needing help from AP Lockheed to get their carbon disc tests going. Then Brembo got up to speed and the team even tried the twin carbon arrangement on Ruggia's 250.**

Honda *(below)* **tried many disc arrangements through the season. Here one bike is fitted with the AP carbon discs and machined calipers with Honda's beautifully crafted shroud. The other bike has Nissin's steel discs and calipers.**

Malcolm Bryan

consider the time taken to 'grow' the disc, and the fact that machining it is more difficult than iron, it is not surprising that the discs are quite expensive. A single disc with its steel carrier costs about £500 compared to £150 for an AP Lockheed cast iron disc. 'That is not cheap, but if you compare it to the Japanese iron discs it is not so bad,' commented Bailey. The factory teams all pay for their discs: the racing development is not a sponsorship but a commercial venture in itself.

Though the Lucky Strike Yamaha and Pepsi Suzuki teams have been long-time users of AP Lockheed equipment, HRC asked them to produce equipment for this season and, during the year, Lawson, Gardner and Doohan have all run a combination of Nissin and Lockheed equipment. Lockheed have provided calipers and discs, both carbon and iron. HRC demanded insulation between the carbon pads and the caliper pistons, but otherwise none is used. The brake fluid used is AP600, which means that it will boil above 600°F (316°C); this is replaced each race and boiling has never been a problem.

There are two different calipers in use, both made from aluminium alloys. The cheaper caliper is cast in two pieces, the more expensive, lighter version is made in one piece, machined from a solid billet on a numerically controlled milling machine.

A glance at the latter caliper leaves one in no doubt that there must be a great deal of swarf left behind after the many different machining processes. The alloy is different and, because the unit is made in one piece, it can be made lighter, by using less material without threatening its stiffness, a most important property. The machined caliper costs about £500 and the cast version £200.

Both calipers have four pistons, one pair 29 mm in diameter, the other 35 mm. The master cylinders are not very complex but Lockheed feel they have gained some advantage from their adjustable leverage ratio system. 'This makes it easier to adjust the brake for rider preference,' Bailey explained. 'The larger, 19-mm bore master cylinder can have its ratio adjusted by a simple screw so that it has the effect of a 16-mm bore cylinder.

'The rider can change the ratio so that the brake feels better at different circuits but I think that Kevin (Schwantz), for instance, only changed it once this season.' The major advantage is that if a rider feels he would like to experiment it can be done in the middle of practice without the need to swap master cylinders and bleed brakes, or swap entire systems.

The Honda riders have been the slowest to convert to carbon discs, even though Lawson used them in Germany, Austria, Yugoslavia and Holland. 'He had a marked change in braking response in one race and after that said that he couldn't afford to carry on using the carbon,' said Bailey. Since then he has used both Nissin and Lockheed iron discs. Honda have had a greater number of braking variations than anyone else this year, with two different manufacturers making three different sizes of iron discs and two different carbons. They have had radially ventilated discs, axially drilled versions, and finally radially ventilated discs with shallow blind holes drilled into the faces: too many variations with too little track time allotted to brake testing to get to the best solution.

All fifteen of the top factory riders have used the carbon discs at some time or other. 'We are not yet at the stage of Formula One racing, where the carbon disc is a permanent fixture. Formula One is always ahead in technology, because they have the budgets to experiment. I am fortunate to be able to benefit from some of their experience, though the subtle temperature variations have a greater effect on motor cycle braking. As I have to explain to the teams with the carbon brakes, the difference between a system that the rider describes as "perfect" and one he says is "terrible" is very small. The iron brake system is much less easily affected.'

Rainey had a brake problem in the middle of the French Grand Prix but, as far as Bailey can ascertain, it had nothing to do with using carbon. 'It is very difficult to analyse what happened in these situations. You have to go on what the rider tells you about precisely how the brake responded. Wayne said that at one point there was almost no power. At the next corner it had half come back and at the next one it worked – he had no more trouble after that. That leads me to think that he had a piston knocked back by a foreign object – something that flew up and knocked the piston back. That has happened and it is one reason we prefer not to run shrouds. If something does get caught up the shroud will hold it there instead of allowing it to be thrown off.

'The shrouds were originally designed for use in the wet, to keep the temperature up in those conditions. We want to get to the point where we do not use them, at least in the dry. We are very close to being able to use the carbon brakes in the wet now; Wayne tried them in practice at Spa and said he could feel no difference.'

The power that is available from the carbon disc will eventually make it essential. 'Niall Mackenzie raced with them for the first time at Donington and he said that, at first, they required a lot of lever pressure but, as the race went on, they got lighter. He was very pleased with them. As the temperature gets up they do not require as much pressure and, of course, they do not fade.'

As for the future, we will see few obvious changes in the carbon brake. The material changes will be subtle but, hopefully, the result will be more consistency and less variation of braking force with temperature. As for servo assistance, or carbon brakes on road bikes, Ray Bailey is less certain. 'We have thought about braking assistance but feel is all-important to the rider, and if you put anything extra between him and the caliper, it tends to affect that feel. These systems tend to get more play in them as they get hot.

'Carbon on road bikes seems a long way off. I hate to say never, because at one time disc brakes seemed improbable. But carbon – I don't know – you would have to be very careful at the first crossroad on a cold morning.'

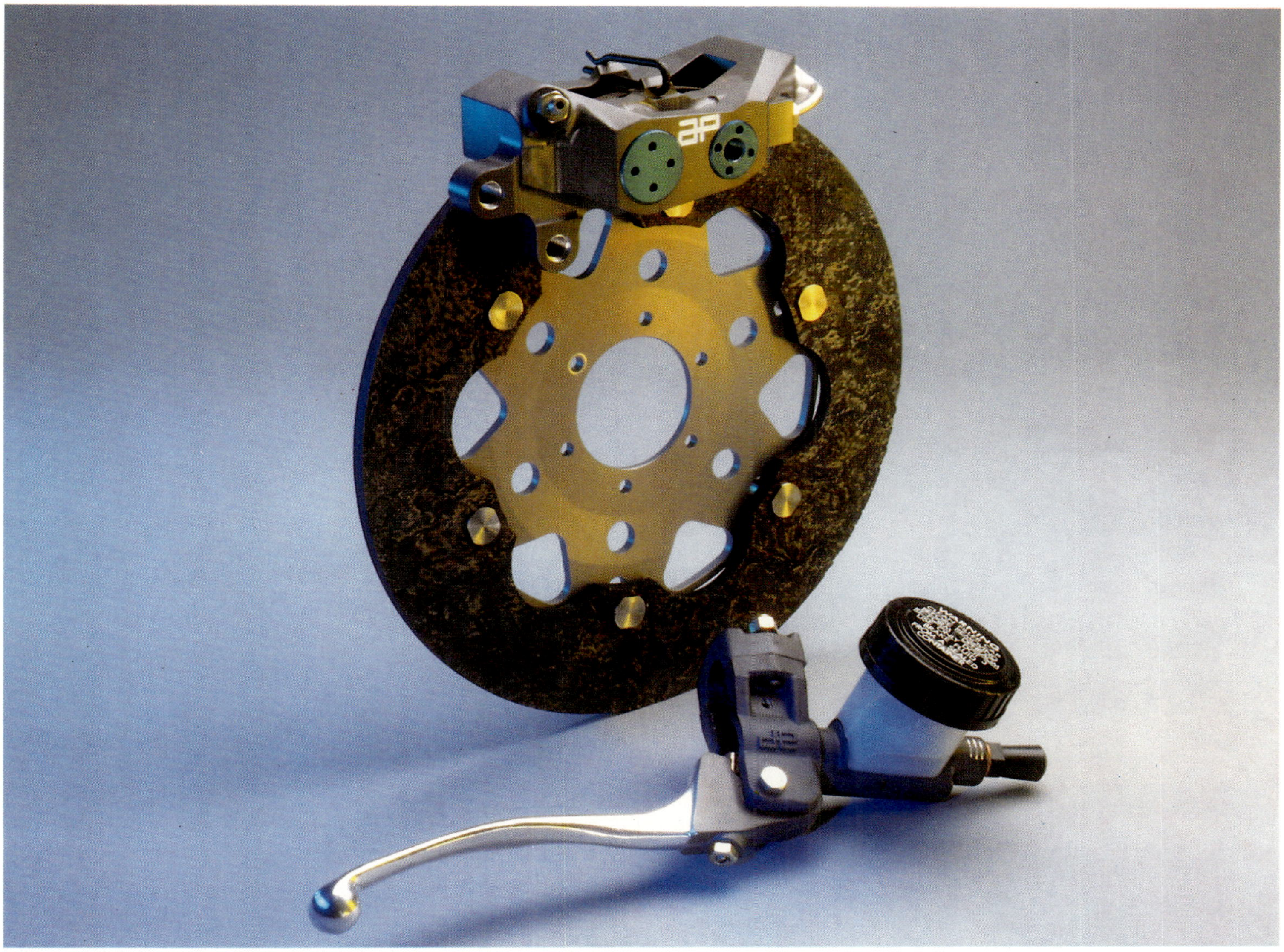

AP Lockheed

1989 500 cc WORLD CHAMPIONSHIP

Japanese GP – 26 March

1.	K. Schwantz	AP
2.	W. Rainey	AP
3.	E. Lawson	Nissin

Australian GP – 9 April

1.	W. Gardner	Nissin
2.	W. Rainey	AP
3.	C. Sarron	Brembo

United States GP – 16 April

1.	W. Rainey	AP *carbon*
2.	K. Schwantz	AP *carbon*
3.	E. Lawson	Nissin

Spanish GP – 30 April

1.	E. Lawson	Nissin
2.	W. Rainey	AP
3.	N. Mackenzie	AP

Italian GP – 14 May

1.	P.F. Chili	Nissin
2.	S. Buckmaster	Nissin
3.	M. Rudroff	Nissin

German GP – 28 May

1.	W. Rainey	AP *carbon*
2.	E. Lawson	AP *carbon*
3.	M. Doohan	Nissin

Austrian GP – 4 June

1.	K. Schwantz	AP *carbon*
2.	E. Lawson	AP *carbon*
3.	W. Rainey	AP *carbon*

Yugoslavian GP – 11 June

1.	K. Schwantz	AP *carbon*
2.	W. Rainey	AP *carbon*
3.	E. Lawson	AP *carbon*

Dutch TT – 24 June

1.	W. Rainey	AP *carbon*
2.	E. Lawson	AP *carbon*
3.	C. Sarron	Brembo

Belgian GP – 2 July

1.	E. Lawson	AP
2.	K. Schwantz	AP
3.	W. Rainey	AP *carbon*

French GP – 16 July

1.	E. Lawson	AP
2.	K. Schwantz	AP *carbon*
3.	W. Rainey	AP *carbon*

British GP – 6 August

1.	K. Schwantz	AP *carbon*
2.	E. Lawson	AP
3.	W. Rainey	AP *carbon*

Swedish TT – 13 August

1.	E. Lawson	Nissin
2.	C. Sarron	Brembo
3.	W. Gardner	AP

Czechoslovak GP – 27 August

1.	K. Schwantz	AP *carbon*
2.	E. Lawson	Nissin
3.	W. Rainey	AP

Brazilian GP – 17 September

1.	K. Schwantz	AP *carbon*
2.	E. Lawson	Nissin
3.	W. Rainey	AP *carbon*

SPECIFICATIONS

Wayne Rainey
498 cc YZR Yamaha
Engine: 56 mm × 50.6 mm, water-cooled, four-cylinder two-stroke; crankcase reed-valve induction; six transfer and three exhaust ports, with electronically controlled cylindrical valve varying exhaust port height; one plain piston ring; roller big ends and needle roller small ends; two pressed cranks, four roller bearings each; dry clutch with five friction and six steel plates, six springs. *Gearbox:* six-speed, nine possible ratios for first, seven for second, six for third and fourth, four for fifth and five for sixth; drum selection. *Carburettors:* 35 mm flat-slide Mikuni.
Frame: Yamaha twin-spar fabricated box-section aluminium, taper roller head bearings; box-section aluminium swing arm, needle roller bearings; lower end-linked rear suspension, one Ohlins unit, coil-spring plus nitrogen pressure, oil damping, adjustable; Ohlins forks, coil-springs, oil-damped, adjustable. *Wheels:* Marvic, commonly used sizes 4.25 in. × 16 in. or 3.50 in. × 17 in. front and 5.50 or 6.00 in. × 17 in. rear (5.50 in. × 19 in. for rain tyres). *Tyres:* Dunlop. *Brakes:* two AP Lockheed carbon (272.5 mm) or cast iron (320 mm) discs at front and a single Yamaha steel (210 mm) at rear; Lockheed aluminium calipers front, Nissin rear; AP Lockheed or Ferodo front and Yamaha rear pads. *Plugs:* NGK. *Gearbox and engine oil:* Motul.

Malcolm Bryan

Malcolm Bryan

Far left: **Paul Treacy, TT and Co. do the carb shuffle on Kevin Magee's Lucky Strike Yamaha during practice for the American Grand Prix.**

Tadahiko Taira crashed his factory Yamaha *(below left)* **during practice in Spain and a fire extinguisher was used on it. That meant stripping it down and cleaning it completely, which also revealed the bare engine and, without the carburettors, the manifolds that lead to the reed valves and into the crankcases. The blue anodised rods connect the exhaust valves for each bank of cylinders and the rocker in the middle is required because there is no straight run between the two, thanks to the engine mount.**

Below: **Suzuki ran a tiny extra radiator, mounted horizontally below the lower cylinder bank to give extra cooling. Though different exhaust pipes and cylinders were tried there were few major developments during the season as the bike was effective from day one.**

Patrick Gosling/Zooom

Kevin Schwantz
498 cc XR75 Suzuki
Engine: 56 mm × 50.7 mm, water-cooled, four-cylinder two-stroke; crankcase reed-valve induction; six transfer and three exhaust ports, with electronically controlled variable exhaust port height; one plain piston ring; needle roller big and small ends; two pressed cranks, four ball bearings each; dry clutch with nine friction and ten steel plates, six springs. *Gearbox:* six-speed, five possible ratios for first, seven for second, fourteen for third and fourth, seven for fifth and sixth gears, five different primary ratios giving a total of 200 possibilities; drum selection. *Carburettors:* 36 mm flat-slide Mikuni.
Frame: Suzuki twin-spar fabricated box-section aluminium, ball roller head bearings in adjustable angle inserts; fabricated aluminium swing arm, needle roller and shims; rocker arm rear suspension, one Kayaba unit, coil-spring, oil damping, adjustable for both high and low speed ranges of compression and rebound; Kayaba OUT forks, coil-springs, oil-damped, externally adjustable for both low and high speed ranges of compression and rebound. *Wheels:* Marchesini, commonly used sizes 3.50 in. × 17 in. front and 5.50, 5.75 or 6.00 in. × 17 in. rear. *Tyres:* Michelin. *Brakes:* two carbon AP Lockheed (272.5 mm) or AP Lockheed cast iron (320 mm) discs at front and a single carbon or iron at rear (210 mm); AP Lockheed aluminium calipers; AP Lockheed or Ferodo pads. *Plugs:* NGK or ND. *Gearbox and engine oil:* Motul.

Malcolm Bryan

Henk Keulemans

Top: **Jim Wood works on the front of Eddie Lawson's Rothmans Honda while Erv Kanemoto concentrates on the left-hand side. The obvious difference between the Honda and the other factory 500s is clear, with the single crankshaft showing the right-hand end which drives the ignition. The massive reinforcing of the main frame rails is obvious from the lengthy welds on the top of the frame tubes.**

This year's Cagiva *(above)* **was not a winner, despite frame and suspension changes during the year. The Italian factory had talked of having a single-crank engine ready for use in 1989. They tested fuel injection, though not at the Grands Prix, and there is again talk of a new single-crank engine for 1990. When Haslam and Magee tested the bike at Rijeka they described the engine as lacking power; Magee even suggested it had holes in the carburation.**

Randy Mamola

498 cc C589 Cagiva

Engine: 56 mm × 50.6 mm, water-cooled, four-cylinder two-stroke; crankcase reed-valve induction; five transfer and three exhaust ports, with electronically controlled cylindrical valve varying exhaust port height; one plain piston ring; roller big ends and needle roller small ends; two pressed cranks, four roller bearings each; dry clutch with seven friction and eight steel plates, six springs. *Gearbox:* six-speed, alternative ratios for all gears; drum selection. *Carburettors:* 35 mm flat-slide Mikuni.

Frame: Cagiva twin-spar fabricated box-section aluminium, taper roller head bearings; box-section aluminium swing arm, needle roller bearings; lower end-linked rear suspension, one Ohlins unit, coil-spring plus nitrogen pressure, oil damping, adjustable; Ohlins forks, coil-springs, oil-damped, adjustable. *Wheels:* Marvic, commonly used sizes 3.50 in. × 17 in. front and 6.00 in. × 17 in. rear. *Tyres:* Michelin. *Brakes:* two AP Lockheed carbon discs at front (272.5 mm) and a single aluminium (190 mm) at rear; AP Lockheed aluminium calipers front and Brembo rear; AP Lockheed and Brembo pads. *Plugs:* NGK. *Gearbox and engine oil:* Agip.

Eddie Lawson

494.6 cc NSR 500 Honda

Engine: 54 mm × 54 mm, water-cooled, four-cylinder two-stroke; crankcase reed-valve induction; five transfer ports and electronically controlled variable-height exhaust port; one piston ring; needle roller big ends and needle roller small ends; one pressed crank, five roller bearings; dry clutch with seven friction and seven steel plates, six springs. *Gearbox:* six-speed, alternative ratios for all gears; drum selection. *Carburettors:* 35 mm cylindrical-slide Keihin with electronic position measurement feeding exhaust valve control system.

Frame: Honda twin-spar rectangular-section aluminium tube, taper roller head bearings; triangulated aluminium swing arm, needle roller bearings; 'Pro-Link' rear suspension, single Showa unit, coil-spring plus nitrogen pressure, adjustable damping; Showa forks, coil-springs, oil-damped, adjustable, mechanical-hydraulic anti-dive. *Wheels:* Honda cast magnesium, commonly used sizes 3.75 in. × 16 in. and 3.50 in. × 17 in. front and 5.50, 5.75, 6.00, 6.125 and 6.25 in. × 17 in. rear. *Tyres:* Michelin. *Brakes:* two AP Lockheed carbon discs (270 or 290 mm) or Nissin or AP Lockheed steel discs (332 or 310 mm) at front and a single Honda carbon fibre at rear (190 mm); AP Lockheed or Nissin calipers; AP Lockheed, Ferodo or Nissin pads. *Plugs:* NGK 9.5. *Gearbox and engine oil:* Shell.

SHOEI
Rothmans
1
NSR
MICHELIN
EDDIE

HONDA
Shell
MICHELIN
NGK
RK
AFAM

Henk Keulemans

Peter Clifford

Sito Pons

247.3 cc RS250R Honda

Engine: 54 mm × 54.5 mm, water-cooled, twin-cylinder two-stroke; reed-valve crankcase; electrically controlled variable height exhaust port; one plain piston ring; needle roller big and small ends; one pressed crank, three ball bearings; dry clutch with five springs. *Gearbox:* six-speed, five possible ratios for first four gears, six for fifth and seven for sixth; drum selection. *Carburettors:* two 38 mm Keihin (the slide has flat sides with rounded ends).

Frame: aluminium twin extruded spars with machined sections in addition, caged ball head bearings; box-section aluminium swing arm, needle roller bearings; 'Pro-Link' rear suspension, one White Power unit, coil-spring, oil damping, adjustable; Showa forks, coil-springs, oil-damped, adjustable. *Wheels:* Marchesini cast magnesium, commonly used sizes 3.25 in. × 17 in. front and 5.00 in. × 17 in. rear. *Tyres:* Michelin. *Brakes:* twin Nissin steel discs at front (275 mm, 280 mm from mid-season) and a single Nissin steel at rear (180 mm); Nissin aluminium calipers; Nissin pads. *Plugs:* NGK 10.5. *Gearbox and engine oil:* Campsa.

(Antonio Cobas was the suspension consultant for the Pons team and designed a revised rear suspension linkage after pre-season tests; Pons used this from the start of the year. He also asked HRC for a special frame with a variable head angle, plus or minus 1.5 degrees from standard. This arrived in time for the Italian Grand Prix at Misano. Pons also had a special rear brake arm fitted.)

Luca Cadalora

249 cc YZR250 Yamaha

Engine: 56 mm × 50.6 mm, water-cooled, twin-cylinder two-stroke; crankcase reed-valve induction; five transfer and three exhaust ports; one plain piston ring; roller big ends and needle roller small ends; one pressed crank, three roller bearings; dry clutch with five friction and six steel plates, six springs. *Gearbox:* six-speed, alternative ratios for all gears; drum selection. *Carburettors:* 38 or 39 mm flat-slide Mikuni.

Frame: Yamaha fabricated box-section twin-spar aluminium, taper roller head bearings; box-section aluminium swing arm, needle roller bearings; lower end-linked rear suspension, one Ohlins unit, coil-spring plus nitrogen pressure, oil damping, adjustable; Yamaha forks, coil-springs, oil-damped, adjustable. *Wheels:* Marchesini, commonly used sizes 3.75 in. × 17 in. front and 5.00 in. × 17 in. rear. *Tyres:* Michelin. *Brakes:* two Yamaha steel discs at front (290 mm) and a single Yamaha at rear (220 mm); Lockheed aluminium calipers front, Nissin rear; Ferodo and Nissin pads. *Plugs:* NGK. *Gearbox and engine oil:* Castrol.

Peter Clifford

Didier de Radiguès
248.6 cc Aprilia

Engine: 54 mm × 54.5 mm, water-cooled, twin-cylinder two-stroke; five transfer and three exhaust ports, vacuum-operated exhaust valve; one plain piston ring; needle roller big ends and small ends; two pressed cranks, two roller bearings; dry clutch with five friction and six steel plates, six springs. *Gearbox:* six-speed, nine possible ratios for first, eight for second, four for third, three for fourth, and five for fifth and sixth; drum selection. *Carburettors:* 38 mm flat-slide Dell' Orto.
Frame: Aprilia fabricated aluminium box-section twin-spar, taper roller head bearings with spherical seating; aluminium swing arm, roller bearings; 'Pro-Link'-style rear suspension, single Ohlins unit, coil-spring, oil damping, adjustable for both compression and rebound; Ohlins OUT forks, coil-springs, oil-damped, adjustable. *Wheels:* Technomagnesio, commonly used sizes 3.5 in. × 17 in. front and 5.00 in. × 17 in. rear. *Tyres:* Michelin. *Brakes:* two Brembo cast steel discs at front (280 mm) and a single aluminium at rear (180 mm); Brembo aluminium calipers; Ferodo pads. *Plugs:* NGK. *Gearbox and engine oil:* Mobil.

Martin Wimmer
249.6 cc Aprilia

Engine: 54 mm × 54.5 mm, water-cooled, twin-cylinder two-stroke; five transfer and three exhaust ports, vacuum operated exhaust valve; one plain piston ring; needle roller big ends and small ends; two pressed cranks, two roller bearings; dry clutch with five friction and six steel plates, six springs. *Gearbox:* six-speed, nine possible ratios for first, eight for second, four for third, three for fourth and five for fifth and sixth; drum selection. *Carburettors:* 35 mm × 42 mm oval flat-slide Dell 'Orto.
Frame: Aprilia fabricated box-section twin-spar aluminium; taper roller head bearings with spherical seating; aluminium swing arm, roller bearings; 'Pro-Link'-style rear suspension, single Ohlins unit, coil-spring, oil damping, adjustable for both compression and rebound; Ohlins OUT forks, coil-springs, oil-damped, adjustable. *Wheels:* Bogl, commonly used sizes 3.5 in. × 17 in. front and 4.50 or 5.00 in. × 17 in. rear. *Tyres:* Michelin. *Brakes:* two Bogl cast iron discs at front (300 mm) and a single aluminium at rear (220 mm); Brembo aluminium calipers; Ferodo pads. *Plugs:* NGK. *Gearbox and engine oil:* Castrol.

The all-powerful NSR250 Honda *(above left)* **had revised frame and suspension for 1989 and that took away the Yamaha's last advantage. This is Reinhold Roth's HB Honda, identical to that used by Pons except for suspension and steering geometry modifications instigated by Antonio Cobas.**

The single-crank Yamaha 250 engine *(left)* **should have been a fitting challenger for the Honda. Unusually for Yamaha the engine proved unreliable as well as slow and, even though there was very little difference, the frame was not as good as the previous year's.**

Above: **The fascinating-looking factory 250 Yamaha of Toshihiko Honma. The aluminium frame featured a thin coating of carbon fibre to aid rigidity. The geometry was standard and this bike, used at the French and British rounds, was not fitted with the electronic fuel injection that Honma had been testing in Japan.**

Far left: **The cylinders from Honma's factory Yamaha, removed during practice in France. Looking up the bore of the nearest cylinder shows the exhaust port on the far side with the guillotine raised. The transfer ports can also be seen on the lower side of the bore.**

Didier de Radiguès rarely had kind words to say about his Aprilia *(right)*. **It handled well enough but it was often slow and rarely reliable. The twin-spar frame was much as it had been in 1988 but the engine was probably slower. The exhaust valve system can be seen protruding up from the rear cylinder, just in front of the seat. The valve is actuated by a vacuum operating against a spring.**

new titles from HAZLETON PUBLISHING *1989-90*

AUTOCOURSE 1989-90

Edited once again by Alan Henry, this thirty-ninth edition of AUTOCOURSE has more pages than ever before and is illustrated throughout in superb full colour.
Detailed Formula 1 race reports combine with feature articles by the sport's leading writers to provide an unrivalled record of the 1989 World Championship, complete with detailed results and statistics.
Also included are Formula 3, Formula 3000, sports car racing and racing in the USA – all vividly recorded and graphically illustrated.

288 pages, over 200 colour photographs
ISBN: 0-905138-62-7
Price: £21.95

MOTOCOURSE 1989-90

For the first time, MOTOCOURSE is illustrated exclusively in full colour throughout its 208 pages. Peter Clifford's penetrating race reports are enhanced by a stunning array of action shots by top photographer Malcolm Bryan. Feature articles include technical developments, personalities and profiles of the year's top ten riders.
MOTOCOURSE also covers the Isle of Man TT, racing in North America, endurance racing and the Superbike, European and National Championships. Detailed results listings add the finishing touch to the year's most complete and lavish motor cycle yearbook.

208 pages, 160 colour photographs
ISBN: 0-905138-63-5
Price: £21.95

RALLYCOURSE 1989-90

Now in its eighth year, RALLYCOURSE provides the enthusiast with a combination of incisive reports and round-by-round results and statistics with maps and stage-times – all illustrated in full colour by the brilliant camera-work of Reinhard Klein.
Feature articles on personalities and developments, colour-illustrated coverage of the British and National Championships and a report on the European Championship complete a top-quality presentation.

176 pages, 140 colour photographs
ISBN: 0-905138-64-3
Price: £21.95

MARCH
THE GRAND PRIX AND INDY CARS

Alan Henry

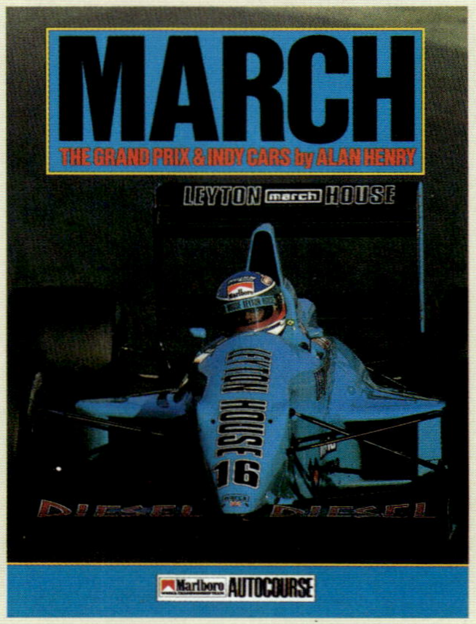

The latest addition to the AUTOCOURSE MARQUE HISTORY series, produced in a larger format to increase the impact of the illustrations. Author Alan Henry has followed the fortunes of the March organisation ever since its inception twenty years ago. Technical developments, races, drivers and the people behind the scenes are all recorded, including a full account of the company's Indy involvement during the 1980s.

256 pages
136 mono plus 34 colour photographs
ISBN: 0-905138-65-1
Price: £19.95

FERRARI
THE GRAND PRIX CARS

Alan Henry

Second edition, updated to take the Ferrari story to the close of the 1988 season. Both in success and failure, Ferrari is always in the forefront of public attention, its name synonymous with drama, controversy and achievement. Here its eventful history is revealed in depth.

352 pages
160 mono plus 32 colour photographs
ISBN: 0-905138-61-9
Price: £17.95

For a complete, fully illustrated catalogue of our books, please write to: HAZLETON PUBLISHING, 3 RICHMOND HILL, RICHMOND SURREY TW10 6RE. Or ask at your local bookshop.

AUTOCOURSE DRIVER PROFILE SERIES

A series of strongly illustrated books on great Formula 1 drivers of past and present. Each volume provides a career history and assessment of its subject driver by a leading motor sport writer, plus results listings and an array of colour and mono plates.

112 pages, 84 mono photos plus 16 pages colour

AUTOCOURSE DRIVER PROFILE 1

NIGEL MANSELL

David Tremayne

ISBN: 0-905138-67-8

Price: £11.95

AUTOCOURSE DRIVER PROFILE 2

NIKI LAUDA

Alan Henry

ISBN 0-905138-68-6

Price: £11.95

AUTOCOURSE DRIVER PROFILE 3

ALAIN PROST

Nigel Roebuck

ISBN: 0-905138-69-4

Price: £11.95

AUTOCOURSE DRIVER PROFILE 4

GILLES VILLENEUVE

Nigel Roebuck

ISBN 0-905138-70-8

Price: £11.95

GRAND PRIX RIDERS

Mick Woollett and Peter Clifford

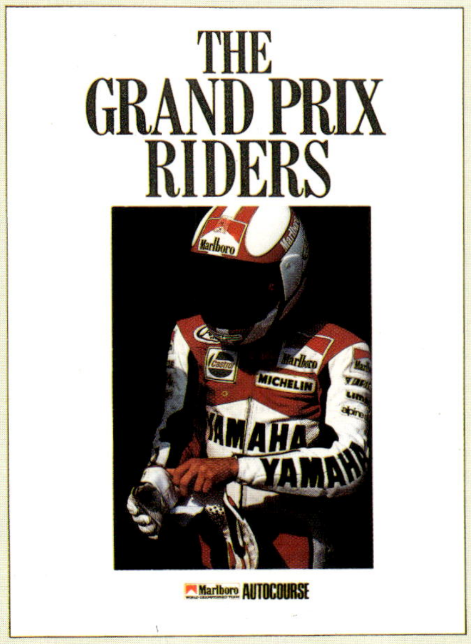

A unique record of the greatest motor cycle racers of the last forty years. Decade by decade, these legendary figures are portrayed in evocative photographs, with their achievements recorded and assessed. Completing this exciting book is a full-colour section on the greatest of the greats.

160 pages
130 mono plus 24 colour photos
ISBN: 0-905138-66-X
Price: £14.95 Hardback

TT

THE MOTOCOURSE HISTORY OF THE ISLE OF MAN TOURIST TROPHY RACES 1907-1989

Nick Harris

This high-quality presentation from the MOTOCOURSE stable captures not only the history but also the unique atmosphere and excitement of the Isle of Man TT. Nick Harris's account of each year's races is complemented by riders' comments, contemporary press reports and a wealth of striking photographs, with a separate detailed results section to complete a truly comprehensive record.

288 pages
160 mono photographs plus 32 pages colour
ISBN: 0-905138-71-6
Price: £19.55

Right: **Even 125 frames are now massively strong, demonstrating that good handling is considered as important as power and weight. Honda expected to win the championship once Derbi had hit such major problems that Martinez was out of the running. Unfortunately Spaan's machine broke down in France.**

Photos: Peter Clifford

Criville's Cobas, showing clearly the nice straight run of the main frame spars from steering head to swing arm pivot. The white plastic mounted behind the carburettor prevents hot air from around the exhaust pipe getting into the carb and stops radiation from the pipe raising the temperature of the carb body itself. The air intake in the fairing feeds an airbox that makes sure that cool fresh air is available to the carburettor. This is now almost universal on all Grand Prix machines, though airbox design is still far from an exact science; Ron Haslam insisted that the top of his Suzuki's airbox be cut off, as he could not cope with the carburation if it remained closed.

Alex Criville
124 cc Cobas

Engine: Rotax 54 mm × 54.5 mm, water-cooled, single-cylinder two-stroke; disc-valve induction; six transfer and three exhaust ports, with electronically controlled port-height exhaust valve; one plain piston ring; needle roller big and small ends; one pressed crank, two ball bearings; dry clutch with five friction and five steel plates, six springs. *Gearbox:* six-speed, seven possible ratios for first, second and third gears, three for fourth, fifth and sixth; drum selection. *Carburettors:* 39 mm flat-slide Dell' Orto.
Frame: Cobas twin-spar fabricated aluminium, taper roller head bearings; aluminium triangulated swing arm, taper roller bearings; progressive-link rear suspension, one White Power unit, coil-spring, oil damping, adjustable; White Power OUT forks, coil-springs, oil-damped, adjustable. *Wheels:* Marchesini, commonly used sizes 2.25 in. × 17 in. front and 2.75 in. × 17 in. rear. *Tyres:* Michelin. *Brakes:* two Zanzani cast steel discs at front (280 mm) and a single Zanzani aluminium disc at rear (180 mm); Brembo aluminium four-piston calipers; Ferodo pads. *Plugs:* NGK. *Gearbox and engine oil:* Repsol.

Hans Spaan
124 cc RS125R Honda

Engine: 54 mm × 54.5 mm, water-cooled, single-cylinder two-stroke; reed-valve induction; five transfer and a single bridged exhaust port; one plain piston ring; needle roller big ends and small ends; one pressed crank, two ball bearings; dry clutch with six friction and five steel plates, five springs. *Gearbox:* six-speed, four possible ratios for first and second, three for third, fourth and fifth, and two for sixth; drum selection. *Carburettor:* 39.5 mm cylindrical-slide Keihin.
Frame: Honda twin extruded aluminium spars, rectangular in section, taper roller head bearings; aluminium rectangular-section triangulated swing arm, plain bearings; cantilever rear suspension, single Ohlins unit; coil-spring, oil damping, adjustable for compression and rebound; Showa forks, coil-springs, oil-damped, adjustable for both compression and rebound. *Wheels:* Technomagnesio, commonly used sizes 2.15 in. × 17 in. front and 3.00 in. × 17 in. rear. *Tyres:* Dunlop. *Brakes:* one Brembo steel disc at front (280 mm) and a single Honda steel at rear (190 mm); Nissin aluminium calipers; Honda pads. *Plugs:* ND. *Gearbox and engine oil:* Shell.

Jorge Martinez
124.5 cc Derbi

Engine: 56 mm × 50.6 mm, water-cooled, single-cylinder two-stroke; disc-valve induction; six transfer ports and one exhaust port; one plain piston ring; needle roller big and small ends; one pressed crank, two roller bearings; dry clutch with seven friction and seven steel plates, seven springs. *Gearbox:* six-speed, three possible ratios for all gears; drum selection. *Carburettors:* 38 mm cylindrical-slide Dell'Orto.
Frame: Derbi truss spine fabricated from straight alloy steel tubes, taper roller head bearings; steel rectangular-section swing arm, roller bearings; rocker arm rear suspension, single White Power unit, coil-spring, oil damping, adjustable for compression and rebound; White Power forks, coil-springs, oil-damped, adjustable for both compression and rebound. *Wheels:* PVM, commonly used sizes 2.25 in. × 17 in. front and 2.75 in. × 17 in. rear. *Tyres:* Michelin. *Brakes:* two Brembo steel discs at front (240 mm) and a single Brembo steel at rear (200 mm); Brembo aluminium calipers; Brembo pads. *Plugs:* Champion. *Gearbox and engine oil:* Castrol.

Peter Öttl's 80 cc Krauser *(below)* **is the official factory machine; Dörflinger claimed that the young German got the better and more powerful engine parts. With the demise of the class the elegant monocoques may be seen no more, as Louis Christen's prototype 125 frame is tubular.**

Bottom: **The factory Derbi, with experimental aluminium monocoque frame. They got it to work so well that Herreros used it for the last race in Czechoslovakia and won the championship.**

Henk Keulemans

Malcolm Bryan

Fausto Gresini
124 cc Aprilia
Engine: Rotax 54 mm × 54.5 mm, water-cooled, single-cylinder two-stroke; disc-valve induction; six transfer and three exhaust ports; one plain piston ring; needle roller big and small ends; one pressed crank, two ball bearings; dry clutch with five friction and five steel plates, six springs. *Gearbox:* six-speed, seven possible ratios for first, second and third gears, three for fourth, fifth and sixth; drum selection. *Carburettors:* 38 mm cylindrical-slide Dell 'Orto.
Frame: Aprilia fabricated aluminium twin-spar, taper roller head bearings; aluminium rectangular-section swing arm, taper roller bearings; rocker arm rear suspension, one Ohlins unit; coil-spring, oil damping, adjustable; White Power forks, coil-springs, oil-damped, adjustable. *Wheels:* Technomagnesio, commonly used sizes 2.75 in. × 17 in. front and 3.25 in. × 17 in. rear. *Tyres:* Michelin. *Brakes:* two Brembo cast steel discs at front (230 mm) and a single Brembo steel disc at rear (210 mm); Brembo aluminium calipers; Brembo pads. *Plugs:* NGK. *Gearbox and engine oil:* Mobil.

Domenico Brigaglia
124.5 cc Garelli
Engine: 56 mm × 50.6 mm, water-cooled, single-cylinder two-stroke; disc-valve induction; six transfer and three exhaust ports; one plain piston ring; needle roller big and small ends; one pressed crank, two roller bearings; dry clutch with six friction and five steel plates, five springs. *Gearbox:* six-speed, three possible ratios for each gear; drum selection. *Carburettor:* 38 mm cylindrical-slide Dell 'Orto.
Frame: Sheet aluminium monocoque, taper roller head bearings; aluminium box-section swing arm, taper roller bearings; single vertical shock, no linkage, rear suspension White Power, coil-springs, oil damping, adjustable; White Power forks, coil-springs, oil-damped, adjustable. *Wheels:* Technomagnesio, commonly used sizes 2.25 in. × 17 in. front and 2.50 in. × 17 in. rear. *Tyres:* Michelin. *Brakes:* two Freni Discacciati cast iron discs at front (240 mm) and a single Zanzani aluminium at rear (180 mm); Brembo aluminium calipers; Brembo pads. *Plugs:* Champion. *Gearbox and engine oil:* Agip.

Stefan Dörflinger
79.6 cc Krauser
Engine: 49 mm × 42.5 mm, water-cooled, single-cylinder two-stroke; disc-valve induction; six transfer and three exhaust ports; one plain piston ring; needle roller big and small ends; pressed cranks, one ball and one roller bearing; dry clutch with five friction and six steel plates, six springs. *Gearbox:* six-speed, three or four possible ratios for each gear; drum selection. *Carburettors:* 38 mm flat-slide Keihin.
Frame: LCR sheet aluminium monocoque, taper roller head bearings; chrome moly box-section swing arm, needle roller bearings; rocker arm rear suspension, single Ohlins unit; coil-spring, oil damping, adjustable; Ceriani forks, coil-springs, oil-damped, adjustable for compression and rebound. *Wheels:* Marvic, commonly used sizes 1.85 in. × 16 in. front and 1.85 in. × 18 in. or 2.15 in. × 17 in. rear. *Tyres:* Michelin. *Brakes:* one Bogl and Braun cast iron disc at front (220 mm) and a single Zanzani aluminium at rear (180 mm); Brembo aluminium calipers; Mozzi Motor pads. *Plugs:* NGK 10.5. *Gearbox and engine oil:* Castrol.

(Peter Öttl's Krauser is similar in most respects but has cantilever rear suspension.)

Manuel Herreros
79.6 cc Derbi
Engine: 48 mm × 44 mm, water-cooled, single-cylinder two-stroke; disc-valve induction; four transfer ports and one exhaust port; one plain piston ring; needle roller big and small end; pressed crank, two ball bearings each; dry clutch with four friction and five aluminium plates, four springs. *Gearbox:* six-speed, four possible ratios for first and sixth gears; drum selection. *Carburettors:* 34 mm cylindrical-slide Dell 'Orto.
Frame: Derbi truss spine fabricated from straight alloy steel tubes, taper roller head bearings; chrome moly box-section swing arm, needle roller bearings; con rod and rocker arm rear suspension, single White Power unit, coil-springs, oil damping, adjustable; White Power forks, coil-springs, oil-damped, non-adjustable. *Wheels:* ADM, commonly used sizes 1.85 in. × 16 in. front and 2.00 in. × 17 in. rear. *Tyres:* Michelin. *Brakes:* two Brembo steel discs at front (220 mm) and a single aluminium at rear (200 mm); Brembo aluminium calipers; Brembo pads. *Plugs:* Champion. *Gearbox and engine oil:* Castrol.

John McKenzie

Left: **Peter 'Shep' Wetters looks for his lunch in the back of the Webster/Hewitt outfit, while Mick Webster tapes the throttles open and the clutch out.**

Egbert Streuer's fuel injection engine *(below)* **uses a modified set of Yamaha crankcases with Honda cylinders grafted on the top. The fuel injection system uses a hot wire in the induction system, to measure the flow of incoming air.**

Below left: **One of Rolf Biland's Krauser engines, sitting in its jig. The fuel pump is hanging loose and that reveals the left-hand end of the cross-shaft which takes the drive from the centre of the crank across to the right-hand side of the engine to drive the crank.**

Harald Bartol *(bottom left)* **sits and thinks about the question of producing enough power from Biland's engine to get him back on terms with Webster. The outfit was never slow, but the lap times that Biland could produce in practice were rarely repeated in the race: the Swiss ace often hit tyre problems trying to run at that speed.**

Henk Keulemans

Steve Webster

498 cc LCR-Krauser

Engine: 56 mm × 50.6 mm, water-cooled, four-cylinder two-stroke; crankcase reed-valve induction; six transfer and three exhaust ports; single plain piston ring; roller big ends and needle roller small ends; two pressed cranks, four needle roller bearings each; dry clutch with seven friction and seven steel plates, six springs. *Gearbox:* six-speed, three possible ratios for first four gears and two for sixth; drum selection. *Carburettors:* 38 mm flat-slide Mikuni.

Chassis: sheet aluminium monocoque, riveted and Araldited; wishbone rear suspension, White Power unit, coil-spring, oil damping, adjustable; parallelogram front suspension, White Power unit, coil-spring, oil-damping, adjustable; no sidecar suspension. *Wheels:* Ronal, 13 in. diameter, commonly used widths 8.2 in. front, 10 in. rear and 9 in. sidecar. *Tyres:* Avon. *Brakes:* cast iron all round, ventilated 254 mm front and rear, 240 mm side; Lockheed calipers; Ferodo pads. *Plugs:* NGK B10EV. *Gearbox and engine oil:* Silkolene.

(Webster, Streuer and Michel swapped from Hummel to Yamaha cylinders for 1989. The Hummel cylinders proved on occasion to be porous. Webster improved the cooling of his engine by machining a water gallery through the cylinder base from front to back so the previously required plumbing over the top of the engine could be avoided. The crankcases are air cooled and there is an oil-cooler for the gearbox.)

Rolf Biland

499 cc LCR-Krauser

Engine: 54 mm × 54.5 mm, water-cooled, four-cylinder two-stroke; crankcase reed-valve induction; seven transfer and three exhaust ports; single plain piston ring; roller big ends and needle roller small ends; two pressed cranks, four needle roller bearings each; dry clutch with seven friction and seven steel plates, six springs. *Gearbox:* six-speed, three possible ratios for first three gears; drum selection. *Carburettors:* 38 mm flat-slide Dell 'Orto.

Chassis: LCR sheet aluminium monocoque, riveted and Araldited, adjustable; wishbone rear suspension, Ohlins unit, coil-spring, oil damping, adjustable; parallelogram front suspension, Ohlins unit, coil-spring, oil damping, adjustable; no sidecar suspension. *Wheels:* BBS, 14 in. diameter, commonly used widths 9 in. front, 11 or 12 in. rear and 10 in. sidecar. *Tyres:* Yokohama. *Brakes:* cast iron all round, ventilated 290 mm front, 240 mm rear and side; Lockheed calipers; Mintex pads. *Plugs:* NGK B10EGV. *Gearbox and engine oil:* Wintershall.

Peter Clifford

John McKenzie

Alain Michel

498 cc LCR-Krauser

Engine: 56 mm × 50.6 mm, water-cooled, four-cylinder two-stroke; crankcase reed-valve induction; six transfer and three exhaust ports; single plain piston ring; roller big ends and needle roller small ends; two pressed cranks, four needle roller bearings each; dry clutch with seven friction and seven steel plates, six springs. *Gearbox:* six-speed, four possible ratios for first three gears and two for sixth; drum selection. *Carburettors:* 38 mm flat-slide Dell'Orto.

Chassis: LCR sheet aluminium monocoque, riveted and Araldited, adjustable; wishbone rear suspension, White Power unit, coil-spring, oil damping, adjustable; parallelogram front suspension, White Power unit, coil-spring, oil damping, adjustable; no sidecar suspension. *Wheels:* Ronal, 13 in. diameter, commonly used widths 9 in. front, 11 or 12 in. rear and 10 in. sidecar. *Tyres:* Avon. *Brakes:* cast iron all round, ventilated 254 mm front and rear, 240 mm side; Lockheed calipers; Mintex pads. *Plugs:* Champion N82. *Gearbox and engine oil:* Elf.

Egbert Streuer

498 cc LCR-Yamaha

Engine: 56 mm × 50.6 mm, water-cooled, four-cylinder two-stroke; crankcase reed-valve induction; six transfer and three exhaust ports; single plain piston ring; roller big ends and needle roller small ends; two pressed cranks, four needle roller bearings each; dry clutch with eight friction and eight steel plates, six springs. *Gearbox:* six-speed, three possible ratios for first three gears; drum selection. *Carburettors:* 38 mm cylindrical-slide Mikuni.

Chassis: LCR sheet aluminium monocoque, riveted and Araldited, adjustable; wishbone rear suspension, White Power unit, coil-spring, oil damping, adjustable; parallelogram front suspension, White Power unit, coil-spring, oil damping, adjustable; no sidecar suspension. *Wheels:* Ronal, 13 in. diameter, commonly used widths 9 in. front, 10 in. rear and sidecar. *Tyres:* Yokohama. *Brakes:* cast iron all round, ventilated 254 mm front, 240 mm rear and side; Lockheed calipers and pads. *Plugs:* NGK. *Gearbox and engine oil:* Valvoline.

(Streuer is also developing a new engine with 54 mm × 54.5 mm bore and stroke with six transfer ports, one bridged into two making seven. This engine has fuel injection.)

THE REVOLUTION

STARTS HERE...

Belstaff bring you a whole range of clothing to suit both the traditional and style conscious biker. Put together in exciting combinations of wax cotton, leather and kevlar, to give pure comfort and maximum protection.

Don't just take our word for it, call in at any of our dealers and check out the Belstaff Revolution for yourself.

NOVUS BLOUSON · Fashion meets practicality ♦ Wadded lining ♦ Leather trim and superb fit complete its stunning good looks.

AMBO · Breathable Aquatex coating ♦ Washable ♦ Detachable liner ♦ Waterproof ♦ Drawstring waist.

CORIUM · Traditional favourite ♦ Superb quality of traditional wax ♦ Leather trim for extra style ♦ Quilted lining.

VIATOR · Classic Belstaff ♦ Drawstring waist ♦ Unbeatable Belflex material ♦ Quilted lining in natural fibres.

SOLARI · Perfect protection ♦ Outstanding resistance to water penetration ♦ High performance thermal wadding.

VERTEX · The ultimate biking suit ♦ Kevlar, leather, H D foam and strong poly cotton combine to give the ultimate in protection, fit and style.

BELSTAFF

BELSTAFF INTERNATIONAL LTD
Caroline Street, Longton,
Stoke-on-Trent ST3 1DD England.
Telephone: (0782) 599261.
Telex: 36500. Fax: (0782) 599065.

GRANDS PRIX
1989

Schwantz arrives inside Rainey at the chicane. The Suzuki was braking and turning so much better than the Yamaha that the Lucky Strike man could offer no antidote.

Malcolm Bryan

WORLD CHAMPIONSHIP · ROUND 1

JAPANESE GRAND PRIX

Each race has a special character and the 500 cc Japanese Grand Prix at Suzuka in 1989 will be remembered for the Schwantz–Rainey ballet. Their *pas de deux* was the most elegant display of skill you could hope to see. It wasn't a heavyweight contest slugged out between old bruisers, or a knife fight where the moves were sudden and violent, it was a piece of artistry that did not have to have a winner to be successful. It was unfortunate that someone had to lose at all and somehow apt that Rainey came second because of a silly error reading the lap counter rather than any lack of skill in machine control.

The pair had been limbering up for their dance-off for a long time. They were vying for the spotlight all through practice, and even before that when various pre-season times were compared, like the first tests at Phillip Island, it was obvious that something had to be settled as soon as the two appeared on stage together.

The fact that the two are old rivals added to the interest. They had first met racing superbikes in America. Then there had been a classic contest at the Anglo-American Match Races early in 1987 which was a brawl, no doubt about it, fairings and elbows clashing and harsh words being exchanged afterwards.

Now things have changed. Both are more experienced, their skills more refined. Superbikes are rough pieces of machinery, used to prove some sort of brutal superiority. The Grand Prix 500 elevates the sport of motor cycle racing to an art form and at Suzuka Rainey and Schwantz demonstrated that they have every right to lead the *corps de ballet*.

That the Grand Prix featured the pair centre stage at all was perhaps unexpected. Eddie Lawson's defection to the Rothmans Honda team monopolised the headlines during the close season and predictions for the coming season had concentrated more on the outcome of the Lawson–Gardner fight on equal machinery than on considering who else might feature in the championship struggle. There were good reasons for this, too, because only Gardner and Lawson had demonstrated the consistency required for a successful season-long campaign. True, both Rainey and Schwantz had won races in 88 and their skill was not in doubt, but neither had been a true championship threat.

The Pepsi Suzuki had not been competitive at some race tracks and while the Lucky Strike Yamaha had been it was let down on more than one occasion by the Dunlop tyres. Team manager Kenny Roberts was under a good deal of pressure to switch to the ubiquitous Michelins at the end of the season, not least from Rainey, who could see his efforts often being wasted because the Dunlops were not lasting the distance. Two flat front tyres at the Brazilian Grand Prix might have been the last straw, but Roberts decided to stand firm.

His reasoning was obvious. Dunlop should be able to get it right if they put the effort in and his prime reason for keeping away from Michelin was still valid: as a Michelin runner all you could hope for was to get as good as the others. With a different tyre company you might get better.

Dunlop responded to his continued confidence by making that effort and the close season saw the Lucky Strike Yamaha team of Rainey and Magee do more testing than perhaps anyone in the history of Grand Prix racing. It was not just the number of tyres that the team tested – they discovered a fundamental point early on that completely changed the effectiveness of the Dunlops. They had been committed to using 18-in. rear tyres, but as soon as they tried the new 17 in. they realised that they had been wasting their time with the larger diameter rims.

'The bike just seems to like the 17-in. tyres,' explained Roberts during practice at Suzuka. 'Last year we could have 50 different 18-in. rears with all different compounds and constructions but there wouldn't be half a second between them on the race track. None of them would be competitive for the race distance. We tried the 17 in. and suddenly we were there. It is hard to believe it could make so much difference. I tried it, so did Wayne and Kevin.

'It is the right size for the bike. Last year with the 18 in. it was easy to see what was wrong, our guys couldn't follow the same line as the bikes with Michelins. It didn't matter what compound we tried, it was no good. We got kind of lost last year but now we are back on track. I am not saying that the Dunlops are better than the Michelins but they are up there and with the 17s the compounds work and we hope they can go the whole race distance. That is the one thing we could not test. We had a lot of track time but we always ran out of daylight or weather, something would stop us doing a full race-distance test on the tyres we had sorted out.'

Tyres were not the only thing that the team had been testing during the winter. During practice at Suzuka they contined to make use of on-board recording equipment. The recorder is housed in a special tank and could track almost any factor of interest. At Suzuka it was being used to relate rpm to gas temperature in order to gain some idea of how combustion chamber temperature varies with engine speed.

Honda also moved a little further into the electronics field, though far behind their Formula One car commitment. They developed a refinement of their Honda Power Port system with an electronic sensor in the carburettor bank reading the throttle position so that the valve opening time could be better matched to engine requirements. Previously the valve was only opened according to engine revs; now both revs and throttle position are used.

Honda also had the chance to use the newly developed Showa outer upper tube forks. After the championship-winning success of the Ohlins forks on the Marlboro Yamaha the previous year no one could afford to ignore the stability advantages of this form of front suspension. Honda obviously intended to leave no stone unturned in trying to make last year's defeated NSR500 into a winner for 1989.

As part of the programme they cancelled Nissin's brake monopoly and tested the Lockheeds that are used almost universally by the Yamaha and Suzuki teams. Honda also did a great deal of

Malcolm Bryan

frame revision and, while changes were not that obvious to the casual observer, by altering design, wall thickness and material a much stiffer frame was built. Even a glance at the rear swing arm would show the changes. A truly massive swing arm would help rear wheel control if section has anything to do with stiffness.

While the factory took care to have a stronger team mechanically, the riders just about took care of themselves. Gardner was in the middle of a two-year contract and World Champion Eddie Lawson almost came on bended knee asking for a ride. Determined to leave the Marlboro Yamaha team he had approached Niall Mackenzie at Spa in July '88, asking him to have a word with Erv Kanemoto about the possibility of riding for Honda.

It was a well-kept secret, particularly from those in the Marlboro team with whom Lawson had worked for six years. Gardner was also in the dark and until the news leaked and appeared in the newspapers in October those that it affected most knew nothing about it. Kel Carruthers was most personally hurt. The team engineer had been such an integral part of Lawson's success and had even flown back from a late season race in Japan sitting beside the World Champion, who said nothing. Carruthers read about the defection on getting home to San Diego and, making matters worse, several press stories reported that one of Lawson's reasons for leaving was disagreement with Kel's wife, Jan. Lawson never tried publicly to reverse this impression and that hurt the Carruthers family.

Racing can be a tough business, where financial, professional and personal considerations often pull in different directions. Personal rivalries between Lawson and Gardner were bound to be increased with both riding the same machines, but Grand Prix newcomer Mick Doohan might well benefit by avoiding the limelight.

The Marlboro Yamaha team were left without a potential World Champion and took the chance of signing Freddie Spencer and Niall Mackenzie. It was a real soap opera script move, because both Spencer and Mackenzie had been riding under Kanemoto's wing until Freddie announced his retirement because of persistent injuries prior to the start of the 1988 season.

After seeing Spencer as the arch enemy for so many years Carruthers was suddenly not only working with him but had to hope that he and Mackenzie could wreak revenge on Lawson. Spencer was unusually candid about their relationship at a Friday afternoon Marlboro press conference. 'I know that Kel used not to like me too much when we were in opposing teams but he is a professional and we both have a job to do. We are developing a good working relationship.'

250 cc

The way the 1989 250 race was run can be traced back to the 1988 event. Although last year's winner Toni Mang has now retired, John Kocinski's win was obviously greatly influenced by what he'd learnt chasing the German World Champion twelve months previously.

Kocinski started from pole position – not a Mang trait – but from that point his ride had all the controlled aggression of the much more experienced champion. The American was sixth on lap one, as Toshihiko Honma on his factory V-twin Yamaha led fellow-Japanese Tadayuki Okada on his NSR250 Honda, with the first Europeans being Jean-Philippe Ruggia, Carlos Cardus and Sito Pons.

Kocinski took his time and, with the confidence of knowing he could lap faster than anyone, picked off an average of one man a lap until he moved into first place on lap five. Second was Honma from Ruggia, Pons and Luca Cadalora on the Marlboro Yamaha. Kocinski had no trouble getting into the lead but he didn't break away at the front. Honma was latched onto the tail of the Yamaha, and the Europeans swapped places behind with neither Pons, Ruggia nor Cadalora able to make an impression on the leader. The pace was too hot for Cardus, who slipped astern, and Okada, who just about hung onto the tail of the leading five.

The next pack were having their own battle with more place-swapping for eighth between Juan Garriga, Jim Filice, Didier de Radiguès and Jacques Cornu. De Radiguès had complained about the handling of the Aprilia all week and eventually dropped from this group to finish fourteenth behind Masahiro Shimizu.

One of the quickest men on the track was Toshinobu Shiomori for, after qualifying twelfth on his V-twin Yamaha, the 28-year-old got a poor start and was down in twenty-sixth place on lap one. His race through the field was rapid and consistent and he finally passed Cardus on the last lap, having recorded a fastest lap over a second quicker than the Spaniard, who had very obvious handling problems with his Repsol Honda.

Almost as impressive was Helmut Bradl who, from a mediocre start from the middle of the grid, was then inspired by the heat of competition to fight his way through from twenty-first to twelfth, closing on Filice who lost his battle with Cornu and Garriga for ninth. It was a good ride from the American after a frustrating practice in which he could not get his '88 NSR to handle well.

Kocinski did not dominate completely, for Honma got back in front briefly on laps six and ten. The American always had an answer, though, and when Cadalora took the lead on lap 11 it was equally short lived. The real Mang touch came on the last two laps when Kocinski, after being completely unrattled by having the others looking over his shoulders for the entire distance, just upped the pace leaving Pons, who was by then the only one with any sort of chance, no opportunity to get alongside.

Cadalora had looked well placed but in the end had his hands full taking third from Honma. 'I had no trouble going at the same speed as the others in the leading group. At the end, when Sito and John started to go away, I tried to go with them but Honma passed me twice on the straight and then held me up in the corners. I

Malcolm Bryan

Left: **Pons, Cadalora and Ruggia.**

Carlos Lavado did not even have two wheels from a factory bike with which to start the year. He was only relieved of the role of spectator during practice by the loan of a machine for one race – hardly the way for a double World Champion to fall into retirement.

TECH
Arai
21

Once more Tadahiko Taira could not match his practice performance in the race. He fought hard from the start but some nasty slides made him realise that it was not to be his day.

Malcolm Bryan

lost touch and that was it. The bike worked well in the race but it just lacked a touch in top speed.'

Kocinski reported few problems once he got off the line. 'I didn't make a very good start, I think the clutch is too stiff. I guess I was about eighth into the first corner. I didn't want to wreck the tyres early on but when I got into the front I tried to go away. I couldn't make the break so I had to wait until the last few laps to get away. It would be great to do the whole season but I just have to think about one race at a time and I don't know how many I will be doing.'

World Champion Sito Pons had repeated his second place finishes of '87 and '88. 'So I am second again. I tried to win but in the last few laps John was going fast and I have to think about the championship more than just one race. John is not planning to do the full season but if he does I will try harder to win next time.'

125 cc

If you wanted elbows and knees locked in a barging battle with little subtlety, then the first Japanese 125 Grand Prix since 1967 had it by the sackful.

There was no battle for the lead, because Ezio Gianola was in front at the first corner and just split from the field. He had set a pole time over a second quicker than World Champion Aspar Martinez, whose Derbi was fourth on the grid behind the Hondas of Masayuki Hirose and Fuyuki Yamazaki.

Gianola was confident as he lined up the factory Honda. 'Last year whenever the Derbi was running well Martinez was fast in practice. I knew that if he was a second slower he was in trouble and not just playing games.'

The Italian had no thoughts about taking it easy, though, and shot away from the start in his usual aggressive manner – and the fact that he was soon out on his own did not cause him to slow down one jot. He kept tucked in from the first lap to lap 16, even though Martinez retired with a broken gear linkage on lap one.

Quickly into second was Hisashi Unemoto, while Yousuke Yamakawa briefly jumped to third on lap two but then crashed. That seemed to set the tone for some pretty wild riding. Hans Spaan used the speed of his Honda to blast past Unemoto down the back straight on lap five, but the Japanese refused to let him secure second. The pair touched on lap eight soon after Domenico Brigaglia changed line suddenly while battling for twenty-fifth and knocked Alex Bedford off the 7Up EMC.

The race got wilder still from lap 10 onwards, as Unemoto and Spaan were joined by Koji Takada and Hirose. Spaan's engine quit on lap 13 but the three-way battle for second went all the way to the line, with the Japanese riders rubbing paint off each other at every other corner. A couple of times the shoulder barging became quite blatant, as first one, then the other thought he was being allowed too little room.

It was probably their season of Grand Prix experience that helped Unemoto and Takada finish in front of Hirose, and it was definitely power that took Unemoto past Takada on the run-in to the line to secure second. The next European after Gianola was Fausto Gresini in eleventh on the Aprilia ahead of the Hondas of Robin Milton and Allan Scott.

500 cc

Wayne Rainey had led Grands Prix before, dominating the early stages of the Portuguese and British Grands Prix in 1988. These races ended very differently: the tyres had packed up in Jerez, but he'd walked away with the event at Donington.

This time his tyres lasted the distance but it was no walk-over. Though Rainey opened up an impressive lead Schwantz was soon giving chase. At first it had been Freddie Spencer in second place on the Marlboro Yamaha, with Taira barging past Schwantz in the middle of the 'S' section behind the pits on lap one. This was a move that did not impress the Texan. Chili slid off at the hairpin when he tried to outbrake Magee but ran out of room and touched the Yamaha.

The Suzuki was fast enough for Schwantz to ease past Taira on the straight during lap two. On the second time round Gardner went straight on at the hairpin and dropped from sixth to fourteenth. Spencer dropped to fourth while Schwantz secured second and set his sights on the by now distant Lucky Strike Yamaha.

Rainey looked to be wrecking the tyres, sliding both wheels on almost every corner. The 1988 Dunlops would have lasted about three laps of that abuse but, as the race wore on, it became obvious that the winter's work had been very fruitful. Rainey certainly was not slowing and while Schwantz had a clear road between him and the Yamaha the gap did not seem to be closing. The Texan later explained that he was probably trying too hard. 'For a long while I didn't seem to get any closer. I was trying but I kept making little mistakes and it took me just about half the race before I caught him.'

It did not take quite half the 22 laps for on lap 10 Schwantz made his move, outbraking Rainey up the inside on the approach to the chicane. He cut past on the right-hander but, as he picked the Suzuki up and tipped it into the left, Rainey made a move to retake him. It was a case of the racer in Rainey over-riding the tactician. There was insufficient room and he had to put the Yamaha up the kerb on the inside to avoid the Suzuki. The error in judgement lost Wayne valuable yards, but he soon made it up and used the Suzuki's slipstream to regain the lead.

Both men were riding their machines quite visibly on the ragged edge. It emerged that the Suzuki was more stable on the brakes for while Rainey was arriving at the corners, especially the chicane, with the rear wheel in the air, fighting to hold the Yamaha on line, Schwantz was able to slip past apparently making less effort.

Rainey was not about to let any such inadequacy force him to settle for second, though, and, pushing as deep into the corners as he dared, he

Malcolm Bryan

John Kocinski showed that he had learnt how to win a Grand Prix from Toni Mang and how to indicate his pleasure from Kevin Schwantz.

would force Schwantz onto a tight line going in so that the Suzuki ran wide on the way out. This gave his Yamaha the chance to accelerate back underneath, laying a wide black brushstroke of rubber on the tarmac.

And so it went on, to and fro, looking at each other down the straight, Rainey edging Schwantz on with a wave of the hand. Both bikes appeared evenly matched in acceleration and top speed. Neither rider could afford to give anything away so when the Yamaha slid a little more than usual, accelerating out of Degner curve, as Rainey tried to pull inside Schwantz, he kept the throttle open. When the rear tyre bit and the front wheel came up he kept accelerating – the wheel kept coming up, but he refused to back off, side by side with his arch rival, until they both had to make the right-hand approach to the chicane.

With neither man able to gain any decisive advantage it began to look as though it would all be decided on a rather desperate outbraking session into the chicane on the last lap. Schwantz would have the advantage there but Rainey would be ready for him and might just block his move.

But it never came to that, because Rainey misjudged the number of laps to go. Racing side by side with Schwantz so often down the start and finish straight he was having difficulty checking his pit board. He started to rely on the huge control tower sign read by the spectators, not realising that it only clicked over to the next lap *after* he'd passed – so at the crucial moment it was reading two laps to go as the leading pair flashed past to start their final circuit.

Schwantz knew that this lap was for the money and went past the Yamaha one more time, up the inside on the brakes at the end of the start and finish straight. He had done it twice before but this time held a tight line and denied Rainey the chance to get back underneath.

The Suzuki led all the way round the final lap but, accelerating out of Spoon curve onto the back straight, the rear Michelin let go and by the time Schwantz had it back in line Rainey was right on his tail. Later he said he would have passed had he realised the situation. At the end of the back straight Rainey did seem to look for a way past but the Yamaha got a little out of shape on the brakes and he tucked in behind.

Schwantz went for the inside at the chicane but Rainey was not close enough even to look at getting past and he must have had a dreadful sinking feeling when he saw the chequered flag waved in front of the Suzuki. Schwantz had won his second Japanese Grand Prix in a row and with the now traditional standing on the footrests and punching the air he let everyone know exactly how he felt about it.

'It was a great race,' said Schwantz. 'We were both pushing the bikes and tyres pretty hard. It was much tougher than last year. I think I only enjoyed it after I had crossed the line!'

Rainey did not whinge about missing the last lap warning. After getting over the disappointment of finishing second he said it was 'the funnest race I have ever had, going that speed and just passing him every time he passed me. Not thinking about what a good show we were putting on, just riding as fast as we could.'

The rest of the field were doing their best too, even though the centre of interest was up front. Spencer had looked good until he ran off the track on lap seven with a mysterious engine surge, the cause of which was never discovered. He struggled on to finish fourteenth.

Marlboro Yamaha team-mate Niall Mackenzie rode very well but fell foul of Wayne Gardner on the Rothmans Honda. The Australian was trying to fight his way forward and barged the Scotsman out of the way. Gardner said he was frustrated at the time it was taking him to get by. His reasoning did not impress Mackenzie.

Gardner was having trouble controlling the Honda. It ran off the track at the hairpin and then, after the ex-champion had fought his way back up to third, it tried to flick him in the biggest possible way through the 'S' section behind the pits. Gardner held onto the bars and landed on the tank, crushing one of his testicles. He was lucky to keep the bike clear of the barrier as he lost third to Lawson, and was fortunate later to avoid amputation of the very swollen and extremely painful testicle. He almost pulled into the pits but fought the pain for the last five laps, finishing fourth.

Lawson's ride was steady and consistent. He was twelfth on lap one but with fast, reserved riding moved forwards as others either made mistakes or proved too slow for the World Champion. He always intended to stay out of trouble, not trusting his injured wrist to cope with the kind of slides that Gardner was prepared for. It was the sort of performance one expects from a World Champion.

Fifth and ahead of Mackenzie was Kevin Magee on the Lucky Strike Yamaha. It was a perfect ride from him, playing himself into the season and avoiding a start to the year that would be anything like the way the previous one had ended.

Grand Prix of Japan, 26 March/statistics
Suzuka International Racing Course, 3.641-mile/5.859-km circuit

500 cc

22 laps, 80.102 miles/128.898 km

Place	Rider	Nat.	Machine	Laps	Time & speed	Practice time	Grid
1	Kevin Schwantz	USA	Suzuki	22	48m 48.374s 98.47 mph/ 158.473 km/h	2m 12.658s	3
2	Wayne Rainey	USA	Yamaha	22	48m 48.801s	2m 12.420s	2
3	Eddie Lawson	USA	Honda	22	49m 19.050s	2m 14.346s	10
4	Wayne Gardner	AUS	Honda	22	49m 23.567s	2m 12.988s	4
5	Kevin Magee	AUS	Yamaha	22	49m 24.798s	2m 13.251s	5
6	Niall Mackenzie	GB	Yamaha	22	49m 27.919s	2m 14.271s	8
7	Christian Sarron	F	Yamaha	22	49m 36.852s	2m 14.437s	11
8	Tadahiko Taira	J	Yamaha	22	49m 36.915s	2m 11.866s	1
9	Norihiko Fujiwara	J	Yamaha	22	49m 57.657s	2m 15.446s	16
10	Shinichi Itoh	J	Honda	22	49m 57.658s	2m 15.212s	12
11	Bubba Shobert	USA	Honda	22	50m 07.366s	2m 15.336s	14
12	Ron Haslam	GB	Suzuki	22	50m 12.257s	2m 15.330s	13
13	Shunji Yatsushiro	J	Honda	22	50m 14.052s	2m 16.156s	19
14	Freddie Spencer	USA	Yamaha	22	50m 14.383s	2m 14.311s	9
15	Kunio Machii	J	Yamaha	22	50m 17.857s	2m 15.431s	15
16	Randy Mamola	USA	Cagiva	22	50m 34.183s	2m 15.672s	17
17	Shinji Katayama	J	Yamaha	22	50m 34.619s	2m 18.194s	22
18	Dominique Sarron	F	Honda	22	51m 00.510s	2m 18.283s	23
19	Katsunori Shinozaki	J	Suzuki	21	49m 33.232s	2m 20.753s	26
20	Marco Gentile	CH	Fior	21	49m 55.199s	2m 21.058s	27
21	Keiji Kinoshita	J	Honda	21	50m 06.956s	2m 21.299s	28
22	Kenmei Matsumoto	J	Honda	20	48m 48.374s	2m 23.948s	30
23	Fernando Gonzalez	E	Honda	20	49m 28.332s	2m 28.357s	31
	Hikaru Miyagi	J	Honda	14	DNF	2m 18.038s	21
	Alessandro Valesi	I	Yamaha	8	DNF	2m 20.071s	24
	Michael Doohan	AUS	Honda	7	DNF	2m 13.989s	6
	Doug Polen	USA	Suzuki	5	DNF	2m 17.749s	20
	Norio Iobe	J	Honda	3	DNF	2m 20.181s	25
	Osamu Hiwatashi	J	Suzuki	3	DNF	2m 15.981s	18
	Pier Francesco Chili	I	Honda	0	DNF	2m 14.071s	7
	Simon Buckmaster	GB	Honda		DNS	2m 22.742s	29

Fastest lap: Schwantz, 2m 11.807s, 98.93 mph/159.22 km/h (record).
Previous record: Niall Mackenzie, GB (Honda), 2m 14.521s, 96.94 mph/156.009 km/h (1988).

World Championship: 1 Schwantz, 20; **2** Rainey, 17; **3** Lawson, 15; **4** Gardner, 13; **5** Magee, 11; **6** Mackenzie, 10; **7** Sarron, 9; **8** Taira, 8; **9** Fujiwara, 7; **10** Itoh, 6; **11** Shobert, 5; **12** Haslam, 4; **13** Yatsushiro, 3; **14** Spencer, 2; **15** Machii, 1.

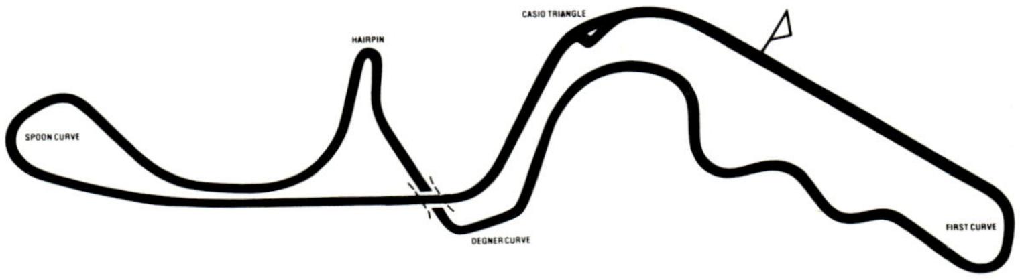

250 cc

20 laps, 72.82 miles/117.18 km

Place	Rider	Nat.	Machine	Laps	Time & speed	Practice time	Grid
1	John Kocinski	USA	Yamaha	20	46m 04.294s 94.83 mph/ 152.617 km/h	2m 17.042s	1
2	Alfonso Pons	E	Honda	20	46m 05.316s	2m 17.748s	4
3	Luca Cadalora	I	Yamaha	20	46m 11.067s	2m 17.787s	5
4	Toshihiko Honma	J	Yamaha	20	46m 11.068s	2m 17.187s	2
5	Jean-Philippe Ruggia	F	Yamaha	20	46m 18.428s	2m 18.430s	7
6	Tadayuki Okada	J	Honda	20	46m 27.292s	2m 17.723s	3
7	Toshinobu Shiomori	J	Yamaha	20	46m 39.931s	2m 19.294s	12
8	Carlos Cardus	E	Honda	20	46m 39.990s	2m 18.846s	9
9	Jacques Cornu	CH	Honda	20	46m 43.983s	2m 18.679s	8
10	Juan Garriga	E	Yamaha	20	46m 45.564s	2m 18.403s	6
11	Jim Filice	USA	Honda	20	46m 48.176s	2m 19.579s	15
12	Helmut Bradl	D	Honda	20	46m 50.786s	2m 20.600s	23
13	Masahiro Shimizu	J	Honda	20	46m 57.039s	2m 19.618s	17
14	Didier de Radiguès	B	Aprilia	20	46m 57.294s	2m 19.869s	20
15	Junya Arai	J	Honda	20	47m 07.463s	2m 19.523s	14
16	Masumitsu Taguchi	J	Honda	20	47m 07.464s	2m 19.772s	18
17	Paolo Casoli	I	Honda	20	47m 10.200s	2m 20.131s	21
18	Masaru Kobayashi	J	Honda	20	47m 11.351s	2m 19.487s	13
19	Loris Reggiani	I	Honda	20	47m 11.614s	2m 21.829s	29
20	Jun Suzuki	J	Honda	20	47m 11.806s	2m 19.159s	11
21	Martin Wimmer	D	Aprilia	20	47m 18.084s	2m 18.984s	10
22	Kyoji Namba	J	Yamaha	20	47m 19.616s	2m 19.608s	16
23	Jochen Schmid	D	Honda	20	47m 29.527s	2m 21.347s	26
24	Daniel Amatriain	E	Honda	20	47m 38.841s	2m 21.855s	30
25	Harald Eckl	D	Aprilia	20	48m 13.458s	2m 22.491s	35
26	Fabio Barchitta	RSM	Aprilia	20	48m 14.418s	2m 24.492s	41
27	August Auinger	A	Yamaha	20	48m 16.760s	2m 22.731s	37
28	Alberto Rota	I	Aprilia	20	48m 17.206s	2m 24.071s	40
29	Jean-François Baldé	F	Yamaha	20	48m 18.953s	2m 22.672s	36
30	Kevin Mitchell	GB	Yamaha	20	48m 30.227s	2m 21.661s	28
31	Gary Cowan	IRL	Assmex	19	46m 19.472s	2m 23.769s	39
	Luis Lavado	YV	Yamaha	19	DNF	2m 23.000s	38
	Ivan Palazzese	YV	Aprilia	12	DNF	2m 22.171s	32
	Andreas Preining	A	Aprilia	8	DNF	2m 22.261s	33
	Yoshinari Hori	J	Honda	7	DNF	2m 21.187s	25
	Patrick van den Goorbergh	NL	Assmex	7	DNF	2m 22.462s	34
	Alexandre Barros	BR	Yamaha	6	DNF	2m 21.587s	27
	Reinhold Roth	D	Honda	5	DNF	2m 19.783s	19
	Fausto Ricci	I	Aprilia	2	DNF	2m 21.926s	31
	Alberto Puig	E	Yamaha	1	DNF	2m 20.391s	22
	Manfred Herweh	D	Yamaha		DNS	2m 21.169s	24
	Jeff Sayle	AUS	Yamaha		DNQ	2m 24.509s	
	Carlos Lavado	YV	Honda		DNQ	2m 24.672s	
	Jean Foray	F	Yamaha		DNQ	2m 24.908s	
	Andy Leisner	USA	Honda		DNQ	2m 25.423s	
	Matt Blair	AUS	Yamaha		DNQ	2m 25.843s	
	Xavier Cardelus	AND	Cobas		DNQ	2m 26.167s	

Fastest lap: Kocinski, 2m 16.720s, 95.86 mph/154.273 km/h (record).
Previous record: Toshihiko Honma, J (Yamaha), 2m 17.95s, 95.00 mph/152.89 km/h (1988).

World Championship: 1 Kocinski, 20; **2** Pons, 17; **3** Cadalora, 15; **4** Honma, 13; **5** Ruggia, 11; **6** Okada, 10; **7** Shiomori, 9; **8** Cardus, 8; **9** Cornu, 7; **10** Garriga, 6; **11** Filice, 5; **12** Bradl, 4; **13** Shimizu, 3; **14** de Radiguès, 2; **15** Arai, 1.

Ezio Gianola and Koji Takada having fun on the rostrum.

125 cc

16 laps, 58.256 miles/93.744 km

Place	Rider	Nat.	Machine	Laps	Time & speed	Practice time	Grid
1	Ezio Gianola	I	Honda	16	39m 20.647s 88.838 mph/ 142.971 km/h	2m 26.981s	1
2	Hisashi Unemoto	J	Honda	16	39m 41.776s	2m 28.744s	5
3	Koji Takada	J	Honda	16	39m 41.916s	2m 29.468s	10
4	Masayuki Hirose	J	Honda	16	39m 42.474s	2m 27.317s	2
5	Kenichi Yoshida	J	Honda	16	39m 49.601s	2m 29.948s	14
6	Masato Shima	J	Honda	16	39m 57.103s	2m 30.226s	18
7	Yutaka Fujiwara	J	Honda	16	40m 10.236s	2m 29.883s	13
8	Kazuaki Yamashita	J	Honda	16	40m 10.476s	2m 29.964s	15
9	Shinichi Fujiyama	J	Honda	16	40m 15.091s	2m 28.998s	7
10	Kazuya Yamada	J	Honda	16	40m 18.756s	2m 29.724s	12
11	Fausto Gresini	I	Aprilia	16	40m 28.314s	2m 32.028s	23
12	Robin Milton	GB	Honda	16	40m 30.213s	2m 32.830s	28
13	Allan Scott	USA	Honda	16	40m 45.821s	2m 33.112s	30
14	Luis Reyes	E	Honda	16	40m 45.917s	2m 31.451s	19
15	Adolf Stadler	D	Honda	16	40m 46.183s	2m 33.623s	33
16	Johnny Wickström	SF	Honda	16	40m 47.799s	2m 34.407s	36
17	Robin Appleyard	GB	Honda	16	40m 49.887s	2m 32.930s	29
18	Corrado Catalano	I	Gazzaniga	16	40m 53.287s	2m 34.711s	38
19	Kazunari Wada	J	Honda	16	40m 53.288s	2m 31.686s	21
20	Heinz Lüthi	CH	Honda	16	40m 53.425s	2m 33.155s	31
21	Kris Galatowicz	GB	Honda	16	40m 54.866s	2m 33.790s	34
22	Lucio Pietroniro	B	Honda	16	41m 00.375s	2m 32.671s	25
23	Gerhard Waibel	D	Honda	16	41m 44.378s	2m 35.802s	41
24	Mike Leitner	A	Honda	16	41m 52.442s	2m 34.841s	40
	Kinya Wada	J	Honda	13	DNF	2m 29.272s	8
	Hans Spaan	NL	Honda	12	DNF	2m 29.679s	11
	Domenico Brigaglia	I	Garelli	12	DNF	2m 34.511s	37
	Julian Miralles	E	Derbi	10	DNF	2m 32.726s	27
	Toshiyuki Okamoto	J	Honda	9	DNF	2m 28.771s	6
	Stefan Dörflinger	CH	Aprilia	9	DNF	2m 34.061s	35
	Bruno Casanova	I	Aprilia	9	DNF	2m 32.013s	22
	Fuyuki Yamazaki	J	Honda	8	DNF	2m 27.432s	3
	Thierry Feuz	CH	Honda	8	DNF	2m 32.690s	26
	Stefan Prein	NL	Honda	8	DNF	2m 31.473s	20
	Herri Torrontegui	E	Honda	6	DNF	2m 30.151s	16
	Alex Bedford	GB	EMC	6	DNF	2m 33.200s	32
	Rafael Roses	E	Cobas	5	DNF	2m 30.194s	17
	Yousuke Yamakawa	J	Honda	1	DNF	2m 29.312s	9
	Jorge Martinez	E	Derbi	1	DNF	2m 28.039s	4
	Emilio Cuppini	I	Garelli		DNS	2m 32.574s	24
	Makoto Moroga	J	Honda		DNS	2m 34.762s	39
	Alex Criville	E	Cobas		DNQ	2m 38.419s	
	Valerio Vivarelli	I	Gazzaniga		DNQ	2m 40.017s	
	Juan Ramon Bolart	E	Honda		DNQ	2m 49.595s	

Fastest lap: Gianola, 2m 26.498s, 89.46 mph/143.975 km/h (record).
Previous record: Masayuki Hirose, J (Honda), 2m 28.08s, 88.505 mph/142.435 km/h.

World Championship: 1 Gianola, 20; **2** Unemoto, 17; **3** Takada, 15; **4** Hirose, 13; **5** Yoshisada, 11; **6** Shima, 10; **7** Fujiwara, 9; **8** Yamashita, 8; **9** Fujiyama, 7; **10** Yamada, 6; **11** Gresini, 5; **12** Milton, 4; **13** Scott, 3; **14** Reyes, 2; **15** Stadler, 1.

WORLD CHAMPIONSHIP · ROUND 2

AUSTRALIAN GRAND PRIX

A crowd of twenty thousand can have one voice. The packed grandstand along the start and finish line raised a single noise, generated by an anxious intake of breath. Gardner was leading Rainey, Sarron and Magee out of the final hairpin on the last lap. Into the first of the last, fast left-handers Gardner was still in front and the collective lungs filled further. They were bursting from the final gasp as Gardner held his advantage through the final curve, and almost drowned the scream of four 500s at 160 mph. The cheer of triumph as it became obvious that Gardner could not be passed created a lastingly special moment, and that memory will send a shiver down the spine for a long time to come.

It was a great privilege to be standing in the pit road then, having walked in from watching most of the race out on the circuit. There was no avoiding the feeling that you had more than witnessed, you had been part of something special. For it was, without doubt, one of the greatest Grands Prix of all time.

If that seems an absurdly expansive statement then consider the straightforward facts. The circuit itself is a great challenge, providing a perfect test of skill and close racing. The run-off provided is sufficient for reasonable safety despite the high-speed nature of many of the corners. Though many were temporary structures, almost all the facilities ranged between adequate and excellent. The organisation was very good, the TV coverage unmatched and the Australian nation's interest in the event greater than Italy ever showed in Uncini and Lucchinelli, or Britain in Barry Sheene. By comparison, no one in America knows who Kenny Roberts is.

After all the build-up to the 500 race, with media attention that was everything from macroscopic to microscopic, practice which provided all the headlines and dramatic pictures any newspaper or television editor could want, the race had to be an anti-climax. No way...no worries mate...it was a boomer.

The fact that there was an Australian Grand Prix at all was down to two people. Thousands played a part, with many putting in a great deal of work and making significant contributions. But if it had not been for Wayne Gardner there would have been no World Championship round, and if Bob Barnard had not been in charge it would have been merely mediocre.

Several of the top teams had used the completely rebuilt Phillip Island circuit for pre-season testing, and even in its raw state the track was impressive. Barnard is a road builder by profession and a motor sports enthusiast by inclination. He was instrumental in putting on the first Adelaide car Grands Prix which were such a success, and he brought the same singleness of purpose and perfectionism to Phillip Island. This was not to be a race track of compromise. He rebuilt the decaying circuit purely as a motor cycle track, making use of the interesting existing layout that Australian racers always said was the best in the country. Budgets are always limited and Barnard spent the money well, solely on the ribbon of tarmac and the pits. He knew from Adelaide that everything else could be erected for the one huge event he was planning and that lesser meetings would be happy to use the permanent portion of the facilities.

The track had been complimented months before the race, by the top teams who tested there before the start of the season. Kenny Roberts suggested that it was perhaps the best Grand Prix track in the world and no one disagreed.

The track is safe, in that it has ample run-off, but the nature of the circuit leaves little room for error. That was demonstrated in practice, as there was no shortage of falls – and there was plenty of publicity as both Gardner and Lawson crashed, though neither could be blamed for the accidents.

Lawson came to grief on Friday afternoon when Kevin Magee's Yamaha seized going onto the Bass straight. The straight is actually a high-speed curve and Magee's Yamaha stood itself up as he pulled in the clutch. Lawson had committed himself to ride round the outside of the Yamaha as it slowed initially, and when the bike picked itself up the Honda hit its rear right-hand side. Magee maintained control but Lawson shot off the track at high speed, feet down, trying to slow on the grass. There is a good deal of run-off there but the World Champion was travelling at such speed that he almost ran out of it before falling. Luckily he was uninjured.

The almost continuously curving track is a great test of rider skill but it makes passing the unpredictable rider difficult, as Gardner found out when looking for a way past Michael Rudroff. 'I waited for about a lap because he was all over the road and then, just when I decided that it was safe to get by and made my move, he suddenly slid under me.' Rudroff lost the front end of his private Honda going into the right-hand hairpin after Lukey Heights and skittled the factory machine. Gardner was furious but unhurt.

Despite the fact that it is a high-speed circuit with two tight corners it puts such an accent on rider ability and maintaining corner speed that handling is much more important than top speed. Even the main straight is approached by such a demanding fast left-hand sweeper that machine speed only comes into play some way down, when the rider is already thinking about the braking point and line into the next, equally demanding, right.

A circuit that put demands on handling was not what Bubba Shobert needed as the 1988 NSR500 was proving to be no friend. It flicked him off in a big way during practice and, to make the point more strongly, landed on top of him, injuring his left ankle and cracking some bones. And it had already done the same to the other ankle in pre-season testing at the circuit.

Kenny Roberts, a great friend of Shobert's and enthusiastic about the Texan's ability to ride any motor cycle, said that he was not surprised he was having trouble with the wicked NSR. 'With a rookie like Bubba riding that bike this was bound to happen. If he can learn to ride the NSR he will be able to ride anything.'

Another rider finding out how much fun an '88 NSR could be was Mal Campbell, having a one-

Malcolm Bryan

The crowd begin to realise that no one is going to pass their man on the last lap and the noise builds to a crescendo. Gardner had given everything and they really appreciated it.

Gianola and Martinez: it was a great race for a while.

Malcolm Bryan

off outing on a bike supplied through his normal employers, Honda Australia. He lacked track time on the bike, as did Michael Dowson on the YZR that he had the use of for one race.

Honda had made big improvements to the 1989 model NSR, but that did not mean that everything was perfect. Different brakes were being tested at Phillip Island, as well as both 16- and 17-in. front wheels. The discs that were being tried had either radial or axial drilling and were all steel as Phillip Island is not tough enough on brakes to make good use of carbon.

It was not only the brakes that failed to get hot at Phillip Island: the temperature was pretty cool and rain threatened to put a damper on things. Suzuki found that they really didn't need their tiny extra rad, mounted horizontally in the bottom of the fairing in front of the lower cylinders.

Schwantz tried to use the 16-in. front, having been told by Michelin that the increased contact patch area would give him more grip. He said he needed it. 'The front keeps sliding away and until you can get that to grip there is no way you can get on the power and start steering with the rear wheel.' He eventually found the grip, but with the old 17-in. front tyre and revised steering geometry generated by raising the rear suspension ride height. It worked well enough to put him on pole, the first time a Suzuki had sat there since Jack Middelburg in the Belgian Grand Prix at Spa in 1982.

Only Gardner was happy enough with the 16-in. front to use it in the race, and Michelin seemed to have a real problem with their front tyres. Some riders preferred older profiles and Juan Garriga said that he was in real trouble until he fitted a standard front for the Sunday morning warm-up.

The front tyre problems that caused Garriga to qualify down in sixth place did not seem to worry Jean-Philippe Ruggia, who put the Gauloises Blondes Yamaha on pole ahead of Sito Pons and Luca Cadalora. Martin Wimmer had the Hein Gericke Aprilia going well and was on the front row in fifth place and quite pleased with the bike. The same could not be said of the official factory Aprilia riders, Didier de Radiguès and Ivan Palazzese, who were ninth and twenty-fifth respectively. They both reported that the bikes were slow and still did not handle.

125 cc

Alex Criville's win was against all the odds. He was not expected to beat Martinez and Gianola with their greater factory backing and, what is more, he had broken his collarbone crashing in Japan. It was wired together so that he could ride in Australia and was hardly strong – but it was good enough to put him fourth on the grid.

The extra help that Criville needed was provided when the early battle for the lead between the only rivals, Gianola and Martinez, ended abruptly. Gianola crashed and Martinez suffered another breakdown, giving him no points from the first two rounds. Gianola put his fall down to

DERBI
DUCADOS
CEPSA

Early on Rainey had a clear lead and Gardner had to work hard to get on terms – chased by Magee, Doohan, Taira, Lawson and Spencer.

Malcolm Bryan

Malcolm Bryan

Left: **Gerry Burgess has a lot of knowledge to impart to Mick Doohan from his winning years with Gardner. Dave Cullen also brought to the team a wealth of experience, having worked with Graeme Crosby, Richard Scott and Shunji Yatsushiro.**

Below: **Pure elation for Wayne Gardner: his Grand Prix, his win.**

the track. 'There was so much mud and dust brought onto the track by the fans who invaded after the 500 race. I was not going that fast.' The Italian remounted to finish fifth, but he was way behind the leading men.

Criville was then in a class of his own, well out in front, and the excitement was centred on the second-place battle between Allan Scott and Robin Milton. The two privateers had ridden well in 1988 but never featured in a battle that would take them onto the rostrum. Scott had briefly diced for third at the French Grand Prix last season only to fall.

There was little to choose between either the two Hondas or their riders but Milton just managed to gain the advantage over the last few laps and Scott was not in a position to make any last-minute effort.

250 cc

The 250 event was not the knock-down, drag-out, all-action bar room brawl that many Australian fans were hoping for after their most recent national meeting, where a pack had decided the race at the last corner. It was, instead, an exciting education for those new to Grand Prix racing as the experienced and reserved Pons controlled the race and held in check the very talented and aggressive Ruggia.

Both men were in superb form and Ruggia took the lead from Jacques Cornu halfway round the first lap. Before the end of that first circuit Pons had moved into second, ahead of Cornu and Cadalora. The other front row man, Martin Wimmer, was out of luck: the Aprilia had bogged on the line and he was way down the field, shades of his days in the Marlboro Yamaha team.

Pons and Ruggia were soon stretching their advantage while Cornu was caught and then passed by Garriga on lap three. Cadalora slipped off the Marlboro Yamaha at the first hairpin on lap two. 'I just braked too hard and the front wheel slid away,' said the Italian. 'I hung on to the bars and kept the engine running so that I could get back in the race.' From that point Cadalora became the man to watch as he fought his way through the field.

Ruggia and Pons were fighting a private duel at the front. Pons tried to get clear away from Ruggia several times, but when he realised that was not possible he moved over to let the Frenchman lead rather than have the younger man breathing down his neck at every turn.

It went on for the entire 26 laps. Towards the end Pons tried a plan that he hoped would bring him victory on the last lap. He moved over once more to let Ruggia past, then tailed him through the fast left-hander onto the start and finish straight. Pulling out of the Frenchman's slipstream he passed the Yamaha comfortably, using the tow and the superior speed of the Campsa Honda.

Pons made sure he was second again on the final lap but Ruggia knew what to expect now, and put in an extra effort going into that final left-hander. It left Pons a yard or two further behind than he'd intended, coming onto the

Malcolm Bryan

straight, and the Honda was struggling to pick up the slipstream. Just before the line the Honda managed to creep past the Yamaha to give Pons the win by a wheel, closer than he wanted, but twenty points were in the bag.

After a good fight between Reinhold Roth and Juan Garriga the pairing was split by the arrival of Cadalora late in the event. The Italian carried on to gain a rostrum position, pulling Garriga away from the German.

The Australians had hoped for a great result from one of their own 250 stars but, with only production bikes to put up against the factory-supported foreigners, they were always up against it. The best result came from Darryl Beattie, who was twelfth on an RS250 Honda run by Honda Australia and fitted with some go-faster parts from HRC (but still no NSR). The quickest true privateer was Roy Leslie, who just missed out on championship points, finishing seventeenth on his TZ 250 Yamaha. Both men are fine riders and know Phillip Island better than the men from overseas, but the 250 class is now the domain of the factory machine and only the very best GP privateers score points.

500 cc

Wayne Rainey made a start that was every bit as good as that in Japan and Tadahiko Taira was second. Schwantz, in third, had been upset in Japan when Taira squeezed past through the 'S' section behind the pits. This time it was the Texan who did the squeezing, under brakes, going into the first left-hand hairpin. 'He wasn't going to give me any room but I kept going and when it was a case of ease off or go on the grass he gave,' recalled Schwantz later, while watching the video.

The next bit he didn't want to watch, though, as the video showed his crash from three different angles. It was at the next hairpin and Schwantz explained what went wrong. 'I tested the rear tyre going out of the first hairpin and it seemed to be fine but when I got on the gas at the next one it just let go.' The slide stopped suddenly and the Pepsi Suzuki rider was flicked over the bars.

Taira was far enough behind to miss him and was ahead of Magee, Gardner and Doohan, who had made a good start but after a nasty practice crash that took the skin of two fingers he was hard pressed to maintain the pace.

Lawson was down in sixth place on the third Rothmans Honda, not enjoying his ride, and soon to come under pressure from Freddie Spencer – who was having his own problems, but trying to make the best of them. 'I was going faster than I had in practice and that put all the gear ratios wrong. I was also pushing the front tyre harder and it was sliding. Because the gearing was wrong I was having trouble getting round Eddie. The Honda was faster so I had to wait until he rolled it off through the fast left, then I went round the outside.'

Sarron also passed Lawson and then both Yamaha riders got by Doohan. Up front Rainey had failed to make the kind of break he had in Japan, and the Australian challenge from Gardner and Magee became stronger towards the end of the first ten laps. By lap ten Gardner was right with Rainey, and soon to close were the Yamahas of Magee and Sarron. The Frenchman was loving the fast corners and riding at his best. Spencer was not quite as impressive but was also closing and was well ahead of Lawson.

In seventh place Ron Haslam had squeezed the Suzuki past Doohan and Taira, but that battle was far from over. The Japanese would get another lease of life in the second half of the race and temporarily take fifth back from Lawson.

The struggles for the lower places were largely ignored by the crowd who had the action they wanted at the head of the field, with their men Gardner and Magee embroiled in a battle for the lead with Sarron and Rainey. It was Rainey and Gardner who spent most of the time in the lead, but Sarron also took a turn. Anyone might have won. Only over the last few laps did it become obvious that Magee was hard pressed to maintain the pace and would not be making a bid for the win.

On the final circuit Gardner made the required extra effort and pulled off the win that sent the crowd wild. Rainey tried to get in front several times in that final lap but Gardner had the line and the speed. The American came closest at the final hairpin but Gardner was in the wrong position and instead of gaining Rainey lost two yards. It was all over. Australia had their winner.

Mamola had retired with crank failure. Chili crashed when touching the front brake through the fast left-hander at Lukey Heights. And Mackenzie had crashed his Yamaha out of eighth place on lap 23, at the same spot as Schwantz.

Australian Grand Prix, 9 April/statistics
Phillip Island, Victoria, 2.765-mile/4.45-km circuit

500 cc

30 laps, 82.95 miles/133.5 km

Place	*Rider*	*Nat.*	*Machine*	*Laps*	*Time & speed*	*Practice time*	*Grid*
1	Wayne Gardner	AUS	Honda	30	48m 15.94s 103.12 mph/ 165.956 km/h	1m 35.77s	3
2	Wayne Rainey	USA	Yamaha	30	48m 16.29s	1m 35.40s	2
3	Christian Sarron	F	Yamaha	30	48m 16.41s	1m 35.93s	5
4	Kevin Magee	AUS	Yamaha	30	48m 17.45s	1m 35.99s	6
5	Eddie Lawson	USA	Honda	30	48m 26.91s	1m 36.02s	7
6	Tadahiko Taira	J	Yamaha	30	48m 28.51s	1m 35.80s	4
7	Ron Haslam	GB	Suzuki	30	48m 48.40s	1m 36.96s	11
8	Michael Doohan	AUS	Honda	30	49m 03.60s	1m 37.03s	12
9	Michael Dowson	AUS	Yamaha	30	49m 43.76s	1m 38.81s	16
10	Dominique Sarron	F	Honda	29	48m 21.88s	1m 38.94s	17
11	Alessandro Valesi	I	Yamaha	29	49m 12.40s	1m 41.23s	19
12	Simon Buckmaster	GB	Honda	29	49m 55.23s	1m 41.82s	20
13	Marco Gentile	CH	Fior	29	50m 15.06s	1m 40.80s	18
14	Niggi Schmassman	CH	Honda	27	48m 23.43s	1m 44.96s	22
15	Michael Rudroff	D	Honda	27	48m 42.82s	1m 44.47s	21
	Randy Mamola	USA	Cagiva	24	DNF	1m 37.88s	14
	Fernando Gonzalez	E	Honda	23	DNF	1m 46.18s	24
	Freddie Spencer	USA	Yamaha	22	DNF	1m 36.23s	8
	Niall Mackenzie	GB	Yamaha	22	DNF	1m 36.46s	9
	Bubba Shobert	USA	Honda	16	DNF	1m 37.79s	13
	Pier Francesco Chili	I	Honda	5	DNF	1m 36.75s	10
	Greg Drew	AUS	PRP	1	DNF	1m 45.18s	23
	Kevin Schwantz	USA	Suzuki	0	DNF	1m 34.99s	1
	James Judd	AUS	Yamaha	0	DNF	1m 47.13s	25
	Malcolm Campbell	AUS	Honda	0	DNF	1m 38.65s	15
	C. Harwood	AUS			DNQ	1m 51.74s	

Fastest lap: Chili, 1m 35.28s, 104.474 mph/168.136 km/h (record).
Previous record: Malcolm Campbell, AUS (Honda), 1m 40.79s, 98.717 mph/158.87 km/h.

World Championship: 1 Rainey, 34; **2** Gardner, 33; **3** Lawson, 26; **4** Magee and Sarron, C., 24; **6** Schwantz, 20; **7** Taira, 18; **8** Haslam, 13; **9** Mackenzie, 10; **10** Doohan, 8; **11** Dowson and Fujiwara, 7; **13** Itoh and Sarron, D., 6; **15** Shobert and Valesi, 5; **17** Buckmaster, 4; **18** Gentile and Yatsushiro, 3; **20** Schmassman and Spencer, 2; **22** Machii and Rudroff, 1.

Freddie Spencer ran strongly until he lost the Yamaha on lap 23.

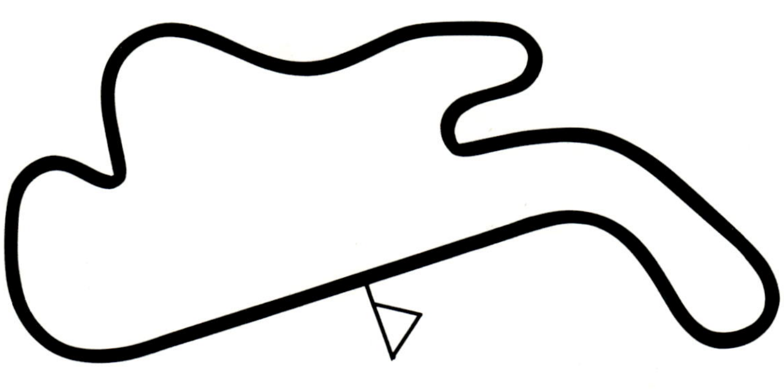

250 cc

26 laps, 71.89 miles/115.7 km

Place	*Rider*	*Nat.*	*Machine*	*Laps*	*Time & speed*	*Practice time*	*Grid*
1	Alfonso Pons	E	Honda	26	43m 16.54s 99.676 mph/ 160.413 km/h	1m 38.91s	2
2	Jean-Philippe Ruggia	F	Yamaha	26	43m 16.67s	1m 38.83s	1
3	Luca Cadalora	I	Yamaha	26	43m 25.29s	1m 39.05s	3
4	Juan Garriga	E	Yamaha	26	43m 28.13s	1m 39.55s	6
5	Reinhold Roth	D	Honda	26	43m 34.67s	1m 39.91s	7
6	Jacques Cornu	CH	Honda	26	43m 46.05s	1m 39.37s	4
7	Carlos Cardus	E	Honda	26	43m 49.58s	1m 40.21s	11
8	Helmut Bradl	D	Honda	26	43m 49.71s	1m 39.99s	8
9	Didier de Radiguès	B	Aprilia	26	44m 09.94s	1m 40.12s	9
10	Alexandre Barros	BR	Yamaha	26	44m 11.33s	1m 41.52s	21
11	Loris Reggiani	I	Honda	26	44m 11.46s	1m 40.30s	12
12	Darryl Beattie	AUS	Honda	26	44m 11.84s	1m 40.13s	10
13	Martin Wimmer	D	Aprilia	26	44m 12.60s	1m 39.41s	5
14	Masahiro Shimizu	J	Honda	26	44m 17.91s	1m 41.65s	26
15	August Auinger	A	Yamaha	26	44m 20.72s	1m 40.68s	13
16	Jochen Schmid	D	Honda	26	44m 20.98s	1m 41.79s	28
17	Roy Leslie	AUS	Yamaha	26	44m 21.30s	1m 41.09s	18
18	Ivan Palazzese	YV	Aprilia	26	44m 36.70s	1m 41.63s	25
19	Fabio Barchitta	RSM	Aprilia	26	44m 36.84s	1m 42.58s	38
20	Harald Eckl	D	Aprilia	26	44m 37.11s	1m 41.61s	22
21	Gary Cowan	IRL	Yamaha	26	44m 37.23s	1m 42.06s	32
22	Xavier Cardelus	AND	Cobas	26	44m 37.49s	1m 41.65s	27
23	Patrick van den Goorbergh	NL	Yamaha	26	44m 37.63s	1m 41.61s	23
24	Daniel Amatriain	E	Honda	26	44m 37.89s	1m 41.62s	24
25	Jean Foray	F	Yamaha	26	44m 38.19s	1m 42.12s	35
26	Jean-François Baldé	F	Yamaha	26	44m 41.60s	1m 42.09s	34
27	Stephen Whitehouse	AUS	Yamaha	26	44m 46.64s	1m 42.71s	39
28	Rene Bongers	AUS	Yamaha	25	43m 23.24s	1m 41.08s	17
29	Darren Milner	AUS	Yamaha	25	43m 24.00s	1m 42.27s	37
30	David Horton	AUS	Yamaha	25	43m 25.79s	1m 42.08s	33
31	Brent Jones	NZ	Yamaha	25	43m 59.26s	1m 42.95s	40
32	Andreas Preining	A	Aprilia	25	44m 04.05s	1m 42.14s	36
33	David Moore	AUS	Yamaha	25	44m 55.73s	1m 41.98s	30
	Paolo Casoli	I	Honda	18	DNF	1m 41.14s	19
	Luis Lavado	YV	Yamaha	14	DNF	1m 41.97s	29
	Jeff Sayle	AUS	Yamaha	13	DNF	1m 41.37s	20
	C. Oldfield	AUS	Yamaha	9	DNF	1m 42.05s	31
	Fausto Ricci	I	Aprilia	6	DNF	1m 40.73s	14
	Alberto Rota	I	Aprilia	4	DNF	1m 40.80s	15
	Alberto Puig	E	Yamaha	4	DNF	1m 41.07s	16
	M. Cocley	AUS	Yamaha		DNQ	1m 43.17s	
	M. Webb	NZ	Yamaha		DNQ	1m 43.57s	
	Andy Leisner	USA	Honda		DNQ	1m 43.72s	
	H. McNicol	AUS	Honda		DNQ	1m 43.87s	
	M. Renfrey	AUS	Honda		DNQ	1m 44.13s	
	C. Stafford	AUS	Yamaha		DNQ	1m 45.28s	
	T. Kingston	AUS	Honda		DNQ	1m 45.83s	
	R. Miller	AUS	Aprilia		DNQ	1m 46.34s	

Fastest lap: Cadalora, 1m 38.49s, 101.069 mph/162.656 km/h (record).
Previous record: Rene Bongers, AUS (Yamaha), 1m 43.60s.

World Championship: 1 Pons, 37; **2** Cadalora, 30; **3** Ruggia, 28; **4** Kocinski, 20; **5** Garriga, 19; **6** Cardus and Cornu, 17; **8** Honma, 13; **9** Bradl, 12; **10** Roth, 11; **11** Okada, 10; **12** de Radiguès and Shiomori, 9; **14** Barros, 6; **15** Filice, Reggiani and Shimizu, 5; **18** Beattie, 4; **19** Wimmer, 3; **20** Arai and Auinger, 1.

125 cc

22 laps, 60.93 miles/97.9 km

Place	*Rider*	*Nat.*	*Machine*	*Laps*	*Time & speed*	*Practice time*	*Grid*
1	Alex Criville	E	Cobas	22	39m 40.04s 92.013 mph/ 148.081 km/h	1m 46.80s	4
2	Robin Milton	GB	Honda	22	39m 48.76s	1m 47.21s	5
3	Allan Scott	USA	Honda	22	39m 53.68s	1m 47.99s	8
4	Stefan Prein	D	Honda	22	39m 57.59s	1m 48.29s	10
5	Ezio Gianola	I	Honda	22	39m 58.93s	1m 46.53s	2
6	Julian Miralles	E	Derbi	22	40m 08.40s	1m 48.94s	15
7	Fausto Gresini	I	Aprilia	22	40m 18.81s	1m 48.38s	13
8	Hans Spaan	NL	Honda	22	40m 21.94s	1m 46.74s	3
9	Luis Reyes	E	Honda	22	40m 32.54s	1m 48.37s	11
10	Adolf Stadler	D	Honda	22	40m 32.71s	1m 49.96s	21
11	Robin Appleyard	GB	Honda	22	40m 33.06s	1m 49.26s	17
12	Lucio Pietroniro	B	Honda	22	40m 34.01s	1m 48.43s	14
13	Ian Saunders	AUS	Honda	22	40m 42.06s	1m 50.41s	24
14	Johnny Wickström	SF	Honda	22	40m 43.68s	1m 49.28s	18
15	Alex Bedford	GB	EMC	22	40m 46.00s	1m 50.62s	25
16	Domenico Brigaglia	I	Garelli	22	40m 46.17s	1m 50.96s	31
17	Peter Galvin	AUS	Honda	22	40m 50.13s	1m 51.09s	34
18	Thierry Feuz	CH	Honda	22	40m 51.27s	1m 50.11s	23
19	Rafael Roses	E	Cobas	22	40m 58.61s	1m 49.74s	20
20	Gerhard Waibel	D	Honda	22	41m 10.68s	1m 50.77s	29
21	Michael Brown	AUS	Honda	22	41m 11.18s	1m 51.15s	35
22	Steve Brouggy	AUS	Honda	22	41m 26.32s	1m 51.77s	37
23	Michael Haisman	AUS	Honda	22	41m 34.03s	1m 52.17s	39
24	Mike Leitner	A	Honda	21	39m 50.45s	1m 50.99s	32
25	Colin Clark	AUS	Honda	21	39m 58.06s	1m 50.69s	28
26	Russell Barker	AUS	Honda	21	40m 15.90s	1m 52.00s	38
27	Alan Bradshaw	AUS	Honda	21	40m 16.27s	1m 49.60s	19
28	Valerio Vivarelli	RSM	Gazzaniga	21	40m 50.38s	1m 53.37s	40
	Trevor Manley	AUS	Rotax	21	DNF	1m 51.26s	36
	Hisashi Unemoto	J	Honda	16	DNF	1m 48.10s	9
	Stefan Dörflinger	CH	Aprilia	15	DNF	1m 50.68s	27
	Kris Galatowicz	GB	Honda	15	DNF	1m 50.09s	22
	Herri Torrontegui	E	Honda	13	DNF	1m 47.52s	6
	Koji Takada	J	Honda	10	DNF	1m 47.56s	7
	Jorge Martinez	E	Derbi	9	DNF	1m 45.53s	1
	Heinz Lüthi	CH	Honda	7	DNF	1m 50.86s	30
	Emilio Cuppini	I	Garelli	5	DNF	1m 51.07s	33
	Bruno Casanova	I	Aprilia	3	DNF	1m 48.38s	12
	Corrado Catalano	I	Gazzaniga	3	DNF	1m 49.08s	16
	Juan Ramon Bolart	E	Cobas		DNS	1m 50.67s	26
	P. McFayden	AUS	Honda		DNQ	1m 53.38s	
	Ian Thornley	AUS	ITB		DNQ	1m 56.79s	
	Martin Hubert	AUS	Rotax		DNQ	2m 05.27s	

Fastest lap: Martinez, 1m 46.53s, 93.44 mph/150.38 km/h (record).
Previous record: Peter Galvin, AUS (Yamaha), 2m 00.89s, 82.306 mph/132.46 km/h.

World Championship: 1 Gianola, 31; **2** Milton, 21; **3** Criville, 20; **4** Scott, 18; **5** Unemoto, 17; **6** Takada, 15; **7** Gresini, 14; **8** Hirose and Prein, 13; **10** Yoshida, 11; **11** Miralles and Shima, 10; **13** Fujiwara and Reyes, 9; **15** Spaan and Yamashita, 8; **17** Fujiyama and Stadler, 7; **19** Yamada, 6; **20** Appleyard, 5; **21** Pietroniro, 4; **22** Saunders, 3; **23** Wickström, 2; **24** Bedford, 1.

WORLD CHAMPIONSHIP · ROUND 3

UNITED STATES GRAND PRIX

A week was too short. Too short to get the bikes from Australia, thanks to an industrial dispute. Too short to forget how good the Australian event was. Too short to recover sufficiently from the jet-lag of a 40-hour day of travel on Monday, crossing the date line, to put up with the frustrations of Laguna Seca. Eddie Lawson said that he would not be surprised if no one ever wanted to come back again.

The circuit had been improved and this year there were no complaints about the surface, which had been so bad the previous season. When initial work was completed with the wrong mix of tarmac the job was redone and the result well worth the effort. Track manager Bo Beresiwsky did his job very effectively too, as always – but unfortunately the track is still dangerous, due to lack of run-off in several places. Riders complained of poor marshalling and an ambulance tending to Gardner during the race stopped right on the edge of the track instead of driving to him across adequate run-off.

Worse than anything, perhaps, was the unprofessionalism of the AMA. How they could run any event from a picnic table set up at the trackside barrier just past the start and finish line – and hope to hear anything by way of radio communications – is unbelievable. No one who wanted a question answered in person could hope to make themselves understood. Even worse was the timekeeping, which was dreadfully late, inaccurate and incomplete. The computer programme failed, but the programmer had only been asked to do the work three weeks before the event.

It was doubly frustrating for IRTA who had wanted SCRAMP, the Laguna Seca promoters, to take the 125 race like the Japanese and Australians. President Michel Metraux said, 'We will not go on like this. The organisers must start to work professionally or they should stop their Grand Prix.' That statement was followed by a letter to the FIM stating that, in furthering the move towards 14 races in a season, the teams would not be attending the Swedish Grand Prix in 1990 and that either Yugoslavia or the USA would also be ignored should they be included on the calendar; the choice between the latter would depend on which of them got their act together.

At least some of the frustration would have been worthwhile if there'd been sufficient media attention. Unfortunately, in America, no one wants to know about Grand Prix motor cycle racing and the event was not energetically promoted. The teams would like nothing better than to be part of an American Grand Prix to which they could invite present and potential sponsors. But, as Pepsi Suzuki team-manager Garry Taylor pointed out, they hoped that the top people from Pepsi International would stay away and come instead to a Grand Prix that shows racing as it should be. This year's event at Laguna Seca might well have been run just so that the top American riders could perform in front of their families. And by the end of the day, with three very popular men in hospital, everyone wished they had gone straight from Australia to Europe.

It was a very different matter for the sidecar crews who started their season in America. Without the comparison of Australia or the frustration of waiting for late freight – and filled with the elation of racing outside Europe for the first time – the crews had few complaints. On the way home, after an excellent second place, Alain Michel spoke for many. 'It was not just that I had a good result, it was a great race. For me the circuit is one of the best. It is not more dangerous than others we use and it is a great test of any rider. There is no rest and you are always having to fight the machine. Like others I was not sure that Lee van Dam would make a good job of organising the trip. I would not say I had trust in him before. It worked perfectly, though, the freighting, everything. After each practice, by the time I had my leathers off, someone was handing me a set of practice times printed from van Dam's own computer in the paddock.'

The most significant thing about the US GP for the 1989 500cc World Championship, though, was not the waiting for practice times, or the tents and containers instead of permanent pits, but the serious injuries sustained by top riders Wayne Gardner and Kevin Magee and the tremendously popular Grand Prix newcomer, Bubba Shobert. None were the fault of the circuit and the gravely injured Shobert was rapidly helicoptered to a suitable hospital.

The crash that finally resulted in Gardner's trip to hospital with a double break of the lower leg was his fifth incident of the meeting – though he did say that it was his own error of judgement rather than the brake problems that had sent him off the track twice in practice and caused two falls.

Last year Laguna Seca had exposed the slightest problem lurking in any brake system, ensuring that neither Niall Mackenzie nor Wayne Gardner stood a chance of winning. Honda's brake problems were never quite as bad elsewhere and, almost a full season later, at the Australian Grand Prix, Gardner pronounced himself more than pleased with brake performance. 'They were perfect, the best I have had in five years of Grand Prix racing, the right feel and power.'

But Phillip Island was not hard on brakes. Carbon discs were not needed and, indeed, there were only two corners that demanded hard braking. Laguna is very different. Almost every corner boils the brakes and there is precious little respite between turns. From perfect the Honda brakes went to near useless in a week.

The first incident occurred at the notorious Corkscrew in practice on Friday, as Gardner was looking for a way past team-mate Mick Doohan. 'The brakes just weren't there. I had nowhere to go, poor Mick,' said Gardner, who had torpedoed the other Rothmans Honda from the inside of the corner as Doohan peeled off, unaware of Gardner's predicament. Doohan was already nursing a hand injured from his Phillip Island crash and, although there was no specific further injury, he and the bike ended up in a heap.

Gardner also escaped to ride again but, on Saturday afternoon, had the brake demons to deal with once more. He ran off the track twice in

Malcolm Bryan

Rainey sweeps down the Corkscrew on his own. Faster through there than anyone else all weekend, he made a wide approach to the left at the top, kept his corner speed up, squirted the Yamaha over the brow going straight ahead with the front wheel two inches off the ground, and lined up perfectly for a great drive down the hill through the right.

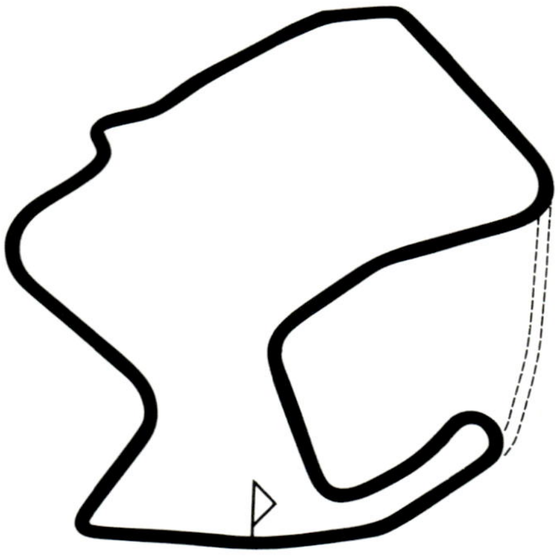

Magee was in third after a long, tough battle with Lawson. Then the Yamaha stuttered, short of fuel, and the Honda swept past. Kevin must have thought *that* was the ruination of his day, but it wasn't.

the same place, as the Nissin calipers and discs faded badly. It was obvious that he would have major troubles trying to race with these, so he returned to the pits and jumped on the bike fitted with the AP Lockheed brakes. The carbon discs had first demonstrated their effectiveness when helping Wayne Rainey to win the British Grand Prix in 1988. As Nissin had failed to improve their brakes sufficiently through the off-season, HRC had approached AP with a request for assistance.

Had Suzuki and Lucky Strike not been using similar equipment so successfully, with few hitches, the disaster that was about to befall Gardner would have been bad publicity and caused quite a hiccup in the development programme. In context, though, the crash must be seen as either a particular problem with the parts fitted to the NSR or Gardner's hurry to get something sorted out that stood a chance of standing the pace, which made him insufficiently cautious.

Carbon discs and their pads, which are made out of the same material, depend upon an elevated temperature to work. Just like tyres, they need warming up and, as they warm, the performance rises sharply, with braking force increasing rapidly even though the rider is maintaining a constant brake pressure. It was this sharp rise that caused Gardner to crash, coming down the hill back to the start and finish line. The front brake performance rose so quickly, as Gardner got into the braking area, that the front wheel locked while he was still going in a straight line and down he went. His leathers and back protector saved him from suffering more than a few scrapes and bruises and, without even calling at the paddock for a change of gear, he walked back to the pits and got on the original steel-braked NSR to complete the session.

The rush caused by lack of practice time could be blamed for Gardner's second crash in two days – and it affected all the solo competitors, because some of the bikes were delayed so long in Australia that they did not arrive at the track until early Friday. It had already been decided by the teams that no one would practise until all the bikes had arrived and those affected given at least some chance to bolt things together. It was reckoned six hours would be enough.

Someone even suggested that at least one of Honda's most important crates should be hidden or they would be out on the track practising as soon as their bikes arrived and to hell with everyone else. Fortunately the AMA agreed with the IRTA majority plan and they changed the practice schedule, avoiding any possibility of a split in the ranks.

So, while the solos sat in tents or in a warehouse in Australia, the sidecars were ready for action. There must have been quite a smirk on the faces

Malcolm Bryan

Wilf Needham finds something to smile about after the second practice crash. The bike required work but his rider had survived again, with the men at Kushitani more than earning their keep.

of Lee van Dam and his men as Thursday was given over entirely to sidecar practice.

The sidecar teams took to the track with great gusto. Historically, the three-wheeled men have been less demanding of track safety and, while the top riders are professional and will not accept outrageously dangerous circuits, they were disinclined to be critical having been invited overseas for a Grand Prix for the first time in history.

World Champions Steve Webster and Tony Hewitt were impressed with the track, finding it demanding and very different from most Grand Prix circuits. Of the much talked about Corkscrew Webster said that it was 'not as hard as we thought it might be, but very tricky to get right. You have to get the left-hander at the top of the hill just perfect. It is tough on the passenger because he is just changing from one side to the other as you go over the edge. If you get the line wrong or he misses his timing he could be in big trouble,' Webster added with a grin.

Webster and Hewitt obviously had their timing right because they headed the table after the first session of official practice and second was the Swiss pair, Markus and Urs Egloff. The Egloffs had never really featured as threats to the top four in the past and this first practice session might have meant little. They started Grand Prix racing in 1984, after four years of national experience, and their best result was second at the Swedish Grand Prix in '86.

As practice went on, though, it became obvious that the Egloff threat would not go away. In the third session they took the lead, being the first outfit to get under 1m 32s. The big four tried but no one could match that performance, and the Egloffs repeated the sub-32s time in the final session. Webster and Hewitt, in second place, were half a second slower and the only other crew under 1m 33s.

Webster explained that the circuit had presented some special problems. 'At first there did not seem to be much grip and, with little abrasion, the track was quite easy on tyres. We thought we were going to have to use soft compounds to get some grip but that changed during practice. The track was a bit slippery at first, like new tarmac normally is, or it could have been dust. We also got more grip from setting up the suspension because we are not used to left-hand circuits.'

The sidecar crews were not the only people doing suspension work, although the new surface had made everyone's life a good deal easier. Almost the entire track had been done, either in the track extension prior to the first GP in 1988 or at the beginning of '89. The most recent resurfacing might have proved a disaster after the rock company supplied the incorrect mix, but the error was discovered just in time to get it reworked with the right mix for the race.

Suspension does more than help the bikes ride over bumps and changes to it usually affect handling and steering. Suspension ride height is often altered to modify steering characteristics or to make up for steering geometry design defects. The Marlboro Yamaha team of Spencer and Mackenzie were trying to lower their bikes, to get them to turn into Laguna's tight corners more quickly. Schwantz was raising his ride height to put more weight on the front wheel so that it would stick better. He had a similar problem at Phillip Island and overcame it in the same way.

The Lucky Strike squad were taking more fundamental measures, to make their bikes steer quicker, and a rash of welds on the rear swing arms showed where they had been shortened. The first experiment had been done after Suzuka when Rainey found that he could not match the lines set by Schwantz on the Pepsi Suzuki.

At Laguna the short arms were considered essential, even though they made the bikes very lively to ride. Shortening the wheelbase will always quicken up a machine's handling, making the angle of lean required for a given corner slightly less; shortening the arm puts more of a weight bias on the rear, helping traction. The disadvantages include easy wheelies and a propensity for tank slappers.

Lively or not, the Lucky Strike Yamaha was quite good enough for Rainey to be fastest in practice. Kevin Schwantz was disappointed to be second on the grid but, as he was less than three-tenths of a second slower than the Californian, there was every chance that the race would be close. Despite his falls and off-road excursions Gardner managed to get the Honda into third place, staying ahead of Magee and Sarron and recording a time seven-tenths faster than Lawson.

The World Champion said that he saw little chance of repeating his impressive 1988 victory and would be happy if he just 'stayed on'. He made no secret of the fact that the Honda was a handful on such a tight circuit and he was not prepared to get in over his head. Lawson is a tactician, and while not winning frustrated him three titles in six years have taught him to look at the broader picture.

Malcolm Bryan

Down in ninth place and the slowest of the factory Yamahas was Freddie Spencer. He was troubled on Saturday by an ear infection. It had started early in the week and treatment that had at first seemed effective wore off. Spencer did not come to the circuit at all on Sunday and later explained that, after having his eardrum burst as a child, the scar tissue occasionally built up and became infected. Most people would have gained sympathy for such a problem but Spencer has exhausted the compassion of many Grand Prix people after problems with wrist, collarbone, back, neck, knee, contact lenses and so forth in recent years.

250 cc

Jim Filice set out to repeat his shattering Grand Prix win of 1988 and managed a better start than he did then. Chased by Cornu for the first two laps Filice then got clear away; Kocinski, on the other hand, made sure that his bike was functioning perfectly before putting in the effort to catch Filice. After qualifying on pole with little apparent difficulty Kocinski had said that his main worry was that things should go as they had done in training and could be maintained for the full race distance. 'I know that we can go the speed to be competitive and I just hope that the bike, the tyres and me can go that speed for all 32 laps. It will be a tough race. It is a long race and I hope I can keep my concentration going.'

Kocinski was behind Spaniards Carlos Cardus and Sito Pons on the opening laps but, after passing Pons with little difficulty on lap two, he took his time looking for a way round Cardus. He could see that Filice was not really getting too far ahead on the Edwin Honda.

One man in a hurry to pass other riders was Luca Cadalora. He had made a terrible start from second place on the grid and was down in eleventh place at the first corner and ninth at the end of lap one. After three laps he was seventh and looking for a way past Pons, which he found at the top of the Corkscrew. He slipped by on the inside under brakes but left it too late and ran wide, up and over the kerb, losing out not only to Pons but to Ruggia as well. The Frenchman had qualified third but his Yamaha was refusing to rev and that would hold him back so that he only finished seventh.

Kocinski eased himself into second and, though Filice knew exactly what was happening, there was little he could do about it. He was using every inch of road and occasionally some of the dirt as well but he had chosen the wrong rear tyre and, as that started to slide around, he had to moderate his pace.

Kocinski could see the trouble he was in and closed for the kill, taking three leisurely laps before deciding to pass at the hairpin. Once in front he quickly opened enough of a lead so that Filice could have no thought of striking back. It was clear to any observer that Kocinski had things under control. Filice had tried, but failed to stem his advance. Last year's winner was going to do no better than second – and suddenly even that was in doubt as Juan Garriga started to close in.

Garriga was only sixth fastest in practice, still sorting out the Yamaha's steering which had troubled him from the start of the year. He was fifth in the opening laps but, after getting past the fading Cornu on lap eight, his riding became more impressive. He went past Cardus on lap 11

Bubba Shobert is a great competitor on any motor cycle, and his post-race accident ruined the meeting for everyone. Wayne Rainey said later that it was as if he had never won the race: if he thought of the US Grand Prix, only Bubba's accident came to mind.

and then started to whittle away at the gap to Filice. The Spaniard could see his chance to cut the points advantage that Pons had gained in the first two races; neither Kocinski nor Filice were World Championship contenders, so any points he could get on Pons were vital. He attacked with his usual zest.

Zestful riding had served him well last year, but this time a touch more reserve would have helped. As he closed to within striking distance of Filice he came upon Jean-François Baldé and looked for a quick way to lap him so as not to lose ground to the man ahead. There were 12 laps to go, time enough to reach Filice, but Garriga decided to jump past Baldé immediately. Accelerating out of the hairpin, trying to pull a tight line inside the Frenchman, the rear tyre of the Ducados Yamaha let go. Garriga tumbled hard and was fortunate to sustain only bad grazes to two fingers.

That did not leave Filice entirely in the clear for, after an inspiring fight with Pons, Cadalora was closing in. Filice could see his advantage over the Italian dwindling and so, while Kocinski was enjoying himself, pulling wheelies for the crowd, Jim fought the sliding Honda and kept the throttle wound on enough to stabilise the gap at about two-and-a-half seconds.

Filice held on to second and was justifiably pleased with his performance. Kocinski said that just about everything was great and Cadalora was content enough to be third for the third time in as many races and only five points behind Pons. The World Champion was not that pleased, maintaining that the Yamahas were hard to beat: 'They out handle and out accelerate us.' He was not looking forward to getting back to Europe for the Spanish Grand Prix at the tight Jerez circuit, and could only hope that he might hang on to his championship lead, or close to it, until he reached the faster circuits where the top speed of the Honda would tell.

500 cc

The race started as a possible replay of the incredible battles in Japan and Australia. Two minutes after it was over the championship was half wrecked, a race to forget even for the winner, Wayne Rainey. Later he would comment that when he remembered the United States Grand Prix he would only think of the terrible accident and injury to his best friend, Bubba Shobert. The points tally said he scored 20 at Laguna Seca but he didn't recall any victory.

The start was the lightning getaway we were coming to expect from Rainey, the rapid first few laps with such obvious confidence in the Dunlop tyres. Schwantz was second off the line but Lawson squeezed past at the first corner; the Texan was determined not to risk any error like that on the first lap at Phillip Island.

Gardner was fourth and Mackenzie, though he started well, was relegated to ninth when the Yamaha's engine stopped coming down the hill to complete the first lap. 'I was about to pull into the pits,' said Mackenzie. 'I thought the race was over but I wanted to see if the engine might start again so I toured onto the start and finish straight. It did start again and ran OK. I don't know why it stopped but there was so much dust about on that first lap it might have sucked something in.'

Lawson was racing on the 16-in. front Michelin for the first ime, but it was his rear tyre that caused trouble on lap two, letting go in a big way as he accelerated out of the first right-hander and allowing Schwantz through to second. Eddie tried to fight back but got into the Corkscrew too hot on the same lap and lost ground, until he was left only just in front of Gardner, Magee and Sarron. Chili was holding off Taira, while Mackenzie remained a distant ninth, comfortably ahead of Mick Doohan who had made a mess of the start. Shobert was chasing Doohan but finding the '88 model NSR little help.

Rainey was setting an impressive pace but Schwantz had not given up hope and, once certain his tyres were not going to play any tricks on him, he put on the pressure. 'I decided to try and close the gap on Wayne and, once I started pushing, my pit boards were telling me I was getting closer. For two or three laps in a row I closed about a tenth of a second and then on one lap it was more. I thought that I could get him, like I did in Japan, because normally when you start closing in on someone you can force him into a few mistakes and that makes it easier.

'That didn't work and he obviously got on the gas because I started losing ground. I realised that I wasn't going to catch him and I couldn't go any faster. The bike was great but I think we had the rear suspension set a little hard because the back was sliding around more than it should.' Schwantz was not that downhearted about second. 'Laguna has never been lucky for me. At least I have 17 points. As far as I can remember these are the first points I have ever won here in any championship.'

Rainey had felt the pressure for a few laps. 'On one lap Kevin cut my lead by quite a bit and I thought, "this is going to be just like Japan." I pushed harder and just kept pushing. I could hold the gap and I only stopped pushing near the end because I was worried about running out of gas. I didn't want to do the sighting lap because of that, but I had to because we needed to scrub in the brand new rear.' Rainey's win meant that

Malcolm Bryan

Dunlop had a memorable double 250/500 victory.

Yamaha had suggested cutting the 40-lap distance because they were concerned about running out of fuel but Honda had scuppered that idea, being confident that the NSRs would go the distance. Hoping that the others would run out of fuel turned out to be the only way that Honda could win and Lawson was having his work cut out holding off Gardner and Magee. At the end of lap four Lawson ran wide going into the tight left onto the start and finish, letting Gardner through on the inside. Magee, with the carbon discs, had been setting up Gardner and, pulling a very tight line, he accelerated early and passed both Hondas on the run up the straight.

Gardner was not going to let Magee get away and set about chasing him. It took the ex-champion four laps to get onto the Yamaha rider's tail. From lap nine the Honda was hounding the Yamaha at every turn and on lap 11 Gardner stole a half chance to get past Magee between the two 90-degree left-handers preceding the climb to the Corkscrew. He managed to get past – but had too little time to regain the racing line before pitching the NSR into the second left. He hit the inside kerb with his foot. 'It wrenched me off the bike. It was my fault, I was off-line,' said Gardner later.

The impact broke Gardner's leg badly and wrecked any chance of him regaining the title in 1989. The ambulance that came to collect him inexplicably stopped only just off the tarmac, rather than drive across the ample run-off to where he lay, but fortunately no one ran wide enough to collide with it.

Magee was handed back third but Lawson, rather than be made warier by watching his fellow-Honda rider crash out, just settled to the task and later rejoined battle with Magee. In the second half of the race the pair passed third backwards and forwards between them. It was an unusual struggle: first one, then the other, would open up a gap of two seconds only to have it eroded in less than a lap. One problem was backmarkers. Rainey had put the first a lap behind after only eight circuits – and Lawson commented later that something would have to be done about qualifying regulations before they caused a serious accident.

With two laps to go Magee genuinely looked to have third secured, but then the Yamaha stuttered, low on fuel. Lawson swept past and Magee could only limp home a frustrated fourth. The last time he was so frustrated was in the Brazilian Grand Prix at the end of 1988. Then he'd stopped for a burn-out on the slowing-down lap, taking his own back on the rear tyre that had let him down. He stopped to do another burn-out this time, on the run up the hill to the Corkscrew, but had not got started when Bubba Shobert smashed into the rear of his Yamaha. Shobert was thrown through the screen and crashed heavily onto the road. Magee sustained a badly broken right ankle.

Shobert had been congratulating Lawson and neither he nor the World Champion were looking ahead. Shobert was helicoptered to hospital in a very serious condition. Unconscious, the surgeons maintained that state until some bleeding of blood capillaries on the brain stopped.

Fifth finisher was Mackenzie who had to work hard to beat Sarron. The Frenchman complained he had chosen a tyre that was too hard and it was obvious that he was not at home away from fast corners. Pier Francesco Chili was a lonely seventh, his first finish of the year. Haslam had been forced to retire with flooding carbs on the second Pepsi Suzuki while Doohan battled on manfully to cross the line eighth, one lap adrift. The badly skinned hand was forcing him to race with a strange grip and his palm was badly blistered at the end.

Sidecars

Steve Webster and Tony Hewitt had every intention of fighting to retain their World Championship crown, but they did not expect it to be easy. They anticipated a fight on their hands from Biland, Streuer and probably Michel. As things turned out none of them caused the slightest worry in the race. Biland and Streuer retired and Michel gave himself too much to do after a bad start.

Webster did not cruise to an easy win, though, because polemen the Egloff brothers were fast off the line. The Swiss made such a run for it that Webster later admitted he was not confident about ever catching them. 'I thought that if they kept that pace up we would never catch them. I try and pace myself. I reckon that if you are fastest in practice and can keep up a pace one-and-a-half seconds slower than that, then you will probably win the race. That is what I try and do. I use the pit board to keep an eye on what pace we are doing. Pacing is important because you have to look after the tyres. You cannot afford to slow down too much because you start using different lines and gears and that can be harder on tyres.'

Webster's experience told in the end, as Markus Egloff later admitted. 'I was too hard on the brakes,' he said. 'I used them too hard and wore them out. I also wore out my foot pressing them too hard!' The Egloffs still finished on the rostrum, but in third place after being overhauled in the closing stages by Alain Michel and Jean-Marc Fresc.

The sidecar race was everything the Americans hoped for, with plenty of action and novelty. The Corkscrew did claim a few victims, however, including Derek Jones and Peter Brown who flipped over and ended up at the bottom of the hill, lucky not to be seriously injured.

United States International Grand Prix, 16 April/statistics

Laguna Seca Raceway, 2.196-mile/3.5136-km circuit

500 cc

40 laps, 87.84 miles/140.544 km

Place	Rider	Nat.	Machine	Laps	Time & speed	Practice time	Grid
1	Wayne Rainey	USA	Yamaha	40	58m 56.179s 85.454 mph/ 137.524 km/h	1m 27.120s	1
2	Kevin Schwantz	USA	Suzuki	40	59m 03.028s	1m 27.404s	2
3	Eddie Lawson	USA	Honda	40	59m 16.091s	1m 28.214s	6
4	Kevin Magee	AUS	Yamaha	40	59m 19.911s	1m 27.908s	4
5	Niall Mackenzie	GB	Yamaha	40	59m 24.402s	1m 28.319s	7
6	Christian Sarron	F	Yamaha	40	59m 26.774s	1m 28.000s	5
7	Pier Francesco Chili	I	Honda	40	60m 26.080s	1m 28.867s	11
8	Michael Doohan	AUS	Honda	39	58m 58.952s	1m 29.193s	12
9	Bubba Shobert	USA	Honda	39	59m 29.709s	1m 29.833s	13
10	Dominique Sarron	F	Honda	39	59m 51.301s	1m 30.714s	15
11	Alessandro Valesi	I	Yamaha	38	58m 57.152s	1m 31.291s	16
12	Marco Gentile	CH	Fior	38	60m 10.996s	1m 31.500s	17
13	Simon Buckmaster	GB	Honda	38	60m 23.113s	1m 33.479s	18
14	Bruno Kneubühler	CH	Honda	37	60m 02.964s	1m 33.962s	19
15	Michael Rudroff	D	Honda	37	60m 09.066s	1m 36.052s	21
16	Fernando Gonzalez	E	Honda	36	59m 23.590s	1m 38.255s	23
17	Vincenzo Cascino	RCH	Honda	36	59m 47.755s	1m 37.798s	22
	Tadahiko Taira	J	Yamaha	34	DNF	1m 28.341s	8
	Niggi Schmassman	CH	Honda	33	DNF	1m 35.886s	20
	Randy Mamola	USA	Cagiva	32	DNF	1m 30.127s	14
	Ron Haslam	GB	Suzuki	20	DNF	1m 28.555s	10
	Eugene Brown	USA	Suzuki	18	DNF	1m 38.361s	24
	Wayne Gardner	AUS	Honda	10	DNF	1m 27.504s	3
	Freddie Spencer	USA	Yamaha		DNS	1m 28.400s	9
	David Busby	USA	Yamaha		DNQ	1m 41.574s	
	Michael Wild	D	Suzuki		DNQ	1m 42.533s	

Fastest lap: Gardner, 1m 28.000s, 89.832 mph/144.572 km/h (record).
Previous record: Wayne Rainey, USA (Yamaha), 1m 29.214s (1988).

World Championship: 1 Rainey, 54; **2** Lawson, 41; **3** Magee and Schwantz, 37; **5** Sarron, C., 34; **6** Gardner, 33; **7** Mackenzie, 21; **8** Taira, 18; **9** Doohan, 16; **10** Haslam, 13; **11** Sarron, D. and Shobert, 12; **13** Valesi, 10; **14** Chili, 9; **15** Buckmaster, Dowson, Fujiwara and Gentile, 7; **19** Itoh, 6; **20** Yatsushiro, 3; **21** Kneubühler, Rudroff, Schmassman and Spencer, 2; **25** Machii, 1.

250 cc

32 laps, 70.272 miles/112.435 km

Place	Rider	Nat.	Machine	Laps	Time & speed	Practice time	Grid
1	John Kocinski	USA	Yamaha	32	48m 19.965s 87.235 mph/ 140.391 km/h	1m 30.163s	1
2	Jim Filice	USA	Honda	32	48m 27.989s	1m 30.486s	4
3	Luca Cadalora	I	Yamaha	32	48m 32.757s	1m 30.248s	2
4	Alfonso Pons	E	Honda	32	48m 37.363s	1m 30.598s	5
5	Carlos Cardus	E	Honda	32	48m 42.191s	1m 30.946s	7
6	Jacques Cornu	CH	Honda	32	48m 42.631s	1m 30.956s	8
7	Jean-Philippe Ruggia	F	Yamaha	32	48m 52.649s	1m 30.331s	3
8	Reinhold Roth	D	Honda	32	49m 13.940s	1m 31.365s	9
9	Loris Reggiani	I	Honda	32	49m 22.666s	1m 31.739s	11
10	Masahiro Shimizu	J	Honda	32	49m 29.349s	1m 32.291s	17
11	Ivan Palazzese	YV	Aprilia	32	49m 38.589s	1m 32.244s	15
12	Alberto Puig	E	Yamaha	31		1m 31.742s	12
13	Jochen Schmid	D	Honda	31		1m 32.867s	20
14	Didier de Radiguès	B	Aprilia	31		1m 33.324s	28
15	Gary Cowan	IRL	Yamaha	31		1m 32.962s	23
16	Alexandre Barros	BR	Yamaha	31		1m 33.000s	25
17	Fabio Barchitta	RSM	Aprilia	31		1m 33.729s	33
18	Stefano Caracchi	RSM	Honda	31		1m 33.636s	31
19	Harald Eckl	D	Aprilia	31		1m 32.923s	22
20	Rich Oliver	USA	Yamaha	31		1m 32.403s	19
21	Fausto Ricci	I	Aprilia	31		1m 33.533s	30
22	Andreas Preining	A	Aprilia	31		1m 32.969s	24
23	Richard Moore	USA	Yamaha	31		1m 33.737s	34
24	Don Greene	USA	Yamaha	31		1m 33.780s	35
25	Jean-François Baldé	F	Yamaha	31		1m 33.800s	36
	Alan Carter	GB	Aprilia	25	DNF	1m 32.393s	18
	Helmut Bradl	D	Honda	22	DNF	1m 32.152s	13
	Alberto Rota	I	Aprilia	21	DNF	1m 31.699s	10
	Martin Wimmer	D	Rotax	20	DNF	1m 32.270s	16
	Juan Garriga	E	Yamaha	19	DNF	1m 30.693s	6
	August Auinger	A	Yamaha	10	DNF	1m 32.218s	14
	Thomas Stevens	USA	Yamaha	8	DNF	1m 33.651s	32
	Xavier Cardelus	AND	Cobas	8	DNF	1m 33.222s	27
	Jean Foray	F	Yamaha	4	DNF	1m 32.890s	21
	Daniel Amatriain	E	Honda	4	DNF	1m 33.003s	26
	Robbie Peterson	ZIM	Aprilia	0	DNF	1m 33.522s	29
	Miguel Duhamel	CAN	Aprilia		DNQ	1m 33.863s	
	Patrick van den Goorbergh	NL	Yamaha		DNQ	1m 33.895s	
	Paolo Casoli	I	Honda		DNQ	1m 33.941s	
	Andy Leisner	USA	Honda		DNQ	1m 34.059s	
	Urs Jucker	CH	Yamaha		DNQ	1m 34.156s	
	Daniel Coe	USA	Yamaha		DNQ	1m 34.158s	
	Doug Brauneck	USA	Yamaha		DNQ	1m 34.348s	
	Luis Lavado	YV	Yamaha		DNQ	1m 34.359s	
	Hans Becker	D	Seel		DNQ	1m 34.520s	
	Steve Crevier	CAN	Aprilia		DNQ	1m 34.709s	
	Jeff Sayle	AUS	Yamaha		DNQ	1m 34.884s	
	Jim DeWitte	CAN	Honda		DNQ	1m 34.979s	
	Lucio Pietroniro	B	Yamaha		DNQ	1m 35.025s	
	Chris D'Aluisio	USA	Yamaha		DNQ	1m 35.229s	
	Jon Cornwell	CAN	Aprilia		DNQ	1m 35.816s	
	David Busby	USA	Honda		DNQ	1m 36.134s	
	Darren Milner	AUS	Yamaha		DNQ	1m 36.389s	
	Eric Kondo	USA	Yamaha		DNQ	1m 36.525s	
	Jose Barresi	YV	Yamaha		DNQ	1m 37.757s	
	James Stephens	USA	Yamaha		DNQ	1m 38.223s	

Fastest lap: Kocinski, 1m 29.195s, 88.631 mph/142.637 km/h (record).
Previous record: Jim Filice, USA (Honda), 1m 32.84s.

World Championship: 1 Pons, 50; **2** Cadalora, 45; **3** Kocinski, 40; **4** Ruggia, 37; **5** Cardus, 28; **6** Cornu, 27; **7** Filice, 22; **8** Garriga and Roth, 19; **10** Honma, 13; **11** Bradl and Reggiani, 12; **13** de Radiguès and Shimizu, 11; **15** Okada, 10; **16** Shiomori, 9; **17** Barros, 6; **18** Palazzese, 5; **19** Beattie and Puig, 4; **21** Schmid and Wimmer, 3; **23** Arai, Auinger and Cowan, 1.

The Egloff brothers *(above left)* **shone on a spectacular overseas debut for the sidecar men.**

The John and Jimmy show ended with a champagne celebration on the rostrum *(right)*.

Sidecars

30 laps, 65.88 miles/105.408 km

Place	Driver & passenger	Nat.	Machine	Laps	Time & speed	Practice time	Grid
1	Steve Webster/ Tony Hewitt	GB GB	LCR- Krauser	30	46m 48.240s 85.454 mph/ 137.525 km/h	1m 32.458s	2
2	Alain Michel/ Jean-Marc Fresc	F F	LCR- Krauser	30	47m 05.558s	1m 33.149s	4
3	Markus Egloff/ Urs Egloff	CH CH	Yamaha	30	47m 12.630s	1m 31.931s	1
4	Masato Kumano/ Markus Fahrni	J CH	LCR- Yamaha	30	48m 15.768s	1m 33.979s	6
5	Barry Brindley/ Grahame Rose	GB GB	LCR- Krauser	30	48m 17.293s	1m 35.417s	9
6	Yoshisada Kumagaya/ Brian Barlow	J GB	Windle- Yamaha	29	46m 50.403s	1m 35.740s	11
7	Fritz Stölzle/ Hubert Stölzle	D D	LCR- Krauser	29	47m 00.893s	1m 36.827s	12
8	Alfred Zurbrügg/ Martin Zurbrügg	CH CH	LCR- Yamaha	29	47m 05.821s	1m 34.102s	7
9	Bernd Scherer/ Thomas Schröder	D D	BSR- Krauser	29	47m 30.295s	1m 36.526s	15
10	René Progin/ Laurent Magnenet	CH CH	LCR- Krauser	28	46m 47.603s	1m 37.194s	17
11	Wolfgang Stropek/ Steve Campbell	A GB	LCR- Krauser	28	47m 06.899s	1m 37.955s	19
12	Judd Drew/ Brian Houghton	GB GB	LCR- JPX	28	47m 29.238s	1m 39.433s	20
13	Tony Baker/ Trevor Hopkinson	GB GB	LCR- Yamaha	28	47m 27.678s	1m 41.046s	22
14	Gary Thomas/ Eckhart Rösinger	GB D	LCR- Krauser	27	47m 18.952s	1m 40.151s	21
15	Derek Jones/ Peter Brown	GB GB	LCR- Yamaha	26	47m 22.251s	1m 36.190s	13
16	Rolf Biland/ Kurt Waltisberg	CH CH	LCR- Krauser	24	37m 44.988s	1m 33.041s	3
17	Steve Abbott/ Shaun Smith	GB GB	LCR- Yamaha	24	38m 34.469s	1m 34.990s	8
	Egbert Streuer/ Bernard Schnieders	NL NL	LCR- Yamaha	16	DNF	1m 33.529s	5
	Ivan Nigrowsky/ Jacques Corbier	F F	LCR- JPX	11	DNF	1m 36.388s	14
	Theo van Kempen/ Simon Birchall	NL GB	LCR- Krauser	9	DNF	1m 37.772s	18
	Tony Wyssen/ Kilian Wyssen	CH CH	LCR- Krauser	5	DNF	1m 37.071s	16
	Rolf Steinhausen/ Bruno Hiller	D D	ADM	0	DNF	1m 35.712s	10
	John Dailey/ Art Dailey	CAN CAN	Yamaha		DNQ	1m 49.877s	
	Ian Fillery/ Steve Earnshaw	CAN CAN	Yamaha		DNQ	1m 53.703s	

Fastest lap: Biland, 1m 30.065s, 87.775 mph/141.26 km/h (record).

World Championship: 1 Webster, 20; **2** Michel, 17; **3** Egloff, 15; **4** Kumano, 13; **5** Brindley, 11; **6** Kumagaya, 10; **7** Stölzle, 9; **8** Zurbrügg, 8; **9** Scherer, 7; **10** Progin, 6; **11** Stropek, 5; **12** Drew, 4; **13** Baker, 3; **14** Thomas, 2; **15** Jones, 1.

Malcolm Bryan

WORLD CHAMPIONSHIP · ROUND 4

SPANISH GRAND PRIX

The pit lane during 500 practice looked relatively empty – no Gardner, no Magee, no Shobert. You could not avoid the feeling that some of the fire had gone out of the World Championship. Lawson had looked rather ordinary in the first three races. Schwantz had been impressive but had crashed at Phillip Island. Rainey was apparently in a class of his own.

This was not the way the season was meant to shape up at all. It was supposed to be a Lawson against Gardner grudge match but, in fact, the two Honda riders get on well enough and Lawson had invited Gardner to stay at his house for a few days after Laguna Seca. The Australian had declined, needing time to sort things out in Europe, but then of course had crashed and put himself out of action.

Without Gardner to carry the flag Honda's cause looked to be in grave trouble, but the World Champion cannot be written off so easily. Lawson's victories do not come from blinding flashes of genius, but are hatched after a long gestation period. There were signs at Jerez that he was incubating something, and he was certainly even more brooding and short-tempered than usual, with Mike Trimby the recipient of an abusive tirade because the new IRTA rules agreed by the teams prohibit any private cars in the paddock. (The walk from the car park to the motorhome must have been at least a hundred yards.)

Lawson was playing himself in with perfect cunning, avoiding the mistakes made by Gardner and Schwantz. He lay second in the championship and, though well behind Rainey, it was not an irreversible situation by any means; as he got the NSR to work better the Yamaha rider was going to have a tougher time.

For the moment, though, Rainey was very much the man to beat. It was a situation the Lucky Strike team had been working towards since the end of the 1988 season. 'We started early,' said Rainey. 'I did, the team did, Dunlop did. The whole team has worked 120 per cent towards getting to this point. Every time I get on the bike it is better. It is always good enough to be right up there, or if it is not we know why and we can fix it. I didn't really think it would go like this. During the winter you fantasise about leading the World Championship with a win and two seconds in the first three races, but then you say to yourself "get real".'

Rainey had certainly not discounted Lawson. 'I thought he would be more competitive but when you think about it the first few races make sense. When he is happy with the bike he will be right there. He just doesn't get in too hard and make mistakes.'

Practice, however, was more of a Schwantz against Rainey battle, just as it had been at the first three races. It wasn't easy for Schwantz to keep pressuring Rainey – the Suzuki was not making life easy for him. Since the beginning of the year the difficulty had been to get enough grip from the front wheel. To do this the rear suspension had been jacked up, putting more weight on the front. Unfortunately this compromised the rear suspension operation and at Jerez, where the bumps make finding drive leaving the corners very difficult, the front end grip problem had to be rethought.

The Pepsi Suzuki team were chasing the solution through practice but, even so, Schwantz was not exactly slow. He was right there with Rainey but said he was having to work hard at doing those times. Many teams were having to revise their suspension adjustments after Laguna Seca, as Ron Haslam explained. 'Laguna Seca is now quite smooth after the resurfacing and this track feels bumpy, especially leaving the corners where you want to have the power on. Getting the rear suspension to work there is not easy. I am also having a bit of trouble with the bike wheelying when we do get the power on.'

Most handling problems were relatively minor compared to Cagiva's. While the Italian factory had made a new frame for Mamola they had had no time to test it before Jerez and practice was taken up in sorting things out. It turned out to be a rather disastrous week for the team who lost one complete session when the engine mounted in the new frame spewed oil all over the rear tyre and then broke again in the race when the ignition rotor fell off. Mamola counted himself very fortunate to have survived the oil-on-tyre incident. 'That was close. It just went sideways and I thought, "Wow, this tyre is taking a long time to warm up", then Ron came past waving his arms and I stopped at the pits.'

Cagiva's chief frame expert is Luigi Botta and he designed the new frame to have greater stiffness and improved drive out of corners. 'The twin spars now each have three internal bulkheads instead of one and the material is thicker in several areas. The swing arm is also stronger and the pivot point in the frame is adjustable,' said the Italian. The adjustable swing arm pivot helped, but Mamola said they had done too little testing; he suspected that the weight distribution was still wrong, with the centre of gravity too low.

Mamola was keeping cheerful despite these frustrations and the fact that old girlfriend Alex had made a one-event comeback, but his absence from the World Championship table was causing him some concern. 'Have you noticed, Simon Buckmaster has more points than I do? Don't laugh, it's serious.'

Cagiva were not the only people making frame modifications. Further down the pit road Honda had some revised designs for Lawson and Doohan to try. It had been obvious since pre-season testing that the handling problems which made the 1988 NSR such a violent motor cycle to ride had not all been sorted out. Several different machines were used through the winter and at Jerez Doohan and Lawson each had a bike featuring changes that would help stiffen the frame and suspension.

Winter developments had followed a strange direction after engineers decided that the 1988 machine's handling problems could be put down to a frame that was too stiff. Last year one Showa suspension technician was heard to say that stiff frames caused sideways wheelspin but frames with flex allowed the spinning wheel to drive the bike forward. To that end a crossbar between the two main frame spars had been cut out in mid-1988 and the upper engine mountings moved back down the spars to give the steering head more leeway to move on its own. Incredibly Honda carried this several steps further and produced an early prototype of the '89 machine. It was after riding this bike that Lawson was quoted as saying they should send the Honda to the crusher.

From that point they made a complete about turn, producing other prototypes in search of more stiffness rather than less, and it was with one of these that Lawson bettered his lap and race times at Goiania in pre-season tests. Carrying the stiffness search further, the Jerez modifications included the addition of the same crossbar that had been removed in the middle of '88. The left-hand front engine mount was stiffened

The 500 race started in front of packed grandstands, with people trying to see from distant hillsides. Over 150,000 spectators were inside the circuit, while some 50,000 were locked outside when the gates were closed.

Malcolm Bryan

by making it a fabricated and welded addition to the main spar rather than a bolted-on unit. The right remained bolted either to aid engine removal or because Honda still think that frame flex is good for right-handers but not for lefts.

The wall thickness of the top tubes of the Showa outer upper tube forks had also been increased, either to aid stiffness or to add weight against wheelies, hence compensating for the carbon fibre handlebars.

For the first winter since the four replaced the very successful triple there was no complete redesign of the engine. There had been some engine modifications to improve power but Mr Ikanoya, Director of HRC, said that they recognised that handling and tyre conservation were now more important than out-and-out power in the 500 class. In fact the changes were minimal. 'We changed ignition timing, exhaust port timing, the exhaust chamber and are making the changes step by step, taking more care of the effect on tyre and overall machine performance than pure power.'

Since the NR500 and 750 projects had been completed there were more engineers working on the Grand Prix machines. Though he would not give actual numbers, Mr Ikanoya said that since the NR projects had been wound up in '87 there has been a 30 per cent increase in the manpower working on the NSR.

Honda have never won the 125, 250 and 500 World Championships in the same season, but with Pons leading the 250, Gianola the 125 and Lawson second in the 500 the possibility of a clean sweep is there. Honda had expected that Derbi would be very hard to beat in the 125 category and had not committed themselves to that class with the same intensity as the 250 and 500. Having made such a great start to the season, though, their interest was increasingly being aroused, especially as the Derbi was proving to be more unreliable and less dominant than in 1988. Martinez was only third fastest in practice, recording a slower time than Alex Criville on the Rotax-engined Cobas and Hans Spaan on his Honda.

The Garellis that had dominated the twin cylinder 125 class for so long continued having problems with their single cylinder layout and had not been brought to Jerez. The factory were working on new frames, hoping for better things at Misano, so Emilio Cuppini and Domenico Brigaglia were nowhere to be seen.

Italy's 500 and 125 teams might be having handling troubles, but there is no shortage of enthusiasm there and the 250 effort of the

Niall Mackenzie lets the front wheel of the Yamaha rise. He was getting to the point where the bike was no enemy to be tamed but a friend that could help him win his first Grand Prix. 'I feel I can do it. When I was riding the Honda I didn't have any idea what I was up to.'

Gazzaniga team had extra weight at Jerez with the Grand Prix comeback of 36-year-old Virginio Ferrari. The 1987 TT Formula 1 champion with Bimota was signed up for a full season on the Rotax-engined machine. Unfortunately neither man nor machine were ready, after only five hours of testing, and Ferrari failed to make the grid, being 44th fastest and nearly seven seconds slower than Cadalora. Ferrari last raced a 250 in 1986. His practice time would easily have put him on the 500 grid, however.

The sluggishness of the bottom third of the 500 field was just as obvious at Jerez as it had been at Phillip Island and Laguna Seca. Many wondered how long the FIM could go on without changing the qualifying regulations. The slowest 500 qualifier was Fabian Pilloud on his Honda, yet at 14 seconds slower than Rainey he was still well within the 15 per cent allowed by the FIM. He was slower than Dörflinger on the 80 cc Krauser (indeed, the first three men on the 80 cc grid would all have made the start in the 500 event). Pilloud was lapped four times in the race.

At least part of the problem is the lack of any machinery that privateers can use in the 500 class. Alessandro Valesi had done well to get a 1988 YZR500 Yamaha out of Agostini and used it to qualify thirteenth, the best privateer and just ahead of Marco Gentile on the Marlboro-backed Fior and Simon Buckmaster on the RS500 Honda.

By comparison the 125 and 250 classes are full of machinery on which a privateer can at least feel he gets a chance to show his paces alongside the factory men. It is a shame that an engine company like Rotax cannot afford to produce a 500, as their 125 and 250 power plants are proving popular and competitive. For their privateers Rotax were pushing forward development of their electronic exhaust valve system (RAVE) which replaced the vacuum-operated valve and aided throttle response and mid-range power.

Aprilia have said that they will produce a 500 for 1990. Of the 250s Wimmer was once more the fastest of the Aprilia men, and was certainly giving the factory Yamaha and Honda riders something to think about. The factory Aprilia team of de Radiguès and Palazzese was, however, becoming something of a joke, with disorganisation and unreliability wrecking their progress.

One privateer at least had little to be thankful for. Harald Eckl had heard that his main sponsor Romer had ceased trading and would probably go into receivership. Reinhold Roth and Jacques Cornu were also affected but only received personal sponsorship from the German helmet company.

Roth was likely to become one of the ever-growing band of Shoei users now serviced by Vince French, the popular Englishman who had been missing from the Grand Prix paddocks since Champion spark plugs stopped their technical support service. Shoei needed a top runner in the 250 category: while their men Rainey and Lawson headed the 500 table, the 250 was dominated by Nolan worn by Sito Pons and Arai with Luca Cadalora and Jean-Philippe Ruggia.

John Kocinski had won two races already for Shoei but was not chasing the 250 crown. His next appearance at a Grand Prix was due to be on a 500 at Misano. Rainey needed help sorting through the large number of available Dunlops but Roberts was not that certain how quickly the youngster would adapt to the power of the 500, having only raced one in Malaysia. (That was when Magee was undergoing a tendonitis operation with the same surgeon who had more recently treated his Laguna Seca injured ankle.) Kocinski had then finished second to Rainey.

Kocinski had his first ride on a 500 at a team tyre test at Laguna Seca in early '87. He also tested the 500 in Japan and at Goiania late last year. Roberts, while obviously pleased with his rider's performances on the 250, is wont to make light of his ability. He tells the story of one of these early rides on the 500, when he was unwilling to let Kocinski loose with the 140 or so bhp normally available. 'We put a bolt against the throttle so that it would only open halfway and still he came in with a white face and shaking his head, saying "Man I never realised they had so much power. No one can ride that." I said was he ready for full throttle yet and he just kept shaking his head.'

Rainey's life during practice was not made any easier when the only other man helping with the testing of Dunlop tyres, Tadahiko Taira, crashed and dislocated his shoulder. The tough Japanese decided to race in spite of his injury, keen not to miss one of the few GP outings on his schedule.

Both Roberts and Rainey had obviously been greatly affected by the Magee–Shobert crash. Not only had it temporarily lost them a team-member, but both are great friends of Shobert. Kenny Roberts was not about to apportion blame, saying that it took two to have the accident. 'This tragedy should and could have been avoided. You can ride round on the slowing-down lap talking to another guy and not looking where you are going a hundred times and nothing will happen. Even if Magee had been doing a burn-out he would normally have missed him.

'It used to be that wheelies and then stoppies were the thing to do on the slowing-down lap to entertain the crowd. After this tragedy perhaps everyone will realise that the racing is spectacular enough for the spectators without any stupid stuff after the race is over. I don't blame anyone. It was the same at Imola last year when Taira was tucked in across the line doing a plug chop and Roche was slowing with a broken engine.'

It was becoming obvious that, while Shobert was recovering, he would not be racing again soon and the Cabin Honda team were forced to look for a replacement. Team-manager Dietmar Maier was at Jerez and said that the team would probably be racing at Misano. 'It is obvious that there are few riders that you can consider. Anyone would draw up the same list – Baldwin, McElnea, Burnett and Lavado. More have been ringing us than we have been ringing them.'

Like Roberts, Maier felt no one was to blame for the accident. 'I don't know who was at fault, that does not matter, but it is very hard to accept. If someone gets hurt racing we have to accept that it is part of the sport. But this was a pointless accident.'

Fortunately Jerez was relatively free from serious injuries, the worst occurring when Dutchman Cees Besseling crashed his 80 cc CJB on Saturday morning and suffered a broken tibia and head injuries. He was rushed to hospital with no chance of being cared for by the Clinica Mobile because it was stuck at Spanish customs, not allowed into the country as it was carrying drugs. Sito Pons is pretty well connected in Spain but even he could not convince the authorities to let the vehicle through.

Last year the race at Jerez was the Portuguese Grand Prix, run only a week after the Spanish Grand Prix at Járama and the crowd, also affected by a petrol strike, was relatively small. This time the Jerez race was the only Grand Prix in Spain and the crowd was huge, the circuit quite obviously packed. The organisers said that there were 120,000 people inside the circuit and they had been forced to close the gates leaving 40,000 outside. The roads were jammed for five miles round the track.

80 cc

The crowd expected a Spanish winner and perhaps they didn't really care who it was. They certainly got their money's worth. Martinez led from the start, just in front of pole position man Stefan Dörflinger, but the sensation of the race, Herri Torrontegui, was about to make his presence felt. He had made a mediocre start from third on the grid which left him sixth at the end of lap one, but after another lap he was diving past Manuel Herreros to take third.

Martinez had been unable to make any use of the clear road ahead of him and by lap three Dörflinger and Torrontegui were on his tail. The Swiss rider realised that Martinez was lapping too slowly and took the lead – but that was not enough to shake the other Spaniard. While Martinez slipped astern Torrontegui took the lead from Dörflinger on lap five as the Swiss made a mistake that temporarily put him back behind the Derbi.

Torrontegui raced away into a clear lead. The only question was regarding his ability to maintain that pace without making a mistake. In fact he just rode quicker and quicker, making his fastest lap of the race the tenth out of eighteen. By that point he had a five-second advantage and was able to ease off.

Martinez slowed and, with the Derbi sounding sicker and sicker, stopped on lap nine with a broken exhaust pipe. Dörflinger had an easy run to second, well clear of Peter Öttl who progressed steadily through the field to take third ahead of Bogdan Nikolov, making it a clean sweep of the top four for Krauser. Factory Krauser man Dörflinger said he could not believe the speed of Torrontegui's private machine. Manuel Herreros might have upset the Krauser domination but for an off-track excursion on lap 12 that dropped him from third to ninth. He eventually clawed his way back to finish fifth.

Marlboro
agv
Castrol
6
Marlboro
Marlboro
MICHELIN
Marlboro

500 cc

The 500 class was run early in the day because the 250 is definitely the race of the moment in Spain, featuring their main stars and displacing the 125 and 80 cc events which historically have been of greater importance. The crush to get into the circuit was so fierce that many of the fans must have missed the 80 and 500 races.

Rainey looked to be favourite. He had been quickest in practice and there was no sign that the tyre problems which lost him the '88 race so disastrously were still present. Schwantz was only a fraction slower, but he did have tyre problems. He went to the line with a cross-ply Michelin fitted to the front after Ron Haslam had tried one in the Sunday morning warm-up and voiced the opinion that it was the only way to cure the front-end problems they had been unable to sort out in practice.

Haslam knew that this tyre might create its own problem. 'The cross-ply is good but at some time in the race the performance will drop off. Because we haven't been able to test during practice we don't know when it will drop off or how much, but the cross-ply normally drops more suddenly than the radial.'

Like Haslam, Schwantz had been unable to make the radial work to his satisfaction and also chose to go with the cross-ply. Even though it is normally considered an unacceptable risk to race with an untried component or adjustment, he considered he had little chance of winning without it and had had enough time on the cross-ply front in the past to know how it would perform.

At the start it looked as though Schwantz had done the right thing for although Rainey jumped into the lead, as he had done at the first three races, he was unable to streak off into the distance. He had every opportunity, too, for Pier Francesco Chili held up Lawson, Schwantz, Mackenzie and Sarron. But when Schwantz jumped to second on lap three Rainey was less than two seconds in front and one more lap cut that to under a second.

Lap five saw Schwantz in front, with Lawson finally getting past Chili who was also overtaken by Mackenzie and Sarron. Rainey held hard to the Suzuki's tail for another eight laps while Lawson inched up on the pair of them. Lapping back-markers broke the bond, though, and Schwantz left Rainey to defend second from Lawson.

That battle went on for three laps, but on lap 16 of the 30 the Rothmans Honda was second and still only five seconds behind the Suzuki. Rainey later explained that he was simply trying as hard as he could. 'The other guys were just riding faster. Without Kevin (Magee) here it is tough to get all the testing you need to do finished so that you have enough laps on all the combinations you might want to race with.' That was Rainey's politic way of saying that something on the bike was not right but that, with the help of a teammate, or more track time himself, it could have been better.

Lawson pressed on, trying to cut the advantage that Schwantz was hanging on to so tenaciously. The gap fluctuated, back-markers hindering first one, then the other, but it hovered at around five seconds and, as the laps were ticked off, that five-second lead looked more and more like a Schwantz victory.

With 24 laps completed the chances of Lawson being able to make up the required second per lap needed to win were obviously slim; Schwantz had just started to think about easing off a fraction when the front end of the Suzuki tucked under. 'It started pushing going into the corner and just kept pushing,' said the Texan later. 'I must have been in la la land or something, I don't know what I was thinking about.'

Schwantz was so furious with himself that he knelt down in the service road and banged his helmeted head on the ground. Lawson and Rainey could hardly believe their luck. It did not make Schwantz feel any better when Lawson later told him that he had given up chasing and accepted that he was going to finish second.

Mackenzie was third, finally getting well clear of Sarron. Both of them were still well in touch with Lawson and Rainey, with roughly a ten-second gap separating each of the top four. Fifth was Spencer who had a good ride after a mediocre start and an off-track excursion when Mick Doohan crashed the Rothmans Honda in front of

Malcolm Bryan

Malcolm Bryan

him on lap four. Sixth was Pier Francesco Chili, but the Italian should have been a place further back, behind Haslam, whom he had pushed off the track on lap 16.

125 cc

Alex Criville took himself to within four points of championship leader Ezio Gianola with a start-to-finish win in the 125 race, setting such a pace that his best lap on the Rotax-engined Cobas was over a second faster than World Champion Aspar Martinez could manage. It was almost two seconds quicker than Gianola, who was fourth behind Koji Takada on another Honda.

While Criville was able to ride his own race Gianola, Martinez, Takada and Spaan were fighting flat out for second. Spaan eventually dropped out on lap 16 but the three-way struggle for second went all the way to the flag. Takada's third was quite an achievement over Gianola in whom Honda placed their championship hopes.

Fausto Gresini also had a great ride on his Team Italia Aprilia. From sixteenth place on lap one he finally eased Allan Scott out of fifth place with just three laps to go.

Ruggia going left, Cardus right and Cadalora in between. Power on, throwing the Yamaha from right to left, the front wheel lifts. Off the ground the right-hand pull on the bars that helped bring the bike upright turns the front wheel further with no contact patch to work against.

Below left: **Spanish youngster Alex Criville dominated on home ground.**

Carlos Cardus *(below)* **often battles with the best. He can do it, but it looks hard work and the speed is difficult to maintain throughout the race. A season without crashes could see the speed come easier, while a fitter Cardus could keep it going.**

250 cc

Another great 250 battle started with Jean-Philippe Ruggia taking an early advantage. 'I couldn't believe it, they seemed to be standing back, waiting for me to go through,' said the Frenchman. Pons tucked in behind on the Campsa Honda with Cardus third, just ahead of Cadalora.

In two laps Cadalora made two identical overtaking moves that made anyone's trip to the south of Spain well worthwhile. There are two very fast right-handers leading back to the start and finish where, normally, a single line is required using every inch of road, white line to white line. Cadalora, however, passed Cardus and then Ruggia by diving inside on the approach some 10 mph faster, then scrubbing off the speed so he was no later getting on the gas but away ahead of the men he had so consummately cleaned up.

'I have never passed anyone there before, but when I saw how they were not so fast there I just went,' said the Italian. He took Pons for the lead on lap five and just kept circulating quickly and consistently until, after 20 of the 25 laps, the World Champion eventually gave up the chase.

'The bike was perfect all the way through the race,' said Cadalora. 'Even at the end the tyres and everything were faultless. I thought I might be able to win the race after practice but then, in the middle, when I could not pull away from Sito, I was not so sure. I thought it was going to be very hard. Then at the end I tried again and did get away.'

Ruggia and Cardus battled for third and while the decision eventually went to the Frenchman it was no easy ride. 'It was like a skating rink out there,' said Ruggia after bringing the Gauloises Blondes Yamaha home nine seconds behind Pons and just three seconds ahead of Garriga. 'Everyone was sliding and I just tried to stay on. It did not help that my rev counter failed on lap two. It may have been part of an ignition problem because the engine was not as good as in practice.'

Garriga gave the crowd a great thrill with his ride from the back of the grid. He had stalled the engine of the Ducados Yamaha coming to the line and was out of position when the race started. From 29th at the end of lap one his rise was meteoric – 24th, 20th, 14th on successive laps – and he kept pressing all the way to the end, finally passing Cardus on lap 24. The jury could well have disqualified him for his start but, for once, good sense prevailed and as he had certainly gained nothing from being out of position the results were allowed to stand.

Sixth was Reinhold Roth. He had a hard ride on the HB Honda after a first-lap mistake. 'I was catching Reggiani and I almost ran into the back of him at one corner. I picked the bike up and ran off the track. I went a long way and by the time I was back on the tarmac many riders had passed and the leaders were long gone.'

Reggiani failed to finish, ending the race with the HB Honda stuck in the gravel after he went straight on when a huge bug or bird committed suicide on his visor. Jacques Cornu crashed the Lucky Strike Honda on lap 19 chasing Ruggia. 'I don't understand what happened because I lost the back end going into the corner,' said the Swiss who hit hard and lay down for a while before walking away from the incident.

Malcolm Bryan

Gran Premio de Espana, 30 April/statistics
Circuito de Jerez, 2.621-mile/4.218-km circuit

500 cc

30 laps, 78.63 miles/126.54 km

Place	Rider	Nat.	Machine	Laps	Time & speed	Practice time	Grid
1	Eddie Lawson	USA	Honda	30	55m 11.26s 85.485 mph/ 137.574 km/h	1m 49.04s	4
2	Wayne Rainey	USA	Yamaha	30	55m 21.43s	1m 48.64s	1
3	Niall Mackenzie	GB	Yamaha	30	55m 28.74s	1m 48.87s	3
4	Christian Sarron	F	Yamaha	30	55m 49.65s	1m 49.22s	5
5	Freddie Spencer	USA	Yamaha	30	56m 02.26s	1m 49.86s	6
6	Pier Francesco Chili	I	Honda	30	56m 31.20s	1m 50.12s	8
7	Ron Haslam	GB	Suzuki	30	56m 40.71s	1m 50.95s	10
8	Tadahiko Taira	J	Yamaha	30	56m 54.70s	1m 50.09s	7
9	Dominique Sarron	F	Honda	30	56m 56.13s	1m 52.43s	12
10	Alessandro Valesi	I	Yamaha	30	57m 05.12s	1m 52.94s	13
11	Massimo Broccoli	I	Cagiva	29	55m 45.76s	1m 54.56s	16
12	Marco Gentile	CH	Fior	29	56m 19.98s	1m 53.73s	14
13	Simon Buckmaster	GB	Honda	29	56m 23.78s	1m 54.18s	15
14	Juan Lopez Mella	E	Honda	28	55m 13.92s	1m 55.06s	17
15	Eddie Laycock	IRL	Honda	28	55m 14.24s	1m 57.95s	21
16	Bruno Kneubühler	CH	Honda	28	55m 14.50s	1m 55.88s	18
17	Claude Albert	F	Suzuki	28	56m 00.79s	1m 58.42s	24
18	Josef Doppler	A	Honda	28	56m 02.06s	1m 58.66s	25
19	Steve Williams	GB	Suzuki	28	56m 16.82s	1m 58.21s	22
20	Michael Rudroff	D	Honda	28	56m 25.91s	1m 58.27s	23
21	Ian Pratt	GB	Honda	28	57m 14.87s	1m 59.91s	27
22	Fabian Pilloud	CH	Honda	26	56m 09.69s	2m 02.96s	29
	Kevin Schwantz	USA	Suzuki	24	DNF	1m 48.84s	2
	Randy Mamola	USA	Cagiva	17	DNF	1m 50.84s	9
	Andreas Leuthe	LUX	Librenti	12	DNF	1m 59.28s	26
	Marco Papa	I	Paton	8	DNF	1m 56.76s	19
	Michael Doohan	AUS	Honda	3	DNF	1m 51.51s	11
	Fernando Gonzalez	E	Honda	3	DNF	2m 00.31s	28
	Niggi Schmassman	CH	Honda	1	DNF	1m 57.72s	20
	Larry Vacondio	YV	Suzuki		DNQ	2m 07.16s	

Fastest lap: Schwantz, 1m 48.79s, 86.73 mph/139.579 km/h (record).
Previous record: Eddie Lawson, USA (Yamaha), 1m 49.29s, 86.33 mph/138.940 km/h (1988).

World Championship: 1 Rainey, 71; **2** Lawson, 61; **3** Sarron, C., 47; **4** Magee and Schwantz, 37; **6** Mackenzie, 36; **7** Gardner, 33; **8** Taira, 26; **9** Haslam, 22; **10** Chili and Sarron, D., 19; **12** Doohan and Valesi, 16; **14** Spencer, 13; **15** Shobert, 12; **16** Gentile, 11; **17** Buckmaster, 10; **18** Dowson and Fujiwara, 7; **20** Itoh, 6; **21** Broccoli, 5; **22** Yatsushiro, 3; **23** Kneubühler, Lopez Mella, Rudroff and Schmassman, 2; **27** Laycock and Machii, 1.

250 cc

25 laps, 65.525 miles/105.45 km

Place	Rider	Nat.	Machine	Laps	Time & speed	Practice time	Grid
1	Luca Cadalora	I	Yamaha	25	46m 46.30s 84.055 mph/ 135.274 km/h	1m 50.52s	1
2	Alfonso Pons	E	Honda	25	46m 48.39s	1m 51.51s	6
3	Jean-Philippe Ruggia	F	Yamaha	25	46m 57.33s	1m 51.15s	3
4	Juan Garriga	E	Yamaha	25	47m 00.17s	1m 50.62s	2
5	Carlos Cardus	E	Honda	25	47m 02.40s	1m 51.59s	7
6	Reinhold Roth	D	Honda	25	47m 29.06s	1m 51.79s	9
7	Masahiro Shimizu	J	Honda	25	47m 36.39s	1m 53.43s	20
8	Martin Wimmer	D	Aprilia	25	47m 41.95s	1m 51.70s	8
9	Gary Cowan	IRL	Assmex	25	47m 49.91s	1m 52.98s	12
10	Wilco Zeelenberg	NL	Honda	25	47m 55.77s	1m 53.17s	14
11	Ivan Palazzese	YV	Aprilia	25	47m 59.56s	1m 53.95s	25
12	Daniel Amatriain	E	Honda	25	48m 02.80s	1m 53.56s	22
13	Jochen Schmid	D	Honda	25	48m 03.06s	1m 53.46s	21
14	Alberto Rota	I	Aprilia	25	48m 04.35s	1m 53.36s	18
15	Stefano Caracchi	RSM	Honda	25	48m 05.34s	1m 53.20s	15
16	Harald Eckl	D	Aprilia	25	48m 11.76s	1m 53.34s	17
17	Andreas Preining	A	Aprilia	25	48m 12.96s	1m 54.64s	32
18	Adrien Morillas	F	Yamaha	25	48m 27.75s	1m 54.98s	36
19	Kevin Mitchell	GB	Yamaha	25	48m 28.01s	1m 54.53s	30
20	Xavier Cardelus	AND	Cobas	25	48m 37.85s	1m 54.63s	31
21	Patrick van den Goorbergh	NL	Yamaha	24	46m 51.19s	1m 54.32s	29
22	Bernard Hänggeli	CH	Yamaha	24	47m 13.12s	1m 54.02s	27
	Jacques Cornu	CH	Honda	18	DNF	1m 51.35s	4
	Loris Reggiani	I	Honda	11	DNF	1m 51.50s	5
	Jean Foray	F	Yamaha	7	DNF	1m 53.89s	24
	Luis Carlos Maurel	E	Yamaha	7	DNF	1m 53.97s	26
	Renzo Colleoni	I	Aprilia	7	DNF	1m 54.86s	34
	Alain Bronec	F	Aprilia	7	DNF	1m 54.69s	33
	Bruno Bonhuil	F	Yamaha	7	DNF	1m 54.25s	28
	Paolo Casoli	I	Honda	6	DNF	1m 53.32s	16
	Fausto Ricci	I	Aprilia	6	DNF	1m 54.93s	35
	Didier de Radiguès	B	Aprilia	4	DNF	1m 53.58s	23
	August Auinger	A	Yamaha	4	DNF	1m 52.93s	11
	Fabio Barchitta	RSM	Aprilia	3	DNF	1m 53.43s	19
	Alberto Puig	E	Yamaha	3	DNF	1m 51.95s	10
	Helmut Bradl	D	Honda	3	DNF	1m 53.00s	13
	Bernhard Schick	D	Yamaha		DNQ	1m 55.52s	
	Urs Jucker	CH	Yamaha		DNQ	1m 55.88s	
	Frédéric Protat	F	Aprilia		DNQ	1m 56.10s	
	Alexandre Barros	BR	Yamaha		DNQ	1m 56.10s	
	Luis Lavado	YV	Yamaha		DNQ	1m 56.16s	
	Andy Leisner	USA	Honda		DNQ	1m 56.65s	
	Engelbert Neumair	A	Rotax		DNQ	1m 57.05s	
	Virginio Ferrari	I	Gazzaniga		DNQ	1m 57.37s	
	Manuel Martin	E	Yamaha		DNQ	1m 57.59s	
	Anselmo Lasaosa	E	Yamaha		DNQ	1m 58.46s	
	Antonio Torralba	E	Cobas		DNQ	1m 59.82s	

Fastest lap: Garriga, 1m 51.08s, 84.942 mph/136.701 km/h (record).
Previous record: Juan Garriga, 1m 51.65s, 84.46 mph/136.004 km/h (1988).

World Championship: 1 Pons, 67; **2** Cadalora, 65; **3** Ruggia, 52; **4** Kocinski, 40; **5** Cardus, 39; **6** Garriga, 32; **7** Roth, 29; **8** Cornu, 27; **9** Filice, 22; **10** Shimizu, 20; **11** Honma, 13; **12** Bradl and Reggiani, 12; **14** de Radiguès and Wimmer, 11; **16** Okada and Palazzese, 10; **18** Shiomori, 9; **19** Cowan, 8; **20** Barros, Schmid and Zeelenberg, 6; **23** Amatriain, Beattie and Puig, 4; **26** Rota, 2; **27** Arai, Auinger and Caracchi, 1.

125 cc

22 laps, 57.662 miles/92.796 km

Place	Rider	Nat.	Machine	Laps	Time & speed	Practice time	Grid
1	Alex Criville	E	Cobas	22	43m 39.38s 79.247 mph/ 127.536 km/h	1m 56.33s	1
2	Jorge Martinez	E	Derbi	22	43m 45.68s	1m 57.68s	3
3	Koji Takada	J	Honda	22	43m 48.55s	1m 59.47s	11
4	Ezio Gianola	I	Honda	22	44m 03.72s	1m 57.93s	4
5	Fausto Gresini	I	Aprilia	22	44m 09.19s	2m 00.06s	17
6	Allan Scott	USA	Honda	22	44m 13.77s	1m 58.71s	5
7	Julian Miralles	E	Derbi	22	44m 14.21s	1m 59.73s	14
8	Hisashi Unemoto	J	Honda	22	44m 14.39s	1m 59.81s	15
9	Herri Torrontegui	E	Honda	22	44m 15.61s	1m 58.84s	6
10	Luis Reyes	E	Honda	22	44m 21.96s	1m 59.10s	7
11	Stefan Prein	D	Honda	22	44m 36.58s	1m 59.50s	12
12	Adolf Stadler	D	Honda	22	44m 36.94s	2m 00.22s	20
13	Robin Milton	GB	Honda	22	44m 37.12s	2m 00.06s	18
14	Lucio Pietroniro	B	Honda	22	44m 38.82s	2m 00.09s	19
15	Taru Rinne	SF	Honda	22	44m 44.57s	2m 00.29s	21
16	Robin Appleyard	GB	Honda	22	44m 46.18s	2m 00.75s	26
17	Antonio Oliveros	E	Honda	22	44m 46.40s	2m 01.56s	34
18	Ricard Jove	E	Cobas	22	44m 52.38s	2m 00.72s	25
19	Johnny Wickström	SF	Honda	22	45m 03.48s	2m 00.87s	27
20	Jean-Claude Selini	F	Honda	22	45m 09.45s	2m 01.63s	36
21	Luis d'Antin	E	Honda	22	45m 09.63s	2m 00.40s	23
22	Reinhard Strack	D	Honda	22	45m 24.82s	2m 01.26s	32
23	Gastone Grassetti	I	Honda	22	45m 32.84s	2m 01.14s	29
24	Mike Leitner	A	Honda	22	45m 38.57s	2m 01.24s	31
	Flemming Kistrup	DK	Honda	18	DNF	2m 00.59s	24
	Hans Spaan	NL	Honda	17	DNF	1m 56.87s	2
	Heinz Lüthi	CH	Honda	17	DNF	2m 01.28s	33
	Othmar Schuler	CH	Honda	13	DNF	2m 00.29s	22
	Antonio Sanchez	E	Cobas	12	DNF	2m 01.59s	35
	Doriano Romboni	I	Honda	11	DNF	2m 00.04s	16
	Thierry Feuz	CH	Honda	10	DNF	2m 00.94s	28
	Manuel Hernandez	E	Honda	7	DNF	1m 59.29s	9
	Rafael Roses	E	Metrakit	6	DNF	1m 59.16s	8
	Bruno Casanova	I	Aprilia	4	DNF	1m 59.43s	10
	Stefan Dörflinger	CH	Aprilia	4	DNF	2m 01.20s	30
	Bady Hassaine	TN	Honda	1	DNF	2m 01.63s	37
	Xavier Debon	E	Cobas		DNS	1m 59.70s	13
	Alfred Waibel	D	Honda		DNQ	2m 01.42s	
	Corrado Catalano	I	Gazzaniga		DNQ	2m 01.50s	
	Hubert Abold	D	Rotax		DNQ	2m 01.75s	
	Xavier Arumi	E	Honda		DNQ	2m 01.82s	
	Hervé Duffard	F	Honda		DNQ	2m 01.87s	
	Manfred Thurmayer	D	Honda		DNQ	2m 01.87s	
	René Dünki	CH	LCR		DNQ	2m 01.93s	
	Serge Julin	B	Honda		DNQ	2m 02.00s	
	Bogdan Nikolov	BG	Honda		DNQ	2m 02.04s	
	Marc Grau	E	Arbizu		DNQ	2m 02.06s	
	Joan Esteve	AND	Honda		DNQ	2m 02.42s	
	Alex Bedford	GB	EMC		DNQ	2m 02.44s	
	Ralf Waldmann	D	Rotax		DNQ	2m 02.87s	
	Antonio Bono	E	Cobas		DNQ	2m 03.04s	
	Andres Marin Sanchez	E	Cobas		DNQ	2m 03.42s	
	Jörg Seel	D	Seel		DNQ	2m 03.59s	
	Jos van Dongen	NL	Honda		DNQ	2m 03.61s	
	Jose Miralles	E	Honda		DNQ	2m 03.63s	
	Trevor Manley	AUS	Honda		DNQ	2m 03.81s	
	Pier Paolo Bianchi	I	Seel		DNQ	2m 04.07s	
	Bert Smit	NL	Honda		DNQ	2m 04.13s	
	Vicente Rocher	E	Honda		DNQ	2m 04.24s	
	Paul Bordes	F	Honda		DNQ	2m 04.55s	
	Alain Guilhat	F	Honda		DNQ	2m 06.52s	
	Manuel Gamez	E	Honda		DNQ	2m 09.34s	
	Carlos Romero	E	Honda		DNQ	2m 10.19s	
	Jose Fombuena	E	Rotax		DNQ	2m 10.64s	
	Gabriele Gnani	I	Gnani		DNQ	2m 11.45s	
	Stuart Edwards	GB	ERM		DNQ	2m 12.37s	
	Juan Munoz	E	Rotax		DNQ	2m 15.74s	

Fastest lap: Criville, 1m 56.61s, 80.914 mph/130.218 km/h (record).
Previous record: Alex Criville, E (Cobas), 1m 56.76s, 80.878 mph/130.161 km/h.

World Championship: 1 Gianola, 44; **2** Criville, 40; **3** Takada, 30; **4** Scott, 28; **5** Gresini and Unemoto, 25; **7** Milton, 24; **8** Miralles, 19; **9** Prein, 18; **10** Martinez, 17; **11** Reyes, 15; **12** Hirose, 13; **13** Stadler and Yoshida, 11; **15** Shima, 10; **16** Fujiwara, 9; **17** Spaan and Yamashita, 8; **19** Fujiyama and Torrontegui, 7; **21** Pietroniro and Yamada, 6; **23** Appleyard, 5; **24** Saunders, 3; **25** Wickström, 2; **26** Bedford and Rinne, 1.

Herri Torrontegui *(above right)* **scored his first Grand Prix win, adding to the delight of the Spanish crowd.**

Right: **Christian Sarron's 500 gets the treatment from the Gauloises Blondes team. As usual they worked hard all through practice, but Sarron was frustrated. 'It is the first time it has happened for a long time, but we made almost no progress through practice. I could not make the bike any better for the race than it was at the start of practice.'**

80 cc

18 laps, 47.178 miles/75.924 km

Place	*Rider*	*Nat.*	*Machine*	*Laps*	*Time & speed*	*Practice time*	*Grid*
1	Herri Torrontegui	E	Krauser	18	37m 12.51s 76.074 mph/ 122.430 km/h	2m 03.65s	3
2	Stefan Dörflinger	CH	Krauser	18	37m 15.36s	2m 02.64s	1
3	Peter Öttl	D	Krauser	18	37m 48.49s	2m 05.50s	6
4	Bogdan Nikolov	BG	Krauser	18	37m 50.36s	2m 05.48s	5
5	Manuel Herreros	E	Derbi	18	37m 53.05s	2m 05.54s	7
6	Jose Saez	E	Krauser	18	37m 53.46s	2m 06.24s	10
7	Antonio Sanchez	E	Cobas	18	37m 54.20s	2m 06.19s	9
8	Ralf Waldmann	D	Seel	18	38m 08.44s	2m 07.01s	13
9	Jaime Mariano	E	Casal	18	38m 10.73s	2m 05.38s	4
10	Gabriele Gnani	I	Gnani	18	38m 43.22s	2m 07.30s	16
11	Paolo Priori	I	Krauser	18	38m 44.53s	2m 10.23s	29
12	Hans Koopman	NL	Ziegler	18	38m 49.02s	2m 07.14s	14
13	René Dünki	CH	LCR	18	38m 56.94s	2m 07.22s	15
14	Jörg Seel	D	Seel	18	39m 02.59s	2m 06.87s	12
15	Bert Smit	NL	Krauser	18	39m 15.94s	2m 08.85s	20
16	Reiner Koster	CH	LCR	17	37m 14.85s	2m 09.55s	22
17	Stefan Brägger	CH	Casal	17	37m 15.04s	2m 09.73s	26
18	Paul Bordes	F	RB	17	37m 15.20s	2m 09.65s	24
19	Joaquin Gali	E	Krauser	17	37m 17.09s	2m 11.92s	35
20	Reiner Scheidhauer	D	Seel	17	37m 35.67s	2m 09.76s	27
21	Mathias Ehinger	D	Seel	17	38m 00.89s	2m 11.54s	34
22	Thomas Engl	D	Esch GP	17	38m 07.78s	2m 11.53s	33
23	Alojz Pavlic	YU	Seel	17	38m 31.89s	2m 10.84s	32
24	Undine Kummer	D	Krauser	17	38m 56.39s	2m 16.70s	37
25	Alberto Fernandez	E	Minarelli	16	38m 32.97s	2m 14.88s	36
	Luis Alvaro	E	Krauser	14	DNF	2m 05.80s	8
	Joaquin Machado	E	Arbizu	14	DNF	2m 09.57s	23
	Günther Schirnhofer	D	Krauser	12	DNF	2m 06.63s	11
	Vicente Rocher	E	Casal	12	DNF	2m 10.83s	31
	Jos van Dongen	NL	Casal	11	DNF	2m 07.98s	18
	Jorge Martinez	E	Derbi	9	DNF	2m 02.81s	2
	Heinz Paschen	D	Casal	9	DNF	2m 07.81s	17
	Jacques Bernard	B	Fantic	7	DNF	2m 08.88s	21
	Janez Pintar	YU	Eberhardt	5	DNF	2m 08.17s	19
	Joaquin Alos	E	Arbizu	4	DNF	2m 09.99s	28
	Xavier Arumi	E	Krauser	1	DNF	2m 09.67s	25
	Cees Besseling	NL	CJB		DNS	2m 10.71s	30
	Antonio Monteiro	P	Casal		DNQ	2m 18.90s	
	Luis Metello	P	Huvo		DNQ	2m 22.66s	
	Manuel Gamez	E	KTH		DNQ	2m 24.50s	
	Anton Gholy	D	Casal		DNQ	2m 27.97s	
	Daniel Pinheiro	P	Casal		DNQ	2m 31.65s	

Fastest lap: Dörflinger, 2m 02.32s, 77.136 mph/124.139 km/h.
Lap record: Alex Criville, E (Derbi), 2m 0.68s, 77.543 mph/124.793 km/h (1987).

World Championship: 1 Torrontegui, 20; **2** Dörflinger, 17; **3** Öttl, 15; **4** Nikolov, 13; **5** Herreros, 11; **6** Saez, 10; **7** Sanchez, 9; **8** Waldmann, 8; **9** Mariano, 7; **10** Gnani, 6; **11** Priori, 5; **12** Koopman, 4; **13** Dünki, 3; **14** Seel, 2; **15** Smit, 1.

Malcolm Bryan

Malcolm Bryan

WORLD CHAMPIONSHIP · ROUND 5

ITALIAN GRAND PRIX

The first third of the season had brought an incredible mix of emotions, from the unbridled pleasure of Phillip Island, through the frustrations and sadness of Laguna Seca to the dead nothingness of post-race Misano. A Grand Prix builds through five days of preparation, testing and practice to a climax on Sunday afternoon. Fortunately the 80, 125 and 250 races were all superb because the 500 was the archetypal damp squib. There was just a feeling of emptiness after the non-race, which happened when the 500 stars decided that racing in the rain at Misano was too dangerous and would not have been a reasonable test of skill.

A Grand Prix is like a nuclear reactor, producing more fissionable material than it consumes. All the paddock participants put their energies into the event and at the same time feed off the energy created. That energy all comes together and is unleashed in the race. No race and the let-down is unbearable.

Practice had been exciting, with the main protagonists in the 500 class all pursuing their very different approaches. Lawson, cautious as ever, was, as one Honda technician pointed out, 'trying to make the Honda handle like his old Yamaha'. To that end the swing arm pivot area of one machine had been reinforced to help stiffen it. It could hardly be said that Honda were pursuing a precise line of development, as in the pre-season tests they had been determined that a more flexible frame was the preferred developmental direction.

The Lucky Strike team's efforts are more measured and have nothing to do with the Japanese Yamaha engineers. The team get the bare bike from Japan but the electronic recording system, brakes, aerodynamics, suspension and tyres are non-factory developments. The latest modification employed at Misano was a pre-load adjuster mounted on the left-hand fork leg. Rainey could adjust the spring pre-load while in motion or the mechanic could do so quickly in the pit. The rear spring had had this facility for several seasons and Ohlins engineer Lars Erikson pointed out that adjusting only the left leg did not create enough of an imbalance to disturb the handling of the bike.

The team had been testing 16-in. front Dunlops the previous week at Paul Ricard but while the 17s were giving no problems they declined to rush them into service. 'I lapped as quick on the 16 as I did on the 17, which is an encouraging start,' said Rainey. Gerry Griffiths, the Dunlop engineer, explained that they might initially have some pattering problems with the 16s so they were not rushing into anything.

During practice at Misano Rainey found himself slightly off the pace and the team were running out of ideas looking for that missing second which would have put him on pole again. He tried the 16 to see if the answer lay there, but that offered no immediate solution. Even with the 17-in. front there was a front-end patter problem that the easy change pre-load adjustment could not help with. 'We've chased those chassis settings all the way round the map,' said Rainey after practice. 'We won't be making any more changes before the race. There aren't any changes left!'

Suzuki found just the right settings but it was more by luck than judgement: Schwantz tried his number two bike just because his favoured machine had flooded its carburettors when being warmed up for Friday afternoon's practice. 'One of Ron's mechanics suggested I go out on my spare bike while my mechanics were sorting out the problem. It did just about everything perfectly. It has slightly different steering geometry. The front tyre stuck and the back didn't slide. I was just riding round and the pit board kept showing 18 seconds and there was quite a lot of traffic about so I thought I must be doing 19s and they had forgotten to change the board. Then I got one clear lap and the board said 17s.'

That put Schwantz a full second faster than Rainey, but in the last moments of practice Lawson put in an extra effort on the Rothmans Honda and recorded a low 18s. It was his fastest lap of the event and while Schwantz recorded at least one sub-18-second time in each of Saturday's two sessions no one else got into that bracket. The last surprise of practice was to come from Pier Francesco Chili who cut almost a second off his time in the final session to take third, only fractionally slower than Lawson. That pushed the fastest Yamaha men – Rainey, Sarron and Mackenzie – back to fourth, fifth and sixth respectively.

Alongside Mackenzie on the second row sat Spencer. He had carburation problems right up to and through the final session, after missing most of the second practice because he crashed on lap two on a cold rear tyre. Kenny Roberts saw the fall. 'He had only done about two laps and I guess the tyre was still cold because, as he gassed it, it just let go. He backed off the throttle and it grabbed again and flicked him.'

The Italian Grand Prix was not turning out to be much fun for Spencer, who received a bang on the head in the fall. The previous day the free training period had seen him run off the track when selecting neutral instead of first. He then got on the second Marlboro Yamaha to perform a plug check. Letting out the clutch when changing down through the gears, the clutch mechanism broke suddenly and jammed the engine in gear. The rear wheel locked and threw Spencer off. In the same session Mackenzie had both bikes seize, so Kel Carruthers and his men had a full evening's work ahead of them.

Spencer was using Lockheed carbon fibre discs for the first time and said they gave him added confidence. 'They work differently, but I had a good idea of what to expect having used the carbon discs on the rear of the Honda. I used the rear disc to control rear wheel slides so I learnt the feel of it and I know you have to work them hard.'

Mackenzie did not get to use the carbon discs. Despite being told at the beginning of the season that he would be on an equal footing with Spencer the first four races had shown that simply not to be true. Carruthers saw to Spencer first, and the American was getting the new equipment when there was only enough for one rider – this despite the fact that Mackenzie had more championship points. Number one and number two riders are a fact of Grand Prix life, but Agostini had been less than frank with Mackenzie when signing him.

Mackenzie slid off the Marlboro Yamaha on Friday, finding the last left-hander onto the start and finish straight very slippery. The track had been ground there in an attempt to smooth it but the grip had been reduced, adding yet another variation to Misano's multitudinous surfaces. The same patch caught Mamola out later in practice and several men on race day.

Misano demands quite a lot from brakes and Lawson had decided that he would persevere with the carbon discs through practice. Lockheed had come up with some new disc material and he did not suffer the same problems as Gardner had at Laguna Seca.

Eddie Lawson was in good form at Misano, enjoying a joke with his fellow-riders. Parked between the impressive Bluebird Wanderlodge of the Schwantz family, complete with new trailer carrying the Suzuki Vitara for local transportation, and the new Mamola $500,000 coach with nightclub-style interior and a golf cart carried in one of the side compartments, Lawson laughed at his embarrassingly old and slightly tatty Foretravel. 'Just a year or two more,' he said, patting her with mock affection, and he even took up Jim Schwantz's offer of some aluminium polish and worked on one wheel, doing just enough to make the rest look even dowdier.

Lawson could not seriously have been feeling poor, but he did tell Mike Trimby that he felt IRTA should be pushing for higher prize money and that the cash spent on the IRTA/Motomedia tractor and trailer unit should have gone to the riders as it was income from television. IRTA's point was that there was little value in pursuing a 10 per cent prize money increase with the FIM and with ROPA when their energies would be better spent getting more TV coverage, which would see everyone's income increase to a far greater extent. Spending money on the tractor and trailer unit was part of building the professional image needed to sell the sport successfully.

There was also discussion over the use of tyre warmers on the grid, banned by IRTA since the Australian Grand Prix. The reason for the ban was that having generators or running mains power lines across the track between the sighting and the warm-up lap lengthened unreasonably the time taken to clear the grid. The riders wanted the tyre warmers saying that, especially at Misano, where the lap is so short and the surface unpredictable, a single warm-up lap could not do the job. The fact that Rainey's Dunlops worked well from lap one and gave him an advantage over the Michelin users might have had something to do with the rider protest headed by Christian Sarron.

The riders did not make much headway in these discussions and were no doubt left with the feeling that someone, sooner or later, was going to be forced to listen to their point of view. They could not have planned that a confrontation would be so soon in coming.

Left: **Michael Rudroff splashes round in the wake of Pier Francesco Chili, who normally laps him easily. It was not the way that Chili or Pirelli wanted to win their first Grand Prix.**

Below left: **Startline dilemma for the mechanics. If the team on the left is changing from intermediates to wets but the team on the right is going from intermediates to slicks, what should we do? The riders were away in Randy's motorhome deciding that no tyres would work in the wet at Misano.**

It is ten years since the riders, then headed by Kenny Roberts, harboured similar feelings of injustice. That was the time of the World Series and the confrontation between 'us', the riders and 'them', the FIM. Mike Trimby had been appointed riders' representative soon afterwards, so the riders had a united voice, a full-time worker who could co-ordinate and plan for them. Their lot improved, mainly through better track safety but also financially and simply because they were taken note of.

Mike Trimby now works for IRTA, as secretary general to the teams association, and ideally he still looks after the interests of the riders as they are part of the teams. Unfortunately IRTA, and particularly Mike Trimby, has now become the closest, most identifiable face of 'them', i.e. those who are responsible when things are not right. The riders are riders, not politicians, and do not care to sort out the various relationships between the FIM, ROPA, IRTA, Motomedia, the circuit owner, the race promoter ... and of all the melange Mike Trimby is the single identifiable, approachable person, so it is to him that people complain.

It would be unrealistic to suggest that Mike Trimby or IRTA are in any way perfect, but what does tend to be forgotten is that the lot of everyone involved on the paddock side of Grand Prix racing is better than it was ten or even five years ago. Memories are short, and many of the riders who were racing ten years ago have retired, but some memories are shorter than they should be. Rob McElnea returned to Grand Prix racing with a few words of sanity, having had a brief foray into the World Superbike Championship. He told Trimby that Superbike racing was just like Grands Prix five or more years ago, when little heed was paid to the riders. He said it made him realise how things at Grands Prix had improved.

McElnea was taking over the Cabin Honda place vacated by Bubba Shobert while the Texan recovered from his Laguna Seca accident. McElnea had tested the 1988 NSR the previous Friday and said he had more respect for Wayne Gardner after riding the machine. He described it as 'interesting'. He had a great deal of work to do through practice, trying to make the Honda work for him, and joked that they had stiffened the suspension so much that they finally had to use springs from the truck.

But McElnea complained about very little. He was just so pleased to be back Grand Prix racing again and determined that, having seen the alternative, he was going to stay.

Less convinced about the swap was Fred Merkel, Superbike World Champion and having one of three proposed Grand Prix outings as number two to Pier Francesco Chili in the HB Gallina team. Riding as number two meant using the '88 NSR. Merkel found life as a small fish in a big pond hard going, especially as he didn't feel he was getting any help. 'I am a second slower now than I was when I first tried the bike last Friday,' said Merkel as practice came to a close. 'Every time I want to change the bike Gallina knows best and changes something completely different.

33
HB
elf
HONDA

2
1
SHOEI
NSR
Rothmans
HONDA
Shell
MICHELIN

Left: **'Flyin' Fred' was not too sure what to make of Grand Prix racing. Used to being a big fish in a small pond and running his own team, he was frustrated to have to work for Roberto Gallina and ride the bike that the Italian thought was best for him.**

Below left: **Doohan was learning fast, following Lawson everywhere. It was a habit he would soon grow out of.**

Bottom: **Martinez is hounded by two Hondas and a Cobas. The Derbi was not up to the challenge and the Italian crowd got the winner they wanted.**

Malcolm Bryan

It doesn't work because I am not allowed to sort it out. The back end is pattering so bad that I am losing all the time going through the left-handers onto the back straight. Round the rest of the track I am up with the pace.'

Another rider making a rare Grand Prix appearance was Raymond Roche. He had crashed the Ducati superbike in Hungary the week before and was still recovering – and he didn't help his recovery by falling twice more in practice.

Loris Reggiani was another notable practice crasher: he fell from the HB Honda in the final session. He had led the table until final practice but was then ousted, first by Martin Wimmer on the Hein Gericke Aprilia, then by Luca Cadalora on the Marlboro Yamaha, and finally by Jean-Philippe Ruggia with the Gauloises Blondes Yamaha and Carlos Cardus on the Repsol Honda. They all recorded times in the high 19s while Reggiani could not better his second session time of 1m 20.033s.

The Italian had been buoyant about the way things were going. 'The early races were hard for me. It took time to get used to the Honda. Now it is all starting to work for me and of course it has been helped by the fact that I know every metre of the track here, every change of surface. I don't think I will just be good here, though, because now I feel I am on top of the bike and I have it working well. I still use the cross-ply front Michelin, though. I cannot get on with the radial at all, I have had too many falls with it to trust it.'

Unfortunately Reggiani wanted so badly to hang on to that pole position that in the last few moments of practice he went out to record one last quick lap. He had been weighing the pros and cons of two rear tyres. One gave him predictable grip while the other hung on longer but let go more suddenly. For the fast lap he chose the second and probably, in his haste, allowed too little time for it to warm up. He was flicked off and suffered a broken bone in his foot – just enough to prevent him from riding on Sunday.

Cadalora said that his half-second improvement in lap time for the final session came from a carburation adjustment that transformed the engine, while Wimmer thanked Michelin for coming up with a good tyre normally reserved for those on the 'A' list.

125 cc

The World Champion ended the day down in thirteenth place in the championship table. Another retirement had left him with only 17 points from four races, while Ezio Gianola headed the chart with 64 points.

Gianola had had to work for those points, though, as Hans Spaan headed the field at the end of lap one, keeping his Honda just in front of Gianola's. The Italian crowd got what they wanted next time round as their man took the lead. Martinez moved to second and Spaan was just in front of Criville.

That group of four soon started to pull away, leaving Fausto Gresini a safe fifth on the Team Italia Aprilia with British privateer Robin Milton slotting himself into sixth place. Milton looked smooth yet deceptively slow. He was riding exceptionally well but the Honda lost revs and no matter how hard he tried he could not prevent himself from being overhauled in the second half of the race.

Martinez took the lead on lap three but never had the pace to break away. On lap six the Derbi sounded sick and stopped at the pits with 'ignition problems'. That left Gianola in the lead once more, with Spaan and Criville climbing all over him.

Spaan was almost brutal in his dealings with Criville and seemed quite prepared to barge past Gianola, but he lacked the speed to capitalise on this position once in front. The two Hondas fought for the lead and Criville looked hard pressed to hang on. As the race neared half-distance Criville seemed close to losing touch but fought back and got in front of Spaan. The Cobas was sliding, with Criville doing everything to stay competitive, but unfortunately his gallant efforts were only rewarded with a fall on lap 24.

That left the win to be decided between Gianola and Spaan. The Dutchman looked prepared to do almost anything to win and set himself up on Gianola's tail for a last-lap effort. The Italian, however, had every move covered and scored a well-deserved victory. Ex-World Champion Gresini was glad to be back on the rostrum after a lean 1988, and Koji Takada had another fine ride to fourth, which jumped him to second in the championship.

250 cc

Cadalora should have won this race. His riding had been consistent and controlled and, after finishing on the rostrum in the first four races, his championship challenge was building nicely. He needed every point before the Hondas were let loose at Hockenheim and the Salzburgring.

But he made a mess of the start and in his anxiety to catch up tried to make up every place he lost off the line in the first lap. He arrived at the last double left onto the start and finish looking to be travelling 20 mph faster than anyone else, riding round the outside of the pack. The speed differential must have been much less, but that was not really the problem. He made it round the two corners but was wide on the exit, trying to accelerate on a little-used patch of tarmac where grit and dust collect. The rear tyre let go, was saved, but went again. Man and machine tumbled up the road and lay in the racing line. Cadalora had gone further and hence was protected. He ran back to pick up the bike as other riders swerved trying to avoid it. Daniel Amatriain and Bernhard Schick collided and crashed. The Spaniard's bike was wrecked and the German suffered an ankle injury.

The Italian crowd had lost their hope of victory, but the race itself was some consolation. Wimmer had led from the start but Ruggia soon took over; the German could not help fading through the 30 laps as the rear Michelin he had been given for the race failed to match the performance of the

Malcolm Bryan

Malcolm Bryan

Left: **Cardus showed great form as he fought to hang on to the lead ahead of Ruggia. Pons was always in the picture, however, keeping himself close to the action but out of trouble.**

Below: **Martinez is chased by local hero Gabriele Gnani – the Italian getting his moment of glory on his home-built machine.**

Malcolm Bryan

tyre he had been allowed for the final practice session.

Ruggia's lead was challenged first by Cardus, who has often ridden well in the opening laps. This time, however, he managed to keep going well almost to the end and was rewarded with fourth place. For much of the distance he no doubt had thoughts of winning, as he and Ruggia traded the lead between them, rarely a metre apart. Sito Pons sat in third and watched. He had a look at getting past but while he could claim second from either Ruggia or Cardus he was not desperate enough on the brakes to get past both and into the lead. For the most part they kept him third and Cornu lay fourth, just a few metres back.

The battle started to boil as the 30-lap race passed half way. Garriga, who had made a mediocre start, closed in on the leading four bringing Roth with him. Pons then realised that, with so many riders in the leading group, the last few laps could well get over-complicated. He extended himself further and took the lead decisively on lap 20, easing past Cardus so assertively that his fellow-Spaniard went well off-line. That let Ruggia and Garriga through as well and Cardus never quite recovered.

Pons led Ruggia and Garriga, cutting through the back-markers, but then on lap 25 Garriga crashed in a carbon copy of his Laguna Seca fall. This time the other man involved was Fabio Barchitta. 'I cannot believe it happened again,' said Garriga. 'It was exactly the same. He was right in the middle of the track not knowing what to do. I had to go to the inside and accelerated too hard.' With only five laps to go the gap created by the Garriga crash could not be closed by Cornu, Cardus and Roth. It was probable that the race would have been decided between Pons and Ruggia in any case, but the incident just removed any doubt.

The win went to Pons for several reasons. The Spaniard put in his fastest lap of the race on the second to last circuit and that coincided with a small mistake made by Ruggia. The Frenchman had all the work to do on the final lap; although he was right on the tail of the Honda at the last corner, Pons had a little something up his sleeve. 'I knew that the last corner was the place that Ruggia would try and pass. It is a Yamaha corner. I had used a false line there all the time I was in front and on the last lap I rode the right line.' Ruggia still managed to get alongside coming out of the corner but the track kinks back a little and he had to give way, just enough to lose the drag race to the line.

80 cc

Stefan Dörflinger started from pole position but was left struggling off the line with what he later complained was a clutch problem. He was eighteenth at the end of lap one. Herri Torrontegui led, but only just, from Martinez, Herreros and Gabriele Gnani. Martinez took the lead on lap two with Torrontegui holding off Gnani and Peter Öttl, who had passed Herreros.

Torrontegui and Öttl tangled on lap four and both ran off the track, giving Martinez and Gnani some breathing space. Herreros held third but Torrontegui was determined to fight his way back from sixth. It took him until lap nine to catch and pass Herreros, and Öttl was not far behind. By lap 14 of the 22 Öttl had also passed the Derbi number two and was looking for revenge on Torrontegui.

The two started to go at it hard and on lap 21 they collided again. This time Öttl got by far the worst of it: he crashed, while Torrontegui merely lost ground to Herreros but managed to repass him on the final circuit. Öttl was quite blunt about what had happened. 'He tee-boned me,' said the German, who saw little compensation in being credited with the fastest lap.

Martinez held off Gnani to win by a comfortable four seconds, while Torrontegui was well behind in third and just a second ahead of Herreros. The rest of the field was well spread out, with Dörflinger working his way to a distant fifth.

Malcolm Bryan

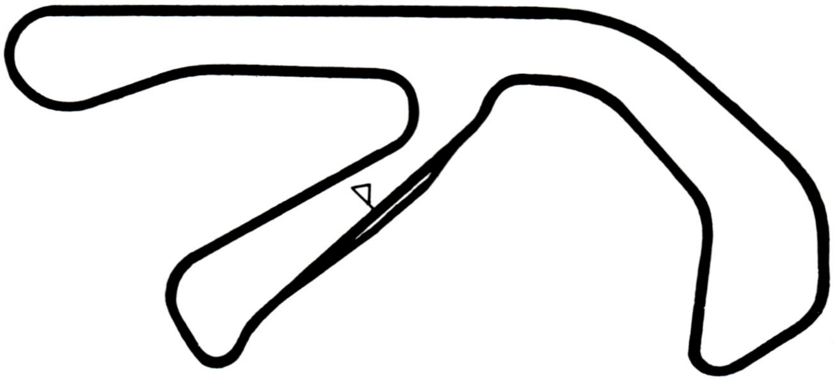

Randy Mamola explains that he and the other top riders are not going to ride. The track is too slippery.

Malcolm Bryan

500 cc

The issue might have been important, but what happened instead of a 36-lap Grand Prix was pretty boring and frustrating compared with a clash of the best riders in the world. It had rained before the scheduled start time, only lightly, but enough to dampen the track and create the most slippery conditions imaginable on any circuit. Too little water to use rain tyres, too slippery for slicks. There was a sighting lap; some riders used slicks, others had switched to patterned tyres, but neither worked.

A group of the leading riders got together in Mamola's motorhome and decided that they would only race once either the track had been allowed to dry or it rained enough to soak the circuit – and then only if they had 15 laps of wet practice. The impromptu committee making that decision comprised Lawson, Schwantz, Rainey, Sarron, McElnea, Mackenzie and Mamola. They sat waiting for the weather to change; most of the rest of the riders waited on the grid. Eventually Mike Trimby went to the motorhome and suggested that they should at least do another sighting lap as the track was drying.

So the riders came out and went for a sighting lap. Lawson led, but returned to the pit lane rather than the grid saying that there were still wet patches where the bridge covered the track in two places. They decided to wait a little longer and then to race only as long as it remained dry.

Eventually the race, scheduled for 15.35, was started soon after 16.55 but the clouds looked grey and threatening. For a few minutes all the arguing and waiting were forgotten as Sarron led from Schwantz, Rainey, Chili, Mamola, Spencer, Haslam and Mackenzie.

Chili said later that he was so churned up by the indecision prior to the race that he was in no fit state to start. By lap two he was seventh; Mamola held fourth but was slipping back from the leading trio, while Spencer and Mackenzie were advancing on him. On lap three they were right behind him.

Lap four saw Rainey leading from Schwantz and Sarron, with Mackenzie fourth ahead of Spencer and Mamola. Halfway round the next lap Schwantz took the lead but, as he did so, he saw spots of rain on his visor. 'I looked back but the others were still racing. I waved to them and they realised what was happening.' Schwantz sprinted ahead and waved his arms to the officials as he approached the start and finish straight. The red flag was put out, stopping the race.

Before a restart could be organised the heavens opened and soaked the circuit. There was no chance of any wet practice, because such a delay would have seen the race run in the dark. So the race was restarted with only Chili and Merkel of the factory men on the grid. Merkel stopped on the first lap with clutch problems but Chili went on to win from Michael Rudroff and Simon Buckmaster. The English rider was promoted to second on aggregate thanks to his better placing in the first four-lapper.

A group of the stars who had boycotted the wet race stood on the finish line and jeered derisively as Chili crossed the line. 'We won't let him forget this,' said Mamola.

Chili's attitude was that the others had messed around so much that he returned to the grid determined to race in the second leg and think about nothing else. 'It is bad enough for me just racing in Italy and being on the front row of the grid. There is tremendous tension. Then all the other guys start saying, "we race", "we don't race", back and forwards. I was completely wrecked before the first start. I made a good start but I was in such a state I couldn't concentrate and if that race had continued I would have been last. After that I decided I would race, ignore everything else and just concentrate on what I was doing. This is not a good day for me or anyone else.'

Schwantz was most obviously the rider with every reason to want to race. He had been fastest in practice and he needed the points; also, he had previously demonstrated just how good he can be in the wet. 'It is a great shame that it has come to this. The biggest problem is that there was no chance to test in the wet and you need a completely different set-up if you are going to ride in the rain. This track is the worst place it could happen at, the surface is so old and slippery that it is hard enough to race here in the dry.

'Both Eddie and I wanted to race today. We need the points to catch Wayne but it just wasn't possible. I think that when Randy Mamola and Christian Sarron don't want to race in the rain there must be something wrong with the surface.'

Schwantz suggested that the united stand taken by the top riders on the point of not racing was the beginning of a new move to stand up and be heard. 'We have been taken to places and made to race at tracks that are just not fit to have Grands Prix. We're tired of being told to shut up and ride the bikes. Finally we are all getting together to do something. Before, that was impossible. There are other tracks which we don't like racing at – Spa, Anderstorp, Salzburg and Laguna Seca. Even the Americans don't like going there.'

Spencer had sided with the majority but was not 100 per cent certain that things had worked out the right way. 'I understand the principle of not racing today, but riders of our standard are supposed to be adaptable. The trouble is that this surface is so bad and very inconsistent. I remember riding here in the damp before and every patch of tarmac is different. Normally we would race in the rain, even if all of practice had been dry. We have done that before, at Silverstone and Hockenheim. I remember choosing completely the wrong tyre at Hockenheim and Christian won but that is fair enough, that's racing.'

Gran Premio delle Nazioni, 14 May/statistics

Autodromo Santamonica, Misano, 2.167-mile/3.488-km circuit

500 cc

33 laps, 71.511 miles/115.104 km

Place	Rider	Nat.	Machine	Laps	Time & speed	Practice time	Grid
1	Pier Francesco Chili	I	Honda	33	59m 21.035s 72.304 mph/ 116.363 km/h	1m 18.181s	3
2	Simon Buckmaster	GB	Honda	33	59m 53.306s	1m 21.849s	17
3	Michael Rudroff	D	Honda	33	59m 53.634s	1m 23.449s	24
4	Marco Gentile	CH	Fior	33	60m 53.486s	1m 22.333s	19
5	Josef Doppler	A	Honda	33	61m 12.155s	1m 23.473s	25
6	Alois Meyer	D	Honda	32	59m 47.329s	1m 25.819s	31
7	Romolo Balbi	I	Honda	32	60m 51.586s	1m 22.992s	23
8	Fernando Gonzalez	E	Honda	32	61m 01.583s	1m 27.396s	32
9	Andreas Leuthe	LUX	Suzuki	31	59m 54.823s	1m 24.095s	28
10	Niggi Schmassman	CH	Honda	31	60m 44.832s	1m 24.194s	29
	Stefan Klabacher	A	Honda	7	DNF	1m 24.665s	30
	Juan Lopez Mella	E	Honda	6	DNF	1m 22.833s	21
	Wayne Rainey	USA	Yamaha	4	DNF	1m 18.286s	4
	Kevin Schwantz	USA	Suzuki	4	DNF	1m 17.424s	1
	Christian Sarron	F	Yamaha	4	DNF	1m 18.606s	5
	Niall Mackenzie	GB	Yamaha	4	DNF	1m 18.902s	6
	Randy Mamola	USA	Cagiva	4	DNF	1m 19.235s	11
	Freddie Spencer	USA	Yamaha	4	DNF	1m 19.036s	7
	Eddie Lawson	USA	Honda	4	DNF	1m 18.147s	2
	Michael Doohan	AUS	Honda	4	DNF	1m 19.180s	9
	Ron Haslam	GB	Suzuki	4	DNF	1m 19.075s	8
	Rob McElnea	GB	Honda	4	DNF	1m 19.701s	12
	Norihiko Fujiwara	J	Yamaha	4	DNF	1m 20.925s	14
	Dominique Sarron	F	Honda	4	DNF	1m 20.061s	13
	Vittorio Scatola	I	Suzuki	4	DNF	1m 22.841s	22
	Raymond Roche	F	Cagiva	4	DNF	1m 22.064s	18
	Massimo Broccoli	I	Cagiva	4	DNF	1m 20.984s	16
	Bruno Kneubühler	CH	Honda	4	DNF	1m 22.477s	20
	Alessandro Valesi	I	Yamaha	4	DNF	1m 20.972s	15
	Marco Papa	I	Paton	2	DNF	1m 23.722s	27
	Larry Vacondio	YV	Suzuki	2	DNF	1m 27.594s	33
	Fred Merkel	USA	Honda	0	DNF	1m 19.232s	10
	Claude Albert	F	Suzuki		DNS	1m 23.522s	26

Fastest lap: Lawson, 1m 19.169s, 98.553 mph/158.607 km/h.
Lap record: Randy Mamola, USA (Yamaha), 1m 18.98s, 98.789 mph/158.987 km/h (1987).

World Championship: 1 Rainey, 71; **2** Lawson, 61; **3** Sarron, C., 47; **4** Chili, 39; **5** Magee and Schwantz, 37; **7** Mackenzie, 36; **8** Gardner, 33; **9** Buckmaster, 27; **10** Taira, 26; **11** Gentile, 24; **12** Haslam, 22; **13** Sarron, D., 19; **14** Rudroff, 17; **15** Doohan and Valesi, 16; **17** Spencer, 13; **18** Shobert, 12; **19** Doppler, 11; **20** Meyer, 10; **21** Balbi, 9; **22** Gonzalez and Schmassman, 8; **24** Dowson, Fujiwara and Leuthe, 7; **27** Itoh, 6; **28** Broccoli, 5; **29** Yatsushiro, 3; **30** Kneubühler and Lopez Mella, 2; **32** Laycock and Machii, 1.

125 cc

26 laps, 56.342 miles/90.688 km

Place	Rider	Nat.	Machine	Laps	Time & speed	Practice time	Grid
1	Ezio Gianola	I	Honda	26	37m 28.518s 90.22 mph/ 145.196 km/h	1m 25.795s	3
2	Hans Spaan	NL	Honda	26	37m 28.649s	1m 25.536s	1
3	Fausto Gresini	I	Aprilia	26	37m 59.463s	1m 25.996s	4
4	Koji Takada	J	Honda	26	38m 01.075s	1m 27.182s	9
5	Julian Miralles	E	Derbi	26	38m 02.289s	1m 26.971s	7
6	Hisashi Unemoto	J	Honda	26	38m 03.597s	1m 27.627s	14
7	Robin Milton	GB	Honda	26	38m 04.628s	1m 27.593s	13
8	Adolf Stadler	D	Honda	26	38m 06.714s	1m 27.736s	17
9	Bruno Casanova	I	Aprilia	26	38m 07.677s	1m 27.142s	8
10	Doriano Romboni	I	Honda	26	38m 07.958s	1m 26.862s	6
11	Luis Reyes	E	Honda	26	38m 08.075s	1m 27.224s	10
12	Herri Torrontegui	E	Honda	26	38m 23.861s	1m 28.174s	23
13	Domenico Brigaglia	I	Garelli	26	38m 26.468s	1m 27.721s	16
14	Robin Appleyard	GB	Honda	26	38m 26.608s	1m 28.275s	25
15	Lucio Pietroniro	B	Honda	26	38m 27.007s	1m 27.459s	11
16	Stefan Prein	D	Honda	26	38m 40.715s	1m 28.103s	22
17	Gastone Grassetti	I	Parilla	26	38m 40.821s	1m 28.315s	26
18	Johnny Wickström	SF	Honda	26	38m 41.372s	1m 28.446s	30
19	Taru Rinne	SF	Honda	26	38m 41.503s	1m 27.844s	18
20	Jean-Claude Selini	F	Honda	26	38m 43.148s	1m 28.092s	21
21	Josef Fischer	A	Honda	26	38m 48.441s	1m 28.462s	31
22	Thierry Feuz	CH	Honda	26	38m 51.996s	1m 27.899s	20
23	Emilio Cuppini	I	Garelli	26	38m 56.776s	1m 28.233s	24
24	Rafael Roses	E	Cobas	25	37m 40.349s	1m 28.852s	35
25	Alfred Waibel	D	Honda	25	37m 49.349s	1m 28.850s	34
26	Mike Leitner	A	Honda	25	37m 49.974s	1m 28.720s	33
	Alex Criville	E	Cobas	23	DNF	1m 26.511s	5
	Hubert Abold	D	Rotax	14	DNF	1m 28.486s	32
	Corrado Catalano	I	Gazzaniga	12	DNF	1m 27.890s	19
	Heinz Lüthi	CH	Honda	9	DNF	1m 28.373s	28
	Stefan Dörflinger	CH	Aprilia	8	DNF	1m 28.404s	29
	Jorge Martinez	E	Derbi	6	DNF	1m 25.775s	2
	Kris Galatowicz	GB	Honda	4	DNF	1m 28.921s	36
	Manuel Hernandez	E	Honda	1	DNF	1m 28.372s	27
	Bady Hassaine	TN	Honda	1	DNF	1m 27.510s	12
	Allan Scott	USA	Honda	1	DNF	1m 27.718s	15
	Jos van Dongen	NL	Honda		DNQ	1m 28.969s	
	Serge Julin	B	Honda		DNQ	1m 29.343s	
	Gerhard Waibel	D	Honda		DNQ	1m 29.386s	
	Othmar Schuler	CH	Honda		DNQ	1m 29.678s	
	Alex Bedford	GB	EMC		DNQ	1m 29.730s	
	Pier Paolo Bianchi	I	Seel		DNQ	1m 29.796s	

Fastest lap: Criville, 1m 25.768s, 90.971 mph/146.404 km/h.
Lap record: August Auinger, A (Bartol), 1m 24.73s, 92.07 mph/148.174 km/h (1986).

World Championship: 1 Gianola, 64; **2** Takada, 43; **3** Criville and Gresini, 40; **5** Unemoto, 35; **6** Milton, 33; **7** Miralles, 30; **8** Scott, 28; **9** Spaan, 25; **10** Reyes, 20; **11** Stadler, 19; **12** Prein, 18; **13** Martinez, 17; **14** Hirose, 13; **15** Torrontegui and Yoshida, 11; **17** Shima, 10; **18** Fujiwara, 9; **19** Yamashita, 8; **20** Appleyard, Casanova, Fujiyama and Pietroniro, 7; **24** Romboni and Yamada, 6; **26** Brigaglia and Saunders, 3; **28** Wickström, 2; **29** Bedford and Rinne, 1.

80 cc

22 laps, 47.674 miles/76.736 km

Place	Rider	Nat.	Machine	Laps	Time & speed	Practice time	Grid
1	Jorge Martinez	E	Derbi	22	33m 31.930s 85.317 mph/ 137.305 km/h	1m 30.205s	2
2	Gabriele Gnani	I	Gnani	22	33m 36.192s	1m 31.385s	4
3	Herri Torrontegui	E	Krauser	22	33m 48.919s	1m 31.612s	5
4	Manuel Herreros	E	Derbi	22	33m 49.835s	1m 32.906s	9
5	Stefan Dörflinger	CH	Krauser	22	34m 00.366s	1m 29.616s	1
6	Jose Saez	E	Krauser	22	34m 07.749s	1m 32.688s	8
7	Giuseppe Ascareggi	I	BBFT	22	34m 09.730s	1m 33.745s	14
8	Antonio Sanchez	E	Cobas	22	34m 16.356s	1m 33.936s	15
9	Roberto Sassone	I	Unimoto	22	34m 16.536s	1m 33.664s	12
10	Paolo Priori	I	Krauser	22	34m 31.196s	1m 33.618s	11
11	Jacques Bernard	B	Fantic	22	34m 40.302s	1m 35.054s	23
12	Hans Koopman	NL	Ziegler	22	34m 41.648s	1m 33.370s	10
13	Stefan Kurfiss	D	Krauser	22	34m 42.089s	1m 34.192s	16
14	Ralf Waldmann	D	Seel	22	34m 45.667s	1m 34.688s	20
15	Jos van Dongen	NL	Casal	21	33m 39.880s	1m 34.275s	18
16	Jaime Mariano	E	Casal	21	33m 40.028s	1m 34.866s	21
17	Janez Pintar	YU	Eberhardt	21	33m 40.184s	1m 35.173s	25
18	Alojz Pavlic	YU	Seel	21	33m 41.575s	1m 35.703s	29
19	Paul Bordes	F	RB	21	33m 55.003s	1m 35.984s	32
20	Stefan Brägger	CH	Casal	21	33m 55.677s	1m 35.345s	27
21	Mathias Ehinger	D	BMC	21	33m 57.576s	1m 36.394s	34
22	Heinz Paschen	D	Casal	21	34m 04.854s	1m 34.904s	22
23	Reiner Koster	CH	LCR	21	34m 09.873s	1m 35.491s	28
24	Undine Kummer	D	Krauser	21	35m 01.290s	1m 37.545s	36
	Peter Öttl	D	Krauser	20	DNF	1m 30.273s	3
	Jörg Seel	D	Seel	17	DNF	1m 32.648s	7
	Bert Smit	NL	Krauser	17	DNF	1m 35.399s	26
	Thomas Engl	D	Esch-GP	17	DNF	1m 35.873s	31
	Xavier Arumi	E	Krauser	14	DNF	1m 36.366s	33
	Bogdan Nikolov	BG	Krauser	10	DNF	1m 32.489s	6
	Zdravko Matulja	YU	Casal	10	DNF	1m 35.859s	30
	Reiner Scheidhauer	D	Seel	9	DNF	1m 35.147s	24
	Janos Szabo	H	Krauser	9	DNF	1m 34.239s	17
	Salvatore Milano	I	Krauser	5	DNF	1m 36.888s	35
	René Dünki	CH	LCR	3	DNF	1m 34.357s	19
	Luis Alvaro	E	CJB	3	DNF	1m 33.682s	13
	Hagen Klein	D	Ziegler		DNQ	1m 37.572s	
	Massimo Piazza	I	Casal		DNQ	1m 38.220s	
	Chris Baert	B	Bultaco		DNQ	1m 39.683s	
	Primoz Sovic	YU	Eberhardt		DNQ	1m 41.087s	
	Giuliano Tabanelli	I	Casal		DNQ	1m 49.651s	

Fastest lap: Öttl, 1m 30.136s, 86.562 mph/139.309 km/h.
Lap record: Pier Paolo Bianchi, I (Seel), 1m 29.65s, 87.018 mph/140.042 km/h (1986).

World Championship: 1 Torrontegui, 35; **2** Dörflinger, 28; **3** Herreros, 24; **4** Gnani, 23; **5** Martinez and Saez, 20; **7** Sanchez, 17; **8** Öttl, 15; **9** Nikolov, 13; **10** Priori, 11; **11** Waldmann, 10; **12** Ascareggi, 9; **13** Koopman, 8; **14** Mariano and Sassone, 7; **16** Bernard, 5; **17** Dünki and Kurfiss, 3; **19** Seel, 2; **20** Smit and van Dongen, 1.

250 cc

30 laps, 65.01 miles/104.64 km

Place	Rider	Nat.	Machine	Laps	Time & speed	Practice time	Grid
1	Alfonso Pons	E	Honda	30	40m 34.485s 96.148 mph/ 154.736 km/h	1m 20.110s	6
2	Jean-Philippe Ruggia	F	Yamaha	30	40m 34.622s	1m 19.866s	3
3	Jacques Cornu	CH	Honda	30	40m 40.600s	1m 20.700s	9
4	Carlos Cardus	E	Honda	30	40m 42.348s	1m 19.974s	4
5	Reinhold Roth	D	Honda	30	40m 42.754s	1m 20.454s	7
6	Marcellino Lucchi	I	Aprilia	30	41m 04.775s	1m 20.905s	11
7	Ivan Palazzese	YV	Aprilia	30	41m 06.933s	1m 21.695s	16
8	Renzo Colleoni	I	Aprilia	30	41m 07.379s	1m 21.458s	13
9	Martin Wimmer	D	Aprilia	30	41m 08.270s	1m 19.845s	2
10	Helmut Bradl	D	Honda	30	41m 13.820s	1m 21.354s	12
11	Masahiro Shimizu	J	Honda	30	41m 19.509s	1m 21.666s	15
12	Harald Eckl	D	Aprilia	30	41m 37.668s	1m 21.867s	18
13	Alberto Rota	I	Aprilia	30	41m 37.920s	1m 22.197s	26
14	Wilco Zeelenberg	NL	Honda	30	41m 38.127s	1m 22.542s	30
15	Alexandre Barros	BR	Yamaha	30	41m 38.799s	1m 22.781s	35
16	Alberto Puig	E	Yamaha	30	41m 38.995s	1m 21.623s	14
17	Gary Cowan	IRL	Yamaha	30	41m 40.051s	1m 22.076s	23
18	Maurizio Vitali	I	Honda	30	41m 43.210s	1m 21.889s	19
19	Jochen Schmid	D	Honda	30	41m 45.942s	1m 22.066s	22
20	Engelbert Neumair	A	Aprilia	30	41m 46.364s	1m 22.637s	32
21	Bernard Hänggeli	CH	Yamaha	29	40m 36.546s	1m 21.978s	20
22	Andreas Preining	A	Aprilia	29	40m 39.838s	1m 22.462s	29
23	Fabio Barchitta	RSM	Aprilia	29	40m 45.185s	1m 22.314s	27
24	Jean Foray	F	Yamaha	29	41m 04.321s	1m 23.014s	36
25	Jean-François Baldé	F	Yamaha	29	41m 04.560s	1m 22.556s	31
	Juan Garriga	E	Yamaha	24	DNF	1m 20.852s	10
	Stefano Caracchi	RSM	Honda	19	DNF	1m 21.809s	17
	August Auinger	A	Yamaha	18	DNF	1m 22.175s	25
	Alain Bronec	F	Aprilia	10	DNF	1m 22.368s	28
	Didier de Radiguès	B	Aprilia	9	DNF	1m 20.622s	8
	Hans Becker	D	Seel	6	DNF	1m 22.647s	33
	Urs Lucker	CH	Yamaha	4	DNF	1m 23.148s	37
	Daniel Amatriain	E	Honda	4	DNF	1m 22.063s	21
	Bernhard Schick	D	Yamaha	4	DNF	1m 22.749s	34
	Luca Cadalora	I	Yamaha	4	DNF	1m 19.751s	1
	Loris Reggiani	I	Honda		DNS	1m 20.033s	5
	Fausto Ricci	I	Aprilia		DNS	1m 22.129s	24
	Adrien Morillas	F	Yamaha		DNQ	1m 23.310s	
	Bruno Bonhuil	F	Yamaha		DNQ	1m 23.351s	
	Virginio Ferrari	I	Gazzaniga		DNQ	1m 23.361s	
	Luis Lavado	YV	Yamaha		DNQ	1m 23.502s	
	Patrick van den Goorbergh	NL	Yamaha		DNQ	1m 23.939s	

Fastest lap. Garriga, 1m 20.342s, 97.114 mph/156.291 km/h (record).
Previous record: Luca Cadalora, I (Yamaha), 1m 21.82s, 95.36 mph/153.469 km/h (1987).

World Championship: 1 Pons, 87; **2** Ruggia, 69; **3** Cadalora, 65; **4** Cardus, 52; **5** Cornu, 42; **6** Kocinski and Roth, 40; **8** Garriga, 32; **9** Shimizu, 25; **10** Filice, 22; **11** Palazzese, 19; **12** Bradl and Wimmer, 18; **14** Honma, 13; **15** Reggiani, 12; **16** de Radiguès, 11; **17** Lucchi and Okada, 10; **19** Shiomori, 9; **20** Colleoni, Cowan and Zeelenberg, 8; **23** Barros, 7; **24** Schmid, 6; **25** Rota, 5; **26** Amatriain, Beattie, Eckl and Puig, 4; **30** Arai, Auinger and Caracchi, 1.

WORLD CHAMPIONSHIP · ROUND 6

GERMAN GRAND PRIX

Malcolm Bryan

Kevin Magee returned to the fold at Hockenheim – thanks to the Misano boycott he had, in fact, only missed one points-scoring chance, at the Spanish Grand Prix. But getting back on the bike was less of a problem than getting to the circuit, because his motorhome wrecked its main bearings on the way down from Holland and had to be towed into the paddock.

Everyone rallied round as usual: Wayne Rainey ordered the parts from America, and Kevin's brother Peter helped take enough of the engine apart to find out what was needed. It could not be fixed on the spot so another motorhome had to be hired while the engine was being repaired. Missed airline connections, lost baggage, motorhome problems – there are more than just hassles on the track to frustrate the Grand Prix racer.

Wayne Gardner remained frustrated, but his problems were purely medical. On the advice of Dr Claudio Costa and Nigel Cobb Gardner had decided against surgery to repair the shattered bone in his leg, but he was depressed when he came to Hockenheim to watch the Grand Prix because the possibility that he might yet need an operation had been raised. But with further X-rays and consultations the likelihood of that receded, so Wayne and Donna could enjoy catching up with friends and the latest gossip.

Gossip is an essential ingredient of paddock life. People live on top of each other for seven months of the year, so there is all the personal stuff about girlfriends, motorhomes, houses, etc. And then there is the racing gossip. At Hockenheim much of the talk revolved around the Misano debacle. There were those who said that they would rather have raced but didn't want to go against Eddie Lawson. There were others who agreed wholeheartedly with the World Champion. And there was every shade of opinion between the two.

The personal disagreement between Lawson and IRTA general secretary Mike Trimby continued to rage; it was mainly confrontational, with little chance of constructive discussion. The politics of Grand Prix racing are becoming ever more complex with the riders feeling increasingly cut off from the decision-making. Being just about as perfect a breeding-ground for gossip and rumour as one can imagine, the stories some were telling about Lawson and others about Trimby or IRTA just added fuel to the flames. Any rumour you care to imagine will surface sooner or later – and there were rumours of bribes, or of another rider demonstration at the start of the 500 race. Hard facts were elusive, though.

It was becoming obvious that the only way that rider frustrations could be sorted out was by appointing a non-riding representative who had the time to co-ordinate their views and an open enough mind to understand some of the wider implications. The riders had to be left to do the main thing that they are good at, and that is to ride a motor cycle.

Lawson had enough troubles with the Rothmans Honda at Hockenheim to occupy all his thinking hours, especially as he had missed

Rainey *(left)* looked every inch a World Champion at Hockenheim.

Roth forces the bars to the left and the HB Honda flicks to the right, ahead of Pons, Cornu, Cardus and Wimmer.

Malcolm Bryan

the free practice session on the Wednesday. All the IRTA teams had agreed that they would not attend this.

Conscious of the cost of keeping their teams at events for four days of practice and racing, IRTA was moving towards axeing untimed practice on Thursdays. In Germany that Thursday was a public holiday and so free training was scheduled for Wednesday. This meant the teams had their men on track for yet another day, and all bar Honda had agreed not to take part in the session. Lawson stayed at home as well, so that only Mick Doohan and Masahiro Shimizu rode. Some privateers and all the top sidecar crews stood with IRTA as well, and the point was made.

Lawson could have done with the practice, though, and engineer Erv Kanemoto would certainly have had him testing on Wednesday, being one of those still wanting to retain free training periods. At the end of the first day of practice the World Champion was more than two seconds off the pace set by Schwantz. Neither Schwantz nor Rainey had ever seen Hockenheim before but both were quicker than the Honda rider. Even Doohan, another first-timer, was ahead, having made use of the free session.

Kanemoto was frustrated. 'We have so much to test here, including new cylinders and pipes. I hate to do things in such a hurry. It is too easy to try something for a few laps and throw it away because it doesn't work immediately, when there are other things to try. You cannot say that it didn't work when you didn't really try it.'

Lawson's Honda was carrying yet more frame weight than it had at Misano, and was now featuring extra tubing welded to the top of the main frame spars, increasing their section by about a quarter. Obviously the search was continuing for an ever stiffer frame. Almost as if the Honda needed to breathe more to lug the extra weight around, the fairing featured larger air intakes, perhaps twice the flow area of the originals.

Kanemoto and Lawson got things sorted out on Saturday and Lawson was quickest in the morning session, even though he did not quite match the time set by Schwantz the previous afternoon.

In the final session everyone went slightly faster still. Rainey moved back to second and settled on using the 16-in. front for the first time. The tyre looked peculiar next to the 17-in. Dunlop. Mounted on a 4.25 by 16 in. rim instead of the normal 3.5 by 17, but with almost exactly the same rolling diameter as the 17, the new Dunlop looked bulky. It obviously weighed more than the 17, and even though the wheel was lighter the combination must have been heavier.

It was also slower to turn, the carcass twist sapping rider input torque and making the feel somewhat sluggish. It offered a good profile for grip, though, and Rainey used it because it got rid of much of the front-end chatter that had been plaguing him. The tall sidewalls soaked up some of the bumps that the suspension could not – or if the chatter was not coming from road bumps the tall sidewalls did not generate as much as the 17-in. front did.

Michelin's 16-in. front had been mounted on a much narrower rim and featured shorter sidewalls. No one was interested in using them at the Hockenheimring, though. Michelin had some new rears to try that seemed promising until at least one of them lost some rubber on the final day of practice and they all had to be recalled.

Kevin Schwantz held pole but by a small enough margin that his chances of running away with the race were slim. He thought it would come down to a battle for the lead on the last lap. 'I don't think Rainey's tyres will last somehow. I think it could be me and Ed on the last lap. There are a couple of places you could pass. The best would be up the inside of the right-hander going into the stadium. I might not be close enough there because the Honda is too fast down the straight, but into the next corner is a possibility. If he is still in front after that and thinks that it is impossible to pass into the last right-hander then he had better watch out for some paint on his fairing!'

The 500 class had three manufacturers locked in a pretty even struggle. The same was not true of the 250 class where the Yamahas were up against the Hondas and the long straights. But it was a challenge that Martin Wimmer's Hein Gericke Aprilia seemed able to rise to. He qualified third, splitting the top four Hondas, taking that place on the Friday behind Helmut Bradl, who was probably the find of the meeting, and the old campaigner, Reinhold Roth. Both were on Schlogl-tuned HB Hondas.

After the first day of practice Wimmer said that things were almost, but not quite, perfect. 'We have a few things to try on the bike but the main thing is that I could ride harder; I was only trying at about 90 per cent.' He had done 15 laps testing at Hockenheim a week before the Grand Prix, so he had some idea that things would go well. 'I expected the bike to go well but not quite this well. When everything is right and I ride harder I think we can go one-and-a-half seconds quicker. In truth you need a slipstream for a really fast lap here. I had Pons's slipstream on that lap, but only for half the straights. We have done a bit of testing; the factories do, so why not us?'

Luca Cadalora could not repeat his recent run of pole positions, finding that the Marlboro Yamaha lacked the necessary speed for Hockenheim. He did well to take sixth place on the grid. It was a one-off, white-knuckle effort that

Right: **Gianola hangs on desperately from ex-champion Gresini, Criville and Taru Rinne.**

Bottom right: **Virginio Ferrari tends to the mortally wounded Ivan Palazzese. The circuit's emergency procedure was a shambles.**

required a tow from one of the fastest bikes on the track on Saturday morning, as the Italian explained. 'I made my best time this morning, chasing Sito Pons and getting a good tow from the Honda. My engine was revving way into the red then, so we thought that gearing up for the afternoon might give some extra speed. It was too much and the engine would not pull the gearing at all. We have to go back to what we had this morning and make do with that.'

The next Yamaha was Ruggia, way down in twelfth place, while Garriga was eighteenth – behind a private TZ Yamaha well ridden by Gary Cowan. The Spaniard was not impressed. 'I don't know why they should be so slow here, but in fifth and sixth our bikes just stop dead.' Ruggia could see no humour in the reaction of Jacques Cornu, who was enjoying the Honda's superiority. 'It is just too slow here on the long straights. Cornu came past this morning and just waved at me. It is very frustrating.'

Even in the 500 class it was only Rainey's Yamaha that was in the thick of the struggle. Spencer was finding it hard going on the Marlboro Yamaha; he was ninth fastest when the bike broke in the final session, leaving him out on the circuit. 'The crankshaft broke and I was stranded and couldn't get back to the pits. The bike was running much stronger than yesterday, as we got the carburation working, but from where I was standing during that session I could see where the Yamahas were suffering. The Suzukis and the Hondas just pick up the revs better as they change gear.'

Team-mate Niall Mackenzie moved to seventh in the final session. 'I wanted a second faster and that is what I got, so I am happy with that, but I have one good engine and the better-handling bike is the other one so we are swapping engines overnight. I was trying in the last session but it certainly wasn't bad and I can run that speed in the race. The times are all pretty close just in front of me.'

Sarron was going even better, in fourth place, but was still not pleased with the way the Gauloises Blondes Yamaha was performing. 'It just has no acceleration. I don't think that I have ever had such a bad practice here. It is a circuit that I normally do well at.' (He won the German Grand Prix at Hockenheim in 1985 on the 500, having won his first-ever Grand Prix at the same circuit in 1977 when riding a 250.)

Rainey moved to second fastest on the Lucky Strike Yamaha in the final session. 'We didn't make any big changes, I was just working into it. The race will probably be run in the twos if three of us get hooked up. I didn't have the chance to compare with the Suzuki or the Honda. I guess I will find out tomorrow.'

Team-mate Kevin Magee slid off in the final session, in the infield section. 'I was going for a faster lap and lost the front. I banged my ankle a bit but I don't think it will stop me racing.' Another faller was Schwantz, who came off the Suzuki in the morning session. He was unhurt and rode the machine back to the pits, where he swapped to the other bike. Kevin blamed his fall on a cold rear tyre.

80 cc

Though the 80 cc class is on its last legs and will be killed off at the end of the season the competition is still fierce – and all the more so for the private little needle match building between Peter Öttl and Herri Torrontegui. This time Öttl had his revenge for, according to him, being run off the track and tee-boned at Misano by Torrontegui. This time there was no exchange of paint. Öttl simply outrode the Spaniard on the similar Krauser as well as Manuel Herreros on the factory Derbi and Stefan Dörflinger on the works Krauser. These four provided an exciting battling display from lap one.

Dörflinger dropped back on the seventh of the eleven laps to finish fifth, behind Antonio Sanchez, the Krauser being slowed by a half-melted spark plug. But that failure did not stop the impressive run of wins by Herbert Ritberger, builder of the 80 cc Krauser, who has won every 50 and 80 cc Grand Prix at Hockenheim since 1977 when he won riding his own machine.

Öttl was inspired as he worked his way into the lead on the final lap. Torrontegui and Herreros did their best to get back past him in the stadium, but were repulsed as the German rider firmly but fairly closed the door every time. 'I worked out through the race where I was faster than them, so I knew exactly what I wanted to do on the last lap. I thought I could win it.'

Aspar Martinez retired on lap six, the Derbi misfiring again with another mysterious ignition problem. He had made a mediocre start and could not close on the leading group.

125 cc

There was no shortage of excitement in this race, and there was the added interest of a relatively new name, Taru Rinne, who looked capable of winning at one point. The Finnish girl had had some good rides in 1988 but never looked like finishing in the top three. At Hockenheim not only did she qualify second but she was right in the thick of the battle for the lead early on.

Even when Rinne dropped back it was a three-way battle, and again it went all the way to the flag. Ezio Gianola on the Honda did most of the leading but, for once, did not come out on top of the scratch to the flag. Julian Miralles was up there on the Derbi, but in the end it was Alex Criville on the Cobas who won the day. He did so on the last lap, by making his mistake first. He braked latest coming into the stadium and led, only to run wide. That gave the advantage to Gianola but he went wide at the Sachs curve, handing the lead to Miralles, who made a similar mistake at the next right-hander.

Hans Spaan had been making up for a slow start and was fourth, with Hisashi Unemoto putting in another good ride to take fifth from Stefan Prein. Seventh was Taru Rinne, and the Finnish girl accepted that she needed to work on her fitness. She faded from second place on lap eight, first because of a mistake as she was breathing down Gianola's neck, then in the closing stages because she ran out of steam.

250 cc

The incident that started the 250 disaster was almost certainly Andreas Preining's Aprilia seizing in the middle of the pack. The Austrian felt someone clip the rear of his machine as it slowed, and Palazzese was thrown over the bars and struck in mid-air by another bike. That was seen by Virginio Ferrari, who stopped rapidly, realising that the Venezuelan rider would need help. Fabio Barchitta and Bruno Bonhuil were also caught in the crashing machinery. Ferrari ran back to give what help he could to Palazzese, clearing his breathing passage before the doctor arrived in the emergency Porsche.

The race so obviously should have been stopped. Men and machines were lying on the track and could not be moved quickly. The ambulances did not stir. Even when shouted to get into action by those who could see how serious the situation was they waited two minutes for orders by radio. Their inaction was due to a lack of direction, as was the ineffective response of the flag marshals who failed to warn the leaders coming round for lap three, two minutes after the crash had occurred.

Only quick thinking and great control by the leading riders saved the already injured men from being run over, and Carlos Cardus had to take to the grass to avoid going into the back of those slowing in front of him.

Palazzese and the other two men suffered their injuries in the initial accident and the organisational disaster afterwards almost certainly had no effect on them – but that didn't change the fact that it might have compounded their suffering. It seems likely that poor Palazzese died at the track, but no announcement was made until he had been taken to hospital. Barchitta suffered serious back injuries and Bonhuil a lengthy list of badly broken bones.

The race was restarted to run the complete distance, and Roth seized an early lead from Cornu and Pons. It was soon obvious that the factory Hondas had the upper hand. Into the stadium on lap three Roth still led from Pons, Cardus, Shimizu, Wimmer on the Aprilia, Cornu, Bradl and the factory Yamahas of Garriga and Ruggia.

The Yamahas had their work cut out just hanging on to the tail of the Honda train. Wimmer's Aprilia was fast enough to mix it with them but unfortunately was not as reliable: the Aprilia seized at the first chicane on lap six with a wrecked crank. Garriga was right on his rear wheel and hit the Aprilia. 'I don't know why I didn't crash,' said Garriga. 'I hit him hard and lost control.'

Garriga managed to hang on to his Yamaha but he and Ruggia both lost ground to the Hondas. They worked to get back on terms and for a couple of laps looked as though they might succeed, but without the slipstream they never really stood much chance. They slipped back to contest seventh between them.

The ninth-place battle was between Loris

Malcolm Bryan

SHOEI
NORDICA
DUNLOP
YAMAHA
ROBERTS
3

SHOEI
EDDIE
HONDA
1
RACING
HRC
NSR
Racing
RACING
HONDA
Shell
MICHELIN
RK
NGK
AFAM

Left: **Wayne Rainey's last-lap victory increased the pressure on his championship rivals.**

Lawson *(below left)* **fought the Honda and *almost* got it to behave.**

Reggiani, who was hampered by his Misano ankle injury, Jochen Schmid on his kitted Honda RS, Luca Cadalora, who never recovered from a bad start on the Marlboro Yamaha, Alain Bronec, having his best ride of the season despite the upset of seeing his good friend Bonhuil injured, Harald Eckl, Wilco Zeelenberg, Hans Becker and Renzo Colleoni. Colleoni was the unlucky one who missed out on scoring any points at the flag.

Up at the front the battle for the lead raged right to the flag. Least likely to win of the six Honda men was Carlos Cardus who obviously had the slowest bike and was forced to some desperate braking manoeuvres just to keep in the middle of the group. In theory Pons did not have to win. His nearest championship rivals, Ruggia and Cadalora, were well out of the picture and the only thing that could harm him would be a DNF. Faintheartedness had not won Pons his first World Championship, though, and it looked like being no part of his second.

Pons won by simply braking at the latest possible moment coming to the end of the last straight before the stadium. Shimizu braked later but he was too late and ran wide, letting Pons come in on the way out. Roth also got past to take second, but at least the Japanese got on to the rostrum for the first time this season.

500 cc

Lawson decided to race with the carbon fibre front wheel for the first time. He had it in front from the start, although that hadn't been the plan. Before the race he had discussed with Kevin Schwantz the likelihood that the Yamahas would be close to running out of fuel over the last few laps, as they had been at Laguna Seca. They had agreed that, as they both needed to see Rainey stop, they would let him run in front and tow them along, thus putting maximum strain on the Yamaha's fuel consumption.

Once the race started Lawson forgot that tactic, reverting to the notion that he had voiced before the Italian Grand Prix, that Hockenheim had a special 'Honda lane' where only the NSRs' superior speed allowed them to run. So the Honda made the running and the Yamaha was able to coast along, saving fuel in the slipstream.

Though Schwantz completed the first lap behind the fast-starting Mick Doohan, he was soon into third and able to pick up the combined slipstream of the Honda and Yamaha. The Suzuki desperately needed the tow, as it lacked the top speed, and though Schwantz sat on pole position it was because of his speed through the chicanes and the stadium section. The Suzuki was a fraction off its best in the race and Schwantz later said he was having to run into the corners harder than he ever did in practice, to make up for what he was losing on the straights. When he was hanging in the slipstream the Suzuki picked up a lot more speed and was over-revving. The American had been advised that the engine could stand it.

The leading trio were pulling steadily away from the pack, which was headed by Doohan on the second Rothmans Honda. He was battling with Christian Sarron on the Gauloises Blondes Yamaha and Pier Francesco Chili on the HB Honda. Ron Haslam was in the midst of that fourth-place battle early on, on the second Pepsi Suzuki, but the machine's weak cush-drive gremlin raised its head and the bike ground to a halt after only three laps. That left Norihiko Fujiwara seventh and on his own for a couple of laps until Kevin Magee settled to the task and closed in, towing with him Freddie Spencer, Dominique Sarron and Niall Mackenzie.

Mackenzie had made a mess of the start because he was worried about running out of fuel. 'I saw that the Lucky Strike bikes did not do the sighting lap. I realised then that they must be worried about running out of fuel,' said the Scot later. 'I did the sighting lap and the warm-up lap in as high a gear as possible. The trouble was when I came to the start the engine was loaded up and it was like a slug off the line.'

Niall was fifteenth on lap one and, to add to his troubles, the Marlboro Yamaha was not running that well after the (theoretically) better engine had been put in the better-handling chassis over night. 'That engine felt stronger in practice but it didn't run as well against the other bikes. It was slow and I got mad with it, trying too hard to make up time round the corners.' Accelerating out of the Sachs curve in the stadium on lap 13 the back end stepped out, wound up the suspension and flicked Mackenzie over the bars. He landed awkwardly, breaking his left kneecap, a little finger and, though it was not found till a week later, he cracked a scaphoid.

Team-mate Freddie Spencer was not doing that much better. He had lost a contact lens just before the start and though he found it on taking his helmet off, wetted it in his mouth and replaced it, vision out of that eye was still a little blurred. It became much worse when the lens popped out again after a few laps. 'I couldn't judge the braking points for the chicanes,' said a disappointed Spencer afterwards.

On lap 15 Schwantz was still hanging on to Lawson and Rainey, but coming into the stadium his engine started to vibrate. It revived and accelerated down the straight but, arriving at the chicane, a crank bearing completed its self-destruction process and the engine stopped. The over-revving had been too much for it.

With no Schwantz to complicate matters the win was a simple battle. Lawson had the speed to stay in front down the straights but could not shake Rainey off; earlier he had almost come to grief trying to get away from the Yamaha. Rainey was braking late for the chicanes but Lawson just decided to go in even later. 'I got in too deep. I was sure it was going to hurt. I bounced off one kerb, then the other, but somehow the bike stayed on its wheels,' recalled Lawson. He might attribute it to good fortune but lesser riders would certainly have been out of luck.

Starting the last lap Lawson was leading but encountering a back-marker gave Rainey a touch of assistance and he tailed the Honda down the four straights through the forest and back to the stadium. Lawson may not have realised how close Rainey was – if he did he made a fundamental tactical error and left the inside line open to the right-hander entering the stadium. To Rainey it was as good as an engraved invitation. He slipped inside the Honda and the crowd cheered in appreciation. Lawson was left with no response. So Rainey won his second Grand Prix of the season, and this time there was nothing to sour his enjoyment.

On the rostrum Lawson made an odd remark about a tail-ender getting in front of him so that he lost the lead. Nonplussed for a second Rainey accepted the point, only later remembering that the back-marker had had no effect on the outcome. Lawson's strange excuse just proved what an important psychological victory it had been for Rainey, who had stopped to give Schwantz a lift back to the pits. Meanwhile his mechanics quickly taped up a sign that said Rainey had found the 'Honda lane', just to rub a little salt into the wound.

Sarron looked to have secured third but the Yamaha ran short of fuel on the last lap and he slipped to fifth behind Doohan and Chili. Fujiwara held off Magee, whose rear tyre had lost several chunks of rubber quite early in the race but held together to finish. Spencer's machine also ran low on fuel and he dropped from seventh to ninth on the last lap.

Doohan may have been a touch fortunate to make the rostrum, but it was a fine ride. Like Rainey, Schwantz and Magee, it was his first visit to the Hockenheimring. Unlike the other three it was also his first Grand Prix season, yet he had been unphased by the high-speed circuit.

Sidecars

The season continued to go perfectly for World Champions Steve Webster and Tony Hewitt – but that did not mean they had an easy time of collecting another 20 points. Quite the opposite. At first it looked as though their old arch-rivals, Rolf Biland and Kurt Waltisperg, would be a great threat. However, the ignition rotor fell off their Krauser engine and it came down to a battle between Webster and Streuer – but what a battle.

There was excitement all the way to the flag as Webster and Streuer fought for the lead. Streuer said later that his new passenger was taking some getting used to; Geral de Haas is 25 kg lighter than Egbert's old passenger, Bernard Schnieders. He also said that his tyres were not right.

Webster and Hewitt went off the track at one chicane, as the two outfits came together. It had looked as though Streuer might have forced Webster off, but the British crew admitted it was their own doing. Not wanting to give way to the Dutchmen they had got into the chicane too hot.

So Webster and Hewitt were still unbeaten and the British pair had extended their championship lead to twelve points over Kumano and Fahrni. Biland had yet to score and the usual challengers, Michel and Streuer, only had one second place apiece against Webster's two wins.

Grosser Preis von Deutschland, 28 May/statistics
Hockenheimring, 4.2183-mile/6.7886-km circuit

500 cc

19 laps, 80.147 miles/128.983 km

Place	Rider	Nat.	Machine	Laps	Time & speed	Practice time	Grid
1	Wayne Rainey	USA	Yamaha	19	39m 14.75s 122.536 mph/ 197.204 km/h	2m 02.82s	2
2	Eddie Lawson	USA	Honda	19	39m 15.02s	2m 02.91s	3
3	Michael Doohan	AUS	Honda	19	39m 35.46s	2m 03.86s	6
4	Pier Francesco Chili	I	Honda	19	39m 40.47s	2m 03.72s	5
5	Christian Sarron	F	Yamaha	19	39m 51.75s	2m 03.46s	4
6	Norihiko Fujiwara	J	Yamaha	19	39m 57.73s	2m 05.39s	11
7	Kevin Magee	AUS	Yamaha	19	39m 58.29s	2m 04.95s	10
8	Dominique Sarron	F	Honda	19	39m 59.73s	2m 06.62s	13
9	Freddie Spencer	USA	Yamaha	19	40m 07.77s	2m 04.84s	9
10	Rob McElnea	GB	Honda	19	40m 23.28s	2m 05.51s	12
11	Ernst Gschwender	D	Suzuki	19	41m 06.14s	2m 07.76s	15
12	Randy Mamola	USA	Cagiva	19	41m 10.64s	2m 06.64s	14
13	Alessandro Valesi	I	Yamaha	18	39m 42.86s	2m 08.97s	16
14	Simon Buckmaster	GB	Honda	18	39m 47.55s	2m 10.76s	18
15	Bruno Kneubühler	CH	Honda	18	40m 03.10s	2m 11.60s	19
16	Hansjorg Bütz	D	Honda	18	40m 06.97s	2m 12.32s	22
17	Rachel Nicotte	F	Chevallier	18	40m 10.65s	2m 11.91s	20
18	Vittorio Scatola	I	Honda	18	40m 22.68s	2m 12.64s	23
19	Juan Lopez Mella	E	Honda	18	40m 25.93s	2m 15.22s	32
20	Peter Schleef	D	Honda	18	40m 31.23s	2m 12.92s	25
21	Michael Rudroff	D	Honda	18	40m 31.80s	2m 10.21s	17
22	Josef Doppler	A	Honda	18	40m 56.18s	2m 13.12s	25
23	Peter Linden	S	Honda	18	41m 03.47s	2m 14.77s	28
24	Stefan Klabacher	A	Honda	17	39m 21.94s	2m 14.99s	30
25	Helmut Schütz	D	Honda	17	39m 23.82s	2m 15.17s	31
26	Hans Klingebiel	D	Suzuki	17	39m 52.25s	2m 15.37s	33
	Kevin Schwantz	USA	Suzuki	15	DNF	2m 02.62s	1
	Georg Jung	D	Honda	15	DNF	2m 12.06s	21
	Niall Mackenzie	GB	Yamaha	12	DNF	2m 04.11s	7
	Martin Trösch	D	Honda	11	DNF	2m 15.76s	36
	Marco Gentile	CH	Fior	7	DNF	2m 14.05s	27
	Alois Meyer	D	Honda	5	DNF	2m 14.90s	29
	Ron Haslam	GB	Suzuki	3	DNF	2m 04.65s	8
	Roland Busch	D	Honda	2	DNF	2m 15.70s	35
	Niggi Schmassman	CH	Honda	2	DNF	2m 13.32s	26
	Karl Dauer	A	Honda	1	DNF	2m 15.68s	34
	Fernando Gonzalez	E	Honda		DNQ	2m 16.08s	
	W. Maier	D	Honda		DNQ	2m 16.15s	
	Andreas Leuthe	LUX	Librenti		DNQ	2m 16.65s	
	Marco Papa	I	Paton		DNQ	2m 16.65s	
	Vincenzo Cascino	RCH	Honda		DNQ	2m 19.48s	

Fastest lap: Schwantz, 2m 02.68s, 123.789 mph/199.220 km/h (record).
Previous record: Wayne Gardner, AUS (Honda), 2m 05.50s, 121.001 mph/194.732 km/h (1987).

World Championship: 1 Rainey, 91; **2** Lawson, 78; **3** Sarron, C., 58; **4** Chili, 52; **5** Magee, 46; **6** Schwantz, 37; **7** Mackenzie, 36; **8** Gardner, 33; **9** Doohan, 31; **10** Buckmaster, 29; **11** Sarron, D., 27; **12** Taira, 26; **13** Gentile, 24; **14** Haslam, 22; **15** Spencer, 20; **16** Valesi, 19; **17** Fujiwara and Rudroff, 17; **19** Shobert, 12; **20** Doppler, 11; **21** Meyer, 10; **22** Balbi, 9; **23** Gonzalez and Schmassman, 8; **25** Dowson and Leuthe, 7; **27** Itoh and McElnea, 6; **29** Broccoli and Gschwender, 5; **31** Mamola, 4; **32** Kneubühler and Yatsushiro, 3; **34** Lopez Mella, 2; **35** Laycock and Machii, 1.

250 cc

16 laps, 67.492 miles/108.617 km

Place	Rider	Nat.	Machine	Laps	Time & speed	Practice time	Grid
1	Alfonso Pons	E	Honda	16	35m 29.34s 114.112 mph/ 183.646 km/h	2m 11.17s	2
2	Reinhold Roth	D	Honda	16	35m 29.70s	2m 11.53s	5
3	Masahiro Shimizu	J	Honda	16	35m 29.82s	2m 12.38s	8
4	Helmut Bradl	D	Honda	16	35m 30.17s	2m 11.04s	1
5	Jacques Cornu	CH	Honda	16	35m 30.51s	2m 11.47s	4
6	Carlos Cardus	E	Honda	16	35m 30.61s	2m 12.44s	9
7	Jean-Philippe Ruggia	F	Yamaha	16	35m 43.76s	2m 13.46s	12
8	Juan Garriga	E	Yamaha	16	35m 44.20s	2m 14.18s	18
9	Loris Reggiani	I	Honda	16	35m 55.66s	2m 14.13s	15
10	Jochen Schmid	D	Honda	16	35m 56.20s	2m 13.59s	14
11	Luca Cadalora	I	Yamaha	16	35m 56.55s	2m 11.82s	6
12	Alain Bronec	F	Aprilia	16	35m 56.66s	2m 15.55s	33
13	Harald Eckl	D	Aprilia	16	35m 57.04s	2m 12.94s	12
14	Wilco Zeelenberg	NL	Honda	16	35m 57.45s	2m 15.21s	27
15	Hans Becker	D	Seel	16	35m 57.57s	2m 12.89s	10
16	Renzo Colleoni	I	Aprilia	16	35m 57.88s	2m 14.41s	21
17	Gary Cowan	IRL	Yamaha	16	36m 37.45s	2m 14.17s	17
18	Bernhard Schick	D	Yamaha	16	36m 37.67s	2m 15.00s	23
19	August Auinger	A	Yamaha	16	36m 44.90s	2m 15.02s	24
20	B. Kassner	D	Yamaha	16	36m 45.02s	2m 15.28s	28
21	Adrien Morillas	F	Yamaha	16	36m 45.30s	2m 14.28s	19
22	Engelbert Neumair	A	Aprilia	16	36m 45.70s	2m 16.43s	37
23	Alberto Puig	E	Yamaha	16	36m 46.00s	2m 15.87s	34
24	Stefano Caracchi	RSM	Honda	16	36m 46.29s	2m 14.85s	22
25	Jean-François Baldé	F	Yamaha	15	35m 38.62s	2m 15.14s	26
	Daniel Amatriain	E	Honda	10	DNF	2m 15.46s	31
	Martin Wimmer	D	Aprilia	5	DNF	2m 11.27s	3
	Nigel Bosworth	GB	Aprilia	5	DNF	2m 15.46s	32
	Bernard Hänggeli	CH	Yamaha	3	DNF	2m 16.26s	35
	Maurizio Vitali	I	Honda	1	DNF	2m 15.46s	30
	Virginio Ferrari	I	Gazzaniga	0	DNF	2m 15.41s	29
	Andreas Preining	A	Aprilia	0	DNF	2m 13.55s	13
	Fabio Barchitta	RSM	Aprilia	0	DNF	2m 14.33s	20
	Ivan Palazzese	YV	Aprilia	0	DNF	2m 15.10s	25
	Bruno Bonhuil	F	Yamaha	0	DNF	2m 16.40s	36
	Didier de Radiguès	B	Aprilia	0	DNF	2m 12.13s	7
	Alberto Rota	I	Aprilia		DNS	2m 14.16s	16
	Jean Foray	F	Yamaha		DNQ	2m 16.46s	
	Massimo Matteoni	I	Yamaha		DNQ	2m 16.59s	
	Andy Leisner	USA	Honda		DNQ	2m 16.65s	
	Manfred Herweh	D	Yamaha		DNQ	2m 16.68s	
	Alexandre Barros	BR	Yamaha		DNQ	2m 16.83s	
	M. Schulten	D	Rotax		DNQ	2m 16.83s	
	Urs Jucker	CH	Yamaha		DNQ	2m 16.84s	
	Frédéric Protat	F	Aprilia		DNQ	2m 17.37s	
	H. Vontobel	CH	Yamaha		DNQ	2m 17.71s	
	Gerhard Häberle	D	Yamaha		DNQ	2m 17.81s	
	Patrick van den Goorbergh	NL	Yamaha		DNQ	2m 17.85s	
	Fausto Ricci	I	Aprilia		DNQ	2m 17.92s	
	Darren Milner	AUS	Yamaha		DNQ	2m 18.06s	
	H. Ruff	D	Rotax		DNQ	2m 18.82s	
	P. Streicher	D	Yamaha		DNQ	2m 18.87s	
	M. Rigattieri	D	WiWa		DNQ	2m 19.38s	
	M. Biegert	D	Yamaha		DNQ	2m 20.06s	
	Hans Koopman	NL	Honda		DNQ	2m 21.98s	
	S. Drazen		Honda		DNQ	2m 30.13s	

Fastest lap: Pons, 2m 10.99s, 115.937 mph/186.583 km/h (record).
Previous record: Carlos Lavado, YV (Yamaha), 2m 14.06s, 113.275 mph/182.298 km/h (1987).

World Championship: 1 Pons, 107; **2** Ruggia, 78; **3** Cadalora, 70; **4** Cardus, 62; **5** Roth, 57; **6** Cornu, 53; **7** Garriga, Kocinski and Shimizu, 40; **10** Bradl, 31; **11** Filice, 22; **12** Palazzese and Reggiani, 19; **14** Wimmer, 18; **15** Honma, 13; **16** Schmid, 12; **17** de Radiguès, 11; **18** Lucchi, Okada and Zeelenberg, 10; **21** Shiomori, 9; **22** Colleoni and Cowan, 8; **24** Barros and Eckl, 7; **26** Rota, 5; **27** Amatriain, Beattie, Bronec and Puig, 4; **31** Arai, Auinger, Becker and Caracchi, 1.

80 cc

11 laps, 46.401 miles/74.674 km

Place	Rider	Nat.	Machine	Laps	Time & speed	Practice time	Grid
1	Peter Öttl	D	Krauser	11	28m 18.84s 98.333 mph/ 158.251 km/h	2m 32.94s	2
2	Manuel Herreros	E	Derbi	11	28m 18.97s	2m 34.43s	4
3	Herri Torrontegui	E	Krauser	11	28m 19.52s	2m 35.92s	5
4	Antonio Sanchez	E	Cobas	11	28m 59.23s	2m 38.01s	8
5	Stefan Dörflinger	CH	Krauser	11	29m 00.69s	2m 32.42s	1
6	Jaime Mariano	E	Casal	11	29m 05.72s	2m 38.43s	10
7	Ralf Waldmann	D	Seel	11	29m 05.92s	2m 38.53s	11
8	Stefan Kurfiss	D	Krauser	11	29m 06.02s	2m 38.74s	12
9	Jörg Seel	D	Seel	11	29m 06.39s	2m 37.27s	6
10	Gabriele Gnani	I	Gnani	11	29m 06.50s	2m 40.62s	20
11	Paolo Priori	I	Krauser	11	29m 06.76s	2m 39.01s	14
12	Janos Szabo	H	Krauser	11	29m 15.32s	2m 37.75s	7
13	Gunther Schirnhöfer	D	Krauser	11	29m 25.65s	2m 40.93s	22
14	Hans Koopman	NL	Ziegler	11	29m 30.48s	2m 38.16s	9
15	Stefan Brägger	CH	Casal	11	29m 33.98s	2m 29.52s	17
16	Heinz Paschen	D	Casal	11	29m 35.24s	2m 39.46s	16
17	Janez Pintar	YU	Eberhardt	11	29m 35.35s	2m 40.96s	23
18	Bert Smit	NL	Krauser	11	29m 35.69s	2m 41.59s	25
19	Alojz Pavlic	YU	Seel	11	29m 47.74s	2m 40.54s	18
20	Maik Stief	D	Casal	11	29m 54.39s	2m 43.07s	32
21	Bernd Völkel	D	Seel	11	29m 54.61s	2m 43.90s	34
22	Zdravko Matulja	YU	Krauser	11	29m 55.05s	2m 42.01s	28
23	Reiner Scheidhauer	D	Seel	11	29m 55.33s	2m 41.78s	27
24	Hagen Klein	D	Ziegler	11	30m 00.63s	2m 43.30s	33
25	Jose Saez	E	Krauser	11	30m 01.42s	2m 40.68s	21
26	Brane Rokavec	YU	Seel	11	30m 10.57s	2m 42.98s	31
27	Paul Bordes	F	RB	11	30m 11.14s	2m 44.22s	35
	Reiner Koster	CH	Kroko	8	DNF	2m 40.58s	19
	Luis Alvaro	E	Krauser	7	DNF	2m 38.83s	13
	Joaquin Gali	E	Krauser	7	DNF	2m 42.68s	29
	Jacques Bernard	B	Krauser	6	DNF	2m 41.03s	24
	Jos van Dongen	NL	Casal	5	DNF	2m 39.23s	15
	René Dünki	CH	LCR	5	DNF	2m 45.97s	36
	Jorge Martinez	E	Derbi	5	DNF	2m 32.96s	3
	Thomas Engl	D	Esch GP	3	DNF	2m 42.89s	30
	Chris Baert	B	Bultaco	2	DNF	2m 41.69s	26
	Cees Besseling	NL	CJB	1	DNF		37

Fastest lap: Öttl, 2m 32.90s, 99.323 mph/159.845 km/h.
Lap record: Stefan Dörflinger, CH (Krauser), 2m 30.72s, 100.755 mph/162.149 km/h (1986).

World Championship: 1 Torrontegui, 50; **2** Herreros, 41; **3** Dörflinger, 39; **4** Öttl, 35; **5** Sanchez, 30; **6** Gnani, 29; **7** Martinez and Saez, 20; **9** Waldmann, 19; **10** Mariano, 17; **11** Priori, 16; **12** Nikolov, 13; **13** Kurfiss, 11; **14** Koopman, 10; **15** Ascareggi and Seel, 9; **17** Sassone, 7; **18** Bernard, 5; **19** Szabo, 4; **20** Dünki and Schirnhöfer, 3; **22** Brägger, Smit and van Dongen, 1.

Sidecars

14 laps, 59.056 miles/95.04 km

Place	Driver & passenger	Nat.	Machine	Laps	Time & speed	Practice time	Grid
1	Steve Webster/ Tony Hewitt	GB GB	LCR-Krauser	14	31m 23.93s 112.855 mph/ 181.623 km/h	2m 12.90s	1
2	Egbert Streuer/ Gerald de Haas	NL NL	LCR-Yamaha	14	31m 24.66s	2m 13.73s	2
3	Masato Kumano/ Markus Fahrni	J CH	LCR-Tec	14	32m 24.66s	2m 15.18s	5
4	Fritz Stölzle/ Hubert Stölzle	D D	LCR-Krauser	14	32m 20.98s	2m 17.45s	11
5	Derek Jones/ Peter Brown	GB GB	LCR-Yamaha	14	32m 21.79s	2m 17.52s	12
6	Rolf Steinhausen/ Bruno Hiller	D D	Schuh-Spezial	14	32m 29.17s	2m 17.75s	13
7	Tony Wyssen/ Kilian Wyssen	CH CH	LCR-Krauser	14	32m 33.95s	2m 20.39s	20
8	Barry Smith/ David Smith	GB GB	Windle-ADM	14	33m 04.39s	2m 20.80s	22
9	Yoshisada Kumagaya/ Brian Barlow	J GB	Windle-Yamaha	14	33m 17.08s	2m 17.29s	9
10	Theo van Kempen/ Simon Birchall	NL GB	Krauser	14	33m 18.61s	2m 18.74s	15
11	Billy Gällros/ Håkan Olsson	S S	Yamaha	14	33m 20.37s	2m 22.42s	29
12	René Progin/ Yves Hunziker	CH CH	LCR	14	33m 20.87s	2m 21.79s	26
13	Clive Stirrat/ Simon Prior	GB GB	LCR	14	33m 21.62s	2m 20.31s	24
14	George Hardwick/ Steve Parker	GB GB	LCR	14	33m 23.66s	2m 22.40s	28
15	Wolfgang Stropek/ Steve Campbell	A GB	Krauser	14	33m 26.77s	2m 21.25s	25
16	Judd Drew/ Bryan Houghton	GB GB	LCR-JPX	13	32m 16.79s	2m 22.76s	30
17	Gary Thomas/ Eckhart Rösinger	GB D	LCR-Krauser	13	32m 16.79s	2m 20.89s	23
18	Jos van Stekelenberg/ Rinie Bettgens	NL NL	LCR	12	33m 48.80s	2m 20.76s	21
19	Ralph Bohnhorst/ Thomas Böttcher	D D	LCR	11	31m 32.97s	2m 20.35s	19
20	Tony Baker/ Trevor Hopkinson	GB GB	LCR-Krauser	11	31m 37.83s	2m 19.82s	17
	Ivan Nigrowsky/ Jacques Corbier	F F	LCR-JPX	10	DNF	2m 19.85s	18
	Ray Gardner/ Tony Stevens	GB GB	LCR	9	DNF	2m 15.68s	6
	Steve Abbott/ Shaun Smith	GB GB	LCR	8	DNF	2m 18.13s	14
	Paul Atkinson/ M. Day	GB GB	LCR-Yamaha	8	DNF	2m 21.92s	27
	Alain Michel/ Jean-Marc Fresc	F F	LCR-Krauser	6	DNF	2m 15.93s	8
	Markus Egloff/ Urs Egloff	CH CH	Yamaha	5	DNF	2m 15.15s	4
	Barry Brindley/ Grahame Rose	GB GB	LCR-Yamaha	5	DNF	2m 18.76s	16
	Rolf Biland/ Kurt Waltisperg	CH CH	LCR-Krauser	3	DNF	2m 15.88s	7
	Alfred Zurbrügg/ Martin Zurbrügg	CH CH	LCR-Yamaha	3	DNF	2m 14.66s	3
	Bernd Scherer/ Thomas Schröder	D D	LCR-Krauser	2	DNF	2m 17.40s	10
	Emil Lauer/ Norbert Wild	D D	Busch-HRC		DNQ	2m 23.24s	
	Raphael Clerc/ Fredy Lueond	CH CH	LCR		DNQ	2m 23.28s	
	Frank Voigt/ Holger Voigt	D D	LCR		DNQ	2m 24.10s	
	Georg Neumann/ Gerhard Lehmann	D D	LCR		DNQ	2m 25.54s	
	Hans Hügli/ Adolf Hänni	CH CH	Sigwa		DNQ	2m 26.07s	
	John Evans/ Ian Gaunt	GB GB			DNQ	2m 26.46s	
	Egon Schons/ Peter Hoess	D D	BSR		DNQ	2m 26.81s	
	K. Hock/ K. Hock	D D	Hock		DNQ	2m 30.36s	

Fastest lap: Streuer, 2m 13.18s, 114.03 mph/183.514 km/h (record).
Previous record: Rolf Biland/Kurt Waltisperg, CH/CH (Krauser), 2m 14.61s, 112.814 mph/181.556 km/h (1986).

World Championship: 1 Webster, 40; **2** Kumano, 28; **3** Stölzle, 22; **4** Kumagaya, Michel and Streuer, 17; **7** Egloff, 15; **8** Jones, 12; **9** Brindley, 11; **10** Progin and Steinhausen, 10; **12** Wyssen, 9; **13** Smith and Zurbrügg, 8; **15** Scherer, 7; **16** Stropek and van Kempen, 6; **18** Gällros, 5; **19** Drew, 4; **20** Baker and Stirrat, 3; **22** Hardwick and Thomas, 2.

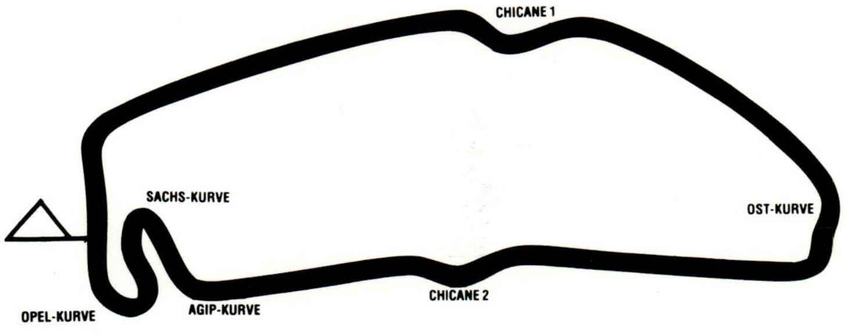

125 cc

14 laps, 59.056 miles/95.04 km

Place	Rider	Nat.	Machine	Laps	Time & speed	Practice time	Grid
1	Alex Criville	E	Cobas	14	33m 57.50s 104.349 mph/ 167.934 km/h	2m 25.14s	4
2	Ezio Gianola	I	Honda	14	33m 57.85s	2m 23.64s	1
3	Julian Miralles	E	Derbi	14	33m 57.96s	2m 26.43s	10
4	Hans Spaan	NL	Honda	14	34m 06.34s	2m 25.54s	6
5	Hisashi Unemoto	J	Honda	14	34m 07.02s	2m 27.68s	22
6	Stefan Prein	D	Honda	14	34m 07.50s	2m 26.86s	12
7	Taru Rinne	SF	Honda	14	34m 07.81s	2m 24.39s	2
8	Adolf Stadler	D	Honda	14	34m 07.92s	2m 27.03s	14
9	Robin Milton	GB	Honda	14	34m 21.73s	2m 26.00s	8
10	Gerhard Waibel	D	Honda	14	34m 40.02s	2m 27.78s	23
11	Alfred Waibel	D	Honda	14	34m 40.46s	2m 27.55s	20
12	Dirk Raudies	D	Honda	14	34m 41.07s	2m 27.98s	25
13	Luis Reyes	E	Honda	14	34m 42.06s	2m 27.41s	17
14	Johnny Wickström	SF	Honda	14	34m 42.43s	2m 26.43s	11
15	Doriano Romboni	I	Honda	14	34m 42.54s	2m 26.99s	13
16	Stefan Dörflinger	CH	Aprilia	14	34m 42.80s	2m 25.98s	7
17	Domenico Brigaglia	I	Garelli	14	34m 43.25s	2m 28.38s	27
18	Klaus Kindle	FL	Honda	14	34m 43.36s	2m 27.51s	19
19	Serge Julin	B	Honda	14	34m 49.90s	2m 28.58s	32
20	Jean-Claude Selini	F	Honda	14	34m 50.02s	2m 28.41s	29
21	Flemming Kistrup	DK	Honda	14	34m 50.66s	2m 28.76s	33
22	Allan Scott	USA	Honda	14	34m 51.53s	2m 27.43s	18
23	Rafael Roses	E	Cobas	14	35m 11.23s	2m 29.13s	36
24	Lucio Pietroniro	B	Honda	14	35m 11.63s	2m 28.07s	26
25	Thierry Feuz	CH	Honda	14	35m 14.74s	2m 27.89s	24
26	Jorge Martinez	E	Derbi	14	35m 20.21s	2m 24.48s	3
27	E. Himmelsbach	D	Honda	14	36m 11.62s	2m 28.82s	34
	Bady Hassaine	TN	Honda	11	DNF	2m 28.57s	31
	Pier Paolo Bianchi	I	Seel	9	DNF	2m 27.63s	21
	Fausto Gresini	I	Aprilia	8	DNF	2m 25.21s	5
	Koji Takada	J	Honda	6	DNF	2m 27.09s	16
	Herri Torrontegui	E	Honda	4	DNF	2m 28.40s	28
	Corrado Catalano	I	Gazzaniga	1	DNF	2m 26.41s	9
	Esa Kytölä	SF	Honda	0	DNF	2m 27.04s	15
	Robin Appleyard	GB	Honda	0	DNF	2m 28.83s	35
	Manfred Fischer	A	Honda	0	DNF	2m 28.55s	30
	J. Amstutz	CH	Honda		DNQ	2m 29.13s	
	Mike Leitner	A	Honda		DNQ	2m 29.23s	
	Gastone Grassetti	I	Honda		DNQ	2m 29.50s	
	Jörg Seel	D	Seel		DNQ	2m 29.56s	
	Reinhard Strack	D	Honda		DNQ	2m 29.60s	
	Alex Bedford	GB	EMC		DNQ	2m 29.88s	
	Jos van Dongen	NL	Honda		DNQ	2m 29.94s	
	Othmar Schuler	CH	Honda		DNQ	2m 30.01s	
	W. Fritz	D	Honda		DNQ	2m 30.03s	
	Hubert Abold	D	Rotax		DNQ	2m 30.08s	
	Emilio Cuppini	I	Garelli		DNQ	2m 30.08s	
	Bruno Casanova	I	Aprilia		DNQ	2m 30.30s	
	Ralf Waldmann	D	Seel		DNQ	2m 30.67s	
	Hervé Duffard	F	Honda		DNQ	2m 31.17s	
	G. Pigue	F	Honda		DNQ	2m 31.20s	
	Bert Smit	NL	Honda		DNQ	2m 31.41s	
	Paul Bordes	F	Honda		DNQ	2m 31.57s	
	O. Kohlinger	D	Honda		DNQ	2m 31.66s	
	Håkan Olsson	S	Rotax		DNQ	2m 31.78s	
	D. Latorre	F			DNQ	2m 31.87s	
	Heinz Lüthi	CH	Honda		DNQ	2m 32.14s	
	Manfred Thurmayer	D	Honda		DNQ	2m 32.59s	
	Trevor Manley	AUS	Honda		DNQ	2m 32.70s	
	Adrie Nijenhuis	NL	Honda		DNQ	2m 33.03s	
	Valerio Vivarelli	RSM	Rotax		DNQ	2m 33.42s	
	H. Litz	D	Honda		DNQ	2m 34.73s	
	Roberto Dova	I	Rotax		DNQ	2m 36.09s	
	Reiner Kurz	D	Siku		DNQ	2m 36.19s	
	Stuart Edwards	GB	Era		DNQ	2m 37.31s	

Fastest lap: Miralles, 2m 24.16s, 105.344 mph/169.536 km/h.
Lap record: Luca Cadalora, I (Garelli), 2m 22.14s, 106.837 mph/171.937 km/h (1986).

World Championship: 1 Gianola, 81; **2** Criville, 60; **3** Unemoto, 46; **4** Miralles, 45; **5** Takada, 43; **6** Gresini and Milton, 40; **8** Spaan, 38; **9** Prein and Scott, 28; **11** Stadler, 27; **12** Reyes, 23; **13** Martinez, 17; **14** Hirose, 13; **15** Torrontegui and Yoshida, 11; **17** Rinne and Shima, 10; **19** Fujiwara, 9; **20** Yamashita, 8; **21** Appleyard, Casanova, Fujiyama, Pietroniro and Romboni, 7; **26** Waibel, G. and Yamada, 6; **28** Waibel, A., 5; **29** Raudies and Wickström, 4; **31** Brigaglia and Saunders, 3; **33** Bedford, 1.

Gianola *(left)* **gave his all on the 125 Honda, but it was Criville who came out the winner.**

Taru Rinne showed her male rivals that they must take her seriously as a potential Grand Prix winner.

Malcolm Bryan

Kevin Schwantz never took any lessons in style from Geoff Duke – but then Manx Nortons didn't viciously spin the rear wheel while lifting the front.

Malcolm Bryan

WORLD CHAMPIONSHIP · ROUND 7

AUSTRIAN GRAND PRIX

The chances of Aspar Martinez repeating his 80 and 125 cc World Championship double were just about non-existent even before the Austrian Grand Prix and half-distance in the series. Ezio Gianola headed the 125 cc table with 81 points while Martinez languished in thirteenth spot with only 17 points. Even if disaster struck the Italian, Criville was up there on 60 – and any doubt at all was removed when Martinez crashed in the Sunday morning warm-up and broke his collarbone after qualifying on pole. He also hurt his thumb, a nasty injury that threatened to keep him out of action for several races.

Derbi just might have been regretting the action they took in sacking Alex Criville from their team because he refused to follow team orders in 1988. Though just 19, the young Spaniard was fast developing into an impressive contender in the 125 class, exhibiting a skill that might well see him go on to race 250s, and maybe even 500s. His second place in the 1988 80 cc World Championship as part of the Derbi factory team had highlighted his tremendous ability, while his wins on the 125 Cobas at the start of this season demonstrated that he is a fast learner.

Criville put much of the early season success down to his pre-season testing. 'We started early, in January, when we went to Calafat for two days. A week later we had three days at Járama, then a month doing more work on the bike before spending a week at Jerez, then flying to Japan for the first race. By the time we left for Japan I knew we had a great bike.'

He had also had the occasional chance to race the 125 cc Derbi last season and hence was able to weigh up what was needed for the Rotax-engined Marlboro Cobas to be competitive. 'The Derbi has more power at the top of the rev range but the Rotax has a better spread and handles better.'

In numbers, at least, most of the 125 opposition comes from factory-supported Hondas. 'The Hondas have the top speed but I can get out of the corners better,' said Criville. Of the riders he rates Martinez, Gianola and Spaan as the main competition but, having beaten them all early in the season, does not see any of them as better bets for the championship than himself. 'I am learning every week. I know I have made mistakes but I do learn and I think I can win the World Championship.'

Practice started wet and miserable. Julian Miralles was fastest on the Derbi with Taru Rinne, starting in Austria as she had left off in Germany, in second place ahead of Martinez and Allan Scott. In his second year of Grand Prix racing the American had changed from an occasionally competitive performer to a regular threat. In the first wet session he was quicker than rain star Gianola, with Spaan sixth ahead of Criville.

The track was still wet for the second session and Martinez went fastest, with Scott second ahead of Gianola. The third session was dry and the times were nearly ten seconds quicker. But any thoughts that the Derbis would prove too fast for the Hondas went out of the window: Gianola and Spaan were heading the table with Criville third and Martinez fourth. In the final session Martinez did find the extra speed to take pole, but with only a second covering the first six it was shaping up to be a close battle, with slipstreaming to even out the lap times in the race.

Only the first session was wet for the 500s and Wayne Rainey was so significantly quicker than anyone else that the Dunlops looked to be in a different class. Michelin were trying some new rain tyres with a hexagonal pattern which they hoped would produce the grip required to match the Dunlops and give improved wear characteristics. They had a number of different compounds and probably constructions to try. In the first and only wet session the top Michelin riders all had different tyres, so there was little chance of getting any hard-and-fast decisions in such a short time.

Christian Sarron and Ruggia had tested the tyres on both the 500 and 250 Yamahas at Le Mans before the season, and both were sure that ultimately the new tyre would be better. But with so little wet practice this season, jumping straight into a wet race was not a pleasant prospect for the Michelin users.

Second quickest in the wet was Randy Mamola on the Cagiva. Though over a second slower than Rainey he was still more competitive than he had been all year. Niall Mackenzie was forced to spectate, thanks to his broken kneecap, and said that Mamola was lapping at such a rate because he was maintaining a higher corner speed than anyone else, whereas Rainey was finding more grip coming out of the corner where he was watching (the 'S' section leading to the start and finish). 'Rainey was getting the best drive. It was sliding but he was controlling it and still going forward. Randy got his good time just by keeping up a high corner speed. Kevin was getting on OK, but Eddie seemed to be struggling.'

Mackenzie hoped to be racing again soon, having heard some good news about his knee. 'I went to Italy on Monday because it seemed that I needed to have the broken kneecap pinned. Dr Costa ordered some new X-rays and he decided that it would mend on its own. I will certainly be fit for Assen and without going through the operation I just might be able to ride in Yugoslavia.'

Team-mate Freddie Spencer eventually qualified ninth, less than half a second slower than Rainey, who was third behind poleman Schwantz and Lawson. Spencer was furious about a story in the Italian sport daily, *Corriere dello Sport*, that suggested he might be in danger of being sacked from the Marlboro Yamaha team.

In truth there was no chance of Spencer actually being sacked, though team-owner and manager Giacomo Agostini had said he was very disappointed with the ex-World Champion's showing. Spencer had tried to talk to Agostini about 1990 and had been told that before they could discuss next season he would have to produce some better results than the fifth he had managed in Spain. The Italian said that unless Spencer got on to the rostrum at the Austrian or Yugoslav rounds then he would start talking to other riders – including, obviously, Gardner, Rainey and Schwantz.

Malcolm Bryan

Spencer said that the kind of reporting that had appeared in the Italian paper was 'the worst thing about this sport'. The man from Louisiana always talks optimistically about what might be achieved, maintaining that the trouble was that the bike was not as competitive as it should be because the Agostini team were doing work during the season that the other Yamaha squads had done in the winter. Certainly Spencer had signed to ride comparatively late and the team was put together well after everyone else knew what they were doing – but it was Spencer who did not turn up for the first test, organised at Jerez, and was a day late for the Phillip Island test session.

Freddie had said prior to the Austrian Grand Prix that he thought the Yamaha would go well at the Salzburgring. 'When I was racing the Honda we always felt that the Yamahas had an advantage here because they accelerated up the hill better, even if the Hondas had the top speed. The single crank Honda was also hard to turn at the top of the hill, though with the change in the corner that problem has gone away.' After practice he admitted that he seemed to have swapped bikes at the wrong time, because he could not get the Yamaha to go anywhere near as fast as the Hondas.

Yamaha were also struggling in the 250 class, where Cadalora had done the same great job as at Hockenheim and qualified fifth, just making the front row. Garriga was ninth and Ruggia twelfth, with Pons fastest on the Campsa Honda and Wimmer second on the Hein Gericke Aprilia. It had transpired that a broken crank had stopped the German at Hockenheim, so two days at the Rotax factory on the dyno on Monday and Tuesday were needed to try to make the improvements that would prevent a recurrence. It was a great deal of work but Wimmer was enjoying running his own team, much more than his period as a full works rider as part of the Marlboro Yamaha set-up.

'I do have to work twice as hard but it is worth it. There are several advantages in running your own team. First, if you need something doing to the bike you can get on with it instantly. We broke a crankshaft in Germany so spent two days testing at Rotax before the next weekend's Austrian Grand Prix. We hope it will not happen again. As a rider in a works team you cannot get things done that quickly.

'In running my own team I also get to keep what I learn for myself. With other riders in a team, or just as one of several riders for one factory, all that you learn goes to the other riders as well. I believe it is not that hard to ride fast; it is harder to develop a machine that can go quicker.'

Wimmer pointed out that he had suffered when he was team-mate to Cadalora. 'There was

Wimmer leads Cadalora, Pons, Cornu, de Radiguès and Bradl.

Below: Garriga had no answers to the Yamaha's lack of power.

one Grand Prix in Sweden in '87 which is a perfect example. I spent the whole of practice trying to sort the bike out, trying different parts. I spent so much time doing that that I was only fifth fastest – so the good bits were given to the other Yamaha riders for the race. That is just one example, but the factory always spreads what one rider learns to the other riders. This way I can keep it to myself.

'I have experience and some feel for development, and as long as we have what is basically a good bike, like the Aprilia, then we can make something very competitive. Last year the TZ Yamaha was just too far off being competitive. We would have had to build a completely new frame to get it to work and it was too late in the year by the time we realised that nothing else would do and we could not have got it sorted out in time.

'I know that we cannot beat the factories completely so I would like to prove myself enough in this way to get factory machinery again, but for my team so I control the development.'

After qualifying second Wimmer was reluctant to make any predictions about the race. 'I have had good practice results before and something seems to go wrong in the race. This time I am going to keep quiet and see what happens.' Wimmer has always been open in courting the press and is the most successful of all the German riders in terms of personal sponsorship and media coverage. That can rub some of the other riders up a little and Reinhold Roth is one of those who occasionally enjoys a lighthearted dig at his fellow-countryman. Roth was only tenth fastest on the HB Honda, with team-mate Bradl eighth. Roth said that this was not the end of the world as he had been working to get the bike going rather than looking for a fast time. He was a second slower than Pons. 'I do not feel the need to be in pole position. My name is not Martin Wimmer.'

Though Wimmer's was quite obviously the fastest Aprilia, the chances of the factory bike ridden by Didier de Radiguès getting into the action looked much stronger with the arrival of a new engineer for the team. Aprilia hired Witteven, the ex-Cagiva motocross man who promptly scrapped all the work they had been doing with special factory engines and went back to the standard units, as used by Wimmer and the rest of the Aprilia privateers.

It had been obvious that something drastic needed to be done for a long time. At the Italian Grand Prix, for example, with Palazzese and de Radiguès riding, the team had wrecked 16 pistons. De Radiguès knew that even Witteven could not turn the bikes into Grand Prix winners overnight. 'We have to start back at the beginning because Wimmer has done a lot of development and his bikes are fast. Our bikes have been slow and they stopped all the time. The faster they went, the quicker they stopped,' said the Belgian, who broke a crank in the warm-up at Hockenheim, then again in the race when the bike was fast for two laps. 'We are now using standard engines which are not as fast as the others but if they can keep going we can gradually make them quicker.'

125 cc

The 125 class has been producing great racing all season. But this one started on a wet track and was a dud, thanks to Martinez crashing in the warm-up and Gianola at the first corner. Others fell, avoiding man and machine, and in all six riders failed to get beyond the first lap, including Taru Rinne, Herri Torrontegui and Koji Takada.

The first-lap shambles left Hans Spaan with a nice lead which he capitalised on superbly. Julian Miralles tried to give chase on the Derbi, but without great success. The third-place battle was more entertaining, with the German Dirk Raudies on his private Honda trying to hold off similarly mounted Stefan Prein and Corrado Catalano on the Gazzaniga. Fausto Gresini tried to pass the trio on lap 12 but after a clash of fairings he almost crashed, fell back to a distant sixth and had to start again.

The track was drying out during the 22-lap race. Spaan judged it perfectly, quickening his pace steadily and holding his advantage over Miralles. Thirty-year-old Spaan was using full wets for his first Grand Prix win, while Miralles was on a wet front and a cut slick rear.

Criville became the man to watch. He was still down in twelfth place on lap 11 but started to get going as the track dried, which suited his cut slicks better. On lap 18 he went from seventh to third in almost one move and quickly stretched his advantage.

The track drying meant that things changed quickly. Casanova charged through the field – eleventh on lap 16, sixth by lap 21 and fourth at the flag. Allan Scott crashed on lap one, remounted, and was sixth by lap six when he fell again. He got back on, in seventeenth place, and finished ninth. It was that sort of race.

Malcolm Bryan

250 cc

This was another great 250 race and another faultless performance from Sito Pons, although he didn't expect his win to be as clear cut as it was. 'This is not the sort of track where you expect to be able to get away from the pack. I thought it would be close right to the finish. But I tried to get away with five laps to go and I was surprised that it worked.'

Pons led off the line but allowed the more aggressive riders to relegate him on the first lap. Last year's winner, Jacques Cornu, took the lead with Cadalora second ahead of Wimmer and Pons. The early laps were not that quick: at around the 1m 27s mark they were almost three seconds slower than Pons would achieve later in the race. Wimmer took the lead on lap two, with Cadalora hanging on grimly and Pons holding on to fourth behind Cornu and ahead of de Radiguès and Bradl.

Garriga and Ruggia had both made appalling starts and their Yamahas were getting blown off

MOTUL
LUCKY STRIKE

Magee and Sarron hide Chili as they charge up the back 'straight'.

Malcolm Bryan

down the straights. On lap two Ruggia was fourteenth, just ahead of Garriga.

As so often happens in Austria, the leading group that had broken up slightly bunched again so that, by lap nine, Pons had worked his way back into the lead. Slipstreaming the Campsa Honda were Cadalora, Wimmer, de Radiguès, Cornu and Bradl.

The next group were just as tightly packed and headed by Roth, who had made a slow start. The German Honda rider was chased by Cardus, Ruggia, Shimizu, Reggiani, and Rota and Preining on their Aprilias. Garriga was out of touch and the Ducados Yamaha stopped after nine laps with a broken piston. Cadalora also started to struggle a little and had slipped to fifth when his bike stopped with the same failure. He had done a remarkable job just to stay with the leaders for so long.

Pons continued to lead with Wimmer, Bradl, Cornu and de Radiguès behind. De Radiguès was hard pressed to maintain the pace and slipped off the back of the pack around lap 17, but he was far enough ahead of the next group to manage a comfortable fifth.

Pons was holding the pace in the low 1m 25s and just beginning to ease away from Wimmer, who had Cornu and Bradl on his tail. It had looked a little as though Cornu might have been playing a waiting game – he had been right with the leading group all the way, without getting mixed up in the fighting. The Swiss rider admitted later that he'd waited just too long and Pons made his break too quickly for an effective retaliation. The World Champion put in his fastest time on lap 21, Cornu equalled that time chasing him, but the one-and-a-half second gap that Pons had seized could not be recovered.

Cornu took second from Wimmer, catching him by surprise, and while the German tried to fight back at the last corner he lost on the run in to the flag. But Wimmer was still pleased to make the rostrum. 'It is very satisfying, to translate practice speed into a race result at last.' Cardus got the better of Roth, Ruggia, Reggiani and Shimizu on the last lap, while Jochen Schmid won his lengthy private battle with Harald Eckl to take eleventh slot.

500 cc

According to speed-trap figures taken during the race, the Suzuki of Kevin Schwantz was some 20 km/h slower than Rainey's Yamaha and Lawson's Honda. Were the story as simple as that, however, Schwantz would never have been able to make the break he did on lap two and hold that advantage to win the race.

The Suzuki might well have been down that much on top speed, but the way it pulled out of the corners and climbed the hill made up for that. Schwantz added his own not inconsiderable skill and made full use of the Suzuki's much-envied handling and steering characteristics – with the result that he set a pace Lawson and Rainey had no chance of beating.

Lawson could almost match Schwantz – indeed he was only two seconds behind at the flag – but he never made any great advances on the Suzuki once his Rothmans Honda had lost the early lead.

Schwantz took the lead on lap two and by the time he started the climb up the back straight on lap three he had a one-second lead. He immediately started lapping in the 19s, and though Rainey took over second he could do no more about the Texan's advantage than Lawson. By lap five the gap was one-and-a-half seconds and Rainey was fighting tooth and nail with Lawson. The Yamaha man had ridden right round the outside of the Honda in the looping right-hander that surrounds the paddock – and Lawson would later accuse his ex-friend of cutting him up.

The pair had drawn well away from the fourth-place contest, where Christian Sarron held sway over Magee, Chili and Doohan in a battle that would prove exciting all the way through the race. Haslam joined in after fighting his way forward from a bad start, taking fourth place on lap 12 with such speed that he might have made it secure. Unfortunately he had used up his front tyre's best performance and was forced to battle every inch of the way to the flag with Sarron, Chili and Magee. Doohan missed out on the contest. He ran onto the gravel at the chicane on lap 13 after being put off-line by a back-marker. Having lost the tail of the group he could not get back on terms and had to settle for eighth, well clear of Spencer who had a lonely ride to ninth.

Schwantz carried on, reeling off the laps in his usual style. The bike was lively, the Texan working at it all the time, playing with his machine as it slid and wobbled. Lawson looked so different, so controlled – fast enough to break away from Rainey from lap 13 but not quite quick enough to catch the Suzuki. So Schwantz had his second win of the year. 'At last I got to show that the guy who sits on pole is the fastest on the race track,' he said, before climbing on to the rostrum.

Eddie Lawson said that a problem early in the race cost him dearly. 'I had a problem with the front tyre early on. It was pushing bad so when Kevin got away there was nothing I could do about it. He rode a real smart race.'

After the awards ceremony the three were on the victory car and, as they approached the sweeping right-hander, Lawson made his accusation that Rainey did not have a clue how to ride and what the ... did he think he was doing? 'Racing,' replied the Lucky Strike rider.

In the end Rainey had been forced to let Lawson get away because the Yamaha started to vibrate terribly. 'The bike was vibrating so badly it was fit to jump out of my hands. It felt as though the tyre may have turned on the rim or a wheel weight fallen off. In the end I just had to ease off because I was sure if I carried on at that speed something would've fallen off.' At the end of the race the front tyre looked a wreck, having run out of balance and overheated. The construction was at fault, and obviously the technical difficulties of making these new 16-in. front tyres had yet to be sorted out.

Haslam cursed as he crossed the line seventh,

Malcolm Bryan

Lawson and Schwantz knew they were in the same boat: Rainey just had too many points. They had schemed at Hockenheim, to let Rainey do all the leading in the hope that he might run out of fuel, but the World Champion had deviated from the plan and towed the Yamaha along. Perhaps if they just prayed that the Yamaha would break down...

having lost out to the group over the last two laps. He felt he should have been fourth. 'I had pushed so hard to make up after I made a mess of the start that the front tyre was finished. It was sliding badly but I thought I could hang on to fourth until Christian nearly had my front wheel away. It was the second to last lap and I was having trouble with the front pushing, as he came round the outside and chopped across me. I nearly hit him and that lost me too much ground to make up on the last lap.' Schwantz said that he too had experienced the front sliding at one point but had altered his line going into the looping right-hander round the pits and that had cured the problem. Later, watching a video of the race, he suggested that Haslam's line was too shallow going in and that put more stress on the front as it forced him to turn more sharply, deep into the curve.

Sarron held fourth from Magee and Chili, with Haslam shaking his head as he crossed the line just yards behind. The Frenchman said his own race had not been easy. 'The bike lost power on the second lap. I think it was the carburation as the weather changed. I couldn't stay with the first three so I just decided to hold on to fourth. I am sorry if Ron feels I passed too close but he was holding me up in that corner. I didn't know he had a problem and it was a very close race for all of us. He passed me very close one time at the top of the hill.'

Magee was happy enough with his fifth. 'I just wanted not to make any mistakes, not get left behind and not do anything spectacular. Chili's bike was faster than mine on the flat but mine pulled like a train up the hill. I had a bit of trouble with my leg, getting through the "S" and the chicane.'

Ninth was not what Spencer needed to answer his critics and afterwards he said that the bike had been disappointing. 'We had to try something to get some more acceleration, so we swapped exhaust pipes this morning. They seemed all right but it was wet. In the race they helped the acceleration a little, but they wouldn't allow the engine to over-rev at all and that made the gearing way too short. Still, we keep trying and next week is another race.'

Spencer's two helpers, his motorhome driver and his trainer, had been doing split times from the chicane to the start of the climb up the back straight and they said his section time for the corners at the western end of the circuit was comparable with the front-runners. Carruthers had Mackenzie's mechanic, Trevor Morris, section timing the climb up the hill. Most bikes took more than seven seconds for the climb. The only machines he recorded under seven seconds were Lawson's Honda and Spencer's Yamaha. If Spencer was losing time, it was somewhere else.

Schwantz piled the pressure on early, setting a new record on lap seven, almost a second and a half faster than the one set in 1988 by Didier de Radiguès. He lapped consistently under the old record and had a four-second lead over Lawson by lap ten. 'I knew where Eddie was and I just held him. I was pretty lucky with the back-markers and didn't get into any trouble there. I didn't take any chances and the bike was working so well it helped a lot.'

Sidecars

Sitting on pole position, with just one-quarter of a second in hand over Alain Michel and nearly half a second over Biland, Webster knew he could win. He also knew that the best way to do it was to make a break at the start so pursuing outfits could not use his slipstream. He was in a hurry to get away, the starter held them up too long ... and he fried the clutch. He had two goes at getting off the line and from there the clutch slipped.

At the end of lap two, when it was obvious that it would not cure itself, he called into the pits. Dragging the fairing off the bike the pit crew threw water over the clutch and put the fairing back on. They worked quickly, but with a lap lasting only a minute and a half most of the field were lapping the World Champions as they pulled out of the pits.

Webster and Hewitt put everything into the remaining 20 laps. They broke the lap record and got up to fifteenth place, scoring what Webster called 'the hardest championship point of my life'.

Up at the front Biland and Waltisperg broke the record again as they fought to hold off Egbert Streuer and Geral de Haas and the Swiss Egloff brothers, Markus and Urs, who were later forced to slow with a slipping clutch. Biland scored his first points of the season and was doubly pleased as practice had been so frustrating. 'To get the bike to go we had changed ignition, carburettors and exhaust. At least it was worth it.'

Webster held the championship lead by two points from fifth-place finisher and consistent scorer, Masato Kumano. Also closing in were Streuer and Michel.

Grosser Preis von Österreich, 4 June/statistics
Salzburgring, 2.636-mile/4.243-km circuit

500 cc

29 laps, 76.444 miles/123.047 km

Place	Rider	Nat.	Machine	Laps	Time & speed	Practice time	Grid
1	Kevin Schwantz	USA	Suzuki	29	38m 39.05s 118.689 mph/ 191.013 km/h	1m 19.23s	1
2	Eddie Lawson	USA	Honda	29	38m 41.18s	1m 19.41s	2
3	Wayne Rainey	USA	Yamaha	29	38m 58.95s	1m 19.67s	3
4	Christian Sarron	F	Yamaha	29	39m 16.88s	1m 20.24s	5
5	Kevin Magee	AUS	Yamaha	29	39m 17.19s	1m 20.94s	7
6	Pier Francesco Chili	I	Honda	29	39m 17.55s	1m 19.95s	4
7	Ron Haslam	GB	Suzuki	29	39m 17.96s	1m 20.42s	6
8	Michael Doohan	AUS	Honda	29	39m 35.82s	1m 21.07s	10
9	Freddie Spencer	USA	Yamaha	29	39m 37.09s	1m 21.04s	9
10	Dominique Sarron	F	Honda	29	39m 42.64s	1m 20.96s	8
11	Rob McElnea	GB	Honda	29	39m 54.22s	1m 21.20s	11
12	Alessandro Valesi	I	Yamaha	28	39m 39.65s	1m 23.51s	14
13	Simon Buckmaster	GB	Honda	28	39m 50.40s	1m 24.26s	15
14	Marco Gentile	CH	Fior	27	38m 49.80s	1m 24.55s	16
15	Bruno Kneubühler	CH	Honda	27	38m 56.21s	1m 25.30s	17
16	Josef Doppler	A	Honda	27	38m 56.84s	1m 25.37s	19
17	Georg Jung	D	Honda	27	39m 04.58s	1m 25.31s	18
18	Stefan Klabacher	A	Honda	27	39m 06.49s	1m 25.70s	21
19	Michael Rudroff	D	Honda	27	39m 06.80s	1m 26.20s	22
20	Karl Dauer	A	Honda	27	39m 43.24s	1m 26.74s	24
21	Niggi Schmassman	CH	Honda	27	40m 06.24s	1m 26.73s	23
22	Fernando Gonzalez	E	Honda	27	40m 07.20s	1m 28.22s	26
23	Pavol Dekanek	CS	Honda	26	38m 44.53s	1m 28.67s	30
24	Rudolf Zeller	A	Manhattan	26	38m 52.72s	1m 28.41s	27
25	Hans Klingebiel	D	Honda	26	38m 53.18s	1m 28.13s	25
26	A. Berghammer	A	Suzuki	26	38m 56.66s	1m 28.63s	29
	Alois Meyer	D	Honda	7	DNF	1m 28.52s	28
	Juan Lopez Mella	E	Honda	7	DNF	1m 25.49s	20
	Randy Mamola	USA	Cagiva	3	DNF	1m 21.44s	12
	Norihiko Fujiwara	J	Yamaha		DNS	1m 21.74s	13
	Larry Vacondio	YV	Suzuki		DNQ	1m 34.83s	

Fastest lap: Schwantz, 1m 19.15s, 119.915 mph/192.985 km/h (record).
Previous record: Didier de Radiguès, B (Yamaha), 1m 20.61s, 117.74 mph/189.490 km/h (1988).

World Championship: 1 Rainey, 106; **2** Lawson, 95; **3** Sarron, C., 71; **4** Chili, 62; **5** Magee and Schwantz, 57; **7** Doohan, 39; **8** Mackenzie, 36; **9** Gardner and Sarron, D., 33; **11** Buckmaster, 32; **12** Haslam, 31; **13** Spencer, 27; **14** Gentile and Taira, 26; **16** Valesi, 23; **17** Fujiwara and Rudroff, 17; **19** Shobert, 12; **20** Doppler and McElnea, 11; **22** Meyer, 10; **23** Balbi, 9; **24** Gonzalez and Schmassman, 8; **26** Dowson and Leuthe, 7; **28** Itoh, 6; **29** Broccoli and Gschwender, 5; **31** Kneubühler and Mamola, 4; **33** Yatsushiro, 3; **34** Lopez Mella, 2; **35** Laycock and Machii, 1.

125 cc

22 laps, 57.992 miles/93.346 km

Place	Rider	Nat.	Machine	Laps	Time & speed	Practice time	Grid
1	Hans Spaan	NL	Honda	22	37m 10.29s 93.624 mph/ 150.673 km/h	1m 33.60s	4
2	Julian Miralles	E	Derbi	22	37m 36.41s	1m 33.79s	8
3	Alex Criville	E	Cobas	22	37m 46.50s	1m 33.32s	5
4	Bruno Casanova	I	Aprilia	22	37m 52.44s	1m 34.91s	23
5	Fausto Gresini	I	Aprilia	22	37m 52.69s	1m 33.62s	7
6	Dirk Raudies	D	Honda	22	37m 53.31s	1m 35.72s	33
7	Domenico Brigaglia	I	Garelli	22	37m 53.56s	1m 34.75s	22
8	Corrado Catalano	I	Gazzaniga	22	37m 55.69s	1m 34.58s	17
9	Allan Scott	USA	Honda	22	37m 55.91s	1m 33.52s	6
10	Robin Milton	GB	Honda	22	37m 56.42s	1m 36.03s	35
11	Jean-Claude Selini	F	Honda	22	38m 08.89s	1m 34.43s	11
12	Thierry Feuz	CH	Honda	22	38m 09.10s	1m 35.12s	26
13	Stefan Prein	D	Honda	22	38m 15.70s	1m 33.11s	3
14	Josef Fischer	A	Honda	22	38m 17.99s	1m 35.68s	31
15	Alfred Waibel	D	Honda	22	38m 20.01s	1m 34.31s	10
16	Gastone Grassetti	I	Honda	22	38m 20.21s	1m 35.37s	28
17	M. Baumann	A	Honda	22	38m 23.87s	1m 34.74s	21
18	Robin Appleyard	GB	Honda	22	38m 37.96s	1m 34.54s	15
19	Flemming Kistrup	DK	Honda	22	38m 41.12s	1m 35.43s	29
20	Heinz Lüthi	CH	Honda	22	38m 42.75s	1m 35.85s	34
21	Bady Hassaine	TN	Honda	22	38m 50.20s	1m 35.64s	30
22	Hisashi Unemoto	J	Honda	22	39m 07.41s	1m 34.49s	13
23	Mike Leitner	A	Honda	21	37m 18.74s	1m 35.69s	32
	Alex Bedford	GB	EMC	20	DNF	1m 35.16s	27
	Stefan Dörflinger	CH	Aprilia	13	DNF	1m 35.02s	24
	Esa Kytölä	SF	Honda	12	DNF	1m 34.73s	20
	Gerhard Waibel	D	Honda	8	DNF	1m 36.15s	36
	Lucio Pietroniro	B	Honda	6	DNF	1m 34.66s	19
	Luis Reyes	E	Honda	6	DNF	1m 35.12s	25
	Adolf Stadler	D	Honda	1	DNF	1m 34.47s	12
	Koji Takada	J	Honda	1	DNF	1m 34.63s	18
	Doriano Romboni	I	Honda	0	DNF	1m 34.53s	14
	Ezio Gianola	I	Honda	0	DNF	1m 32.61s	2
	Taru Rinne	SF	Honda	0	DNF	1m 34.07s	9
	Herri Torrontegui	E	Honda	0	DNF	1m 34.57s	16
	Jorge Martinez	E	Derbi		DNS	1m 32.58s	1
	Pier Paolo Bianchi	I	Seel		DNQ	1m 36.49s	
	Xavier Debon	E	Cobas		DNQ	1m 36.55s	
	Janez Pintar	YU	Honda		DNQ	1m 37.25s	
	Johnny Wickström	SF	Honda		DNQ	1m 37.29s	
	Rafael Roses	E	Cobas		DNQ	1m 37.33s	
	Klaus Kindle	FL	Honda		DNQ	1m 37.44s	
	Jos van Dongen	NL	Honda		DNQ	1m 37.60s	
	Emilio Cuppini	I	Garelli		DNQ	1m 37.73s	
	Othmar Schuler	CH	Honda		DNQ	1m 37.78s	
	Trevor Manley	AUS	Honda		DNQ	1m 37.99s	
	Håkan Olsson	S	Rotax		DNQ	1m 38.70s	

Fastest lap: Criville, 1m 38.13s, 96.721 mph/155.658 km/h.
Lap record: Fausto Gresini, I (Garelli), 1m 30.58s, 104.78 mph/168.633 km/h (1987).

World Championship: 1 Gianola, 81; **2** Criville, 75; **3** Miralles, 62; **4** Spaan, 58; **5** Gresini, 51; **6** Milton and Unemoto, 46; **8** Takada, 43; **9** Scott, 35; **10** Prein, 31; **11** Stadler, 27; **12** Reyes, 23; **13** Casanova, 20; **14** Martinez, 17; **15** Raudies, 14; **16** Hirose, 13; **17** Brigaglia, 12; **18** Torrontegui and Yoshida, 11; **20** Rinne and Shima, 10; **22** Fujiwara, 9; **23** Catalano and Yamashita, 8; **25** Appleyard, Fujiyama, Pietroniro and Romboni, 7; **29** Waibel, A., Waibel, G. and Yamada, 6; **32** Selini, 5; **33** Feuz and Wickström, 4; **35** Saunders, 3; **36** Fischer, 2; **37** Bedford, 1.

250 cc

24 laps, 63.264 miles/101.832 km

Place	Rider	Nat.	Machine	Laps	Time & speed	Practice time	Grid
1	Alfonso Pons	E	Honda	24	34m 29.14s 110.089 mph/ 177.172 km/h	1m 24.69s	1
2	Jacques Cornu	CH	Honda	24	34m 31.18s	1m 25.02s	3
3	Martin Wimmer	D	Aprilia	24	34m 31.40s	1m 24.73s	2
4	Helmut Bradl	D	Honda	24	34m 33.57s	1m 25.46s	8
5	Didier de Radiguès	B	Aprilia	24	34m 39.68s	1m 25.31s	6
6	Carlos Cardus	E	Honda	24	34m 45.25s	1m 25.02s	4
7	Reinhold Roth	D	Honda	24	34m 45.47s	1m 25.67s	10
8	Jean-Philippe Ruggia	F	Yamaha	24	34m 45.71s	1m 25.86s	12
9	Loris Reggiani	I	Honda	24	34m 46.03s	1m 25.79s	11
10	Masahiro Shimizu	J	Honda	24	34m 46.26s	1m 25.32s	7
11	Jochen Schmid	D	Honda	24	35m 09.55s	1m 26.10s	15
12	Harald Eckl	D	Aprilia	24	35m 11.08s	1m 26.38s	16
13	Renzo Colleoni	I	Aprilia	24	35m 23.51s	1m 26.54s	19
14	Maurizio Vitali	I	Honda	24	35m 23.82s	1m 27.42s	33
15	Wilco Zeelenberg	NL	Honda	24	35m 24.36s	1m 26.88s	25
16	Bernhard Schick	D	Yamaha	24	35m 24.57s	1m 27.16s	29
17	Jean-François Baldé	F	Yamaha	24	35m 24.87s	1m 26.76s	22
18	Daniel Amatriain	E	Honda	24	35m 25.08s	1m 26.70s	20
19	Alexandre Barros	BR	Yamaha	24	35m 25.64s	1m 26.98s	28
20	B. Kassner	D	Yamaha	24	35m 26.25s	1m 26.87s	24
21	Gary Cowan	IRL	Yamaha	24	35m 29.10s	1m 26.71s	21
22	Alberto Puig	E	Yamaha	24	35m 33.99s	1m 26.91s	27
23	Andy Leisner	USA	Honda	24	35m 36.07s	1m 26.89s	26
24	August Auinger	A	Yamaha	24	35m 45.11s	1m 26.85s	23
25	Manfred Herweh	D	Yamaha	23	34m 34.38s	1m 27.19s	30
26	Kevin Mitchell	GB	Yamaha	23	34m 37.22s	1m 27.68s	34
27	Jean Foray	F	Yamaha	23	34m 37.43s	1m 27.92s	36
28	Virginio Ferrari	I	Gazzaniga	23	34m 39.47s	1m 26.44s	17
29	Fausto Ricci	I	Aprilia	23	34m 40.64s	1m 27.71s	35
	Luca Cadalora	I	Yamaha	16	DNF	1m 25.09s	5
	Andreas Preining	A	Aprilia	16	DNF	1m 26.07s	14
	Alberto Rota	I	Aprilia	16	DNF	1m 25.95s	13
	Juan Garriga	E	Yamaha	9	DNF	1m 25.46s	9
	Adrien Morillas	F	Yamaha	7	DNF	1m 27.21s	31
	Hans Becker	D	Seel	6	DNF	1m 26.49s	18
	Alain Bronec	F	Aprilia	2	DNF	1m 27.40s	32
	Engelbert Neumair	A	Aprilia		DNQ	1m 27.89s	
	Patrick van den Goorbergh	NL	Yamaha		DNQ	1m 28.14s	
	Josef Hutter	A	Honda		DNQ	1m 28.22s	
	K. Dambauer	A	Rotax		DNQ	1m 28.22s	
	Doug Milner	AUS	Yamaha		DNQ	1m 29.73s	
	Martin Sraj	YU			DNQ	1m 31.74s	

Fastest lap: Pons, 1m 24.69s, 112.071 mph/180.361 km/h (record).
Previous record: Jacques Cornu, CH (Honda), 1m 24.82s, 111.89 mph/180.085 km/h (1988).

World Championship: 1 Pons, 127; **2** Ruggia, 86; **3** Cardus, 72; **4** Cadalora and Cornu, 70; **6** Roth, 66; **7** Shimizu, 46; **8** Bradl, 44; **9** Garriga and Kocinski, 40; **11** Wimmer, 33; **12** Reggiani, 26; **13** de Radiguès and Filice, 22; **15** Palazzese, 19; **16** Schmid, 17; **17** Honma, 13; **18** Colleoni, Eckl and Zeelenberg, 11; **21** Lucchi and Okada, 10; **23** Shiomori, 9; **24** Cowan, 8; **25** Barros, 7; **26** Rota, 5; **27** Amatriain, Beattie, Bronec and Puig, 4; **31** Vitali, 2; **32** Arai, Auinger, Becker and Caracchi, 1.

Sidecars

22 laps, 57.992 miles/93.346 km

Place	Driver & passenger	Nat.	Machine	Laps	Time & speed	Practice time	Grid
1	Rolf Biland/ Kurt Waltisperg	CH CH	LCR- Krauser	22	31m 47.35s 109.48 mph/ 176.191 km/h	1m 26.21s	3
2	Egbert Streuer/ Geralde Haas	NL NL	LCR- Yamaha	22	31m 48.88s	1m 27.38s	7
3	Alain Michel/ Jean-Marc Fresc	F F	LCR- Krauser	22	32m 07.57s	1m 26.07s	2
4	Alfred Zurbrügg/ Martin Zurbrügg	CH CH	LCR- Yamaha	22	32m 08.19s	1m 26.36s	4
5	Masato Kumano/ Markus Fahrni	J CH	LCR- Tec	22	32m 12.19s	1m 26.79s	6
6	Markus Egloff/ Urs Egloff	CH CH	Yamaha	22	32m 15.19s	1m 26.53s	5
7	Barry Brindley/ Grahame Rose	GB GB	LCR- Yamaha	22	32m 26.11s	1m 27.42s	8
8	Rolf Steinhausen/ Bruno Hiller	D D	Schuh	22	32m 34.58s	1m 28.06s	9
9	Fritz Stölzle/ Hubert Stölzle	D D	LCR- Krauser	22	32m 45.45s	1m 28.39s	12
10	Tony Wyssen/ Kilian Wyssen	CH CH	LCR- Krauser	22	32m 45.66s	1m 28.36s	11
11	Steve Abbott/ Shaun Smith	GB GB	LCR	22	33m 00.50s	1m 29.19s	16
12	Theo van Kempen/ Simon Birchall	NL GB	LCR- Krauser	21	31m 58.86s	1m 29.45s	17
13	Tony Baker/ Trevor Hopkinson	GB GB	LCR- Krauser	21	32m 04.15s	1m 31.02s	21
14	Ivan Nigrowsky/ Jacques Corbier	F F	LCR- JPX	21	32m 05.39s	1m 28.90s	15
15	Steve Webster/ Tony Hewitt	GB GB	LCR	21	32m 23.76s	1m 25.79s	1
16	Klaus Klaffenboeck/ Christian Parzer	A A	LCR	21	32m 29.61s	1m 30.87s	20
17	René Progin/ Yves Hunziker	CH CH	LCR	21	32m 42.43s	1m 30.67s	18
18	Billy Gällros/ Håkan Olsson	S S	Yamaha	18	32m 05.62s	1m 30.73s	19
	Derek Jones/ Peter Brown	GB GB	LCR	16	DNF	1m 28.74s	14
	Wolfgang Stropek/ Steve Campbell	A GB	Krauser	7	DNF	1m 31.31s	23
	Bernd Scherer/ Thomas Schröder	D D	LCR- Krauser	6	DNF	1m 28.44s	13
	Yoshisada Kumagaya/ Brian Barlow	J GB	Windle		DNS	1m 28.30s	10
	Ray Gardner/ Tony Strevens	GB GB	LCR		DNS	1m 31.04s	22
	George Hardwick/ Steve Parker	GB GB	LCR		DNQ	1m 32.44s	
	Gary Thomas/ Eckhart Rösinger	GB D	LCR		DNQ	1m 32.94s	

Fastest lap: Biland, 1m 25.17s, 111.439 mph/179.344 km/h (record).
Previous record: Rolf Biland/Kurt Waltisperg, CH/CH (LCR-Krauser), 1m 25.87s, 110.531 mph/177.883 km/h (1988).

World Championship: 1 Webster, 41; **2** Kumano, 39; **3** Streuer, 34; **4** Michel, 32; **5** Stölzle, 29; **6** Egloff, 25; **7** Zurbrügg, 21; **8** Biland and Brindley, 20; **10** Steinhausen, 18; **11** Kumagaya, 17; **12** Wyssen 15; **13** Jones, 12; **14** Progin and van Kempen, 10; **16** Smith, 8; **17** Scherer, 7; **18** Baker and Stropek, 6; **20** Abbott and Gällros, 5; **22** Drew, 4; **23** Stirrat, 3; **24** Hardwick, Nigrowsky and Thomas, 2.

WORLD CHAMPIONSHIP · ROUND 8

YUGOSLAVIAN GRAND PRIX

Hearing that the deaths of Phil Mellor and Steve Henshaw had brought the total fatalities in the Isle of Man to five generated a breadth of reaction in the paddock. Many people have become somewhat immune to news from the TT, knowing that it will always be bad. They try to ignore it, writing it off as nothing to do with motor cycle racing. Those who are not hardened to it and find any racing death upsetting were angered by the stupidity of the TT, while everyone who knew those charming people was deeply saddened.

For many the TT is now a distant irrelevance and its only relationship to Grand Prix racing is that it devalues all motor cycling in the eyes of the general public. The few trade people and journalists still involved with both Grand Prix racing and the TT arrived late in Yugoslavia, talking about how things must change – but it has all been said before, and the Grand Prix cynics know that next June the same news, all bad, will be heard again.

While sadness was being generated in the Isle of Man on Wednesday the fastest men in Grand Prix racing spent the day flying from Trieste, on the Italian side of the Yugoslav border, to Amsterdam and back for a press conference to publicise the Dutch TT. Wayne Rainey, Kevin Schwantz and Kevin Magee spent some time discussing the state of the championship and swapping tales of past adventures both on and off the track.

A more serious by-product of the trip was that it gave Lucky Strike mechanic Trevor Tilbury the chance to pick up a new frame from Yamaha in Amsterdam. It just fitted in the back of the six-seater Learjet. In fact it was not so much a new frame as a special version of the standard frame, built by the factory and tested by the team in the winter. It featured a revised swing arm position and head angle. No one was saying in exactly what way the frame had been modified but it looked as though the swing arm pivot had been raised and moved forward about 8 mm and the head angle increased so that the front wheel was moved forward perhaps 25 mm. (This is purely a visual guess, using the rather unreliable comparison of distances between front wheel and fairing on each machine.)

Pushing the front wheel forward demanded the use of different fork yokes to reduce the trail and had the advantage of lessening the percentage of the bike's weight running on the front wheel. This helped the bike turn more quickly, something it needed thanks to the 16-in. front Dunlop being slower to steer than the 17. The 16's taller sidewalls were flexing and absorbing Rainey's handlebar-applied steering force.

The 16 was proving advantageous, though, because that same flexing was helping the suspension cope with small bumps. Some of the pattering that had been causing Rainey a number of problems disappeared when the 16 was used. These advantages and disadvantages are not what using the 16 was supposed to be all about: it was designed to improve grip and steering by being closer in profile to the very successful 17-in. rear. Tyre design, as much as any other branch of racing, is an unpredictable science but, for whatever reason, the Dunlops were working. Rainey was right on the pace as usual, faster than any other Yamaha, faster than the Hondas and bettered only by Schwantz on the Suzuki.

Even Schwantz did not dominate practice quite as crushingly as he has done on some occasions. The fact that he took pole position without any apparent difficulty was accepted as quite normal. The only surprising thing was that he was not fastest in every session. He set the pace in the first practice period and bettered his own time in the second. That was to be the pole time and while Rainey could not quite match it he did cut the deficit to under a second on Saturday and was quicker than Schwantz in both sessions.

Lawson was obviously struggling to get the Honda round Rijeka and did well to get within half a second of the Suzuki's time. If he was beginning to doubt the wisdom of abandoning Yamaha in favour of Honda he refused to show any sign of it. It was becoming something of a joke in the paddock that Lawson, who had always been so ready to complain about the Yamaha's poor carburation or lack of speed, would now say nothing ill of the Honda. The World Champion was refusing to give anyone the chance of saying 'Ha ha, I told you so'.

Wayne Gardner was saying it anyway – if not in exactly those words, then with precisely the same sentiment. Gardner was spectating at Rijeka, frustrated because Dr Costa had suggested the plaster might come off that weekend but, when it came to an X-ray, Dr C. said that another ten days would be needed. The Australian had never actually thought he was going to race in Yugoslavia but ten more days would be very close to his intended return at Assen, and his restricted exercise programme up to that point would make racing in Holland more difficult.

Even though he was frustrated by the delay, Gardner was very impressed with Costa's skill at getting his leg to mend so well after the spiral fractures it had sustained. The bone was healing without an operation and to almost precisely the right length. 'He is right to be proud of what he has done without operating, because it was a mess,' said Wayne. 'Apparently the leg can twist ten or twenty degrees without breaking, but mine went further and just exploded like an Italian bread stick. It was catching my foot on the kerb that did it. I won't make that mistake again.'

Gardner was certain that what he had been saying over the last two years about the difficulties of riding the Honda had been proved now that Lawson was riding it and not winning anything like the number of races he had with the Yamaha. Far from saying that Lawson wasn't trying Gardner maintained that the World Champion was trying as hard as he felt was reasonable, but with the Honda that was not enough to win.

'I have been telling Honda for a long time that the bike didn't handle, but people thought I was just whingeing. Now they believe me because Eddie is having the same problems. He won eight races last year but so far this season he has only won one and that was luck, because Schwantz crashed.

'Eddie doesn't ride like I do, he is a different character and maybe that is the smart thing as far as the championship goes. I was out to win at Phillip Island but he just rode round steadily and collected some points. The way things worked out that is the way to win the championship this year and I might have to think about how far I push it in the future.

'I still think that I'm faster than Eddie but he is more consistent. We are different human beings. Maybe I'm wrong and he is right. I certainly made a mistake at Laguna Seca and I've made no excuses for that.

'Consistency could win Eddie the championship this year. I think that the Yamaha is a better bike but the Dunlop tyres aren't as good as the Michelins from what I can see. In a way I don't care who wins the championship; I just want to get racing and winning again myself.'

Lawson said that his attitude had been vindicated by Gardner's Laguna Seca crash. 'You have to give him credit for trying so hard. I wasn't prepared to do that. I just wanted to ride as hard as I could and I needed more track time on the bike.'

When it was suggested to Lawson that he had changed his style, now that he was riding the Honda, he denied it. 'No, I ride exactly the same as I always have.' Pressed on the point by the observer, Mat Oxley from *Motor Cycle News*, who said that when comparing still photographs or videos of Lawson riding the Yamaha and the Honda he was hanging off the latter much more, the World Champion stuck to his point. 'I've seen the photos and the videos, and there is no difference that I can see.'

It was almost as though he was being bloody-minded about it, refusing to be drawn into a situation where he might have to criticise the Honda for forcing him to hang off more. Privately he joked about just how far he was hanging off, how he was looking more and more like Yatsushiro had in his two Grand Prix seasons, hanging off so much that he looked to be heading in a completely different direction to the bike.

As Wayne Gardner's two-year contract with Honda was coming to a close there were many rumours that he would replace Freddie Spencer in the Marlboro Yamaha team, especially as Agostini was so publicly dissatisfied with the American's performance. Asked about the possibility Gardner was coy. 'Can I answer with a smile? For more information you will have to speak to Harris Barnett' (Gardner's manager).

Gardner was more direct about Spencer's riding. 'He is just not the same as he was in '85, when everyone called him Fast Freddie. Now he is just Freddie Spencer and it is hard to believe it is the same person. He has been pretty disappointing this season. I thought he would start off slow but be riding with the best in the middle of the season. Instead he has got slower. I have watched him in practice and he only ever puts in a couple of laps and is never hard on the gas. He just seems full of excuses. I think he's finished.'

If that was not enough Spencer's own team-manager, Giacomo Agostini, had some pretty hard words to say. 'I think Freddie is worn out. He

Herreros had a clear run at the head of the 80 field but Ötti would come from nowhere to take the win.

is only 27 but he has been racing since he was 13 and he has no more drive left. Cornu and Roth are ten years older than him but they still have hunger and determination. Freddie Spencer is not hungry. He is two seconds off the pace and never riding at full speed. Life is hard.'

Spencer himself maintained that, while he found the lack of results frustrating, it was all down to getting the bike to work and once that was sorted out he would be competitive. The latest step was to use the 16-in. front again. He had tried it at the beginning of the season but, like the other Michelin users, had gone back to the more fully developed 17.

'The only place that I have been happy with the handling of the bike this year has been Australia. I realised after last week that I needed to make the 16-in. front work for me. We have been sorting that out here and it is pretty close to being right. The rest of the bike is good and I am happier with my own performance (he qualified eighth). We have changed the bike somewhat to suit me. I have adapted a little for the bike and we are meeting in the middle. It's a happy compromise.'

The other Michelin riders have given up on the 16-in. front, though Gardner won on a 16 at Phillip Island. 'That was the old tyre,' said Spencer. 'The new tyre is different, but I think if Gardner was riding he would be using it.'

The Marlboro team were in a bit of a sorry state all round, as Mackenzie was unlikely to set the world on fire with his disabling knee injury. In one respect it was questionable whether he should have been riding anyway, as he was all but unable to change direction on the machine, but he very much wanted to get back on the bike. It was not just the broken kneecap that was slowing him down; his riding was also affected by the broken finger in his right hand and cracked scaphoid in his left wrist. 'It is better than watching,' he said, but admitted riding was a painful experience. 'Braking at the end of the straight hurts my finger, turning into the corner hurts my wrist and then my knee.'

At least the team's 250 rider, Luca Cadalora, was fully fit. The bike was his handicap, for it was proving unreliable as well as uncompetitive and had thrown him off in practice when it seized. He still managed to qualify fourth, not bad in itself, but disappointing at a circuit that the Yamaha riders thought would show their bikes in a better light.

Juan Garriga was particularly frustrated with seventh place, just slower than Ruggia. The Spaniard had convinced his team to modify one of the frames because he was certain that the bike did not handle as well as the '88 model. 'I have been saying since the beginning of the season that there is something wrong with the handling. Cadalora and Ruggia didn't believe me when I said that the frame was too weak. They are fast riders but I am a chassis man and we tested this year's frame on a jig and found that it was only two-thirds as stiff as last year's.' The team welded in a crossbeam between the two main frame spars, much like the modification made to Lawson's Honda for Jerez.

'None of the Yamahas are lapping as fast as I did here last year,' said Garriga. 'My bike is so slow that I can't get away from Puig's TZ. I paid 20 million pesetas for mine and he paid 1 million. As for a tuned TZ like Becker's, that just goes past me. I have had three years of struggling with lack of horsepower and it is making me old. Here, when I come onto the front straight, accelerating side by side with a Honda, he has 20 metres on me by the end of the straight. Where can you make that up and for how many laps? It is hard on a rider's morale. You can ride over the limit for one or two races but at the third you crash.'

It was particularly galling for Garriga to see fellow-Spaniard Sito Pons leading the championship so convincingly. With Pons talking of a switch to the 500 class Garriga was already entertaining the idea of changing to Honda at the end of the season.

Pons was continually being asked about his plans for 1990. It was early days, but then he already looked to have this year's championship wrapped up. 'I would like just to think about this year and this race, but already a lot of people have been making approaches about next season, asking what bike I would like to ride. I have to say that it is 95 per cent certain that it will be

SHOEI
5
MOTUL
SHOEI
LUCKY STRIKE
3
LUCKY STRIKE
Rothman
1

Jad Sherif/International Press Agency

Ron Haslam hated Yugoslavia. He felt that way before he tried the Suzuki, and a long and fearful front-wheel slide early in practice merely confirmed his opinion.

a 500 and 95 per cent certain that it will be a Honda.'

Pons rode a 500 Suzuki for the HB Gallina team in 1985, finishing twelfth, so what makes him think he can do better now? 'I have more experience. I realise what is involved and what it takes. I thought I was fast when I rode in '85, but looking back I can see how much I still had to learn. I know it will not be easy. The 500 class is very competitive and I will have to ride very differently, but I am prepared to make the changes. If riding a 500 means riding, standing on the seat on one leg, I will learn to ride like that!'

As for the key to his success on the 250 he was not expansive but admitted to having thought everything through very carefully. 'I think that the secret is consistency. I was fortunate at the start of the season because all the races went well for me and the others had trouble at one place or another. We have never taken the success for granted and my team work very hard all the time. We are always trying something, testing different engine parts, steering geometry, brakes, suspension and frame ideas. We started early in the year with pre-season testing and we have kept it up. Honda have helped us by making a good bike and they keep developing it.'

80 cc

Stefan Dörflinger had pole position by less than half a second from Peter Öttl. The Swiss veteran had done well in practice at all the rounds, but so often bad starts wasted his advantage. This race was another case in point, although Öttl was also slow off the line. It was left to Manuel Herreros to take the lead, after being fourth fastest in practice. Julian Miralles was backing him up on the other Derbi as team-leader Aspar Martinez could not ride because of the thumb and shoulder injury sustained in Austria. Miralles had been seventh fastest in practice but did not make a good start either, so second place went to Bogdan Nikolov ahead of Luis Alvaro and Herri Torrontegui.

By the end of lap one Torrontegui was up to second behind Herreros and the two started a battle for the lead that took them away from third-placed Alvaro. By lap two Dörflinger was still well back in eleventh place but Öttl had climbed to seventh, just ahead of Miralles. By lap five Öttl was fourth and flying, having passed Nikolov and Jörg Seel, who was riding the wheels off his father's machine. Dörflinger was ninth but right on the tail of Miralles and Paolo Priori, both of whom he passed on the next lap.

The struggle between Herreros and Torrontegui had given them quite a lead, but there was little doubt that Öttl would catch them at the speed he was going. On lap eight he was 10 metres behind, in third place, but by the end of lap nine he was at the front, flying past the two Spaniards with speed to spare. Torrontegui then woke up and chased after him, leaving the Derbi behind. By lap 12 Dörflinger was fourth, while Torrontegui continued to shadow Öttl.

Suddenly, on lap 19, Torrontegui was missing. The battery of his Krauser had run flat but unfortunately he stopped on the track side of the pit wall to have it replaced. Repairs made in places other than the pits count as outside assistance and that meant that Torrontegui was disqualified, even though he got going again and finished in eighth position, and would have scored some useful points.

This left Öttl with a comfortable win over Herreros and Dörflinger, while Miralles just beat Nikolov to the line after fighting for the last ten laps of the race. The Spaniard said afterwards that he preferred to stick to the 125 class, maintaining that there was little he could do to help Herreros in his bid for the 80 cc title.

250 cc

Yamaha should have been strong in Yugoslavia, for Rijeka is a course that rewards rider skill plus machine handling and flexibility rather than out and out power and top speed. But it was a disaster for them, another race totally dominated by Honda.

Not all the Honda men had done well in practice, though. Masahiro Shimizu could not start the race after suffering a whiplash injury in the neck from a car accident. Carlos Cardus was down in eleventh place and unlikely to star in the race but three Hondas in the hands of Pons, Roth and Cornu headed the table. The Yamahas had hit more reliability problems in practice, with Cadalora's bike suffering two crankshaft failures, one of which had thrown him off. But he was still fourth quickest.

The race was a fair reflection of practice, with Pons leading off the line from Roth. Daniel Amatriain got a flyer from the third row and was briefly third while Garriga, coming off the second row, was swallowed up by the pack; he later accused them of jumping the start.

Didier de Radiguès had been only tenth fastest in practice but was inspired once the race started, joining the Hondas at the head of the field. Roth took the lead early on lap one and de Radiguès followed with Pons, Cornu, Bradl, Reggiani and Cadalora soon making it a seven-man pack at the front. Cardus was eighth by lap two but the leaders were already stretching their advantage and the Spaniard had his work cut out dealing with Ruggia. Lap four saw Garriga still back in seventeenth place but working hard to cut his way to the front.

Roth continued to lead, but only by a metre or two, while those behind swapped places several times at each corner. On lap six Reggiani slid off unhurt; he rejoined the race but the incident cut the leading group to six. Cardus and Ruggia continued to contest seventh, with Jochen Schmid having probably his best ride of the season behind them. Amatriain crashed on lap seven, forcing Wilco Zeelenberg onto the dirt, but the Dutch rider fought back to finish ninth behind Adrien Morillas, the French superbike rider who is just beginning to make an impression as a Grand Prix privateer.

Lap nine saw de Radiguès retire just after Cadalora had collided with Bradl. Cadalora said afterwards that Bradl had tried to run into the corner underneath him and was too late on the brakes; Bradl said that the Italian had seen him on the inside, let off the brakes and then turned into him. Neither was hurt but both went out of the race.

That left only three men at the front. Pons had just taken the lead from Roth while Cornu lost a little ground when Bradl and Cadalora did their thing. But it only took him a couple of laps to catch up. By lap 11 all three were nose to tail again – and there were still 15 laps to go. Ruggia had pulled away from Cardus, who had to watch out for Garriga. The Spanish Yamaha rider had finally fought his way clear of the pack and was closing from behind.

The most crucial events in the second half of the race were that Garriga eventually got ahead of Cardus and the battle for the lead came right down to the last lap.

Pons is often said to have the fastest bike of all the Hondas. That may be so, but he also makes it look good by getting onto the straights so well. The back straight at Rijeka was a perfect example because the World Champion took his time through the first right and left in the gully and gave himself a better run than Roth through the next right and up the hill onto the straight. Even when Pons led Roth the German either did not pick this up or did not have the gearing to be able to make use of it.

In fact Roth almost won because a back-marker, Massimo Matteoni, appeared at precisely the right time to give him a break from Pons. Going onto the last lap he had half a second over the Spaniard but, unfortunately, the advantage all went away in that final circuit. Down the back straight Pons closed right up onto the tail of the HB Honda. Roth still held the lead round the far loop and through the right-hander onto the start and finish straight, but Pons was closing all the while. 'I held the inside line onto the straight,' said Roth, 'but Sito just came round the outside. His bike had more speed.' Once more Pons had shown what an incredible performer he is, so much more certain of winning than in 1988.

Roth was furious with himself for giving the race away on the final lap and Cornu was a little frustrated that back-markers had made his life more difficult in third place. He also said that after his engine had seized in the morning warm-up Jörg Moller had enriched the carburation slightly and the engine was not quite as sharp as it had been in practice.

Gary Cowan had a good ride into eleventh place on his Docshop Yamaha and Kevin Mitchell got the better of a very hard struggle with Patrick van den Goorbergh and Andreas Preining to take twelfth on his Gallacher-backed Yamaha.

Martin Wimmer retired early after his gear-change lever broke at the first corner. It had been swapped over after a practice crash left him with broken bones in his normal gearchange foot. Typically philosophical, the German said, 'It is better that it happened on the first corner rather than the last but it is annoying that it happened at all as I was tenth fastest in the warm-up this morning.'

PEPSI
SUZUKI
Arai

Jad Sherif/International Press Agency

500 cc

Schwantz led the charge off the line but, at the first corner, Rainey was right beside him and took the lead. The Suzuki rider had no plans to repeat the excesses of his first lap at Phillip Island, and Lawson also slipped past him in the first half-lap.

Rainey led Lawson, Schwantz and Magee by the narrowest of margins onto lap two but the Australian misjudged his braking with a full fuel load and ran off the track, dropping to eighth. Christian Sarron took over fourth ahead of Chili, Doohan and Haslam. Rainey was well into gear while his pursuers were still feeling their way and by the end of lap two his lead was 1.85 seconds. By the bottom of the gulley, half-way round the next lap, it was 2.29s but Lawson and Schwantz held it at that for the remainder of the lap.

A pattern was established with Rainey having the advantage over the first half of each lap, where all the corners are, while Lawson caught up down the straight and Schwantz made up a tremendous amount of ground at the far loop where he was so much faster than both his opponents.

Lap four saw the gap at three seconds, but that was as big as it got. 'I didn't plan to split like that. I just wanted to ease the tyres into the race. I was surprised to be pulling away and it wasn't hard. I thought I was lapping at around 1m 31s, but in fact I was doing 29s. Then I started to lose side grip and had to ease off. I still thought I might make a break for it with five laps to go but I couldn't get away. I would have had to make a break but I was losing time round the double left.'

Lawson and Schwantz were closing from lap five onwards, but the gains they made were still uneven, with Rainey holding them at bay for the first half-lap only to have them close on the second. That went on until lap ten, with both Lawson and Schwantz looking for a way past Rainey, when back-markers began complicating the issue. Then, on the second half of lap 13, Lawson blasted past and into the lead.

It did not last long. As the World Champion tried to make use of the clear track ahead the unwieldy Honda refused to oblige and the front tyre slid away from him. 'It tucked under on me going into the corner (the first of the double rights leading away from the left off the start and finish straight). My knee was under the bike, my foot off the footrest and I just pushed the bike upright again.' Lawson ran onto the dirt but regained control. 'It was better than hitting the guard rail.' After that, though, he felt that the front tyre was suspect and both Rainey and Schwantz started to get away. An initial gap of four-and-a-half seconds to Rainey went to five-and-a-half in three laps.

Schwantz did not even realise that Lawson had gone off the track. The Texan was right on Rainey's tail, slightly to the inside, unsighted, and was only aware that Lawson had run wide, letting them both through. He then dived past Rainey and into the lead but the Suzuki did not get clear away. Later Schwantz admitted that when he had been following Lawson early on he thought that his chances of winning were slim. 'I was going as fast as I could,' he said. 'I didn't think we were going to catch him.'

Once in front, though, Schwantz just kept forcing the pace and in the end Rainey could barely hang onto the tail of the Suzuki. When two back-markers needed passing on the last lap that just gave Rainey a little bit more of a handicap he couldn't deal with, and the deficit that had varied between one second and half a second went to just over a second. Schwantz had the win in the bag.

Lawson cruised home a distant third but well ahead of Magee on the second Lucky Strike Yamaha. He had fought all race to catch and pass Christian Sarron on the Gauloises Blondes Yamaha. The Frenchman was slowed by his right hand, injured in free practice on Thursday. 'It got to the point where I was not controlling the bike properly,' said Sarron.

Magee said that it was his mistake that made the race so difficult. 'I was right behind Lawson but with a full tank of gas I went into a corner too deep and ran wide. The rear tyre was spinning a bit but once the performance had dropped off it was pretty consistent. I caught up to Christian, then in one corner lost all that I had made up because of some back-markers. I caught him again but I thought he might have been saving himself for the end.'

The point where Magee came upon the back-markers, as he was looking for a way past Sarron, was a very close-run thing. The best of the privateers, Simon Buckmaster, was himself lapping Fernando Gonzalez as Magee came to lap Buckmaster for the first time and Gonzalez for the third time. Buckmaster needed to use all the road to get round the unpredictable Spaniard and there was no room at all for Magee.

In sixth place was Mick Doohan on the second Rothmans Honda. He had started well, was seventh on lap one and moved to sixth as Magee went off the track. He then passed Chili but was too far behind Sarron to make any impression and was later passed by Magee. 'I was pleased with the start and to get some good points, but I wanted a better result. The tyres went off and I couldn't hold Kevin when he got in front.'

Randy Mamola looked like death as he got off the Cagiva after finishing seventh, having fought a debilitating sickness that gave him a swollen throat and a raging temperature. 'I could keep going OK. It wasn't fun but the only time that I thought I wasn't going to get any points was when Ron did his thing in front and I hit him.' Ron Haslam, who finished eighth, had almost crashed the Pepsi Suzuki at two-thirds distance while battling with Mamola. 'I lost the front and the back, the bike threw me over the screen and then Randy ran into the back of me.' Somehow both men stayed on, though they ran off the track.

A careful twelfth was Niall Mackenzie on the Marlboro Yamaha, keeping himself out of trouble as much as possible with his injuries, but he couldn't avoid running up the kerb and onto the dirt at the first left-hander because he could not get across the bike in time to turn it. Team-mate Freddie Spencer pulled out on lap one saying that his bike would not run and that he suspected a problem with the fuel supply.

Grand Prix de Yougoslavie, 11 June/statistics
Rijeka, 2.590-mile/4.168-km circuit

500 cc

30 laps, 77.7 miles/125.04 km

Place	Rider	Nat.	Machine	Laps	Time & speed	Practice time	Grid
1	Kevin Schwantz	USA	Suzuki	30	45m 10.967s 103.176 mph/ 166.045 km/h	1m 29.164s	1
2	Wayne Rainey	USA	Yamaha	30	45m 12.159s	1m 29.257s	2
3	Eddie Lawson	USA	Honda	30	45m 26.637s	1m 29.603s	3
4	Kevin Magee	AUS	Yamaha	30	45m 52.512s	1m 29.745s	4
5	Christian Sarron	F	Yamaha	30	45m 52.640s	1m 30.154s	6
6	Michael Doohan	AUS	Honda	30	46m 16.703s	1m 30.982s	10
7	Randy Mamola	USA	Cagiva	30	46m 23.889s	1m 30.131s	5
8	Ron Haslam	GB	Suzuki	30	46m 33.420s	1m 30.924s	9
9	Pier Francesco Chili	I	Honda	30	46m 42.894s	1m 30.255s	7
10	Dominique Sarron	F	Honda	29	45m 18.781s	1m 31.356s	11
11	Rob McElnea	GB	Honda	29	45m 22.297s	1m 31.757s	12
12	Niall Mackenzie	GB	Yamaha	29	45m 43.454s	1m 32.189s	13
13	Massimo Broccoli	I	Cagiva	29	46m 06.670s	1m 33.919s	16
14	Simon Buckmaster	GB	Honda	29	46m 27.271s	1m 34.100s	17
15	Michael Rudroff	D	Honda	29	46m 44.850s	1m 35.341s	19
16	Bruno Kneubühler	CH	Honda	29	46m 45.001s	1m 35.509s	21
17	Marco Papa	I	Paton	28	45m 59.966s	1m 35.467s	20
18	Stefan Klabacher	A	Honda	27	45m 15.395s	1m 35.767s	25
19	Fernando Gonzalez	E	Honda	27	45m 15.732s	1m 39.627s	27
20	Niggi Schmassman	CH	Honda	27	45m 48.660s	1m 37.511s	24
21	Rudolf Zeller	A	Manhattan	27	45m 57.837s	1m 39.868s	28
	Vittorio Scatola	I	Honda	22	DNF	1m 34.906s	18
	Michael Kaplan	A	Honda	11	DNF	1m 39.077s	26
	Marco Gentile	CH	Fior	9	DNF	1m 33.459s	15
	Alessandro Valesi	I	Yamaha	8	DNF	1m 32.942s	14
	Andreas Leuthe	LUX	Librenti	3	DNF	1m 35.776s	22
	Freddie Spencer	USA	Yamaha	0	DNF	1m 30.797s	8
	Claude Albert	F	Suzuki		DNS	1m 36.892s	23
	Donato Battistoni	I			DNQ	1m 45.720s	
	Helmut Schütz	D	Honda		DNQ	1m 46.988s	

Fastest lap: Rainey, 1m 29.289s, 104.419 mph/168.047 km/h (record).
Previous record: Christian Sarron, F (Yamaha), 1m 30.57s, 102.943 mph/165.672 km/h (1988).

World Championship: 1 Rainey, 123; **2** Lawson, 110; **3** Sarron, 82; **4** Schwantz, 77; **5** Magee, 70; **6** Chili, 69; **7** Doohan, 49; **8** Mackenzie, 40; **9** Haslam and Sarron, D., 39; **11** Buckmaster, 34; **12** Gardner, 33; **13** Spencer, 27; **14** Gentile and Taira, 26; **16** Valesi, 23; **17** Rudroff, 18; **18** Fujiwara, 17; **19** McElnea, 16; **20** Mamola, 13; **21** Shobert, 12; **22** Doppler, 11; **23** Meyer, 10; **24** Balbi, 9; **25** Broccoli, Gonzalez and Schmassman, 8; **28** Dowson and Leuthe, 7; **30** Itoh, 6; **31** Gschwender, 5; **32** Kneubühler, 4; **33** Yatsushiro, 3; **34** Lopez Mella, 2; **35** Laycock and Machii, 1.

250 cc

26 laps, 67.34 miles/108.368 km

Place	Rider	Nat.	Machine	Laps	Time & speed	Practice time	Grid
1	Alfonso Pons	E	Honda	26	40m 37.119s 99.466 mph/ 160.076 km/h	1m 31.766s	1
2	Reinhold Roth	D	Honda	26	40m 37.270s	1m 32.059s	2
3	Jacques Cornu	CH	Honda	26	40m 38.639s	1m 32.220s	3
4	Jean-Philippe Ruggia	F	Yamaha	26	40m 59.893s	1m 32.503s	6
5	Juan Garriga	E	Yamaha	26	41m 13.195s	1m 32.629s	7
6	Carlos Cardus	E	Honda	26	41m 16.730s	1m 33.405s	11
7	Jochen Schmid	D	Honda	26	41m 17.009s	1m 33.767s	16
8	Adrien Morillas	F	Yamaha	26	41m 23.503s	1m 34.994s	32
9	Wilco Zeelenberg	NL	Honda	26	41m 23.962s	1m 33.733s	15
10	Renzo Colleoni	I	Aprilia	26	41m 24.167s	1m 33.695s	14
11	Gary Cowan	IRL	Yamaha	26	41m 37.047s	1m 34.117s	18
12	Kevin Mitchell	GB	Yamaha	26	41m 46.774s	1m 34.282s	23
13	Patrick van den Goorbergh	NL	Yamaha	26	41m 46.975s	1m 34.210s	22
14	Andreas Preining	A	Aprilia	26	41m 47.096s	1m 34.407s	26
15	Alexandre Barros	BR	Yamaha	26	41m 48.634s	1m 34.780s	29
16	Jean Foray	F	Yamaha	26	42m 01.652s	1m 35.250s	35
17	August Auinger	A	Yamaha	26	42m 01.799s	1m 34.132s	21
18	Massimo Matteoni	I	Yamaha	25	40m 44.178s	1m 35.047s	33
19	Alain Bronec	F	Aprilia	25	40m 47.591s	1m 35.203s	34
	Didier de Radiguès	B	Aprilia	9	DNF	1m 33.256s	10
	Fausto Ricci	I	Aprilia	9	DNF	1m 34.865s	30
	Helmut Bradl	D	Honda	8	DNF	1m 32.718s	9
	Luca Cadalora	I	Yamaha	8	DNF	1m 32.324s	4
	Daniel Amatriain	E	Honda	7	DNF	1m 33.475s	12
	Martin Wimmer	D	Aprilia	5	DNF	1m 32.339s	5
	Alberto Puig	E	Yamaha	5	DNF	1m 33.830s	17
	Urs Jucker	CH	Yamaha	5	DNF	1m 35.578s	36
	Hans Becker	D	Seel	5	DNF	1m 34.904s	31
	Jean-François Baldé	F	Yamaha	5	DNF	1m 33.693s	13
	Stefano Caracchi	RSM	Honda	5	DNF	1m 34.450s	27
	Maurizio Vitali	I	Honda	5	DNF	1m 34.347s	24
	Harald Eckl	D	Aprilia	5	DNF	1m 34.120s	19
	Loris Reggiani	I	Honda	5	DNF	1m 32.689s	8
	Masahiro Shimizu	J	Honda		DNS	1m 34.382s	25
	Alberto Rota	I	Aprilia		DNS	1m 34.132s	20
	Bernhard Schick	D	Yamaha		DNS	1m 34.709s	28
	Virginio Ferrari	I	Gazzaniga		DNQ	1m 35.614s	
	Andy Leisner	USA	Yamaha		DNQ	1m 35.720s	
	Manfred Herweh	D	Yamaha		DNQ	1m 35.938s	
	Martin Sraj	YU	Yamaha		DNQ	1m 36.904s	
	Darren Milner	AUS	Yamaha		DNQ	1m 37.163s	
	Zdravkden Leljak	YU	Honda		DNQ	1m 41.122s	
	Drazen Srdoc	YU	Honda		DNQ	1m 45.835s	

Fastest lap: Cadalora, 1m 32.260s, 101.057 mph/162.636 km/h.
Lap record: Juan Garriga, E (Yamaha), 1m 32.184s, 101.14 mph/162.770 km/h (1988).

World Championship: 1 Pons, 147; **2** Ruggia, 99; **3** Cornu, 85; **4** Roth, 83; **5** Cardus, 82; **6** Cadalora, 70; **7** Garriga, 51; **8** Shimizu, 46; **9** Bradl, 44; **10** Kocinski, 40; **11** Wimmer, 33; **12** Reggiani and Schmid, 26; **14** de Radiguès and Filice, 22; **16** Palazzese, 19; **17** Zeelenberg, 18; **18** Colleoni, 17; **19** Cowan and Honma, 13; **21** Eckl, 11; **22** Lucchi and Okada, 10; **24** Shiomori, 9; **25** Barros and Morillas, 8; **27** Rota, 5; **28** Amatriain, Beattie, Bronec, Mitchell and Puig, 4; **33** van den Goorbergh, 3; **34** Preining and Vitali, 2; **36** Arai, Auinger, Becker and Caracchi, 1.

80 cc

22 laps, 56.98 miles/91.696 km

Place	Rider	Nat.	Machine	Laps	Time & speed	Practice time	Grid
1	Peter Öttl	D	Krauser	22	37m 43.794s 90.607 mph/ 145.819 km/h	1m 42.258s	2
2	Manuel Herreros	E	Derbi	22	37m 57.238s	1m 43.633s	4
3	Stefan Dörflinger	CH	Krauser	22	38m 11.484s	1m 41.893s	1
4	Julian Miralles	E	Derbi	22	38m 23.495s	1m 44.348s	7
5	Bogdan Nikolov	BG	Krauser	22	38m 27.488s	1m 45.092s	10
6	Jörg Seel	D	Seel	22	38m 34.633s	1m 43.979s	5
7	Paolo Priori	I	Krauser	22	38m 37.506s	1m 44.764s	9
8	Gabriele Gnani	I	Gnani	22	39m 01.349s	1m 45.554s	12
9	Hans Koopman	NL	Ziegler	22	39m 12.183s	1m 44.614s	8
10	Jos van Dongen	NL	Casal	22	39m 24.288s	1m 46.198s	14
11	Zdravko Matulja	YU	Casal	21	37m 51.621s	1m 48.496s	23
12	Janez Pintar	YU	Eberhardt	21	37m 51.771s	1m 46.979s	17
13	Thomas Engl	D	Esch	21	38m 14.194s	1m 47.983s	21
14	Matthias Ehinger	D	BMC	21	38m 14.472s	1m 48.712s	24
15	Xavier Arumi	E	Krauser	21	38m 34.956s	1m 46.578s	16
16	Heinz Paschen	D	Casal	21	38m 50.271s	1m 47.181s	18
17	Primoz Sovic	YU	Eberhardt	20	38m 27.792s	1m 52.374s	27
18	Andres Sanchez	E	Cobas	18	38m 35.802s	1m 45.115s	11
	Herri Torrontegui	E	Krauser	22	DSQ	1m 42.769s	3
	Reiner Koster	CH	LCR	19	DNF	1m 47.363s	20
	Ralf Waldmann	D	Seel	14	DNF	1m 45.582s	13
	Hagen Klein	D	Ziegler	13	DNF	1m 50.325s	26
	Luis Alvaro	E	CJB	11	DNF	1m 44.119s	6
	Günther Schirnhofer	D	Krauser	10	DNF	1m 46.516s	15
	Brane Rokavec	YU	Seel	8	DNF	1m 49.092s	25
	Stefan Brägger	CH	Casal	5	DNF	1m 47.351s	19
	Anton Goehly	D	Bartol		DNQ	1m 58.818s	
	Sreten Vasic	YU	Sever		DNQ	1m 59.479s	
	Miljenko Nervo	YU	Sever		DNQ	1m 59.699s	
	Miroslav Lesicki	YU	Sever		DNQ	2m 01.735s	

Fastest lap: Öttl, 1m 41.373s, 91.972 mph/148.015 km/h.
Lap record: Jorge Martinez, E (Derbi), 1m 40.16s, 93.087 mph/149.808 km/h (1986).

World Championship: 1 Herreros, 58; **2** Öttl, 55; **3** Dörflinger, 54; **4** Torrontegui, 50; **5** Gnani, 37; **6** Sanchez, 30 **7** Priori, 25; **8** Nikolov, 24; **9** Martinez and Saez, 20; **11** Seel and Waldmann, 19; **13** Koopman and Mariano, 17; **15** Miralles, 13; **16** Kurfiss, 11; **17** Ascareggi, 9; **18** Sassone and van Dongen, 7; **20** Bernard and Matulja, 5; **22** Pintar and Szabo, 4; **24** Dünki, Engl and Schirnhofer, 3; **27** Ehinger, 2; **28** Arumi, Brägger and Smit, 1.

Jad Sherif/International Press Agency

Cadalora fell from the Marlboro Yamaha in practice when it seized and then again in the race when he had a disagreement with Helmut Bradl over who owned a certain piece of road.

Opposite page: **Dominique Sarron** *(left)* **had some difficulty beating Rob McElnea on the year-old NSR Honda.**

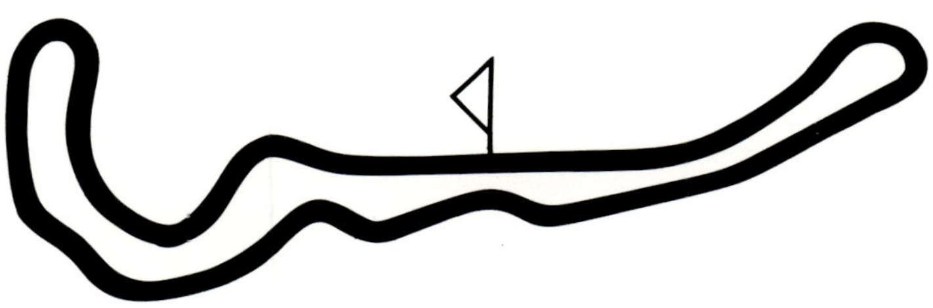

WORLD CHAMPIONSHIP · ROUND 9

DUTCH TT

Three Grands Prix on successive weekends had worn everyone out, but the week off prior to the Dutch TT was a chance to recharge the batteries before the start of the second half of the season. Fifteen races a year is hard work but, running directly contrary to the requests and demands from IRTA, the teams' organisation, the FIM announced at Assen that they were planning a 16-round calendar for 1990. It would include the Yugoslav, Swedish and American rounds that were under threat, according to IRTA, with the addition of a new Hungarian Grand Prix. IRTA has been campaigning for several years to reduce the number of Grands Prix to 14, but FIM Road Racing Commission President, Joe Zegwaard, has consistently refused to listen. Zegwaard and IRTA have been running head to head on almost every issue and the FIM had finally thrown down the gauntlet to see how IRTA would react.

One positive move at Assen was the quashing of the fines that had been imposed on the riders who had refused to race in the rain at Misano. They had been accused of withdrawing from the meeting without informing the clerk of the course, but a hearing found that there were no grounds on which to take action against them. Indeed, politics failed to make much of an impact at Assen, which was just as well: the race meeting is superb and, in the middle of the season, the championship battles should be the most important consideration.

A look at the tables showed that the title races were in very different states. Sito Pons was storming away with the 250: a string of four wins in a row had brought his total to five wins in eight races, which put him 48 points ahead of nearest rival Jean-Philippe Ruggia. This meant that Pons could even afford to fail to finish two races in the second half of the year and still hold a healthy lead in the championship. With the reliability of the Hondas running at an all-time high, and Pons never looking like making the sort of mistakes he had in 1988, that two-race cushion looked ample.

His lead looked doubly comfortable considering the frailty of the factory Yamahas. They had already let Garriga and Cadalora down during races as well as causing numerous problems for all three factory men during practice. But what made Pons's lead so impressive was that the four riders behind him – Ruggia, Cornu, Roth and Cardus – had all been scoring consistently. Roth and Cornu had been getting the rostrum places and finishing within seconds of Pons, sometimes less, yet they were nowhere near him in the championship.

The 500 table, on the other hand, looked very different. Rainey held the lead by just 13 points from Lawson, even though he had beaten the World Champion five out of seven times. It was all too clear that one DNF from Rainey would swing the championship Lawson's way: the scoring system that awards 20 points for a win and only three less for second and two fewer for third makes finishing races of prime importance.

Lawson is a past master at finishing races and the Honda, which had let Gardner down twice so crucially in 1988, was not failing at all in '89 – not in the races, and only rarely in practice. Could it be that Lawson is much easier on the machine than other riders? He is certainly the smoothest man on the track, and since Freddie Spencer took his place at Yamaha the Marlboro bikes have been stopping left, right and centre. Kel Carruthers and the mechanics had certainly not forgotten how to put them together, so it was becoming increasingly obvious that the combination of Lawson, Carruthers and the Yamaha had been something special. Carruthers could build a bike with which Lawson could win races. Lawson had not valued that sufficiently when he left to go to Honda. But there is no doubt that he can ride the Honda superbly, and his easy style probably helped it to finish races, more reliably than it had with Gardner, although Lawson was not actually winning on it.

Kevin Schwantz had won more races than anyone, as many as Lawson and Rainey put together, but his three wins were only accompanied by a single second place. He was sixth in the championship, with little practical hope of winning, but even if Schwantz was not going to be World Champion he continued to be the fastest man on the circuit. From the first timed session at Assen he set a standard that was obviously going to be hard to match. His lap time of 2m 9.85s was a full second quicker than Rainey could manage and over a second better than Christian Sarron's pole-position time from the previous year. Schwantz had bettered Wayne Gardner's lap record by almost a second and a half.

Gardner was unlikely to retain his lap record. He was making his comeback after nine weeks' convalescence, during which time he'd missed five Grands Prix. Dr Costa had only removed the plaster on Monday, replacing it with a light plaster that would offer some measure of protection against knocks. The Australian could not afford to fall off, though, and would not be taking any chances. It was great to see him racing again and the Australian media thought it was newsworthy enough for Channel Nine, who take all the races live, to send a news crew just to film Gardner stepping down from the Clinica Mobile and then talking about his comeback.

Gardner had his first ride on the Rothmans Honda during free practice on Wednesday and, while he didn't try to pretend that the leg was not painful, he said he was determined to race. After the first timed session on Thursday he was twelfth fastest, only fractionally slower than Lawson and Doohan, and he was smiling broadly as he sat on the tyre trolley in the pits. 'It hurts....The enjoyment outweighs the pain though. It is great to work up a sweat again, it's been a long time.' Gardner had touched the knee of his injured leg on the grass, which caused a jolt of pain. 'It is slowing me down, about two seconds a lap. I am surprised how easy the riding feels, though, as if I have never been away. I am not going to be doing any winning or anything like that here. I just want to work back into it.'

After four sessions he had cut over a second off his time and was ninth quickest, less than a second slower than Lawson, who was sixth. He was obviously not his usual self yet – he looked uncomfortable moving around on the bike, and that made him use some slightly strange lines – but there was no denying that he was fast.

Gardner's race engineer, Stuart Shenton, had already weighed up what Gardner should ride. Rather than start with the latest version of the NSR being used by Lawson, with the massive reinforcement of the twin spar, Gardner would first try one of the slightly earlier frames with the crossbar between the twin spars and reinforcement of the swing arm pivot, but only on the left-hand side where the chain pull acts. There had already been many variations on the reinforcement theme, after Lawson had the cross-tube version at Jerez with the fabricated front engine mount on the left side. Since then the right side mount had become a permanent fixture as well, and this was to be seen on Gardner's frame too.

Not every Honda team looked upon total rigidity as their main aim, and the teams using leased machines – HB Gallina and Elf ROC – did not get the updated versions anyway. Gallina was actually trying more flexible engine mounting, using only two bolts on each front engine mount instead of three. 'We have had some carburation problems that seem to be associated with engine vibration and using one less bolt seems to help,' said Gallina. 'We know that it might not help the handling but that doesn't seem to be a problem.'

Gallina had Chili's two machines set up differently, one with the two-bolt version and the other with three bolts, so that carburation difficulties and possible handling problems could be isolated. Whatever they were doing was certainly working. Chili was right on the pace all through practice, ending up third fastest behind Schwantz and Rainey and ahead of Sarron, Magee and Lawson – no mean feat to be the fastest Honda rider and the best part of a second quicker than the World Champion.

It was not the first time that Chili's practice performance had been impressive. Some of the other 500 men have commented that the Italian spends too much time tailing them to pick up a fast time, but at Assen he was having to do most of it on his own – too few other riders were fast enough. However, his practice times have not so far been translated into race performances and some observers have made noises about qualifying tyres. The notion that because Formula One car racing uses qualifying tyres then they must exist in Grand Prix motor cycle racing too is rather daft. There is so little to be gained from moving forward a few places or even a row on a motor cycle grid that the time wasted setting up the bike to run a tyre of such superior performance to that which will be used in the race would be much better apportioned to some other line of improvement or development.

Pirelli's chief race engineer, ex-Dunlop man Peter Ingley, was quite adamant that there was no such thing as a 'qualifying tyre', even if not every tyre was a race possibility. 'We have to make a choice between two rear tyres for the race. They would both go the distance. We never

Left: **Roth got the win he'd been waiting for. Yamaha piston failure saved him from having to deal with Cadalora on the last lap, but he saw off Pons and Cornu.**

In front of his home crowd Hans Spaan rode uncompromisingly to resist the challenge of Alex Criville.

make qualifying tyres. Certainly not every tyre you make would go the distance, but that is why you test them. We have tyres at the track that would probably not last a Grand Prix here, but they have not been on the motor cycle this week.'

It was great to see three different makes of tyre and machine filling the first three places on the grid. Lawson was one of those who'd said that the race would not reflect practice performance – but then he was starting from the second row. 'I have won races from the second row before. I don't care about practice, the race will be very different. It is interesting to see that both Wayne and Kevin crashed in practice. I think there is a lot of pressure on them.'

After spending most of the season practising, and certainly racing, almost exclusively on the 17-in. front Michelin, Lawson committed himself to the 16-in. front wheel from the start of practice at Assen. 'We spent the Monday in Yugoslavia trying different tyres and steering geometry so that we got the 16 working well,' he commented.

There was a time when Lawson's only rival was Freddie Spencer, but that seemed a long time ago. At Assen Spencer was closer in practice, only just over half a second slower than Lawson, and he said things were starting to come together. 'Two things make me feel good about the way things are going. The 16-in. front wheel is really starting to work for me. I have always needed something that will do more than hold a line round the corner. I need a bike that I have to control how much it turns in by the throttle, or on the Honda with the rear brake. The second thing is that towards the end of the session I came across a lot of traffic. I dropped back and then went again and was right up to speed in one lap.'

But being eighth fastest in practice was not enough to quell the rumours of just how dissatisfied Agostini was with Spencer. The Italian press had been getting ever more excited about the idea that Ago was about to make some incredible mid-season *coup*. After the Yugoslav Grand Prix Giancarlo Galavotti wrote a long article in the daily *Gazzetta dello Sport* suggesting that Marlboro had reached an agreement with Rothmans to buy out Wayne Gardner's Honda contract so that he could join the Marlboro Yamaha team. According to the story, Gardner would be racing in Marlboro colours at either Assen or Spa. The only real basis for the story was that Agostini had made no secret of the fact that he was not thrilled with Spencer's performance.

Gardner wasn't riding a Yamaha at Assen and Marlboro held a press conference to try and clear the air. Agostini said that there would be no termination of Spencer's contract. 'We have a contract for this season and of course I am going to respect that contract. We want to win races, that is what we are here for, and we are all working for that.' When asked if there might be another rider on the team before the end of the season he replied, 'I don't think so. We have enough work to do to get the results we want with the riders we have.'

Not surprisingly the press were less aggressive when face to face with Spencer than they

had been in print, but he was asked if he was disappointed with his own performance. 'Of course I am disappointed. I have won World Championships and a lot of championship races, and anything less than winning is disappointing. All I can say is that the team is working 100 per cent towards winning and every time I go out on the bike, this afternoon, tomorrow or next week, I give 100 per cent.' It was also suggested that he must be feeling under a great deal of pressure to get better results. 'I have been racing a long time and there has always been pressure. I put more pressure on myself than anyone else does. I want to win more than anyone.'

If Lawson no longer had to concern himself with Spencer, and for the moment at least not with Gardner either, he had plenty of opposition in the form of Rainey and Schwantz. The Texan was full of confidence after his pace-setting in the first session, even though he'd slid off the Suzuki. 'It was not that hard. I think I can go faster. I think it is possible to do eights here. Eddie says I shouldn't, but we'll see,' said Schwantz. And commenting on the fall: 'It was at the tight 90-degree right-hander that gives everyone trouble. The engine just bogged a little, then cut in and spun the bike round. It was no big deal.'

His prediction about getting into the eights was never realised because, as he explained later, 'It is possible to go quicker but it would have meant trying pretty hard and there was a bit too much wind in the afternoon sessions on Thursday and Friday. The track is narrow and the wind isn't the same everywhere. There is one place in the middle of the last left-hander, coming back to the start and finish, where there is a gap in the banking to let the ambulance through. You can feel the bike move across the track there, and there is not a lot of room to let that happen.

'The only trouble we had through practice was on Friday morning when the number one bike wouldn't go and I had to use the spare. That worried me a little but it was all sorted out for the afternoon.'

Schwantz's fall was not big news; it was a little more surprising to see repair work being performed on Rainey's machine on Friday. 'We were testing a new front tyre. It was chattering and we tried to fix that by changing the suspension but it didn't work.' It was only Rainey's third fall in two years. He did not hurt himself and, as practice continued, he managed to cut his lap-time deficit to Schwantz to half a second.

Less than a tenth of a second separated the two men at the top of the 250 table and Sito Pons only took pole by finding almost a second in the final period. 'The bike was more or less the same; I rode harder. I do want to win tomorrow because I have never won here, but it will be a very fast, hard race. Roth and Ruggia have done a lot of fast laps in practice and they will be very hard to beat. The pace of the race will be fast, 15.5 or 16,' predicted the World Champion, his pole-position time being 2m 15.10s.

The Campsa Honda was fitted with special vertical throat carbs during practice, as had been used in a single session in Yugoslavia, but the bike did not have them to set the pole time. Masahiro Shimizu had been testing the carbs all through the season and, while the operation was top secret, they were said to operate in a very special fashion. They have flat slides and needles but some sort of electronic fuel metering.

Roth was only just squeezed down to second place by Pons. The fastest Yamaha man throughout practice was Jean-Philippe Ruggia. He was quickest after two sessions and then slipped to third on the final day, even though he found another second. The Gauloises Blondes team had spent three days working on the test bench at their workshop beside Orly airport in Paris, trying a variety of possibilities and new parts from Japan including cylinders, heads, exhaust pipes and ignition. 'The engine is stronger, certainly. I am not sure how much faster because I have not been able to try it against the factory Hondas yet,' said Ruggia after the first day. The engine was quicker but not reliable enough, stopping on the last lap of the Friday morning session. Rebuilt for the afternoon it was not quite as strong. 'That is a shame because I think I could have gone under 2m 15s,' asserted Ruggia.

Cadalora had carburation trouble with his Yamaha and his team were trying out new parts at the track. The mechanics were reluctant to make the needle changes that would help the carburation, as that set-up had previously caused seizures, but they finally did so without problems.

Garriga's team were not so lucky, and he would start the race from the middle of the third row.

Gardner was back but taking every opportunity to sit down. The leg was only just healed enough for him to ride.

'The bike runs well in one session, then not in the next, and we have no idea why. When it is going like this it is impossible to sort out suspension, gearbox, or get in a fast lap.'

Hopes of local success in the 250 class hinged on Wilco Zeelenberg and Patrick van den Goorbergh. Van den Goorbergh had qualified better (nineteenth as opposed to Zeelenberg's twenty-third place), but Zeelenberg's Grand Prix performances on his private Honda had been much more consistent. He was currently seventeenth in the championship.

Of course the Dutch fans were hoping for a sidecar win from Egbert Streuer and Geral de Haas, but they had a new hero too. Hans Spaan displayed his determination to win the 125 class by qualifying seven-tenths faster than second man, Alex Criville. The 125 class was getting more interesting all the time, even if the 80 cc stalwarts were wearing 'T' shirts saying '80 cc forever'. They demonstrated their feelings at the start of their own race, although the top 80 men like Stefan Dörflinger are committed to the move. 'I enjoy riding the 80 more because I have a more competitive bike, but the 125 is the future. We only need one small class.'

Dörflinger took pole again on the 80 cc Krauser, and Krausers filled the first three places. But even Krauser is switching its attention to the 125 class, and the new bike made its debut at Assen. Michael Krauser has been looking for German riders to back, and hence it is young star Peter Öttl who gets the best 80 cc Krauser equipment and gave the 125 its first outing.

Herbert Ritberger has built a single cylinder disc-valve engine very similar to his successful 80 cc design but with the cylinder pointing up a little more, at 33 degrees to the horizontal. The 56 by 50.7 mm engine breathes through a disc valve and 39 mm Keihin carb. It is mounted in the first tubular LCR chassis. Though this is a departure from the usual monocoque design that Louis Christen uses for sidecars and solos the Swiss engineer denied that he was having any great change of faith. 'I don't care what method is used to make a frame as long as it is the right one. The monocoque is good if it suits the engine. Herbert needs some flexibility because he wants to try a reed-valve version.'

Ritberger said that the machine weighed 67 kg with its 18-in. wheels, Ohlins rear shock and Forcella Italia front fork. The German engineer said he was surprised how well the engine performed. 'It produces 40–42 bhp and we have had no technical problems at all so far. It has done an hour and a half on the bench and 200 km of testing at Hockenheim and Assen.' Krauser had already spent DM 500,000 on the project and was committed to an all-out 1990 125 championship attempt with two riders.

80 cc

Stefan Dörflinger started from his fifth pole position in a row, set the fastest lap of the race by seven-tenths of a second but finished third behind Peter Öttl and Manuel Herreros.

Both Öttl and Dörflinger made a mess of the start, so Herreros was away with a clear road in front of him. Luis Alvaro was temporarily second, having made a great start from the second row, sitting behind Herreros. Unfortunately the Spaniard regressed later in the race thanks to engine problems, finishing seventeenth.

Soon into second place was Torrontegui, and he had taken the lead before the end of the first lap. Herreros fought back to regain the advantage late in lap two, while Öttl jumped from eleventh to seventh and Dörflinger from thirteenth to tenth. Indeed, the most important aspect of this race was the progress made by these two. By lap four Öttl was second and Dörflinger fifth and, although Herreros had quite a lead, from lap five they were together and closing on the Spaniard. It was actually Dörflinger who caught him first, after setting the fastest lap of the race on lap six.

From lap seven to the eleventh and final circuit the three men were locked together, well clear of Miralles who was fourth after being well placed from the beginning. Öttl manoeuvred himself into second but was having a hard time finding a way past the Derbi. Then, only five corners from home, Herreros went into a big slide and the young German nipped inside on the factory Krauser.

250 cc

Reinhold Roth had been so frustrated with himself for losing the Yugoslav Grand Prix on the last lap that he later admitted to having been on the point of tears after the race. He was absolutely determined that the same mistake would not happen again. 'There will be no more "slow" last laps,' he said. And at Assen he exacted sweet revenge.

The race was another Honda clean sweep but it was a disaster for Yamaha as none of their men finished. Jean-Philippe Ruggia had been the quickest of them in practice but he crashed the Gauloises Blondes Yamaha on the first lap, colliding with the rear of Cadalora's machine. The Frenchman accused the Italian of cutting across him but that was just a flash of frustration from Ruggia. As the whole pack funnelled into the Strubben, the long, looping right-hander that begins the run along the back of the paddock, there was the usual first-lap juggling for position and Ruggia was simply unlucky.

Juan Garriga was outside the top ten on lap one and was still struggling to fight his way forwards when the V-twin expired on lap 15 with a broken piston. Luca Cadalora, on the other hand, was very much in the hunt and fought for the lead all the way. He was leading Roth by the tiniest margin when his piston collapsed with only a lap and a half to go.

Pons was in front off the line but Roth got past him before the end of the first lap. The World Champion was then pushed back to third by fellow-countryman Carlos Cardus, but Cardus started to suffer from his carpal tunnel problem and was forced to slow. He spent most of the race holding Martin Wimmer at bay and the pair finished fourth and fifth.

Roth ran at the front with Cadalora and Pons swapping second between them and Cornu shadowing in fourth on the Lucky Strike Honda. Cadalora was certainly not playing a waiting game behind Roth, though, and on lap six was second and looking for a way past the German. At the start and finish, going on to lap seven, he was right in the slipstream of the HB Honda and he passed Roth on the brakes, at the end of the front straight. But the German fought back and was soon in front again. The leading four then pulled away slightly from Cardus and Wimmer. They formed two pairs, with Cadalora sitting right on Roth's shoulder and Cornu doing the same to Pons.

The 'if only' of Cadalora's bike keeping going to the end would certainly have given the last-lap battle an added dimension, but it was not to be. The unlucky Italian was left forlornly slumped over the tank of his Yamaha as the three Hondas sped away from the Strubben on the second to last lap.

Roth's job was thus made simpler, but it was still no easy task. He had been planning what he would do for the final circuit. 'I thought after practice that it might come down to a last-lap battle with Sito,' said Roth, who had been quickest in the final session of practice until the very last moment. 'I was using the same tyre all through the final session, I had 19 laps on it, and Sito went out with a new tyre just for a quick time.

'I thought before the race that I might have to have something in hand for the last lap. I wasn't going to let there be a repeat of Yugoslavia. I knew where he might pass me and that was inside into the last double left. I went straight from the previous right-hander to the inside of the left so that he would have to go round the outside. At the chicane I just closed all the doors and there was no way he was going to get past.'

Roth's win was the end of a rather long dry period for him. Although always a front-runner, his only other Grand Prix win was in the rain at Le Mans in 1987. At that time he had been fighting for the championship lead, and he ended the year second. By comparison 1988 had not been a very successful year but, as he explained, it had taken him most of the season to recover from a serious crash and a badly broken leg. 'The Fuji crash in October '87 was in my brain deeper than I realised. When it takes you a year and a half to get over such an injury it must have an effect. It is behind me now though.' But 36-year-old Roth has been well served by tuner Sepp Schlogl, for in 38 Grands Prix the HB Honda had not stopped once.

Pons accepted that he had been beaten fair and square. 'The bike was great. My only problem today was Reinhold Roth. He rode well and deserved to win. I tried hard on that last lap but there was nothing I could do. I am happy, of course, that I increased my lead in the World Championship. When my team-manager signalled on the second lap that Ruggia was out I could be more relaxed, but I was still trying to win.

Gentile and Buckmaster had their own entertaining battle but it ended in the sandpit.

'During the last lap I remembered what happened last year (Pons and Dominique Sarron became locked together going into the chicane and ended up in the sandpit). I was not going to let that happen again. I was also thinking about Cornu behind and not letting him past.'

Cornu saw Roth and Pons manoeuvring on the last lap. He was on hand to take advantage of any last-lap mistakes but said he saw little chance of winning. 'I didn't have too much hope of winning but I was certainly trying to get past Sito. I had a look at the end of the back straight and then tried to ride round the outside before the finish, but there was no way.'

Wimmer said that, considering he was still recovering from his Rijeka practice injury, he was pleased with fifth on the Hein Gericke Aprilia. 'The bike was great, but my foot hurt enough to slow me down,' he said. 'It was not the broken bone but the blisters caused by my changing gear with my toe instead of the middle of the foot where the break is.'

125 cc

German Stefan Prein jumped into the lead from the start and held off Alex Criville and Hans Spaan for the first lap. Spaan was obviously the crowd's favourite so they loved it when he moved to second behind Criville on lap two and Prein was displaced to third. They went wild when he took the lead on lap three. Gianola was third and though Prein briefly hung on to the trio he could not match their pace. Later he had his work cut out when under pressure from Miralles on the Derbi, and the Spaniard eventually got the better of him.

It was a very tough race at the front, with no quarter being asked or given. The trio battling for the lead looked evenly matched, but Ezio Gianola crashed his Honda on lap 14 of the 16 leaving local hero Spaan on the Samson Honda to rub fairings – almost literally – with Criville on the Marlboro Cobas. The last lap was obviously going to be a heart-stopper. Criville braked as late as he dared at the tight right-hander at the end of the back straight. The Cobas had its rear wheel in the air but Spaan just slid up the inside. The pair went through the turn side by side but Spaan let the Honda drift wide on the exit and forced Criville to back off. It was hard riding and only just fair.

Gianola's departure meant that Miralles won a rostrum place by defeating Prein, while Hisashi Unemoto finally overcame Fausto Gresini to take fifth.

500 cc

Disbelief was the general reaction when Kevin Schwantz failed to make it past the pits to start the last lap. A con rod on the Pepsi Suzuki broke while he had a two-and-a-half second lead over Wayne Rainey and the Lucky Strike Yamaha. That gave Eddie Lawson second place on the Rothmans Honda with Christian Sarron completing the rostrum positions on the Gauloises

Malcolm Bryan

Rolf Biland and Kurt Waltisperg had so much trouble in practice that they only recorded times in two of the four sessions. They still took pole position, but a few of the gremlins returned in the race and they had no chance of catching Streuer and Webster.

Blondes Yamaha.

It would have been the third win in a row for Schwantz and the Texan, who had turned 25 at the beginning of the week, certainly deserved victory. 'Everything had been going fine up to then,' said Kevin, who led off the line. 'Wayne came past at the end of the first lap and I followed him for a while but he was already spinning the tyre, laying rubber everywhere, and that gave me more confidence. I was just flicking it in, turning and driving without any problems. I got back in front and just ran at my own pace, which was pretty easy. I thought I would see if it was fast enough for me to get away. He stayed with me, though.

'Closer to the end I thought, "Well, let's see how fast he can go." I felt he was probably riding pretty close to the limit when we were doing high nines, and when we went faster I did start getting away,' said Schwantz, who set the fastest lap of the race with three to go.

Three wins and a second left him sixth in the championship at the end of the day, while Rainey extended his lead to 16 points with another great ride. He had attempted to make his usual break early on but, after opening up an advantage of a few metres on lap two, Schwantz was soon on his tail again with Pier Francesco Chili looking over *his* shoulder. So it was the same group that had headed practice.

Schwantz got back in front on lap four but he did not storm away either. Lawson closed up on Chili, making it a four-man string with Sarron and Magee only a fraction behind. There was then a slightly bigger gap before the incredible sight of Gardner easing his Rothmans Honda past Doohan, the Australian pair heading Haslam and Mackenzie. They eventually finished in front of Doohan, who had a very frustrating first visit to Assen. 'I never felt I was getting to grips with the track, or getting the bike sorted out through practice,' he said. Doohan had slid off the Honda once in training: 'I just wasn't able to make the front end work and it was the same in the race. Every time I started to work the front hard it would start skipping across the road and be about to tuck under. I decided that it was better just to finish and not do anything silly.'

Up front Rainey kept the pressure on and, had he not done so, Schwantz might well have finished. If he had been able to throttle back and use less revs the Suzuki might well have gone the distance but, with Rainey still within striking distance, Schwantz had to keep the bike hurrying along.

Lawson relegated Chili to fourth on lap nine, by which time the Italian had used the best of his tyres. He quickly lost fourth to Sarron and then another place to Magee. Lawson never got close enough to Rainey to mount a challenge and he was soon under pressure from behind, as Sarron arrived on his tail.

For several laps it was obvious that Lawson was holding Sarron up, yet the Frenchman could not find a way past. 'Assen is so tight and narrow that it is hard enough to overtake when you come up to a back-marker and you are six seconds a lap faster. I was only a second a lap faster than Lawson and that was too hard, especially as the Honda jumped off the corners slightly quicker than the Yamaha.'

Sarron lacked the confidence to barge past Lawson the way the World Champion would have done had the positions been reversed and, with a couple of laps to go, Lawson opened up just enough of a gap to prevent Sarron from thinking about a final effort. But the Frenchman was not that dispirited by the result. 'The bike was perfect and I am very pleased with third, even if I have to accept that I was lucky. My only problem was that I had to use the steel instead of the carbon brake because my hand is still not strong and the heavier brake discs make the bike slower to turn.'

Lawson's Honda had looked a big lump to keep between the narrow borders of the track but he made no criticism of it after the race. 'The bike was real fast but I lost touch with the other two and that was it. I guess they were going a little too fast. Wayne is riding real consistent and holding onto the championship is going to be hard, but you never give up.'

Rainey, less surprisingly, had nothing but praise for the Yamaha. It has never let him down and has been so consistently competitive that he has been on every rostrum since the start of the year. 'I rode the best I could but in the end Kevin started pulling away. I guess everyone wins a race like this once in a while. The bike worked well and it finished the race.' The championship leader was much less willing to comment on the ultimate outcome of the season. 'I learnt a valuable lesson today, watching Kevin. It's never over till the flag drops!'

Team-mate Magee, very little fitter than Gardner, did well to finish fourth. 'It is a matter of fitness now. I can ride OK but I have got to be fitter to go hard for the full race.'

Rainey, Lawson and Gardner had all used the 16-in. front wheels, as had Spencer. The ex-triple champion did not have a good ride, however, finishing thirteenth and a lap behind after the engine seized twice. 'It started to be a little sluggish, then as I changed down at the end of the straight it just quit. I turned around and restarted, but in some places it was obviously not pulling as strongly as it should. We had had problems in the last session, when we had made steering geometry changes, so I decided to carry on riding just to get some more time to test the ideas. The bike is better and it was worth carrying on even though it seized again.'

Gardner's return was very impressive. It was quite obviously not yet the old Gardner, but he was still very fast and quite pleased with the way things went. 'It was all right, I was happy to put in a 10.5, which isn't too bad. I wasn't leaning it over, though, I couldn't and I was scared to. I got going a bit towards the end and when I saw Chili ahead I thought I'd get away from Haslam and have a go at him. I got alongside on the last lap but we touched fairings and he wasn't going to let me past so that'll wait till next time.'

Haslam was a little frustrated with seventh. He was getting better tyres from Michelin but these were producing the same sort of machine balance problems that Schwantz had experienced at the beginning of the year, with more grip on the rear pushing the front. Rob McElnea was tenth on the Cabin Honda, ahead of Randy Mamola who was riding with a sore leg and a damaged bike after crashing on the sighting lap when pulling a wheelie for the crowd.

Sidecars

The crowd at Assen are always patriotic, and they fell silent at the result of the sidecar race. But it was such a great contest between Webster and Streuer that a polite ripple of applause could be heard in places. Some fans were decidedly displeased, though, and Webster's father, Mick, reported that a local had kicked the bike as he was wheeling it away. '"Bloody bike" he said, and gave it a bit of a kick. I was thinking we might have to paint out the name on the van to get out of the country,' said Webster senior with a grin.

Webster and Hewitt and Streuer and de Haas put on a great display, and were nose to tail all the way. The lead was with Streuer for the last three laps but Webster was closing every time on the run through the series of corners onto the back straight. He could never quite get past before being cut off by Streuer at the last kink but, on the final lap, Webster pulled out that extra bit that only champions can find and seized the lead. Then, approaching the chicane just before the finish, Streuer pulled alongside Webster again. The Dutchman was off-line and going too fast to make the corner but, in a desperate attempt to win, he took to the grass, trying to reach the correct side of the track for the better line.

Webster had covered any possible move that Streuer might try, but he could not have foreseen such tactics. However, the Dutch crew failed to gain from their move, and Webster and Hewitt won. Had Streuer succeeded he would have been disqualified, but as the result was unchanged he was not censured.

Passenger Tony Hewitt didn't see what happened. 'I have my head down there, tucked in behind the fairing. All I know is that on the previous laps we would get to the kink and Steve would slam the brakes on as Egbert cut across us. That pushed my helmet into the fairing and squeezed all the sweat out of the padding into my eyes. This time there was no braking and when I looked up to get across for the next corner there was no Egbert.'

Rolf Biland was third, saying he had numerous problems. The ex-champion had completed so few laps in the second and third practice sessions that his times were only quoted for the first and fourth sessions. He still went faster than anyone in that final period.

Alain Michel and Jean-Marc Fresc were a steady fourth. The best battle behind the leaders was that between Steinhausen and Hiller, Abbott and Smith, and Kumano and Fahrni. The Japanese/Swiss crew faded in the last few laps, to finish eighth behind Scherer and Schröder, but Steinhausen had to fight all the way to the line to take fifth from Abbott.

Grote Prijs van Nederland, 24 June/statistics
Circuit van Drenthe, Assen, 3.812-mile/6.134-km circuit

500 cc

20 laps, 76.24 miles/122.68 km

Place	Rider	Nat.	Machine	Laps	Time & speed	Practice time	Grid
1	Wayne Rainey	USA	Yamaha	20	43m 42.08s 106.177 mph/ 170.876 km/h	2m 10.34s	2
2	Eddie Lawson	USA	Honda	20	43m 49.05s	2m 11.33s	6
3	Christian Sarron	F	Yamaha	20	43m 51.92s	2m 10.66s	4
4	Kevin Magee	AUS	Yamaha	20	44m 04.19s	2m 10.95s	5
5	Pier Francesco Chili	I	Honda	20	44m 12.16s	2m 10.59s	3
6	Wayne Gardner	AUS	Honda	20	44m 12.40s	2m 12.20s	9
7	Ron Haslam	GB	Suzuki	20	44m 13.19s	2m 11.46s	7
8	Niall Mackenzie	GB	Yamaha	20	44m 31.63s	2m 12.73s	12
9	Michael Doohan	AUS	Honda	20	44m 37.92s	2m 13.06s	13
10	Rob McElnea	GB	Honda	20	45m 07.51s	2m 13.27s	14
11	Randy Mamola	USA	Cagiva	20	45m 47.04s	2m 12.42s	10
12	Alessandro Valesi	I	Yamaha	19	43m 43.23s	2m 15.13s	15
13	Freddie Spencer	USA	Yamaha	19	43m 58.96s	2m 11.87s	8
14	Marco Gentile	CH	Fior	19	44m 07.02s	2m 17.83s	18
15	Kees Doorakkers	NL	Honda	19	44m 36.90s	2m 18.72s	22
16	Bruno Kneubühler	CH	Honda	19	44m 37.44s	2m 19.13s	23
17	Michael Rudroff	D	Honda	19	44m 40.77s	2m 19.28s	26
18	Michele Valdo	I	Honda	19	44m 52.08s	2m 19.23s	25
19	Simon Buckmaster	GB	Honda	19	45m 04.27s	2m 17.32s	17
20	Marco Papa	I	Paton	19	45m 07.25s	2m 18.66s	21
21	Peter Schleef	D	Honda	19	45m 10.94s	2m 22.53s	35
22	Martin Trösch	D	Honda	19	45m 22.80s	2m 21.45s	33
23	Niggi Schmassman	CH	Honda	19	45m 26.04s	2m 20.40s	29
24	F. Beck	CH	Honda	19	45m 26.37s	2m 20.72s	30
25	Alois Meyer	D	Honda	18	43m 45.19s	2m 23.46s	36
	Kevin Schwantz	USA	Suzuki	18	DNF	2m 09.85s	1
	Stéphane Mertens	B	Honda	18	DNF	2m 15.96s	16
	Eddie Laycock	IRL	Honda	18	DNF	2m 18.43s	20
	Andreas Leuthe	LUX	Librenti	12	DNF	2m 20.84s	31
	Pavol Dekanek	CS	Honda	12	DNF	2m 21.94s	34
	Karl Truchsess	A	Honda	11	DNF	2m 19.15s	24
	Juan Lopez Mella	E	Honda	7	DNF	2m 21.03s	32
	Peter Linden	S	Honda	3	DNF	2m 18.39s	19
	Josef Doppler	A	Honda	3	DNF	2m 19.45s	27
	Dominique Sarron	F	Honda		DNS	2m 12.73s	11
	Rachel Nicotte	F	Honda		DNS	2m 19.72s	28
	Fernando Gonzalez	E	Honda		DNQ	2m 23.74s	
	Ian Pratt	GB	Honda		DNQ	2m 24.99s	
	Tony Carey	IRL	Spondon		DNQ	2m 42.08s	

Fastest lap: Schwantz, 2m 09.16s, 106.235 mph/170.969 km/h (record).
Previous record: Wayne Gardner, AUS (Honda), 2m 11.28s, 104.52 mph/168.208 km/h (1988).

World Championship: 1 Rainey, 143; **2** Lawson, 127; **3** Sarron, C., 97; **4** Magee, 83; **5** Chili, 80; **6** Schwantz, 77; **7** Doohan, 56; **8** Haslam and Mackenzie, 48; **10** Gardner, 43; **11** Sarron, D., 39; **12** Buckmaster, 34; **13** Spencer, 30; **14** Gentile, 28; **15** Valesi, 27; **16** Taira, 26; **17** McElnea, 22; **18** Mamola and Rudroff, 18; **20** Fujiwara, 17; **21** Shobert, 12; **22** Doppler, 11; **23** Meyer, 10; **24** Balbi, 9; **25** Broccoli, Gonzalez and Schmassman, 8; **28** Dowson and Leuthe, 7; **30** Itoh, 6; **31** Gschwender, 5; **32** Kneubühler, 4; **33** Yatsushiro, 3; **34** Lopez Mella, 2; **35** Doorakkers, Laycock and Machii, 1.

250 cc

18 laps, 68.616 miles/110.412 km

Place	Rider	Nat.	Machine	Laps	Time & speed	Practice time	Grid
1	Reinhold Roth	D	Honda	18	41m 03.89s 101.055 mph/ 162.633 km/h	2m 15.18s	2
2	Alfonso Pons	E	Honda	18	41m 04.28s	2m 15.10s	1
3	Jacques Cornu	CH	Honda	18	41m 04.67s	2m 16.18s	6
4	Carlos Cardus	E	Honda	18	41m 15.47s	2m 15.75s	4
5	Martin Wimmer	D	Aprilia	18	41m 17.48s	2m 16.38s	7
6	Didier de Radiguès	D	Aprilia	18	41m 19.35s	2m 16.84s	10
7	Alberto Puig	E	Yamaha	18	41m 41.19s	2m 16.62s	9
8	Wilco Zeelenberg	NL	Honda	18	41m 41.43s	2m 18.58s	23
9	Marcellino Lucchi	I	Aprilia	18	41m 47.33s	2m 17.88s	18
10	Carlos Lavado	YV	Aprilia	18	41m 52.14s	2m 17.80s	17
11	Masahiro Shimizu	J	Honda	18	41m 58.82s	2m 17.55s	14
12	Stefano Caracchi	RSM	Honda	18	41m 59.99s	2m 19.53s	31
13	Patrick van den Goorbergh	NL	Yamaha	18	42m 00.34s	2m 17.96s	19
14	Harald Eckl	D	Aprilia	18	42m 04.87s	2m 18.93s	26
15	Alberto Rota	I	Aprilia	18	42m 05.17s	2m 19.60s	32
16	August Auinger	A	Yamaha	18	42m 05.49s	2m 18.43s	21
17	Andreas Preining	A	Aprilia	18	42m 08.41s	2m 18.96s	27
18	Fausto Ricci	I	Aprilia	18	42m 10.28s	2m 18.54s	22
19	Bernard Hänggeli	CH	Yamaha	18	42m 16.73s	2m 18.73s	24
20	Daniel Amatriain	E	Honda	18	42m 43.33s	2m 18.30s	20
21	Bernhard Schick	D	Yamaha	18	42m 47.25s	2m 19.65s	33
22	René Delaby	LUX	Yamaha	18	42m 57.60s	2m 20.11s	36
23	Jean-François Baldé	F	Yamaha	18	43m 25.27s	2m 20.07s	35
	Luca Cadalora	I	Yamaha	16	DNF	2m 15.90s	5
	Juan Garriga	E	Yamaha	14	DNF	2m 17.00s	12
	Hans Becker	D	Seel	11	DNF	2m 19.10s	29
	Helmut Bradl	D	Honda	10	DNF	2m 16.93s	11
	Gary Cowan	IRL	Yamaha	7	DNF	2m 17.48s	13
	Adrien Morillas	F	Yamaha	6	DNF	2m 18.82s	25
	Maurizio Vitali	I	Honda	3	DNF	2m 17.64s	15
	Engelbert Neumair	A	Aprilia	2	DNF	2m 19.37s	30
	Nigel Bosworth	GB	Aprilia	2	DNF	2m 19.84s	34
	Alexandre Barros	BR	Yamaha	1	DNF	2m 17.69s	16
	Loris Reggiani	I	Honda	1	DNF	2m 16.58s	8
	Renzo Colleoni	I	Aprilia	0	DNF	2m 18.97s	28
	Jean-Philippe Ruggia	F	Yamaha	0	DNF	2m 15.44s	3
	Jean Foray	F	Yamaha		DNQ	2m 19.78s	
	Xavier Cardelus	AND	Yamaha		DNQ	2m 20.27s	
	Andy Leisner	USA	Honda		DNQ	2m 20.33s	
	Kevin Mitchell	GB	Yamaha		DNQ	2m 20.58s	
	Alain Bronec	F	Aprilia		DNQ	2m 21.04s	
	Virginio Ferrari	I	Gazzaniga		DNQ	2m 21.37s	
	Manfred Herweh	D	Yamaha		DNQ	2m 21.49s	
	Massimo Matteoni	I	Yamaha		DNQ	2m 21.84s	
	Urs Jucker	CH	Yamaha		DNQ	2m 21.92s	
	Hans Koopman	NL	Honda		DNQ	2m 24.40s	
	Luis Lavado	YV	Yamaha		DNQ	2m 28.00s	

Fastest lap: Pons, 2m 15.09s, 101.571 mph/163.464 km/h (record).
Previous record: Anton Mang, D (Honda), 2m 16.00s, 100.892 mph/162.371 km/h (1988).

World Championship: 1 Pons, 164; **2** Roth, 103; **3** Cornu, 100; **4** Ruggia, 99; **5** Cardus, 95; **6** Cadalora, 70; **7** Shimizu and Garriga, 51; **9** Bradl and Wimmer, 44; **11** Kocinski, 40; **12** de Radiguès, 32; **13** Reggiani, Schmid and Zeelenberg, 26; **16** Filice, 22; **17** Palazzese, 19; **18** Colleoni and Lucchi, 17; **20** Cowan, Eckl, Honma and Puig, 13; **24** Okada, 10; **25** Shiomori, 9; **26** Barros and Morillas, 8; **28** Lavado, Rota and van den Goorbergh, 6; **31** Caracchi, 5; **32** Amatriain, Beattie, Bronec and Mitchell, 4; **36** Preining and Vitali, 2; **38** Arai, Auinger and Becker, 1.

Sidecars

16 laps, 60.99 miles/98.14 km

Place	Driver & passenger	Nat.	Machine	Laps	Time & speed	Practice time	Grid
1	Steve Webster/ Tony Hewitt	GB GB	LCR	16	37m 07.67s 99.271 mph/ 159.762 km/h	2m 17.84s	3
2	Egbert Streuer/ Geral de Haas	NL NL	LCR- Yamaha	16	37m 08.11s	2m 17.75s	2
3	Rolf Biland/ Kurt Waltisperg	CH CH	LCR- Krauser	16	37m 38.76s	2m 17.42s	1
4	Alain Michel/ Jean-Marc Fresc	F F	LCR- Krauser	16	37m 42.59s	2m 19.25s	5
5	Rolf Steinhausen/ Bruno Hiller	D D	Schuh Spezial	16	38m 08.30s	2m 21.35s	9
6	Steve Abbott/ Shaun Smith	GB GB	Windle- Yamaha	16	38m 11.68s	2m 20.52s	8
7	Bernd Scherer/ Thomas Schröder	D D	BSR- Krauser	16	38m 28.48s	2m 22.84s	12
8	Masato Kumano/ Markus Fahrni	J CH	LCR	16	38m 29.98s	2m 20.46s	7
9	Theo van Kempen/ Simon Birchall	NL GB	LCR- Yamaha	16	38m 35.31s	2m 23.37s	14
10	Ivan Nigrowsky/ Jacques Corbier	F F	LCR- JPX	16	38m 39.91s	2m 23.93s	16
11	Fritz Stölzle/ Hubert Stölzle	D D	LCR- Krauser	16	38m 43.76s	2m 23.05s	13
12	Derek Jones/ Peter Brown	GB GB	LCR- Yamaha	16	38m 44.11s	2m 21.41s	10
13	Yoshisada Kumagaya/ Peter Linden	J S	Windle- KS	16	38m 51.33s	2m 23.95s	17
14	René Progin/ Yves Hunziker	CH CH	LCR- Krauser	16	38m 56.49s	2m 23.93s	15
15	Tony Baker/ Trevor Hopkinson	GB GB	LCR- Krauser	16	38m 57.62s	2m 24.88s	19
16	Barry Smith/ David Smith	GB GB	Windle- ADM	15	37m 23.68s	2m 24.10s	18
	Alfred Zurbrügg/ Martin Zurbrügg	CH CH	LCR- Yamaha	11	DNF	2m 19.19s	4
	Jos van Stekelenburg/ Rinie Bettgens	NL NL	LCR- Yamaha	10	DNF	2m 24.90s	20
	Barry Brindley/ Grahame Rose	GB GB	Fowler- Yamaha	4	DNF	2m 22.64s	11
	Markus Egloff/ Urs Egloff	CH CH	SM-SI- Yamaha	2	DNF	2m 20.12s	6
	Billy Gällros/ Håkan Olsson	S S	Yamaha		DNQ	2m 25.09s	
	Paul Atkinson/ Phil Coombes	GB GB	LCR- Krauser		DNQ	2m 25.17s	
	Wolfgang Stropek/ Steve Campbell	A GB	Mibag Krauser		DNQ	2m 25.48s	
	George Hardwick/ Gary Irlam	GB GB	LCR		DNQ	2m 26.45s	
	Gary Thomas/ Eckhart Rösinger	GB GB	LCR		DNQ	2m 26.78s	

Fastest lap: Streuer, 2m 17.75s, 99.61 mph/160.307 km/h.
Lap record: Rolf Biland/Kurt Waltisperg, CH/CH (LCR-Krauser), 2m 17.35s, 99.9 mph/160.775 km/h (1988).

World Championship: 1 Webster, 61; **2** Streuer, 51; **3** Kumano, 47; **4** Michel, 45; **5** Biland, 35; **6** Stölzle, 34; **7** Steinhausen, 29; **8** Egloff, 25; **9** Zurbrügg, 21; **10** Brindley and Kumagaya, 20; **12** van Kempen, 17; **13** Jones and Scherer, 16; **15** Abbott and Wyssen, 15; **17** Progin, 12; **18** Nigrowsky and Smith, 8; **20** Baker, 7; **21** Stropek, 6; **22** Gällros, 5; **23** Drew, 4; **24** Stirrat, 3; **25** Hardwick and Thomas, 2.

Malcolm Bryan

Above: **Öttl's battle with Dörflinger and Herreros was a classic.**

Spaan's epic win was cause for national celebration at the track and front-page photographs next day in the papers.

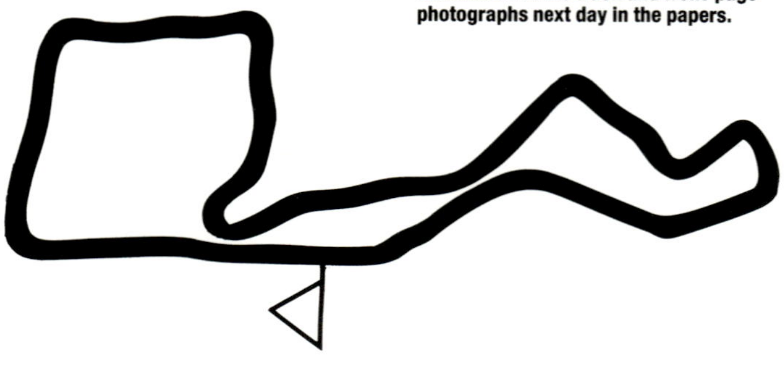

125 cc

16 laps, 60.99 miles/98.14 km

Place	Rider	Nat.	Machine	Laps	Time & speed	Practice time	Grid
1	Hans Spaan	NL	Honda	16	38m 57.68s 94.642 mph/ 151.140 km/h	2m 25.20s	1
2	Alex Criville	E	Cobas	16	38m 57.88s	2m 25.92s	2
3	Julian Miralles	E	Derbi	16	39m 17.33s	2m 27.53s	7
4	Stefan Prein	D	Honda	16	39m 18.01s	2m 27.07s	5
5	Hisashi Unemoto	J	Honda	16	39m 40.65s	2m 28.71s	13
6	Fausto Gresini	I	Aprilia	16	39m 40.66s	2m 27.91s	9
7	Jorge Martinez	E	Derbi	16	39m 49.11s	2m 26.68s	4
8	Taru Rinne	SF	Honda	16	39m 55.30s	2m 28.36s	11
9	Koji Takada	J	Honda	16	40m 04.09s	2m 28.81s	15
10	Alfred Waibel	D	Honda	16	40m 04.43s	2m 28.58s	12
11	Thierry Feuz	CH	Honda	16	40m 05.12s	2m 29.27s	21
12	Lucio Pietroniro	B	Honda	16	40m 05.46s	2m 28.86s	16
13	Gabriele Debbia	I	Aprilia	16	40m 06.46s	2m 27.82s	8
14	Allan Scott	USA	Honda	16	40m 08.66s	2m 30.36s	31
15	Dirk Raudies	D	Honda	16	40m 16.00s	2m 29.70s	27
16	Domenico Brigaglia	I	Garelli	16	40m 21.81s	2m 29.07s	18
17	Doriano Romboni	I	Honda	16	40m 22.02s	2m 29.88s	29
18	Flemming Kistrup	DK	Honda	16	40m 22.57s	2m 28.97s	17
19	Hubert Abold	D	Rotax	16	40m 22.99s	2m 29.13s	19
20	Manfred Fischer	A	Honda	16	40m 32.31s	2m 29.53s	23
21	Adrie Nijenhuis	NL	Honda	16	40m 34.44s	2m 30.58s	34
22	Heinz Lüthi	CH	Honda	16	40m 34.69s	2m 29.56s	24
23	Othmar Schuler	CH	Honda	16	41m 19.31s	2m 30.68s	35
24	Herri Torrontegui	E	Honda	16	41m 31.78s	2m 28.76s	14
	Ezio Gianola	I	Honda	13	DNF	2m 26.05s	3
	Emilio Cuppini	I	Garelli	13	DNF	2m 29.46s	22
	Robin Appleyard	GB	Honda	9	DNF	2m 30.41s	33
	Bruno Casanova	I	Aprilia	7	DNF	2m 27.11s	6
	Stefan Dörflinger	CH	Aprilia	5	DNF	2m 29.67s	25
	Robin Milton	GB	Honda	3	DNF	2m 29.68s	26
	Jean-Claude Selini	F	Honda	3	DNF	2m 30.71s	36
	Luis Reyes	E	Honda	2	DNF	2m 29.18s	20
	Peter Öttl	D	Krauser	1	DNF	2m 28.28s	10
	Adolf Stadler	D	Honda	1	DNF	2m 30.41s	32
	Alex Bedford	GB	EMC	1	DNF	2m 30.18s	30
	Corrado Catalano	I	Rotax	0	DNF	2m 29.85s	28
	Bert Smit	NL	Honda		DNQ	2m 30.92s	
	Johnny Wickström	SF	Honda		DNQ	2m 30.96s	
	Bady Hassaine	TN	Honda		DNQ	2m 31.46s	
	Gastone Grassetti	I	Honda		DNQ	2m 31.49s	
	Håkan Olsson	S	Rotax		DNQ	2m 31.55s	
	Pier Paolo Bianchi	I	EGA		DNQ	2m 31.92s	
	Mike Leitner	A	Honda		DNQ	2m 32.31s	
	Jos van Dongen	NL	Honda		DNQ	2m 32.55s	
	Trevor Manley	AUS	Honda		DNQ	2m 34.41s	
	Kris Galatowicz	GB	EMC		DNQ	2m 34.43s	
	Rafael Roses	E	Cobas		DNQ	2m 36.56s	
	Valerio Vivarelli	RSM	Rotax		DNQ	2m 36.64s	

Fastest lap: Gianola, 2m 24.84s, 94.734 mph/152.460 km/h.
Lap record: Fausto Gresini, I (Garelli), 2m 24.02s, 95.27 mph/153.323 km/h (1987).

World Championship: 1 Criville, 92; **2** Gianola, 81; **3** Spaan, 78; **4** Miralles, 77; **5** Gresini, 61; **6** Unemoto, 57; **7** Takada, 50; **8** Milton, 46; **9** Prein, 44; **10** Scott, 37; **11** Stadler, 27; **12** Martinez, 26; **13** Reyes, 23; **14** Casanova, 20; **15** Rinne, 18; **16** Raudies, 15; **17** Hirose, 13; **18** Brigaglia and Waibel, A., 12; **20** Pietroniro, Torrontegui and Yoshida, 11; **23** Shima, 10; **24** Feuz and Fujiwara, 9; **26** Catalano and Yamashita, 8; **28** Appleyard, Fujiyama and Romboni, 7; **31** Waibel, G. and Yamada, 6; **33** Selini, 5; **34** Wickström, 4; **35** Debbia and Saunders, 3; **37** Fischer, 2; **38** Bedford, 1.

80 cc

11 laps, 41.932 miles/67.474 km

Place	Rider	Nat.	Machine	Laps	Time & speed	Practice time	Grid
1	Peter Öttl	D	Krauser	11	28m 30.78s 89.356 mph/ 143.321 km/h	2m 34.81s	3
2	Manuel Herreros	E	Derbi	11	28m 31.12s	2m 35.03s	4
3	Stefan Dörflinger	CH	Krauser	11	28m 31.35s	2m 33.35s	1
4	Julian Miralles	E	Derbi	11	28m 48.67s	2m 35.50s	5
5	Jaime Mariano	E	Casal	11	29m 00.63s	2m 39.19s	13
6	Bogdan Nikolov	BG	Krauser	11	29m 07.27s	2m 39.66s	17
7	Hans Koopman	NL	Ziegler	11	29m 07.48s	2m 38.01s	10
8	Bert Smit	NL	Krauser	11	29m 07.97s	2m 39.41s	16
9	Paolo Priori	I	Krauser	11	29m 08.22s	2m 39.35s	15
10	Bernd Völkel	D	Seel	11	29m 16.55s	2m 39.32s	14
11	Herri Torrontegui	E	Krauser	11	29m 17.94s	2m 34.81s	2
12	Ralf Waldmann	D	Seel	11	29m 34.02s	2m 39.09s	12
13	Stefan Brägger	CH	Casal	11	29m 44.08s	2m 41.68s	28
14	Jos van Dongen	NL	Casal	11	29m 50.07s	2m 40.93s	22
15	Stefan Kurfiss	D	Krauser	11	29m 52.38s	2m 40.96s	23
16	René Dünki	CH	LCR	11	29m 52.90s	2m 41.20s	25
17	Luis Alvaro	E	Krauser	11	29m 53.27s	2m 37.47s	8
18	Günther Schirnhofer	D	Krauser	11	29m 53.74s	2m 40.38s	19
19	Janez Pintar	YU	Eberhardt	11	29m 54.03s	2m 41.04s	24
20	Reiner Koster	CH	Kroko	11	30m 07.05s	2m 41.38s	26
21	Joaquin Gali	E	Krauser	11	30m 08.59s	2m 41.58s	27
22	Heinz Paschen	D	Casal	11	30m 11.26s	2m 43.72s	32
23	Thomas Engl	D	Esch GP	11	30m 11.49s	2m 41.97s	29
24	Zdravko Matulja	YU	Casal	11	30m 12.02s	2m 44.16s	35
25	Matthias Ehinger	D	Krauser	10	28m 47.25s	2m 44.15s	34
26	Janos Szabo	H	Krauser	9	30m 37.49s	2m 40.44s	20
	Antonio Sanchez	E	Cobas	10	DNF	2m 37.51s	9
	Undine Kummer	D	Krauser	6	DNF	2m 43.56s	31
	Roberto Sassone	I	Unimoto	3	DNF	2m 39.07s	11
	Jose Saez	E	Krauser	2	DNF	2m 37.41s	7
	Jorg Seel	D	Seel	2	DNF	2m 36.68s	6
	Gabriele Gnáni	I	Gnani	2	DNF	2m 39.97s	18
	Maik Stief	D	Casal	1	DNF	2m 44.11s	33
	Jacques Bernard	B	Fantic		DNS	2m 40.84s	21
	Xavier Arumi	E	Krauser		DNS	2m 43.19s	30
	Manuel Duarte	P	Fareel-Zündapp		DNS	2m 44.76s	36
	Chris Baert	B	Bultaco		DNQ	2m 45.44s	
	Paul Bordes	F	RB		DNQ	2m 46.27s	
	Alojz Pavlic	YU	Seel		DNQ	2m 46.51s	
	Emilio Palencia	E	Arbizu		DNQ	2m 50.43s	
	Fabrice Roy	F	Tyl		DNQ	2m 51.90s	
	Claude Gourdon	F	DGM		DNQ	2m 54.35s	

Fastest lap: Dörflinger, 2m 32.84s, 89.775 mph/144.480 km/h (record).
Previous record: Peter Öttl, D (Krauser), 2m 33.98s, 89.11 mph/143.411 km/h (1988).

World Championship: 1 Herreros and Öttl, 75; **3** Dörflinger, 69; **4** Torrontegui, 55; **5** Gnani, 37; **6** Nikolov, 34; **7** Priori, 32; **8** Sanchez, 30; **9** Mariano, 28; **10** Koopman and Miralles, 26; **12** Waldmann, 23; **13** Martinez and Saez, 20; **15** Seel, 19; **16** Kurfiss, 12; **17** Ascareggi, Smit and van Dongen, 9; **20** Sassone, 7; **21** Völkel, 6; **22** Bernard and Matulja, 5; **24** Brägger, Pintar and Szabo, 4; **27** Dünki, Engl and Schirnhofer, 3; **30** Ehinger, 2; **31** Arumi, 1.

WORLD CHAMPIONSHIP · ROUND 10

BELGIAN GRAND PRIX

Malcolm Bryan

If you were at the Belgian Grand Prix you would know that Wayne Rainey won the 500 race. There'd be no doubt in your mind, because you'd seen him chasing Schwantz along the rain-soaked tarmac, the Lucky Strike Yamaha sliding and aquaplaning even more than the Pepsi Suzuki. You'd know that Schwantz crashed on the last lap so Rainey mounted the rostrum as the winner.

If you'd only read about the race, or watched edited highlights on television, you might feel there was some confusion over the result. A jury of men, who were after all present at the race, somehow decided that the riders who'd performed so brilliantly in the rain had wasted their time. They decreed that the race result would be judged on the total time of the two club race-type sprints that were truncated by the riders when it started to rain.

The jury decided that Eddie Lawson was the winner of the Belgian Grand Prix because he had a better time for the two races – not as they were stopped, but for the lap before the red flag was shown each time. You see those are the rules, or at least the rules as the FIM jury applied them to a situation they were never meant to cover. The clerk of the course started the race for the third time. The jury president, Max Deubel, had told him he could not do that. Both men represent the FIM. The first has the power to make something happen, the second to make out that it hadn't happened.

No one looked good on Sunday evening. The spectators looked wet and miserable, the leading 500 riders looked ill informed and unprofessional, the team-managers looked to have no management skills, the FIM looked to have no control whatever over the sport and the press looked stupid submitting stories that changed during the evening. The sport looked like all of the above.

So the jury had Lawson winning from Schwantz and Rainey after five- and three-lap legs gave Lawson the advantage by 0.92 seconds over Schwantz and 1.52 seconds over Rainey. Half-points were awarded. For the rest of us, Rainey won the Grand Prix over a total of 17 laps by 15.29 seconds with Lawson second and John Kocinski third.

It was a most dismal end to what had been a very pleasant week. The weather in Belgium had been quite un-Spa like, with the sun following us down from Assen. The trip wasn't the usual Sunday dash, because major alterations to the paddock at Spa were late being completed. But the paddock was opened on Tuesday and quickly started to fill up.

There were the usual games of golf, cycling and running round the circuit. Most people took a look at the circuit improvements, which were considerable. The largest changes had been made to the two very fast left-handers leading to La Source. The hill on the inside had been

Opposite: **Rainey had just run the toughest race of his life. The smile was well earned but the win was not there to be savoured.**

Ezio Gianola had been the rain star of the 125 class. At Spa Hans Spaan wrenched the title from him.

Malcolm Bryan

pushed back to improve visibility and a great deal more run-off had been provided, thanks to additional landfill into the valley on the right of the track. This made a repeat of Kevin Wrettom's fatal accident most unlikely and virtually ruled out the chance of another crash like last year's Wimmer–Reggiani one. The run-off at the first left ended rather too early, but an extension was promised for 1990 when the land could be purchased.

Less significant increases to the run-off had been created at the exit of the 'bus stop' chicane and to the Raidillon, the fast-climbing right and left after the start and finish. The circuit remained imperfect in the eyes of some, but it was undoubtedly greatly improved.

The meeting was being promoted by Bernie Ecclestone, the dictator of Formula One car racing. There have been rumours of his imminent involvement in motor cycle racing for many years and they were circulating again at Spa. Ecclestone would also be taking over the running of the Brazilian Grand Prix in 1990, moving it from Goiania to the armco-lined circuit at Rio de Janeiro. He was said to have paid 700 million Belgian francs for the commercial rights to the Belgian Grand Prix for a three-year period. He ensured that the safety improvements demanded by the riders were made to the circuit and would presumably see to the required improvements at Rio as well.

Ecclestone's system of paddock marshalling worked much better than the total confusion that normally reigns at Spa and, for most of the time, the paddock and especially the pit lane were clear of non pass-holders. Things got out of hand a little on Saturday evening and Sunday but, up to that point, there'd been a significant improvement. Bernie Ecclestone only visited the event briefly and was not there for race day, but it does not require much imagination to visualise what he would have thought of the organisational shambles created by the FIM and the Belgian federation.

Free practice on Thursday saw Rainey quickest ahead of Schwantz and Lawson, so it was business as usual. Pier Francesco Chili started off well and was fourth fastest, but he would not maintain that position during his next two troubled days of practice. The Italian team had paid 20 million lire for new exhaust pipes and cylinders for the NSR and said that the parts had improved both the mid-range power and the top end of the rev band. What held Chili back was the search for rear-wheel grip. After chasing his tail through the range of Pirellis the Italian ended practice with the thought that the problem probably did not lie with the tyre at all, but with the rear suspension. Seventh place on the grid was not bad, but it hardly matched his third at Assen.

Rainey still held the advantage when timed practice started on Friday morning but by the end of the afternoon session Schwantz had moved ahead. The Texan stayed ahead of the field and took his sixth pole position in a row, and his seventh of the season. Next quickest was Rainey. The time-keepers had Doohan third but there'd been an error and the Australian was actually a second slower. Schwantz and Rainey were over a second quicker than anyone else and Lawson was down in fifth place behind Christian Sarron.

Eighth fastest was John Kocinski, having his first Grand Prix ride on a 500. Indeed, it was practically his first race on a 500. His previous experience amounted to little more than a ride round in Malaysia when Magee's bike was vacant because he was having an operation in the off-season. 'That was just a demonstration ride,' said Kenny Roberts. 'This is just about his first ride.'

Kocinski was rather frustrated by the fact that the wrist he had injured racing the 250 in America, which had already delayed his 500 debut, was still restricting his performance. 'I know that I'm not up to going at Wayne (Rainey)'s pace yet, but the wrist sure isn't helping.'

Having won two 250 Grands Prix for Yamaha early in the season it would have been interesting to see how Kocinski fared at Spa on the little V-twin. The regular Yamaha men – Cadalora, Ruggia and Garriga – were having a dismal run after their bright start to the season, when their bikes had looked to have the edge over the Hondas. In the first five races, up to and including the Italian Grand Prix at Misano, Yamahas had taken every pole position and every lap record. Kocinski had won in Japan and America, Cadalora in Spain, while Ruggia was second in Australia and Italy.

From that point on, though, they had had no rostrum positions, no pole positions and no lap records. Honda had begun their clean sweep, thanks to both superior performance and reliability. At Assen Cadalora and Garriga had both stopped with broken pistons, as they had in Austria. Ruggia fell on the first lap but was an unlikely finisher anyway, having had three engine failures in practice.

Ruggia had made it to the front row this time, but only just. Pole position went to local hero Didier de Radiguès on the Aprilia, in a last-minute achievement. 'There were just four laps of practice to go and I didn't want to stay on the third row of the grid. I got down to riding harder, flat out. The only changes we made to the bike today were to put new pistons in it. It has been a good bike for the last week, but in Assen I was sick so I couldn't do it justice. It is great to be on pole, I haven't been there for years. The closest I came last year was at Imola on the Marlboro Yamaha, when I just missed out.'

Schwantz might be going well, but team-mate Ron Haslam was out of luck. The British rider crashed in the final session going into the very fast downhill double left-hander. He managed to get a lift back to the pits through the infield and went out on the second bike for two laps. Pulling into the pits he had to admit that he could not hold on to the bars. A visit to the Clinica Mobile revealed that both thumbs were broken and he had torn ligaments in his right hand, so he was obviously out of the race. It was hard to believe he'd managed those two laps.

125 cc

It was a first-class race at the beginning with Ezio Gianola heading the field fractionally from Hans Spaan in wet and difficult conditions. Hisashi Unemoto and Allan Scott were third and fourth and made up ground over lap two to be right behind Gianola and Spaan.

Spaan took the lead from Gianola at the end of lap three, outbraking Gianola at the hairpin. Scott was right with them but had to retire on the next lap with a broken gear linkage. 'It is disappointing,' said the American. 'At least I showed what I could do. I was feeling comfortable, not having to try too hard, just waiting to see what would happen. I wasn't going to try and take the lead because I knew that the others had faster bikes and would just come past me again.'

The excitement faded after that. Alex Criville had charged up to sixth but the Cobas slowed and he slipped to seventh behind Derbi man Miralles. Then the bike stopped completely on lap five as the engine seized.

Spaan kept up a pace that Gianola could not match and the Dutchman later accepted that his Dunlop tyres had probably given him a slight advantage. Unemoto was a good and consistent third, using his speed in the early laps to good effect and successfully defending his advantage from Julian Miralles. Fausto Gresini had impressively worked his way through to fourth, only to have the engine slow in the last three laps. He finished seventh.

250 cc

On a drying track the choice of tyres was absolutely crucial. It was Jacques Cornu who got it right and the Swiss rode the tightrope between the slippery patches of tarmac with speed and style. 'I had some very good information about the weather so I put an intermediate tyre on the front for safety but chose a slick for the rear. For the first four or five laps it was very tricky and there were quite a few wet patches but then the dry line got wider and I was able to ride harder.

'At first I had a couple of slides, but once the track was fully dry I could attack without any problem. On the last few laps, when I was in front and Pons was trying to catch me, I looked back at the downhill section to check that he could not catch me and then once more just before La Source (the last hairpin).'

That other nearly-man of the year, Carlos Cardus, charged off the line on the Repsol Honda but Jean-Philippe Ruggia (another nearly-man) cut through from fourth to lead by the end of lap one. He was looking very strong but the Yamaha wasn't and it expired on lap two: a main bearing had failed and locked, throwing the Frenchman

Malcolm Bryan

John Kocinski demonstrated that the capacity of his steed matters little – and the state of the circuit was equally unimportant.

onto a wet patch and spitting him over the bars.

Cornu was handed back the lead but he still had Cardus behind, ahead of Roth, with Pons fifth just behind Wimmer's Aprilia. Roth had obviously been inspired by his Assen win and soon scythed past Cardus to tail Cornu. At the top of the hill, at the end of the long straight, Roth pulled alongside Cornu and moved into the lead. In half a lap he had a one-second advantage.

Roth set about establishing himself as the unchallengeable leader while behind him Cardus took second back from Cornu. Halfway through the 14-lap race Roth looked strong, with an almost three-second lead over Cardus and Cornu. 'I knew then that the men with the slick tyres were on their way. I was praying for a little light rain,' said the German, who had intermediate Michelins front and rear. 'Pons had almost the same tyres but with less cuts in the rear. Because there was a dry line the tyre was getting too hot and I had to slow down.'

Roth's lead dwindled. On lap eight he only had a one-second lead, and a lap later Cardus and Cornu were all over him. Lap ten saw Pons join in. It was total Honda domination again, with Helmut Bradl a distant fifth, slowing with overheated tyres but still ahead of Luca Cadalora, the fastest surviving Yamaha man.

Martin Wimmer fell from the Hein Gericke Aprilia on lap nine while contesting third place with Pons and Bradl. 'My visor misted up. I just couldn't see,' he said later.

At the beginning of lap 11 Cornu pulled out of the slipstream of the HB Honda on the high-speed climb away from Eau Rouge. Pons saw his move and was quickly into second place but the Swiss ace managed to hang on till the flag. Roth was finally forced back to fourth by Cardus.

Cadalora took fifth from Helmut Bradl on the last lap. 'It was the only good thing about the race. The clutch started slipping from about lap three and from then on I had to change without the clutch. The engine sounded terrible, I don't know what it was but I didn't think it would finish. I used intermediate tyres. I think it was the right choice because slicks would have been too risky at the start.'

Local hero and poleman Didier de Radiguès fell unhurt from the Aprilia at the hairpin, as he completed lap one in the leading pack.

500 cc

How does one write about a race that didn't happen? For the spectators, the Belgian Grand Prix was decided in the rain, because the first two races had only just started to boil when they were stopped. However...

The first scheduled start was slightly delayed after the sighting lap, when the riders arrived at La Source to find that cement dust laid during the last laps of the 250 race had not been swept up. After that was done the race got underway. All the riders were using slicks as it had not rained since the 250 race and there were hardly any damp patches remaining.

Lawson led the charge down to Eau Rouge and up the hill but Rainey seized the lead halfway round lap one and Schwantz soon demoted the World Champion to third. Christian Sarron was right with the leading group, and the four pulled away from the pack. It had all the makings of a great Grand Prix and, after a mediocre practice, Lawson was clearly not going to accept defeat readily. No one had an obvious advantage and all three Americans had a turn at leading, sometimes all of them at the same corner, with Sarron only inches behind. The order was changing at every other corner, and Rainey went from first to fourth in a single lap. That was no slur on his riding ability, though, for he could reverse the situation in the same distance.

Schwantz was leading when it started to rain on lap five. He had a big slide through the ultra-fast lefts leading to the 'bus stop' chicane and Lawson overtook. Sarron also went past so that when Schwantz raised his hand to stop the race before the end of lap five only Rainey saw him. But Lawson also reacted to the spots of rain and slowed, although Sarron did not and raced on.

The Frenchman slid off halfway round lap six arriving at the very fast double left. There was some disagreement afterwards as to whether the track was damp there or not. Sarron said he had not noticed the rain and suddenly the track was slippery. Some of the fast men could not believe that Sarron had not seen the rain while others said that the downhill section was not wet and Sarron had just got carried away, finding himself in front. Whatever the truth of the matter, the red flag was shown at the end of lap six and the result counted from the end of lap five. That meant that Sarron was able to restart on his spare machine.

The rain shower was light and short-lived so that when the field lined up for a restart they were still on slicks. This time Sarron got a terrible start but the other three renewed their battle as if nothing had happened. If anything, it was even more aggressive. On lap three Schwantz tried to get inside Lawson, who was leading, in the middle of the very fast downhill double left. The pair almost collided and both wandered off-line. Rainey saw his chance and almost squeezed between the two of them, braking for the next corner.

When the rain came again, after only four laps, it completely soaked the circuit. The second leg was counted after just three laps and the time for each rider added to the time from the first race. That had Lawson ahead of Schwantz, Rainey and Sarron. With less than two seconds covering the first three the winner out of the American trio would almost certainly be the man who crossed the line first at the end of the remaining nine-lap leg, if he could build any sort of lead at all. Just to complicate things a little further Doohan and Kocinski had collided as they slowed at the end of the second leg. Kocinski had no spare bike to use but the clerk of the course, Claude Danis, allowed him to make use of Magee's number two machine.

Danis was keen to get the event rolling again. He was receiving advice and demands from all quarters, and later said that the police had told him there would be a riot if the race was not resumed. (Someone pointed out later that cold, wet, bedraggled people do not riot.) The FIM jury maintained that Mr Danis had been informed by president Max Deubel that the rules did not allow the running of a third race. 'The rules say "two parts"; if the words "or more" were added it would be fine, but they are not,' said Deubel.

Danis would later maintain that he had not been told this, plus he had the police pressure. The fact is that he did start the third leg and the riders tried their very hardest. Any notion that they were limp-wristed pansies went out of the window as the bikes slid and aquaplaned every few yards – and the same men that were fastest in the dry and had stopped the races twice were also fastest in the wet.

Rainey led off the line but Schwantz was right on his tail. The pair traded places several times on the first lap, which ended with the man from

Schwantz, Rainey, Lawson and Sarron used every inch of road, every conceivable line and every trick in the book, even though the first leg only lasted five laps.

Houston in front. He just kept the pace fast and a touch desperate and started to pull away from Rainey, who looked a touch more desperate in his attempt to prevent it. The Californian had not opened up an impressive lead in the World Championship by being faint-hearted and despite, as he admitted later, 'being scared', he kept the pressure on. He cut the Suzuki's advantage from ten to just over five seconds on lap seven and it remained at that for the final lap.

That gap would still have given Schwantz the overall win but approaching the tight downhill 180-degree right-hander the front wheel of the Suzuki locked and the bike simply fell on its side. Schwantz had no chance to counter the move.

'I just fell down,' said a sad, wet Schwantz as he walked back to his motorhome, having received a lift to the pits from Eddie Lawson. Incredibly, an hour later, he was quite willing to relive that dark moment for the innumerable media representatives who sought him out. 'I went pretty fast early on in the rain because I wanted to open up a lead. Once I had done that I eased off and was just cruising. I let the gap close and was just trying to control the race.

'I hadn't had any trouble locking the front all race and I don't know if I hit a slick patch or what,' said Schwantz. 'It was so sudden.'

Mechanical failure had handed Rainey the win just eight days before, although this time it was probably human error. Nothing could be found wrong with the brakes, although Schwantz had felt the wheel lock more suddenly than could be explained by other than a mechanical occurrence.

Take nothing from Rainey's performance, he had ridden perfectly, keeping the pressure on Schwantz as much as he could all the way through the demanding last leg. He had also ridden just as hard in the first two legs. 'All I know is that I rode as fast as I could in the wet. We were trying a brand new rear tyre and it was pretty scary. It worked great this morning but it wasn't so wet then. In the race the puddles were so big it was aquaplaning.'

Dunlop had produced a new 18-in. rear rain tyre to replace the previously used 19, in an attempt to rationalise the wheel-size choice that included 17-, 18- and 19-in. rims. The new tyre was tried for the first time in the wet morning warm-up, the only wet session of the week.

Rainey: 'I had no idea if I was going faster towards the end; I thought he was slowing down. All I knew for sure was I was catching. It was the hardest race of my life. No one could see where they were going and with the tyre situation it was tough.'

As for the confusion created by stopping the race twice and running it over a two-and-a-half hour period that wrecks television schedules, never mind crazy cancellations of nine-lap legs, Rainey was not sure of an answer – not on Sunday evening, anyway. 'It is hard to know what to do,' he said. 'No one wants to stop but if we are out there leading and it starts to rain, what choice do we have? Kevin got a hell of a slide and we could see that there were rain spots on our screens. I was sliding all through the "bus stop" and Eddie was shaking his head. Christian told me he didn't see the rain at all and he crashed. That shows what will happen. We are on slick tyres, we are going to crash. I saw no warning flags. No one else was going to stop the race, so we had to.'

Rainey and Schwantz had the crowd's attention riveted to the front of the race – but after they had torn past, smashing the spray aside, it was John Kocinski who made jaws drop again. He had ridden superbly in the dry but it was the wet that allowed him to reveal genuinely stunning skill. The little guy from Arkansas was only ninth at the end of lap one and, with clouds of spray hindering vision, forward progress was difficult. Kocinski was not deterred, though, and in two laps he had passed McElnea, Magee, Chili, Sarron and even Mick Doohan who had also been moving forward pretty rapidly. Not satisfied with that he reeled in Lawson at an incredible speed, passing him with no regard at all for the Californian's three world titles and almost seven years of Grand Prix experience.

In three Grand Prix outings this year Kocinski had made the rostrum each time and, before the jury made their move, he was given the third-place trophy for finishing behind Lawson on total time. 'It's been a great week. The mechanics have worked hard for me the whole time and I can hardly believe the way it worked out.'

Roberts said he had no fear for his rider, even though Kocinski had never ridden the 500 in the rain before. 'He has a great feel for the rain. He has ridden a couple of wet races in Japan on a 250. I knew that once he settled in and started to get the feedback from the tyres he would be fine.' This did not mean that Kocinski would be racing a Grand Prix 500 in 1990. 'It is just another piece of experience to log into the computer. It will be useful whatever he rides.'

Malcolm Bryan

Randy Mamola had a fine wet ride on the Cagiva, even though he finished well down in thirteenth place in the total results because a primary gear had broken in the first leg. 'The wet race was a good test for us. Michelin gave me a front tyre that had never been tried before. I said I would give it a go as I had nothing to lose. The worst thing about the race was the lack of visibility. If there were more than two people in front of you it was impossible even to see the corner at the bottom of the start and finish. I just waited until the pack got strung out a bit so that I could see, then I got going.' Mamola crossed the line fifth in the rain and right on Doohan's tail. 'I thought about passing him on the last lap but he was pulling away on acceleration and though I was getting real close on the brakes I thought I had better not risk dorking him.'

It might seem strange that Mamola had been able to take part in the second race at all, as the Cagiva had not been running at the end of the first leg. The obliging Mr Danis, however, wanted as many riders as possible and let him start.

Wayne Gardner watched most of the race from the Rothmans hospitality bus, after retiring early in the first leg. On lap two one of the front discs exploded. 'I was going through the flat-out left-handers and suddenly there was a bang. I thought my front tyre had exploded as a silver thing shot through the air ahead of me. I picked the bike up and couldn't believe I was still in control. I looked down at the front wheel and there was no disc. I am one very lucky boy.'

Sidecars

The rain that soaked the 500 men all but drowned the sidecar competitors. More importantly, with the sun invisibly sliding towards the horizon and the air full of spray, visibility that would have had airliners flying on instruments made racing little short of impossible. You would not have known it, though, to see the speed and attack of Streuer and Co

Egbert Streuer and Geral de Haas took full advantage of the clear road and better visibility, taking the lead from the start. 'In these conditions it is important to get in front because you can see. We opened up a lead and could then cut the revs and look after the engine.'

Webster and Hewitt did what they could but after missing a couple of gears they lost the slipstream and sight of the Dutch outfit. The pair were frozen at the finish and Webster said he'd never realised that it was Biland behind him. The Swiss crew had been right there, but Biland never got past. 'I think that I was faster than Steve but there was so much spray I could not get close enough to get past. I just couldn't see.'

Grand Prix de Belgique, 2 July/statistics
Spa-Francorchamps Circuit, 4.312-mile/6.940-km circuit

500 cc

8 laps, 34.496 miles/55.52 km

Place	Rider	Nat.	Machine	Laps	Time & speed	Practice time	Grid
1	Eddie Lawson	USA	Honda	8	19m 46.26s 104.694 mph/ 168.489 km/h	2m 26.46s	5
2	Kevin Schwantz	USA	Suzuki	8	19m 47.18s	2m 24.65s	1
3	Wayne Rainey	USA	Yamaha	8	19m 47.78s	2m 25.02s	2
4	Christian Sarron	F	Yamaha	8	19m 57.69s	2m 26.44s	4
5	John Kocinski	USA	Yamaha	8	20m 01.48s	2m 27.24s	8
6	Pier Francesco Chili	I	Honda	8	20m 05.13s	2m 26.55s	7
7	Kevin Magee	AUS	Yamaha	8	20m 06.98s	2m 26.50s	6
8	Michael Doohan	AUS	Honda	8	20m 13.49s	2m 26.33s	3
9	Freddie Spencer	USA	Yamaha	8	20m 14.11s	2m 27.27s	9
10	Niall Mackenzie	GB	Yamaha	8	20m 19.10s	2m 27.56s	11
11	Rob McElnea	GB	Honda	8	20m 19.23s	2m 28.90s	13
12	Marco Gentile	CH	Fior	8	21m 11.72s	2m 35.12s	16
13	Kees Doorakkers	NL	Honda	8	21m 20.72s	2m 37.96s	21
14	Eddie Laycock	IRL	Honda	8	21m 23.32s	2m 37.39s	20
15	Simon Buckmaster	GB	Honda	8	21m 23.85s	2m 35.55s	17
16	Josef Doppler	A	Honda	8	21m 26.08s	2m 38.28s	22
17	Bruno Kneubühler	CH	Honda	8	21m 27.62s	2m 36.27s	18
18	Marco Papa	I	Paton	8	21m 49.29s	2m 36.95s	19
19	Niggi Schmassman	CH	Honda	8	22m 00.66s	2m 38.45s	23
20	Hans Klingebiel	D	Suzuki	8	22m 17.63s	2m 42.28s	26
21	Fernando Gonzalez	E	Honda	8	22m 22.25s	2m 41.91s	25
22	Mark Phillips	GB	Suzuki	8	22m 53.31s	2m 40.67s	24
23	Randy Mamola	USA	Cagiva	7	19m 45.63s	2m 29.16s	14
	Alessandro Valesi	I	Yamaha	2	DNF	2m 32.24s	15
	Wayne Gardner	AUS	Honda	2	DNF	2m 27.42s	10
	Pavol Dekanek	CS	Honda	2	DNF	2m 42.56s	27
	Ron Haslam	GB	Suzuki		DNS	2m 28.00s	12
	Patrick Chavanne	B	Honda		DNQ	2m 45.93s	

Fastest lap: Schwantz, 2m 26.11s, 106.251 mph/170.994 km/h (record).
Previous record: Eddie Lawson, USA (Yamaha), 2m 28.35s, 104.647 mph/168.412 km/h (1987).

World Championship: 1 Rainey, 150.5; **2** Lawson, 137; **3** Sarron, C., 103.5; **4** Magee, 87.5; **5** Schwantz, 85.5; **6** Chili, 85; **7** Doohan, 60; **8** Mackenzie, 51; **9** Haslam, 48; **10** Gardner, 43; **11** Sarron, D., 39; **12** Buckmaster, 34.5; **13** Spencer, 33.5; **14** Gentile, 30; **15** Valesi, 27; **16** Taira, 26; **17** McElnea, 24.5; **18** Mamola and Rudroff, 18; **20** Fujiwara, 17; **21** Shobert, 12; **22** Doppler, 11; **23** Meyer, 10; **24** Balbi, 9; **25** Broccoli, Gonzalez and Schmassman, 8; **28** Dowson and Leuthe, 7; **30** Itoh, 6; **31** Kocinski, 5.5; **32** Gschwender, 5; **33** Kneubühler, 4; **34** Yatsushiro, 3; **35** Doorakkers, 2.5; **36** Laycock and Lopez Mella, 2; **38** Machii, 1.

250 cc

14 laps, 60.368 miles/97.16 km

Place	Rider	Nat.	Machine	Laps	Time & speed	Practice time	Grid
1	Jacques Cornu	CH	Honda	14	34m 45.58s 98.541 mph/ 158.587 km/h	2m 32.43s	3
2	Alfonso Pons	E	Honda	14	36m 46.16s	2m 32.68s	7
3	Carlos Cardus	E	Honda	14	36m 48.51s	2m 31.85s	2
4	Reinhold Roth	D	Honda	14	36m 55.26s	2m 32.65s	6
5	Luca Cadalora	I	Yamaha	14	37m 11.05s	2m 33.50s	11
6	Helmut Bradl	D	Honda	14	37m 14.52s	2m 32.43s	4
7	Juan Garriga	E	Yamaha	14	37m 26.63s	2m 34.44s	13
8	Fausto Ricci	I	Aprilia	14	37m 36.65s	2m 36.41s	23
9	Masahiro Shimizu	J	Honda	14	37m 41.95s	2m 36.41s	24
10	Alain Bronec	F	Aprilia	14	37m 43.46s	2m 37.28s	32
11	Daniel Amatriain	E	Honda	14	37m 43.93s	2m 35.49s	16
12	Renzo Colleoni	I	Aprilia	14	37m 44.61s	2m 36.22s	21
13	Alberto Puig	E	Yamaha	14	37m 45.06s	2m 33.30s	10
14	Harald Eckl	D	Aprilia	14	37m 48.65s	2m 35.60s	18
15	Carlos Lavado	YV	Aprilia	14	37m 50.86s	2m 34.02s	12
16	Bernard Hänggeli	CH	Yamaha	14	37m 51.18s	2m 36.56s	27
17	Hans Becker	D	Seel	14	38m 08.91s	2m 36.44s	26
18	Maurizio Vitali	I	Honda	14	38m 09.58s	2m 36.36s	22
19	Wilco Zeelenberg	NL	Honda	14	38m 22.96s	2m 36.16s	20
20	Andreas Preining	A	Aprilia	14	38m 27.03s	2m 37.83s	35
21	Luis Lavado	YV	Yamaha	14	38m 27.35s	2m 38.06s	36
22	Bernhard Schick	D	Yamaha	14	38m 36.09s	2m 36.82s	29
23	Manfred Herweh	D	Yamaha	14	39m 10.89s	2m 37.18s	31
24	Laurent Naveau	B	Yamaha	13	37m 19.11s	2m 37.67s	34
	Martin Wimmer	D	Aprilia	8	DNF	2m 32.74s	8
	Gary Cowan	IRL	Yamaha	8	DNF	2m 36.41s	25
	Alexandre Barros	BR	Yamaha	7	DNF	2m 35.14s	14
	Alberto Rota	I	Aprilia	6	DNF	2m 37.05s	30
	Adrien Morillas	F	Yamaha	6	DNF	2m 36.58s	28
	Loris Reggiani	I	Honda	5	DNF	2m 33.27s	9
	Stefano Caracchi	RSM	Honda	5	DNF	2m 35.73s	19
	Andy Leisner	USA	Honda	5	DNF	2m 35.35s	15
	Patrick van den Goorbergh	NL	Yamaha	4	DNF	2m 37.33s	33
	August Auinger	A	Yamaha	2	DNF	2m 35.59s	17
	Jean-Philippe Ruggia	F	Yamaha	1	DNF	2m 32.55s	5
	Didier de Radiguès	B	Aprilia	1	DNF	2m 31.79s	1
	Massimo Matteoni	I	Yamaha		DNQ	2m 38.38s	
	Jean Foray	F	Yamaha		DNQ	2m 38.52s	
	Paolo Casoli	I	Honda		DNQ	2m 38.56s	
	Urs Jucker	CH	Yamaha		DNQ	2m 38.78s	
	Virginio Ferrari	I	Gazzaniga		DNQ	2m 39.50s	
	Jean-François Baldé	F	Yamaha		DNQ	2m 40.91s	
	Kevin Mitchell	GB	Yamaha		DNQ	2m 41.53s	
	Mario Houssin	B	Yamaha		DNQ	2m 41.56s	
	Darren Milner	AUS	Yamaha		DNQ	2m 41.97s	
	Woolsey Coulter	IRL	Aprilia		DNQ	2m 42.42s	
	Alain Kempener	B	Aprilia		DNQ	2m 43.68s	

Fastest lap: Pons, 2m 33.53s, 101.115 mph/162.730 km/h.
Lap record: Anton Mang, D (Honda), 2m 32.06s, 102.09 mph/164.304 km/h (1988).

World Championship: 1 Pons, 181; **2** Cornu, 120; **3** Roth, 116; **4** Cardus, 110; **5** Ruggia, 99; **6** Cadalora, 81; **7** Garriga, 60; **8** Shimizu, 58; **9** Bradl, 54; **10** Wimmer, 44; **11** Kocinski, 40; **12** de Radiguès, 32; **13** Reggiani, Schmid and Zeelenberg, 26; **16** Filice, 22; **17** Colleoni, 21; **18** Palazzese, 19; **19** Lucchi, 17; **20** Puig, 16; **21** Eckl, 15; **22** Cowan and Honma, 13; **24** Bronec and Okada, 10; **26** Amatriain and Shiomori, 9; **28** Barros, Morillas and Ricci, 8; **31** Lavado, 7; **32** Rota and van den Goorbergh, 6; **34** Caracchi, 5; **35** Beattie and Mitchell, 4; **37** Preining and Vitali, 2; **39** Arai, Auinger and Becker, 1.

125 cc

13 laps, 56.056 miles/90.220 km

Place	Rider	Nat.	Machine	Laps	Time & speed	Practice time	Grid
1	Hans Spaan	NL	Honda	13	38m 38.49s 87.047 mph/ 140.088 km/h	2m 43.54s	2
2	Ezio Gianola	I	Honda	13	38m 50.89s	2m 43.47s	1
3	Hisashi Unemoto	J	Honda	13	39m 16.80s	2m 46.46s	9
4	Julian Miralles	E	Derbi	13	39m 27.69s	2m 46.06s	8
5	Lucio Pietroniro	B	Honda	13	39m 36.41s	2m 44.38s	5
6	Stefan Prein	D	Honda	13	39m 40.00s	2m 47.45s	15
7	Fausto Gresini	I	Aprilia	13	39m 40.35s	2m 45.09s	6
8	Adolf Stadler	D	Honda	13	39m 41.15s	2m 46.66s	11
9	Koji Takada	J	Honda	13	39m 41.51s	2m 46.47s	10
10	Thierry Feuz	CH	Honda	13	39m 42.10s	2m 47.25s	13
11	Domenico Brigaglia	I	Garelli	13	39m 47.59s	2m 48.72s	27
12	Doriano Romboni	I	Honda	13	39m 48.26s	2m 47.65s	18
13	Dirk Raudies	D	Honda	13	39m 53.41s	2m 48.76s	28
14	Jean-Claude Selini	F	Honda	13	39m 53.82s	2m 48.40s	24
15	Hubert Abold	D	Rotax	13	39m 54.65s	2m 47.47s	16
16	Alex Bedford	GB	EMC	13	40m 02.60s	2m 48.71s	26
17	Robin Milton	GB	Honda	13	40m 07.94s	2m 48.91s	29
18	Luis Reyes	E	Honda	13	40m 27.81s	2m 48.26s	22
19	Peter Öttl	D	Krauser	13	40m 49.94s	2m 47.92s	19
20	Gastone Grassetti	I	Honda	13	40m 50.93s	2m 49.04s	30
21	Flemming Kistrup	DK	Honda	13	40m 52.04s	2m 47.55s	17
22	Håkan Olsson	S	Rotax	13	41m 11.12s	2m 49.16s	32
23	Johnny Wickström	SF	Honda	13	41m 11.65s	2m 49.53s	36
24	Serge Julin	B	Honda	12	38m 55.85s	2m 48.37s	23
25	Manfred Fischer	A	Honda	12	38m 57.99s	2m 49.54s	37
	Alfred Waibel	D	Honda	10	DNF	2m 46.86s	12
	Emilio Cuppini	I	Garelli	7	DNF	2m 49.13s	31
	Corrado Catalano	I	Rotax	6	DNF	2m 45.12s	7
	Alex Criville	E	Cobas	4	DNF	2m 43.59s	4
	Allan Scott	USA	Honda	4	DNF	2m 47.32s	14
	Stefan Dörflinger	CH	Aprilia	3	DNF	2m 48.69s	25
	Bady Hassaine	TN	Honda	2	DNF	2m 48.26s	21
	Jorge Martinez	E	Derbi	2	DNF	2m 43.56s	3
	Robin Appleyard	GB	Honda	2	DNF	2m 49.23s	33
	Bruno Casanova	I	Aprilia	1	DNF	2m 48.20s	20
	Taru Rinne	SF	Honda		DNS	2m 49.31s	34
	Heinz Lüthi	CH	Honda		DNS	2m 49.46s	35
	Herri Torrontegui	E	Honda		DNQ	2m 49.84s	
	Paul Bordes	F	Honda		DNQ	2m 49.87s	
	Ralf Waldmann	D	Cobas		DNQ	2m 50.19s	
	Rafael Roses	E	Cobas		DNQ	2m 50.86s	
	Othmar Schuler	CH	Honda		DNQ	2m 51.36s	
	Mike Leitner	A	Honda		DNQ	2m 51.68s	
	Klaus Kindle	FL	Honda		DNQ	2m 51.77s	
	Alan Patterson	IRL	Honda		DNQ	2m 52.33s	
	Trevor Manley	AUS	Honda		DNQ	2m 52.68s	
	Jacky Bernard	B	Rotax		DNQ	2m 54.95s	
	Alain Kempener	B	Honda		DNQ	2m 55.23s	
	Kris Galatowicz	GB	EMC		DNQ	3m 02.23s	

Fastest lap: Spaan, 2m 55.74s, 88.337 mph/142.165 km/h.
Lap record: August Auinger, A (Monnet), 2m 45.36s, 93.882 mph/151.088 km/h (1985).

World Championship: 1 Gianola and Spaan, 98; **3** Criville, 92; **4** Miralles, 90; **5** Unemoto, 72; **6** Gresini, 70; **7** Takada, 57; **8** Prein, 54; **9** Milton, 46; **10** Scott, 37; **11** Stadler, 35; **12** Martinez, 26; **13** Reyes, 23; **14** Pietroniro, 22; **15** Casanova, 20; **16** Raudies and Rinne, 18; **18** Brigaglia, 17; **19** Feuz, 15; **20** Hirose, 13; **21** Waibel, A., 12; **22** Romboni, Torrontegui and Yoshida, 11; **25** Shima, 10; **26** Fujiwara, 9; **27** Catalano and Yamashita, 8; **29** Appleyard, Fujiyama and Selini, 7; **32** Waibel, G. and Yamada, 6; **34** Wickström, 4; **35** Debbia and Saunders, 3; **37** Fischer, 2; **38** Abold and Bedford, 1.

The 250s stream past the pits and into La Source hairpin.

Sidecars

12 laps, 51.744 miles/83.28 km

Place	Driver & passenger	Nat.	Machine	Laps	Time & speed	Practice time	Grid
1	Egbert Streuer/ Geral de Haas	NL NL	LCR- Yamaha	12	34m 52.03s 89.048 mph/ 143.310 km/h	2m 36.08s	3
2	Steve Webster/ Tony Hewitt	GB GB	LCR- Krauser	12	35m 10.48s	2m 35.25s	1
3	Rolf Biland/ Kurt Waltisperg	CH CH	LCR- Krauser	12	35m 11.47s	2m 35.56s	2
4	Rolf Steinhausen/ Bruno Hiller	D D	Schuch	12	35m 28.44s	2m 38.89s	8
5	Derek Jones/ Peter Brown	GB GB	LCR- Yamaha	12	35m 49.27s	2m 39.57s	9
6	Bernd Scherer/ Thomas Schröder	D D	BSR- Krauser	12	35m 56.39s	2m 40.92s	13
7	Barry Brindley/ Grahame Rose	GB GB	Fowler- Yamaha	12	35m 58.58s	2m 41.68s	17
8	Alain Michel/ Jean-Marc Fresc	F F	LCR- Krauser	12	36m 23.98s	2m 36.52s	4
9	Markus Egloff/ Urs Egloff	CH CH	Yamaha	12	36m 25.60s	2m 36.95s	5
10	Fritz Stölzle/ Hubert Stölzle	D D	LCR- Krauser	12	36m 26.55s	2m 39.60s	10
11	Yoshisada Kumagaya/ Phil Coombes	J GB	KS- Windle	12	36m 29.11s	2m 41.47s	14
12	Ivan Nigrowsky/ Jacques Corbier	F F	LCR- JPX	12	36m 29.96s	2m 39.83s	11
13	Theo van Kempen/ Simon Birchall	NL GB	LCR- Yamaha	12	37m 20.43s	2m 40.35s	12
14	Kenny Howles/ Steve Pointer	GB GB	LCR- Krauser	12	37m 27.75s	2m 44.51s	26
15	Billy Gällros/ Håkan Olsson	S S	Yamaha	12	37m 28.53s	2m 43.55s	22
16	George Hardwick/ Gary Irlam	GB GB	LCR- Yamaha	12	37m 34.19s	2m 44.14s	23
17	Ralph Bohnhorst/ Thomas Böttcher	D D	LCR	12	37m 37.94s	2m 41.66s	16
18	Hans Hügli/ Adolf Hänni	CH A	Sigwa	12	37m 38.27s	2m 42.76s	20
19	Masato Kumano/ Markus Fahrni	J CH	LCR- Tec	12	37m 46.49s	2m 38.30s	6
20	Wolfgang Stropek/ Steve Campbell	A GB	Krauser	12	37m 54.17s	2m 44.23s	24
21	Klaus Klaffenböck/ Christian Parzer	A A	LCR	11	35m 03.03s	2m 44.43s	25
22	Clive Stirrat/ Simon Prior	GB GB	LCR	11	35m 27.23s	2m 43.00s	21
	Barry Smith/ David Smith	GB GB	ADM	7	DNF	2m 42.18s	18
	René Progin/ Yves Hunziker	CH CH	Krauser	3	DNF	2m 42.46s	19
	Steve Abbott/ Shaun Smith	GB GB	Windle- Yamaha		DNS	2m 38.53s	7
	Tony Baker/ Trevor Hopkinson	GB GB	Yamaha		DNS	2m 41.57s	15
	Gary Thomas/ Eckhart Rösinger	GB D	Krauser		DNQ	2m 44.57s	
	Jos van Stekelenburg/ Rinie Bettgens	NL NL	LCR- Yamaha		DNQ	2m 44.79s	
	Paul Atkinson/ J. Tailford	GB GB	LCR- Yamaha		DNQ	2m 47.58s	
	Frank Voigt/ Holger Voigt	D D	LCR		DNQ	2m 48.35s	
	Judd Drew/ Bryan Houghton	GB GB	LCR- Krauser		DNQ	2m 48.88s	
	Egon Schons/ Peter Höss	D D	BSR- Yamaha		DNQ	2m 50.76s	

Fastest lap: Streuer, 2m 51.53s, 90.505 mph/145.654 km/h.
Lap record: Egbert Streuer/Bernard Schnieders, NL/NL (LCR-Yamaha), 2m 36.05s, 99.483 mph/160.102 km/h (1985).

World Championship: 1 Webster, 78; **2** Streuer, 71; **3** Michel, 53; **4** Biland, 50; **5** Kumano, 47; **6** Steinhausen, 42; **7** Stölzle, 40; **8** Egloff, 32; **9** Brindley, 29; **10** Jones, 27; **11** Scherer, 26; **12** Kumagaya, 25; **13** Zurbrügg, 21; **14** van Kempen, 20; **15** Abbott and Wyssen, 15; **17** Nigrowsky and Progin, 12; **19** Smith, 8; **20** Baker, 7; **21** Gällros and Stropek, 6; **23** Drew, 4; **24** Stirrat, 3; **25** Hardwick, Howles and Thomas, 2.

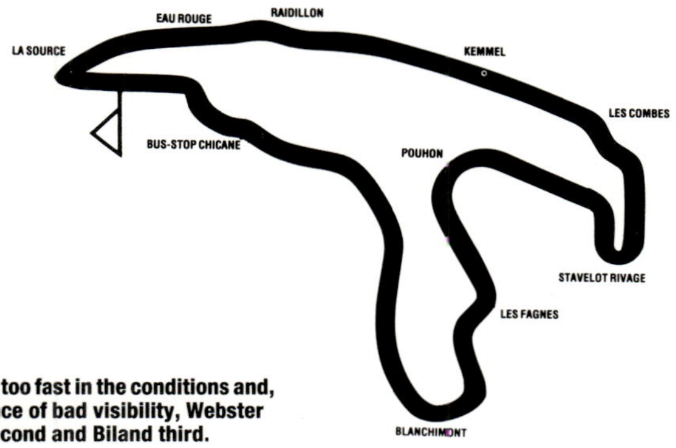

Streuer was just too fast in the conditions and, with the hindrance of bad visibility, Webster had to accept second and Biland third.

Malcolm Bryan

Malcolm Bryan

FRENCH GRAND PRIX

Christian Sarron is perhaps the most universally popular of the 500 stars and it would have been a perfect two-hundredth anniversary celebration of Bastille Day had the man from Clermont-Ferrand won his own Grand Prix. It was not to be. He was on the pace early in practice but a fall at the end of the first session knocked his confidence and he never matched those times. The cheers he raised from the crowd every time he took to the circuit, however, left no doubt as to his popularity.

There were cheers, too, for his brother, Dominique, who has done so many laps of Le Mans on endurance machines, but he was most unlikely to be as competitive on the 500 as he had not yet recovered from a shoulder injury sustained in the Sunday warm-up at Assen. Because Sarron never thought he would be 100 per cent fit to ride Adrien Morillas, also from Clermont-Ferrand, was glad to be given a chance on the Elf-backed NSR, even if there was little hope of it leading to a full factory place. Better known as a superbike rider, Morillas has had several Grand Prix outings on his own 250 Yamaha.

Serge Rosset had become almost desperate in his search for a top-class rider and the finance to run a team after Elf told him they were reducing their budget for 1990. Rosset claimed that he had been near to signing Lawson at one point in the closed season but Elf would not accept dual billing with Rothmans and the deal fell through. Elf wanted a French rider and hence Dominique was signed. It was a little much to expect him to be an instant success on a 500, and he was just starting to show some promise when he was injured at Assen.

Another Frenchman getting a chance on a Grand Prix 500 was 28-year-old Parisian, Thierry Crine. He was using the same factory Suzuki that Doug Polen had ridden at Suzuka and Ernst Gschwender at Hockenheim; it was also the bike that Schwantz had ridden at Macau at the end of '88.

The French are desperately searching for a replacement for Christian Sarron, who had been saying that he would probably retire at the end of the season. However, he had been enjoying his riding so much that he'd started to talk about one more year. At Le Mans he announced formally that he would race again in 1990 – and his Gauloises Blondes team revealed that they would be running two factory 500s, the second being for Jean-Philippe Ruggia. Ruggia had been making plenty of noise about going elsewhere for a competitive 250, as the Yamaha continued to give trouble. His team offered him the 500 to keep him from leaving but he had refused to sign on the spot. The équipe said that if Ruggia did leave they would still run a second 500, even if it meant signing a foreigner.

There were plenty of Frenchmen in the 500 race, with Raymond Roche having another outing on the second Cagiva, but none of them were likely to put on a performance to equal Christian Sarron's. At least the French were well represented. Other European nations looked poor.

The Italians only had Chili to cheer for and the British Mackenzie and McElnea; Haslam was still out of action with the broken thumbs he had sustained at Spa. He had tried to ride his ATC round the farm, at home in Derbyshire, but found he could not hang on at all. 'I took the plaster off the left hand to see if I could use it but I couldn't even pull in the clutch. I knew that I would not be able to use the brake. The hospital said that both thumbs would take four weeks to heal so I will be fit for Donington.'

The Gauloises team also announced their connection with the Zenith computer company, with whom they would be working on the development of electronic measurement systems. Rosset's team were trying engine measurement at Le Mans too, sending information from the bike by radio to a reception computer in the pits, as opposed to the Lucky Strike team's method of storing information on the bike.

The factory Yamaha teams had the option of trying a new fairing design, featuring repositioned air intakes. The normal intake position is below the radiator side intakes, but the airflow is disturbed there by the air coming round the front wheel. Moving the intakes to above the radiator gave them undisturbed air and hence they could be smaller than the originals. The air is ducted to the carb airbox through the fairing dividers between the central radiator intake and the side intakes. The Lucky Strike team tested them at Le Mans.

Ending the four sessions just tenth quickest, Wayne Gardner was not at all impressed with himself. His engineer Stuart Shenton explained: 'He expects so much of himself and when he can't win races it is very frustrating. We have to accept that the others have done a lot of work since he has been injured. The bikes are better developed and they have been riding every weekend.'

Gardner wasn't blaming anyone but himself. 'I just don't seem to be able to go into the corners hard enough. I am braking 50 metres too early. I am getting out of the corners OK but I just can't rush into the corners like I should. It will come but I didn't think it would take this long. All the time I was off racing I was sure I would just get back on and be as fast as I was before but that hasn't happened.'

Gardner was testing the fully reinforced aluminium frame and he used it for the race. Both he and Lawson had carbon fibre silencers but, surprisingly, neither was using the carbon discs. Gardner tested them for the first time since his Laguna Seca practice fall, when they had locked on him. Lawson had used the discs previously but, after testing at Le Mans in the week prior to the Grand Prix, had decided to go back to the steel discs for race week. Lockheed were working on some new components for Honda and until these were ready Lawson was using Nissin equipment.

Lawson had the use of some new suspension components and that made the Rothmans Honda handle much better. Eddie had been very critical of the circuit after his test and was widely quoted in France as saying that the track was terrible, the surface rough and slippery. It is certainly not a good place to go for a Grand Prix and, with luck, the circus will make fewer trips there in future: the 1990 event is due to be held at the completely rebuilt Magny Cours and the date should then alternate between that new venue and Paul Ricard.

Eddie Lawson was displeasing more than just the owners of the Bugatti circuit during practice. He had unpleasant exchanges with both Kevin Schwantz and Kevin Magee.

The disagreement with Magee occurred during Friday practice, when Lawson felt that the Australian had held him up on a fast lap. 'I didn't realise he was behind me,' said Magee. 'I was just doing my thing. I passed Gardner and when I saw the nose of a Rothmans bike I thought it was Wayne and I just expected him to come past, because he's normally pretty fast into the corners. It didn't come past and I kept going. At the end of the back straight the bike came alongside. I saw it was Lawson and I braked to go into the corner behind him. He kept braking, going slower and slower until we got into the corner and he forced me to go on a strange line. Then he was just shaking his head and wobbling through the corner in front of me. He squirted down to the next corner and did the same thing.'

Practice finished and Magee stopped next to Schwantz, expecting Lawson to chat to Schwantz as usual. This time Lawson stopped beside Rainey and ignored Magee's invitation to come over. Magee pushed his bike across to the Honda and asked Lawson what he thought he was doing, whereupon he was told that he had stopped Lawson putting in a good lap time.

At the end of qualifying Magee was 0.36 of a second slower than Lawson. It is by no means the first time that Lawson has let it be known that other riders should clear the track for him. He had ranted at Dominique Sarron in the pit lane at Jerez, after the Frenchman committed some alleged misdemeanour in practice, and he often indicates his displeasure at privateers, many of whom, he feels, certainly don't have the machinery to warrant being on the circuit, while some do not have the ability either.

On that Friday evening at Le Mans Lawson had a dinner engagement with the boss of Dainese leathers. Kevin Schwantz was also present and the poor Italian ended up trying to referee a shouting match between the two riders. Lawson's abuse of Schwantz related to the discussion that had taken place at the riders' meeting with the clerk of the course earlier that afternoon, concerning the action to be taken if it rained during the race. (It had been decided that at the first drop of rain the clerk of the course would stop the race. After 30 minutes it would be restarted and any change in the weather after that would be ignored. That is largely in keeping with the FIM rules.) Lawson maintained that the race should be stopped as many times as was necessary for changes in the weather and he told Schwantz the decision was stupid. He was the only one of the top riders who had not turned up to the meeting – but that did not stop him disagreeing with the result.

One of Lawson's main opponents said that he

Eddie Lawson tested the Rothmans Honda the week before the Grand Prix and it started to go exactly where he put it.

Malcolm Bryan

was in no way surprised by Eddie's attitude to the other riders. 'He has to work himself up to hate everyone. That is his way of trying to win.' Whether it was the new suspension parts, the pre-race testing or animosity towards several or all of his opponents, the fact was that Lawson ended practice in pole position, his and Honda's first of the season.

Suzuki and Yamaha had been dominating 500 practice before the French Grand Prix, but in the 250 class everything had been going Honda's way. The French broke their run with Ruggia fastest, just easing out European newcomer Toshihiko Honma who was the sensation of practice.

In the 125 class Jorge Martinez was back in his old position at the head of the practice table, having got over the nasty hand injury sustained in Austria. His nearest rivals were Spaan on the Honda and Criville on the Cobas with Gianola, who had started the year as very much Honda's best chance of success, down in fourth place though only three-tenths of a second slower than the Derbi.

Gianola was trying a new rear suspension system in an attempt to redress the advantage Spaan seemed to have. Replacing the cantilever system and White Power suspension unit on one bike was a rocker-arm system and Ohlins unit. The frame had been modified to mount the nose of the unit on the right-hand main frame spar, up close to where the seat rail is also mounted. The forward end of the rocker arm pivoted on the right-hand side of the frame, the rearward end was connected to the suspension unit, while the centre of the rocker was connected via a rod to the swing arm. The front suspension on both Gianola's bikes was still being cared for by White Power OUT (Outer Upper Tube) forks; Ohlins do not make OUT forks that small.

250 cc

This race had all the makings of yet another brilliant win for Pons, who led early on and was always right in contention – but this time the laurels went to fellow-Spaniard Carlos Cardus on the Repsol Honda. It was the first-ever Grand Prix win for the popular Cardus. He has never enjoyed the same adoration in Spain as Pons, Garriga and Martinez – he has never had the results of these three either – but his win confirmed Spain's position as the strongest nation in the class and put paid to Cardus's reputation as a man who could lead, put in a few good laps, but who lacked that special combination of concentration, skill and stamina that wins Grands Prix.

Cardus's win came after a battle between seven men that any one of them might have won. At the end of lap one Honma was second to Pons with Ruggia, Cardus, Roth, Cornu and Shimizu right there. Next came Wimmer on the Hein Gericke Aprilia; he hung on to the seven for the first four laps but then fell back to face pressure from de Radiguès and Garriga, who had not made a good start. Worst off was Luca Cadalora, who had made a disastrous getaway from the outside of the first row. 'It was my fault, I let the clutch out too quickly and the engine started to die. I tried again but then I had too many revs and that was no good. Catching up from there is hard. You lose so much time in the first laps. After I got clear I was doing the same lap times as the leading group but I wasn't catching them.'

By lap three Cardus was up to second place, having displaced Honma, and Ruggia went past the Japanese a lap later as Cardus seized the lead from Pons. Pons had led races before and let him get on with it, as Honma and Ruggia battled behind. The French had expected great things of their man after he took pole but his best engine had been wrecked in the morning warm-up and the second bike was, said Ruggia, 'a second a lap slower'.

On lap six Ruggia was pushed back to fifth by the rise of Cornu. There was still the group of seven men at the front, but it was obvious that the Swiss was looking menacing. Cardus opened up a fraction of a lead, not as much as a second, but there was daylight between him and Pons. The World Champion was too wise to let his fellow-Honda rider make any more of it and, as Cornu moved to third, the leading trio closed up again.

Laps 12 and 13 had the crowd on their feet as Ruggia tried once more to attack the front. He got past Cornu but Pons held him off for five laps. On lap 19 it was back to fourth again for Ruggia, thanks to Cornu.

It looked for all the world as though Pons was lining himself up for a late run on Cardus but, just at the time when the championship leader should have been making a move, Cornu squeezed past and from lap 22 of the 24 it was Cardus leading from Cornu, Pons and Honma. Cornu had a look at taking the lead but Cardus kept the pace up and the Swiss could not chance a pass. 'It was the best, most enjoyable race we have had all year. I thought about trying to pass Carlos on the last lap but to do so would have been very risky so I settled for second,' said Cornu.

Pons was nowhere near as ready to accept third. 'Of course I am not satisfied,' he said later. 'I thought that the race was going OK but when I tried to force the pace a little towards the end I started to have some stability problems. When Cornu came past it was impossible to retake him.'

Cardus could hardly speak for emotion after his first Grand Prix victory. Later, when he'd collected his thoughts, he explained that he had been confident of winning, even with Pons and Cornu breathing down his neck. 'Even before the last lap I knew that I could win. I just concentrated on making no mistakes. The tyres were sliding a bit but today is so hot I knew all the other riders must be having the same trouble.'

Honma took fourth: it had been a great ride but slightly disappointing to the Japanese ace after being second quickest in practice. 'I did think I might do better but it was a great experience. One thing I learnt is that the other riders are so good that you should not allow yourself to be passed because it is so hard to get in front of them again.'

Behind Ruggia was Roth who, while in the leading group all the way, never threatened and later complained that he lacked strength after suffering a stomach infection earlier in the week. 'I thought that I was well over it but halfway through the race I just had nothing left to give. It was time to speed up and improve my position but I didn't have the strength. The bike and the tyres were perfect. It was just me.'

Shimizu was seventh and frustrated still to be hindered by the sore back and neck that he had sustained in his Yugoslav car crash. For Juan Garriga eighth place was a mediocre result that merely reflected the way the season had been going. 'It was not a good start and then I got held up by de Radiguès and Wimmer. When I got past them I could do the same lap times as the guys at the front but I could not catch them. Even passing Wimmer and de Radiguès was not easy. About the only place I could make up time was on the brakes.'

125 cc

Reigning World Champion Aspar Martinez won his first 125 race of the season – he was quite a clear winner in the end – but only after a lengthy battle to stay ahead of Alex Criville and Ezio Gianola. And the championship advantage swung back to Gianola for, although the Italian only finished third, it was enough to take the lead from Hans Spaan, who stopped on lap 17 with loss of water from his Honda due to a cracked cylinder head.

The race started with four men at the front, Spaan taking the lead from Martinez, but after nine laps the Honda was overheating so much that the Dutchman had to rush into the pits for water. He rejoined the action but eventually the engine blew all the water out again and Spaan was forced to retire.

Martinez held the advantage by a second on lap 16, then put in a burst of speed in an attempt to drop Criville. The Cobas rider was three seconds up on Gianola, whose Honda was losing power. Criville fought back and closed again on Martinez, cutting his advantage to under a second. It was obvious now that the win would be decided between the two Spaniards and, going onto the last lap, Martinez forced the gap to just over a second. Criville made up ground on that final circuit but not enough to be in a passing position, even though he gained 10 metres going into the last corner.

Gianola was a comfortable third. The fourth-place battle between Takada, Gresini and Unemoto that had been going on throughout the race was only decided at the last double right. It ended with the nearest thing to a crash Hisashi Unemoto will ever experience without actually parting company with his machine. He had just got the better of a race-long battle with Fausto Gresini and Koji Takada, but then suffered a vicious slide exiting the last left-hander. Unemoto fell across the petrol tank and smashed the screen as he fought for control and, while he was thus occupied, Gresini and Takada came past.

While he was still only half in control but heading in the right direction Unemoto wobbled into the back of either Gresini's or Takada's machine (they were side by side). Touching at least one of their rear wheels sent Unemoto's bike out of control again and off the track to the right. His two opponents carried on and turned right as he cut the corner, running through a gravel pit. He intersected the track and crossed

Malcolm Bryan

PROFILE – TOSHIHIKO HONMA

The 22-year-old from Nagoya saw his first Grand Prix outside Japan at Donington Park when he attended the 1988 British Grand Prix as a spectator, travelling with Tadahiko Taira. This year saw Honma finish fourth in the Japanese Grand Prix at Suzuka, but as reigning Japanese 250 champion he had to concentrate on retaining his title and could do no more World Championship rounds until the French, the eleventh of the series.

Honma was right on the pace the moment that practice started at Le Mans, with fifth-fastest time in the first session and only a second slower than the much more experienced Juan Garriga on the similar factory Yamaha, who headed the practice table on Friday morning.

Honma's previous race meeting had been at the tight Tscuba circuit. While the Bugatti circuit at Le Mans is also tight with slow corners, Honma said that it was very different from what he was used to. 'The surface is very rough here. Back in Japan the circuits have much better surfaces. They tend to be more consistent, too, and give much better grip. Here the track is bumpy and slippery, and there are a lot of different tarmac patches. I have never experienced wheelspin in a straight line before but the track is so slippery that just accelerating out of the corner makes the wheel spin.'

On Saturday Honma chopped more than a second off his time and then, that afternoon, he went half a second quicker again. That took him to the head of the practice leaderboard, an achievement that stunned many in the pit lane. In the last seconds of practice, though, French hero Jean-Philippe Ruggia went quicker and stole pole position away from Honma.

Honma would have liked to be on pole, but second was better than he expected. 'I never thought that it was possible to do this well when I came racing in Europe. It is quite a surprise to me,' said the rider, who has been a Yamaha man since he started racing, aged 16, on a TZ250.

He believes in his own ability, of course, but for a little extra luck he had the factory V-twin Yamaha fitted with the fairing used by John Kocinski to win the Japanese and American Grands Prix. The fairing still had the two scrutineering stickers on it.

Honma had made very few changes to the bike through practice. 'We left the internal ratios the same as at Tscuba and I just concentrated on learning the circuit. I changed the steering head angle and made some adjustment to the suspension to cope with the bumps but apart from that the bike has been good from the start.'

The bike had a very special experimental frame, whose difference was quite obvious from the shiny black coating over the normal aluminium. It was made from thinner-gauge aluminium sheet, but to the same form as the standard factory bikes, then covered in a carbon fibre layer about 2 mm thick. The normal aluminium lugs are used in the frame for the engine mounts and the rear engine mount and swinging arm pivot sections are standard and substantial. The fabricated box section is certainly thinner walled, though, and may well be foam filled.

The frame appeared very smooth and obviously great care had been taken to grind the seam welds flat. A coating of carbon fibre and laminate is then added all over the fabricated twin spar frame just leaving the standard lugs and the swing arm pivot section protruding.

The method of construction is quite unusual and, while the engineers claimed that the carbon added to the stiffness, the combination of two materials bonded together in this way means that the less ductile of the two, the carbon, must be taking the greater share of the load. Under maximum stress, if the carbon alone is not strong enough to take the loadings, it will start to fail. If the carbon is strong enough on its own the aluminium might just be there as a captive mould and jig to hold the lugs in position. It is a lower-cost way of producing small numbers of frames as it avoids the need for expensive moulds.

Honma's machine featured normal carburation but the engineers confirmed that they had been testing fuel injection on another bike. The injection fires into the inlet tract rather than direct into the combustion chamber. They added that the injection system was still considerably inferior to carburation when it came to setting up the engine for top performance.

Honma surprised some of the Italian journalists by the fact that he wore a small Ferrari pin badge on his shirt. He explained that he owned a 328 and when asked how he managed to use the performance of the car on the crowded roads of Japan he replied, 'It is not easy. I spend most of my time cleaning and polishing it.' He also enjoys playing golf and said that he had a great time travelling in Europe and would obviously hope to do the full World Championship season in 1990. 'I want to do all the Grands Prix but of course it depends on Yamaha,' said Honma, who also mentioned that his hero was Kenny Roberts and that his ambition was to emulate him.

Having decided that he would continue to race in 1990, Christian Sarron was keen to show that he remained as competitive as ever.

Below right: **Cardus had looked this good before but at last kept the effort going for the entire Grand Prix distance.**

just behind the pair – but, still not in control enough to stop or turn, he carried on crossing the track and went into the outer gravel pit. As the bike slowed he began to master it again, lucking upon the car 24-hour circuit so that he could turn and rejoin the common start and finish straight. He crossed the line without losing another place, in sixth.

500 cc

It was a great victory for Lawson and he summed things up with his post-race comment: 'We needed that, we really needed that. I can't believe it. The bike was so fast, Erv and the guys did a great job and that made so much difference on this track. It is miserable, the back-markers are just ridiculous.'

Rainey, Lawson and Freddie Spencer were quickest away from the line and it was the Lucky Strike Yamaha that got to the first chicane in front. Rainey held that advantage for lap one while Spencer dropped from third to fifth and then completely out of the running, to retire after three laps saying that the stomach bug that had hindered him throughout practice had left him with vision problems.

Schwantz had got away badly and had to battle past McElnea and Mackenzie to complete the first lap in seventh place. By lap two the Texan was fifth, behind Sarron and Chili. Rainey and Lawson already had a two-second lead; Rainey had attempted his usual early break but could not secure it. Schwantz took third from Chili going into the last double right at the end of lap three and was then three seconds behind Rainey.

Lawson had had enough time in second place by now and he took the lead on lap five. Schwantz was inching closer and Magee looked a very strong fourth as Chili was passed by Sarron. The Suzuki was closing in on the leading machines, its job made easier on lap ten as Rainey and Lawson were held up by back-markers. From that point it was the three fastest men on the three fastest bikes, with the back-markers acting as mobile chicanes, just to add some random variables to the equation. Lap 14 saw Schwantz being given an opening. As the trio approached the double right leading to the start and finish a back-marker made Rainey hesitate. Lawson went inside and, incredibly, Schwantz passed his two opponents and the back-marker, forcing Lawson to ease over as both headed for the first apex.

Magee was no longer a threat to the top three, having run off the track at the last double right ending lap six. That dropped him behind Sarron and Chili. By lap ten the Australian was back to fourth but some distance down on the leaders. Sarron was still sixth but Chili was clearly having an exciting time on the HB Honda and having trouble holding the Frenchman at bay.

Schwantz later admitted that the ease with which he had taken the lead made him think he could win, especially as Rainey suddenly dropped out of contention with brake problems. 'Suddenly the front brake lever came right back to the bars. It was so sudden, it was as though the brake hose had broken. I had to slow but then the brake started to come back after about half a lap. After that it was fine. I have no idea what happened but I had lost contact and couldn't catch up.'

Within two laps Rainey was two seconds behind and, though he held it at that for several laps, he never got any closer. Schwantz realised that the win wouldn't come easily on lap 18. 'Lawson just blew past up the front straight and I knew then it would be tough,' said Schwantz. 'He had the jump out of the corners and there was hardly anywhere I could make ground. I could catch a little on the brakes here and there but there was no place where I was really making it up.'

Lawson, on the other hand, was not getting away either and with four laps to go Schwantz decided to make the big push. 'I decided that I had to work at getting up with him for the last lap and it took me all that time to do it. I got balked a little on the last lap and, at the time, I didn't think that much of it. I still thought I could get by but at the last corner I was still a bit too far behind.'

Schwantz made his play anyway – he was very late on the brakes – and if Lawson had been a little cautious the Suzuki would have appeared underneath him. But Lawson was not cautious. He knew Schwantz would be eyeing up that move and he went in deep on the brakes himself. Arriving at the corner, almost with Lawson, Schwantz was forced to turn hard; the rear tyre broke traction and, for a moment, it looked as though the Suzuki was getting away from its rider. But, almost before you could think that, Kevin had reacted and saved the situation.

Lawson's victory brought life back into the championship – how much life depended on the final outcome of the Spa debacle. If Lawson remained the winner in Belgium, Rainey's advantage would be just eight-and-a-half points. If the FIM came to their senses and gave the win back to Rainey he would still be 14 points ahead, while if they scrubbed the results in Belgium completely he would be 11 ahead.

Rainey said that his only problem had been the front brake, but Lawson wouldn't have it. 'Nah, your tyre went off, I saw it,' he said, as soon as they finished the race. He also thanked Schwantz for letting him win. Surely he realised that the Texan had tried everything to get past? More likely it was just part of Lawson's psychological battle with Rainey, making Rainey think that Schwantz was helping him, putting Rainey under more pressure. Schwantz was insulted but that didn't worry Lawson: he had won the race and he would make use of anything he could to put one over on his opponents.

Magee was passed by Sarron with five laps still to go and the Frenchman kept the speed up right to the end, to make sure the Australian had no chance to alter that situation. 'I made my fastest lap of the race on the last lap because I thought Magee was going to try and get past,' said the Gauloises Blondes rider. 'Earlier on we had been so close together that we almost collided. I had to back off and that lost me a lot of ground. It was a struggle then to catch Chili and finally Magee.'

Magee celebrated his twenty-seventh birthday with a fine ride. 'The rear tyre started to slide quite a bit towards the end and Christian was getting more grip than me coming out of the corners so there was not too much I could do about it. I had a big front-end slide at the fast right, past the start and finish. It left a big black mark and I was slower through there after that.' The Australian was using a new Dunlop rear with more vertical sidewalls; it was thought this would provide more consistent grip. The tyre had seemed to work well during practice but was perhaps not as successful in the race.

Mackenzie fought through to seventh on the Marlboro Yamaha and might have done better but for a problem early on. He was eighth at the end of lap one but on lap four dropped well behind Mick Doohan. 'The front slid away and I ran off the track,' said the British rider. 'When I got back on I had a lot of work to do. I didn't have any confidence in the front, though, and I had quite a few more slides. I had to change my lines to use the back more and not lean over as much.'

The new men, Morillas and Crine, did quite well without stunning anyone. The Elf Honda crossed the line tenth after getting the worst of a lengthy fight with the year-older NSR ridden by Rob McElnea. The Cabin rider had brake problems from the start but still pushed hard going into the corners. 'In the end I got past Morillas because I was better on the brakes, even though they warped on the warm-up lap and were juddering all through the race,' said McElnea. 'His bike had a better drive out of the corners so it wasn't easy to get past.' Morillas explained that he had run out of stamina. 'It was going quite well but in the second half of the race I could not keep the pace up. I was exhausted.'

Sidecars

Steve Webster and Tony Hewitt started the season with a pair of wins that demonstrated how good they are. Along with those wins went some misfortune for the opposition that left the British pair with a healthy championship lead. Four races further on the struggle looked a lot closer, as Rolf Biland and Kurt Waltisperg won their second race of the year and moved to within 25 points of Webster and Hewitt. They, in turn, slightly increased their advantage over Streuer and de Haas by finishing ahead of them in second place.

Biland set off from pole position and soon took the lead from Webster. It was very hot and the British crew saw the sense in accepting second place, as they were informed that Streuer was well behind. 'We were sliding around quite a lot, it was so hot and hard on the tyres,' said Webster. 'We were well ahead of Eggy so I thought it made sense not to take any chances.'

Streuer had made a disastrous start and had his work cut out to fight through the field on a track that allows few opportunities for passing. Alain Michel and Jean-Marc Fresc had been third but eventually Streuer overhauled them.

GAULOISES
BLONDES
YAMAHA
MICHELIN
Mobil 1
Arai
SONAUTO
CHRISTIAN SARRON
brembo
FACOM

Arai
REPSOL
NOLAN
Campsa

Grand Prix de France, 16 July/statistics

Circuit Bugatti, Le Mans, 2.635-mile/4.240-km circui

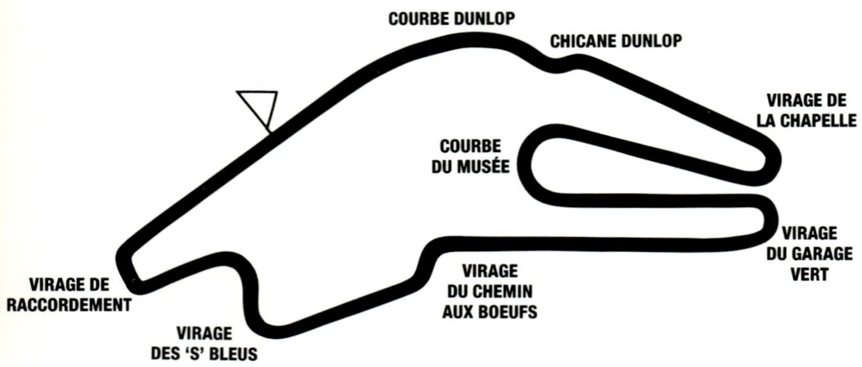

500 cc

29 laps, 76.42 miles/122.96 km

Place	Rider	Nat.	Machine	Laps	Time & speed	Practice time	Grid
1	Eddie Lawson	USA	Honda	29	50m 16.94s 95.254 mph/ 153.298 km/h	1m 42.33s	1
2	Kevin Schwantz	USA	Suzuki	29	50m 17.71s	1m 42.59s	2
3	Wayne Rainey	USA	Yamaha	29	50m 32.47s	1m 42.59s	3
4	Christian Sarron	F	Yamaha	29	50m 40.53s	1m 43.24s	5
5	Kevin Magee	AUS	Yamaha	29	50m 41.15s	1m 42.69s	4
6	Pier Francesco Chili	I	Honda	29	50m 53.94s	1m 43.91s	7
7	Niall Mackenzie	GB	Yamaha	29	51m 10.48s	1m 43.46s	6
8	Michael Doohan	AUS	Honda	29	51m 16.06s	1m 44.19s	8
9	Rob McElnea	GB	Honda	29	51m 43.23s	1m 45.38s	11
10	Adrien Morillas	F	Honda	29	51m 48.40s	1m 45.91s	15
11	Randy Mamola	USA	Cagiva	28	50m 18.52s	1m 45.60s	13
12	Thierry Crine	F	Suzuki	28	50m 39.28s	1m 46.73s	16
13	Alessandro Valesi	I	Yamaha	28	51m 02.76s	1m 48.93s	19
14	Simon Buckmaster	GB	Honda	28	51m 57.64s	1m 50.12s	21
15	Fabio Biliotti	I	Honda	27	50m 21.16s	1m 51.48s	27
16	Eddie Laycock	IRL	Honda	27	50m 22.43s	1m 49.67s	20
17	Bruno Kneubühler	CH	Honda	27	50m 35.58s	1m 50.41s	22
18	Juan Lopez Mella	E	Honda	27	50m 54.86s	1m 50.95s	26
19	Claude Albert	F	Suzuki	27	51m 00.17s	1m 50.42s	23
20	Jean-Paul Lecointe	F	Suzuki	27	51m 05.13s	1m 51.92s	28
21	Niggi Schmassman	CH	Honda	27	51m 42.86s	1m 53.03s	31
22	Pascal Seguela	F	Honda	27	51m 52.21s	1m 53.45s	34
23	Bernard Gitton	F	Fior	26	50m 28.06s	1m 53.64s	35
24	Fernando Gonzalez	E	Honda	26	51m 21.36s	1m 55.00s	36
25	Kees Doorakkers	NL	Honda	22	51m 14.55s	1m 50.51s	24
	Bernard Andrault	F	Honda	19	DNF	1m 53.03s	32
	Patrick Salles	F	Honda	11	DNF	1m 52.85s	30
	Wayne Gardner	AUS	Honda	9	DNF	1m 44.99s	10
	Raymond Roche	F	Cagiva	9	DNF	1m 47.93s	17
	Marco Papa	I	Paton	8	DNF	1m 50.63s	25
	Fred Merkel	USA	Honda	6	DNF	1m 45.55s	12
	Andreas Leuthe	LUX	Suzuki	5	DNF	1m 53.07s	33
	Freddie Spencer	USA	Yamaha	3	DNF	1m 44.92s	9
	Marco Gentile	CH	Fior	3	DNF	1m 48.42s	18
	Patrick Leruste	F	Fior	1	DNF	1m 52.36s	29
	Dominique Sarron	F	Honda		DNS	1m 45.72s	14

Fastest lap: Schwantz, 1m 42.97s, 96.237 mph/154.880 km/h (record).
Previous record: not available.

World Championship: 1 Rainey, 165.5; **2** Lawson, 157; **3** Sarron, C., 116.5; **4** Schwantz, 102.5; **5** Magee, 98.5; **6** Chili, 95; **7** Doohan, 68; **8** Mackenzie, 60; **9** Haslam, 48; **10** Gardner, 43; **11** Sarron, D., 39; **12** Buckmaster, 36.5; **13** Spencer, 33.5; **14** McElnea, 31.5; **15** Gentile and Valesi, 27; **17** Taira, 26; **18** Mamola, 23; **19** Rudroff, 18; **20** Fujiwara, 17; **21** Shobert, 12; **22** Doppler, 11; **23** Meyer, 10. **24** Balbi, 9; **25** Broccoli, Gonzalez and Schmassman, 8; **28** Dowson and Leuthe, 7; **30** Itoh and Morillas, 6; **32** Kocinski, 5.5; **33** Gschwender, 5; **34** Crine and Kneubühler, 4; **36** Yatsushiro, 3; **37** Doorakkers, 2.5; **38** Laycock and Lopez Mella, 2; **40** Biliotti and Machii, 1.

Malcolm Bryan

250 cc

24 laps, 63.24 miles/101.76 km

Place	Rider	Nat.	Machine	Laps	Time & speed	Practice time	Grid
1	Carlos Cardus	E	Honda	24	43m 21.12s 91.434 mph/ 147.149 km/h	1m 47.25s	3
2	Jacques Cornu	CH	Honda	24	43m 21.47s	1m 47.89s	8
3	Alfonso Pons	E	Honda	24	43m 22.11s	1m 47.73s	7
4	Toshihiko Honma	J	Yamaha	24	43m 23.51s	1m 47.12s	2
5	Jean-Philippe Ruggia	F	Yamaha	24	43m 23.79s	1m 46.76s	1
6	Reinhold Roth	D	Honda	24	43m 26.09s	1m 47.37s	4
7	Masahiro Shimizu	J	Honda	24	43m 28.61s	1m 48.54s	13
8	Juan Garriga	E	Yamaha	24	43m 42.15s	1m 47.72s	6
9	Didier de Radiguès	B	Aprilia	24	43m 43.61s	1m 48.36s	11
10	Helmut Bradl	D	Honda	24	43m 44.42s	1m 48.34s	10
11	Luca Cadalora	I	Yamaha	24	43m 45.47s	1m 47.48s	5
12	Martin Wimmer	D	Aprilia	24	43m 53.88s	1m 48.48s	12
13	Daniel Amatriain	E	Honda	24	43m 57.57s	1m 49.25s	16
14	Alberto Puig	E	Yamaha	24	43m 57.95s	1m 48.77s	15
15	Gary Cowan	IRL	Yamaha	24	44m 11.63s	1m 50.56s	24
16	Alberto Rota	I	Aprilia	24	44m 11.97s	1m 50.59s	25
17	Renzo Colleoni	I	Aprilia	24	44m 12.39s	1m 49.84s	17
18	Carlos Lavado	YV	Aprilia	24	44m 17.41s	1m 48.68s	14
19	Paolo Casoli	I	Honda	24	44m 28.15s	1m 50.05s	18
20	Andreas Preining	A	Aprilia	24	44m 35.16s	1m 50.31s	21
21	Alain Bronec	F	Aprilia	24	44m 35.62s	1m 50.60s	26
22	Frédéric Protat	F	Aprilia	24	44m 36.06s	1m 50.73s	28
23	Xavier Cardelus	AND	Yamaha	24	44m 48.34s	1m 50.88s	31
24	Jean Foray	F	Yamaha	24	44m 50.44s	1m 50.99s	32
25	Patrick van den Goorbergh	NL	Yamaha	24	45m 00.39s	1m 51.00s	33
26	Hans Becker	D	Seel	24	45m 07.96s	1m 50.74s	29
27	Luis Lavado	YV	Yamaha	24	45m 12.03s	1m 51.16s	36
28	Kevin Mitchell	GB	Yamaha	24	45m 12.29s	1m 51.04s	34
29	Maurizio Vitali	I	Honda	19	43m 30.76s	1m 51.07s	35
	Harald Eckl	D	Aprilia	17	DNF	1m 50.26s	20
	Jochen Schmid	D	Honda	17	DNF	1m 50.55s	22
	August Auinger	A	Yamaha	13	DNF	1m 50.55s	23
	Fausto Ricci	I	Aprilia	9	DNF	1m 50.68s	27
	Wilco Zeelenberg	NL	Honda	5	DNF	1m 50.06s	19
	Loris Reggiani	I	Honda	2	DNF	1m 48.13s	9
	Alexandre Barros	BR	Yamaha	1	DNF	1m 50.75s	30
	Bernhard Schick	D	Yamaha		DNQ	1m 51.18s	
	Urs Jucker	CH	Yamaha		DNQ	1m 51.18s	
	Jean-François Baldé	F	Yamaha		DNQ	1m 51.34s	
	René Delaby	LUX	Yamaha		DNQ	1m 51.46s	
	Michel Bodeâu	F	Yamaha		DNQ	1m 52.10s	
	Manfred Herweh	D	Yamaha		DNQ	1m 52.17s	
	Virginio Ferrari	I	Gazzaniga		DNQ	1m 52.19s	
	Bruno Vecchioni	F	Yamaha		DNQ	1m 53.08s	
	Guy Olla	F	Yamaha		DNQ	1m 53.57s	
	Didier Bordeaux	F	Honda		DNQ	1m 54.68s	
	Darren Milner	AUS	Yamaha		DNQ	1m 55.39s	
	Daniel Pauget	F	Honda		DNQ	1m 56.81s	

Fastest lap: Pons, 1m 47.30s, 92.354 mph/148.630 km/h (record).
Previous record: Bruno Bonhuil, F (Yamaha), 1m 52.73s, 86.54 mph/139.273 km/h.

World Championship: 1 Pons, 196; **2** Cornu, 137; **3** Cardus, 130; **4** Roth, 126; **5** Ruggia, 110; **6** Cadalora, 86; **7** Garriga, 68; **8** Shimizu, 67; **9** Bradl, 60; **10** Wimmer, 48; **11** Kocinski, 40; **12** de Radiguès, 39; **13** Honma, Reggiani, Schmid and Zeelenberg, 26; **17** Filice, 22; **18** Colleoni, 21; **19** Palazzese, 19; **20** Puig, 18; **21** Lucchi, 17; **22** Eckl, 15; **23** Cowan, 14; **24** Amatriain, 12; **25** Bronec and Okada, 10; **27** Shiomori, 9; **28** Barros, Morillas and Ricci, 8; **31** Lavado, 7; **32** Rota and van den Goorbergh, 6; **34** Caracchi, 5; **35** Beattie and Mitchell, 4; **37** Preining and Vitali, 2; **39** Arai, Auinger and Becker, 1.

Malcolm Bryan

Top: **Still hampered by the shoulder injury he had sustained at Assen, Dominique Sarron elected not to start his home race. The transition to the 500 class was proving frustrating.**

There was no shortage of French talent on display but, despite the efforts of Jean-Philippe Ruggia *(above)*, **no home victory for the crowd to celebrate.**

125 cc

22 laps, 57.97 miles/93.28 km

Place	Rider	Nat.	Machine	Laps	Time & speed	Practice time	Grid
1	Jorge Martinez	E	Derbi	22	42m 37.94s 85.229 mph/ 137.163 km/h	1m 55.42s	1
2	Alex Criville	E	Cobas	22	42m 38.83s	1m 55.58s	3
3	Ezio Gianola	I	Honda	22	42m 54.50s	1m 55.74s	4
4	Koji Takada	J	Honda	22	43m 06.32s	1m 56.64s	7
5	Fausto Gresini	I	Aprilia	22	43m 06.70s	1m 56.29s	5
6	Hisashi Unemoto	J	Honda	22	43m 13.54s	1m 57.53s	11
7	Flemming Kistrup	DK	Honda	22	43m 24.74s	1m 57.45s	10
8	Luis Reyes	E	Honda	22	43m 25.09s	1m 58.38s	20
9	Domenico Brigaglia	I	Garelli	22	43m 32.63s	1m 58.36s	18
10	Alfred Waibel	D	Honda	22	43m 33.04s	1m 58.36s	19
11	Adolf Stadler	D	Honda	22	43m 35.77s	1m 56.88s	8
12	Jean-Claude Selini	F	Honda	22	43m 37.30s	1m 57.75s	14
13	Jean-Pierre Jeandat	F	Honda	22	43m 40.41s	1m 57.72s	13
14	Corrado Catalano	I	Gazzaniga	22	43m 56.43s	1m 59.31s	35
15	Hervé Duffard	F	Honda	22	43m 59.91s	1m 58.50s	22
16	Johnny Wickström	SF	Honda	22	44m 02.41s	1m 59.26s	33
17	Manuel Hernandez	E	Honda	22	44m 02.96s	1m 59.12s	31
18	Xavier Debon	E	Cobas	22	44m 04.19s	1m 58.72s	25
19	Emilio Cuppini	I	Garelli	22	44m 07.76s	1m 58.57s	23
20	Hubert Abold	D	Krauser	22	44m 25.48s	1m 59.00s	29
21	Robin Appleyard	GB	Honda	22	44m 26.00s	1m 58.20s	16
22	Håkan Olsson	S	ESV	22	44m 39.74s	1m 59.21s	32
23	Serge Julin	B	Honda	21	42m 40.48s	1m 59.27s	34
24	Mike Leitner	A	Honda	17	43m 18.76s	1m 59.12s	30
	Allan Scott	USA	Honda	18	DNF	1m 57.71s	12
	Hans Spaan	NL	Honda	16	DNF	1m 55.45s	2
	Herri Torrontegui	E	Honda	10	DNF	1m 58.40s	21
	Bady Hassaine	TN	Honda	10	DNF	1m 58.73s	27
	Bruno Casanova	I	Aprilia	8	DNF	1m 58.72s	26
	Doriano Romboni	I	Honda	8	DNF	1m 57.21s	9
	Alex Bedford	GB	EMC	6	DNF	1m 58.84s	28
	Lucio Pietroniro	B	Honda	5	DNF	1m 58.67s	24
	Stefan Prein	D	Honda	4	DNF	1m 56.56s	6
	Trevor Manley	AUS	Honda	3	DNF	1m 59.31s	36
	Thierry Feuz	CH	Honda	2	DNF	1m 58.32s	17
	Julian Miralles	E	Derbi	2	DNF	1m 58.10s	15
	Rafael Roses	E	Cobas		DNQ	1m 59.37s	
	Stefan Dörflinger	CH	Aprilia		DNQ	1m 59.50s	
	Peter Öttl	D	Krauser		DNQ	1m 59.52s	
	Robin Milton	GB	Honda		DNQ	1m 59.71s	
	Gastone Grassetti	I	Honda		DNQ	1m 59.65s	
	Jos van Dongen	NL	Honda		DNQ	1m 59.67s	
	Olivier Prion	F	Honda		DNQ	1m 59.79s	
	Heinz Luthi	CH	Honda		DNQ	2m 00.07s	
	René Dünki	CH	LCR		DNQ	2m 00.23s	
	Michel le Garrec	F	Honda		DNQ	2m 00.60s	
	Paul Bordes	F	Honda		DNQ	2m 00.77s	
	Xavier Arumi	E	Honda		DNQ	2m 02.17s	
	Othmar Schuler	CH	Honda		DNQ	2m 02.18s	
	Alain Guilhat	F	Honda		DNQ	2m 02.23s	
	Stuart Edwards	GB	ERM		DNQ	2m 03.03s	
	Valerio Vivarelli	RSM	Rotax		DNQ	2m 03.60s	
	Pascal Serra	F	Honda		DNQ	2m 04.58s	
	Pierre Micciarelli	CH	Honda		DNQ	2m 05.13s	

Fastest lap: Martinez, 1m 55.24s, 85.99 mph/138.389 km/h (record).
Previous record: Jean-Pierre Jeandat, F (Honda), 2m 00.67s, 81.128 mph/130.654 km/h.

World Championship: 1 Gianola, 113; **2** Criville, 109; **3** Spaan, 98; **4** Miralles, 90; **5** Unemoto, 82; **6** Gresini, 81; **7** Takada, 70; **8** Prein, 54; **9** Martinez and Milton, 46; **11** Stadler, 40; **12** Scott, 37; **13** Reyes, 31; **14** Brigaglia, 24; **15** Pietroniro, 22; **16** Casanova, 20; **17** Raudies, Rinne and Waibel, A., 18; **20** Feuz, 15; **21** Hirose, 13; **22** Romboni, Selini, Torrontegui and Yoshida, 11; **26** Catalano and Shima, 10; **28** Fujiwara and Kistrup, 9; **30** Yamashita, 8; **31** Appleyard and Fujiyama, 7; **33** Waibel, G. and Yamada, 6; **35** Wickström, 4; **36** Debbia, Jeandat and Saunders, 3; **39** Fischer, 2; **40** Abold, Bedford and Duffard, 1.

Sidecars

22 laps, 57.97 miles/93.28 km

Place	Driver & passenger	Nat.	Machine	Laps	Time & speed	Practice time	Grid
1	Rolf Biland/ Kurt Waltisperg	CH CH	LCR- Krauser	22	40m 59.26s 88.649 mph/ 142.667 km/h	1m 49.44s	1
2	Steve Webster/ Tony Hewitt	GB GB	LCR- Krauser	22	41m 07.77s	1m 49.99s	2
3	Egbert Streuer/ Geral de Haas	NL NL	LCR- Yamaha	22	41m 27.75s	1m 50.69s	3
4	Alain Michel/ Jean-Marc Fresc	F F	LCR- Krauser	22	41m 43.36s	1m 51.81s	6
5	Masato Kumano/ Markus Fahrni	J CH	LCR- Tec	22	41m 49.37s	1m 51.43s	5
6	Derek Jones/ Peter Brown	GB GB	LCR- Yamaha	22	41m 56.63s	1m 53.13s	9
7	Steve Abbott/ Shaun Smith	GB GB	LCR	22	42m 01.96s	1m 51.94s	7
8	Barry Brindley/ Grahame Rose	GB GB	Fowler- Yamaha	22	42m 11.11s	1m 53.21s	10
9	Fritz Stölzle/ Hubert Stölzle	D D	LCR- Krauser	22	42m 21.38s	1m 53.30s	11
10	Theo van Kempen/ Simon Birchall	NL GB	Krauser	22	42m 23.79s	1m 53.96s	13
11	Tony Wyssen/ Kilian Wyssen	CH CH	LCR- Krauser	22	42m 26.90s	1m 54.38s	18
12	Markus Egloff/ Urs Egloff	CH CH	Yamaha	22	42m 34.27s	1m 50.98s	4
13	René Progin/ Yves Hunziker	CH CH	LCR	22	42m 44.47s	1m 53.58s	12
14	Barry Smith/ David Smith	GB GB	Windle- ADM	22	42m 48.63s	1m 55.27s	20
15	Billy Gällros/ Håkan Olsson	S S	Yamaha	21	41m 06.48s	1m 55.59s	21
16	Paul Güdel/ Charly Güdel	CH CH	LCR- Yamaha	21	41m 16.58s	1m 54.20s	15
17	Kenny Howles/ Steve Pointer	GB GB	LCR- Krauser	21	41m 32.86s	1m 56.92s	25
18	Yoshisada Kumagaya/ Phil Coombes	J GB	Windle	21	41m 40.21s	1m 54.33s	17
19	Ray Gardner/ Tony Strevens	GB GB	LCR- Krauser	21	41m 47.38s	1m 54.42s	19
20	Clive Stirrat/ Simon Prior	GB GB	LCR	21	41m 54.83s	1m 56.58s	23
21	Gary Thomas/ Eckhart Rösinger	GB D	LCR	21	42m 20.37s	1m 57.14s	26
	Bernd Scherer/ Thomas Schröder	D D	BSR- Krauser	15	DNF	1m 54.02s	14
	George Hardwick/ Gary Irlam	GB GB	LCR	6	DNF	1m 56.19s	22
	Ivan Nigrowsky/ Jacques Corbier	F F	LCR- JPX	3	DNF	1m 54.28s	16
	Rolf Steinhausen/ Bruno Hiller	D D	Schuh	3	DNF	1m 52.33s	8
	Raphael Clerc/ Fredy Lueond	CH CH	LCR		DNS	1m 56.91s	24
	Tony Baker/ Trevor Hopkinson	GB GB	LCR- Krauser		DNQ	1m 57.28s	
	Wolfgang Stropek/ Steve Campbell	A GB	Mibag- Krauser		DNQ	1m 57.48s	
	Jacques Heriot/ Jean-Louis Heriot	F F	Yamaha		DNQ	1m 58.11s	
	Hans Hügli/ Wolfgang Bock	CH D	Sigwa		DNQ	1m 58.38s	
	Yann Hansen/ J. Gosnet	F F	Suzuki		DNQ	2m 01.96s	
	John Evans/ Ian Gaunt	GB GB	Yamaha		DNQ	2m 02.59s	

Fastest lap: Biland, 1m 50.28s, 89.859 mph/144.614 km/h (record).
Previous record: not available.

World Championship: 1 Webster, 95; **2** Streuer, 86; **3** Biland, 70; **4** Michel, 66; **5** Kumano, 58; **6** Stölzle, 47; **7** Steinhausen, 42; **8** Brindley and Jones, 37; **10** Egloff, 36; **11** Scherer and van Kempen, 26; **13** Kumagaya, 25; **14** Abbott, 24; **15** Zurbrügg, 21; **16** Wyssen, 20; **17** Progin, 15; **18** Nigrowsky, 12; **19** Smith, 10; **20** Baker and Gällros, 7; **22** Stropek, 6; **23** Drew, 4; **24** Stirrat, 3; **25** Hardwick, Howles and Thomas, 2.

Rolf Biland and Kurt Waltisperg took a commanding victory from pole position.

Malcolm Bryan

WORLD CHAMPIONSHIP · ROUND 12

BRITISH GRAND PRIX

Malcolm Bryan

The sensation of the first few days of the British Grand Prix was the news that Freddie Spencer had been sacked from the Marlboro Yamaha team. Different words were used to explain why the triple World Champion, a man many still regard as the greatest talent of the 1980s, would not be riding for the rest of the season. The official statement was careful to imply that there had been mutual agreement, and that Spencer was only discontinuing his racing season rather than retiring from the sport, but there was no real secret. Giacomo Agostini had suggested to Spencer that he should not ride in the last four races of the season.

The Italian team-manager said as much at the Friday press conference. 'The final agreement was made over the phone but we had had discussions at Le Mans. I told him that I thought that it was better if he did not race any more this season. He has been a great champion and there was no point in him racing for eighth place.'

Rumours had been rife since mid-season that Spencer would be replaced, though Agostini had denied this at Assen. No one will ever know the exact words that passed between them, but it seems that at first Spencer wanted to continue racing. Agostini eventually convinced him otherwise – and Freddie would receive most if not all of his contract fee, despite missing the final quarter of the year. His departure came at the end of a desperately disappointing season for all those concerned with his return, and for everyone who had seen his genius at work earlier in the decade.

Agostini said that he had no intention of replacing Spencer immediately. 'We are thinking about next year now. Luca is testing the 500 to see how he likes it but there is no point in having another rider in the team unless it was just to test for one race and we have no plans for that at the moment.'

Agostini was roundly criticised for picking Spencer when Lawson departed for the Rothmans Honda team. It is difficult to say whether he was largely to blame for the team losing Lawson in the first place, as the motives behind the World Champion's defection have never been clear. As team-manager Ago must carry the can but, having seen Lawson go, there were precious few options available to him. He signed Spencer out of semi-retirement as the best chance of finding a Grand Prix winner.

As Leo de Graffenried, Marlboro's on-track representative said, they'd expected Spencer to be able to make an impressive comeback. 'We thought he would be able to do something like Niki (Lauda); he won his third race when he made the comeback for McLaren.' Lauda also went on to win the World Championship again.

However, if Spencer was as dedicated to making a triumphal return as Lauda it certainly did not show in his public preparations. He missed test sessions in Spain, Italy and Japan and arrived a day late for a test in Australia. He was thinner at the beginning of the season than he had been at the winter press conference announcing his signing for the team, but he never looked as lean and hungry as his competitors. He seemed simply to have underestimated what was required, and as someone who had known him intimately since his international career took off commented, 'His own image of himself no longer reflects reality'. Spencer had been the best racer in the world, but a return to that position now seemed an unattainable goal. The overriding reaction to his departure was sadness – no one likes to see heroes humbled – and although Freddie insisted that the announcement only related to this season, that he might race again, most hoped he would not try.

In an interview with Mark Graham for the following week's *Motor Cycle News*, Kenny Roberts voiced his opinion, obviously more valid than most. 'I don't think Freddie's problem is one we know too much about. Freddie's had such a goofy history that you can't predict what he's going to do. The problem is that he's not the Freddie Spencer I rode with.

'Somewhere along the line he has gone adrift at drawing out that ability that he had, drawing out that desire. You can't do it just by getting paid money. You can't push things past the limit just because someone's paying you to be there. If your heart's not there, your inside's not there and your desire's not there. You're just not going to do it. And he wasn't there.'

If the old adage that 'there is no such thing as bad publicity' is true then Marlboro should have been happy, for not only were they gaining column inches with the Spencer story but there had already been headlines about the rumoured three million dollar offer to Wayne Rainey that Agostini was said to have made after the French Grand Prix. In truth the offer was closer to two million dollars, but it still went a long way towards doubling the going rate for a top 500 rider and was a good deal more than double what Rainey had been earning at Lucky Strike for each year of his two-year tenure.

Kenny Roberts was forced to raise his offer considerably and was not pleased with the step Agostini had taken. 'It is mad, the sport can't stand that sort of increase. We are not trying to keep riders' wages down but when you get that sort of jump in one year it wrecks everyone's plans. Budgets have already been set and sponsors are not impressed when you go back to them and ask for more money.'

Roberts did not say whether he had matched Agostini's offer, but he did confirm that an agreement had been reached that would see Rainey riding for the Lucky Strike team again in 1990. That left Agostini with a major problem about what to do for a top rider for next season. He had wanted Schwantz, but the Texan was well advanced with negotiations to stay with Suzuki (he'd had a meeting with them on the Monday after the Suzuka Eight Hour and then flown to Donington for the Grand Prix).

Wayne Gardner had also been approached by Agostini but looked set to stay with Honda – as long as he could negotiate a satisfactory contract that saw him as their number one rider. That put HRC in a difficult position, as Lawson was obviously the man with the better results this season and he would not accept second-class machinery. Honda had already separated Lawson from Gardner by having the Rothmans Kanemoto team distinct from the Rothmans HRC team of Gardner and Doohan.

With Cabin wanting a more competitive team for the coming season HRC had suggested that they take over the Kanemoto–Lawson set-up. That certainly had an appeal to Cabin but not, of course, to Rothmans, especially if Lawson had the number one plate. Rothmans had an agreement with HRC that only they would get the top factory machinery. With Gardner and Rothmans thinking they should get the best and Lawson unlikely to settle for anything less negotiations were likely to be long and hard.

Gardner's manager, Harris Barnett, had more talks with Agostini at Donington – but if Gardner did stay at Honda Agostini was fast running out of possibilities. He did not have a grip on any of 1989's four Grand Prix winners (Lawson, Gardner, Rainey and Schwantz), and with five big sponsors (Marlboro, Cabin, Rothmans, Lucky Strike and Pepsi) all wanting to run major teams, someone was going to be left short of a current Grand Prix winner.

The situation put up Kevin Magee's value. He was returning to form after his injury and had won a Grand Prix more recently than anyone else outside the 'big four'. Agostini, Lucky Strike, Cagiva and Suzuki were all showing an interest in his services.

Serge Rosset was also keen to have Magee as a rider, if he could find sponsorship. However, it was a fairly big 'if' as Elf, Rosset's main backer since he started competing in the 500 class, was planning to reduce its input to 30 per cent and leave him with a great deal of cash to find. Rosset had been after Cabin money but was not receiving much encouragement. He also entertained a top representative from Martini at Donington and, although all the right noises were being made, Rosset is far too experienced to think that a deal was close at hand.

It seemed that Freddie Spencer *(left)* had made his last appearance on the Grand Prix stage. His ignominious exit gave Luca Cadalora *(below)* a chance to claim a place among the stars of the 500 class.

Right: **Reinhold Roth had another competitive race but there was no stopping Pons.**

Hisashi Unemoto *(below right)* **took fifth place in the 125 race after his fellow-countryman Koji Takada fell on the last lap.**

Rosset was feeling quite frustrated, especially as he had never agreed with Elf's suggestion that Dominique Sarron was the right choice to lead their 500 team. It was asking too much of Sarron, who had no 500 experience, and if Elf were disappointed it should not have reflected on Rosset. It hardly helped matters that Sarron had had his best ride of the season the week before, winning the Suzuka Eight Hour with Alex Vieira – because Dominique had been riding for HRC, not for Rosset.

It is always hard for riders to forget about money and negotiations at this time of the year and concentrate on racing. Schwantz had been badly affected the year before and that was one of the reasons he wanted to stay put. For Gardner it was just one more thing on his mind. He was concerned with regaining his lost form and had hoped that the Suzuka race would help, being on a bike for an extended period.

'I do feel better about things after the Eight Hour. I wanted a result but the riding did me good anyway. It is more important to show myself I can do it on a Grand Prix bike, though.' After the first free practice session Gardner said he did feel measurably more comfortable. 'I felt much better. I was sliding the back end everywhere, and not worrying about it.'

Gardner and his engineer Stuart Shenton still had development work to catch up with after the Australian's mid-season absence. New things were arriving all the time, the latest being a new steel disc brake. The Honda men were not totally enamoured with the Lockheed carbon discs. Lawson said that he did not like the feel and Gardner was still wary after carbon discs had helped him to slide down the road at Laguna Seca.

Honda had produced sets of the ventilated discs with shallow blind holes to aid cooling. Kanemoto said that they seemed to be the answer. 'The air must flow in and around the holes because they certainly cool down quicker. Eddie says that he can feel them taking time to heat up at the next corner, but there's not as much delay as you get with the carbons, just a little of the same effect.'

Donington is hard on brakes. Not only are there the dead-stop hairpins but there's a good deal of high-speed braking with little respite between. Niall Mackenzie liked the carbon discs and decided to race with them for the first time on the Marlboro Yamaha. The other teams using the Lockheed discs, like Lucky Strike and Suzuki, all ran with the normal covers off, because they were getting so hot.

Lawson was happy with the drilled discs but did not have enough time to test fully all the things that HRC made available for him, including a third bike with a revised swing arm pivot position. Having a third bike had been useful for pre-Donington testing. One machine had gone overland to Sweden so that the team could fly there for a day of testing, after spending a day at Donington in the week prior to the Grand Prix.

The day in Sweden was not that successful as the track was wet, but the work at Donington certainly paid off. The Lucky Strike team were affected both practically and psychologically. Lawson had won at Le Mans after gaining an advantage from pre-race testing and, throughout practice at Donington, Rainey was frustrated by not being able to string together the laps he needed to sort the bike out.

Roberts said later that losing the British Grand Prix could be blamed on the Suzuka Eight Hour. 'I know that, you know that. Everyone knows that except the people at Lucky Strike and Yamaha who wanted us to do the Eight Hour. It is up to me and the rest of us to do the best with what we have got.

'The problem at Donington was that we were not able to get a good six- or seven-lap run on the tyre that we were going to race. Every time we went out we had either a brake problem with the carbons, or we had a tyre out of round, or the wheel would not fit on the bike we wanted to use. There was always something that stopped Wayne stringing the laps together. He was just not able to assess a race combination. That was one of the few races where Wayne wasn't able to put together a race pace in practice on any tyre combination. I don't know about France, I wasn't there.'

It was a far cry from the previous year when Michelin had been in trouble all week with the new surface and Dunlop had totally dominated the event. One of Dunlop's problems was that they could not use the winning tyre from '88 as they had since swapped from 18- to 17-in. rear rims. Rainey managed the third-quickest practice time behind Schwantz and Lawson but was more concerned with choosing a tyre that would last the race distance and a frame geometry and suspension set-up that would turn and handle the way he wanted. A final experiment in the Sunday morning warm-up did not help.

Schwantz said that the Suzuki was good right from the start of the week. He had tested at Donington the previous Tuesday but had missed the team's Thursday test because he was in Japan. Schwantz tried a titanium RK chain on the 500 but it was not used for the race. The same sort of chain had been used on the Yoshimura Suzuki for the Eight Hour, saving 150g in weight – not a huge amount, because only the outer plates are made of titanium, but worthwhile considering the way the weight flails around.

Schwantz had been complimentary all season about the Suzuki, but at Donington he found that the quick-handling machine enabled him to follow whatever line he wished on a circuit where so many of the corners run together. From the first right-hander at Redgate to the last right-hander at Coppice that leads onto the main straight there is little chance to vary the line with most machines – and especially after Redgate, when the bike is committed to the downhill right-handers that lead into the left and straight towards the tight right-handed old hairpin. Kevin reported that the Suzuki allowed him unusual flexibility there. 'You can be wide going through the right-handers and down the hill but still get back on line for the left and the old hairpin.'

Strangely, things went a little awry for Schwantz in the final session and, even on reflection, he found it hard to explain. 'The bike had been good all week but in that last session it felt as though it went to pieces. I don't know if I was riding differently, or trying too hard, but the bike seemed completely different from the morning to the afternoon session.

'I was a bit confused about that on Saturday night and didn't sleep real well. On Sunday morning, during the warm-up, the bike seemed back to perfect again. The tyres worked great and the bike seemed to work the way it had before so I kind of blame most of it on me riding it differently, trying too hard and not riding smooth. It had been as if all the testing we had done was out the window, nothing was right.

'On Sunday it was back to being good again and that showed in the race, how smooth it was everywhere and how easy it looked. It wasn't easy by any means but it probably looked like it.'

Schwantz was, as usual, impressive in practice but the sensation was Luca Cadalora, having his first race on the 500 Yamaha. He quickly got used to the bike and was fifth fastest, just elbowing team-mate Mackenzie off the front row in the last moments of practice.

The Italian said that he did not find the 500 that hard to ride. 'The engine is very flexible and that makes it easy but many places here you must accelerate while the bike is well leaned over. I am not yet sure just how hard you can accelerate. I still have to find the limit.' Coping with the speed and power of the 500 made riding the 250 seem easy. 'There are places where I used to just roll off the throttle slightly, now I am flat out wishing the bike would go faster.' Cadalora topped the 250 table ahead of Juan Garriga, showing Yamahas in a better light than they'd been for a couple of months.

Cadalora was down for just two 500 rides, trying the Yamaha at Donington and Anderstorp to see what he wanted to do for 1990. He preferred, he said, to stick with the 250 class as long as he could get a competitive machine. In all likelihood that would mean switching to Honda as Yamaha had yet to show the required determination to make their V-twin consistently competitive. Cadalora had already received an offer that looked inviting, to join Jacques Cornu in the Lucky Strike Elf Honda team.

It had not been a very lucky year for Yamaha and the final blow to their chance of a top-three championship finish was dealt at Donington, when Jean-Philippe Ruggia crashed in practice for the second time. The first fall happened when he lost the front wheel during free practice. He was unhurt but then crashed more heavily during the first session of timed practice and dislocated his hip. He was quickly operated on but looked likely to miss most if not all the remaining races as he needed at least three weeks in traction.

His 250 Gauloises Blondes Yamaha was offered to Adrien Morillas on Sunday morning but, only hours later, Morillas was also offered Dominique Sarron's 500 Elf Honda after Sarron crashed in the 500 race and broke his wrist. Morillas decided to take the 500 ride.

SHOEI
SHOEI
5
5
Castrol
SHOEI
NGK

Arai
Arai
Arai
DUNLOP

Winning his second World Championship at his 100th Grand Prix showed Pons *(right)* **to be a faultless professional. It was a triumph of his riding skill but also a result of his abilities as a team organiser and negotiator, for his machine proved to be more competitive than even the other factory Hondas.**

Garriga *(below)* **had plenty to think about. The Yamaha was not as disadvantaged at Donington as at most tracks but motivation was now difficult. The bike had let him down so many times that his thoughts were already on next season and a switch to either Honda or the 500 class.**

Below left: **Alex Criville is able to show his ex-Derbi team-mate Jorge Martinez a thing or two. Many were starting to think of him as much more than a 125 specialist.**

Bryn Williams/Creative Pictures

125 cc

The 125 class is so competitive that it was a real shock when Hans Spaan was more than a second faster than anyone else in practice. It was not just a one-off lap time either – the 30-year-old Dutchman was clearly faster than anyone else in each session and the next five men were covered by one second. Spaan put in more laps than any of the other top riders and had no doubt that his tyres would last the distance. He was using the new 17-in. rear Dunlop that he had first tried at Le Mans, and it obviously worked.

The weather had been gradually warming up all morning, but Spaan still had tape on his radiator when he set off on the sighting lap. The temperature of the Honda rose and Spaan ripped the tape off on the line. He later reported that he was still worried about a repeat of his French Grand Prix boil over after the start, but the temperature gradually came back to normal.

It was Ezio Gianola who got the jump off the line but Spaan dived past at the first corner and was then in charge. Gianola chased him hard for the first two laps, followed in turn by Alex Criville and Aspar Martinez, but by lap three Spaan was clearly pulling away. Fifth place was contested just as hotly as second, with Allan Scott swapping places with Stefan Prein.

Criville was riding at 100 per cent as usual and squeezed past Gianola, only to have the Italian fight back. These two were, if anything, slowing each other down in front of Martinez. Prein and Scott took the opportunity to close in so that, by lap six, it was a five-man battle for second place, three seconds behind Spaan.

Seventh was Fausto Gresini but he was having to push hard to stay in front of Hisashi Unemoto, Koji Takada, Robin Milton and Herri Torrontegui. Gresini ran off the track on lap ten and

Malcolm Bryan

went from seventh to sixteenth.

By lap 12 Spaan was looking even more comfortable, with a five-second lead, and Criville had finally inched away from Gianola and Martinez. Prein and Scott ultimately proved unequal to the faster four and dropped back. The American kept riding hard but fell at the chicane on lap 17 of the 24.

By that time Takada and Unemoto's fierce private battle had taken them clear of the field and Gresini had worked his way back up to eighth. The ex-World Champion had used a great deal of energy and tyre rubber getting there, though, and never got clear of five riders who were determined to get back in front of him. Domenico Brigaglia and Doriano Romboni both succeeded.

On lap 20 the factory Derbi of Martinez started to falter yet again and then stopped. That left Gianola a clear third, well ahead of Prein. The excitement continued, though, in the battle for fifth between the two Japanese. It boiled over at the chicane on the last lap when Takada went up the inside but fell. Unemoto was fifth; Takada remounted to take eleventh.

Malcolm Bryan

250 cc

It was Sito Pons's 100th Grand Prix – and it resulted in his fourteenth win and his second World Championship. In all he had been on the rostrum 39 times with 15 seconds and 10 thirds. Racing against four other factory Hondas could never be described as easy, especially as two of the factory Yamahas were also quicker in practice, but even if Pons didn't make it look easy he left no doubt about who was in charge. A worthy champion.

Pons was sixth on lap one as Reinhold Roth charged into the lead on the HB Honda, passed on the following lap by Loris Reggiani on his similar machine. Masahiro Shimizu and Jacques Cornu made it four Hondas up front and these men would give Pons a hard time. But the World Champion passed Martin Wimmer on lap two and on lap three moved to third as Cornu took the lead ahead of Roth. Reggiani had run off on to the grass and relegated himself to sixth, just ahead of Gary Cowan.

The Yamahas were well out of the picture. Cadalora had jumped the start slightly, then stopped. He was left struggling as the field swept past. He tried to catch up but later pulled in when told by his pit board that he had been given a one-minute penalty for jumping the lights. Juan Garriga had made another of his disastrous starts and was still down in tenth place at the end of lap four, just behind Helmut Bradl, who was likewise having to fight his way up through the field. Yamaha's other hope, Toshihiko Honma, was even further behind in nineteenth place.

Up front the five Honda men went marching on, with Cornu leading and trying to put some distance between himself and Roth. Pons saw what the Swiss was trying to do and eased past Roth on lap six. Pons was not going to take any chances, but he had to finish in front of Cornu to seal the championship. No one else was a title threat.

Pons reeled the Lucky Strike Honda in and on lap eight outbraked Cornu at the chicane to take the lead. The pair had pulled away from Roth,

who had to concentrate on keeping Reggiani and Shimizu behind him. Garriga had just passed Bradl to take sixth place, with Wimmer eighth ahead of Cowan, Carlos Lavado and Didier de Radiguès. Pons said later that he had never intended to go for the win but Cornu gave him no choice. Both men broke the lap record repeatedly, then Roth got another lease of life, seeing that Cornu was no longer able to pull away.

By lap 13 of the 26 Pons had upped the speed to a point which none of the others could match. It was Cornu's fastest lap, but Pons had still more to give and finally set a new record on lap 17 as he jumped clear of Cornu and Roth. He continued to inch away, always smooth but very fast.

From that point the win was secure, but there was plenty of excitement in the battle for second. Reggiani had had another big moment. 'The back wheel slid and tried to flick me off. I landed across the tank and screen.' The Italian lost most of the screen but it did not seem to slow him down at all. He and Shimizu closed on Roth and Cornu so that it was a thrilling four-man fight for second place for the last ten laps, with Garriga sixth. The Ducados Yamaha man rode hard but was not fast enough to make an impression on the Honda pack.

Then Reggiani got in over his head again, on the second to last lap, in an incident that determined the rostrum positions. The four Hondas were swapping places every few corners and, with Roth in front, they headed for the right-hand hairpin at the bottom of the short hill behind the pits. Reggiani went for the inside and looked as though he had forgotten to brake. He committed himself to passing Shimizu and the Japanese ace decided to go inside Cornu at the same moment. There was almost nowhere for Reggiani to go, and he nearly clipped the back of Roth's machine as he headed straight on across the bows of Shimizu and Cornu. Both had to take avoiding action.

That gave Roth breathing space for the last lap, so second was secure. Reggiani had lost enough ground to put himself out of the picture, hence third would be decided between Cornu and Shimizu. The Swiss rider had been having brake troubles during the second part of the race. He got ahead of Shimizu at that same hairpin on the last lap, but not far enough ahead because Shimizu got back at the last corner, the left-hand hairpin. 'It couldn't have been closer, we touched,' said Cornu later.

Garriga was a lonely sixth, the only factory Yamaha to finish after Honma had crashed and knocked himself out on lap 22. He had climbed up to eighth but was riding on the ragged edge, having literally barged Lavado out of the way when he dived inside the ex-World Champion at the left-hand hairpin on lap 13.

Malcolm Bryan

500 cc

The crowd did not go to Donington expecting to see a British winner. They might hope for one, but the reality of the American/Australian domination is plain for all to see. The fact that Niall Mackenzie led the race for half a lap, after catching and passing the all-powerful American triumvirate, however, made it the most memorable British Grand Prix for many years.

Schwantz was very much the pre-race favourite (his disquiet over his machine's performance in the final session was not generally known), so Rainey and Lawson might have been content to let him run away with the lead and fight their own private championship battle. But both went for the 20 points, both hoping to put Schwantz between himself and his arch-rival.

Rainey won the charge to the first corner, just holding off Schwantz. Christian Sarron then slotted into second, ahead of Eddie Lawson and Wayne Gardner. Mackenzie was sixth ahead of Magee, Cadalora, Haslam, McElnea and Dominique Sarron. In getting past Gardner Mackenzie lost ground to the leading four and, with Schwantz taking the lead from Rainey, catching the fastest man in the world seemed a tall order for the Scot.

Lap three, however, demonstrated that Mackenzie was doing exactly that as he rapidly gained on the leading quartet. At the front Rainey got back ahead on lap five, then Schwantz went later on the brakes at the end of the straight and retook the lead. Mackenzie used the same trick to get past Sarron and, three corners later, starting lap six, sent the crowd wild as he went inside Lawson at Redgate. In the middle of that lap he cut under Rainey and was then right on the tail of the Pepsi Suzuki.

Mackenzie was looking for a way past Schwantz, who had said that the Suzuki handled well at Donington. So often the Yamahas and Hondas have looked cumbersome by comparison, but this time Mackenzie was flicking his bike from side to side with alacrity, probing for a gap either side of the Suzuki. 'I found I was faster than them just about everywhere,' said Mackenzie later. 'I could gain going into the corners and I was faster through the corner and could still get the gas on.'

One of the obvious passing places at Donington is the approach to Redgate. It was where Mackenzie had gone under Lawson. He used it again on Schwantz. The Texan said he knew Mackenzie was about to pass him as he braked at the end of the start and finish straight: 'I saw the crowd on their feet, arms in the air, and I thought, "Here comes Niall".'

Schwantz was not about to make a race of it for the crowd. Half a lap later he went by the Yamaha on the brakes at the end of the main straight and, with the Suzuki holding the inside line, Mackenzie had to let him go. 'I couldn't say that getting in front was that exciting. I was concentrating so hard I wasn't thinking about it,' said Mackenzie who, for the next six laps, looked as though he might repeat the move but could never quite accomplish it. Then the total faith in his front tyre that he had been demonstrating obviously started to wane and Mackenzie was forced to think more of those behind.

Gardner had dropped back and retired on lap 12 with an odd ignition fault. 'The engine was pretty bad from the start,' he said. 'It is a problem that has happened before and they don't know why. I guess it is one of those years.'

Lawson had realised that it was not possible to race Schwantz all the way to the line. He had

Left: **Mackenzie was the man of the moment, getting into the midst of the American triumvirate and bringing the crowd to their feet when he took the lead. He had the Marlboro Yamaha working perfectly, and Lawson and Schwantz were hard pressed to deal with it.**

Webster and Hewitt *(below)* **rounded off a perfect Shell British Grand Prix with a decisive win. It now looked unlikely that anyone could stop them taking their third World Championship.**

certainly not slowed up and, in fact, never dropped that far behind the Suzuki. His priority was Rainey and, having got in front of his fellow-Californian when Mackenzie took the lead, the World Champion paced himself perfectly and started to inch away from the Lucky Strike Yamaha.

The leading trio had opened a two-second advantage over Rainey and Sarron. Then, on lap 17, Lawson made one of his calm, calculated manoeuvres and eased past Mackenzie into second place, just as it had become obvious that the Scot was starting to lose ground to Schwantz. Mackenzie found the situation frustrating: he tried to tail the Honda but could not flick the Yamaha around as he had early on. His fastest lap of the race was his third, but Schwantz and Lawson were both fastest on lap 20, with Lawson taking the record. Rainey was quickest on lap 18.

Getting on the rostrum would have been a reasonable reward for Mackenzie's efforts, but the Yamaha started to run low on fuel. A couple of coughs were enough to let Rainey by and put Mackenzie fourth, but well clear of Sarron who had been forced to slow after some nasty moments early on. 'The tyres seemed great at first but then suddenly I had some big slides and had to be more careful.'

Schwantz eased off over the last few laps but could not afford to coast; Lawson was less than a second behind him at the flag. Schwantz complimented Mackenzie on his effort: 'I was glad to see him up there. He rode well. I enjoyed the race, the bike was perfect and I was pretty confident that I could win.'

Before the race Schwantz had an agonising tyre decision. 'There were two tyres I could have used, one was the "L" that Lawson used, which is also the tyre we raced with at Suzuka, both for the Grand Prix and the Eight Hour. The other was the "T", which is supposed to come in a bit quicker. There is also the "S" which is the same compound as the "T" but the construction of the "T" is a little stiffer so it keeps going a bit longer. I could have used the "T" or the "L" and as I don't think anyone had raced with the "T" before I was inclined to go with the "L", but when we looked back at the notes my comments on the "L" were that it didn't offer quite the same grip. The bike was so good today, though, that I think I could have won on the "L" or the "T".

'The only problem I had was when I got in a little deep a couple of times on the brakes, but that only made me wide by one or two bike widths. The bike made it easy for me. I think I rode very differently today from the way I ever have before. Instead of being real hard on the gas between every corner, right up to the braking point, I was smoother. Through the section where the corners all run together I was using less revs, driving it real smooth and easy. It worked. It was a great race with a great atmosphere. The crowd were all over the track at the end of the race.'

Lawson made his usual modest remarks about the race. 'Kevin just went faster. I couldn't keep up. It was one of those days. I had fun today, though; Christian, Niall, all the guys rode well and it was a great race.' It had been another perfect, championship-aimed performance from the Californian.

The race was a disappointing one for Kevin Magee, who looked to be tailing Mackenzie and capable of catching the leaders until his front wheel started vibrating badly. The tyre had turned on the rim. Rob McElnea also had tyre trouble. His rear went completely out of shape soon after the start, so finishing tenth was a minor triumph.

Ron Haslam eventually won a lengthy struggle with Luca Cadalora. Haslam was slowed by the torn tendons in his right hand, which had still not healed from the Spa crash. He could barely hold the throttle open, never mind brake. Cadalora got in front of him but could not get away. 'I still have to learn how to control a 500 when the tyres go off,' he said honestly. Haslam gritted his teeth and repassed the Yamaha for the last time with four laps to go.

Dominique Sarron was flicked off the Elf Honda when he was in tenth place on lap three and broke his wrist. Pier Francesco Chili ran off the track early on, and though he fought his way up to ninth the tyres were well past their best by then and the other factory machines too far ahead.

Sidecars

It was the third British Grand Prix win in a row for Steve Webster and Tony Hewitt. The pair took the lead from Rolf Biland and Kurt Waltisperg on the second lap but, unlike the previous year's duel to the flag, this was a clear-cut victory. After the second lap Webster had a one-second lead and then settled down to lap consistently under the lap record for the first half of the race.

Ten seconds behind, Biland had other things to worry about. His tyres were past their best and he never got close to his pole-position practice time. The Swiss outfit was eventually passed by Egbert Streuer and Geral de Haas and was forced to race hard right to the line to stay ahead of Alain Michel and Jean-Marc Fresc.

Webster later explained that his thoughts of winning had not been knocked by the fact that Biland was faster in practice. 'I thought we could win it because we could do pretty consistent lap times in practice while Rolf could do just one fast lap. When I was still in front with eight laps to go and had an 11-second lead I realised that I could ease off and as long as there were no mechanical problems, we were going to win.

Malcolm Bryan

'There is quite a tyre war going on at the moment between those who use Avons, like us, and those who use Yokohamas, like Rolf. He has even gone to bigger wheels so that he can use a different type of tyre, to try and get round the problems. The big problem is vibration through right-handers. What is happening is that everyone goes like hell from the start for five or six laps and then the tyres start to vibrate.

'If you keep going flat out the tyres can't stand it so everyone has to slow down to a pace that saves the tyres. Then everyone is watching what the others are doing, to see how hard they can push their tyres. The Avons are a harder tyre than the Yokohama so they don't have quite the grip for one fast lap, but they will stand the abuse better.'

Webster had his Avons fitted without the use of the liquid soap that is normally employed so that the tyre slides onto the rim more easily. The thinking was that the soap might be contributing to the imbalance, and even allowing the tyre to creep on the rim. The tyres were also blown up with nitrogen to keep their temperature more stable.

Shell British Grand Prix, 6 August/statistics

Donington Park Race Circuit, 2.5-mile/4.02-km circuit

500 cc

30 laps, 75 miles/120.69 km

Place	Rider	Nat.	Machine	Laps	Time & speed	Practice time	Grid
1	Kevin Schwantz	USA	Suzuki	30	47m 45.67s 94.21 mph/ 151.61 km/h	1m 34.05s	1
2	Eddie Lawson	USA	Honda	30	47m 46.64s	1m 34.30s	2
3	Wayne Rainey	USA	Yamaha	30	47m 54.27s	1m 34.84s	3
4	Niall Mackenzie	GB	Yamaha	30	47m 56.61s	1m 35.10s	6
5	Christian Sarron	F	Yamaha	30	48m 13.98s	1m 34.89s	4
6	Kevin Magee	AUS	Yamaha	30	48m 24.16s	1m 35.60s	8
7	Ron Haslam	GB	Suzuki	30	48m 33.03s	1m 35.69s	9
8	Luca Cadalora	I	Yamaha	30	48m 37.44s	1m 35.05s	5
9	Pier Francesco Chili	I	Honda	30	49m 13.38s	1m 35.44s	7
10	Rob McElnea	GB	Honda	29	48m 10.14s	1m 36.90s	11
11	Fred Merkel	USA	Honda	29	48m 27.69s	1m 38.59s	14
12	Roger Burnett	GB	Honda	29	48m 28.25s	1m 37.73s	13
13	Marco Gentile	CH	Fior	29	49m 16.40s	1m 39.09s	15
14	Fabio Biliotti	I	Honda	29	49m 26.86s	1m 40.73s	20
15	Simon Buckmaster	GB	Honda	28	47m 51.42s	1m 40.34s	17
16	Marco Papa	I	Paton	28	47m 54.93s	1m 41.44s	23
17	Robert Holden	NZ	Honda	28	48m 08.72s	1m 41.90s	26
18	Bruno Kneubühler	CH	Honda	28	48m 19.35s	1m 42.21s	27
19	Claude Albert	F	Suzuki	28	48m 23.99s	1m 41.32s	22
20	Andreas Leuthe	LUX	Suzuki	28	48m 59.82s	1m 43.11s	30
21	Josef Doppler	A	Honda	28	49m 15.38s	1m 43.05s	29
22	Fernando Gonzalez	E	Honda	28	49m 25.41s	1m 43.99s	31
23	Peter Graves	GB	Honda	27	48m 23.46s	1m 47.53s	36
	Kees Doorakkers	NL	Honda	28	DNF	1m 40.64s	19
	Niggi Schmassman	CH	Honda	20	DNF	1m 41.84s	25
	Mark Phillips	GB	Suzuki	14	DNF	1m 44.46s	32
	Ian Pratt	GB	Honda	13	DNF	1m 45.28s	33
	Wayne Gardner	AUS	Honda	12	DNF	1m 35.72s	10
	Rachel Nicotte	F	Honda	8	DNF	1m 39.77s	16
	Alessandro Valesi	I	Yamaha	8	DNF	1m 40.74s	21
	John Mossey	GB	Suzuki	8	DNF	1m 46.13s	34
	Alan Carter	GB	Honda	7	DNF	1m 40.37s	18
	Juan Lopez Mella	E	Honda	6	DNF	1m 41.83s	24
	David Crampton	GB	Suzuki	3	DNF	1m 46.44s	35
	Dominique Sarron	F	Honda	2	DNF	1m 37.01s	12
	Andy McGladdery	GB	Honda		DNS	1m 43.03s	28
	Larry Vacondio	YV	Suzuki		DNQ	1m 50.08s	
	Eddie Laycock	IRL	Honda		DNQ	2m 24.93s	

Fastest lap: Lawson, 1m 34.51s, 95.22 mph/153.24 km/h (record).
Previous record: Christian Sarron, F (Yamaha), 1m 36.21s, 93.54 mph/150.54 km/h (1988).

World Championship: 1 Rainey, 180.5; **2** Lawson, 174; **3** Sarron, C., 127.5; **4** Schwantz, 122.5; **5** Magee, 108.5; **6** Chili, 102; **7** Mackenzie, 73; **8** Doohan, 68; **9** Haslam, 57; **10** Gardner, 43; **11** Sarron, D., 39; **12** Buckmaster and McElnea, 37.5; **14** Spencer, 33.5; **15** Gentile, 33; **16** Valesi, 30; **17** Taira, 26; **18** Mamola, 23; **19** Rudroff, 18; **20** Fujiwara, 17; **21** Shobert, 12; **22** Doppler, 11; **23** Meyer, 10; **24** Balbi, 9; **25** Broccoli, Cadalora, Gonzalez and Schmassman, 8; **29** Dowson and Leuthe, 7; **31** Itoh and Morillas, 6; **33** Kocinski, 5.5; **34** Gschwender and Merkel, 5; **36** Burnett, Crine and Kneubühler, 4; **39** Biliotti and Yatsushiro, 3; **41** Doorakkers, 2.5; **42** Laycock and Lopez Mella, 2; **44** Machii, 1.

125 cc

24 laps, 60 miles/96.48 km

Place	Rider	Nat.	Machine	Laps	Time & speed	Practice time	Grid
1	Hans Spaan	NL	Honda	24	42m 10.64s 85.35 mph/ 137.35 km/h	1m 43.75s	1
2	Alex Criville	E	Cobas	24	42m 19.43s	1m 44.98s	2
3	Ezio Gianola	I	Honda	24	42m 23.31s	1m 45.14s	3
4	Stefan Prein	D	Honda	24	42m 26.86s	1m 45.84s	6
5	Hisashi Unemoto	J	Honda	24	42m 57.99s	1m 46.13s	7
6	Domenico Brigaglia	I	Garelli	24	43m 07.85s	1m 47.15s	15
7	Doriano Romboni	I	Honda	24	43m 08.12s	1m 47.05s	12
8	Fausto Gresini	I	Aprilia	24	43m 08.56s	1m 46.75s	9
9	Adolf Stadler	D	Krauser	24	43m 09.66s	1m 47.16s	16
10	Robin Appleyard	GB	Honda	24	43m 10.27s	1m 47.01s	11
11	Koji Takada	J	Honda	24	43m 18.46s	1m 46.81s	10
12	Luis Reyes	E	Honda	24	43m 25.89s	1m 48.44s	36
13	Dirk Raudies	D	Honda	24	43m 27.50s	1m 48.21s	30
14	Bady Hassaine	TN	Honda	24	43m 29.35s	1m 47.95s	24
15	Flemming Kistrup	DK	Honda	24	43m 37.87s	1m 47.28s	17
16	Julian Miralles	E	Derbi	24	43m 38.31s	1m 47.95s	25
17	Steve Patrickson	GB	Honda	24	43m 38.82s	1m 47.75s	20
18	Heinz Lüthi	CH	Honda	24	43m 42.40s	1m 47.92s	23
19	Herri Torrontegui	E	Honda	24	43m 42.65s	1m 46.56s	8
20	Josef Fischer	A	Honda	24	43m 57.62s	1m 48.37s	32
21	Manuel Hernandez	E	Honda	23	42m 11.81s	1m 48.07s	27
22	Hervé Duffard	F	Honda	23	42m 11.99s	1m 48.12s	29
23	Rob Orme	GB	Honda	23	42m 12.28s	1m 48.39s	33
24	Johnny Wickström	SF	Honda	23	42m 13.39s	1m 48.41s	34
25	Hubert Abold	D	Krauser	23	42m 14.49s	1m 48.10s	28
26	Mike Leitner	A	Honda	23	42m 19.13s	1m 47.99s	26
27	Alan Patterson	IRL	Honda	20	43m 13.61s	1m 48.21s	31
	Jorge Martinez	E	Derbi	20	DNF	1m 45.33s	4
	Robin Milton	GB	Honda	17	DNF	1m 47.12s	14
	Allan Scott	USA	Honda	16	DNF	1m 45.57s	5
	Bruno Casanova	I	Aprilia	8	DNF	1m 47.87s	21
	Alex Bedford	GB	EMC	7	DNF	1m 47.12s	13
	Stefan Dörflinger	CH	Aprilia	5	DNF	1m 47.90s	22
	Corrado Catalano	I	Rotax	3	DNF	1m 47.74s	19
	Ralf Waldmann	D	Cobas	2	DNF	1m 47.29s	18
	Taru Rinne	SF	Honda		DNQ	1m 48.48s	
	Serge Julin	B	Honda		DNQ	1m 48.49s	
	Emilio Cuppini	I	Garelli		DNQ	1m 48.52s	
	Lucio Pietroniro	B	Honda		DNQ	1m 48.54s	
	Alfred Waibel	D	Honda		DNQ	1m 48.81s	
	Thierry Feuz	CH	Honda		DNQ	1m 49.12s	
	Othmar Schuler	CH	Honda		DNQ	1m 49.24s	
	Kris Galatowicz	GB	EMC		DNQ	1m 49.26s	
	Stuart Edwards	GB	Honda		DNQ	1m 49.26s	
	Peter Öttl	D	Krauser		DNQ	1m 49.33s	
	Rafael Roses	E	Cobas		DNQ	1m 49.65s	
	Jos van Dongen	NL	Honda		DNQ	1m 49.95s	
	Kazuya Yamada	J	Honda		DNQ	1m 50.75s	
	Klaus Kindle	FL	Honda		DNQ	1m 51.08s	
	Gastone Grassetti	I	Honda		DNQ	1m 51.21s	
	Ray Murphy	GB			DNQ	1m 51.83s	
	Valerio Vivarelli	RSM	Rotax		DNQ	1m 51.94s	

Fastest lap: Spaan, 1m 44.67s, 85.98 mph/138.37 km/h (record).
Previous record: Ezio Gianola, I (Honda), 1m 45.76s, 85.09 mph/136.94 km/h (1988).

World Championship: 1 Gianola, 128; **2** Criville, 126; **3** Spaan, 118; **4** Unemoto, 93; **5** Miralles, 90; **6** Gresini, 89; **7** Takada, 75; **8** Prein, 67; **9** Stadler, 47; **10** Martinez and Milton, 46; **12** Scott, 37; **13** Reyes, 35; **14** Brigaglia, 34; **15** Pietroniro, 22; **16** Raudies, 21; **17** Casanova and Romboni, 20; **19** Rinne and Waibel, A., 18; **21** Feuz, 15; **22** Appleyard and Hirose, 13; **24** Selini, Torrontegui and Yoshida, 11; **27** Catalano, Kistrup and Shima, 10; **30** Fujiwara, 9; **31** Yamashita, 8; **32** Fujiyama, 7; **33** Waibel, G. and Yamada, 6; **35** Wickström, 4; **36** Debbia, Jeandat and Saunders, 3; **39** Fischer and Hassaine, 2; **41** Abold, Bedford and Duffard, 1.

With the top sponsors chasing a handful of leading riders, Niall Mackenzie gave a timely reminder of his talent by battling with Schwantz *(left)* **and Rainey** *(right)*.

Malcolm Bryan

250 cc

26 laps, 65 miles/104.52 km

Place	Rider	Nat.	Machine	Laps	Time & speed	Practice time	Grid
1	Alfonso Pons	E	Honda	26	43m 06.81s 90.22 mph/ 145.20 km/h	1m 38.66s	4
2	Reinhold Roth	D	Honda	26	43m 13.46s	1m 39.13s	6
3	Masahiro Shimizu	J	Honda	26	43m 14.19s	1m 39.34s	8
4	Jacques Cornu	CH	Honda	26	43m 14.44s	1m 38.73s	5
5	Loris Reggiani	I	Honda	26	43m 19.87s	1m 38.62s	3
6	Juan Garriga	E	Yamaha	26	43m 21.08s	1m 38.55s	2
7	Helmut Bradl	D	Honda	26	43m 26.36s	1m 39.52s	11
8	Carlos Lavado	YV	Aprilia	26	43m 44.65s	1m 39.76s	14
9	Gary Cowan	IRL	Yamaha	26	43m 45.69s	1m 39.37s	9
10	Wilco Zeelenberg	NL	Honda	26	43m 47.88s	1m 40.19s	20
11	Martin Wimmer	D	Aprilia	26	43m 50.96s	1m 39.43s	10
12	Stefano Caracchi	RSM	Honda	26	43m 54.13s	1m 40.12s	19
13	Alexandre Barros	BR	Yamaha	26	43m 57.04s	1m 40.46s	25
14	Jochen Schmid	D	Honda	26	43m 57.67s	1m 40.65s	29
15	Adrien Morillas	F	Yamaha	26	43m 57.88s	1m 40.54s	26
16	Alberto Puig	E	Yamaha	26	43m 58.60s	1m 39.70s	13
17	Daniel Amatriain	E	Honda	26	44m 05.23s	1m 40.97s	33
18	Hans Becker	D	Seel	26	44m 17.07s	1m 40.41s	23
19	Harald Eckl	D	Aprilia	26	44m 18.54s	1m 40.63s	28
20	Alain Bronec	F	Aprilia	26	44m 21.47s	1m 41.47s	37
21	August Auinger	A	Yamaha	26	44m 21.75s	1m 41.23s	34
22	Manfred Herweh	D	Yamaha	26	44m 38.98s	1m 39.94s	16
23	Andreas Preining	A	Aprilia	26	44m 40.06s	1m 40.62s	27
24	Patrick van den Goorbergh	NL	Yamaha	26	44m 40.75s	1m 41.41s	35
25	Bernard Hänggeli	CH	Yamaha	25	43m 11.49s	1m 40.78s	30
26	Maurizio Vitali	I	Honda	25	43m 12.30s	1m 40.79s	31
27	Jean-François Baldé	F	Yamaha	25	44m 02.33s	1m 41.45s	36
	Didier de Radiguès	B	Aprilia	22	DNF	1m 39.69s	12
	Toshihiko Honma	J	Yamaha	21	DNF	1m 40.11s	18
	Paolo Casoli	I	Honda	20	DNF	1m 40.24s	22
	Fausto Ricci	I	Aprilia	18	DNF	1m 40.22s	21
	Kevin Mitchell	GB	Yamaha	16	DNF	1m 40.94s	32
	Luca Cadalora	I	Yamaha	15	DNF	1m 38.31s	1
	Renzo Colleoni	I	Aprilia	6	DNF	1m 39.80s	15
	Carlos Cardus	E	Honda	2	DNF	1m 39.15s	7
	Alberto Rota	I	Aprilia	0	DNF	1m 40.44s	24
	Jean-Philippe Ruggia	F	Yamaha		DNS	1m 40.00s	17
	Nigel Bosworth	GB	Aprilia		DNQ	1m 41.50s	
	Virginio Ferrari	I	Gazzaniga		DNQ	1m 41.60s	
	Jean Foray	F	Yamaha		DNQ	1m 41.97s	
	Woolsey Coulter	IRL	Aprilia		DNQ	1m 42.06s	
	Luis Lavado	YV	Yamaha		DNQ	1m 42.73s	
	Martyn Jupp	GB			DNQ	1m 43.00s	
	Ian McConnachie	GB	Yamaha		DNQ	1m 43.46s	
	Andy Leisner	USA	Honda		DNQ	1m 43.69s	
	Darren Milner	AUS	Yamaha		DNQ	1m 43.99s	
	Engelbert Neumair	A	Aprilia		DNQ	1m 44.08s	
	Urs Jucker	CH	Yamaha		DNQ	1m 44.68s	
	Massimo Matteoni	I	Yamaha		DNQ	1m 53.43s	
	René Delaby	LUX	Yamaha		DNQ	7m 28.37s	

Fastest lap: Pons, 1m 38.33s, 91.52 mph/147.29 km/h (record).
Previous record: Juan Garriga, E (Yamaha), 1m 38.87s, 91.02 mph/146.48 km/h (1988).

World Championship: 1 Pons, 216; **2** Cornu, 150; **3** Roth, 143; **4** Cardus, 130; **5** Ruggia, 110; **6** Cadalora, 86; **7** Shimizu, 82; **8** Garriga, 78; **9** Bradl, 69; **10** Wimmer, 54; **11** Kocinski, 40; **12** de Radiguès, 39; **13** Reggiani, 37; **14** Zeelenberg, 32; **15** Schmid, 28; **16** Honma, 26; **17** Filice, 22; **18** Colleoni and Cowan, 21; **20** Palazzese, 19; **21** Puig 18; **22** Lucchi, 17; **23** Eckl and Lavado, 15; **25** Amatriain, 12; **26** Barros, 11; **27** Bronec and Okada, 10; **29** Caracchi, Morillas and Shiomori, 9; **32** Ricci, 8; **33** Rota and van den Goorbergh, 6; **35** Beattie and Mitchell, 4; **37** Preining and Vitali, 2; **39** Arai, Auinger and Becker, 1.

Malcolm Bryan

Malcolm Bryan

Sidecars

24 laps, 60 miles/96.48 km

Place	Driver & passenger	Nat.	Machine	Laps	Time & speed	Practice time	Grid
1	Steve Webster/ Tony Hewitt	GB GB	LCR- Krauser	24	40m 20.90s 89.22 mph/ 143.57 km/h	1m 39.40s	2
2	Egbert Streuer/ Gerald de Haas	NL NL	LCR- Yamaha	24	40m 31.42s	1m 39.99s	3
3	Rolf Biland/ Kurt Waltisperg	CH CH	LCR- Krauser	24	40m 34.67s	1m 38.87s	1
4	Alain Michel/ Jean-Marc Fresc	F F	LCR- Krauser	24	40m 36.84s	1m 40.39s	4
5	Markus Egloff/ Gavin Simmons	CH GB	LCR- Yamaha	24	41m 24.65s	1m 40.43s	5
6	Fritz Stölzle/ Hubert Stölzle	D D	LCR- Krauser	24	41m 28.22s	1m 42.02s	9
7	Barry Brindley/ Graham Rose	GB GB	Fowler- Yamaha	24	41m 54.42s	1m 41.44s	7
8	René Progin/ Yves Hunziker	CH CH	LCR- Krauser	24	41m 58.32s	1m 42.30s	15
9	Billy Gällros/ Julian Tailford	S GB	Yamaha	23	40m 23.41s	1m 43.70s	22
10	Theo van Kempen/ Simon Birchall	NL GB	LCR- Krauser	23	40m 25.40s	1m 43.53s	20
11	Ray Gardner/ Tony Strevens	GB GB	LCR- Krauser	23	40m 28.61s	1m 43.83s	23
12	Kenny Howles/ Steve Pointer	GB GB	LCR- Krauser	23	40m 32.08s	1m 44.31s	24
13	Ivan Nigrowsky/ Jacques Corbier	F F	LCR- JPX	23	40m 45.43s	1m 42.61s	16
14	Wolfgang Stropek/ Steve Campbell	A GB	Mibag- Krauser	23	40m 52.48s	1m 43.35s	19
15	Tony Baker/ Trevor Hopkinson	GB GB	LCR- Krauser	23	40m 57.69s	1m 44.62s	26
16	Clive Stirrat/ Simon Prior	GB GB	LCR- Krauser	23	40m 58.18s	1m 44.36s	25
17	Alfred Zurbrügg/ Martin Zurbrügg	CH CH	LCR- Yamaha	23	41m 32.86s	1m 42.05s	10
18	Derek Jones/ Peter Brown	GB GB	LCR- Yamaha	23	41m 37.01s	1m 42.27s	14
19	Yoshisada Kumagaya/ Phil Coombes	J GB	Windle- KS	23	41m 40.33s	1m 42.08s	12
20	Paul Güdel/ Charly Güdel	CH CH	LCR- Yamaha	22	41m 20.76s	1m 42.95s	17
	Barry Smith/ David Smith	GB GB	Windle- ADM	21	DNF	1m 43.55s	21
	Bernd Scherer/ Thomas Schröder	D D	BSR- Krauser	14	DNF	1m 41.86s	8
	Tony Wyssen/ Kilian Wyssen	CH CH	LCR- Krauser	10	DNF	1m 43.10s	18
	Rolf Steinhausen/ Bruno Hiller	D D	Schuh	6	DNF	1m 42.14s	13
	Steve Abbott/ Shaun Smith	GB GB	LCR- Yamaha	5	DNF	1m 40.54s	6
	Masato Kumano/ Markus Fahrni	J CH	LCR- Yamaha		DNS	1m 42.07s	11
	George Hardwick/ Gary Irlam	GB GB	LCR		DNQ	1m 44.83s	
	Michael Burcombe/ Nick Roche	GB GB	LCR		DNQ	1m 44.83s	
	Gary Thomas/ Eckhart Rösinger	GB D	LCR- IMI		DNQ	1m 44.91s	
	Judd Drew/ Bryan Houghton	GB GB	LCR- JPX		DNQ	1m 45.60s	
	Paul Atkinson/ Steve Parker	GB GB	LCR		DNQ	1m 46.38s	
	John Evans/ Ian Gaunt	GB GB	LCR		DNQ	1m 47.87s	

Fastest lap: Webster, 1m 39.34s, 90.59 mph/145.79 km/h (record).
Previous record: Rolf Biland/Kurt Waltisperg, CH/CH (LCR-Krauser), 1m 40.05s, 89.95 mph/144.76 km/h (1988).

World Championship: 1 Webster, 115; **2** Streuer, 103; **3** Biland, 85; **4** Michel, 79; **5** Kumano, 58; **6** Stölzle, 57; **7** Egloff, 47; **8** Brindley, 46; **9** Steinhausen, 42; **10** Jones, 37; **11** van Kempen, 32; **12** Scherer, 26; **13** Kumagaya, 25; **14** Abbott, 24; **15** Progin, 23; **16** Zurbrügg, 21; **17** Wyssen, 20; **18** Nigrowsky, 15; **19** Gällros, 14; **20** Smith, 10; **21** Baker and Stropek, 8; **23** Howles, 6; **24** Gardner, 5; **25** Drew, 4; **26** Stirrat, 3; **27** Howles and Thomas, 2.

Malcolm Bryan

Masahiro Shimizu *(far left)* **took third place from Jacques Cornu at the last corner but the latest 250 star to emerge from Japan, Toshihiko Honma** *(far left below)*, **suffered a nasty fall.**

Rainey *(left)* **thinks of tyres and lines, carburation and apexes, suspension, braking points and Lawson.**

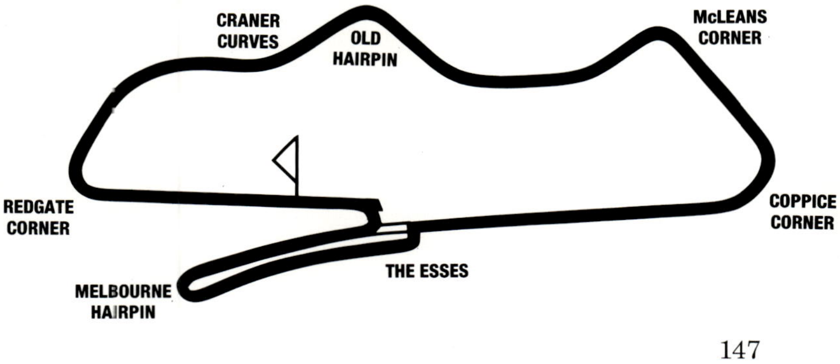

After his surprise move to Honda Eddie Lawson had worked steadily throughout the season to ensure that he retained his World Championship.

WORLD CHAMPIONSHIP · ROUND 13

SWEDISH TT

A World Championship season is made up of thousands of incidents, interactions and – mostly subconscious – decisions. All form a vital part of the picture, yet a few are pinpointed as momentous. The twenty-seventh lap of the 500 race in Sweden, when Wayne Rainey was thrown off the Lucky Strike Yamaha, was an obvious turning point. And it's impossible to say whether the pressure of an ever-diminishing points lead so increased the tension that Rainey made a mistake, or whether it was merely the distraction of a confusing pit signal that generated a moment's loss of concentration by the American.

Lawson's performances on the Rothmans Honda had been improving steadily since early in the season, but the start of his year was hardly auspicious. He crashed during pre-season testing in Japan and then, at the Grand Prix at Suzuka, finished an average third after Gardner lost ground fighting his Rothmans Honda – and that was followed by a dismal fifth at Phillip Island, where Gardner won. Eddie later admitted that with the Australian Grand Prix result he doubted that he could win the championship. 'It sure didn't seem very likely at that point. We were a long way off.'

Erv Kanemoto never shared his opinion. 'I honestly feel that Phillip Island would not have been all that bad, but physically he was in bad shape. The crash in Japan and then the crash during practice in Australia when he got beat up pretty bad – it was a high-speed crash, pretty hard. He was hurting all over, his leg was giving him trouble, his back and his wrist were giving him trouble from the crash in Japan. I felt that the bike wasn't perfect by any means, but it was probably better than it was at Laguna Seca because there we did have problems. I think we would have finished better had he been fit.'

According to Kanemoto things improved markedly the next week in America for, although Lawson was only third again and a long way behind Rainey and Schwantz, the understanding between rider and engineer moved on several steps. 'Until that time he would say things, and we were reacting to what he was saying, but at Laguna Seca we could see what the bike was doing in relationship to his comments. At that point we started to understand and then we went to Jerez. At Laguna, from Saturday evening to Sunday morning, we made a change which seemed to work in the warm-up but we had to stay pretty conservative for the race. When we got to Jerez I remember Eddie saying, after the first practice, that it was beginning to feel like a bike. From there we were still quite a long way off but we could start to see where we were going. We knew what we could do to help him.'

Lawson may have the reputation among his fellow-riders of being hard to get along with, but Kanemoto has nothing but praise for his rider. 'Working with Eddie has been a pleasure. I know I have said that so many times, but it is so true. Any time we ask him to do another few laps at the end of the day – I know he is beat, it has been a long day – he will go out and do two five-lap stints for a back-to-back test. He will do it, no question. He is so good for us.'

Kanemoto not only appreciated Lawson's dedication to the cause, he also never doubted his ability to turn the points situation around. 'I have felt all through that we could win the championship. The main thing was not to make any mistakes and, by finishing and trying to learn more from each race, we would have a chance.

'At first I knew that the bike was way wrong for him, because you could see that his style changed dramatically. Where he was sitting, the way he was positioned, you could understand what the bike was doing, why and how he was trying to compensate for it. But at that point we really didn't know what to do to put it right.

'Eddie may not agree, but I think that he has developed the bike to where it is now through testing and feedback, but I believe that he has also been able to utilise some of the characteristics of the Honda. We talked about the problem, that we could change the bike, but we would have to take away its strong point. We could maybe make it perform the way he wanted, but not for free. We would have to give perhaps twice as much to get what he wanted. We worked out some of the basic handling problems and I think that he has adjusted slightly himself. I feel that.

'The bike's strongest point is acceleration and top speed, when it is set up right. The handling – we are a little weak in the steering, the side-to-side movement seems to be a little slow. At this moment I think that the basic design of the whole machine kind of dictates that, the engine layout. That is why, when I talked to Eddie, I said that if we did try and correct the big problems, the problems he would like corrected, then we would have to give up too much.

'I am able to talk to Eddie a lot more freely lately. It is hard for me to get to know someone, he is three-times World Champion, and it is hard for me to say or suggest things. I really don't want to create a barrier between the two of us because we do have to have a good working relationship and I respect him so much. From my side I have been going kind of slow at things and that is my basic way.'

Going slow at things is also Lawson's way, but he maintains his cautious approach has been vindicated when you look at what happened to Gardner. 'Wayne was pushing real hard from the start of the year. In Japan he ran off the track a couple of times, then in Australia he made a couple of mistakes but won, and then he crashed at Laguna. I was not prepared to push that hard. I thought I might fall off and break something, so I just rode as hard as I felt I could and worked at getting the bike better. I was thinking, "Well, I can push harder and go faster right now but I don't want to take the risk of falling down." You have to give Wayne a lot of credit for trying so hard. It is difficult to say which attitude is best, but I was looking at the long season.'

It had undoubtedly been a long season and while the first half of it very much belonged to Wayne Rainey, his advantage had been eroded in the second part.

The Lucky Strike team had started the year with the best machines, after very successful pre-season testing in Brazil and Australia. However, for months the Roberts team had had very little new to test and no time to make anything or get track time on it. Roberts readily accepted that Honda were doing all the work and were catching up. 'Obviously all the testing hurts us. There is not a whole lot we could do about that, because we had the Suzuka Eight Hour thrown in on us. But we are not Honda. We are only Lucky Strike. There are times when I feel we could do better if we did not have manpower restrictions. I'm not going to say money, because we don't actually have a money problem. It is more of a manpower problem. Honda have so many engineers working on their development. I have people in America, and some people in Europe that can assist us, but we are not engineers. We do not have the personnel to make stuff for us. It is difficult to hire engineers for two or four weeks, to make things for us. Honda have those people full time, all year round.

'That is the biggest problem for us. If the Honda team here phones Japan they can get this or that built. If I was to phone Japan and ask Yamaha for something, they would have to build enough parts for everybody, because of the way the teams are structured – and I had something to do with that, so I'm not complaining about it. We are just trying to keep things in perspective. You can't just go out and hire Learjets to fly people around the world, getting special parts made.

'We can massage the motor cycle but we can't engineer a new one. We decided the combination at the beginning of the season, that we all felt was better than the standard Yamaha by quite a bit. That is what we are still running today. To get it any better it wouldn't just be a case of modifying what we have got. It would be a case of designing something different from scratch.

'We only have so much manpower so, when the season started, the development couldn't go on at the same pace because we have racing and testing to do – and only so many people to do the work. We still have a lot of tyre testing to do and we don't have the resources that we have in the off-season. The lead time to get pieces made that are better in the engine is just too long to make mid-season changes. This time last year we knew what pieces we needed to start this season with, and we already know what we need for next year, but we can't get them made any quicker. We are starting now for next year.'

Roberts felt that Rainey was doing a great job of withstanding the pressure. 'It will get tougher, this is nothing yet, but he has been good. There are good races and bad races for any rider. He is going to have some races where he feels much more confident than others. The big deciding factors are tyres, motor cycle, lap times – they all contribute to his willingness to go past the 100 per cent mark. So there have been races where we honestly felt that we had no advantages and there are races where we have felt we were ahead. Obviously it all plays a big part in how the rider feels.'

With a lead of just six-and-a-half points (assuming that the FIM continued to discount the third leg at Spa), Rainey could not afford to be

Right: **From the start Pons leads Wimmer and Roth on the completely resurfaced Anderstorp circuit.**

Malcolm Bryan

Martinez heads Spaan and Takada in a great 125 battle.

Malcolm Bryan

second to Lawson for the last three races. Roberts said that they were changing their strategy after a team meeting following the British Grand Prix. 'We are going out to race for it. We have all been going at it a little conservatively up to this point, but now we are going to have to push it.'

Much of the practice was wet, and a wet race would have suited Rainey well, but he was quickest in the dry too. He was almost a second faster than Schwantz, with Lawson slightly slower, but the Roberts team were not making too much of practice times. The fastest times were snatched on a dry track at the beginning of the third session, before it started to rain again, and were unlikely to be a fair reflection of race times. The best thing to come out of practice, as far as Rainey was concerned, was that Lawson had very little time to sort out the Honda; Kanemoto commented that they needed at least another half-hour on a dry track to get their bike ready.

The 250 grid was no more representative, with very little dry track time. Carlos Cardus was fastest ahead of Luca Cadalora and Reinhold Roth. Cardus was also quickest in the wet, with Cadalora not far behind. The young Italian had already demonstrated his ability to ride the 500 on a wet track, finishing ninth fastest, before deciding that he would not ride the bigger bike in the race. 'I have had too little time to set the 500 up to ride it well here. I always said that the 250 was my priority and I want to concentrate on that.'

Despite his impressive outings on the 500, Cadalora was still of the opinion that he would probably ride a 250 again in 1990 and had had serious talks with Michel Metreux about joining the Lucky Strike Honda team as a partner to Jacques Cornu.

125 cc

If Wayne Rainey was feeling the pressure of Lawson closing in on his points lead, Ezio Gianola was under the crushing weight of a two-man attack in the 125 class. After the German Grand Prix he had held a 21-point lead over Alex Criville, with Hans Spaan a further 22 points behind. Since then things had been going wrong for the Italian and, with just two races to go, the Spanish youngster was just two points behind and the Dutchman ten.

Gianola finally blew it in Sweden, outbraking himself at the end of the straight on lap three while locked in battle with Spaan, Criville, Koji Takada and Jorge Martinez. The four of them continued their battle a little way ahead of Fausto Gresini, who was having to work hard to hold fifth place from Stefan Prein and Allan Scott. The dice for the lead was desperate and it was not until halfway through the 23 laps that the decisive move was made. Then, between laps 11 and 12, Criville made the break. Martinez was second at that point but could not match his fellow-countryman's effort.

'My bike was not as good as the Honda out of the slow corners,' said Criville later. 'I could not let the battle go to the end so I had to get clear and far enough in front so that they could not pick up my slipstream. Once I got away I could hold the distance.'

Martinez, Spaan and Takada continued their fight while Prein and Gresini contested fifth, having dropped Scott who was not happy with the way his bike was running. It had broken a reed petal in the morning warm-up.

Over the last four laps the fight between Spaan and Takada proved too much for Martinez, who lost ground slightly. Spaan finally had just enough speed to get in front of Takada when it mattered, even though the Japanese had ridden the wheels off his Honda and repeatedly attacked the Dutchman round the outside of Sweden's looping right-handers.

500 cc

With Rainey, Lawson and Schwantz right together from the start the scene was set for another classic battle. Kevin Magee was fourth ahead of Christian Sarron and Pier Francesco Chili. Rainey did his initial disappearing trick over the early laps and by lap six was ahead by three seconds. Lawson waited for the front tyre to warm and Schwantz sat on his tail, happy to watch and not wanting to slow Lawson down by getting in front.

'There was no point in passing Eddie,' said Schwantz later. 'He knows his way round here

and I could pick up his lines. This track is very hard on front tyres and I could see that Eddie was working at saving his, braking more in a straight line, not running in deep on the brakes.'

Rainey's early advantage did not concern either of his two rivals unduly and, from lap eight, the gap began to close again. The Lucky Strike rider was still lapping in the mid-32-second bracket but Lawson and Schwantz were going slightly quicker. The fastest man on the circuit, though, was Christian Sarron. Only the Frenchman broke the 32-second barrier as he closed on Schwantz and Lawson, who in turn were catching Rainey.

Lap 13 should have seen all four in a pack – but suddenly there was no Schwantz. He toured into the pits to retire the Suzuki, saying that it had started to vibrate badly. The engine had pulled a piston apart in Holland before the rod broke and cut the engine in half. This time Schwantz stopped before the destruction became so complete.

Lawson took the lead on lap 16 but still had Rainey and Sarron looking over his shoulder. Sarron might have passed Rainey but was not keen to get involved in the championship struggle. 'The bike was perfect today,' he commented later. 'The tyres and the suspension were better than I have ever had and the engine was fast. I have never leaned over so far as I did today, my elbow was in the grass. I could have got past Rainey but I did not want to get in the middle. If I could have got past both of them in one go I would have but that was not really possible so I stayed behind.'

Over the last five laps Sarron's Yamaha started to misfire and he dropped back slightly. Rainey had looked capable of passing Lawson at the tight left-hander before the pit straight: he was quicker than the World Champion round the long, slightly banked right-hander leading to it, and looked at diving up the inside a couple of times. He might have favoured a test of braking at the end of the back straight where there would have been just two corners to go for the end of the lap, but no matter how he tried he could not get out of the preceding corner and onto the back straight hard enough to gain from the Honda's slipstream. He needed that if he was to pull out at the end of the straight and pass on the brakes.

Rainey, however, was working on another plan, encouraged by his observation of the way Lawson's bike was working. 'I felt his front tyre was going off, that is what I thought. I thought, good, I'll just keep pushing and find a place to go past. Into the long right before the pit straight he was running wide going in and I could catch him there coming around the outside and get up the inside into the next tight left. I had a look and it seemed possible. So I thought that would be a good place to pass him on the last lap.

Left: **Arcs of spin from Lawson, Rainey and Sarron. Schwantz has already dropped out with engine failure and it was from this distance that Sarron was trying to weigh up whether or not he could pass both men in front in one go.**

Haslam in front of Chili – but with his hand injury he could not do justice to his ability.

'I would slow him down in the left, take him out wide and squirt it down to the next right. I could then square that off and he would have to pass me on the outside down the back straight and I could outbrake him at the end because I was getting in a little better. I had to be in front of him going onto the back straight because he was getting a better drive there and I was trying different lines but not being able to hold him.

'I was watching my pit boards that were going L9, L8, L7, L6, then they started going L4.5, L3.5, L2.5. I didn't realise what they were showing. I wondered if it was the gap to Christian behind. (In fact the team were showing half-laps to go as the pit and signalling station is half a lap from the finish at Anderstorp.) They had forgotten to tell me that is what they were going to do, they thought of it just as I was riding out to the line.

'As it got to L2.5 I was thinking, "Is this the lap I have got to make the move on, or the next one?" Going into the corner that is what I was thinking about, not concentrating on what I was doing.

'I highsided in the middle of the corner, not coming out. It had gone away and come back before I thought, "I'm crashing". I screwed up.'

The first that Lawson knew about Rainey's disappearance was a lap later, when his sign board said WR OUT. From that point he only had a lap and a half to go to take the championship lead, so he throttled back and coasted. Sarron was far enough back to pose no threat.

After the race Lawson explained that while the bike ran well he did not feel it was that much faster than Rainey's; it was the performance of his rear tyre that had given him the advantage. 'It was the tyre, I think, that won the race for me,' he explained. 'The heat was on right from the start of the race and I had no strategy for the end of the race. There isn't much you can do with a strategy when the board keeps saying plus zero. I think it would have been pretty exciting on the last lap – it could well have come down to the last couple of corners. I was just hoping it didn't turn out like '83, when Freddie and Kenny both went off the track. I don't know if I had a horsepower advantage but, if I did, it wasn't much because I couldn't get away.'

Wayne Gardner was a comfortable third, happy to be back on the rostrum but not claiming that it was a return to anything like his best form. 'I feel better and now I have got to do more work on the bike, get it handling better.'

Niall Mackenzie was fourth, held back early on by the front tyre which took time to warm up. 'I got away fine but I knew the front tyre would not work well early on and I got passed by everyone on the first lap. I just had to wait until it warmed up and then I started to overtake a few people. I also smacked my knee on a kerb. I couldn't see the beginning of the kerb because it was hidden by grass. It hurt so much that I couldn't concentrate for a couple of laps. I lost ground and, by that time, the leaders were too far ahead.'

Mackenzie caught and passed Magee on lap 22. The Australian was having his own tyre problems: the rear tyre turned on its rim and from

Malcolm Bryan

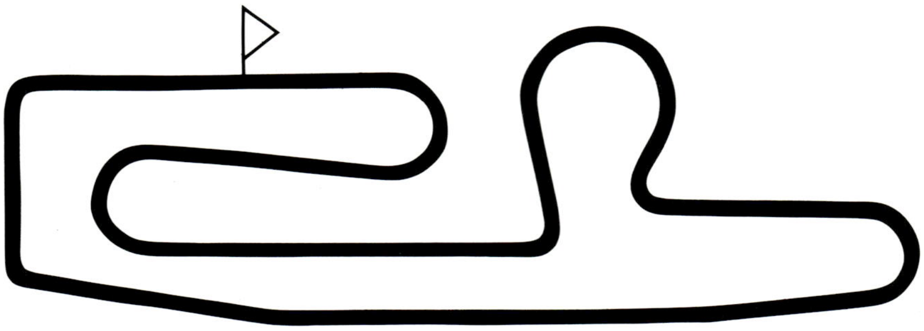

Alain Michel and Jean-Marc Fresc had their best race for some time, taking second place ahead of Webster and Hewitt.

Malcolm Bryan

then on it vibrated so badly he could not run at full speed.

Haslam had to contend with the hand trouble that still lingered from Spa, and a vicious slide while he was chasing Mackenzie early on wrenched it again. After that he had to battle with Pier Francesco Chili and Adrien Morillas for sixth, but got the better of them on the last lap.

250 cc

Martin Wimmer led the first-lap charge but, on lap two, Toshihiko Honma took over. Then it was time for Cardus to hit the front, and he tried to establish himself as Roth moved in behind. Honma was third ahead of Wimmer, Pons and Cornu. From lap six Cardus and Roth started to get away from Honma and Wimmer.

Pons saw that happening, slipped past Honma and Wimmer into third and, in just two laps, he'd caught the leading duo. Cornu matched his move a few laps later. Honma headed the fourth-place group from Helmut Bradl, Wimmer, Masahiro Shimizu, Didier de Radiguès and Luca Cadalora.

The two groups were equally close, with the leading four being perhaps slightly more reserved. Pons took the lead from Roth on lap 12 and Cardus moved into second. Bradl continued to head the fourth-place pack but could not shake off Shimizu and the rest.

There was another lead change on lap 16 when Roth hit the front but he could not get away and traded places with Pons several times. On the last lap Pons stole just enough of an advantage to stop Roth trying any late braking chances.

'Sito was getting more drive than I was out of the rear tyre,' Roth said later, sitting on his mountain bike in the paddock. As he was sitting there, Pons's mechanics were wheeling the Campsa Honda back to the truck. The German stopped them for a look at the rear tyre and the compound number, then shook his head. 'That is much softer than the tyre I used. I never would have believed that would last the distance.'

Cornu was third, so Cardus missed out on a rostrum place and blamed it on the slothfulness of his Repsol Honda. Bradl was still heading the fifth-place group on the last lap but, under increasing pressure from Cadalora, crashed on the last lap.

Cadalora missed him, as did Honma, who had de Radiguès on his tail and looking for a way past. 'I saw the bike and thought he might be lying in the road but I could not see because of Honma,' explained de Radiguès. 'I slowed just in case and there he was. It wasn't worth taking the chance but it cost me the opportunity to pass Honma.'

Sidecars

The battle between Rolf Biland and Alain Michel was the high point of the Frenchman's season, even though he and Jean-Marc Fresc eventually finished second by just over half a second. 'It was a good feeling to be racing for the lead with Rolf. You know that he will always ride hard, and I enjoyed every minute of it. People might ask why I didn't overtake him on the last lap. That's easy to say but it is not so easy to do and there was just no way past.'

Biland thought he had blown it on the last lap. 'I was having a slight problem with the gear-change and it jumped out of gear. For a moment we lost drive and I thought that Alain might get by, but we got going again,' said Biland, who recorded his fifty-fifth Grand Prix win.

Only slightly astern of the leading outfits were Webster and Hewitt, who were well ahead of Egbert Streuer and Geral de Haas, the only pair that could catch them in the championship. 'The hardest part was trying to do some mental arithmetic while we were going round,' said Steve Webster. 'I knew that third was good enough to put Rolf out of the hunt, but just finishing in front of Egbert was not sufficient, so we still have to finish in Czecho. I didn't have any troubles in the race at all. The only problems were Biland and Michel!'

Swedish TT, 13 August/statistics
Anderstorp Circuit, 2.505-mile/4.031-km circuit

500 cc

30 laps, 75.15 miles/120.93 km

Place	Rider	Nat.	Machine	Laps	Time & speed	Practice time	Grid
1	Eddie Lawson	USA	Honda	30	46m 31.95s 96.889 mph/ 155.929 km/h	1m 33.44s	3
2	Christian Sarron	F	Yamaha	30	46m 37.60s	1m 33.93s	4
3	Wayne Gardner	AUS	Honda	30	46m 56.98s	1m 39.05s	14
4	Niall Mackenzie	GB	Yamaha	30	47m 03.58s	1m 34.20s	6
5	Kevin Magee	AUS	Yamaha	30	47m 23.50s	1m 34.08s	5
6	Ron Haslam	GB	Suzuki	30	47m 27.40s	1m 34.60s	8
7	Pier Francesco Chili	I	Honda	30	47m 27.61s	1m 34.48s	7
8	Adrien Morillas	F	Honda	30	47m 27.79s	1m 36.48s	12
9	Rob McElnea	GB	Honda	30	48m 05.45s	1m 35.45s	10
10	Tadahiko Taira	J	Yamaha	29	46m 45.13s	1m 36.15s	11
11	Alessandro Valesi	I	Yamaha	29	47m 46.49s	1m 39.28s	15
12	Simon Buckmaster	GB	Honda	29	48m 05.85s	1m 42.08s	21
13	Fabio Biliotti	I	Honda	28	46m 34.70s	1m 40.55s	19
14	Bruno Kneubühler	CH	Honda	28	46m 43.16s	1m 45.78s	26
15	Juan Lopez Mella	E	Honda	28	46m 56.81s	1m 40.48s	18
16	Niggi Schmassman	CH	Honda	28	47m 17.73s	1m 41.57s	20
17	Timo Paavilainen	SF	Suzuki	28	47m 56.43s	1m 46.30s	27
	Wayne Rainey	USA	Yamaha	27	DNF	1m 32.49s	1
	Peter Linden	S	Honda	19	DNF	1m 38.92s	13
	Kevin Schwantz	USA	Suzuki	12	DNF	1m 33.39s	2
	Torbjorn Bastiansen	N	Suzuki	4	DNF	1m 44.78s	25
	Alan Carter	GB	Honda	1	DNF	1m 42.60s	22
	Andreas Leuthe	LUX	Librenti	1	DNF	1m 43.61s	24
	Rachel Nicotte	F	Honda	0	DNF	1m 40.12s	17
	Luca Cadalora	I	Yamaha		DNS	1m 35.19s	9
	Marco Gentile	CH	Fior		DNS	1m 39.81s	16
	Josef Doppler	A	Honda		DNS	1m 43.00s	23
	Fernando Gonzalez	E	Honda		DNQ	1m 46.43s	
	Ake Dahli	S	Honda		DNQ	1m 47.14s	
	Ian Pratt	GB	Suzuki		DNQ	1m 49.57s	

Fastest lap: Sarron, 1m 31.99s, 98.021 mph/157.751 km/h (record).
Previous record: Eddie Lawson, USA (Yamaha), 1m 34.43s, 95.49 mph/153.676 km/h (1988).

World Championship: 1 Lawson, 194; **2** Rainey, 180.5; **3** Sarron, C., 144.5; **4** Schwantz, 122.5; **5** Magee, 119.5; **6** Chili, 111; **7** Mackenzie, 86; **8** Doohan, 68; **9** Haslam, 67; **10** Gardner, 58; **11** McElnea, 44.5; **12** Buckmaster, 41.5; **13** Sarron, D., 39; **14** Valesi, 35; **15** Spencer, 33.5; **16** Gentile, 33; **17** Taira, 32; **18** Mamola, 23; **19** Rudroff, 18; **20** Fujiwara, 17; **21** Morillas, 14; **22** Shobert, 12; **23** Doppler, 11; **24** Meyer, 10; **25** Balbi, 9; **26** Broccoli, Cadalora, Gonzalez and Schmassman, 8; **30** Dowson and Leuthe, 7; **32** Biliotti, Itoh and Kneubühler, 6; **35** Kocinski, 5.5; **36** Gschwender and Merkel, 5; **38** Burnett and Crine, 4; **40** Lopez Mella and Yatsushiro, 3; **42** Doorakkers, 2.5; **43** Laycock, 2; **44** Machii, 1.

250 cc

25 laps, 62.63 miles/100.78 km

Place	Rider	Nat.	Machine	Laps	Time & speed	Practice time	Grid
1	Alfonso Pons	E	Honda	25	40m 37.68s 92.476 mph/ 148.825 km/h	1m 37.51s	4
2	Reinhold Roth	D	Honda	25	40m 39.33s	1m 37.16s	3
3	Jacques Cornu	CH	Honda	25	40m 39.82s	1m 37.59s	5
4	Carlos Cardus	E	Honda	25	40m 41.51s	1m 36.74s	1
5	Luca Cadalora	I	Yamaha	25	40m 47.25s	1m 36.89s	2
6	Toshihiko Honma	J	Yamaha	25	40m 50.10s	1m 38.24s	12
7	Didier de Radiguès	B	Aprilia	25	40m 50.47s	1m 38.04s	9
8	Martin Wimmer	D	Aprilia	25	41m 02.39s	1m 37.82s	8
9	Alexandre Barros	BR	Yamaha	25	41m 11.33s	1m 36.69s	29
10	Juan Garriga	E	Yamaha	25	41m 11.62s	1m 37.71s	6
11	Jochen Schmid	D	Honda	25	41m 12.13s	1m 38.46s	15
12	Wilco Zeelenberg	NL	Honda	25	41m 17.92s	1m 38.23s	11
13	Harald Eckl	D	Aprilia	25	41m 18.19s	1m 39.59s	26
14	Andreas Preining	A	Aprilia	25	41m 19.05s	1m 39.08s	18
15	Alain Bronec	F	Aprilia	25	41m 36.75s	1m 39.53s	23
16	Gary Cowan	IRL	Yamaha	25	41m 37.30s	1m 39.28s	19
17	Manfred Herweh	D	Yamaha	25	41m 45.06s	1m 39.69s	28
18	Patrick van den Goorbergh	NL	Yamaha	25	41m 45.47s	1m 39.55s	24
19	Hans Becker	D	Seel	25	41m 45.76s	1m 39.67s	27
20	Peter Linden	S	Yamaha	25	42m 00.78s	1m 39.43s	22
21	Jean Foray	F	Yamaha	24	40m 52.44s	1m 39.86s	32
22	Johan Svaerdgren	S	Yamaha	24	40m 57.57s	1m 39.98s	36
23	Alberto Rota	I	Aprilia	24	41m 04.01s	1m 39.37s	21
24	August Auinger	A	Yamaha	24	41m 13.18s	1m 39.88s	34
	Helmut Bradl	D	Honda	24	DNF	1m 37.76s	7
	Alberto Puig	E	Yamaha	21	DNF	1m 38.28s	13
	Masahiro Shimizu	J	Honda	18	DNF	1m 38.40s	14
	Bernard Hänggeli	CH	Yamaha	16	DNF	1m 39.86s	31
	Stefano Caracchi	RSM	Honda	11	DNF	1m 38.72s	17
	Daniel Amatriain	E	Honda	10	DNF	1m 39.94s	35
	Carlos Lavado	YV	Aprilia	4	DNF	1m 38.11s	10
	Fausto Ricci	I	Aprilia	2	DNF	1m 39.86s	30
	Jean-François Baldé	F	Yamaha	1	DNF	1m 40.03s	37
	Maurizio Vitali	I	Garelli	0	DNF	1m 39.33s	20
	Paolo Casoli	I	Honda	0	DNF	1m 38.47s	16
	Andy Leisner	USA	Honda		DNS	1m 39.55s	25
	Loris Reggiani	I	Honda		DNS	1m 39.88s	33
	Renzo Colleoni	I	Aprilia		DNQ	1m 40.24s	
	Virginio Ferrari	I	Gazzaniga		DNQ	1m 41.05s	
	Harri Kallio	SF	Honda		DNQ	1m 41.43s	
	Luis Lavado	YV	Yamaha		DNQ	1m 41.47s	
	Massimo Matteoni	I	Yamaha		DNQ	1m 41.55s	
	Urs Jucker	CH	Yamaha		DNQ	1m 42.13s	
	Sandy Berlin	S	Yamaha		DNQ	1m 43.63s	

Fastest lap: Pons, 1m 36.36s, 93.576 mph/150.597 km/h (record).
Previous record: Reinhold Roth, D (Honda), 1m 38.39s, 91.655 mph/147.506 km/h (1988).

World Championship: 1 Pons, 236; **2** Cornu, 165; **3** Roth, 160; **4** Cardus, 143; **5** Ruggia, 110; **6** Cadalora, 97; **7** Garriga, 84; **8** Shimizu, 82; **9** Bradl, 69; **10** Wimmer, 61; **11** de Radiguès, 48; **12** Kocinski, 40; **13** Reggiani, 37; **14** Honma and Zeelenberg, 36; **16** Schmid, 33; **17** Filice, 22; **18** Colleoni and Cowan, 21; **20** Palazzese, 19; **21** Barros, Eckl and Puig, 18; **24** Lucchi, 17; **25** Lavado, 15; **26** Amatriain, 12; **27** Bronec, 11; **28** Okada, 10; **29** Caracchi, Morillas and Shiomori, 9; **32** Ricci, 8; **33** Rota and van den Goorbergh, 6; **35** Beattie, Mitchell and Preining, 4; **38** Vitali, 2; **39** Arai, Auinger and Becker, 1.

125 cc

23 laps, 57.61 miles/92.713 km

Place	Rider	Nat.	Machine	Laps	Time & speed	Practice time	Grid
1	Alex Criville	E	Cobas	23	39m 56.09s 86.554 mph/ 139.296 km/h	1m 43.61s	1
2	Hans Spaan	NL	Honda	23	39m 58.86s	1m 44.34s	2
3	Koji Takada	J	Honda	23	39m 59.10s	1m 44.92s	7
4	Jorge Martinez	E	Derbi	23	39m 59.34s	1m 44.65s	4
5	Fausto Gresini	I	Aprilia	23	40m 27.03s	1m 45.82s	13
6	Stefan Prein	D	Honda	23	40m 27.32s	1m 44.91s	6
7	Allan Scott	USA	Honda	23	40m 42.89s	1m 44.67s	5
8	Flemming Kistrup	DK	Honda	23	40m 44.55s	1m 45.78s	12
9	Hubert Abold	D	Krauser	23	40m 48.35s	1m 45.32s	9
10	Johnny Wickström	SF	Honda	23	40m 50.25s	1m 46.79s	22
11	Dirk Raudies	D	Honda	23	40m 50.75s	1m 47.52s	32
12	Mike Leitner	A	Honda	23	40m 52.00s	1m 45.95s	14
13	Stuart Edwards	GB	ERM	23	40m 52.71s	1m 46.37s	17
14	Herri Torrontegui	E	Honda	23	40m 55.61s	1m 47.42s	30
15	Taru Rinne	SF	Honda	23	40m 59.58s	1m 46.77s	21
16	Heinz Lüthi	CH	Honda	23	41m 01.45s	1m 47.65s	33
17	Robin Milton	GB	Honda	23	41m 11.42s	1m 45.75s	11
18	Alfred Waibel	D	Honda	23	41m 11.91s	1m 47.19s	29
19	Ralf Waldmann	D	Rotax	23	41m 12.35s	1m 46.43s	18
20	Bady Hassaine	TN	Honda	23	41m 13.19s	1m 46.11s	15
21	Bruno Casanova	I	Aprilia	23	41m 13.52s	1m 46.92s	26
22	Emilio Cuppini	I	Garelli	23	41m 17.78s	1m 47.44s	31
23	Hervé Duffard	F	Honda	23	41m 18.01s	1m 47.77s	35
24	Alex Bedford	GB	EMC	23	41m 18.34s	1m 46.85s	23
25	Jukka Vainio	SF	Honda	23	41m 40.08s	1m 47.71s	34
	Manuel Hernandez	E	Honda	16	DNF	1m 47.06s	27
	Peter Ött	D	Krauser	13	DNF	1m 47.14s	28
	Robin Appleyard	GB	Honda	9	DNF	1m 46.89s	25
	Thierry Feuz	CH	Honda	9	DNF	1m 46.50s	19
	Julian Miralles	E	Derbi	6	DNF	1m 46.86s	24
	Serge Julin	B	Honda	6	DNF	1m 47.81s	36
	Hisashi Unemoto	J	Honda	4	DNF	1m 44.64s	3
	Ezio Gianola	I	Honda	2	DNF	1m 45.13s	8
	Adolf Stadler	D	Honda	2	DNF	1m 45.74s	10
	Doriano Romboni	I	Honda	0	DNF	1m 46.66s	20
	Corrado Catalano	I	Rotax		DNS	1m 46.22s	16
	Luis Reyes	E	Honda		DNQ	1m 47.81s	
	Domenico Brigaglia	I	Garelli		DNQ	1m 47.87s	
	Håkan Olsson	S	Rotax		DNQ	1m 48.32s	
	Klaus Kindle	FL	Honda		DNQ	1m 48.41s	
	Othmar Schuler	CH	Honda		DNQ	1m 48.71s	
	Kazuya Yamada	J	Honda		DNQ	1m 48.82s	
	Rafael Roses	E	Cobas		DNQ	1m 48.85s	
	Gastone Grassetti	I	Honda		DNQ	1m 49.45s	
	Stefan Dörflinger	CH	Aprilia		DNQ	1m 50.04s	

Fastest lap: Criville, 1m 42.77s, 87.74 mph/141.204 km/h (record).
Previous record: Fausto Gresini, I (Garelli), 1m 43.79s, 86.88 mph/139.817 km/h (1987).

World Championship: 1 Criville, 146; **2** Spaan, 135; **3** Gianola, 128; **4** Gresini, 100; **5** Unemoto, 93; **6** Miralles and Takada, 90; **8** Prein, 77; **9** Martinez, 59; **10** Stadler, 47; **11** Milton and Scott, 46; **13** Reyes, 35; **14** Brigaglia, 34; **15** Raudies, 26; **16** Pietroniro, 22; **17** Casanova and Romboni, 20; **19** Rinne, 19; **20** Kistrup and Waibel, A., 18; **22** Feuz, 15; **23** Appleyard, Hirose and Torrontegui, 13; **26** Selini and Yoshida, 11; **28** Catalano, Shima and Wickström, 10; **31** Fujiwara, 9; **32** Abold and Yamashita, 8; **34** Fujiyama, 7; **35** Waibel, G. and Yamada, 6; **37** Leitner, 4; **38** Debbia, Edwards, Jeandat and Saunders, 3; **42** Fischer and Hassaine, 2; **44** Bedford and Duffard, 1.

Sidecars

23 laps, 57.61 miles/92.713 km

Place	Driver & passenger	Nat.	Machine	Laps	Time & speed	Practice time	Grid
1	Rolf Biland/ Kurt Waltisperg	CH CH	LCR- Krauser	23	37m 52.90s 91.246 mph/ 146.846 km/h	1m 38.93s	2
2	Alain Michel/ Jean-Marc Fresc	F F	LCR- Krauser	23	37m 53.48s	1m 39.29s	3
3	Steve Webster/ Tony Hewitt	GB GB	LCR- Krauser	23	37m 54.69s	1m 38.43s	1
4	Egbert Streuer/ Geral de Haas	NL NL	LCR- Yamaha	23	38m 08.92s	1m 44.90s	18
5	Steve Abbott/ Shaun Smith	GB GB	Windle- Yamaha	23	38m 47.77s	1m 40.15s	5
6	Barry Brindley/ Grahame Rose	GB GB	Fowler- Yamaha	23	38m 53.50s	1m 41.10s	6
7	Markus Egloff/ Urs Egloff	CH CH	Yamaha	23	38m 54.16s	1m 40.12s	4
8	Rolf Steinhausen/ Bruno Hiller	D D	Schuh	23	39m 04.97s	1m 41.28s	7
9	Yoshisada Kumagaya/ Phil Coombes	J GB	Windle- KS	23	39m 08.46s	1m 42.65s	9
10	Fritz Stölzle/ Hubert Stölzle	D D	LCR- Krauser	23	39m 13.26s	1m 42.58s	8
11	Bernd Scherer/ Thomas Schröder	D D	BSR- Krauser	23	39m 19.14s	1m 43.16s	13
12	René Progin/ Yves Hunziker	CH CH	LCR- Krauser	23	39m 23.97s	1m 43.33s	14
13	Ivan Nigrowsky/ Jacques Corbier	F F	LCR- JPX	23	39m 25.32s	1m 42.90s	11
14	Tony Wyssen/ Kilian Wyssen	CH CH	LCR- Krauser	23	39m 25.48s	1m 43.09s	12
15	Wolfgang Stropek/ Steve Campbell	A GB	Mibag- Krauser	22	37m 56.26s	1m 43.93s	15
16	Gary Thomas/ Eckhart Rösinger	GB D	LCR	22	37m 57.16s	1m 44.91s	19
17	Billy Gällros/ Julian Tailford	S GB	Yamaha	22	38m 58.33s	1m 44.35s	17
	Theo van Kempen/ Simon Birchall	NL GB	LCR- Yamaha	13	DNF	1m 42.87s	10
	Derek Jones/ Peter Brown	GB GB	LCR- Yamaha	5	DNF	1m 45.07s	20
	Alfred Zurbrügg/ Martin Zurbrügg	CH CH	LCR- Yamaha	1	DNF	1m 44.15s	16

Fastest lap: Michel, 1m 37.51s, 92.473 mph/148.821 km/h (record).
Previous record: Rolf Biland/Kurt Waltisperg, CH/CH (LCR-Krauser), 1m 38.66s, 91.395 mph/ 147.087 km/h (1988).

World Championship: 1 Webster, 130; **2** Streuer, 116; **3** Biland, 105; **4** Michel, 96; **5** Stölzle, 63; **6** Kumano, 58; **7** Brindley and Egloff, 56; **9** Steinhausen, 50; **10** Jones, 37; **11** Abbott, 35; **12** Kumagaya and van Kempen, 32; **14** Scherer, 31; **15** Progin, 27; **16** Wyssen, 22; **17** Zurbrügg, 21; **18** Nigrowsky, 18; **19** Gällros, 14; **20** Smith, 10; **21** Stropek, 9; **22** Baker, 8; **23** Howles, 6; **24** Gardner, 5; **25** Drew, 4; **26** Stirrat, 3; **27** Hardwick and Thomas, 2.

WORLD CHAMPIONSHIP · ROUND 14

CZECHOSLOVAK GRAND PRIX

Malcolm Bryan

There were riots in Prague early in the week as Czechoslovakia remembered the twenty-first anniversary of the invasion of Warsaw Pact troops. The Czechs who have made friends with the Grand Prix population over the years commented that things were improving for them under *perestroika*, not so much in financial terms but by way of freedoms. The East Germans who make the journey to Brno in their tens of thousands were less hopeful about their future: the most they could do was enjoy the increased liberalism of Czechoslovakia for a few days during the Grand Prix.

But the best part of the weekend for the East Germans was Reinhold Roth's victory in the 250 race, and the opportunity to sing their old national anthem. The low point perhaps was Peter Öttl's last-lap crash, which robbed him of the chance to win the 80 cc World Championship.

That fall raised gasps and groans from the crowd but, in the press room, the Spanish corps watching on television were leaping in the air and screaming as though their national team had just scored a World Cup-winning goal. It may not have been an exhibition of sportsmanship, but the size of the Spanish press and their excitement were an indication of the high level of interest in Grand Prix racing within Spain. News of Herreros's 80 cc World Championship win, and that of Alex Criville on the 125, filled the front pages of both Spain's biggest dailies.

Angel Nieto was the first Spanish road racer to achieve true superstar status but it has been Sito Pons who has spearheaded the move out of the smallest classes and into the big league. Spain can now claim to have as great an influence on the world championships as the USA. And Pons has not done it alone by any means, for Juan Garriga and Carlos Cardus aided Spain's strength in the 250 class, while Jorge Martinez, Manuel Herreros, Alex Criville, Herri Torrontegui and Julian Miralles made sure they are still the strongest force on the smaller machines. The Spaniards won the 80 cc, 125 cc and 250 cc World Championships in 1988 as well as in '89.

Pons is Spain's spokesman as far as the world at large is concerned. Not only has he dominated the 250 class for two years but he also speaks excellent English and is prepared to work, apparently tirelessly, to promote the cause of motor cycle racing in general and Sito Pons in particular.

Sito is a remarkable character, as he controls every aspect of his racing programme. He is certainly his own PR man, talking with an open professionalism that comes across as friendliness. He organises his own sponsorship, making personal deals and arrangements with Campsa and Coca-Cola, and has obviously done the job very well. He manages his own team, at least to the point of hiring all the people and setting up the structure during the winter so that, he says, once the season starts he can concentrate on riding the bike and not worry about the operation of the team. In the winter he also manages to find time to work in his father's business as an architect.

'I enjoy doing everything,' says Pons. 'I seem to have that sort of mind, so that I can concentrate on one thing at a time. I believe that it is important to concentrate entirely on what you are doing. I do not think that I am clever enough to think about two things at the same time. You have to concentrate completely so that you make the right decisions when you are negotiating a business deal. You also have to remain cool and let your mind control what goes on, not your heart. The same is true of racing. If you don't, you make a difficult thing impossible.'

In Czechoslovakia Pons was in the process of finalising his plans for a switch to the 500 class. Typically, he was not rushing into it, blind with passion, and, while he wanted to ride a 500, would only do so if he could be certain of having the use of the right machines and tyres. 'I have no illusions about the 500 class. I know that it will not be easy and without the right equipment, bikes and tyres it will be impossible. I want to ride a 500 but I want to have the same equipment as Lawson and Gardner. I want to win races and I cannot do that without the same material.'

While negotiating the right situation for his move to the 500 class Pons continued to act as riders' representative and made some telling comments on the achievements of the previous winter. 'We had to get four tracks improved, Salzburg, Laguna Seca, Spa and Anderstorp. All these changes the riders got done, no one else. Now there is a lot of cohesion between the riders. We work together. That is what makes it possible for me to go to a track and say, "If you don't do this, we cannot race". I know that the other riders will back me. Without that it would be impossible. I have help from some of the other riders and if anyone else wants to take the job I would be happy to let them but I think that it is important and at the moment I can do it.

'It is not just for the riders that we do this. It is for the sport. It improves things for everybody, the journalists, sponsors, everyone who is interested in motor cycling. The priority is safety, of course: this is important because if someone crashes and gets hurt unnecessarily then it makes our sport look bad to the people outside and the sponsors don't want to be involved. We lose our prestige in this way.

'As for running my own team, I am very fortunate because I have been able to get my own sponsors since 1986, thanks to the fact that racing is the second or third most popular sport in Spain. This has meant that the sponsors are willing to put in the big budget and promotion that we need to run a first-class team. There is a great deal of publicity in Spain and that also helps us get good bikes. The sport is very strong and we have more and more good riders coming up through the ranks and it just gets stronger and stronger.

'I like talking to sponsors and doing negotiations. Of course, I have a lot of people working with me on these things but it is my character to enjoy being involved in the business side of things. I like to control and oversee all that is going on with my team.'

Pons was training as an architect when he decided that he would turn his attention to racing full time. 'I realised that I could not do both properly. I was only going to have one chance to make it as a professional racer but I could go back to architecture later.'

Perhaps because he could so obviously make a living at other things one wonders why Pons is so committed to racing. 'I could stop racing now and still make enough money in architecture. But racing still has something special for me. The competition is so complex. It is not like running, where one guy is simply faster than the other. In our sport it depends on so many things and that makes it even more interesting. It is the same in 500 and 250. Of course I think I am the best but then so do the other riders – Cardus, Cadalora, Schwantz, Lawson, they all think they are the best. If I didn't think I could beat the other riders when I go to 500 for sure I wouldn't be going. I wouldn't waste my time. I know it is difficult and I must work a lot. I think I can beat them in the

Shimizu looks over his shoulder to see what threat there is from behind, before attacking Roth on the last lap.

future. I am the type of man that doesn't like to spend my time for no reason. If I go to 500 it is because I think I can do the best for my career and the sport.'

Having won the Swedish Grand Prix, even after clinching the championship, Pons was obviously going to be one of the race favourites in Czechoslovakia and he qualified third fastest. Second quickest was Jacques Cornu, with Reinhold Roth on pole. The German ace has always said that practice times are relatively unimportant but, for the second half of the season, he was making more of an attempt to gear himself up and this time took a rare pole position, only the second of his Grand Prix career. 'The last time was at the German Grand Prix at Hockenheim in '87. It is not something that I try for. I just ride round in practice trying to get the best out of the machine. It happens that this time that has put me in pole position. It is our team that is fastest. Helmut (Bradl) and I have been fastest all the time.

'I think that it will be possible to do 2m 08s laps in the race, but only if it is cool. Otherwise it will be about 2m 09s laps. It would be good if I was doing the eights and everyone else the nines,' concluded Roth, one of the pleasantest people you could hope to meet, with his usual broad grin.

Once again Yamaha were not putting on much of a show. Jean-Philippe Ruggia was making a welcome return, having recovered from his British Grand Prix hip injury, and was all set to ride the 500 Gauloises Blondes Yamaha as well as the 250. Then he crashed the smaller machine in the first session, breaking his forearm.

Things were looking increasingly dismal but, in the final session, Cadalora sorted out some handling problems and jumped up the table. 'Ohlins checked the rear shock and that and a new rear tyre got rid of the chattering – but the faster lap just came from riding right on the limit. I don't know how fast I will be able to go in the race, because the Hondas are just faster on every straight and, if they get in the way at the corners, there is not much I can do.'

The Italian had decided against racing the 500 Marlboro Yamaha again and had turned down an offer from Agostini to race the 500 in 1990. He preferred to go for the 250 championship again but was intent on riding a Honda, having given up on Yamaha as being uncompetitive. He had an offer from the Lucky Strike Honda team to join Jacques Cornu but was also part of the incredible Rothmans – Cabin – HRC – Kanemoto – Lawson – Gardner *mélange* as a possible team-mate for Lawson in the Kanemoto team, to be painted in either Cabin or Rothmans colours.

1
DUCADOS
CEPSA
DERBI
30
ATOMIC
PICHLER
KRAUSER
MICHELIN

3
HONDA

Left: **Jorge Martinez chases Peter Öttl. The Spaniard did all he could to help his Derbi team-mate, Manuel Herreros, take the 80 cc title.**

Below left: **The battle for the 125 World Championship: Spaan leads Criville, Gianola, Takada and Unemoto.**

Kanemoto was looking for a second rider. 'Eddie is not going to retire tomorrow, but we have thought about another rider so that there is someone to take over when he decides to stop. We could have another rider on a 500 but a second rider always feels that he is getting second machinery or attention, even if everything is exactly the same. It is probably best to have a second rider on a 250, at least for the first year, and then he can learn. Eddie would be able to help him make the change to a 500 when it is the right time.'

Garriga had also had enough of not succeeding with the 250 Yamaha and was on the point of deciding either to swap to the 500 class or to a 250 Honda – so Yamaha would be short of 250 competitors. That worked well with Kenny Roberts's plan to have John Kocinski ride a lone and very special 250 factory Yamaha. Unfortunately they needed a second sponsor for this effort and it was proving very hard to find one. Roberts was facing a situation where he would be forced to let Magee leave the team and run both Kocinski and Rainey on 500s because that was the only combination he could finance.

More pressing for Roberts was the question of winning the current World 500 cc Championship. Rainey was not having an easy time of it. If losing the championship lead in Sweden was disastrous, then practice at Brno did nothing to make the team optimistic about turning the situation around with just two races to go. Rainey was not even the quickest Yamaha rider. He was sitting fourth on the grid, behind Christian Sarron, with Kevin Schwantz on pole for the ninth time. Eddie Lawson was second quickest, a second and a half faster than Rainey.

Lawson did not need any help from Rothmans Honda team-mate Wayne Gardner, which was just as well as the ex-champion had crashed in the first timed session and did not make the race. He practised in the second session but was in considerable pain, having traumatised the leg break without rebreaking the bone. Dr Costa advised him not to ride, as he was not fighting for the World Championship.

Rainey said that, for the first time in his career, he was hoping for a wet race as his only chance of being competitive. It would rain on Sunday – but two-and-a-half hours too late.

80 cc

Herri Torrontegui won his second race of the season– he had also won the first – but, thanks to his flat battery in Yugoslavia, was not in the running for the last 80 cc world title. The fact that he was quickly beyond striking range at the beginning of the race centred interest on Peter Öttl and Manuel Herreros, who were tied on points, and Stefan Dörflinger, who was six points behind them. Dörflinger was on pole once more but, yet again, made a disastrous start and was down in fourteenth place at the end of lap one.

That put all the title interest in the fight between Öttl and Herreros, because the one who finished in front would be champion. Öttl was seventh at the end of lap one but it did not take him long to get among the factory Derbis of Herreros and surrendering World Champion, Aspar Martinez.

Battle was soon joined as Martinez guarded Herreros's tail. Öttl took two more laps to get past Jörg Seel and into fourth place, but he had known full well, before the start of the race, that Aspar would play the team game and try to help Herreros as much as possible. It takes a skilled rider to do that but who could doubt Aspar's ability?

'He kept himself in front of me as much as possible,' said Öttl later. 'He would ride slow in the middle of the corners and accelerate out so that Herreros could get away.'

Even working together, the Derbi men had their work cut out and could not stop Öttl getting up to second. He could not get clear of the Derbis, though, and had to resign himself to making it a last-lap effort. 'I got in front on the last lap but then both wheels slid away together and there was nothing I could do to save it,' said the disappointed German, who was unhurt.

Herreros crossed the line second with Martinez on his tail. Dörflinger had got in front of Seel but lost out on the run to the line, even though both were given the same finish time. Eleven points for fifth was enough to lift Dörflinger to second place in the championship, even though neither he nor Herreros had won a single race. Öttl had scored three wins and a third, with two crashes, when he tangled with Torrontegui in Italy and then overstepped the limit at Brno.

The '80 cc forever' supporters had had a race to promote their cause, however futile their protests. It had been an exciting battle with a full field and no one was lapped. The same could not be said of the 500 race.

125 cc

Sixth place would have been good enough to secure the championship for Alex Criville, even if Hans Spaan was to win his fifth race of the twelve-round season. The Dutchman started well enough and jumped into a slight lead over Gianola, Criville, Unemoto, Martinez, Prein, Scott and Takada but could not extend his advantage. He only just kept in front of the other seven as the group pulled away from the rest of the field.

Criville might have wanted a quiet race, and accepted third or fourth behind Spaan. But with a pack of eight men trading places several times at every corner there was going to be no peace anywhere near where he needed to finish to make certain of his championship. So, on lap eight, Criville jumped from third into the lead, the only place where he was going to have clear space around him. After three laps he was over three seconds in front of Stefan Prein, who was heading the second-place group.

Koji Takada had been second fastest to Criville in practice and by lap 11 had worked his way into second. From there he broke away from the group and started to close on Criville, getting to within two seconds of the Spaniard, but then his exhaust pipe split and he lost power. He faded rapidly and eventually finished seventh, with just the slight compensation of recording the fastest lap. Unfortunately that left him sixth in the championship, two places behind fellow-Japanese and arch-rival Unemoto, who crossed the line fifth at Brno.

Criville completed the race without further threat, while Hans Spaan just managed to get the better of Stefan Prein for second, and second overall in the championship. They were well ahead of the fourth-place battle between Martinez, Unemoto and Gianola: that went down to the line.

250 cc

With Pons already champion by a mile the points interest lay in the battle between Cornu and Roth for second. There was every reason to expect Pons to feature in the race, though, as he had still taken the win in Sweden.

Cornu made another of his excellent starts but had to overtake Daniel Amatriain, who was leading a Grand Prix for the first time. The 23-year-old from Barcelona led for half a lap and then regressed steadily to finish fourteenth.

In three laps the leading group had started to sort itself out. Cornu was still in front with Roth on his tail and just ahead of Pons. Shimizu had worked his way into fourth and was soon in the middle of the leading group as Pons took the lead on lap six. Then it was Roth's turn to lead, but they were not pulling away from the field.

The Yamahas were well back, having both contrived to make poor starts. However, Garriga and Cadalora steamed through the field together and by lap eight they were eighth and ninth, and only just over five seconds behind Roth. They cut almost a second off that on the next lap but were then slowed while trying to pass Cardus, who held sixth behind Bradl. They never got the gap to under four seconds and they never progressed past sixth, even though Garriga recorded the fastest lap of the race on lap ten.

Bradl could not quite catch the leading quartet either and it was down to them to sort out the rostrum positions. Roth's lead was never more than a few yards and it was Shimizu who tailed him closest, with Cornu third and Pons fourth. Later the World Champion complained he had chosen the wrong tyre.

On the last lap Shimizu stole the lead – which surprised the German. 'I didn't even know it was him behind, I kept expecting Jacques to come past.' Roth rode round the outside of Shimizu at the last corner and cut in so tightly that the pair touched. The German was ahead for his second win of the season, and with Cornu crossing the line third, the pair were tied on points at the end of the day.

Pons was fourth and Bradl only just held off Cadalora on the run in to the line. Garriga was a little further back, complaining that his rear tyre did not match Cadalora's for drive and he had lost his rear brake over the last few laps. Carlos Lavado had a good run to ninth, making him the best privateer and demonstrating that he can still do the job. Alexandre Barros was tenth, looking as impressive as he had done at Anderstorp.

Rothmans

Left: **Gardner's year did not get any better in Czechoslovakia.**

Niall Mackenzie *(below)* **suffered from front tyre difficulties once more, having to choose a hard front that took too long to warm up.**

Malcolm Bryan

500 cc

Wayne Rainey went into the race knowing that he was very much up against it. He did what he could, leading from the start. In most races he had been able to open up a lead over the first few laps while the Michelin riders waited for their tyres to reach optimum operating temperature. This time there was no such advantage to be gained, and on lap two Lawson and Schwantz were sitting on his tail.

Schwantz went from third to first on lap three. At the same time Christian Sarron was closing on the leading trio, leaving Magee fifth and soon to come under pressure from Haslam. Lawson got past Rainey without any apparent difficulty and then took Schwantz. On lap five Rainey had one last fling and got past Schwantz again, but the Dunlops were just not up to the task at Brno. Soon the Lucky Strike rider was back to third and having to press on to keep in front of Sarron.

Schwantz had only Lawson ahead of him and caught up quickly – it looked almost casual, but the Texan would say later that it was hard work. A back-marker gave Schwantz a little assistance and by lap 11 he was in front.

Sarron had a spell in third, but if he had been playing a waiting game, hoping that his fellow-Yamaha rider might still get on terms with Lawson, then he had waited too long. The Frenchman was then too far behind Lawson to make any impression and, after trying for five laps, he settled back behind Rainey.

Up front Schwantz strolled away from Lawson. If the Californian could have done anything about it, he would have: a win, with Rainey fourth, would have wrapped up the championship there and then. But it was down to the last race in Brazil.

The fifth-place battle was more entertaining, for Haslam had been unable to get clear away from Magee as his front tyre had faded. Pier Francesco Chili and Niall Mackenzie joined Haslam and Magee in a race to the finish. On the last lap Chili held sway over Mackenzie, while Magee managed to stay in front of Haslam. Tadahiko Taira was a lonely and disappointing ninth ahead of Adrien Morillas on the Elf Honda. The Frenchman had successfully held off Mamola on the Cagiva and Rob McElnea on the Cabin Honda, who'd had to slow over the last few laps as his bike overheated.

Thirteenth was Alberto Rota having a one-off ride on the Marlboro Yamaha to make up the numbers as the team had dispensed with Spencer. He had fought with Alessandro Valesi on the 1988 V-four Honda in the early laps but then eased clear.

Sidecars

Steve Webster and Tony Hewitt led at the end of lap one but could not get away from Egbert Streuer and Geral de Haas. The Dutch team took the lead on lap two and the British outfit was pushed back to third on the same lap by Frenchmen Alain Michel and Jean-Marc Fresc.

Things got pretty hectic at the front, as the Egloff and the Zurbrügg brothers also got in on the act. It was time to take a back seat, as Webster later explained. 'We set out just to see how the race would develop. Things got a bit too close, and there was no point in making a race of it, so we dropped back and had no problems at all.

'It was the hardest title to win. The first one seemed pretty straightforward. The second we had given up all hope of but, with this, the pressure was on almost all the way through the year.'

The Egloffs took the lead on lap four and looked possible winners but, in the end, Streuer proved too clever and won his second Grand Prix of the season. It was not enough to stop Webster and Hewitt winning their third consecutive world title, though, with a comfortable third place.

Malcolm Bryan

Grand Prix CSSR, 27 August/statistics
Autodromo Brno, 3.35-mile/5.394-km circuit

500 cc

23 laps, 77.05 miles/124.062 km

Place	*Rider*	*Nat.*	*Machine*	*Laps*	*Time & speed*	*Practice time*	*Grid*
1	Kevin Schwantz	USA	Suzuki	23	48m 20.649s 95.674 mph/ 153.973 km/h	2m 03.167s	1
2	Eddie Lawson	USA	Honda	23	48m 25.926s	2m 03.180s	2
3	Wayne Rainey	USA	Yamaha	23	48m 46.700s	2m 04.943s	4
4	Christian Sarron	F	Yamaha	23	48m 46.705s	2m 04.216s	3
5	Pier Francesco Chili	I	Honda	23	49m 11.802s	2m 06.715s	9
6	Niall Mackenzie	GB	Yamaha	23	49m 11.807s	2m 06.141s	5
7	Kevin Magee	AUS	Yamaha	23	49m 13.580s	2m 06.459s	7
8	Ron Haslam	GB	Suzuki	23	49m 15.720s	2m 06.171s	6
9	Tadahiko Taira	J	Yamaha	23	49m 39.827s	2m 06.743s	10
10	Adrien Morillas	F	Honda	23	49m 46.434s	2m 07.847s	13
11	Randy Mamola	USA	Cagiva	23	49m 48.722s	2m 07.481s	12
12	Rob McElnea	GB	Honda	23	50m 11.426s	2m 06.953s	11
13	Alberto Rota	I	Yamaha	22	48m 26.724s	2m 10.418s	15
14	Alessandro Valesi	I	Yamaha	22	48m 31.876s	2m 10.167s	14
15	Peter Linden	S	Honda	22	48m 59.016s	2m 11.945s	17
16	Juan Lopez Mella	E	Honda	22	48m 59.884s	2m 11.330s	16
17	Eddie Laycock	IRL	Honda	22	49m 01.571s	2m 12.260s	18
18	Bruno Kneubühler	CH	Honda	22	49m 10.069s	2m 13.447s	25
19	Fabio Biliotti	I	Honda	22	49m 16.243s	2m 13.052s	24
20	Michael Rudroff	D	Honda	22	49m 17.763s	2m 12.687s	22
21	Simon Buckmaster	GB	Honda	22	49m 23.089s	2m 12.466s	20
22	Stefan Klabacher	A	Honda	22	49m 39.827s	2m 12.779s	23
23	Andreas Leuthe	LUX	Librenti	22	49m 40.317s	2m 13.495s	26
24	Josef Doppler	A	Honda	22	50m 08.689s	2m 15.011s	28
25	Fernando Gonzalez	E	Honda	21	48m 41.317s	2m 16.227s	32
26	Vincenzo Cascino	RCH	Suzuki	21	48m 41.446s	2m 16.221s	31
27	Rudolf Zeller	A	Honda	21	48m 45.453s	2m 16.583s	33
28	Pavol Dekanek	CS	Honda	21	48m 46.806s	2m 15.578s	29
29	Dario Marchetti	I	Honda	21	49m 09.211s	2m 17.310s	36
30	Harry Heutmekers	D	Suzuki	21	49m 09.583s	2m 17.342s	37
31	Michael Kaplan	A	Honda	21	50m 24.555s	2m 16.660s	34
	Marco Papa	I	Paton	19	DNF	2m 12.263s	19
	Helmut Schütz	D	Honda	5	DNF	2m 17.070s	35
	Kees Doorakkers	NL	Honda	4	DNF	2m 13.691s	27
	Niggi Schmassman	CH	Honda	3	DNF	2m 12.655s	21
	Karl Dauer	A	Honda	1	DNF	2m 15.754s	30
	Wayne Gardner	AUS	Honda		DNS	2m 06.648s	8
	Marian Troliga	CS	Suzuki		DNQ	2m 18.076s	
	Peter Graves	GB	Honda		DNQ	2m 19.662s	
	Anton Berghammer	A	Suzuki		DNQ	2m 20.198s	
	Hans Klingebiel	D	Honda		DNQ	2m 21.596s	
	Norbert Heiles	D	Suzuki		DNQ	2m 34.742s	
	Tony Carey	IRL	Spondon		DNQ	2m 35.234s	

Fastest lap: Schwantz, 2m 04.408s, 96.987 mph/156.086 km/h (record).
Previous record: Wayne Gardner, AUS (Honda), 2m 06.24s, 95.579 mph/153.821 km/h (1988).

World Championship: 1 Lawson, 211; **2** Rainey, 195.5; **3** Sarron, C., 157.5; **4** Schwantz, 142.5; **5** Magee, 128.5; **6** Chili, 122; **7** Mackenzie, 96; **8** Haslam, 75; **9** Doohan, 68; **10** Gardner, 58; **11** McElnea, 48.5; **12** Buckmaster, 41.5; **13** Sarron, D. and Taira, 39; **15** Valesi, 37; **16** Spencer, 33.5; **17** Gentile, 33; **18** Mamola, 28; **19** Morillas, 20; **20** Rudroff, 18; **21** Fujiwara, 17; **22** Shobert, 12; **23** Doppler, 11; **24** Meyer, 10; **25** Balbi, 9; **26** Broccoli, Cadalora, Gonzalez and Schmassman, 8; **30** Dowson and Leuthe, 7; **32** Biliotti, Itoh and Kneubühler, 6; **35** Kocinski, 5.5; **36** Gschwender and Merkel, 5; **38** Burnett and Crine, 4; **40** Lopez Mella, Rota and Yatsushiro, 3; **43** Doorakkers, 2.5; **44** Laycock, 2; **45** Linden and Machii, 1.

250 cc

20 laps, 67 miles/107.88 km

Place	*Rider*	*Nat.*	*Machine*	*Laps*	*Time & speed*	*Practice time*	*Grid*
1	Reinhold Roth	D	Honda	20	43m 33.888s 92.322 mph/ 148.578 km/h	2m 08.508s	1
2	Masahiro Shimizu	J	Honda	20	43m 33.889s	2m 09.404s	6
3	Jacques Cornu	CH	Honda	20	43m 34.145s	2m 08.593s	2
4	Alfonso Pons	E	Honda	20	43m 34.732s	2m 08.748s	3
5	Helmut Bradl	D	Honda	20	43m 39.582s	2m 09.253s	5
6	Luca Cadalora	I	Yamaha	20	43m 39.649s	2m 08.964s	4
7	Juan Garriga	E	Yamaha	20	43m 44.077s	2m 09.885s	8
8	Carlos Cardus	E	Honda	20	43m 50.505s	2m 09.472s	7
9	Carlos Lavado	YV	Aprilia	20	44m 01.699s	2m 10.368s	11
10	Alexandre Barros	BR	Yamaha	20	44m 07.229s	2m 10.496s	13
11	Wilco Zeelenberg	NL	Honda	20	44m 14.384s	2m 10.792s	16
12	Paolo Casoli	I	Honda	20	44m 14.473s	2m 11.089s	21
13	Didier de Radiguès	B	Aprilia	20	44m 14.891s	2m 10.207s	10
14	Daniel Amatriain	E	Honda	20	44m 15.365s	2m 10.779s	15
15	Manfred Herweh	D	Yamaha	20	44m 20.043s	2m 10.911s	18
16	Alberto Puig	E	Yamaha	20	44m 27.051s	2m 10.861s	17
17	Gary Cowan	IRL	Yamaha	20	44m 31.214s	2m 10.936s	19
18	Maurizio Vitali	I	Honda	20	44m 31.449s	2m 12.042s	27
19	Alain Bronec	F	Aprilia	20	44m 31.717s	2m 11.465s	23
20	Harald Eckl	D	Aprilia	20	44m 34.652s	2m 11.447s	22
21	Jochen Schmid	D	Honda	20	44m 34.872s	2m 10.947s	20
22	Patrick van den Goorbergh	NL	Yamaha	20	44m 49.272s	2m 11.974s	24
23	Renzo Colleoni	I	Aprilia	20	44m 49.348s	2m 11.975s	25
24	August Auinger	A	Yamaha	20	44m 57.795s	2m 12.526s	29
25	Luis Lavado	YV	Yamaha	20	44m 58.714s	2m 13.660s	32
26	Bernhard Schick	D	Yamaha	20	44m 58.929s	2m 13.043s	30
27	Virginio Ferrari	I	Gazzaniga	20	45m 10.543s	2m 13.666s	33
28	Frédéric Protat	F	Aprilia	20	45m 10.543s	2m 13.999s	35
29	Jean Foray	F	Yamaha	20	45m 34.074s	2m 14.225s	36
30	Urs Jucker	CH	Yamaha	20	45m 44.141s	2m 14.517s	38
31	Jean-François Baldé	F	Yamaha	19	44m 11.395s	2m 13.885s	34
32	Arpad Harmati	H	Yamaha	19	44m 11.558s	2m 16.185s	39
33	Andreas Preining	A	Aprilia	19	44m 24.107s	2m 11.982s	26
	Fausto Ricci	I	Aprilia	13	DNF	2m 13.394s	31
	Stefano Caracchi	RSM	Honda	11	DNF	2m 12.166s	28
	Martin Wimmer	D	Aprilia		DNS	2m 10.002s	7
	Loris Reggiani	I	Honda		DNS	2m 10.411s	12
	Jean-Philippe Ruggia	F	Yamaha		DNS	2m 10.758s	14
	Alberto Rota	I	Aprilia		DNS	2m 14.275s	37
	Hans Becker	D	Seel		DNQ	2m 17.114s	
	Istvan Lovasi	H	Yamaha		DNQ	2m 17.860s	
	Marian Troliga	CS	Yamaha		DNQ	2m 19.575s	
	Darren Milner	AUS	Yamaha		DNQ	2m 20.547s	
	Jiri Pertlicek	CS	Rotax		DNQ	2m 22.868s	

Fastest lap: Garriga, 2m 09.670s, 93.052 mph/149.752 km/h (record).
Previous record: Juan Garriga, E (Yamaha), 2m 09.79s, 92.965 mph/149.614 km/h (1988).

World Championship: 1 Pons, 249; **2** Cornu and Roth, 180; **4** Cardus, 151; **5** Ruggia, 110; **6** Cadalora, 107; **7** Shimizu, 99; **8** Garriga, 93; **9** Bradl, 80; **10** Wimmer, 61; **11** de Radiguès, 51; **12** Zeelenberg, 41; **13** Kocinski, 40; **14** Reggiani, 37; **15** Honma, 36; **16** Schmid, 33; **17** Barros, 24; **18** Filice and Lavado, 22; **20** Colleoni and Cowan, 21; **22** Palazzese, 19; **23** Eckl and Puig, 18; **25** Lucchi, 17; **26** Amatriain, 14; **27** Bronec, 11; **28** Okada, 10; **29** Caracchi, Morillas and Shiomori, 9; **32** Ricci, 8; **33** Rota and van den Goorbergh, 6; **35** Beattie, Casoli, Mitchell and Preining, 4; **39** Vitali, 2; **40** Arai, Auinger, Becker and Herweh, 1.

Malcolm Bryan

Left **Adrien Morillas stood in for the injured Dominique Sarron once again, finishing tenth.**

It was another frustrating race for Rob McElnea *(above)* **with the Cabin Honda.**

Juan Garriga *(right)* **set the fastest lap of the race but, having made a poor start, could only finish seventh.**

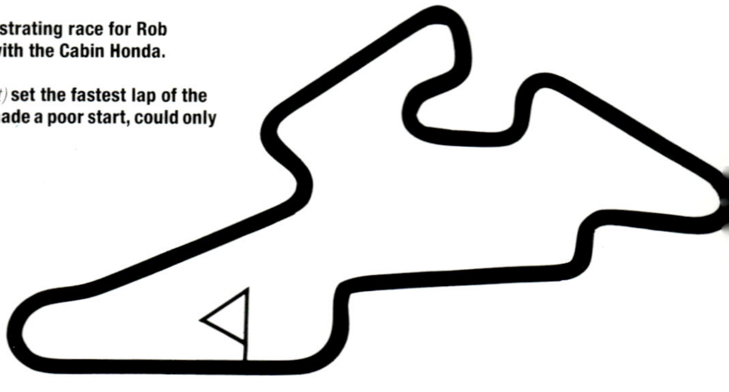

125 cc

17 laps, 56.95 miles/91.698 km

Place	Rider	Nat.	Machine	Laps	Time & speed	Practice time	Grid
1	Alex Criville	E	Cobas	17	39m 28.521s 86.603 mph/ 139.375 km/h	2m 16.371s	1
2	Hans Spaan	NL	Honda	17	39m 33.060s	2m 17.048s	3
3	Stefan Prein	D	Honda	17	39m 34.732s	2m 18.870s	9
4	Jorge Martinez	E	Derbi	17	39m 41.860s	2m 19.299s	13
5	Hisashi Unemoto	J	Honda	17	39m 41.861s	2m 18.150s	4
6	Ezio Gianola	I	Honda	17	39m 42.147s	2m 18.430s	7
7	Koji Takada	J	Honda	17	39m 46.619s	2m 16.947s	2
8	Allan Scott	USA	Honda	17	39m 48.175s	2m 18.667s	8
9	Alfred Waibel	D	Honda	17	39m 53.113s	2m 18.243s	5
10	Adolf Stadler	D	Krauser	17	39m 53.986s	2m 19.737s	17
11	Robin Appleyard	GB	Honda	17	39m 54.765s	2m 19.120s	11
12	Taru Rinne	SF	Honda	17	39m 55.794s	2m 19.202s	12
13	Dirk Raudies	D	Honda	17	39m 55.906s	2m 20.304s	23
14	Fausto Gresini	I	Aprilia	17	40m 03.876s	2m 20.400s	25
15	Heinz Lüthi	CH	Honda	17	40m 03.965s	2m 20.129s	20
16	Robin Milton	GB	Honda	17	40m 04.034s	2m 19.332s	14
17	Lucio Pietroniro	B	Honda	17	40m 04.203s	2m 19.047s	10
18	Flemming Kistrup	DK	Honda	17	40m 04.203s	2m 19.725s	16
19	Mike Leitner	A	Honda	17	40m 26.603s	2m 19.542s	15
20	Stuart Edwards	GB	Honda	17	40m 29.658s	2m 20.865s	31
21	Emilio Cuppini	I	Garelli	17	40m 35.003s	2m 20.493s	26
22	Johnny Wickström	SF	Honda	17	40m 40.135s	2m 20.152s	21
23	Hubert Abold	D	Rotax	17	40m 40.525s	2m 20.183s	22
24	Bruno Casanova	I	Aprilia	17	40m 50.424s	2m 21.029s	35
25	Hervé Duffard	F	Honda	17	41m 08.789s	2m 21.012s	34
26	Rafael Roses	E	Cobas	17	41m 35.787s	2m 20.549s	27
	Manuel Hernandez	E	Honda	15	DNF	2m 20.346s	24
	Ralf Waldmann	D	Cobas	12	DNF	2m 19.910s	18
	Alex Bedford	GB	EMC	12	DNF	2m 20.893s	33
	Thierry Feuz	CH	Honda	11	DNF	2m 20.012s	19
	Herri Torrontegui	E	Honda	10	DNF	2m 20.792s	28
	Håkan Olsson	S	ESM	9	DNF	2m 21.380s	37
	Domenico Brigaglia	I	Garelli	7	DNF	2m 21.083s	36
	Doriano Romboni	I	Honda	6	DNF	2m 20.828s	30
	Corrado Catalano	I	Gazzaniga	3	DNF	2m 18.400s	6
	Luis Reyes	E	Honda		DNS	2m 20.883s	32
	Imrich Majoros	CS	Honda		DNS	2m 21.529s	38
	Jos van Dongen	NL	Honda		DNQ	2m 21.667s	
	Julian Miralles	E	Derbi		DNQ	2m 21.694s	
	Jean-Claude Selini	F	Honda		DNQ	2m 21.806s	
	Xavier Debon	E	Cobas		DNQ	2m 21.997s	
	Attila Gsost	H	Honda		DNQ	2m 22.092s	
	Othmar Schuler	CH	Honda		DNQ	2m 22.169s	
	Manfred Thurmayer	D	Honda		DNQ	2m 22.339s	
	Gerhard Waibel	D	Aprilia		DNQ	2m 22.622s	
	Gastone Grassetti	I	Semprucci		DNQ	2m 22.699s	
	Serge Julin	B	Honda		DNQ	2m 22.773s	
	Marco Cipriani	I	Honda		DNQ	2m 22.787s	
	Stefan Dörflinger	CH	Aprilia		DNQ	2m 23.066s	
	Janos Szabo	H	Rotax		DNQ	2m 23.619s	
	Kazuya Yamada	J	Honda		DNQ	2m 23.691s	
	Valerio Vivarelli	I	Honda		DNQ	2m 24.427s	
	Bohumil Stasa	CS	Honda		DNQ	2m 25.772s	
	Xavier Arumi	E	Honda		DNQ	2m 26.336s	
	Jörg Seel	D	Seel		DNQ	2m 27.183s	

Fastest lap: Takada, 2m 17.252s, 87.91 mph/141.479 km/h (record).
Previous record: Bruno Casanova, I (Garelli), 2m 18.18s, 87.26 mph/140.53 km/h (1987).

Final 125 cc World Championship points: see page 200.

80 cc

13 laps, 43.55 miles/70.122 km

Place	Rider	Nat.	Machine	Laps	Time & speed	Practice time	Grid
1	Herri Torrontegui	E	Krauser	13	31m 30.370s 82.977 mph/ 133.539 km/h	2m 26.005s	2
2	Manuel Herreros	E	Derbi	13	31m 49.151s	2m 27.148s	5
3	Jorge Martinez	E	Derbi	13	31m 49.548s	2m 26.186s	3
4	Jörg Seel	D	Seel	13	31m 51.860s	2m 27.549s	6
5	Stefan Dörflinger	CH	Krauser	13	31m 51.860s	2m 24.605s	1
6	Luis Alvaro	E	Krauser	13	32m 02.860s	2m 28.628s	10
7	Paolo Priori	I	Krauser	13	32m 03.831s	2m 29.067s	15
8	Gabriele Gnani	I	Gnani	13	32m 05.804s	2m 29.307s	20
9	Bernd Völkel	D	Seel	13	32m 08.312s	2m 28.993s	14
10	Bogdan Nikolov	BG	Krauser	13	32m 15.462s	2m 28.140s	8
11	Jaime Mariano	E	Casal	13	32m 15.558s	2m 29.509s	21
12	Jos van Dongen	NL	Casal	13	32m 17.694s	2m 28.007s	7
13	Bert Smit	NL	Krauser	13	32m 17.803s	2m 29.769s	23
14	Janos Szabo	H	Krauser	13	32m 41.445s	2m 29.939s	24
15	Heinz Paschen	D	Casal	13	32m 44.192s	2m 30.327s	26
16	Jose Saez	E	Krauser	13	32m 44.564s	2m 29.255s	18
17	Gunther Schirnhöfer	D	Krauser	13	32m 44.565s	2m 28.888s	13
18	René Dünki	CH	LCR	13	32m 44.908s	2m 28.805s	11
19	Ralf Waldmann	D	Seel	13	32m 44.909s	2m 28.812s	12
20	Janez Pintar	YU	Eberhardt	13	32m 45.231s	2m 29.699s	22
21	Antonio Sanchez	E	Cobas	13	32m 50.103s	2m 29.138s	17
22	Stefan Brägger	CH	Casal	13	32m 53.660s	2m 32.412s	30
23	Reiner Koster	CH	LCR	13	33m 09.419s	2m 29.112s	16
24	Matthias Ehinger	D	Krauser	13	33m 14.092s	2m 35.050s	37
25	Thomas Engl	D	Esch	13	33m 25.480s	2m 31.932s	28
26	Zdravko Matulja	YU	Casal	13	33m 37.656s	2m 32.715s	31
27	Chris Baert	B	Bultaco	13	33m 58.501s	2m 34.449s	34
28	Maik Stief	D	Casal	13	33m 59.125s	2m 34.903s	35
	Peter Öttl	D	Krauser	12	DNF	2m 27.123s	4
	Hans Koopman	NL	Ziegler	7	DNF	2m 28.522s	9
	Paul Bordes	F	RB	6	DNF	2m 33.481s	33
	Roberto Sassone	I	Unimoto	5	DNF	2m 30.984s	27
	Jacques Bernard	B	Fantic	5	DNF	2m 29.270s	19
	Joaquin Gali	E	Krauser	4	DNF	2m 33.067s	32
	Xavier Arumi	E	Krauser	2	DNF	2m 32.028s	29
	Stefan Kurfiss	D	Krauser	2	DNF	2m 30.249s	25
	Jan Vanecek	CS	Krauser		DNS	2m 35.021s	36
	Alojz Pavlic	YU	Seel		DNQ	2m 35.344s	
	Otto Krmicek	CS	Casal		DNQ	2m 35.617s	
	Undine Kummer	D	Krauser		DNQ	2m 35.937s	
	Otto Machinek	A	Eigenbau		DNQ	2m 43.123s	
	Eduard Klimek	CS	RB		DNQ	2m 43.511s	
	Anton Gohly	D	Bari		DNQ	2m 46.362s	
	Kvetoslav Samak	CS	Casal		DNQ	2m 55.487s	
	Fernando Gonzalez	E	Krauser		DNQ	3m 15.805s	

Fastest lap: Torrontegui, 2m 24.435s, 83.539 mph/134.443 km/h.
Lap record: Stefan Dörflinger, CH (Krauser), 2m 24.02s, 83.78 mph/134.831 km/h (1987).

Final 80 cc World Championship points: see page 200.

Sidecars

17 laps, 56.95 miles/91.698 km

Place	Driver & passenger	Nat.	Machine	Laps	Time & speed	Practice time	Grid
1	Egbert Streuer/ Geral de Haas	NL NL	LCR- Yamaha	17	37m 33.835s 91.010 mph/ 146.467 km/h	2m 10.329s	4
2	Markus Egloff/ Urs Egloff	CH CH	Yamaha	17	37m 36.395s	2m 10.297s	3
3	Steve Webster/ Tony Hewitt	GB GB	LCR- Krauser	17	37m 42.088s	2m 10.241s	2
4	Alain Michel/ Jean-Marc Fresc	F F	LCR- Krauser	17	37m 43.371s	2m 10.916s	5
5	Steve Abbott/ Shaun Smith	GB GB	LCR	17	38m 02.200s	2m 11.984s	7
6	Alfred Zurbrügg/ Martin Zurbrügg	CH CH	LCR- Yamaha	17	38m 09.277s	2m 11.640s	6
7	Masato Kumano/ Sindus	J	LCR	17	38m 25.365s	2m 12.671s	10
8	Bernd Scherer/ Thomas Schröder	D D	BSR- Krauser	17	38m 27.349s	2m 12.962s	12
9	Rolf Steinhausen/ Bruno Hiller	D D	Schuh	17	38m 27.504s	2m 13.061s	13
10	Fritz Stölzle/ Hubert Stölzle	D D	LCR- Krauser	17	38m 28.782s	2m 13.191s	15
11	Yoshisada Kumagaya/ Phil Coombes	J GB	Windle- Yamaha	17	38m 30.614s	2m 13.090s	14
12	Gary Thomas/ Eckhart Rösinger	GB D	LCR- Krauser	17	38m 31.005s	2m 12.566s	9
13	Tony Wyssen/ Kilian Wyssen	CH CH	LCR- Krauser	17	38m 46.091s	2m 13.456s	17
14	Theo van Kempen/ Simon Birchall	NL GB	Krauser	17	38m 53.492s	2m 13.806s	19
15	Tony Baker/ Trevor Hopkinson	GB GB	LCR- Krauser	17	39m 06.950s	2m 15.965s	21
16	Clive Stirrat/ Simon Prior	GB GB	LCR	17	39m 17.562s	2m 15.760s	20
17	George Hardwick/ Gary Irlam	GB GB	LCR	17	39m 43.278s	2m 16.241s	22
18	Judd Drew/ Bryan Houghton	GB GB	LCR	17	39m 43.383s	2m 17.211s	24
19	Wolfgang Stropek/ Wolfgang Bock	A D	Mibag	17	39m 49.601s	2m 17.293s	25
20	Paul Atkinson/ T. Atkinson	GB GB	LCR- Yamaha	16	37m 42.935s	2m 18.006s	26
21	G. Arlati/ V. Montanelli	I I	LCR- Krauser	16	39m 00.861s	2m 19.763s	28
22	Egon Schons/ Peter Hess	D D	BSR- Yamaha	16	39m 01.252s	2m 21.330s	29
	Barry Brindley/ Grahame Rose	GB GB	Fowler- Yamaha	15	DNF	2m 12.803s	11
	René Progin/ Yves Hunziker	CH CH	LCR	8	DNF	2m 13.316s	16
	Hans Hügli/ Adolf Hänni	CH CH	Sigwa- Yamaha	4	DNF	2m 19.177s	27
	Ivan Nigrowsky/ Jaques Corbier	F F	LCR- JPX	2	DNF	2m 13.691s	18
	Derek Jones/ Peter Brown	GB GB	LCR	1	DNF	2m 12.356s	8
	Rolf Biland/ Kurt Waltisperg	CH CH	LCR- Krauser	1	DNF	2m 08.418s	1
	Klaus Klaffenböck/ Christian Parzer	A A	Yamaha		DNS	2m 16.423s	23

Fastest lap: Streuer, 2m 11.182s, 91.979 mph/148.026 km/h.
Lap record: Egbert Streuer/Bernard Schnieders, NL/NL (LCR-Yamaha), 2m 10.47s, 92.48 mph/148.834 km/h (1988).

Final Sidecar World Championship points: see page 201.

Malcolm Bryan

It's early in the race, and Lawson leads from Rainey and Schwantz. The World Champion did not take the careful route to his fourth title, he raced from the start.

Malcolm Bryan

WORLD CHAMPIONSHIP · ROUND 15

BRAZILIAN GRAND PRIX

No racer can look forward to an event when winning the World Championship depends on the other guy breaking down or falling off. Wayne Rainey was a little subdued all week – and the fact that he was fastest in practice only added to his frustration. It did not help that, at the last Grand Prix of the season, his Dunlop tyres were providing drive equal or superior to the Michelins. They had let him down too often, in his opinion, and if they were working at the last race that was too late. He would need more than that to be champion.

Rainey talked quite frankly about swapping to Michelins for the 1990 season. 'Two years on Dunlops is enough. There have been too many times when the tyres have not been consistent. We have missed practices because tyres are out of round or something else was wrong with them. You cannot even set up the carburation, never mind the suspension, if the tyres are not working. If I go to Michelin I might have tyre problems from time to time, but at least I will be in the same situation as everyone else. If I am not fast enough then, I will know it is down to me.'

The change to Michelin was no foregone conclusion, however. The French company had declined to supply tyres to the Lucky Strike team for the present season because they had committed themselves to Freddie Spencer as the fourth Grade One supported rider alongside Wayne Gardner, Eddie Lawson and Kevin Schwantz. There would be no Spencer in 1990, but Michelin were facing other demands. Mr Chatard, Michelin's chief Grand Prix representative, said that they would again be confining the 'A' list to four names but that the list had yet to be finalised. Assuming that three of the riders would be Lawson, Gardner and Schwantz, the fourth place was still open. Sito Pons has always said that he would only swap to the 500 class if given the same tyres as the top men – and Michelin Spain would be putting a great deal of pressure on head office. There would be more pressure from within France, too, for Christian Sarron to get the best equipment.

Michelin even had reason to keep Rainey on Dunlop, because they had to have someone to beat. There would be little publicity to be gained from beating only themselves. Assuming they could feel confident in their continued superiority, then Rainey might again provide the perfect foil.

For the moment, though, Wayne Rainey was having to explain why he was actually faster than the Michelin men. 'At last we have got some drive. We are still sliding and bouncing around all over the place, but we happen to be going faster than anyone else. Give the others some of our problems for one race and they start complaining.'

Dunlop and the Lucky Strike team had done a great deal of pre-season testing at Goiania which no doubt helped them to be so well prepared and competitive. The question that then sprang to mind was: 'Had tuning the tyres to the rough, coarse surface of Goiania made them too specialised?' Winter testing had also been done at Phillip Island, but the initial 17-in. rear tyre tests had been done at Goiania and that, obviously, had had a great deal of influence on the course of development.

There is no doubt that Michelin had their problems during the season as well, failing to win a race at Laguna Seca or at Spa (if you reckon on the three-leg 500 event). These tracks were dominated by Dunlop, but Michelin still held sway at the majority – and the World Championship is all about consistency.

With Lawson expected to go for safe World Championship points, Schwantz was Michelin's best hope of a win in the last race, even though Suzuki had not tested at Goiania. This led to some frustration for the Texan during practice. 'Friday was OK but when we tried to improve the bike on Saturday we just went backwards. We could not even get back to the point we were at on Friday. It was a worse situation than we had been in at Donington. The bike was running wide in the corners and nothing that we did to the suspension made it any better.

'An overnight change for the Sunday morning warm-up provided the answer, altering the head angle and the triple clamp offset. Now it turns in and holds the line like it should,' said Schwantz.

That still left Rainey on pole ahead of Schwantz and Lawson, with Magee fourth on the second Lucky Strike Yamaha. The Australian felt that practice had been a success, even though he had missed the free training on Thursday thanks to a mechanical problem delaying his flight – as it had done the previous year. 'The bike was not bad from the start of practice and each session we could make some steady progress,' said Magee. 'We are getting some drive from the tyres and, of course, that helps.'

Practice looked good for Dunlop in the 250 class as well, with both Carlos Cardus and Jacques Cornu going well. Brazil was particularly crucial for Cornu, because second place in the World Championship hung in the balance. He was on equal points with Reinhold Roth for that second place and the fact that the lanky Swiss veteran qualified third, though only a tenth quicker than Roth in sixth place, was just the boost he needed going into the race.

Loris Reggiani was fastest, and accepted that he was probably the only rider to be happy with his suspension set-up. 'It is very difficult to get the bike set up here because there are bumps everywhere but we had some help from the Showa engineer. He helped us with the settings from Eddie's 500 and that worked for us,' said the Italian, who was looking forward to possibly his last Grand Prix. 'I want to go on racing, but only with factory machines. At the moment Honda have not told me that I can have factory bikes for next year and I must assume that I will not get them, so it looks as though I shall be retiring.'

Reggiani's quandary was typical of the situation most teams and riders found themselves in at Goiania. There were incredible rumours of machine, rider and sponsor swaps that kept the gossip cauldron boiling over all week.

It had been assumed all season, for instance, that Lawson had a two-year agreement to stay with the Rothmans Honda team. This, it

Agip
Arai
12
CAGIVA
AGRALE

Not a great year for Mamola *(left)*, **whose exuberance was slightly dampened after the wheelie crash at Assen. The sport would be dull without him, though, and the Brazilians appreciate his showmanship.**

Nice gloves, Kev.

Malcolm Bryan

transpired, either never existed or was not binding so a second Lawson move in two seasons became a real possibility. It was not difficult to imagine that the notion of winning the 1990 World Championship on a Suzuki appealed to Lawson, giving him a unique title hat-trick on three different machines.

The possibility was also being mentioned of Marlboro giving its backing to the Suzuki or Roberts Yamaha teams: Agostini looked unlikely to get the best factory bikes in 1990, even though he left Brazil with a commitment from Kevin Schwantz to ride for him if he could be assured of equal machinery with Rainey.

The silly season had been longer and sillier than ever – and the contest for the final points of the year seemed almost tame compared with the wheeling, dealing and back-stabbing going on behind the scenes.

500 cc

There was no reason to believe that the last Grand Prix of the season would be a classic. Lawson only needed to finish the race to be champion, and if he stopped Rainey only needed second to take the championship. One might have expected Schwantz to run away with the win, with Rainey taking a cautious second ahead of an even more cautious Lawson.

It did not work out like that at all. The race was a three-way battle for the win right from the start, and the fourth-place contest was just as exciting.

Lawson took an early lead, with Rainey sitting on his tail just ahead of Schwantz. Doohan was fourth and, though well placed, was not quite able to match the speed of the triumvirate. Sarron was fifth – but not for long. The delightful Frenchman had been complaining all through practice that he had been unable to make any progress sorting the bike out and so was little faster in the final session than he had been in free practice on Thursday.

Lap two saw the Americans start to pull away. Doohan came under increased pressure, briefly from Sarron, but more seriously from Magee, who was just ahead of Gardner and Chili. The fourth-place battle was soon sorted out, as much by what was right or wrong with the machines as by rider skill. Chili soon lost touch, as his tyres started to play up. Magee looked impressive, but his front brakes would not stand the pace. Sarron was battling his whole machine. Only Doohan was happy with both the bike and himself.

Magee took fourth on lap four, keeping in front of Doohan for three laps, but he soon started to run out of brakes. 'I wanted to use the steel discs instead of the carbons, because I can't get on with the feel of the carbons braking into the corner. You leave it late and they are stopping harder and harder as you need to be easing off, because you are getting deep into the corner. I can do that with the steel discs but, in the race, they ran out of power. I suppose I should have used the carbons.' It is easy to be wise after the event: Magee ended the race with his pads worn well through to the metal. The backing plate had been worn away so much, in fact, that what was left slipped down out of the caliper and started to rub on the disc retainers.

Up front Lawson still held the advantage, with Rainey watching his every move just inches behind – and hoping that something would go wrong with the Honda. Schwantz just sat there, apparently not wanting to get involved in this all-important championship battle, but he said later that that was not the case. 'I was riding flat out from the start and I couldn't get past Rainey at first. I wasn't taking it easy.'

All three men were sliding around well, fighting for grip over the bumps. It almost looked as though Lawson was pushing his luck – but he stayed in the saddle. After 15 laps Rainey was visibly having trouble holding on to the Honda, as his tyres ceased to give him the drive he needed.

He dropped back slightly and Schwantz jumped past. Rainey did not want to give way but, after the Texan had slid underneath him going into the first, tighter, segment of the double right that leads onto the start and finish straight, the Lucky Strike rider responded. Schwantz had gone in a little fast and drifted out. Rainey got back underneath and on the gas early so that the pair ran through the rest of the corner together, the Suzuki inches ahead and squeezing Rainey towards the second apex. No quarter was given by either man, but Rainey could not hold out for long. On the next lap Schwantz was ahead and quickly closing on Lawson. Two laps later he was right in the wheel tracks of the Honda, and lap 22 saw him ahead.

With Rainey dropping steadily astern Lawson might have considered honour served and accepted a safe second. He didn't. He kept on at the Suzuki, pushing hard, and by lap 25 the two men had a three-second advantage over Rainey.

'I wanted to win it,' said Lawson later. 'I went after it, but Kevin was riding well and I guess I realised in the last couple of laps that it was not worth doing anything dumb.' Schwantz felt the pressure too. 'It didn't get any easier when I was in front. I was not sure I was going to win until the last couple of laps. Then I got slightly ahead and I realised that Eddie was not going to take any chances trying to get by on the last lap.'

By mid-race Doohan looked pretty secure in fourth, his bike apparently handling more predictably than most. He was hanging the rear end out on long, perfect, power slides. 'The bike was working great. The rear tyre was sliding predictably. I was just hanging it out there until it started to grip, then I'd hook the next gear. I thought that the tyre performance would drop off with that much abuse, but it kept up.'

Fifth place went to Ron Haslam, who had a spectacular run through from the back of the field after a disastrous start. The man who'd led so many charges to the first corner when Honda mounted had failed to make the same starts on the Suzuki – and the last race of the season was his worst. 'I made a complete mess of it and it was my own fault. On the Hondas I just used to hold the throttle open and feed in the clutch and feel

Below left: **Come back in anger. Doohan's finger was well on the mend and his last race of the season was one of his best.**

Right: **Roth looked like he was out to win the race as the most certain way of beating Cornu but slackened his pace when informed of his opponent's position. Cadalora would probably have won anyway. It was a day when no one could stay in front of him.**

A great deal of life in the old dog. Carlos Lavado *(below)* **proved that he should still be on a factory bike, while Bradl and Cornu were not happy with the way they finished the season.**

Malcolm Bryan

it bite. The Suzuki has a rev-limiter and when you hold the throttle open that cuts in and stops the spark. That floods the engine.

'To make a good start you have to hold the revs below the limiter, and I can do that in practice. On the grid I seem to forget: the rev-limiter cut in, the engine wouldn't clear and I was last away. At the first corner I just had to go round the outside. I wasn't too sure about that, because it is dirty out there, but I stayed on.'

Haslam quickly cut his way through the field to join the group chasing Doohan for fourth, but his troubles were not over. 'Three times I knocked the gear lever and the engine jumped into neutral. I don't know if I was sitting on the bike differently, or why I did it, but I lost ground every time.' Ron did not give up, but it took a long time before he could get clear of Magee. He then spent the last ten laps slowly closing on Doohan but ran out of time before he could ask the Australian if he had anything left to give.

Kevin Magee was left in sixth place, ahead of Sarron and Gardner who were having their own lengthy contest. Magee's brakes were getting sicker and sicker and, in the last four laps, Gardner saw his fellow-Australian within striking distance and suddenly jumped ahead of Sarron. The ex-World Champion spent the last lap looking for a way past the Lucky Strike rider; he pulled out of the Yamaha's slipstream on the run to the line but could not get alongside.

'I didn't know it was the last lap,' said Gardner later. 'I knew it was getting close to the end and I tried to pull past, but the bike wouldn't do it. I was glad to finish the race in one piece and forget about this season. The bike was working OK at the beginning of the race but midway through it seemed to lose power and I couldn't get past the Yamahas.'

Niall Mackenzie finished ninth on the Marlboro Yamaha – not his best result of the season, but an improvement after being twelfth in practice. 'Michelin gave us a good rear tyre for the race and that made a difference, but it was still pretty disappointing.'

Pier Francesco Chili pulled into the pits after discovering the Pirellis were no match for the Goiania surface. He could not be caught in the championship and, with no chance of gaining points over Magee with the way his bike was sliding, he retired with a shredded front tyre.

Adrien Morillas was the only one of the Elf men to finish, after Dominique Sarron was thrown off his Honda on lap 23. It was a hard, high-speed fall and Sarron was fortunate to suffer nothing more than a twisted ankle – and he was not sad to be saying goodbye to the 500.

Randy Mamola was eleventh, after a demonstration of rear-wheel sliding that almost equalled his 1988 performance. It was less spectacular, though, because the Michelins refused to smoke. He finished in front of Rob McElnea, who had ridden the Cabin Honda hard and, initially, been tenth but was forced to relinquish successive places as his front tyre faded.

250 cc

Brazil was Yamaha's consolation prize for a dismal season. Despite a promising start to the year they ended up without a man in the World Championship top four. The race was perhaps more of a triumph for Luca Cadalora than it was for his machine, however, as the Italian was quite clearly riding the wheels off the Marlboro Yamaha.

Cadalora is not known for his great starts and was back in ninth place at the end of lap one. Roth led from Cornu, Cardus, Shimizu, Carlos Lavado, Wimmer and Reggiani. Roth kept up a good pace but had not been serious about his pre-race claim. 'If I get in front no one will have the speed or the guts to get past,' the German had said in jest. Though he did lead he later explained that it was not, in fact, the plan.

'I did not go out to win the race and even when I was leading we were not going that fast. What I was interested in was beating Cornu, and I just kept looking for my pit signals which were telling me his position. When a few guys passed me I just kept checking that I was well in front of him, so I knew I didn't have to go any faster. I lost a lot of ground passing a back-marker later on and I couldn't catch the leaders after that.'

Roth lost the lead to Cardus on lap seven but was back in front briefly on lap nine before the Spaniard once more took over. Cadalora, meanwhile, had been working his way forward as fast as he could, and on lap 11 he pushed Cardus out of the way.

'I never waited for a second,' said Cadalora after the race. 'I just raced flat out from the start. If there was half a chance to pass someone I did it – and I kept riding like that all the way to the end. Even when I was in front I never thought about those behind. I just rode as fast as I could, every lap.'

When Cadalora hit the front Reggiani took second ahead of Cardus, Roth and Shimizu. That group of five had pulled away from the pack, but World Champion Sito Pons was closing in on them, having fought his way through from a very bad start. He had been fourteenth at the end of lap one, but his climb through the field was so spectacular he looked a possible winner. It was not to be, however, because of the effort he had expended making progress. 'By the time I caught the leading group I had used up the best of the rear tyre. I couldn't do any more.'

If Pons had used the best of his tyres Cardus was in an even worse state. His Dunlops, like those of Cornu, and Rainey in the 500 race, were spent by two-thirds distance. He faded quickly after lap 16 and by lap 21 was dropping astern of the leading group, still headed by Cadalora from Reggiani, Shimizu and Pons.

Roth was looking good for the number two spot in the championship because Cornu had slipped back to seventh and was working hard to keep ahead of Bradl and Carlos Lavado. The Swiss later commented, 'The tyres were not that good and the bike was not that fast. Together that made it difficult.'

On lap 23 Reggiani and Shimizu had a coming together: that offered Cadalora a fractional breathing space and he never lost it. Shimizu clung to second and Reggiani retained third. The Japanese rider's second good result in two races gave him the possibility of another Grand Prix season. Prior to that second place in Czechoslovakia he had been told he'd be staying home in 1990.

SHOEI
Castrol
YAMAHA
Marlboro

RUDY PROJECT

Grande Premio do Brasil, 17 September/statistics
Autodromo de Goiania, 2.383-mile/3.835-km circuit

500 cc

32 laps, 76.258 miles/122.72 km

Place	Rider	Nat.	Machine	Laps	Time & speed	Practice time	Grid
1	Kevin Schwantz	USA	Suzuki	32	46m 44.390s 97.887 mph/ 157.535 km/h	1m 26.148s	2
2	Eddie Lawson	USA	Honda	32	46m 46.096s	1m 26.614s	3
3	Wayne Rainey	USA	Yamaha	32	46m 55.607s	1m 25.447s	1
4	Michael Doohan	AUS	Honda	32	47m 03.518s	1m 27.254s	8
5	Ron Haslam	GB	Suzuki	32	47m 08.643s	1m 26.777s	5
6	Kevin Magee	AUS	Yamaha	32	47m 17.810s	1m 26.727s	4
7	Wayne Gardner	AUS	Honda	32	47m 18.021s	1m 26.945s	6
8	Christian Sarron	F	Yamaha	32	47m 23.000s	1m 27.063s	7
9	Niall Mackenzie	GB	Yamaha	32	47m 51.032s	1m 28.010s	12
10	Adrien Morillas	F	Honda	32	47m 54.406s	1m 28.895s	14
11	Randy Mamola	USA	Cagiva	32	47m 56.044s	1m 28.128s	13
12	Rob McElnea	GB	Honda	32	47m 56.822s	1m 27.935s	11
13	Alessandro Valesi	I	Yamaha	31	47m 47.490s	1m 30.345s	15
14	Simon Buckmaster	GB	Honda	31	48m 10.993s	1m 32.293s	17
15	Juan Lopez Mella	E	Honda	30	47m 16.756s	1m 32.244s	16
16	Fernando Gonzalez	E	Honda	29	47m 02.361s	1m 36.338s	20
17	Niggi Schmassman	CH	Honda	29	48m 24.000s	1m 33.254s	18
	Vincenzo Cascino	RCH	Suzuki	27	DNF		
	Dominique Sarron	F	Honda	22	DNF	1m 27.788s	10
	Pier Francesco Chili	I	Honda	12	DNF	1m 27.386s	9
	Marco Gentile	CH	Fior		DNS	1m 35.194s	19
	Peter Graves	GB	Honda		DNQ	1m 37.505s	

Fastest lap: Lawson, 1m 26.980s, 98.627 mph/158.726 km/h (record).
Previous circuit record: Eddie Lawson, USA (Yamaha), 1m 27.81s, 97.706 mph/157.243 km/h (1988).

Final 500 cc World Championship points: see page 198.

250 cc

27 laps, 64.339 miles/103.545 km

Place	Rider	Nat.	Machine	Laps	Time & speed	Practice time	Grid
1	Luca Cadalora	I	Yamaha	27	40m 46.149s 94.688 mph/ 152.387 km/h	1m 29.534s	4
2	Masahiro Shimizu	J	Honda	27	40m 46.380s	1m 29.833s	9
3	Loris Reggiani	I	Honda	27	40m 46.945s	1m 28.989s	1
4	Alfonso Pons	E	Honda	27	40m 47.506s	1m 29.557s	5
5	Carlos Cardus	E	Honda	27	40m 53.948s	1m 29.143s	2
6	Reinhold Roth	D	Honda	27	40m 59.104s	1m 29.618s	6
7	Carlos Lavado	YV	Aprilia	27	41m 06.753s	1m 29.772s	8
8	Helmut Bradl	D	Honda	27	41m 07.146s	1m 29.769s	7
9	Jacques Cornu	CH	Honda	27	41m 07.557s	1m 29.503s	3
10	Alexandre Barros	BR	Yamaha	27	41m 24.183s	1m 30.791s	16
11	Juan Garriga	E	Yamaha	27	41m 24.352s	1m 30.146s	10
12	Gary Cowan	IRL	Yamaha	27	41m 40.333s	1m 30.252s	12
13	Jochen Schmid	D	Honda	27	41m 40.545s	1m 31.383s	20
14	Luis Lavado	YV	Yamaha	27	41m 41.166s	1m 31.056s	19
15	Martin Wimmer	D	Aprilia	27	41m 43.115s	1m 30.422s	13
16	Harald Eckl	D	Aprilia	27	41m 49.348s	1m 30.764s	15
17	Alain Bronec	F	Aprilia	27	42m 03.339s	1m 31.912s	22
18	Renzo Colleoni	I	Aprilia	27	42m 03.583s	1m 31.020s	18
19	Miguel Gonzalez	YV	Yamaha	26	40m 48.362s	1m 32.011s	23
20	Jose Barresi	YV	Yamaha	26	40m 49.838s	1m 31.814s	21
21	Jean-François Baldé	F	Yamaha	26	41m 59.268s	1m 34.013s	24
22	Eduardo Aleman	YV	Yamaha	25	42m 22.869s	1m 35.493s	25
23	Francisco Incoruai	RA	Yamaha	24	41m 43.387s	1m 38.898s	26
	Alberto Puig	E	Yamaha	12	DNF	1m 30.553s	14
	Ricardo Blanco	RA	Yamaha	12	DNF	1m 39.344s	28
	Paolo Casoli	I	Honda	11	DNF	1m 30.949s	17
	Eduardo Amen	RA	Yamaha	10	DNF	1m 39.182s	27
	Didier de Radiguès	B	Aprilia	1	DNF	1m 30.225s	11
	Daniel Rosich	ROU	Cobas		DNQ	1m 42.605s	

Fastest lap: Cadalora, 1m 29.262s, 96.106 mph/154.668 km/h (record).
Previous circuit record: Luca Cadalora, I (Yamaha), 1m 30.09s, 95.233 mph/153.263 km/h (1988).

Final 250 cc World Championship points: see page 199.

It could all have ended here, even on the last lap, but Lawson was far enough away from the back-marker not to be involved.

Malcolm Bryan

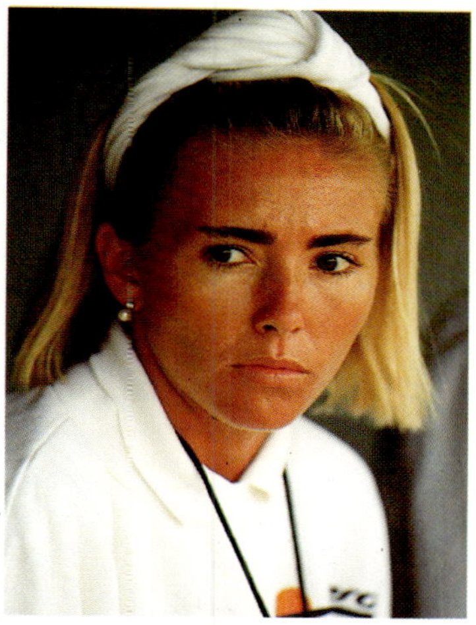

Malcolm Bryan

Left: **Mrs Sylvie Cardus: one of the most charming people in the paddock, as well as one of the prettiest.**

Below: **Just good friends. Wayne, Eddie and a lady from Australia. Eddie's girl, that is – he met her while visiting Mick Doohan at Surfers Paradise, honest Donna.**

Malcolm Bryan

Malcolm Bryan

Above: **So good looking, so strong, so manly, so statuesque, so muscular, so Randy: Mr Brazil 1989.**

Left: **Jean-François Baldé, still going strong after 200 events.**

Malcolm Bryan

1989 CIRCUIT REPORT

	Possible score	JAPAN Suzuka	AUSTRALIA Phillip Island	USA Laguna Seca	SPAIN Jerez	ITALY Misano	GERMANY Hockenheim	AUSTRIA Salzburg	YUGOSLAVIA Rijeka	HOLLAND Assen	BELGIUM Spa	FRANCE Le Mans	GREAT BRITAIN Donington Park	SWEDEN Anderstorp	CZECHOSLOVAKIA Brno	BRAZIL Goiania
1. Circuit safety																
a) Natural safety of circuit	20	12	18	7	14	10	14	6	14	16	9	12	17	14	17	17
b) Temporary safety provisions	20	16	18	8	14	10	15	13	11	16	10	15	17	12	16	16
c) Clerk of the Course/race direction	10	8	5	4	6	3	3	8	6	8	2	6	7	6	7	7
d) Marshals	10	7	8	4	7	6	2	6	6	8	4	7	6	5	8	6
e) First aid and ambulances	10	6	6	3	6	6	4	6	5	7	4	6	7	4	7	6
2. Facilities																
a) Paddock size	10	6	6	5	6	5	7	5	6	7	6	5	7	5	8	7
b) Paddock amenities	10	6	5	2	5	5	5	5	4	5	4	5	8	4	6	6
c) Sanitary arrangements	10	7	3	2	6	5	6	6	4	6	5	4	6	5	5	5
d) Paddock security	10	8	5	5	6	1	7	6	4	8	5	5	7	2	5	7
e) General working conditions	10	8	6	2	7	4	7	4	4	6	6	4	7	3	7	6
3. Organisers' co-operation																
a) From organisers/promoters	20	17	18	9	14	8	9	15	12	13	12	12	18	13	15	14
4. Spectator facilities																
a) Viewing	10	6	8	7	8	6	7	6	5	8	6	6	8	5	8	6
b) Facilities (amenities/catering)	10	6	8	6	5	5	6	8	4	7	4	5	7	4	7	4
5. Location and scheduling																
a) Circuit location/travel hassle	10	5	4	3	5	6	7	7	4	7	6	6	5	4	5	3
b) Practice and race schedules	10	6	8	5	6	6	3	6	5	5	5	5	7	2	6	7
6. Media																
a) Press facilities (photo/reporting)	10	7	9	4	6	6	6	5	4	8	6	6	9	5	6	5
b) TV coverage and volume	10	7	9	5	8	5	6	6	4	8	7	7	8	3	4	4
Grand total per Grand Prix	200	138	144	81	129	97	114	118	102	143	101	116	151	96	137	126

Photos: Malcolm Bryan

Excellent support for the press and media – just one of the reasons for the British Grand Prix taking the top slot in 1989.

GRAND PRIX RANKINGS

RESULTS 1984 – 89

RANK	1984	1985	1986	1987	1988	1989
1.	BRITAIN Silverstone	GERMANY Hockenheim	GERMANY Nürburgring	HOLLAND Assen	JAPAN Suzuka	BRITAIN Donington
2.	HOLLAND Assen	BRITAIN Silverstone	HOLLAND Assen	BRITAIN Donington	BRITAIN Donington	AUSTRALIA Phillip Island
3.	GERMANY Nürburgring	AUSTRIA Salzburg	BRITAIN Silverstone	JAPAN Suzuka	HOLLAND Assen	HOLLAND Assen
4.	AUSTRIA Salzburg	HOLLAND Assen	SPAIN Járama	SPAIN Jerez	PORTUGAL Jerez	JAPAN Suzuka
5.	FRANCE Paul Ricard	SAN MARINO Misano	AUSTRIA Salzburg	GERMANY Hockenheim	BRAZIL Goiania	CZECHOSLOVAKIA Brno
6.	SAN MARINO Mugello	SWEDEN Anderstorp	YUGOSLAVIA Rijeka	BRAZIL Goiania	ITALY Imola	SPAIN Jerez
7.	ITALY Misano	SOUTH AFRICA Kyalami	SWEDEN Anderstorp	SAN MARINO Misano	AUSTRIA Salzburg	BRAZIL Goiania
8.	SOUTH AFRICA Kyalami	YUGOSLAVIA Rijeka	SAN MARINO Misano	FRANCE Le Mans	GERMANY Nürburgring	AUSTRIA Salzburg
9.	SWEDEN Anderstorp	ITALY Mugello	BELGIUM Spa	AUSTRIA Salzburg	CZECHOSLOVAKIA Brno	FRANCE Le Mans
10.	YUGOSLAVIA Rijeka	BELGIUM Spa	FRANCE Paul Ricard	CZECHOSLOVAKIA Brno	BELGIUM Spa	GERMANY Hockenheim
11.	BELGIUM Spa	SPAIN Járama	ITALY Monza	YUGOSLAVIA Rijeka	SPAIN Járama	YUGOSLAVIA Rijeka
12.	SPAIN Járama	FRANCE Le Mans	–	SWEDEN Anderstorp	USA Laguna Seca	BELGIUM Spa
13.	–	–	–	PORTUGAL Járama	FRANCE Paul Ricard	ITALY Misano
14.	–	–	–	ITALY Monza	YUGOSLAVIA Rijeka	SWEDEN Anderstorp
15.	–	–	–	ARGENTINA Buenos Aires	SWEDEN Anderstorp	USA Laguna Seca

1989 GRAND PRIX RANKING

1
BRITAIN
DONINGTON PARK

Runner-up for the last two years, Donington finally takes the title. The event is superbly promoted and organised by Robert Fearnall and his team, and this year we saw genuine attempts by the ACU to improve their co-operation with the teams.

2
AUSTRALIA
PHILLIP ISLAND

Were it not for a few shortcomings in facilities and the location of this superb circuit then Bob Barnard's Grand Prix would have gone straight to the top of our poll.

Phillip Island: a great circuit.

3
HOLLAND
ASSEN

The Dutch event always figures among the favourite Grands Prix. The Speedweek concept may be popular with the fans but it puts pressure on the facilities and schedules and drags down the score for Assen.

NOTES ON RESULTS

The rankings of the Grands Prix are the result of a poll conducted among a selection of IRTA members, riders, managers, technicians, etc. The winners are awarded the title 'Best Grand Prix' and are presented with a trophy at the IRTA annual meeting.

4
JAPAN
SUZUKA

The increase to three races with the corresponding increase in competitors and support crews put a strain on the Suzuka facilities. No doubt the Japanese will be planning to overcome these problems and recover the title they held last year.

5
CZECHOSLOVAKIA
BRNO

Brno has worked its way up the rankings. It is a splendid circuit and the Czechs try hard to accommodate the wishes of the teams. If it wasn't for the harassment that is dished out by the local police it would be even more popular.

6
SPAIN
JEREZ

A good facility with co-operative organisers, but the track could be safer and the utilities in the paddock need improving.

7
BRAZIL
GOIANIA

This Grand Prix, probably the last in Goiania, has slipped down the rankings because the new promoters completely screwed up the teams' travel arrangements. The event itself is well run and the teams enjoy the end-of-season, party atmosphere in this friendly city.

8
AUSTRIA
SALZBURGRING

While dramatically improved for 1989 the circuit is still the most frightening on the calendar. More work on safety will need to be done to ensure the long-term survival of this event.

9
FRANCE
LE MANS

The riders don't like the new circuit layout which, although much safer, consists of lots of slow corners. Also some of the paddock facilities are still not adequate.

10
GERMANY
HOCKENHEIM

Once again the organisation of the German GP fell apart when things started to go wrong. The German organisers are unresponsive to the wishes of the teams and riders, and the event will continue to go down the rankings until they change their attitude.

Grand Prix racing is so much safer than it was ten years ago that there are thankfully few serious accidents. No one needs reminding that racing is still dangerous, however, although the terrible accident at Hockenheim that resulted in the death of Ivan Palazzese *(above)* **and the serious injuries of Fabio Barchitta and Bruno Bonhuil had nothing to do with circuit safety.**

The fact that the reaction of the circuit organisation was disastrous had no bearing on their injuries either, but it was pure luck that the confusion did not make things a great deal worse. It rightly focused the attention on the need for more professional executives at Grands Prix and reminded us all that racing safety is still more important than scrabbling for political power.

11
YUGOSLAVIA
RIJEKA

Finally we got our bigger paddock – but the promised new pits didn't materialise. The cash-starved Yugoslavs do their best with limited resources, but marshalling and facilities let the event down.

12
BELGIUM
SPA

It seems unfair that this event should slip down the rankings due to the farcical actions of the International Jury. The fact is that the decision on the 500 cc race result was morally wrong and tainted views of the whole event. Improvement of safety at this circuit is still a major priority.

13
ITALY
MISANO

Back to normal for a Flammini promotion. Absolutely no paddock security, negligible co-operation with the teams and riders, and complete amazement, followed by shouted threats, when the riders say enough is enough. The Italian fans deserve better than this but probably won't get it until we have a promoter who is sympathetic to the needs of the teams.

Misano: same old problems.

14
SWEDEN
ANDERSTORP

A new surface and improved safety drags the Swedish event off the bottom of the rankings. IRTA have declared they will not go to Anderstorp again.

15
USA
LAGUNA SECA

The inaugural American event was bad and everyone hoped the organisers would learn from their mistakes. They didn't – and many of the teams voted not to go back in 1990. As it is the Americans have been given strict conditions and one last chance to make the event work.

Steve Hislop confirmed his status as the new idol of the Isle of Man fans with a dominant win in the Senior TT, but the race was overshadowed by the disaster in the 1300 Production event.

ISLE OF MAN TT
By PAUL FOWLER

The great Joey Dunlop has stamped his authority so effectively on the TT that it seemed inconceivable that he would have to sit out the 1989 event. The Irish certainly thought so!

Following his Easter crash at Brands Hatch, Yer Maun was in a hell of a state. He could hardly walk with two elbow crutches, let alone unaided, and his weak right wrist was devoid of strength. Anyone could see at a glance that Dunlop was in no fit state to be out and about, let alone going for his seventh straight F1 win and a record-equalling fourteenth TT victory. Yet, days before the event, Irish doctors apparently passed him fit to compete...only in Ireland! To everyone's massive relief the official ACU medics thought otherwise and the 40,000 TT fans were rightly denied the opportunity of seeing Dunlop make a fool of himself on the 37.73-mile Mountain Course.

Dunlop's determination to race probably had something to do with the fact that Honda had cause to celebrate this year. Exactly 30 years ago the Japanese factory had made their first appearance in the Isle of Man. Everyone had laughed at them then. Not any more!

Honda badly wanted to win this time and, even with Dunlop out, they were favourites for a clean sweep of the F1, Senior, Production 750, Supersport 600 and Junior races. And one man could conceivably win them all, earning himself a unique place in the record books. No one had ever won four races in a week, let alone five.

With Dunlop sitting it out, the burden of responsibility rested on the slight Scottish shoulders of Steve Hislop. Hislop had proved his worth after a lengthy TT apprenticeship, winning the F2 in 1987 and adding the 750 Production a year later.

With dramatic improvements to the course, lap times were expected to improve in equally dramatic fashion – but few were prepared for the incredible exploits of Steve Hislop as he prepared for an historic TT.

PRACTICE

We didn't have to wait long for Hislop to prove he was going to be the man to beat. While the Island early arrivals were still reeling from the nightmare of the Steam Packet and bleary-eyed at the first middle-of-the-night practice of the year, Hislop was rewriting his own records.

The 600 Supersport was the first to fall, as Hislop fired his Honda around at 111.87 mph on a second-hand set of tyres which had already seen service at the North West 200. By the end of the day the 27-year-old Scottish Borderer had clipped another 11 seconds from that time and upped the lap speed to 112.83 mph. His time of 20m 03.8s was never bettered in practice.

A pretty good start to the week you might think – but our Stevie was just warming up. He finished the Monday night session not only top of the leaderboard in the Supersport 600 but also in the 750 Production and Formula One categories. His standing-start F1 lap of 118.21 mph was just nine seconds outside Steve Cull's outright lap record. Suddenly the first sub-19-minute TT lap and the first 120 mph average seemed real possibilities.

Both barriers fell together on Tuesday evening, when Hislop climbed aboard the RVF750 Honda which Dunlop had been scheduled to ride. The bike was far from correctly set up for the Scot, yet his lap at 120.89 mph ensured him a place in the history books.

With standard forks from his own RC30 Honda, a different rear shock and a set of floating discs, Hislop lined up for Thursday night's session determined to up the record further. And that's just what he did, lopping almost half a minute from Cull's record time as he completed the 37.73-mile circuit in an incredible 18m 33.4s – 121.99 mph.

'It didn't really seem that fast,' said Hislop. 'Tuesday night's lap was much more hairy – the bike was all over the place – but on Thursday everything was smooth and though I knew I'd put in a quick one I had no idea at all it was as fast as that.'

Hislop wasn't about to waste the perfect conditions of that Thursday practice session by merely cracking the 120 mph barrier and smashing the outright and F1 lap records. He had the Junior to think about too. The landmark here was the 114 mph mark and that fell as he bettered Joey Dunlop's old record by 7.2 seconds to put himself top in a third class.

The only one to elude him was the 750 Production. In the same Thursday session he had beaten the lap record in that too, only to see Yamaha's Dave Leach spoil his clean sweep by putting in a lap just 3.4 seconds quicker.

It wasn't as if any of his rivals were hanging about, either. In the Formula One, Brian Morrison, Nick Jefferies, Graeme McGregor, Leach and reigning World Champion, Carl Fogarty, had all lapped at over 117 mph. It seemed, however, that Hislop could do no wrong.

The return of the 125 cc TT after an absence of 15 years gave the Dunlop family a chance to shine as Joey's younger brother, Robert, topped the leaderboard with a lap at 102.84 mph on his single-cylinder Honda, setting himself up for a unique family double. No two brothers have ever won solo TT races, but Robert certainly looked odds on to join Joey on the TT winners' list in the two-lap tiddler race.

In the 1300 Production class another rider with a famous brother – Loctite Yamaha's Nick Jefferies – was also looking for his first TT win. Jefferies headed a Yorkshire Yamaha one-two ahead of Leach, with the Yamaha FZR1000 taking four of the top five places.

On top in the 400 Supersport class with the 1990 version of their TZR250, ridden by Barry Woodland, Yamaha was the only maker in with a realistic chance of spoiling that Honda celebration party. Between them Honda and Yamaha topped the leaderboard in all the solo classes, leaving the newly Durex-sponsored Suzuki team and the Team Green Kawasaki boys to wonder whether either was destined for any TT success.

The much-touted possibility of a 350 cc sidecar limit became more of a likelihood when two sidecar competitors died in separate incidents during the same Tuesday evening practice session. Driver John Mulcahy, a Scot who lived in Newcastle-upon-Tyne, was killed when his Suzuki outfit crashed into a hedge at the top of Barregarrow. And 27-year-old Italian passenger Marco Fattorelli died in a crash at Gorse Lea, Greeba.

Manxman Phil Hogg, the fastest Islander ever on the TT course, was killed instantly on Friday morning when he crashed his TZR250 Yamaha on the flat-out Ballagarey right-hander near Glen Vine. These fatalities – particularly the death of Phil Hogg, who was a popular local – cast a dark shadow over the practice proceedings. But worse was to come during the races themselves.

SUPERSPORT

To say Hislop was not a hot favourite to lift the first Supersport 600 TT would be like saying Frank Bruno was in with a fighting chance against Tyson. Despite a practice time which put him only a couple of seconds ahead of Yamaha's Leach, the Scot was, in reality, in a class apart.

It wasn't a long wait before he proved just how determined he was. By Ballacraine – seven miles out on lap one – Hislop was an amazing four seconds clear. By the end of the first lap that gap had grown to more than 15 seconds. He was already home and dry. From a standing start the amazing, spiky-haired Hislop had fired off a lap of 113.15 mph – and his second lap was even quicker. Leach didn't have a chance.

At the end of four laps Leach, who was later to suffer a race-threatening misfire, trailed by 28.8 seconds, victim of Hislop's go-for-it-from-the-start tactics. 'I planned to do a Dunlop – get away fast and put the pressure on in the first two laps. It worked a dream,' said Hislop, whose average for the 150.92 miles was 112.58 mph.

It had been a lonely ride for the Honda man who hardly saw a soul once he had passed first men away, Brian Morrison and Nick Jefferies. They took fifth and sixth places after a tremendous battle on the roads which remained undecided until Signpost on the final lap when Morrison outbraked his Yorkshire rival and headed him over the line by just 1.4 seconds. Suzuki's James Whitham took third spot, despite worries that his thirsty GSX-FK600 would run out of gas, after overhauling his team-mate Phil Mellor. 'I caught Phil – who started 10 seconds ahead – and then used him for a tow to save fuel,' said Whitham, who finished ten seconds ahead of his Durex Suzuki team-mate.

Mellor had a trouble-free ride until after the finish line, when he crashed turning into the paddock as his throttle stuck open. The incident left him wincing with pain from a couple of bruised ribs. He wasn't the only one in the wars. Geoff Johnson had to have an inch-long sliver of flint removed from his shoulder after clipping a wall at Glen Helen on his Loctite Yamaha. That put him out for the rest of the week. And Scot Jim Moodie was also sidelined after crashing and injuring his arm at Creg-ny-Baa.

With Honda-Yamaha-Suzuki making up the

PHIL MELLOR

Phil Masters

Phil Mellor was simply the nicest man in road racing. In a macho sport like motor cycling there are few who, it can be said, were loved by all. Phil – Mez to everyone who knew him personally and to the fans who knew only his undoubted talent as a rider – was unique.

In the 11 years I knew him I can honestly say I never heard of anyone with a bad word to say about the Yorkshire painter and decorator turned pro-racer. And I never heard Mez say a bad word about anyone else.

Phil, who died in hospital after losing control of his 1100 Suzuki at Doran's Bend on the second lap of the 1300 Production TT, never made an enemy in a sport where enemies are not difficult to make.

He first shot to prominence when he won the 250 cc Newcomers race in the 1978 Manx Grand Prix. He was a three-times TT winner and captured no fewer than 11 national titles in his distinguished career.

As a rider he was respected and admired by everyone in the sport as he achieved success on the roads and the short circuits. He loved the TT and the Mountain Course above all others, regarding it as the ultimate challenge in his beloved sport.

And as a man his invariably cheerful approach to everything he did earned him the love of everyone who knew him. In a poll for the best-liked rider in Britain, Mez would have come out on top every time.

The night before he lost his life, at the age of 35, I came across Mez and his baby son Thomas in the Imperial Hotel in Douglas. Beaming his infectious grin as he cradled the four-month-old baby in his arms he said: 'I'll bet you never thought you'd see me like this, Paul – in charge of a baby instead of a bike.' The real tragedy is that I never will again.

PAUL FOWLER

one-two-three, only Kawasaki missed out. Ray Swann, who had survived an horrific practice moment which saw him being dragged both-legs-one-side along the road at 120 mph, went out when his engine ran out of sparks at Ballacraine on the opening lap.

Hislop had led all the way. And it was a similar story in the 400 class as mild-mannered Dubliner, Eddie Laycock, took his 1990-spec RGV250 Suzuki to a runaway win over similarly mounted Aussie Graeme McGregor by 1m 19.6s.

'The only problem all the way was a rabbit which dashed in front of me at Governors Bridge. Other than that it went like a dream,' said Eddie, after picking up his second TT win.

McGregor also had trouble at Governors, falling at about one mph before leaping back on and heading fastest qualifier Barry Woodland home by a healthy nine seconds. Neil Tuxworth was the first four-stroke home on his FZR400 Yamaha in fourth place, just ahead of ex-winner Mat Oxley.

Kawasaki's KR1 had been in contention in the hands of Kevin Mawdsley, who was lying fifth before a high-speed crash at Glen Helen put him out.

Nick Jefferies, TT expert, was second in the 1300 Production race on his 1000 Yamaha. He chased Dave Leach all the way but could not match his record-breaking speed.

FORMULA ONE

After his Supersport win, Hislop reckoned he was well set up for an F1 victory. How right he was! Six laps, 226.38 miles and just 1 hour 53 minutes 47.4 seconds after setting off, Hislop had won the fastest race in TT history.

Record after record had gone out of the window as Hislop earned himself a permanent place in the TT Hall of Fame. He put in the first-ever sub-19-minute and first 120 mph racing lap from a *standing start*. On his second lap he upped the outright lap record to 121.13 mph. And his record-breaking race average of 119.36 mph was faster than the old *lap* record.

Course improvements might have helped, but Hislop's stunning achievement simply can't be underestimated. Journalists were already running out of superlatives – and Hislop was still in with a chance of three more wins!

Steve's tactics were just the same as they had been in the 600 race – crucify them on the first lap and the rest of the race is a piece of cake. While the others were dithering over tyres Hislop picked slicks straight away and his opening lap sent shock waves through the Island. He piloted the RVF750 around the 37.73-mile circuit in 18m 43.2s at a speed of 120.92 mph to establish a 25.8 second lead over Honda team-mate Morrison.

Morrison is no slouch himself, but he just wasn't in the game. Imagine putting in a 120.03 mph lap and still being second! But that's what happened to Morrison on the second lap as Hislop pulled even further away.

This time the race wasn't exactly trouble-free for Steve. He had one heart-stopping moment at Kirk Michael when he forgot to pump his brakes and ended up on the pavement. 'I had just caught Morrison and Jefferies when it happened. I had to run up the kerb and along the path. I just kicked it down a gear and plopped it back onto the road by the pub.'

There were other problems, too. He'd been so nervous before the 2 p.m. start that he had been unable to face eating anything. That resulted in a leg cramp which lasted for three laps. 'I was dragging my leg all the way down the Sulby Straight – God knows what people must have thought,' he said.

Petrol proved another bugbear. Not fuel consumption – that was fine – but petrol splashed in his eyes during the Honda man's 26-second stop for fuel and a new rear tyre. Only one thought spoiled Hislop's victory party. 'I wish I had been out there racing with a fit Joey Dunlop. That would have been a hell of a race.'

At the flag Hislop was 1m 42.8s in front of fellow-Scot Morrison, who'd surrendered second only once – when he couldn't close his filler cap at the fuel halt and Jefferies briefly went through.

Jefferies was 24.8 seconds adrift in third after struggling with a duff steering damper throughout, while World F1 Champion Carl Fogarty was fourth despite a string of incidents. He hit the kerb at Ballacraine, broke an exhaust bracket and clouted a back-marker in Parliament Square, Ramsey, but still managed to become only the third member of the sub-19-minute club with a final lap of 119.52 mph.

Fogarty's final lap put him 25 seconds ahead of McGregor, who had brake troubles with his Honda in the early stages. McGregor in turn was seven seconds ahead of Whitham on the first of the Suzukis. His team-mate Mellor had retired at Parliament Square with a bad oil leak.

The much-vaunted British challenge from the two JPS Nortons had come to nothing. Trevor Nation expired at the Mountain Box on lap two while Steve Cull, who had been holding a top ten place, went out with gearbox problems.

Hislop aside, the ride of the day award undoubtedly went to the unlucky Dave Leach. His Yamaha clutch cable snapped on the line and he missed his starting slot. Setting off at the back of the field, he was sixty-fifth at the end of lap one. He raced through heavy traffic to haul his way up to nineteenth at the finish, earning himself a bronze replica.

125 cc

As expected, Robert Dunlop kept the famous family in the winners' circle with a start-to-finish victory in the first 125 race for 15 years. After shrugging off a first-lap challenge from Fogarty, Dunlop raced away, beating Welshman Ian Lougher by 15.8 seconds. Fogarty was forced to settle for third.

Not surprisingly, Dunlop set new lap and race records, slicing 35.6 seconds from the late Bill Ivy's 1968 standard, set on a four-cylinder Yamaha, to boost the record to 103.02 mph.

750 PRODUCTION

The three top men all had something to prove as they lined up for the four-lap 750 Production race. Hislop was out for win number three, to prove he was on an equal footing with Dunlop. Leach desperately wanted to make up for the disappointment of his F1 debacle. And Fogarty was out to prove he could compete on equal terms with Hislop.

It turned out to be a classic as the three slugged it out, short-circuit style, to clock the fifth-closest finish in TT history. And it was Fogarty the gambler who was victorious: his decision to go two laps before a fuel stop paid off by giving him a tantalising 1.8-second win over Leach. 'I didn't decide to try for two laps until the start – and I was running out as I cruised to a halt at the end of the second – but it paid off and that's all that matters,' said the F1 champ.

Hislop led after the first lap but, as Fogarty roared past the pits, he knew it was all over for him. 'There was no way I could have gone two laps on one tank and that cost me the race,' said Steve. Leach was disappointed too, as he finished the race with the exhaust hanging off his Yamaha. 'I thought I would be black-flagged on the last lap but I just made it,' he said.

After the last set of stops Fogarty, Hislop and Leach found themselves together on the roads with 30 miles of the race remaining. Hislop,

LOCTITE
DUNLOP

whose Honda never ran quite right, backed off to make sure Fogarty could give Honda another win, and that left Fogarty and Leach to fight it out. Time and again they swapped the lead but, as the Leach exhaust began to flap, Fogarty dived ahead at Brandish to lead over the line by a matter of yards.

JUNIOR

The runaway success story of Steve Hislop came crashing down to earth as he made his bid for the third part of his TT triple, in the Junior. And his misfortune cost Eddie Laycock the chance of his second TT win in a week.

Hislop made one of his now customary lightning starts in the four-lapper, but it all went wrong as he went into Quarry Bends for the second time with an eight-second lead. 'I must have been trying too hard, the front end tucked under. The bike went one way over a bank and I slid backwards up the road. I was lucky to get away with just a bang on the ankle as I flipped up the kerb at over 100 mph,' he said.

Laycock, following hard on the heels of the Scot, saw it all. 'I was convinced it had been a bad one and it really screwed my mind for the next two laps. I backed right off.' Two laps later, when Laycock saw Hislop sitting on the bank, giving him the thumbs-up sign, he got his head down and went for it again – but it was too late.

By then Ulster's Johnny Rea had taken a commanding lead and was heading towards a dream first win in his sixth year of trying. At the halfway stage Rea held a 16-second advantage over Laycock and though the Dubliner whittled that down to a mere six seconds at the Bungalow on the final lap he had been left with too much to do.

Laycock never gave up, though, and the gap at the grandstand was a mere 2.8 seconds. Rea could hardly believe it. 'My Yamaha was misfiring badly on the last lap and I never thought I would be able to hang on,' he said.

1988 Manx GP winner Steve Hazlett took third place on his ex-Laycock EMC when McGregor's in-line twin 350 Kawasaki stuck in first gear and Steve Williams's Yamaha seized on lap three. Fogarty took fourth place despite suffering a bust fork oil seal which sprayed oil all over his screen, a broken steering damper and a last-lap power loss.

It had been another record-breaking TT, with Laycock upping Joey Dunlop's old record to 114.04 mph on lap four and Rea just bettering the race record with an average of 112.12 mph.

1300 PRODUCTION

Dave Leach finally made up for his previous disappointments and clinched the TT victory that his talent deserved, but it was a sombre rostrum party that received their laurels in an atmosphere full of sadness, following the tragic deaths of two of the Island's most staunch supporters. Phil Mellor and Steve Henshaw had died in separate incidents just nine miles apart on a fateful second lap of a race hitherto untainted by the bitter taste of tragedy.

It was a bleary-eyed Leach who lined up for the start of the four-lap race, knowing it was his best chance of adding to his single TT success. He had been so nervous that he hadn't slept a wink the night before the race. Once he was flagged off down the Glencrutchery road, though, all trace of nerves disappeared and the Yorkshire Yamaha rider led every lap, beating his own record with a lap of 115.65 mph from a standing start. A lap later he set another new record at 117.25 mph. But Nick Jefferies was right on his tail, poised to take advantage of any mistakes his rival might make.

Leach, starting just behind Jefferies, was always in control, however. His only hitch came at the halfway fuel stop, when a delay in shutting the fuel cap cost him a vital second and Jefferies momentarily went ahead.

By this time tragedy had struck twice. Mellor's 1100 Suzuki crashed at the 110 mph Doran's Bend and he hit a wall. He died later in hospital. His team-mate Whitham crashed at Quarry Bends. Henshaw and Mike Seward touched as they attempted to avoid the debris dislodged by Whitham's accident, Henshaw was killed instantly and Mike Seward badly hurt. Several riders, including Brian Morrison who had stopped to help, pulled in when they saw the incident, but the race went ahead.

Leach and Jefferies battled it out over the Mountain on the last lap but Halifax welder Leach had judged it perfectly and Jefferies was again denied that elusive first TT win. Londoner Alan Batson, drafted into the Loctite Yamaha line-up following Geoff Johnson's injury, amply repaid the team's faith by racing to a fine third place ahead of Scot Howard Selby.

SENIOR

Hislop finally joined Joey Dunlop and Mike Hailwood in the TT Triple Club with another record-breaking win in the Senior TT. And once again it was Jefferies who was the bridesmaid after trailing in 38 seconds behind the new darling of the TT crowds.

Several top men, including Morrison, Kawasaki's Ray Swann and Whitham, stayed

Left: **Steve Hislop's second victory came in the Formula One race. He lapped at record-breaking speed on his way to an emphatic win over Brian Morrison (2) and Nick Jefferies (1).**

It took Johnny Rea *(below)* **six years to win a TT, but the waiting was worthwhile for the Ulsterman. He had a hard job retaining his lead over Eddie Laycock on the last lap, as his Yamaha was misfiring badly.**

away following Wednesday's tragedy, but it would have made no difference to the result. Hislop proved he was the new Lord of the Island in no uncertain fashion.

By the end of the second lap he had a healthy 35-second advantage and, from then on, there was never the remotest chance of failure. 'This was the icing on the cake. The one I really wanted was the Formula One but, after that, three in a week was the target,' he beamed afterwards. 'The events of the other day certainly made me take things a little more easily – I went out to win at the slowest speed possible.' Despite those reservations Hislop still managed to put in two 120 mph-plus laps and they were all over 115 mph.

With the weather looking uncertain, most of the field had picked intermediate fronts with slick rears. As it turned out, slicks all round would have been the correct choice. 'I would definitely have been better with a slick on the front,' said Hislop. 'The first couple of laps were very ragged and, after falling there on Wednesday, I took great care not to push the front at Quarry Bends.'

Despite a couple of slides – at Waterworks and Quarry Bends – Jefferies was only troubled by the wind on the Mountain as he cruised to a well-controlled second ahead of McGregor, one of the only top men to have gambled on a front slick. He came from fifth on lap one to finish ahead of Robert Dunlop.

Laycock was the first two-stroke man home, fifth on his ageing NS500 Honda, despite running throughout with no brakes. Fogarty's hopes of a double were dashed when his Honda shed a breather pipe and the engine covered him with oil, causing him to pull out at the end of lap five.

The luckless Leach was in the wars again, too. He was black-flagged on lap four and forced to limp back to the pits for adjustments. Rejoining minus his Yamaha fairing, he finished sixteenth, just missing out on a silver replica.

And the chequered flag hero was JPS Norton's Steve Cull. Eighth at the beginning of the last lap, his chain snapped at Governors and, to the cheers of the crowd, he pushed the last mile to finish a heroic twenty-third.

Steve Hislop was undoubtedly the star of this TT but, after the events of Black Wednesday, most agreed that this was a TT that they were glad to go home from.

SIDECARS

Mick Boddice and Chas Birks were the hottest of hot favourites for both the two sidecar races but their fortunes in the two three-lap races could hardly have been more different.

Their first outing was over after just a couple of miles when a split in a 50p fuel line sidelined them at Snugborough – and left the field wide open.

Kenny Howles and Steve Pointer led for two laps and were looking set for victory when it was cruelly snatched from them through little fault of their own. Because of a timing mix-up, the pair were getting inaccurate signals through the last lap – had they had the right ones, they could possibly have won. As it was, local men Dave Molyneux and Colin Hardman became the first Manx winners for more than 20 years, after being handed victory by just 1.2 seconds.

Howles, who lost his clutch halfway round lap one, started five seconds adrift of his allotted time and the information his signallers had been relying on was consequently out by that margin. It was only when the timekeepers made their adjustment at the end that Molyneux, much to his surprise, came out on top.

In the Formula Two 'race within a race' Dave Saville and Richard Crossley dominated, just missing out on a 100 mph circuit with a lap at an amazing 99.23 mph.

When Boddice makes up for a disappointment, he certainly does it in style. Without even bothering to strip their outfit, save replacing the split pipe, Boddice and Birks set off at an incredible pace in the second sidecar race, to show the opposition a clean pair of wheels. From a standing start they shattered Jock Taylor's 'unbeatable' lap record with a sub-21-minute lap of 20m 54s – 108.31 mph – and though they slowed after that amazing time, they won the race by over a minute from Scots Dennis Brown and Bill Nelson.

'I'm happy to have the record but I hope I never have to go that fast again,' said Mick, whose seventh TT win – his sixth with Birks in the chair – makes him the most successful sidecar rider ever on the Mountain Circuit.

Saville completed the double, taking thirteenth overall in the race, which is now certain to go F2 only in 1990.

STEVE HENSHAW

Steve Henshaw never won the glittering prizes of motor cycle racing but the likeable and popular Nottinghamshire man was one of the most respected of British competitors throughout his 15-year career.

Henshaw, 35, quit a partnership in a bike dealership to turn full-time professional racer and consistently made a living from the sport through his dedicated and committed approach to the business of racing.

Twice winner of the Scarborough Gold Cup, Henshaw was a journeyman-racer who could turn his hand to any type of track, but who excelled on pure road circuits, from the Isle of Man to Macau.

He was killed instantly when he crashed trying to avoid debris dislodged by an earlier accident at Quarry Bends, on the second lap of the 1300 Production TT.

I got to know Steve well through many trips to Macau in the Far East where he amused all as he refused to make any compromises to the exotic location. While others would make forays to the adventurous eating houses and night clubs of the colony, Steve refused resolutely to eat anything other than English food. The first item he packed for the trip was always his stock of English tea-bags.

His professionalism, winning smile and willingness to do a good turn for anyone will be sadly missed.

PAUL FOWLER

Two Plus Two

US ROAD RACING

By JOHN ULRICH · AMERICAN ROADRACING

Superbike racing seasons in America have frequently been marked by epic battles between a pair of riders, corner after corner, lap after lap, race after race. Eddie Lawson and Freddie Spencer in 1982. Wayne Rainey and Mike Baldwin in 1983. Fred Merkel and Rainey in 1986. Rainey and Kevin Schwantz in 1987. Bubba Shobert and Doug Polen in 1988. That wasn't the case in 1989. There have been other years when no battle between a pair of riders defined the season; 1984 and 1985 largely belonged to Merkel alone, being the only man on a factory bike backed by a factory team for those entire seasons.

But the 1989 Superbike season in America was like no other. There was no defining battle – no dominance by one rider – and the championship was won by a slow-spoken 28-year-old from Louisiana who kept his eye on the goal and stayed out of trouble while his competitors crashed, broke down and generally threw away their chances.

Not that Calby 'Jamie' James didn't run at the front: he did, winning one out of the six races that constituted the abbreviated AMA Superbike season, finishing second in another, third in another, and fourth and fifth in the other two of the five races he finished; he crashed out of the sixth while racing his team-mate for the lead, and the team-mate fell, too, after they collided.

In six races, five different men on four different brands of motor cycle won, marking the most diverse season in recent memory. Three of the six wins were straight-up racing triumphs; three were inherited victories.

When the season started, four men were considered most likely to win races and the championship: James, 28, and team-mate Scott Russell, 25, on Yoshimura R & D of America Suzukis; Dave Sadowski, 26, on a Vance & Hines Suzuki; and Doug Chandler, 23, on the Muzzy Racing Kawasaki. Sadowski didn't win a single race, being let down by his machine at every single event, twice while leading. Chandler missed two races because he didn't feel well, the under-development Kawasaki broke in two others, but Doug did win the last two events. Russell flat-out blew it, winning one race but making mistakes that cost him his chance to win two others and the championship as well. And James, keeping his eye on the goal, keeping the big picture in mind, became 1989 Superbike Champion.

More remarkable than that was the fact that the racing series that used to transform championship-winning riders into rich men with $100,000 bonuses and offers of Grand Prix rides ended with the new Superbike Champion living at the home of his long-time girlfriend's parents and trying to figure out how he could actually make some money racing in 1990. Instead of pulling down huge purses and a healthy salary with win bonuses, new champion James paid Yoshimura R & D of America $5000 cash and 40 per cent of his earnings (about another $15,000) for the privilege of winning the 1989 AMA Superbike Championship. The Yoshimura team, which receives factory bikes and monetary support from Suzuki under contract, also kept all the money received from team sponsors like Michelin and EBC, with James only allowed to sign for and personally collect money from his helmet sponsor, Arai.

In fairness, James was reluctant to talk about his arrangement with Yoshimura; but the team had interviewed enough other riders – and offered them a ride under those terms – that finding out what the deal was constituted no trouble. James's team-mate, Scott Russell, had a similar arrangement, but didn't pay $5000 up front, that payment instead being deducted from his winnings during the season. Sadowski's deal with Vance & Hines (theoretical arch-rival to Yoshimura but, in terms of 1989 reality, merely a well-dressed, well-equipped exercise in spending money with no results to speak of) was better only because Sadowski didn't have to pay the team money and was allowed to keep all of whatever he won. Never mind that he rarely finished a race, and never had an entire event without a mechanical problem.

John Flory

The best deal in AMA Superbike racing in 1989 belonged to Doug Chandler, riding a Rob Muzzy-prepared Kawasaki ZX-7, a machine with its own teething problems during early season development but which turned into the only two-race winner by season's end. For riding the green machine Chandler was paid a modest contract fee (rumoured to be about $30,000), making him the only paid rider in a class that used to boast half a dozen fully salaried and supported riders in any given season.

John Flory

Why did men like James, Russell and Sadowski agree to pay to ride, or at best ride for free, to risk life and limb for nothing but what they could win? Because all were, before their chance to ride for Yoshimura or Vance & Hines, self-supporting privateers. All had had the chance – and took it – to spend every dime of their money (and anybody else's they could get their hands on) racing on their own bikes, getting lapped by the guys with the works bikes, all the time chasing the dream that someday they'd have bikes like those, would win big races and

Jamie James won the Superbike Championship but did not get rich doing so. Americans have a stronger grip than ever on the World Championship and their club racing scene is very strong, but between them the National title is floundering.

Scott Russell *(bottom left)* **was team-mate to James in the Yoshimura squad. Between them they had a strong grasp on the championship; the only thing that went wrong was knocking each other out of contention at Elkhart Lake.**

become famous racing stars. And if, by the time they got good enough to be offered a ride on a good bike, the rules and the situation had altered, that didn't change the fact that the alternative was to keep riding their own bikes on their own dime.

These are men who have struggled for their shot at racing success. James went racing on a Yamaha FZ750 sponsored by his girlfriend's father in 1987, who estimated they spent $100,000 with no results to speak of, James learning the hard way just about every way not to do well. He had his brilliant rides, the year before he tried a Superbike, riding instead a Yamaha RZ350 and being the only kid who could run with Kevin Schwantz when Schwantz raced an RZ350 too. A badly broken femur kept James out of serious racing for almost a season, and it took another season for his confidence to return enough so that he was competitive. By the end of 1987, though, he was a hard charger again, but he didn't crash a lot like he had before. Asked about that he'd say something about being in traction for months making a fellow not want to crash much.

In 1988 James rode for Team Hammer, logging over 5000 miles in endurance and sprint races, and winning his share. By the end of the year he was one of the best riders in the country, two other top up-and-comers being Scott Russell (who James often had to race in 1988 endurance events) and Dave Sadowski (who had James's Team Hammer ride two years earlier).

The situation was one long in coming, an extreme example of why it is that top American stars leave the country to race overseas as fast as they master their trade. The American motor cycle market was a shadow of its former self in 1989: the big factory teams were all gone, replaced by three contracted independent teams, two racing Suzukis, one Kawasakis.

There were fewer races, the year's schedule starting out with seven events listed and ending up with just six Superbike races, Sears Point opting for a cheaper race with only Supersport and 250 cc classes.

There was less money to be won with a Superbike, Camel having abandoned its sponsorship of the entire AMA series and, instead, opting to sponsor a few races; Camel also didn't renew the lucrative five-lap, $10,000-to-win Camel Challenges that served as big pay-days for top pilots in 1987 and 1988.

Complaints and proposed solutions abounded. Most complainants pointed to the lack of television coverage of AMA events and what seemed to be an emphasis on collecting back-gate entry fees from more and more riders by adding classes run in conjunction with Superbike Nationals. But there were bright spots as well. While overall

Rich Oliver *(right)* was fast and consistent, but chasing Kocinski is a risky proposition at any time.

It was some consolation for competitors who knew they were not in the same league as John Kocinski that the man from Arkansas could go to the World Championship and demonstrate that very few of *those* riders could race him either.

John Flory

John Flory

motor cycle sales were down in the US, sportsbike sales as a percentage of the market were increasing in importance; only the hard-core, dedicated motor cycle enthusiasts were still buying motor cycles, although selling motor cycles through racing still had its appeal.

Spectator attendance was up for most events, perhaps due to interest in road racing being stimulated by the US Grand Prix and the US round of the Superbike World Championship. But, mostly, things were simply different from what they had been. It used to be that there were Superbike riders, and guys who rode in the supporting Supersport races for close-to-stock Production bikes. In 1989 the guys who ran at the front in the Superbike races also ran at the front in the Supersport events. And most Superbike privateers supported their racing largely with contingency money won with Supersport-class machines at local, non-National races across the country.

Average race speeds were generally down in Superbike events, the races being everywhere slower than they were in 1988, except at Road Atlanta. But they were no less amusing, confounding, impossible to predict.

The newspapers called for Doug Polen to win at Daytona, and he agreed, figuring he'd lap the field. His Yoshimura Suzuki sprung an oil leak, while he was in the lead. Russell's effort never got off the grid; he stalled his bike on the start and got hit from behind by another rider, causing a race red flag and damaging his bike so that, while he made the restart, he was never a factor. Sadowski led, and his bike broke. Rich Arnaiz led on his Yamaha FZR750, and crashed. Dale Quarterley led on a Ducati 851, but his bike broke. James led for a long time in the closing stages of the race, then pitted three laps from the finish when his bike started missing, James thinking it was out of fuel; he got a splash of gas and finished second, but his bike's problem turned out to be a broken spark plug. And John Ashmead won on a 1986 Honda VFR750, his first notable racing success since winning a Superbike race at Laguna Seca in 1985. Kevin Rentzell was third on a ratty privateer Suzuki; 250 cc Grand Prix regular Martin Wimmer was sixth on an internally stock GSXR750 streetbike barely illegal for Supersport classes. Chandler (who at one time was sponsored by Freddie Spencer Racing) didn't ride the Kawasaki, saying he was too ill with the 'flu.

Russell managed to get off the grid with the field at Road Atlanta, and won. Sadowski raced James for second most of the event, and took the position despite a slipping clutch; James had his own problems, being forced to use a stock (and legal) swing arm when the trick (and illegal) works swing arm originally on his race bike broke. Chandler's bike broke in the opening stages of the race, while he led.

Russell crashed his Supersport bike hard at Loudon, breaking a collarbone; the race was between Sadowski, James and Quarterley, Sadowski's bike breaking while he barely led James, James finally pulling away from Quarterley, whose Ducati overheated. In an amazing demonstration of pure desire, Russell talked a doctor into giving him a medical release and raced, finishing third on the demanding, 10-turn, 1.8-mile Loudon course. Chandler had

Doug Chandler started to feature on the improving Kawasaki and won the last two rounds.

John Flory

retired his Kawasaki with an oil leak.

A week later, at Elkhart Lake, Russell led on the last lap; James, having closed up from a deficit of 20 bike-lengths to right behind Russell, tried to go around his team-mate entering a turn. But Russell swung wide to set up for the turn, and James and Russell collided, their bikes locking together and both running off the track and crashing in a cloud of dust. While they squared off, with Russell looking ready to throw fists at any moment, Arnaiz cruised past, unaware of what had happened. Arnaiz was shocked when he arrived at the winner's circle and found himself the winner; he thought he had finished third! Sadowski's bike quit on the grid, with a wiring harness problem; Quarterley's Ducati was out with a crankshaft problem. Chandler didn't start, being beaten up in a Supersport class collision and crash involving Sadowski, who knocked James into Chandler. James and Chandler both fell, but Sadowski escaped without crashing.

At Mid-Ohio, Chandler and the Muzzy Kawasaki won. Russell was second, coming from the back of the grid after stalling in his heat race, and out-of-retirement Dan Chivington was third on George Vincensi's VFR750F Honda.

James was fifth at Mid-Ohio, mindful of the way the chance of winning the Superbike Championship had been thrown away in crashes at the slippery track by Polen (1988), Schwantz (1987) and Rainey (1986). James wanted nothing to do with that type of trouble, and he was nervous. Forget the championship, Yoshimura R & D of America boss Suehiro Watanabe told him. Win the race. James rejected the advice.

That left the final race, at a new track, Heartland Park, constructed in Topeka, Kansas, in the centre of America's wheat-growing bread-basket. James was nervous in Topeka, too – even more so when he discovered on the warm-up lap that something was terribly wrong with the front end of his race bike. Somehow a bent front wheel had been installed, the mechanics and Michelin tyre technicians not catching the damage from some earlier crash and, instead, installing a new tyre and bolting the wheel up to James's Suzuki. James wasn't sure what the problem was, only knowing that his bike chattered terribly on the brakes.

Maybe it's a brake disc, and maybe it'll explode, James thought to himself. He used the brakes gingerly, gently, then speeded up when nothing bad happened. Arnaiz, the only man close enough to James to be a threat at this point, caught and passed him, so James speeded up again. He finished fourth, behind Chandler, Russell and Quarterley – and became Superbike Champion. Then he started thinking about the possibility of not just having a ride on a good bike, but actually making a living from racing.

John Kocinski had an easier time of it in the 250 cc class, being paid well by Kenny Roberts to ride a Team Viceroy TZ250 Yamaha tuned by Bud Aksland. Kocinski won six out of eight races and tied up the championship before the season even ended, despite missing one race with a broken wrist and riding hurt in two others. Every 250 cc race except one (at slippery Mid-Ohio) was won with a higher average speed than the corresponding race in 1988, and Kocinski shattered lap records and demoralised the competition throughout the season. What used to be the most competitive, closest racing in the country turned into a one-man demonstration: anybody who can win 250 cc Grands Prix on a Yamaha can win the AMA 250 cc Championship, easily.

Kocinski won at Daytona. But he fell at Road Atlanta while leading his heat race, low-siding and sliding to a halt unhurt. As he stood up, his back to the track, however, Richard Moore also crashed, and Moore's bike slid into him, sending Kocinski head over heels, backwards. When he landed his right wrist broke – and this a week before his scheduled 500 cc Grand Prix debut.

Rich Oliver won at Road Atlanta, and then won again at Brainerd, a 250 cc National race being held there in conjunction with the Superbike World Championship round. Kocinski rode at Brainerd and finished second to Oliver, only four weeks after the crash at Road Atlanta, and just a few days after cutting off his cast; his injured wrist was supported by a special brace.

At that point Oliver, riding a TZ250 for Randy Mamola Racing (Mamola's answer to Roberts's team, but on a smaller, more informal scale), led the 250 cc points standings. But Oliver's lead evaporated when he crashed at Loudon, and Kocinski won. Kocinski won again at Elkhart Lake, with Oliver second. And again at Mid-Ohio, Oliver sixth. And at Sears Point, Oliver crashing again. Kocinski's crushing, runaway victory at Topeka was simply a demonstration of his skill, and of the superiority of Grand Prix Dunlop tyres as opposed to the for-sale Dunlops used by Oliver and the rest of the field. Run as hard as Kocinski, have GP potential, and we'll supply you with the good stuff, too, a Dunlop tyre technician told Oliver.

Oliver could take some comfort in a $10,000 cheque from Castrol, the 250 cc series sponsor, issued for being the highest-placed rider to use and endorse Castrol oil. Kocinski, for the third straight year, wasn't eligible because he's sponsored by another oil company.

WORLD SUPERBIKE CHAMPIONSHIP

By NICK HARRIS

The single most important factor for the World Superbike Championship in 1989 was the simple fact that it survived. Despite losing its major backer on the eve of the first round of the 11-round championship, the series staggered on towards a brighter financial future under Italian racing mogul Maurizio Flammini.

Six days before the opening round in Britain, the New Zealand-based promoters, Sports Marketing Company, ceased trading. They'd lost an estimated one million pounds supporting the series in its first year, in 1988. Failure to secure a major sponsor to a series that had been a great success in that first season was the major reason for the company's collapse. SMC had implemented a travel fund to pay the expenses of the top 25 riders from last year's championship. When SMC disappeared from the scene there was nobody left to pay that money and prospects looked bleak as the field lined up on the Donington grid in late March. The FIM stepped in and paid the fund for the opening round; the riders and the teams were then left largely to their own devices. They were paid travelling expenses to go to the American, Canadian and Japanese rounds, but for the remainder of the races they had to find the money.

The riders and teams stuck together, however, and went on to provide some superb racing. In September they were duly rewarded when Flammini and the FIM eventually signed a three-year deal. Flammini already promotes the Italian, Yugoslav and Czechoslovakian Grands Prix so his latest acquisition makes him a very powerful force in world motor cycle racing. The Japanese advertising agency, Dentsu, who manage the accounts for all four of the major Japanese manufacturers – Honda, Yamaha, Suzuki and Kawasaki – had been interested in backing the series but they kept the nervous FIM waiting too long and Flammini stepped in.

It would have been a tragedy if the World Superbike series had gone under, because the silhouette formula provided some breathtaking sport which enabled the manufacturers to put their products in the shop window under racing conditions. That first round at Donington Park was a perfect example of what the series was all about: just 4.17 seconds split the 40-strong field, with five of the six manufacturers taking part in the series on the front two rows. Honda, Yamaha, Suzuki and Kawasaki were all represented by importer teams while Ducati and Bimota provided works machinery from Italy.

American Fred Merkel was committed to the complete series and determined to retain his title, riding an Italian-sponsored RC30 Honda. Davide Tardozzi, who missed out on the title last year after crashing in the final round, repeated that performance at Donington, crashing his private Bimota in practice and missing the race. His place in the works Bimota team had been taken by new Italian sensation Giancarlo Falappa, who joined former Grand Prix rider Fabio Biliotti. The latest YB4EI Bimota was very quick and used more carbon fibre to comply with FIM weight regulations. It also featured inverted Ohlins forks and a triangulated bracing section on the swing arm. Falappa was to prove just how competitive the machine was, when he won the second Donington heat.

Ducati only had time to prepare two machines for former Grand Prix star, Raymond Roche. This left young Italian Baldassarre Monti without a Ducati to ride, but plenty was to be seen of this young man later in the series. The new Ducati V-twin was a beauty and Roche was fastest in both qualifying sessions as well as posting quickest lap time in the second heat. Like the Bimota, it sported inverted Ohlins forks, a stronger swing arm, new-style exhausts – and Roche reported extra bhp from the 883 cc engine.

World Endurance Champions in 1988, the French pair of Hervé Moineau and Thierry Crine rode Minolta Suzuki France GSXR750s, while Kawasaki were represented by former Grand Prix rider Patrick Igoa and Christophe Bouheben, riding their rather overweight Kawasaki France ZXR750s.

Yamahas were scattered throughout the entry, with Britain's Terry Rymer riding the Loctite-sponsored machine with the latest factory parts, an obvious threat to the established stars,

Kel Edge

Kel Edge

together with Swedish ace Anders Andersson with his superbly prepared OWO1. Last year's runner-up, Italian Fabrizio Pirovano, returned on the FJ Valli/Belgarda Yamaha OWO1.

Throw in the likes of former British champion and Grand Prix star Roger Burnett on the Honda Britain-prepared RC30, West Germans Peter Rubatto and Ernst Gschwender and Swiss ace Andreas Hofmann and the series seemed to have no problem in producing the goods out on the track. Meanwhile the problems went on behind the scenes.

Another former Grand Prix rider, the Belgian Stéphane Mertens, missed the Donington round, but his arrival later in the series, on an RC30 from Honda Belgium, had a major bearing on the final outcome of the championship. At the time of going to press there are two rounds of the series left, in Australia and New Zealand, but the title looks to be securely on its way back to

Fred Merkel gets the jump on the rest of the field at Mosport but saw his championship lead whittled away towards the end of the season.

Stéphane Mertens *(opposite)* proved increasingly consistent on the Honda Belgium bike, making him a stronger championship threat than he had been in '88.

Honda. The two Ms, Merkel and Mertens, have fought a tremendous duel at the front, with Merkel on his way to the Antipodes hanging onto a slender two-point lead.

Things looked very different at that opening round in England, in some unusual March sunshine. After two cracking races Brits Terry Rymer and Roger Burnett headed the championship table with 32 points apiece, after some typical Italian indiscretions. Pirovano won the first leg, riding 30 superb laps which had the 20,000 crowd on their feet. The heat developed into an Italy versus Britain battle, with Pirovano and Falappa meeting Rymer and Burnett head on. Falappa and his Bimota tried to prise open a gap, overtaking a back-marker who was not there, and disappeared into the gravel on the twenty-second lap, at McLeans. He returned to the fray, but out of the points in nineteenth place. Pirovano, who'd only been road racing three years after a successful motocross career, kept the Italian flag flying with a famous victory. Burnett was second, despite being sprayed with oil from Falappa's breather pipe, and Rymer was third. Champion Merkel, using Pirelli tyres for the first time, had his problems but still managed to finish fourth. Roche had gone out on the first lap with ignition troubles.

The second race was even better, with Frenchman Crine leading for the opening couple of laps until he exited in spectacular style at Coppice. Falappa, desperate to make up for his first-leg excursion, gradually pulled away from the chasing pack of Rymer, Burnett and Pirovano. With seven laps remaining Pirovano made his move, pulling away from the British duo, but they fought back and hauled in his advantage. With just two laps remaining the Italian went wide at the old hairpin and crashed. Falappa made no mistakes this time and won from Rymer, who pipped Burnett for second place. Scottish TT star Steve Hislop was a creditable fourth, in front of Andersson and Merkel.

Fiery Fred Merkel fought back in the best possible way at the second round at the Hungaroring. His aggressive style, plus the perfect combination of his RC30 Honda and its Pirelli tyres, proved ideal partners for the tricky circuit and the opposition never saw which way he went. He won both legs comfortably, to snatch the lead in the championship. It was a disappointing day for the early series leaders from Britain. Ironically, Rymer and Burnett collided in the first race: Burnett went down and then missed the second leg after discovering an oil leak on the warm-up lap. Rymer, seventh in that first leg, could only manage ninth in the second and slipped to third in the championship table.

Pirovano had briefly led the first race, until Merkel charged by. Behind Fred the battle then

Kel Edge

Raymond Roche *(left)* **made little secret of the fact that he wanted to return to the Grands Prix, but he still made a first-class job of racing the Ducati.**

Fabrizio Pirovano *(centre)* **was Yamaha's strongest contender.**

The uncompromising riding style of Bimota's Giancarlo Falappa *(bottom)* **made him a hit with the fans, even if he was not quite as popular with some of his fellow-competitors.**

Kel Edge

Kel Edge

raged between Pirovano, Ducati-mounted Roche, British Grand Prix star Rob McElnea, riding the OWO1 Yamaha, and Mertens, making his first Superbike appearance of the season. Roche eventually pushed Pirovano back to third, in front of McElnea and Mertens.

They were at it again in the second leg, with Falappa and young Baldassarre Monti joining in the fun too. But Roche crashed out on the first lap, and Pirovano moved into second place in the championship after finishing second in front of McElnea (who then departed to the Grands Prix with Cabin Honda), Falappa, Monti and Mertens.

Despite its uncertain future the series then crossed the Atlantic for the first time, for the third round at Mosport Park in Canada. The racing turned into a battle between the locals and the established stars, with Merkel winning the first leg, in front of the biggest crowd at a Canadian motor cycle race for over 20 years. Honda-mounted Canadian Rueben McMurter overtook him on the seventh lap but eventually dropped back to third behind Roche, with Mertens fourth.

The crowd got their reward in the second leg, though, when McMurter pushed Merkel back to third on the last bend. The race was won by Falappa. After a false start the race distance was reduced by one lap and, on the very last bend, Merkel tried to outbrake Falappa. They touched fairings, the American star nearly crashed, then ran wide and that gave McMurter the chance to squeeze his Honda into second. Pirovano retained his second place in the championship by finishing fourth, in front of Mertens.

The teams then faced a long drive to Brainerd in Minnesota for the fourth round, where Roche and the Ducati really came into their own. The gritty Frenchman won both legs, but Merkel hung onto his championship lead with fourth and third places respectively. It was here that Mertens began to look threatening, moving into fourth place in the championship with a third behind Roche and Pirovano in the first leg, and second behind Roche in the second heat. Rymer also bounced back to form, returning to third place in the table following his two fifth-place finishes in America.

Endurance ace Alex Vieira made his first Superbike appearance of the season at the fifth round, at the Österreichring in Austria – and what a debut! Riding an RC30 Honda he won the first leg following a ten-man battle that lasted the complete distance and whose outcome was in doubt right up to the chequered flag. Amidst all the outbraking, slipstreaming and fairing-bashing, Roche emerged in second place, in front of Mertens, who led the Italian trio of Ducati-mounted Massimo Broccoli, Pirovano on the Yamaha, and Monti on another Ducati. Merkel never became involved and finished a lowly eleventh. He was much happier in the second leg, ending up third behind Mertens and Pirovano, with Broccoli fourth.

Merkel thus held a 13-point lead going into the next round at Paul Ricard in France at the end of July. Despite a relatively unsuccessful day he increased that lead by another seven

Close action at the Österreichring. Broccoli leads Mertens, Roche (hidden), Monti, Pirovano and Vieira.

points in the French sunshine, but Mertens now moved into second place. The Belgian Honda rider won the first leg, which was delayed by 20 minutes following an accident on the warm-up lap. Two laps from the finish Mertens raced past former Grand Prix star, American Mike Baldwin, riding the works Bimota, with local hero Roche third in front of early leader Terry Rymer. Merkel was a disappointing eighth but had a better ride in a cracking second leg. Falappa was the eventual winner of that race, ahead of Roche and Mertens with Merkel in fourth.

The only real winner at the seventh round in Japan was the weather. A typhoon battered the Sugo race track, spelling bad news for the regulars who were given a hard time in the rain by 'guest' riders. In steady drizzle American Doug Polen won the first leg on his Yoshimura Suzuki ahead of Australians Michael Dowson and Rob Phillis, Falappa restoring some European pride in fourth place with Pirovano seventh and Mertens eighth. Merkel slipped and slid his way to sixteenth and no points. Then the heavens opened for the second leg. In these appalling conditions Dowson displayed great skill, piloting his Yamaha to victory in front of Japanese ace Kenichiro Iwahashi on a Honda with Falappa a very worthy third. Mertens closed to within eight points of Merkel in the table after finishing eighth – four places in front of the championship leader.

Fred Merkel lost his lead to Mertens at the eighth round, at Hockenheim in West Germany, although the day actually belonged to Raymond Roche. Riding the Ducati the Frenchman won both hotly contested legs – but Mertens's consistency was beginning to pay off. In the first leg Roche and Mertens had fought a titanic duel around the ultra-fast circuit. They got tangled up with the pace car going into the last lap, Roche taking full advantage, with Vieira third and Merkel down in eighth. The second leg saw even better racing, with Roche, Falappa and Mertens contesting every inch of the circuit. Merkel managed fourth, but his effort was not enough to prevent Mertens leading the championship for the first time, by just three points.

That three-point lead evaporated in the Sicilian sunshine, at the last round in Europe. New championship leader Mertens looked in brilliant form and won the opening race after a head-to-head confrontation with Merkel, who was second. But the Belgian rider's luck disappeared in the second leg: he dropped from the leading group when his Honda went onto three cylinders and finally stuttered over the line in seventh place. Roche won, but a determined Merkel was second, which was enough to give him a two-point lead going into the last two rounds.

Next year, hopefully, the World Superbike Championship will have the financial stability it deserves. The riders have produced the goods out on the track over the last two years and it's due to their belief in the series that the future looks so good.

FIM ENDURANCE CUP

By MAT OXLEY · MOTOR CYCLE NEWS

An unexpected posse of Portuguese press and TV crews turned up at September's Bol d'Or 24 Hours. The country's media, which doesn't have too many sporting heroes to cheer, had just discovered a Portuguese World Champion – or at least the winner of the newly titled FIM Endurance Cup.

They could be forgiven their earlier ignorance, for Alex Vieira, born in Portugal and now a French resident with a Portuguese passport, has never been a self-publicist.

But, alongside the GP demigods, Vieira rates as one of the true heroes of the 1989 season. The 32-year-old won all four rounds of the endurance series, putting in some 2500 faultless miles in 28 aching hours of track time. Now good luck may be a *sine qua non* in endurance racing but devotees of the long-distance haul know you make your own luck: Vieira hardly put a wheel out of line as he evaded the Le Mans oil slicks, outlasted the GP superstars at Suzuka, groped his way through the pitch darkness of Spa and survived a typically chaotic Bol to come out ahead every time.

With Honda putting in its most dedicated endurance effort since a title hat-trick completed in 1986, the outcome of the championship should not perhaps have been in doubt. But the sport's special attraction is the fragility of foregone conclusions – even when Vieira and factory Honda RVF750s are involved.

In April, beneath the towering grandstands of Le Mans, the official Suzuki and Kawasaki tried their best but, as all the know-alls knew, their efforts were eventually fruitless as chain-smoking Honda France chief, Jean-Louis Guillou, orchestrated the RVF's fourth successive Le Mans victory.

Guided by Vieira, Roger Burnett and Jean-Michel Mattioli, the number one RVF led virtually throughout the 24 hours despite a leisurely start which at least allowed the opposition a short-lived dose of the limelight.

Vieira's unhurried move into the lead spelt the beginning of the end for the rest and, before three hours had passed, World Champion Hervé Moineau's hard-pressed GSX-R punched a con rod through its casings, ending Suzuki's hopes. Two hours later a hundred smoky camp fires heralded the Le Mans dusk and a growing lead for Vieira, chased by the factory Kawasaki ZXR7 of Patrick Igoa, Christophe Bouheben and Pierre Bolle.

A second Honda RVF, piloted by the intriguing trio of tough Australian Mal Campbell and the moustachioed sons of legendary Canadian Yvon DuHamel, Mario and Miguel, held third ahead of the first all-Japanese team to tackle the French classic – Takahiro Sohwa, Kiyokazu Tada and Shouichi Tsukamoto on another ZXR7.

Vieira's supremacy wavered in the darkness as ex-Honda teamster Igoa put in a heroic session to pull the ZXR7 to within one lap of the leaders before the Kawasaki faltered with a persistent ignition fault. That put the DuHamels into second and, when the leading Honda snapped its chain at dawn, the number two RVF swept into the lead.

Alex Vieira *(left)* **became the first man ever to win the 'Grand Slam' – Le Mans, Suzuka, Spa and the Bol d'Or. He dominated the endurance championship and, despite the need to be conservative, to protect his title lead at Suzuka, his speed against the Grand Prix men was impressive.**

Slick pit stops are vital to success in endurance racing. This rapid rider change *(right)* **helped the all-French crew of Monneret/de Puiriet/Bertin take fifth place at Le Mans.**

Below: **Shouichi Tsukamoto and his fellow-Japanese riders became heroes in Japan for their third place at Le Mans. Kawasaki have not been competitive in the endurance championship since the ROC Performance team pulled out. The factory Kawasaki still needed more speed – but at least they were making the effort again.**

Colorsport

It fell to Burnett, riding with broken bones in both feet, to push the paralysed Honda back to the pits. But his team was saved the effort of a gruelling counter-attack against the DuHamels when Mario highsided his RVF shortly afterwards.

From then on the number one Honda cruised luxuriously to the flag, followed at a respectful distance by Igoa, while the Japanese ZXR7 and Campbell's battered RVF wrestled for the last rostrum spot. The Japanese came out on top when Miguel DuHamel slipped off the Honda, leaving his team fourth.

Almost three months later battle resumed at Suzuka, Japan. In the stifling Japanese summer heat the Suzuka Eight Hours was a race apart, with 15 factory bikes entered and few of the European privateers making the trip. Myriad GP stars were flown in to contest the event which Honda put second on their list of priorities to winning the 500 world title.

Victory at Suzuka means more for Honda than increased bike sales: the circuit is owned by the giant company and defeat by Yamaha in the previous two years had been a humiliating experience. This year no chances were taken. The RVF had been transformed, with Rothmans GP rookie Mick Doohan twice flown away from his GP commitments in Europe to test the bike he was to share with Wayne Gardner at Suzuka.

In the second outing he'd shattered the lap record so it was no surprise when Doohan established an easy race lead over '88 winner Wayne Rainey on a Lucky Strike YZF750 shared with Kevin Magee. But Suzuka '89 was to be a disastrous affair for the favourites. Honda had planned to let Doohan and Gardner set an unbearable pace to overstretch the opposition and, for a while, the strategy worked.

Less than a minute behind the RVF, Magee went out in the fourth hour when his YZF sheared a sump plug bolt, belching oil over the bike. Now defending a massive lead Honda became victims of their own tactics when Doohan collided an hour later with a slower rider, ending his race. Doohan's exit was bad but it wasn't that bad – for Dominique Sarron and Vieira on another RVF inherited the lead.

The battle was still a two-way Honda/Yamaha duel, though. Just 40 seconds behind the Frenchmen were John Kocinski and Tadahiko Taira on another YZF but the precocious American parked the bike in the seventh hour with valve trouble.

Running a sensibly sustainable pace, Sarron and Vieira weren't threatened from that moment on. Shoji Miyazaki and Tadashi Ohshima were one lap down on another RVF when the flag came out, followed by an earth-shaking fireworks display, with privateer Yamaha OW01 pilots Peter Goddard and Shingo Katoh a fine third.

The opposition was less intense when Vieira returned to Europe to man the lone RVF in the Spa 24 Hours in mid-August – just one factory Suzuki and one factory Kawasaki to deal with. This time there was a definite scent of inevitability in the cool Ardennes air as Vieira and team-mates Burnett and Stéphane Mertens – deputising for injured Mattioli – began to walk away with the lead.

Their task was made that much easier when the Kawasaki ran out of fuel and Michel Graziano aquaplaned the Suzuki into the bales at high speed during a brief Saturday afternoon downpour.

Honda's race wasn't without worries, however. A holed radiator threatened the RVF's healthy lead when the replacement rad suffered an air lock. To prevent overheating Guillou prescribed a lower rev limit and that was enough to safeguard the RVF's lead.

With the other factory bikes recovering from their own problems the British That's Racing team established itself in second, despite minor early race troubles. New teamster Steve Chambers had qualified on pole in drizzly timed qualifying and brilliantly led partners Mat Oxley and Steve Manley. Chambers was the fastest man on the track at night and the team often found themselves overtaking the three factory bikes on their private RC30. And the That's squad kept their second place, resisting late pressure from Suzuki and Kawasaki, who upped the pace from Sunday morning as they contested third.

Kel Edge

Suzuki took third as Igoa suffered alternator problems while the Dutch Yamaha OW01 of Dirk Brand, Gerard Van Der Wal and Kees Doorakkers held fifth – the first time an OW had managed to hold together for more than 12 hours.

Vieira's three-lap winning margin was enough to make him first recipient of the FIM Endurance Cup with one round still to go – the legendary Bol d'Or.

For the second year running Yamaha opted out of flying a factory YZF to the Circuit Paul Ricard to contest September's Bol. Cynics suggested that Yamaha knew it was hopeless trying to beat the RVFs in a 24-hour race and, if that was the case, they were probably right.

Vieira's free practice performance should have been enough to convince Kawasaki and Suzuki that they were once again to play a secondary role in the race. Vieira lapped at 2m 01.68s – a time which would have put him on the third row of the '88 500 GP grid at Ricard, alongside Kevin Schwantz's Suzuki. Vieira smiled at suggestions that he'd been overlooked by GP team-managers anxious to discover a new star.

Sharing with his Le Mans team-mates – Burnett and Mattioli – Vieira's main threat to a third Bol win was the second RVF, this time piloted by Mertens, Mario DuHamel and last-minute signing Fred Merkel. The aggressive Californian Superbike champ was spoiling for a first-hour fight with Vieira but the Portuguese amply demonstrated his unsung talent by leaving Merkel for dead after a close first few laps.

From then on Vieira and his RVF were never headed. Using their significant speed advantage on the Mistral straight, they amassed a lead which allowed them to replace exhaust and water pipe components without surrendering their advantage.

Merkel, meanwhile, had to contend with a serious challenge for second from Igoa's Kawasaki. The ZXR crept ahead in the early hours when the second RVF needed the same exhaust surgery, but the green effort ended at 4.30 a.m. when Bouheben destroyed the ZXR, falling at the fearsome 120 mph Signes corner.

Memories of the curtailed '88 Bol were evoked when dense fog halted the race for an hour at dawn but, at the restart, Vieira was as commanding as ever. In the last hours the gap between the two RVFs shrank but Guillou wouldn't allow potentially disastrous Honda in-fighting and the two bikes flew in formation round the tortuous Ricard turns, with Moineau's Suzuki in a safe third.

Swiss RC30 privateers Urs Meier, Robi Schläfi and Bernard Hänggeli took fourth after ex-GP winner Guy Bertin's National Motos RC broke its chain in the last hour and was then disqualified after mechanics threw a split link over the fence to the stranded Bertin. The French crew's crime also promoted That's Racing's trio of Oxley, Chambers and Brian Morrison to fifth, to retain the team's mantle of top series privateers.

Honda's omnipotence in the championship was verging on the boringly predictable by the end of the Bol. But Honda were unrepentant for building a bike as invincible as the RVF. 'We see no other solution,' was one Japanese Honda staffman's simple explanation of his employer's ruthless domination of endurance racing.

FORMULA ONE WORLD CHAMPIONSHIP

By JOHN CUTTS · SUPERBIKE MAGAZINE

In 1989, World Championship TT Formula One racing returned to its roots and its public roads. It was a backwards but largely inevitable step. Overshadowed for a second year by its glamorous counterpart, the World Superbike series, Formula One found itself left with only those circuits the Superbikers didn't care to race at. In this respect, its fortunes had come full circle. Originally conceived just to keep a World Championship race on the Isle of Man, the Formula One series had enjoyed a period of growth and development that culminated in 1987 when Virginio Ferrari and Bimota took the crown without contesting a single round on closed roads. But, with Superbike up and running, this year the Formula One title-hunt reverted to type. Four of the six races were run on street circuits – the highest proportion of public-road outings in the shortest fixture list for years – and the series was handed back to its traditional exponents, the ranks of British and Irish road racers.

Before the season got under way there were some interesting developments. On the political front, Formula One's world status for '89 was cast in doubt when only five circuits applied to stage rounds and the Italian federation complained loudly that this fell one short of FIM requirements. Fortunately, the Assen promoters, who'd originally contemplated running a World Superbike race during Assen speed week, changed their minds and saved the day.

Moreover, the FIM confirmed support for Formula One (again, much to the annoyance of the Italians) by deciding that the Norton rotary would be eligible on a one-year experimental basis. The twin-rotor Norton RCW588 was rated as a 1000 cc twin by the FIM, who imposed a factor of 1.7:1 to its nominal capacity. Norton had attracted considerable sponsorship from one of their old racing associates, Imperial Tobacco and John Player Special (JPS). Kitted out in stark black and gold JPS livery, there seemed every reason to think that Norton could once again be a force on the world stage. The bike was light and powerful – 320 lb and 135 hp. Over the winter they'd worked on improving the handling by running the engine higher in the twin-spar aluminium Spondon frame, by shortening the wheelbase and by getting White Power specialists to set up the suspension. They were stuck with a rather agricultural five-speed gearbox but they had everything else, including a first-rate rider in Trevor Nation.

Before the opening round at Sugo there was one final development – a personal one involving the five-times Formula One World Champion, Joey Dunlop. During the Easter Eurolantic races at Brands Hatch, Dunlop was involved in a serious crash, breaking a thigh, a wrist and several ribs. He predicted he'd be fit by the Isle of Man TT, but things didn't look promising when the troublesome wrist had to be rebroken and reset several weeks after the accident.

Although the major manufacturers claim that Formula One is vital to their ongoing R & D, it's only at the opening round, held in their own backyard at Sugo, that you see works bikes on the grid in depth. Sugo is a bit of an anomaly in the championship, being too far away and too expensive for most of the regular Formula One competitors. Last year not a single Sugo points scorer contested any of the other rounds. This year, two British boys with an eye on the title were in attendance and intent on making the long journey pay in points. One was Trevor Nation, on the factory Norton; the other was the reigning Formula One World Champion, Carl Fogarty, armed with a factory-supported and kitted Honda RC30.

Practice, held in dismal conditions of rain and fog, was dominated by the Japanese works teams led by Doug Polen on a Yoshimura Suzuki and Michael Dowson on a YZF Yamaha. Nation and the Norton were going well until someone protested that their new water-cooled machine hadn't been homologated (which was true). Fortunately, team-boss Brian Crighton had taken a set of the old air-cooled cases along with him and these were hurriedly fitted. The air-cooled bike was a shade slower but Nation still put in thirteenth on the grid. Fogarty qualified thirtieth, admitting difficulties in coming to grips with the big curves on this fast track.

On race day Sugo was covered in low cloud but, after a delay, the race was flagged away in the best conditions anybody had seen since they'd arrived. As expected, the 50-lap, 117-mile race was a factory showdown. Polen got a bad start he was unable to recover from. Dowson got a flier and used it to full advantage. Nation was in sixth after 19 laps when he ran off the track and crashed, damaging the exhaust. He rejoined the race only to find the oil temperature gauge soaring so, rather than continuing and possibly dropping oil on the track, he parked the Norton at the far end of the pits and pushed in down the exit road. This earned him an immediate disqualification – not that it mattered much.

Dowson had the race sewn up from half-distance and cantered to the win. He was followed home by Nagai (Yamaha), Ohshima (Suzuki), Rob Phillis (Kawasaki), Iwahashi (Honda) and Polen (Suzuki). The names are mere details. The important fact is the spread of machines – every manufacturer got a result of sorts (it was Honda's worst result of the season by far). Carl Fogarty battled bravely and impressed everybody with a gritty performance to finish thirteenth and collect two points towards retaining his title.

The F1 troops were back on familiar ground on the Isle of Man for the next round. Joey Dunlop arrived with a note from his own doctor saying he was fit to race. Two ACU doctors examined him and found he had nowhere near enough strength in his right arm to control the bike over this most arduous of courses. So Dunlop's specially-prepared and ultra-quick RC30, complete with £20,000 factory carbs, was given to Steve Hislop. He rocked the island in practice week, becoming the first man to lap at over 120 mph.

As expected, Steve Hislop crowned a speed-happy TT by leading throughout the F1 race. He posted a new outright lap record of 121.34 mph and was so quick that even his six-lap average speed, including two fuel stops, was higher than the old outright lap record. Brian Morrison was second in an impressive display on a kitted RC30 without trick carbs and *his* second lap time made him the only other rider in TT history to lap above 120 mph. Nick Jefferies, a model of consistency on the Isle of Man, was third on the Loctite Yamaha OWO1 while Carl Fogarty was fourth, having raised his individual pace from a previous TT best of 115.8 mph to 119.5 mph. En route, Foggy collected a Ducati back-marker at Parliament Square, hit a kerb at Appledene and broke an exhaust bracket. Two Nortons were entered but neither of them finished. Nation ran out of fuel, and possibly out of engine, early on, while Steve Cull, the 1988 outright lap record holder signed up especially for the event, went out with a dodgy gearbox.

A few weeks later, on the narrow but safer turns of Assen, Carl Fogarty turned in a performance befitting a World Champion. Fastest in every practice, he led the race from the line, established an early lead, then took command from the front. He set a record fastest lap and didn't even lose the lead when he pitted to refuel. An anticipated race-long dice with Hislop, on equal machinery, never materialised. Hislop was running solidly near the front until his gas stop, when the fuel filler valve jammed. Worse, it then flew open once he'd rejoined the track. His enthusiasm doused by escaping petrol, Hislop slipped further and further back, eventually finishing eleventh. In terms of points, Assen ruined Hislop's chances.

One place ahead of him in tenth was the Norton of Trevor Nation. He would have been several places higher but for a protracted fuel stop that took 30 seconds instead of 10. While Nation was collecting the Norton's first World Championship points their other rider, Steve Cull, was wondering aloud whether he should be collecting stamps at his fuel stop, which took well over a minute.

An honourable mention should go to Roger Burnett, making a one-off Formula One appearance. His regular loyalties were with Superbike and endurance racing, but Burnett turned up at Assen because he likes the circuit and had won the race in 1988, setting a class lap record. For reasons unknown the ACU did not have Burnett on their Formula One grading list and refused to authorise his entry. Roger spent two days camped outside the circuit before the ACU saw fit to mend their bureaucratic ways. In haste, and with minimal practice, Burnett qualified and then ran an impressive third in the race, just beaten to the wire by course expert, Andreas Hoffman (Honda), who'd finished second to Burnett in the race last year.

The Formula One regulars like going to Portugal because it means a holiday in the sun before or after the race. Hardly anybody except the locals likes the circuit, though – it's a hilly run through the houses and walls on dirty, oil-stained roads. There's no run-off (just a couple of level-crossings) and, because of the heat (130 degrees in the shade), they have to start the race at 5 p.m. Liquid and carbohydrate loading is necessary to ward off dehydration and sheer exhaustion. The race tends to go to the brave and

Carl Fogarty did a good job of retaining his title, scoring in every round and winning twice. He sees the need for just one four-stroke championship, and he would be a serious contender.

the fit – and the Formula One points leaders, Carl Fogarty and Steve Hislop, showed they were both in fighting condition.

Fogarty was fastest in practice. Hislop was fastest in the race and won it in a perfectly measured display. It was becoming obvious that there was little to choose between the two of them but the more dangerous the circuit, the more Hislop seemed to turn and power it on. Brian Morrison was third, making it another rostrum benefit for Honda. Nine of the top ten places went to British riders and, in the table, Fogarty now led Hislop by eight points.

Norton gave Portugal a miss after Nation was injured in a crash at Cadwell Park. Realising that all chance of World Championship honours had vanished, they missed the next round at Kouvola in Finland too.

No one goes to Finland for a racing holiday except the Formula One boys. It's a long drive involving several ferries and when you finally get there, some 60 miles inside the Russian border, you know that you've left Central Europe a long way behind. Still, a race track is a race track and Kouvola's 1.98 miles of closed roads is not without attraction, especially if you like a lot of right-handers. Fogarty clearly did and won the race in style from a hard-charging Hislop, lapping everybody up to third-place man, Jari Suhonen.

Carl Fogarty journeyed to Dundrod and the final round at the Ulster GP knowing he needed only a sixth place or better in order to retain his title and that Hislop was the only opponent with a mathematical chance of wresting it from him. In practice, Fogarty ran an unofficial outright lap record of 122.25 mph, but he was not alone in going quick. Finally, at the end of the year, everybody seemed to be going really fast – Hislop, Morrison, even the Nortons of Cull and Nation.

The race proved a classic Dundrod encounter. The 7.4-mile public road course was wet in parts yet dry for most of the lap. Fogarty led early on until Cull put the Norton's nose briefly in front (the first time a Norton had led the Ulster GP in over 25 years). Despite taking to the grass right in front of the packed grandstand, Fogarty regained and established enough of a lead to pit, refuel and rejoin still with an advantage. Nation had retired early with ignition problems. Cull was still second, Robert Dunlop third and Hislop a strangely cautious fourth. Hislop had chosen not to refuel and the order remained much the same until the dying stages, when Hislop decided he had nothing to lose and turned up the wick. His late charge just paid off. He overhauled Fogarty in the sprint to the line by 9/100ths of a second. The championship was Fogarty's and Hislop was left to rue the events at Assen, when a tiny fuel valve had cost him a large number of points. Cull was third, 30 seconds in arrears but by far the best showing the Norton had made all season.

Joey Dunlop, making an emotional Formula One comeback in front of an army of adoring fans, finished twentieth and exhausted. He said he was in extreme pain from half-distance and only the supporters had kept him going. The 37-year-old Dunlop also said he was going to have one last crack at the championship next year.

No such commitment came from the 24-year-old World Champion, Carl Fogarty. He was the only rider to contest all six rounds this year, but didn't consider the rewards were enough to justify the huge outlay. In his moment of triumph he was refreshingly frank about the value of the series. 'There just isn't room for two 750 cc World Championships. They should put the Formula One on good short circuits leaving the TT and Ulster as optional rounds. Then standards would rise.'

Standards had risen in 1987, at the peak of Formula One's popularity, the year before World Superbikes arrived and stole much of the good work Formula One had pioneered. At the moment, it's a championship that persists rather than survives. To flourish it needs more dates, and particularly more rounds away from the closed road courses that have always been its hallmark but which severely restrict its appeal.

EUROPEAN CHAMPIONSHIP

By CHRIS HERRING

Kel Edge

The series which has already given Grand Prix racing the names of Chili, Ruggia and Bradl has again announced a potential 250 cc contender from the 1989 European campaign.

After taking second place at Zolder in round two Italian Andrea Borgonovo remained in control of the quarter-litre series throughout. If the opposition had any doubts regarding the consistency of 'Borgo' they received sufficient warning of his intention when he scored three successive victories early in the series. The Salzburgring, Anderstorp and Most rounds left the talented 25-year-old privateer in total command with a 23-point cushion between himself and Marcellino Lucchi, the first of the Team Italia Aprilia runners. The first seven rounds had seen the eccentric 'Borgo' take six top-three finishes, with a fourth place at Assen. In Yugoslavia and France, in July, he suffered his only breakdowns, with piston trouble on both occasions, but at the following round at Donington Park the Italian was guaranteed the title after he watched fellow-countryman Lucchi crash while leading the British round.

Austrian Engelbert Neumair completed the Aprilia domination with third place in the series, highlighted with a single second place at the opening Spanish round. Tremendous consistency throughout the season kept Neumair ahead of Yamaha-mounted Swiss rider Bernard Hänggeli, and he retained third place in the championship by a slender three-point margin.

Eventually to finish seventh in the championship Gilberto Gambelli looked impressive early on, following his victory in Spain. Sadly the Team Italia rider lacked the experience to capitalise on his win, but he will be back next year, and is a good prospect to take the title.

Team Italia had their investment rewarded in the 125 cc series through Aprilia-mounted Gabriele Debbia. While the Italian Federation were celebrating the success of Debbia after his victory in the opening two rounds, however, the rest of the European circus was more interested in the progress of another tiddler sensation. Loris Capirossi, at 16 years of age, had taken his private Honda to second place in the series with fourth and third finishes. A late-starting Alessandro Gramigni finally notified the opposition of his arrival, with victory in round three at Zolder in Belgium, just ahead of team-mate Debbia. Capirossi could only manage a lowly thirteenth place here, but up into second place in the championship came Britain's leading contender, Steve Patrickson, with third spot at the Belgian circuit.

Debbia maintained his lead with victory at the Salzburgring and in Sweden, but Capirossi welcomed the challenge and won in Czechoslovakia to close on his rival. The turning point in the series was undoubtedly at Assen, where Debbia was the victor with Capirossi a disappointed thirteenth-place finisher. Adding to the young Italian's frustrations were West German Dirk Raudies and Gramigni, now closing in as the championship moved to Misano.

Capirossi hit back with victory in the Italian round, from Raudies and Gramigni, with Debbia finishing a lowly tenth, while at round nine in Yugoslavia it was the turn of Raudies to secure his first victory of a thrilling series from Gramigni and young Loris. Debbia, meanwhile, was quite prepared to take a back-seat sixth place: he still held a 23-point advantage over Capirossi with three rounds remaining.

When Capirossi failed to score at Paul Ricard Raudies took over second place in the championship; he had finished fifth at the French venue. Spaniard Josep Volta and his Arbizu won the race, and again Debbia was happy with a tactical seventh place to extend his overall lead to 28 points.

Capirossi bounced back once more to take his third win of the championship at Donington Park and promote himself to second in the series again. Gramigni held off Patrickson by four-hundredths of a second to finish second in the British round. And, once again, Debbia sat in a lower leaderboard eighth place to ensure that the title was his.

At Hockenheim, for the final round, Raudies took his second victory to guarantee third place overall, but Gramigni's second place in Germany and Capirossi's failure to finish gave the Team Italia outfit the 1–2 they had longed for. Capirossi finished fourth in the championship – with the consolation for him being that he could win the title for the next five years, by which time he would be an experienced veteran of 21!

The curtain came down on the 500 cc European Championship after nine years of competition, with Swedish all-rounder Peter Linden the final victor. Despite 44 different points-scorers in the 8 rounds, compared with 50 names in the 11-round 250 cc series, Linden confirmed the interest, or lack of it, in the once premier category by not even bothering to attend the final leg because his title was already secure.

Phil Masters

Phil Masters

Kel Edge

Opposite page: **A successful motor cycle all-rounder, Peter Linden races all sorts of machines from 250 and 500 cc Grand Prix bikes to production Superbikes and endurance machines, as well as passengering sidecars. Even though he does not quite make it as a Grand Prix ace, he was a convincing European Champion.**

The star of the year was Italian Andrea Borgonovo *(left)* **on his private 250 Aprilia. He will be a man to watch when he goes Grand Prix racing.**

Below left: **At only sixteen, Capirossi was sensational on his Honda. Here he leads fellow-Italian Alessandro Gramigni and Britain's Steve Patrickson at Donington.**

The 125 champion was Gabriele Debbia *(bottom left)*, **another who has to thank the enthusiasm of Team Italia for his success.**

Linden took individual race victories in the Honda-dominated series in Portugal, Sweden and Czechoslovakia. Ironically the final year for the 500s proved to be one of the best, with second to sixth places in the championship being decided in the final race at Rijeka.

British GP privateer Simon Buckmaster doesn't seem able to resist the temptation of competing in the Euro series. The 28-year-old from Potters Bar took in four races and won three, in Austria, Holland and Italy, and finished second to Linden at Anderstorp, to give him sixth place in the championship.

Consistent West German Hansjorg Butz finished runner-up in the series. He scored no victories and only one second place, at Most, but he did, needless to say, finish in every round but one and never outside the top six. Frenchman Rachel Nicotte won in Spain and Yugoslavia to assist his cause, and he eventually achieved third place overall and a guaranteed Grand Prix start in 1990.

In the six-round 80 cc class Spaniards Jaime Mariano and Jose Saez were level on points after two rounds, with a win and a second place apiece. Casal-mounted Mariano took the honours in Portugal and Krauser-mounted Saez in Spain but both were overpowered in Belgium. West German Ralf Waldmann ensured three different winners on three different machines when he rode his 80 cc Seel to victory at Zolder. Both Mariano and Saez failed to score in Czechoslovakia, where Hungarian rider Janos Szabo took victory from West Germany's Stefan Kurfiss.

Saez took the championship advantage in Holland by finishing second to Italian Roberto Sassone on a Unimoto, with Mariano a lowly eighth.

The 80 cc riders then had a three-month break before the Hockenheim decider. Saez held an 11-point advantage over Mariano before the last round. If Mariano won in West Germany Saez needed at least sixth place to secure the title. The Casal rider had little doubt about where he would finish and took his second victory in the series, but for Saez a disastrous seventh place meant the two were level on points – and Mariano was European Champion, having won two races to Saez's one. Kurfiss finished third at Hockenheim on his Krauser, and took a well-deserved third in the series after finishing in all six races.

The ACU were again well represented in the sidecar class, with nearly half the final championship table belonging to Britain. Four of the six rounds were won by British teams but, unfortunately, the title went to West Germany's Ralph Bohnhorst and Thomas Böttcher.

The series got under way in Portugal, where Kenny Howles and Steve Pointer beat Mick Burcombe and John Gibbard, the West German LCR of Bohnhorst and Böttcher coming home in third place.

In Czechoslovakia, for round two, the British pairing of Barry and David Smith were the victors, with Bohnhorst second and the Swiss Güdel brothers third. Howles had to retire minus a clutch. So Bohnhorst led the charge after round two, seven points in front of Burcombe, with the British outfits of Reddington third, Knight fourth and Smith and Howles equal fifth.

The Swiss pairing of René Progin and Yves Hunziker arrived on the scene to win the third round at Assen from Smith and Bohnhorst. The Germans now led the Smiths by ten points, with Gary Knight and Malcolm Jackson third, a further eight points adrift.

Smith got the victory he needed at Paul Ricard in round four, where Bohnhorst could only take sixth. Howles finished fourth and Knight fifth behind the Güdels and Swedish driver Billy Gällros. The sidecar championship was warming up, with Smith and Bohnhorst now level on points, the Güdels third, Knight a close fourth and Howles fifth.

Donington Park gave Howles his second victory from Güdel, Gällros and Bohnhorst. The Smith brothers were struggling with carburation trouble on their ADM motor, and only managed fifth. Approaching the final round Bohnhorst led Smith by just two points with Güdel a further eight points behind. Howles was in fourth and seven points adrift of the Swiss crew.

At Hockenheim Progin appeared once more, to take his second victory of the series. Bohnhorst's second place gave him the title but not without a strong challenge from the Smiths: the British pairing finished third to end the season in second place, just four points short of a European title. Howles finished fourth in Germany but, more importantly, with Güdel twelfth, promoted himself to third in the championship by two points. Knight ended the campaign in equal fifth place with Gällros, and Burcombe came seventh.

Ralph Bohnhorst and Thomas Böttcher had won the title without winning a race but, none the less, had displayed a relentless dedication to the cause, finishing every race and depriving the Smiths of overall success.

BRITISH NATIONAL RACING
By ROLAND BROWN

Phil Masters

The story of British racing in 1989 was undoubtedly the return to victory of the Norton. Riding an all-black JPS-sponsored rotary that fully lived up to its promise of the season before, Steve Spray roared to win after win to take two major championships amid much patriotic programme-waving.

The British bike's success – coupled with some very exciting racing in many classes, and a healthy dose of television exposure – gave domestic racing an invaluable shot in the arm. Crowds were up almost everywhere: they'd seen the action on TV the week before, or perhaps they'd watched Niall Mackenzie's stirring ride in the Donington Grand Prix, and increasing numbers of them took advantage of the never-ending summer sunshine to stand on grassy racetrack banks from Knockhill to Thruxton.

With the Norton there to cheer, it seemed to matter less that Mackenzie and our other Grand Prix men (let alone the foreign stars) were rarely, if ever, seen on home tarmac again. Even the opposition were glad to see the rotaries, or almost. 'I get a bit fed up when the Nortons come past on the straight throwing flames at me,' admitted Mitsui Yamaha's Terry Rymer, reluctantly interrupting his World Superbike effort to take in a late-season Cadwell national. 'But it certainly keeps the crowd happy. This has been one of the best British seasons for years.'

Unfortunately by no means everything was good, however. Yet again the format of the major domestic championships was changed, this time to a combination of multi-round British Championship and five-round Shell Oils Supercup. One had the more prestigious title; the other gave vital television coverage at every round – so which champions really had the right to call themselves the best in Britain?

With guaranteed television coverage, at least for the Supercup, there should have been no problem finding a big-money sponsor from outside the sport. A big cash introduction could have been distributed throughout national-level racing to benefit those who badly needed it – the riders. But what money Shell did introduce certainly didn't find its way onto the grid.

Back in 1983, it's interesting to note, the ACU British Formula One Championship paid £1000 for a win at each of ten rounds. Six years later the winner of a British Championship F1 round received a pitiful £250, a 75 per cent *reduction* at a time when in some classes the cost of a bike alone is well into five figures.

With a total of nine manufacturer- or importer-backed riders entered at the Cadwell Park F1 round, for example, the brave privateer who battled his way to tenth spot on his £13,000 Yamaha would have been rewarded with a princely £35. 'The prize money situation is a bloody insult and something has got to be done about it,' said newly crowned champion Steve Spray, not forgetting that a year earlier he had been just another struggling privateer.

'The riders have got to get together and say we're just not going to ride for this sort of money. I know you'll always have guys riding for the love of the sport, but others are having to give up.' By mid-season current F1 champion Darren Dixon had done just that, abandoning the defence of his title due to what he described as 'joke' prize money.

The other classes were even less well rewarded. 'You get £150 for a win in the 250 cc class, which is less than the price of a pair of tyres,' said Ian McConnachie, who nevertheless enjoyed his successful return to national racing after five years in Grands Prix. 'We normally use two pairs, if you include practice. Then you've got to get to the circuit; the entry fees are high; the bike costs £10,500 plus VAT...'

Luckily for McConnachie, he was one of the well-sponsored few who could afford it. Grids were remarkably full, considering the financial rewards, but the lack of young riders coming through to Grand Prix level in the smaller classes can only be a reflection on the lack of support they receive at home.

If the fact that there was any racing at all was largely down to the riders' determination and the generosity of sponsors – some of whom had to resort to buying tickets to get into meetings – then equally the increased crowds owed more to the quality of racing and the Nortons' return than to circuit-owners' inspired promotion. 'Some people are all too ready to slap themselves on the back and say attendances are up, but they couldn't have gone down much more or there would have been nobody there at all,' reflected Harris Performance partner Steve Harris, enthusiast, businessman and long-time sponsor.

'Some circuits like Brands have made a big effort with facilities but at the moment most tracks are still in the 1950s and '60s, when we were prepared to stand on a muddy bank at Mallory Park getting wet but just happy to see the

Phil Masters

Opposite page: **Steve Spray was the most successful of the Norton men and his home-grown wins helped make the season one of the best for many years.**

Equally impressive was Steve Patrickson *(left)*, **who won both the 125 and 250 classes. It is hard to imagine how anyone can mount a serious effort with such terrible prize money available. The riders, organisers and spectators have team-sponsors to thank for the fact that the sport keeps going.**

Below: **The sort of action that kept spectators and television viewers happy: Steve Spray leads Steve Chambers and Trevor Nation at Thruxton.**

Bottom: **Kevin Mitchell, another rider who benefits from a tremendously enthusiastic sponsor.**

bikes go past. That amateurish outlook used to be the same in all sports – tennis, cricket or whatever – but most have changed. Whether it's for better or worse they have changed, and motor cycling will have to change too or it will get left behind.'

It was Brands Hatch Leisure, the company that owns not only the Kent track but Cadwell, Oulton Park and Snetterton too, that threatened to do most to change British racing in the future. As we went to press, Brands, frustrated by what managing director John Webb described as ACU interference and by the rash decision to award Donington Park the next five British Grands Prix, was planning to split from the governing body to promote its own championships. Ironically, such a desperate move could be just what is needed to drag British bike racing into the 1990s.

Phil Masters

Barry Brindley and Grahame Rose *(right)* get faster all the time and may soon be challenging the top Grand Prix teams.

Right: **Mike Edwards leading a pack of Supercup 600 men at Thruxton. He threw the championship away by crashing at the last round and it was seized by Rodney Knapp from Wanganui, New Zealand, who has followed Richard Scott's lead in travelling from that town on the other side of the world to the top of British racing.**

Below right: **Dave Fern gets a touch of the limelight as he organises the prize-giving at Donington. The recipients are Nigel Bosworth, Steve Patrickson and Ian McConnachie. All three have shown the ability to compete against the Europeans but currently lack the backing to mount a full-time effort.**

BRITISH CHAMPIONSHIPS

While the little bikes kicked off their British title chase at Brands on May Day, the first Formula One round was held three weeks later on Norton's doorstep at Mallory Park – and it showed. Steve Spray used his circuit knowledge and his bike's power to perfect advantage, shadowing Terry Rymer and his Loctite Yamaha OWO1 before barrelling past on the back straight on the last lap to the delight of the crowd.

Phil Mellor took third for Suzuki, ahead of the Hondas of Steve Chambers and Carl Fogarty. John Reynolds and his Team Green Kawasaki finished one place behind Ray Stringer (Yamaha), putting five different makes in the top seven places. But the day was all about Norton, and at Donington's next round it was again Spray – this time taking advantage of Terry Rymer's crash and shoulder injury – who took the win, from Fogarty and Suzuki's James Whitham.

Rymer got his revenge at the tighter Knockhill circuit, where the aggressive Whitham charged through from last off the line to steal second from Spray near the end. But at Snetterton there was again no stopping the Nortons. Spray won from temporary team-mate Ray Stringer (replacing the injured Trevor Nation that day, and consistently fast all year before ending his season with a crash at Mallory's notoriously dangerous Devil's Elbow) to take a commanding 22-point lead in the championship. Rymer could manage only fifth, after getting the worst of a race-long battle with Steve Chambers (Honda) and Whitham.

At Snetterton the JPS Nortons had simply hoovered everything else up on the straights but at the next round – on Cadwell Park's ridiculously tight 0.85-mile Woodland circuit – Spray had no such advantage and won it the hard way, coming from behind to beat Whitham, Gary Thrush (Honda) and Nation. Back on Cadwell's full circuit, two months later, he took a cool second place behind Carl Fogarty to secure a historic British Championship for Norton with two rounds still to go.

Last year's F1 title had been won by Darren Dixon's Suzuki RG500 but this season – with the exception of Norton's fish-nor-fowl Wankel – was a four-stroke benefit. In the other four-stroke classes Suzuki's James Whitham was impressive until injuring his ankle in an Ulster Grand Prix crash, leading the 1300 cc Production class and lying second behind 21-year-old Sheffield rider Paul Brookes in the Supersport 600.

Brookes, arguably the find of the season on his FZR Yamaha, was left to battle out a close-fought 600 championship with similarly mounted Mike Edwards, Rodney Knapp and Gary Weston and, as *Motocourse* went to press, Brookes needed only two points from the final round to take the title. The burly Kiwi Knapp was again in contention in the Yamaha-dominated big proddy class, along with Dean Ashton (who led him by ten points going into the last round) and veteran Scot Howard Selby.

If the larger Supersport class belonged to the 600 cc four-strokes, then the 400 Supersport catered entirely for roadster-based 250 cc two-strokes. One man dominated both that and the 'proper' 250 cc British Championship: Ian McConnachie. The little red-haired man from Derbyshire, who in 1986 became the first Briton to win a home solo GP (the 80 cc event) since the TT was a World Championship round, was back in national racing and putting his Grand Prix experience to good effect.

McConnachie won the first three rounds of the Supersport championship on his KR1 Kawasaki, each time from Dave Heal, then took a second and two thirds – behind winners Paul Booler (Suzuki), John Reynolds (Kawasaki) and Reynolds again – to put one hand on the crown. His fifth place at the penultimate round at Donington was enough to clinch the title. And with the likes of Steve Patrickson, Kevin Mitchell and Nigel Bosworth missing abroad for most of the season, McConnachie's march to the 250 cc crown was equally smooth.

Patrickson won the Brands opener in fine style but in the Yorkshireman's absence McConnachie, who finished second on his Yamaha, took Mallory's next round ahead of Matt Llewellyn, who would be his closest challenger throughout the year. Nigel Bosworth won at Donington and Snetterton; McConnachie twice more, at Knockhill and Cadwell, before taking the championship at Donington with one round to go.

Steve Patrickson also took an opening-round win in the revived and increasingly competitive Honda-dominated 125 cc class. But it was the man who finished second at Brands, Rob Orme, who emerged to battle for the title with Steve Mason. Orme took two second places to Mason's pair of sevenths but then crashed at Donington, where Mason's win put him back in the hunt.

Mason won again at Snetterton but missed several races after a Thruxton crash. Orme came back with victories in July at Mallory and Cadwell, then closed the gap further with a third at Cadwell. They went into the last round equal on points, after Mason failed to score in the Donington round, to bring the championship to an exciting conclusion.

In the absence of World Champions Webster and Hewitt (apart from their win at Donington), the two sidecar championships looked like becoming a benefit for the Brindley family from Bawtry, on the Yorkshire/Notts border. Big brother Barry led the way, winning six rounds out of six to take the Open title with passenger Grahame Rose. Closest challengers Robert Fisher and Trevor Crone got some good starts on their Suzuki 1100-powered outfit but the four-stroke was no match for Brindley's lighter 500 Yamaha.

In the F2 class brother Derek, passengered by Nick Roche, was almost as dominant, and held a seemingly comfortable 22-point lead with three rounds to go. But the pair's spin at Cadwell's September meeting, where closest challengers Dave Saville and Richard Crossley won, set up a thrilling finish, compounded by a Brindley–Saville 1–2 at Donington. They went into the final leg with Brindley's lead down to ten points.

SHELL OILS SUPERCUP

Its one-day format may have been less than ideal and its prize money nothing special, but the Shell Oils Supercup at least offered the unmissable chance to star on television – and the BBC must have been delighted with the result. Almost every race shown was exciting, often in marked contrast to the car race broadcast on the same Sunday afternoon, and many were simply breathtaking.

Some of the thrills were a little stage-managed, it's true. World Sidecar champs Webster and Hewitt took in four of the five rounds and had the class not only to win but to make each victory look much more dramatic than it actually was. Barry Brindley, who finished second each time, knew he had little chance but was happy enough to watch and learn from Webster.

Steve Patrickson certainly wasn't playing around as he rode to a hard-fought double in the 250 and 125 cc classes. Two previous wins in each meant he could settle for fourth and second respectively in the Brands Hatch finale, but Patrickson had to come up with some inspired riding on the way.

In the 250s Kevin Mitchell notched up two wins and finished only three points behind Patrickson, but was always struggling after his Yamaha had packed up on the line at Donington's first round. In the 125s Patrickson's main threat was his team-mate, Rob Orme, who just got the better of a superb fairing-bashing battle at Mallory Park but ended the year two points behind the Shipley rider.

New Zealander Rodney Knapp took the 600 Supersport title by limping home eighth in the final round with a burst oil seal. Mike Edwards, winner of two rounds and a point ahead before Brands, crashed out on the first lap. Brian Morrison, the Scot who was almost unbeatable in 1988, salvaged something from a disappointing year by taking the 750 cc Superbike championship in which five different riders – himself, Roger Burnett, Carl Fogarty, Ray Stringer and Terry Rymer – won rounds.

Norton's rotary was ineligible for Superbikes but ran in the F1 class, where Steve Spray once again used its power to good effect. The 26-year-old from Nottingham won only one of the first four rounds but his consistency, with three third places, paid off. At Brands Spray knew exactly what he had to do: he cruised to a comfortable fourth to take the title and set the seal on a season in which, for all its problems, he and Norton had given British racing plenty to smile about.

72
8
2
10
METZ

DUNLOP
PAYNES
PJ1
STEVE
DUNLOP
CLARKE
PRO-TEK
BODY ARMOUR
BEL-RAY

RESULTS · 1989

500 cc World Championship

Position	Rider	Nationality	Machine	Japan	Australia	USA	Spain	Italy	Germany	Austria	Yugoslavia	Holland	Belgium	France	Great Britain	Sweden	Czechoslovakia	Brazil	TOTAL
1	**Eddie Lawson**	USA	Honda	15	11	15	20	-	17	17	15	17	10	20	17	20	17	17	**228**
2	**Wayne Rainey**	USA	Yamaha	17	17	20	17	-	20	15	17	20	7.5	15	15	-	15	15	**210.5**
3	**Christian Sarron**	F	Yamaha	9	15	10	13	-	11	13	11	15	6.5	13	11	17	13	8	**165.5**
4	**Kevin Schwantz**	USA	Suzuki	20	-	17	-	-	-	20	20	-	8.5	17	20	-	20	20	**162.5**
5	**Kevin Magee**	AUS	Yamaha	11	13	13	-	-	9	11	13	13	4.5	11	10	11	9	10	**138.5**
6	**Pier Francesco Chili**	I	Honda	-	-	9	10	20	13	10	7	11	5	10	7	9	11	-	**122**
7	**Niall Mackenzie**	GB	Yamaha	10	-	11	15	-	-	-	4	8	3	9	13	13	10	7	**103**
8	**Ron Haslam**	GB	Suzuki	4	9	-	9	-	-	9	8	9	-	-	9	10	8	11	**86**
9	**Michael Doohan**	AUS	Honda	-	8	8	-	-	15	8	10	7	4	8	-	-	-	13	**81**
10	**Wayne Gardner**	AUS	Honda	13	20	-	-	-	-	-	-	10	-	-	-	15	-	9	**67**
11	**Rob McElnea**	GB	Honda	-	-	-	-	-	6	5	5	6	2.5	7	6	7	4	4	**52.5**
12	**Simon Buckmaster**	GB	Honda	-	4	3	3	17	2	3	2	-	0.5	2	1	4	-	2	**43.5**
13	**Alessandro Valesi**	I	Yamaha	-	5	5	6	-	3	4	-	4	-	3	-	5	2	3	**40**
14=	**Dominique Sarron**	F	Honda	-	6	6	7	-	8	6	6	-	-	-	-	-	-	-	**39**
14=	**Tadahiko Taira**	J	Yamaha	8	10	-	8	-	-	-	-	-	-	-	-	6	7	-	**39**
16	**Freddie Spencer**	USA	Yamaha	2	-	-	11	-	7	7	-	3	3.5	-	-	-	-	-	**33.5**
17=	**Marco Gentile**	CH	Fior	-	3	4	4	13	-	2	-	2	2	-	3	-	-	-	**33**
17=	**Randy Mamola**	USA	Cagiva	-	-	-	-	-	4	-	9	5	-	5	-	-	5	5	**33**
19	**Adrien Morillas**	F	Honda	-	-	-	-	-	-	-	-	-	-	6	-	8	6	6	**26**
20	**Michael Rudroff**	D	Honda	-	1	1	-	15	-	-	1	-	-	-	-	-	-	-	**18**
21	**Norihiko Fujiwara**	J	Yamaha	7	-	-	-	-	10	-	-	-	-	-	-	-	-	-	**17**
22	**Bubba Shobert**	USA	Honda	5	-	7	-	-	-	-	-	-	-	-	-	-	-	-	**12**
23	**Joseph Doppler**	A	Honda	-	-	-	-	11	-	-	-	-	-	-	-	-	-	-	**11**
24	**Alois Meyer**	D	Honda	-	-	-	-	10	-	-	-	-	-	-	-	-	-	-	**10**
25	**Romolo Balbi**	I	Honda	-	-	-	-	9	-	-	-	-	-	-	-	-	-	-	**9**
26=	**Massimo Broccoli**	I	Cagiva	-	-	-	5	-	-	-	3	-	-	-	-	-	-	-	**8**
26=	**Luca Cadalora**	I	Yamaha	-	-	-	-	-	-	-	-	-	-	-	8	-	-	-	**8**
26=	**Fernando Gonzalez**	E	Honda	-	-	-	-	8	-	-	-	-	-	-	1	-	-	-	**8**
26=	**Niggi Schmassman**	CH	Honda	-	2	-	-	6	-	-	-	-	-	-	-	-	-	-	**8**
30=	**Michael Dowson**	AUS	Yamaha	-	7	-	-	-	-	-	-	-	-	-	-	-	-	-	**7**
30=	**Andreas Leuthe**	LUX	Suzuki	-	-	-	-	7	-	-	-	-	-	-	-	-	-	-	**7**
32=	**Fabio Biliotti**	I	Honda	-	-	-	-	-	-	-	-	-	-	1	2	3	-	-	**6**
32=	**Shinichi Itoh**	J	Honda	6	-	-	-	-	-	-	-	-	-	-	-	-	-	-	**6**
32=	**Bruno Kneubühler**	CH	Honda	-	-	2	-	-	1	1	-	-	-	-	-	2	-	-	**6**
35	**John Kocinski**	USA	Yamaha	-	-	-	-	-	-	-	-	-	5.5	-	-	-	-	-	**5.5**
36=	**Ernst Gschwender**	D	Suzuki	-	-	-	-	-	5	-	-	-	-	-	-	-	-	-	**5**
36=	**Fred Merkel**	USA	Honda	-	-	-	-	-	-	-	-	-	-	-	5	-	-	-	**5**
38=	**Roger Burnett**	GB	Honda	-	-	-	-	-	-	-	-	-	-	-	4	-	-	-	**4**
38=	**Thierry Crine**	F	Suzuki	-	-	-	-	-	-	-	-	-	-	4	-	-	-	-	**4**
38=	**Juan Lopez Mella**	E	Honda	-	-	-	2	-	-	-	-	-	-	-	-	1	-	1	**4**
41=	**Alberto Rota**	I	Yamaha	-	-	-	-	-	-	-	-	-	-	-	-	-	3	-	**3**
41=	**Shunji Yatsushiro**	J	Honda	3	-	-	-	-	-	-	-	-	-	-	-	-	-	-	**3**
43	**Kees Doorakkers**	NL	Honda	-	-	-	-	-	-	-	-	1	1.5	-	-	-	-	-	**2.5**
44	**Eddie Laycock**	IRL	Honda	-	-	-	1	-	-	-	-	-	1	-	-	-	-	-	**2**
45=	**Peter Linden**	S	Honda	-	-	-	-	-	-	-	-	-	-	-	-	-	1	-	**1**
45=	**Kunio Machii**	J	Yamaha	1	-	-	-	-	-	-	-	-	-	-	-	-	-	-	**1**

Past 500 cc World Champions

			(Wins/ Races)
1949	Les Graham, GB	AJS	(2/6)
1950	Umberto Masetti, I	Gilera	(2/6)
1951	Geoff Duke, GB	Norton	(4/8)
1952	Umberto Masetti, I	Gilera	(2/8)
1953	Geoff Duke, GB	Gilera	(4/8)
1954	Geoff Duke, GB	Gilera	(5/8)
1955	Geoff Duke, GB	Gilera	(4/8)
1956	John Surtees, GB	MV-Agusta	(3/6)
1957	Libero Liberati, I	Gilera	(3/6)
1958	John Surtees, GB	MV-Agusta	(6/7)
1959	John Surtees, GB	MV-Agusta	(7/7)
1960	John Surtees, GB	MV-Agusta	(5/7)
1961	Gary Hocking, RSR	MV-Agusta	(7/10)
1962	Mike Hailwood, GB	MV-Agusta	(5/8)
1963	Mike Hailwood, GB	MV-Agusta	(7/8)
1964	Mike Hailwood, GB	MV-Agusta	(7/9)
1965	Mike Hailwood, GB	MV-Agusta	(8/10)
1966	Giacomo Agostini, I	MV-Agusta	(3/9)
1967	Giacomo Agostini, I	MV-Agusta	(5/10)
1968	Giacomo Agostini, I	MV-Agusta	(10/10)
1969	Giacomo Agostini, I	MV-Agusta	(10/12)
1970	Giacomo Agostini, I	MV-Agusta	(10/11)
1971	Giacomo Agostini, I	MV-Agusta	(8/11)
1972	Giacomo Agostini, I	MV-Agusta	(11/13)
1973	Phil Read, GB	MV-Agusta	(4/11)
1974	Phil Read, GB	MV-Agusta	(4/10)
1975	Giacomo Agostini, I	Yamaha	(4/10)
1976	Barry Sheene, GB	Suzuki	(5/10)
1977	Barry Sheene, GB	Suzuki	(6/11)
1978	Kenny Roberts, USA	Yamaha	(4/11)
1979	Kenny Roberts, USA	Yamaha	(5/12)
1980	Kenny Roberts, USA	Yamaha	(3/8)
1981	Marco Lucchinelli, I	Suzuki	(5/11)
1982	Franco Uncini, I	Suzuki	(5/12)
1983	Freddie Spencer, USA	Honda	(6/12)
1984	Eddie Lawson, USA	Yamaha	(4/12)
1985	Freddie Spencer, USA	Honda	(7/12)
1986	Eddie Lawson, USA	Yamaha	(7/11)
1987	Wayne Gardner, AUS	Honda	(7/15)
1988	Eddie Lawson, USA	Yamaha	(7/15)

Past 350 cc World Champions

			(Wins/ Races)
1949	Freddie Frith, GB	Velocette	(5/5)
1950	Bob Foster, GB	Velocette	(3/6)
1951	Geoff Duke, GB	Norton	(5/8)
1952	Geoff Duke, GB	Norton	(4/7)
1953	Fergus Anderson, GB	Guzzi	(3/7)
1954	Fergus Anderson, GB	Guzzi	(4/9)
1955	Bill Lomas, GB	Guzzi	(4/7)
1956	Bill Lomas, GB	Guzzi	(3/6)
1957	Keith Campbell, AUS	Guzzi	(3/6)
1958	John Surtees, GB	MV-Agusta	(6/7)
1959	John Surtees, GB	MV-Agusta	(6/6)
1960	John Surtees, GB	MV-Agusta	(2/5)
1961	Gary Hocking, RSR	MV-Agusta	(4/7)
1962	Jim Redman, RSR	Honda	(4/6)
1963	Jim Redman, RSR	Honda	(5/7)
1964	Jim Redman, RSR	Honda	(8/8)
1965	Jim Redman, RSR	Honda	(4/9)
1966	Mike Hailwood, GB	Honda	(6/10)
1967	Mike Hailwood, GB	Honda	(6/8)
1968	Giacomo Agostini, I	MV-Agusta	(7/7)
1969	Giacomo Agostini, I	MV-Agusta	(8/10)
1970	Giacomo Agostini, I	MV-Agusta	(9/10)
1971	Giacomo Agostini, I	MV-Agusta	(6/11)
1972	Giacomo Agostini, I	MV-Agusta	(6/12)
1973	Giacomo Agostini, I	MV-Agusta	(4/11)
1974	Giacomo Agostini, I	Yamaha	(5/10)
1975	Johnny Cecotto, YV	Yamaha	(4/10)
1976	Walter Villa, I	Harley-Davidson	(4/10)
1977	Takazumi Katayama, J	Yamaha	(5/11)
1978	Kork Ballington, ZA	Kawasaki	(6/11)
1979	Kork Ballington, ZA	Kawasaki	(5/11)
1980	Jon Ekerold, ZA	Yamaha	(3/6)
1981	Anton Mang, D	Kawasaki	(5/8)
1982	Anton Mang, D	Kawasaki	(1/9)

250 cc World Championship

Position	Rider	Nationality	Machine	Japan	Australia	USA	Spain	Italy	Germany	Austria	Yugoslavia	Holland	Belgium	France	Great Britain	Sweden	Czechoslovakia	Brazil	TOTAL
1	**Alfonso Pons**	E	Honda	17	20	13	17	20	20	20	20	17	17	15	20	20	13	13	**262**
2	**Reinhold Roth**	D	Honda	-	11	8	10	11	17	9	17	20	13	10	17	17	20	10	**190**
3	**Jacques Cornu**	CH	Honda	7	10	10	-	15	11	17	15	15	20	17	13	15	15	7	**187**
4	**Carlos Cardus**	E	Honda	8	9	11	11	13	10	10	10	13	15	20	-	13	8	11	**162**
5	**Luca Cadalora**	I	Yamaha	15	15	15	20	-	5	-	-	-	11	5	-	11	10	20	**127**
6	**Masahiro Shimizu**	J	Honda	3	2	6	9	5	15	6	-	5	7	9	15	-	17	17	**116**
7	**Jean-Philippe Ruggia**	F	Yamaha	11	17	9	15	17	9	8	13	-	-	11	-	-	-	-	**110**
8	**Juan Garriga**	E	Yamaha	6	13	-	13	-	8	-	11	-	9	8	10	6	9	5	**98**
9	**Helmut Bradl**	D	Honda	4	8	-	-	6	13	13	-	-	10	6	9	-	11	8	**88**
10	**Martin Wimmer**	D	Aprilia	-	3	-	8	7	-	15	-	11	-	4	5	8	-	1	**62**
11	**Loris Reggiani**	I	Honda	-	5	7	-	-	7	7	-	-	-	-	11	-	-	15	**52**
12	**Didier de Radiguès**	B	Aprilia	2	7	2	-	-	-	11	-	10	-	7	-	9	3	-	**51**
13	**Wilco Zeelenberg**	NL	Honda	-	-	-	6	2	2	1	7	8	-	-	6	4	5	-	**41**
14	**John Kocinski**	USA	Yamaha	20	-	20	-	-	-	-	-	-	-	-	-	-	-	-	**40**
15=	**Toshihiko Honma**	J	Yamaha	13	-	-	-	-	-	-	-	-	-	13	-	10	-	-	**36**
15=	**Jochen Schmid**	D	Honda	-	-	3	3	-	6	5	9	-	-	-	2	5	-	3	**36**
17	**Carlos Lavado**	YV	Aprilia	-	-	-	-	-	-	-	-	6	1	-	8	-	7	9	**31**
18	**Alexandre Barros**	BR	Yamaha	-	6	-	-	1	-	-	1	-	-	-	3	7	6	6	**30**
19	**Gary Cowan**	IRL	Yamaha	-	-	1	7	-	-	-	5	-	-	1	7	-	-	4	**25**
20	**Jim Filice**	USA	Honda	5	-	17	-	-	-	-	-	-	-	-	-	-	-	-	**22**
21	**Renzo Colleoni**	I	Aprilia	-	-	-	-	8	-	3	6	-	4	-	-	-	-	-	**21**
22	**Ivan Palazzese**	YV	Aprilia	-	-	5	5	9	-	-	-	-	-	-	-	-	-	-	**19**
23=	**Harald Eckl**	D	Aprilia	-	-	-	-	4	3	4	-	2	2	-	-	3	-	-	**18**
23=	**Alberto Puig**	E	Yamaha	-	-	4	-	-	-	-	-	9	3	2	-	-	-	-	**18**
25	**Marcellino Lucchi**	I	Aprilia	-	-	-	-	10	-	-	-	7	-	-	-	-	-	-	**17**
26	**Daniel Amatriain**	E	Honda	-	-	-	4	-	-	-	-	-	5	3	-	-	2	-	**14**
27	**Alain Bronec**	F	Aprilia	-	-	-	-	-	4	-	-	-	6	-	-	1	-	-	**11**
28	**Tadayuki Okada**	J	Honda	10	-	-	-	-	-	-	-	-	-	-	-	-	-	-	**10**
29=	**Stefano Caracchi**	RSM	Honda	-	-	-	1	-	-	-	-	4	-	-	4	-	-	-	**9**
29=	**Adrien Morillas**	F	Yamaha	-	-	-	-	-	-	-	8	-	-	-	1	-	-	-	**9**
29=	**Toshinobu Shiomori**	J	Yamaha	9	-	-	-	-	-	-	-	-	-	-	-	-	-	-	**9**
32	**Fausto Ricci**	I	Aprilia	-	-	-	-	-	-	-	-	-	8	-	-	-	-	-	**8**
33=	**Alberto Rota**	I	Aprilia	-	-	-	2	3	-	-	-	1	-	-	-	-	-	-	**6**
33=	**Patrick van den Goorbergh**	NL	Yamaha	-	-	-	-	-	-	-	3	3	-	-	-	-	-	-	**6**
35=	**Darryl Beattie**	AUS	Honda	-	4	-	-	-	-	-	-	-	-	-	-	-	-	-	**4**
35=	**Paolo Casoli**	I	Honda	-	-	-	-	-	-	-	-	-	-	-	-	-	4	-	**4**
35=	**Kevin Mitchell**	GB	Yamaha	-	-	-	-	-	-	-	4	-	-	-	-	-	-	-	**4**
35=	**Andreas Preining**	A	Aprilia	-	-	-	-	-	-	-	2	-	-	-	-	2	-	-	**4**
39=	**Luis Lavado**	YV	Yamaha	-	-	-	-	-	-	-	-	-	-	-	-	-	-	2	**2**
39=	**Maurizio Vitali**	I	Honda	-	-	-	-	-	-	2	-	-	-	-	-	-	-	-	**2**
41=	**Junya Arai**	J	Honda	1	-	-	-	-	-	-	-	-	-	-	-	-	-	-	**1**
41=	**August Auinger**	A	Yamaha	-	1	-	-	-	-	-	-	-	-	-	-	-	-	-	**1**
41=	**Hans Becker**	D	Seel	-	-	-	-	-	1	-	-	-	-	-	-	-	-	-	**1**
41=	**Manfred Herweh**	D	Yamaha	-	-	-	-	-	-	-	-	-	-	-	-	-	1	-	**1**

Past 250 cc World Champions

			(Wins/ Races)
1949	Bruno Ruffo, I	Guzzi	(1/4)
1950	Dario Ambrosini, I	Benelli	(3/4)
1951	Bruno Ruffo, I	Guzzi	(2/5)
1952	Enrico Lorenzetti, I	Guzzi	(2/6)
1953	Werner Haas, D	NSU	(2/7)
1954	Werner Haas, D	NSU	(5/7)
1955	Hermann-Peter Müller, D	NSU	(1/5)
1956	Carlo Ubbiali, I	MV-Agusta	(5/6)
1957	Cecil Sandford, GB	Mondial	(2/6)
1958	Tarquinio Provini, I	MV-Agusta	(4/6)
1959	Carlo Ubbiali, I	MV-Agusta	(2/6)
1960	Carlo Ubbiali, I	MV-Agusta	(4/6)
1961	Mike Hailwood, GB	Honda	(4/11)
1962	Jim Redman, RSR	Honda	(6/10)
1963	Jim Redman, RSR	Honda	(4/10)
1964	Phil Read, GB	Yamaha	(5/11)
1965	Phil Read, GB	Yamaha	(7/13)
1966	Mike Hailwood, GB	Honda	(10/12)
1967	Mike Hailwood, GB	Honda	(5/13)
1968	Phil Read, GB	Yamaha	(5/10)
1969	Kel Carruthers, AUS	Benelli	(3/12)
1970	Rod Gould, GB	Yamaha	(6/12)
1971	Phil Read, GB	Yamaha	(3/12)
1972	Jarno Saarinen, SF	Yamaha	(4/13)
1973	Dieter Braun, D	Yamaha	(4/11)
1974	Walter Villa, I	Harley-Davidson	(4/10)
1975	Walter Villa, I	Harley-Davidson	(5/11)
1976	Walter Villa, I	Harley-Davidson	(7/11)
1977	Mario Lega, I	Morbidelli	(1/12)
1978	Kork Ballington, ZA	Kawasaki	(4/12)
1979	Kork Ballington, ZA	Kawasaki	(7/12)
1980	Anton Mang, D	Kawasaki	(4/10)
1981	Anton Mang, D	Kawasaki	(10/12)
1982	Jean-Louis Tournadre, F	Yamaha	(1/12)
1983	Carlos Lavado, YV	Yamaha	(4/11)
1984	Christian Sarron, F	Yamaha	(3/12)
1985	Freddie Spencer, USA	Honda	(7/12)
1986	Carlos Lavado, YV	Yamaha	(6/11)
1987	Anton Mang, D	Honda	(8/15)
1988	Alfonso Pons, E	Honda	(4/15)

125 cc World Championship

Position	Rider	Nationality	Machine	Japan	Australia	Spain	Italy	Germany	Austria	Holland	Belgium	France	Great Britain	Sweden	Czechoslovakia	TOTAL
1	**Alex Criville**	E	Cobas	-	20	20	-	20	15	17	-	17	17	20	20	**166**
2	**Hans Spaan**	NL	Honda	-	8	-	17	13	20	20	20	-	20	17	17	**152**
3	**Ezio Gianola**	I	Honda	20	11	13	20	17	-	-	17	15	15	-	10	**138**
4	**Hisashi Unemoto**	J	Honda	17	-	8	10	11	-	11	15	10	11	-	11	**104**
5	**Fausto Gresini**	I	Aprilia	5	9	11	15	-	11	10	9	11	8	11	2	**102**
6	**Koji Takada**	J	Honda	15	-	15	13	-	-	7	7	13	5	15	9	**99**
7	**Stefan Prein**	D	Honda	-	13	5	-	10	3	13	10	-	13	10	15	**92**
8	**Julian Miralles**	E	Derbi	-	10	9	11	15	17	15	13	-	-	-	-	**90**
9	**Jorge Martinez**	E	Derbi	-	-	17	-	-	-	9	-	20	-	13	13	**72**
10	**Allan Scott**	USA	Honda	3	15	10	-	-	7	2	-	-	-	9	8	**54**
11	**Adolf Stadler**	D	Honda	1	6	4	8	8	-	-	8	5	7	-	6	**53**
12	**Robin Milton**	GB	Honda	4	17	3	9	7	6	-	-	-	-	-	-	**46**
13	**Luis Reyes**	E	Honda	2	7	6	5	3	-	-	-	8	4	-	-	**35**
14	**Domenico Brigaglia**	I	Garelli	-	-	-	3	-	9	-	5	7	10	-	-	**34**
15	**Dirk Raudies**	D	Honda	-	-	-	-	4	10	1	3	-	3	5	3	**29**
16	**Alfred Waibel**	D	Honda	-	-	-	-	5	1	6	-	6	-	-	7	**25**
17	**Taru Rinne**	SF	Honda	-	-	1	-	9	-	8	-	-	-	1	4	**23**
18	**Lucio Pietroniro**	B	Honda	-	4	2	1	-	-	4	11	-	-	-	-	**22**
19=	**Bruno Casanova**	I	Aprilia	-	-	-	7	-	13	-	-	-	-	-	-	**20**
19=	**Doriano Romboni**	I	Honda	-	-	-	6	1	-	-	4	-	9	-	-	**20**
21=	**Robin Appleyard**	GB	Honda	-	5	-	2	-	-	-	-	-	6	-	5	**18**
21=	**Flemming Kistrup**	DK	Honda	-	-	-	-	-	-	-	-	9	1	8	-	**18**
23	**Thierry Feuz**	CH	Honda	-	-	-	-	-	4	5	6	-	-	-	-	**15**
24=	**Masayuki Hirose**	J	Honda	13	-	-	-	-	-	-	-	-	-	-	-	**13**
24=	**Herri Torrontegui**	E	Honda	-	-	7	4	-	-	-	-	-	-	2	-	**13**
26=	**Jean-Claude Selini**	F	Honda	-	-	-	-	-	5	-	2	4	-	-	-	**11**
26=	**Kenichi Yoshida**	J	Honda	11	-	-	-	-	-	-	-	-	-	-	-	**11**
28=	**Corrado Catalano**	I	Gazzaniga	-	-	-	-	-	8	-	-	2	-	-	-	**10**
28=	**Masato Shima**	J	Honda	10	-	-	-	-	-	-	-	-	-	-	-	**10**
28=	**Johnny Wickström**	SF	Honda	-	2	-	-	2	-	-	-	-	-	6	-	**10**
31	**Yutaka Fujiwara**	J	Honda	9	-	-	-	-	-	-	-	-	-	-	-	**9**
32=	**Hubert Abold**	D	Rotax	-	-	-	-	-	-	-	1	-	-	7	-	**8**
32=	**Kazuaki Yamashita**	J	Honda	8	-	-	-	-	-	-	-	-	-	-	-	**8**
34	**Shinichi Fujiyama**	J	Honda	7	-	-	-	-	-	-	-	-	-	-	-	**7**
35=	**Gerhard Waibel**	D	Honda	-	-	-	-	6	-	-	-	-	-	-	-	**6**
35=	**Kazuya Yamada**	J	Honda	6	-	-	-	-	-	-	-	-	-	-	-	**6**
37	**Mike Leitner**	A	Honda	-	-	-	-	-	-	-	-	-	-	4	-	**4**
38=	**Gabriele Debbia**	I	Aprilia	-	-	-	-	-	-	3	-	-	-	-	-	**3**
38=	**Stuart Edwards**	GB	ERM	-	-	-	-	-	-	-	-	-	-	3	-	**3**
38=	**Jean-Pierre Jeandat**	F	Honda	-	-	-	-	-	-	-	-	3	-	-	-	**3**
38=	**Ian Saunders**	AUS	Honda	-	3	-	-	-	-	-	-	-	-	-	-	**3**
42=	**Josef Fischer**	A	Honda	-	-	-	-	-	2	-	-	-	-	-	-	**2**
42=	**Bady Hassaine**	TN	Honda	-	-	-	-	-	-	-	-	-	2	-	-	**2**
44=	**Alex Bedford**	GB	EMC	-	1	-	-	-	-	-	-	-	-	-	-	**1**
44=	**Hervé Duffard**	F	Honda	-	-	-	-	-	-	-	-	1	-	-	-	**1**
44=	**Heinz Lüthi**	CH	Honda	-	-	-	-	-	-	-	-	-	-	-	1	**1**

80 cc World Championship

Position	Rider	Nationality	Machine	Spain	Italy	Germany	Yugoslavia	Holland	Czechoslovakia	TOTAL
1	**Manuel Herreros**	E	Derbi	11	13	17	17	17	17	**92**
2	**Stefan Dörflinger**	CH	Krauser	17	11	11	15	15	11	**80**
3	**Peter Öttl**	D	Krauser	15	-	20	20	20	-	**75**
4	**Herri Torrontegui**	E	Krauser	20	15	15	-	5	20	**75**
5	**Gabriele Gnani**	I	Gnani	6	17	6	8	-	8	**45**
6	**Paolo Priori**	I	Krauser	5	6	5	9	7	9	**41**
7	**Bogdan Nikolov**	BG	Krauser	13	-	-	11	10	6	**40**
8	**Jorge Martinez**	E	Derbi	-	20	-	-	-	15	**35**
9	**Jaime Mariano**	E	Casal	7	-	10	-	11	5	**33**
10	**Jörg Seel**	D	Seel	2	-	7	10	-	13	**32**
11	**Antonio Sanchez**	E	Cobas	9	8	13	-	-	-	**30**
12=	**Hans Koopman**	NL	Ziegler	4	4	2	7	9	-	**26**
12=	**Julian Miralles**	E	Derbi	-	-	-	13	13	-	**26**
14	**Ralf Waldmann**	D	Seel	8	2	9	-	4	-	**23**
15	**Jose Saez**	E	Krauser	10	10	-	-	-	-	**20**
16=	**Jos van Dongen**	NL	Casal	-	1	-	6	2	4	**13**
16=	**Bernd Völkel**	D	Seel	-	-	-	-	6	7	**13**
18=	**Stefan Kurfiss**	D	Krauser	-	3	8	-	1	-	**12**
18=	**Bert Smit**	NL	Krauser	1	-	-	-	8	3	**12**
20	**Luis Alvaro**	E	Krauser	-	-	-	-	-	10	**10**
21	**Giuseppe Ascareggi**	I	BBFT	-	9	-	-	-	-	**9**
22	**Roberto Sassone**	I	Unimoto	-	7	-	-	-	-	**7**
23	**Janos Szabo**	H	Krauser	-	-	4	-	-	2	**6**
24=	**Jacques Bernard**	B	Fantic	-	5	-	-	-	-	**5**
24=	**Zdravko Matulja**	YU	Casal	-	-	-	5	-	-	**5**
26=	**Stefan Brägger**	CH	Casal	-	-	1	-	3	-	**4**
26=	**Janez Pintar**	YU	Eberhardt	-	-	-	4	-	-	**4**
28=	**René Dünki**	CH	LCR	3	-	-	-	-	-	**3**
28=	**Thomas Engl**	D	Esch	-	-	-	3	-	-	**3**
28=	**Gunther Schirnhöfer**	D	Krauser	-	-	3	-	-	-	**3**
31	**Matthias Ehinger**	D	BMC	-	-	-	2	-	-	**2**
32=	**Xavier Arumi**	E	Krauser	-	-	-	1	-	-	**1**
32=	**Heinz Paschen**	D	Casal	-	-	-	-	-	1	**1**

Past 125 cc World Champions

			(Wins/ Races)
1949	Nello Pagani, I	Mondial	(2/3)
1950	Bruno Ruffo, I	Mondial	(1/3)
1951	Carlo Ubbiali, I	Mondial	(1/4)
1952	Cecil Sandford, GB	MV-Agusta	(3/6)
1953	Werner Haas, D	NSU	(3/6)
1954	Rupert Hollaus, A	NSU	(4/6)
1955	Carlo Ubbiali, I	MV-Agusta	(5/6)
1956	Carlo Ubbiali, I	MV-Agusta	(5/6)
1957	Tarquinio Provini, I	Mondial	(3/6)
1958	Carlo Ubbiali, I	MV-Agusta	(4/7)
1959	Carlo Ubbiali, I	MV-Agusta	(3/7)
1960	Carlo Ubbiali, I	MV-Agusta	(4/5)
1961	Tom Phillis, AUS	Honda	(4/11)
1962	Luigi Taveri, CH	Honda	(6/11)
1963	Hugh Anderson, NZ	Suzuki	(6/12)
1964	Luigi Taveri, CH	Honda	(5/11)
1965	Hugh Anderson, NZ	Suzuki	(7/12)
1966	Luigi Taveri, CH	Honda	(5/10)
1967	Billy Ivy, GB	Yamaha	(8/12)
1968	Phil Read, GB	Yamaha	(6/9)
1969	Dave Simmons, GB	Kawasaki	(8/11)
1970	Dieter Braun, D	Suzuki	(4/11)
1971	Angel Nieto, E	Derbi	(5/11)
1972	Angel Nieto, E	Derbi	(5/13)
1973	Kent Andersson, S	Yamaha	(5/12)
1974	Kent Andersson, S	Yamaha	(5/10)
1975	Paolo Pileri, I	Morbidelli	(7/10)
1976	Pier Paolo Bianchi, I	Morbidelli	(7/9)
1977	Pier Paolo Bianchi, I	Morbidelli	(7/12)
1978	Eugênio Lazzarini, I	MBA	(4/12)
1979	Angel Nieto, E	Minarelli	(8/13)
1980	Pier Paolo Bianchi, I	MBA	(2/10)
1981	Angel Nieto, E	Minarelli	(8/12)
1982	Angel Nieto, E	Garelli	(6/12)
1983	Angel Nieto, E	Garelli	(6/11)
1984	Angel Nieto, E	Garelli	(6/8)
1985	Fausto Gresini, I	Garelli	(3/10)
1986	Luca Cadalora, I	Garelli	(4/11)
1987	Fausto Gresini, I	Garelli	(10/11)
1988	Jorge Martinez, E	Derbi	(9/11)

Past 50 cc/*80 cc World Champions

			(Wins/ Races)
1962	Ernst Degner, D	Suzuki	(4/10)
1963	Hugh Anderson, NZ	Suzuki	(2/9)
1964	Hugh Anderson, NZ	Suzuki	(4/8)
1965	Ralph Bryans, IRL	Honda	(3/8)
1966	Hans-Georg Anscheidt, D	Suzuki	(2/6)
1967	Hans-Georg Anscheidt, D	Suzuki	(3/7)
1968	Hans-Georg Anscheidt, D	Suzuki	(3/5)
1969	Angel Nieto, E	Derbi	(2/10)
1970	Angel Nieto, E	Derbi	(5/10)
1971	Jan de Vries, NL	Kreidler	(5/9)
1972	Angel Nieto, E	Derbi	(3/8)
1973	Jan de Vries, NL	Kreidler	(5/7)
1974	Henk van Kessel, NL	Kreidler	(6/10)
1975	Angel Nieto, E	Kreidler	(6/8)
1976	Angel Nieto, E	Bultaco	(5/9)
1977	Angel Nieto, E	Bultaco	(3/7)
1978	Ricardo Tormo, E	Bultaco	(5/7)
1979	Eugênio Lazzarini, I	Kreidler	(5/7)
1980	Eugênio Lazzarini, I	Kreidler/Iprem	(2/6)
1981	Ricardo Tormo, E	Bultaco	(6/8)
1982	Stefan Dörflinger, CH	Kreidler	(3/6)
1983	Stefan Dörflinger, CH	Kreidler	(3/7)
1984*	Stefan Dörflinger, CH	Zundapp	(4/8)
1985*	Stefan Dörflinger, CH	Krauser	(2/7)
1986*	Jorge Martinez, E	Derbi	(4/9)
1987*	Jorge Martinez, E	Derbi	(7/10)
1988*	Jorge Martinez, E	Derbi	(6/7)

Past Sidecar World Champions

			(Wins/ Races)
1949	Eric Oliver, GB/ Denis Jenkinson, GB	Norton	(2/3)
1950	Eric Oliver, GB/ Lorenzo Dobelli, I	Norton	(3/3)
1951	Eric Oliver, GB/ Lorenzo Dobelli, I	Norton	(3/5)
1952	Cyril Smith, GB/ Bob Clements, GB	Norton	(1/5)
1953	Eric Oliver, GB/ Stanley Dibben, GB	Norton	(4/5)
1954	Wilhelm Noll, D/ Fritz Cron, D	BMW	(3/6)
1955	Wilhelm Faust, D/ Karl Remmert, D	BMW	(3/6)
1956	Wilhelm Noll, D/ Fritz Cron, D	BMW	(3/6)
1957	Fritz Hillebrand, D/ Manfred Grunwald, D	BMW	(3/5)
1958	Walter Schneider, D/ Hans Strauss, D	BMW	(3/4)
1959	Walter Schneider, D/ Hans Strauss, D	BMW	(2/5)
1960	Helmut Fath, D/ Alfred Wohligenmuth, D	BMW	(4/5)
1961	Max Deubel, D/ Emil Horner, D	BMW	(3/6)
1962	Max Deubel, D/ Emil Horner, D	BMW	(3/6)
1963	Max Deubel, D/ Emil Horner, D	BMW	(2/5)
1964	Max Deubel, D/ Emil Horner, D	BMW	(2/6)
1965	Fritz Scheidegger, CH/ John Robinson, GB	BMW	(4/7)
1966	Fritz Scheidegger, CH/ John Robinson, GB	BMW	(5/5)
1967	Klaus Enders, D/ Ralf Engelhardt, D	BMW	(5/8)
1968	Helmut Fath, D/ Wolfgang Kallaugh, D	URS	(3/6)
1969	Klaus Enders, D/ Ralf Engelhardt, D	BMW	(4/7)
1970	Klaus Enders, D/ Wolfgang Kallaugh, D	BMW	(5/8)
1971	Horst Owesle, D/ Peter Rutterford, GB	URS-Fath	(3/8)
1972	Klaus Enders, D/ Ralf Engelhardt, D	BMW	(4/8)
1973	Klaus Enders, D/ Ralf Engelhardt, D	BMW	(7/8)
1974	Klaus Enders, D/ Ralf Engelhardt, D	Busch-BMW	(2/8)
1975	Rolf Steinhausen, D/ Josef Huber, D	Busch-König	(3/7)
1976	Rolf Steinhausen, D/ Josef Huber, D	Busch-König	(3/7)
1977	George O'Dell, GB/ Kenny Arthur, GB Cliff Holland, GB	Yamaha	(-/7)
1978	Rolf Biland, CH/ Kenny Williams, GB	Yamaha	(3/8)
1979	*B2A* Rolf Biland, CH/ Kurt Waltisperg, CH	Yamaha	(3/7)
	B2B Bruno Holzer, CH/ Karl Meierhans, CH	Yamaha	(-/6)
1980	Jock Taylor, GB/ Benga Johansson, S	Yamaha	(4/8)
1981	Rolf Biland, CH/ Kurt Waltisperg, CH	Yamaha	(7/10)
1982	Werner Schwärzel, D/ Andreas Huber, D	Yamaha	(-/9)
1983	Rolf Biland, CH/ Kurt Waltisperg, CH	Yamaha	(6/8)
1984	Egbert Streuer, NL/ Bernard Schnieders, NL	Yamaha	(3/7)
1985	Egbert Streuer, NL/ Bernard Schnieders, NL	LCR-Yamaha	(3/6)
1986	Egbert Streuer, NL/ Bernard Schnieders, NL	LCR-Yamaha	(5/8)
1987	Steve Webster, GB/ Tony Hewitt, GB	LCR-Yamaha	(3/8)
1988	Steve Webster, GB/ Tony Hewitt, GB	LCR-Krauser	(3/9)

Sidecar World Championship

Position	Driver & passenger	Nationality	Machine	USA	Germany	Austria	Holland	Belgium	France	Great Britain	Sweden	Czechoslovakia	TOTAL
1	**Steve Webster/ Tony Hewitt**	GB GB	LCR-Krauser	20	20	1	20	17	17	20	15	15	**145**
2	**Egbert Streuer/ Geral de Haas**	NL NL	LCR-Yamaha	-	17	17	17	20	15	17	13	20	**136**
3	**Alain Michel/ Jean-Marc Fresc**	F F	LCR-Krauser	17	-	15	13	8	13	13	17	13	**109**
4	**Rolf Biland/ Kurt Waltisperg**	CH CH	LCR-Krauser	-	-	20	15	15	20	15	20	-	**105**
5	**Markus Egloff/ Urs Egloff**	CH CH	Yamaha	15	10	–	7	4	11	9	17	-	**73**
6	**Fritz Stölzle/ Hubert Stölzle**	D D	LCR-Krauser	9	13	7	5	6	7	10	6	6	**69**
7	**Masato Kumano/ Markus Fahrni**	D CH	LCR-Tec	13	15	11	8	-	11	-	-	9	**67**
8	**Rolf Steinhausen/ Bruno Hiller**	D D	Schuh	-	10	8	11	13	-	-	8	7	**57**
9	**Barry Brindley/ Grahame Rose**	GB GB	Fowler-Yamaha	11	-	9	-	9	8	9	10	-	**56**
10	**Steve Abbott/ Shaun Smith**	GB GB	LCR-Yamaha	-	-	5	10	-	9	-	11	11	**46**
11	**Bernd Scherer/ Thomas Schröder**	D D	BSR-Krauser	7	-	-	9	10	-	-	5	8	**39**
12=	**Derek Jones/ Peter Brown**	GB GB	LCR-Yamaha	1	11	-	4	11	10	-	-	-	**37**
12=	**Yoshisada Kumagaya/ Brian Barlow Peter Linden Phil Coombes**	J GB S GB	Windle-KS	10	7	-	3	5	-	-	7	5	**37**
14	**Theo van Kempen/ Simon Birchall**	NL GB	LCR-Krauser	-	6	4	7	3	6	6	-	2	**34**
15	**Alfred Zurbrügg/ Martin Zurbrügg**	CH CH	LCR-Yamaha	8	-	13	-	-	-	-	-	10	**31**
16	**René Progin/ Laurence Magnenet Yves Hunziker**	CH CH CH	LCR-Krauser	6	4	-	2	-	3	8	4	-	**27**
17	**Tony Wyssen/ Kilian Wyssen**	CH CH	LCR-Krauser	-	9	6	-	-	5	-	2	3	**25**
18	**Ivan Nigrowsky/ Jacques Corbier**	F F	LCR-JPX	-	-	2	6	4	-	3	3	-	**18**
19	**Billy Gällros/ Håkan Olsson Julian Tailford**	S S GB	Yamaha	-	5	-	-	1	1	7	-	-	**14**
20	**Barry Smith/ David Smith**	GB GB	Windle-ADM	-	8	-	-	-	2	-	-	-	**10**
21=	**Tony Baker/ Trevor Hopkinson**	GB GB	LCR-Yamaha	3	-	3	1	-	-	1	-	1	**9**
21=	**Wolfgang Stropek/ Steve Campbell Wolfgang Bock**	A GB D	Mibag-Krauser	5	1	-	-	-	-	2	1	-	**9**
23=	**Kenny Howles/ Steve Pointer**	GB GB	LCR-Krauser	-	-	-	-	2	-	4	-	-	**6**
23=	**Gary Thomas/ Eckhart Rösinger**	GB D	LCR-IMI	2	-	-	-	-	-	-	-	4	**6**
25	**Ray Gardner/ Tony Strevens**	GB GB	LCR-Krauser	-	-	-	-	-	-	5	-	-	**5**
26	**Judd Drew/ Bryan Houghton**	GB GB	LCR-JPX	4	-	-	-	-	-	-	-	-	**4**
27	**Clive Stirrat/ Simon Prior**	GB GB	LCR	-	3	-	-	-	-	-	-	-	**3**
28	**George Hardwick/ Steve Parker Gary Irlam**	GB GB GB	LCR	-	2	-	-	-	-	-	-	-	**2**

Isle of Man Tourist Trophy Races, 29 May-9 June
Isle of Man Tourist Trophy Course, 37.73-mile/60.72-km circuit

TT Formula 1 race

6 laps, 226.38 miles/364.32 km

Place	No.	Rider	Nat.	Machine	Time & speed
1	6	Steve Hislop	GB	750 Honda	1h 53m 47.4s 119.36 mph/ 192.091 km/h
2	2	Brian Morrison	GB	750 Honda	1h 55m 30.2s
3	1	Nick Jefferies	GB	750 Yamaha	1h 55m 55.0s
4	12	Carl Fogarty	GB	750 Honda	1h 56m 25.8s
5	32	Graeme McGregor	AUS	750 Honda	1h 56m 50.6s
6	20	James Whitham	GB	750 Suzuki	1h 56m 57.4s
7	21	Robert Dunlop	GB	750 Honda	1h 56m 59.2s
8	15	Andy McGladdery	GB	750 Honda	1h 57m 34.8s
9	19	Sam McClements	IRL	750 Honda	1h 58m 57.2s
10	50	Colin Gable	GB	750 Honda	1h 59m 12.2s
11	51	Charlie Corner	GB	750 Honda	2h 00m 06.8s
12	17	Steve Ward	GB	750 Honda	2h 00m 13.6s
13	36	Tony Moran	GB	750 Yamaha	2h 00m 55.2s
14	53	Bob Jackson	GB	750 Honda	2h 01m 14.2s
15	34	Phillip McCallen	GB	750 Honda	2h 01m 15.8s
16	31	Dennis Ireland	NZ	750 Honda	2h 01m 30.4s
17	43	Ray Swann	GB	750 Kawasaki	2h 01m 36.4s
18	14	Steve Henshaw	GB	750 Honda	2h 01m 51.6s
19	7	Dave Leach	GB	750 Yamaha	2h 02m 38.2s
20	54	Richard Rose	GB	750 Kawasaki	2h 03m 06.8s
21	49	Kenny Harrison	GB	750 Yamaha	2h 04m 43.2s
22	41	Phil Nicholls	GB	750 Honda	2h 04m 44.0s
23	55	Eric Galbraith	IRL	750 Honda	2h 04m 47.0s
24	105	John Reynolds	GB	750 Kawasaki	2h 07m 33.4s
25	56	Derek Chatterton	GB	750 Yamaha	2h 07m 52.6s
26	66	Dave Woolams	GB	750 Kawasaki	2h 08m 10.2s
27	86	Steve Boyes	GB	750 Suzuki	2h 09m 03.8s

Fastest lap: Hislop, 18m 39.4s, 121.34 mph/195.278 km/h (record).

Senior TT

6 laps, 226.38 miles/364.32 km

Place	No.	Rider	Nat.	Machine	Time & speed
1	6	Steve Hislop	GB	750 Honda	1h 54m 52.6s 118.23 mph/ 190.272 km/h
2	1	Nick Jefferies	GB	750 Yamaha	1h 55m 30.6s
3	32	Graeme McGregor	AUS	750 Honda	1h 56m 42.4s
4	21	Robert Dunlop	GB	750 Honda	1h 57m 44.2s
5	11	Eddie Laycock	IRL	500 Honda	1h 58m 11.0s
6	15	Andy McGladdery	GB	750 Honda	1h 58m 18.4s
7	19	Sam McClements	IRL	750 Honda	1h 58m 36.4s
8	46	Ian Young	GB	750 Honda	1h 59m 28.6s
9	50	Colin Gable	GB	1000 Yamaha	2h 00m 03.8s
10	49	Kenny Harrison	GB	1000 Yamaha	2h 01m 11.6s
11	53	Bob Jackson	GB	750 Honda	2h 01m 37.4s
12	31	Dennis Ireland	NZ	750 Honda	2h 01m 56.6s
13	41	Phil Nicholls	GB	750 Honda	2h 02m 16.6s
14	39	Iain Duffus	GB	750 Suzuki	2h 02m 25.0s
15	74	Brian Raynor	GB	1000 Yamaha	2h 02m 25.8s
16	7	Dave Leach	GB	750 Yamaha	2h 02m 42.6s
17	34	Phillip McCallen	GB	750 Honda	2h 02m 53.4s
18	48	Stephen Johnson	GB	1000 Yamaha	2h 03m 10.2s
19	54	Richard Rose	GB	750 Kawasaki	2h 03m 12.2s
20	40	Howard Selby	GB	750 Yamaha	2h 04m 00.8s
21	55	Eric Galbraith	IRL	750 Honda	2h 04m 05.2s
22	115	Rory Thomson	GB	750 Yamaha	2h 04m 38.0s
23	8	Steve Cull	GB	588 Norton	2h 04m 42.6s
24	70	Derrick Bates	GB	750 Honda	2h 05m 20.0s
25	56	Derek Chatterton	GB	1000 Yamaha	2h 05m 22.6s
26	77	Paul Davies	GB	1000 Yamaha	2h 06m 47.2s
27	75	Alan Dugdale	GB	1300 Yamaha	2h 06m 50.0s

Fastest lap: Hislop, 18m 45.4s, 120.69 mph/194.231 km/h (record).

Junior TT

4 laps, 150.92 miles/242.88 km

Place	No.	Rider	Nat.	Machine	Time & speed
1	5	Johnny Rea	GB	250 Yamaha	1h 20m 45.8s 112.12 mph/ 180.439 km/h
2	1	Eddie Laycock	IRL	250 Yamaha	1h 20m 48.6s
3	19	Steve Hazlett	IRL	250 EMC	1h 21m 35.4s
4	4	Carl Fogarty	GB	250 Honda	1h 22m 23.6s
5	20	Ian Young	GB	350 Yamaha	1h 22m 50.0s
6	7	Barry Woodland	GB	250 Yamaha	1h 23m 15.8s
7	24	Derek Chatterton	GB	350 Yamaha	1h 24m 10.8s
8	29	Richard Coates	GB	350 Yamaha	1h 24m 54.6s
9	28	Richard Swallow	GB	250 Honda	1h 25m 12.6s
10	56	Robbie Boland	IRL	350 Yamaha	1h 25m 48.8s
11	27	Gary Radcliffe	GB	350 Yamaha	1h 26m 34.8s
12	21	James Hodson	GB	250 CCM	1h 27m 06.4s
13	49	Mike Booys	GB	350 Yamaha	1h 27m 12.8s
14	43	Mark Westmoreland	GB	250 Yamaha	1h 27m 28.0s
15	55	Jeremy Thrush	GB	250 Honda	1h 27m 37.0s
16	51	Sammy Henry	GB	250 Honda	1h 27m 39.8s
17	39	Alan 'Bud' Jackson	GB	350 Yamaha	1h 28m 12.6s
18	53	Mick Chatterton	GB	350 Yamaha	1h 29m 57.2s
19	74	Mark Langton	GB	250 Suzuki	1h 30m 59.0s

Fastest lap: Laycock, 19m 51.0s, 114.04 mph/183.529 km/h (record).

Sidecar TT: Race A

3 laps, 113.19 miles/182.16 km

Place	No.	Driver & passenger	Nat.	Machine	Time & speed
1	7	Dave Molyneux/ Colin Hardman	GB GB	750 Bregazzi-Yamaha	1h 04m 57.0s 104.56 mph/ 168.273 km/h
2	1	Kenny Howles/ Steve Pointer	GB GB	700 Ireson-Yamaha	1h 04m 58.2s
3	15	Neil Smith/ Dave Wood	GB GB	700 Yamaha	1h 05m 29.0s
4	9	Dennis Brown/ Bill Nelson	GB GB	750 Yamaha	1h 05m 45.8s
5	10	Lars Schwartz/ Leif Gustavsson	S S	750 Ireson-Yamaha	1h 05m 56.0s
6	2	Derek Plummer/ Anthony Darby	GB GB	700 Yamaha	1h 06m 56.8s
7	37	Victor Jefford/ Peter Hill	GB GB	700 Baker-Yamaha	1h 07m 22.8s
8	6	Artie Oates/ Edda Oates	GB GB	700 Yamaha	1h 07m 37.8s
9	17	Geoff Bell/ Julian Tailford	GB GB	700 Yamaha	1h 07m 53.6s
10	28	David Low/ Janet Low	GB GB	1170 Jacobs-Suzuki	1h 08m 29.4s
11	26	Dave Saville/ Richard Crossley	GB GB	350 Sabre (F2)	1h 09m 11.4s
12	21	John Phillips/ Malcolm Hollis	GB GB	750 Yamaha	1h 09m 14.4s
13	43	Goronwy Davies/ Pete Smethurst	GB GB	700 Yamaha	1h 09m 32.8s
14	57	Bob Munro/ Colvin Denholm	GB GB	1000 Rumble-Suzuki	1h 10m 19.4s
15	78	Brian Gray/ Stuart Graham	GB GB	750 Yamaha	1h 10m 40.8s

Fastest lap: Howles, 21m 25.6s, 105.65 mph/170.027 km/h.

Sidecar TT: Race B

3 laps, 113.19 miles/182.16 km

Place	No.	Driver & passenger	Nat.	Machine	Time & speed
1	3	Mick Boddice/ Chas Birks	GB GB	700 Ireson-Yamaha	1h 03m 22.0s 107.17 mph/ 172.473 km/h
2	9	Dennis Brown/ Bill Nelson	GB GB	750 Yamaha	1h 04m 23.2s
3	7	Dave Molyneux/ Colin Hardman	GB GB	750 Bregazzi-Yamaha	1h 04m 31.2s
4	4	Geoff Rushbrook/ Jim Cochrane	GB GB	700 Ireson-Yamaha	1h 04m 46.0s
5	5	Dave Hallam/ John Gibbard	GB GB	700 Windle-Yamaha	1h 05m 39.8s
6	17	Geoff Bell/ Julian Tailford	GB GB	700 Yamaha	1h 05m 56.4s
7	10	Lars Schwartz/ Leif Gustavsson	S S	750 Ireson-Yamaha	1h 06m 09.2s
8	14	Eric Cornes/ Graham Wellington	GB GB	700 Ireson-Yamaha	1h 07m 17.6s
9	12	Derek Rumble Jnr/ Gareth Keep	GB GB	700 Rumble-Yamaha	1h 07m 18.8s
10	6	Artie Oates/ Edda Oates	GB GB	700 Yamaha	1h 07m 25.6s
11	21	John Phillips/ Malcolm Hollis	GB GB	750 Yamaha	1h 07m 31.8s
12	23	Ian Pugh/ David Samuel	GB GB	750 Yamaha	1h 08m 26.8s
13	26	Dave Saville/ Richard Crossley	GB GB	350 Sabre (F2)	1h 08m 54.0s
14	15	Neil Smith/ Dave Wood	GB GB	700 Yamaha	1h 09m 13.6s
15	18	Rod Bellas/ Geoff Knight	GB GB	750 Yamaha	1h 09m 26.4s

Fastest lap: Boddice, 20m 54.0s, 108.31 mph/174.308 km/h (record).

125 cc TT

2 laps, 75.46 miles/121.44 km

Place	No.	Rider	Nat.	Machine	Time & speed
1	106	Robert Dunlop	GB	125 Honda	44m 08.0s 102.58 mph/ 165.086 km/h
2	108	Ian Lougher	GB	125 Honda	44m 23.8s
3	104	Carl Fogarty	GB	125 Honda	44m 41.8s
4	109	Ian Newton	GB	125 Honda	44m 46.2s
5	107	Michael McGarrity	IRL	125 Honda	45m 21.6s
6	112	Richard Swallow	GB	125 Honda	45m 40.2s
7	103	Phillip McCallen	GB	125 Honda	45m 49.4s
8	119	David Nobbs	GB	125 Honda	47m 37.2s
9	105	Steve Ward	GB	125 Morbidelli	47m 44.8s
10	142	Dave Shields	GB	125 Honda	48m 21.4s
11	127	Reg Lennon	GB	125 Honda	48m 28.0s
12	120	Steve Mason	GB	125 Honda	48m 32.8s
13	126	Christopher Barton	GB	125 Honda	48m 54.4s
14	139	Tim Salveson	GB	125 MBA	49m 07.4s
15	123	Michael Topping	GB	125 Honda	49m 16.2s

Fastest lap: Dunlop, 21m 58.4s, 103.02 mph/165.794 km/h (record).

Supersport 600

4 laps, 150.92 miles/242.88 km

Place	No.	Rider	Nat.	Machine	Time & speed
1	6	Steve Hislop	GB	600 Honda	1h 20m 25.8s 112.58 mph/ 181.179 km/h
2	7	Dave Leach	GB	600 Yamaha	1h 20m 54.6s
3	12	James Whitham	GB	600 Suzuki	1h 21m 05.6s
4	10	Phil Mellor	GB	600 Suzuki	1h 21m 16.2s
5	2	Brian Morrison	GB	600 Honda	1h 21m 36.2s
6	1	Nick Jefferies	GB	600 Yamaha	1h 21m 37.6s
7	26	Ian Young	GB	600 Honda	1h 22m 28.8s
8	21	Howard Selby	GB	600 Yamaha	1h 22m 33.8s
9	18	Alan Batson	GB	600 Yamaha	1h 22m 54.0s
10	15	Johnny Rea	GB	600 Honda	1h 23m 05.4s
11	17	Steven Linsdell	GB	600 Yamaha	1h 23m 16.4s
12	23	Iain Duffus	GB	600 Yamaha	1h 23m 27.4s
13	24	Phil Nicholls	GB	600 Honda	1h 24m 19.2s
14	36	Brian Raynor	GB	600 Yamaha	1h 24m 31.0s
15	20	Ian Simpson	GB	600 Suzuki	1h 24m 37.2s
16	33	Phil Armes	GB	600 Honda	1h 24m 59.0s
17	28	Stephen Johnson	GB	600 Honda	1h 25m 29.4s
18	45	Dean Ashton	GB	600 Honda	1h 25m 44.4s

Fastest lap: Leach, 19m 55.6s, 113.60 mph/182.821 km/h (record).

Supersport 400

4 laps, 150.92 miles/242.88 km

Place	No.	Rider	Nat.	Machine	Time & speed
1	81	Eddie Laycock	IRL	250 Suzuki	1h 26m 01.0s 105.27 mph/ 169.415 km/h
2	87	Graeme McGregor	AUS	250 Suzuki	1h 27m 21.4s
3	86	Barry Woodland	GB	250 Yamaha	1h 27m 30.2s
4	94	Neil Tuxworth	GB	400 Yamaha	1h 29m 04.6s
5	83	Mat Oxley	GB	250 Yamaha	1h 29m 38.6s
6	118	Mark Langton	GB	250 Suzuki	1h 31m 27.6s
7	99	Derek Glass	GB	250 Suzuki	1h 31m 36.4s
8	95	Neil Crawford	GB	250 Kawasaki	1h 31m 58.4s
9	123	John Reynolds	GB	250 Kawasaki	1h 32m 27.4s
10	119	Ian McMillan	GB	250 Suzuki	1h 32m 59.2s

Fastest lap: Laycock, 21m 10.6s, 106.90 mph/172.038 km/h (record).

Production 750 cc

4 laps, 150.92 miles/242.88 km

Place	No.	Rider	Nat.	Machine	Time & speed
1	8	Carl Fogarty	GB	750 Honda	1h 18m 57.6s 114.68 mph/ 184.559 km/h
2	7	Dave Leach	GB	750 Yamaha	1h 18m 59.4s
3	6	Steve Hislop	GB	750 Honda	1h 19m 13.8s
4	1	Nick Jefferies	GB	750 Yamaha	1h 19m 48.4s
5	2	Brian Morrison	GB	750 Honda	1h 20m 11.0s
6	26	Ian Young	GB	750 Honda	1h 20m 52.4s
7	28	Bob Jackson	GB	750 Honda	1h 21m 15.6s
8	27	Kenny Harrison	GB	750 Yamaha	1h 21m 17.2s
9	10	Phil Mellor	GB	750 Suzuki	1h 21m 41.2s
10	15	Mark Farmer	GB	750 Kawasaki	1h 22m 12.6s
11	31	Gary Thrush	GB	750 Honda	1h 22m 35.6s
12	25	Phil Nicholls	GB	750 Honda	1h 22m 35.6s
13	32	Gary Radcliffe	GB	750 Yamaha	1h 22m 40.0s
14	21	Dennis Ireland	NZ	750 Kawasaki	1h 24m 24.8s

Fastest lap: Leach, 19m 21.8s, 116.91 mph/188.148 km/h (record).

Production 1300 cc

4 laps, 150.92 miles/242.88 km

Place	No.	Rider	Nat.	Machine	Time & speed
1	7	Dave Leach	GB	1000 Yamaha	1h 18m 19.4s 115.61 mph/ 186.056 km/h
2	1	Nick Jefferies	GB	1000 Yamaha	1h 18m 29.4s
3	18	Alan Batson	GB	1000 Yamaha	1h 19m 40.4s
4	22	Howard Selby	GB	1000 Yamaha	1h 19m 46.2s
5	28	Colin Gable	GB	1000 Yamaha	1h 20m 36.0s
6	27	Kenny Harrison	GB	1000 Yamaha	1h 20m 41.0s
7	26	Steve Hazlett	GB	1000 Yamaha	1h 20m 55.2s
8	11	Andy McGladdery	GB	1000 Yamaha	1h 21m 26.2s
9	23	Iain Duffus	GB	1000 Suzuki	1h 21m 47.4s
10	8	Steve Ward	GB	1000 Kawasaki	1h 22m 11.4s
11	17	Nigel Barton	GB	1000 Yamaha	1h 22m 18.6s
12	6	Barry Woodland	GB	1000 Yamaha	1h 22m 29.8s
13	31	Richard Rose	GB	1000 Yamaha	1h 22m 43.0s
14	36	Robert Holden	NZ	1100 Suzuki	1h 22m 50.0s
15	54	Dean Ashton	GB	1100 Suzuki	1h 23m 35.6s
16	43	Rory Thomson	GB	1000 Yamaha	1h 23m 48.4s
17	34	Derek Chatterton	GB	1000 Yamaha	1h 23m 58.8s
18	69	David Goodley	GB	1100 Suzuki	1h 23m 59.0s

Fastest lap: Jefferies, 19m 18.2s, 117.27 mph/188.727 km/h (record).

US Road Racing

AMA National Championship Road Race Series (Superbike)

DAYTONA INTERNATIONAL SPEEDWAY, Daytona Beach, Florida, 12 March 1989. 203 miles/326.69 km
1 John Ashmead (Honda), 2h 06m 24s, 96.323 mph/154.117 km/h.
2 Jamie James (Suzuki); **3** Kevin Rentzell (Suzuki); **4** Ottis Lance (Suzuki); **5** Mike Harth (Suzuki); **6** Martin Wimmer (Suzuki); **7** Keith Pinkstaff (Suzuki); **8** Rich Schlachter (Honda); **9** Joe Pittman (Suzuki); **10** Jay Springsteen (Yamaha).

ROAD ATLANTA, Braselton, Georgia, 7 May 1989. 60 miles/96.56 km
1 Scott Russell (Suzuki), 35m 43s, 101.611 mph/162.578 km/h.
2 Dave Sadowski (Suzuki); **3** Jamie James (Suzuki); **4** Rich Arnaiz (Yamaha); **5** Rueben McMurter (Honda); **6** Tom Kipp (Yamaha); **7** Mike Harth (Suzuki); **8** Donald Jacks (Suzuki); **9** John Eidenberger (Suzuki); **10** Keith Pinkstaff (Suzuki).

NEW HAMPSHIRE INTERNATIONAL SPEEDWAY, Loudon, New Hampshire, 18 June 1989. 60.8 miles/97.85 km
1 Jamie James (Suzuki), 44m 33s, 81.890 mph/131.024 km/h.
2 Dale Quarterley (Ducati); **3** Scott Russell (Suzuki); **4** Rich Arnaiz (Yamaha); **5** Jeff Heino (Suzuki); **6** Mark Bougas (Suzuki); **7** Donald Jacks (Suzuki); **8** Mike Harth (Suzuki); **9** Tom Kipp (Yamaha); **10** Marc Smith (Suzuki).

ROAD AMERICA RACEWAY, Elkhart Lake, Wisconsin, 25 June 1989. 60 miles/96.56 km
1 Rich Arnaiz (Yamaha), 36m 23s, 98.988 mph/158.381 km/h.
2 Jeff Farmer (Yamaha); **3** Donald Jacks (Suzuki); **4** John Ashmead (Honda); **5** Tom Kipp (Yamaha); **6** Mark Chin (Yamaha); **7** Joe Pittman (Suzuki); **8** Scott Zampach (Suzuki); **9** Eric Moe (Suzuki); **10** Carry Andrew (Suzuki).

MID-OHIO SPORTS CAR COURSE, Lexington, Ohio, 6 August 1989. 57.6 miles/92.16 km
1 Doug Chandler (Kawasaki), 40m 55s, 87.975 mph/140.76 km/h.
2 Scott Russell (Suzuki); **3** Dan Chivington (Honda); **4** Rueben McMurter (Honda); **5** Jamie James (Suzuki); **6** Rich Arnaiz (Yamaha); **7** Donald Jacks (Suzuki); **8** Kurt Hall (Yamaha); **9** Deiter Lane (Suzuki); **10** Dave Sadowski (Suzuki).

HEARTLAND PARK, Topeka, Kansas, 3 September 1989. 60 miles/96.56 km
1 Doug Chandler (Kawasaki); **2** Scott Russell (Suzuki); **3** Dale Quarterley (Ducati); **4** Jamie James (Suzuki); **5** Rich Arnaiz (Yamaha); **6** Tom Kipp (Yamaha); **7** Mike Harth (Suzuki); **8** Deiter Lane (Suzuki); **9** Donald Jacks (Suzuki); **10** Phil Kress (Yamaha).

Final points

1	Jamie James	70
2	Scott Russell	65
3	Rich Arnaiz	61
4	Donald Jacks	42
5	Doug Chandler	40

6 John Ashmead, 37; **7** Mike Harth, 35; **8** Tom Kipp, 34; **9** Dale Quarterley, 29; **10** Dave Sadowski and Rueben McMurter, 21.

AMA Castrol 250 GP Series

DAYTONA INTERNATIONAL SPEEDWAY, Daytona Beach, Florida, 12 March 1989. 64.08 miles/103.12 km
1 John Kocinski (Yamaha), 36m 02s, 106.706 mph/170.730 km/h.
2 Rich Oliver (Yamaha); **3** Richard Moore (Yamaha); **4** Donny Greene (Yamaha); **5** Danny Coe (Yamaha); **6** Alan Carter (Aprilia); **7** Chris D'Aluisio (Yamaha); **8** Miguel DuHamel (Yamaha); **9** Jon Cornwell (Aprilia); **10** Steve Crevier (Aprilia).

ROAD ATLANTA, Braselton, Georgia, 7 May 1989. 50 miles/80.47 km
1 Rich Oliver (Yamaha), 30m 06s, 100.452 mph/160.723 km/h.
2 Jim Filice (Honda); **3** Robbie Petersen (Aprilia); **4** Miguel DuHamel (Yamaha); **5** Donny Greene (Yamaha); **6** Alan Carter (Aprilia); **7** Danny Coe (Yamaha); **8** Doug Brauneck (Yamaha); **9** Steve Crevier (Aprilia); **10** Richard Moore (Yamaha).

BRAINERD INTERNATIONAL RACEWAY, Brainerd, Minnesota, 11 June 1989. 42 miles/67.2 km
1 Rich Oliver (Yamaha), 24m 50s, 101.499 mph/162.398 km/h.
2 John Kocinski (Yamaha); **3** Robbie Petersen (Aprilia); **4** Doug Brauneck (Yamaha); **5** Donny Greene (Yamaha); **6** Richard Moore (Yamaha); **7** Danny Coe (Yamaha); **8** Thomas Stevens (Yamaha); **9** Chris D'Aluisio (Yamaha); **10** Al Salaverria (Yamaha).

NEW HAMPSHIRE INTERNATIONAL SPEEDWAY, Loudon, New Hampshire, 18 June 1989. 51.2 miles/82.40 km
1 John Kocinski (Yamaha), 36m 51s, 83.356 mph/133.370 km/h.
2 Donny Greene (Yamaha); **3** Miguel DuHamel (Yamaha); **4** Thomas Stevens (Yamaha); **5** Alan Carter (Aprilia); **6** Danny Coe (Yamaha); **7** Doug Brauneck (Yamaha); **8** James Stephens (Yamaha); **9** Robbie Petersen (Aprilia); **10** Cam Roos (Yamaha).

ROAD AMERICA RACEWAY, Elkhart Lake, Wisconsin, 25 June 1989. 52 miles/83.68 km
1 John Kocinski (Yamaha), 31m 15s, 99.834 mph/159.734 km/h.
2 Rich Oliver (Yamaha); **3** Alan Carter (Aprilia); **4** Thomas Stevens (Yamaha); **5** Chris D'Aluisio (Yamaha); **6** Doug Brauneck (Yamaha); **7** Danny Coe (Yamaha); **8** Robbie Petersen (Aprilia); **9** Donny Greene (Yamaha); **10** Cam Roos (Yamaha).

MID-OHIO SPORTS CAR COURSE, Lexington, Ohio, 6 August 1989. 50.4 miles/80.64 km
1 John Kocinski (Yamaha), 34m 17s, 88.207 mph/141.131 km/h.
2 Thomas Stevens (Yamaha); **3** Robbie Petersen (Aprilia); **4** Donny Greene (Yamaha); **5** Doug Brauneck (Yamaha); **6** Rich Oliver (Yamaha); **7** James Stephens (Yamaha); **8** Chris D'Aluisio (Yamaha); **9** Richard Moore (Yamaha); **10** Cam Roos (Yamaha).

SEARS POINT INTERNATIONAL RACEWAY, Sonoma, California, 13 August 1989. 50 miles/80.51 km
1 John Kocinski (Yamaha), 35m 08s, 85.399 mph/136.638 km/h.
2 Thomas Stevens (Yamaha); **3** Robbie Petersen (Yamaha); **4** Jim Filice (Honda); **5** Donny Greene (Yamaha); **6** Doug Brauneck (Yamaha); **7** Richard Moore (Yamaha); **8** James Stephens (Yamaha); **9** Danny Coe (Yamaha); **10** Al Salaverria (Yamaha).

HEARTLAND PARK, Topeka, Kansas, 3 September 1989. 50 miles/80.51 km
1 John Kocinski (Yamaha), 36m 10s, 82.935 mph/132.696 km/h.
2 Robbie Petersen (Aprilia); **3** Thomas Stevens (Yamaha); **4** Rich Oliver (Yamaha); **5** Donny Greene (Yamaha); **6** Chris D'Aluisio (Yamaha); **7** Al Salaverria (Yamaha); **8** Doug Brauneck (Yamaha); **9** Danny Coe (Yamaha); **10** Cam Roos (Yamaha).

Final points

1	John Kocinski	136
2	Rich Oliver	92
3	Donny Greene	84
4	Robbie Petersen	81
5	Thomas Stevens	74

6 Doug Brauneck, 61; **7** Danny Coe, 57; **8** Chris D'Aluisio, 43; **9** Alan Carter and Richard Moore, 41.

World Superbike Championship

DONINGTON PARK CIRCUIT, Great Britain, 27 March. 1.96-mile/3.136-km circuit. World Superbike Championship, round 1 (2 × 30 laps, 58.8 miles/94.08 km)

Heat 1
1 Fabrizio Pirovano, I (Yamaha), 37m 14.42s, 94.6 mph/152.24 km/h.
2 Roger Burnett, GB (Honda); **3** Terry Rymer, GB (Yamaha); **4** Fred Merkel, USA (Honda); **5** Thierry Crine, F (Suzuki); **6** Anders Andersson, S (Yamaha); **7** Carl Fogarty, GB (Honda); **8** Brian Morrison, GB (Honda); **9** Andreas Hofmann, CH (Honda); **10** Patrick Igoa, F (Kawasaki); **11** Ernst Gschwender, D (Suzuki); **12** Mark Phillips, GB (Yamaha); **13** Peter Rubatto, D (Bimota); **14** Hervé Moineau, F (Suzuki); **15** Christophe Bouheben, F (Kawasaki).
Fastest lap: Burnett, 1m 13.62s, 95.69 mph/153.998 km/h.

Heat 2
1 Giancarlo Falappa, I (Bimota), 37m 16.1s, 94.51 mph/152.099 km/h.
2 Terry Rymer, GB (Yamaha); **3** Roger Burnett, GB (Honda); **4** Steve Hislop, GB (Honda); **5** Anders Andersson, S (Yamaha); **6** Fred Merkel, USA (Honda); **7** Ernst Gschwender, D (Suzuki); **8** Peter Rubatto, D (Bimota); **9** Mark Phillips, GB (Yamaha); **10** Patrick Igoa, F (Kawasaki); **11** Andy McGladdery, GB (Honda); **12** Paul Iddon, GB (Yamaha); **13** Carl Fogarty, GB (Honda); **14** Rene Rasmussen, DK (Suzuki); **15** René Delaby, LUX (Honda).
Fastest lap: Raymond Roche, F (Ducati), 1m 13.26s, 96.16 mph/154.75 km/h.
Championship points: **1** Burnett and Rymer, 32; **3** Merkel, 23; **4** Andersson, 21; **5** Falappa and Pirovano, 20.

HUNGARORING, Hungary, 30 April. 2.494-mile/4.013-km circuit. World Superbike Championship, round 2 (2 × 25 laps, 62.365 miles/100.325 km)

Heat 1
1 Fred Merkel, USA (Honda), 46m 29.67s, 79.54 mph/128.01 km/h.
2 Raymond Roche, F (Ducati); **3** Fabrizio Pirovano, I (Yamaha); **4** Rob McElnea, GB (Yamaha); **5** Stéphane Mertens, B (Honda); **6** Anders Andersson, S (Yamaha); **7** Terry Rymer, GB (Yamaha); **8** Ernst Gschwender, D (Suzuki); **9** Giancarlo Falappa, I (Bimota); **10** Brian Morrison, GB (Honda); **11** Andreas Hofmann, CH (Honda); **12** Rene Rasmussen, DK (Suzuki); **13** Patrick Igoa, F (Kawasaki); **14** Jari Suhonen, SF (Yamaha); **15** Malcolm Campbell, AUS (Honda).
Fastest lap: Roche, 1m 49.70s, 80.908 mph/130.21 km/h.

Heat 2
1 Fred Merkel, USA (Honda), 44m 14.57s, 80.24 mph/129.14 km/h.
2 Fabrizio Pirovano, I (Yamaha); **3** Rob McElnea, GB (Yamaha); **4** Giancarlo Falappa, I (Bimota); **5** Baldassarre Monti, I (Ducati); **6** Stéphane Mertens, B (Honda); **7** Anders Andersson, S (Yamaha); **8** Rene Rasmussen, DK (Suzuki); **9** Terry Rymer, GB (Yamaha); **10** Peter Rubatto, D (Bimota); **11** Jari Suhonen, SF (Yamaha); **12** Malcolm Campbell, AUS (Honda); **13** Brian Morrison, GB (Honda); **14** Andreas Hofmann, CH (Honda); **15** Patrick Igoa, F (Kawasaki).
Fastest lap: Merkel, 1m 49.20s, 81.28 mph/130.81 km/h.
Championship points: **1** Merkel, 63; **2** Pirovano, 52; **3** Rymer, 48; **4** Andersson and Falappa, 40; **6** Burnett, 32.

MOSPORT PARK, Ontario, Canada, 4 June. 2.458-mile/3.957-km circuit. World Superbike Championship, round 3

Heat 1 (25 laps, 61.45 miles/98.925 km)
1 Fred Merkel, USA (Honda), 36m 35.506s, 100.792 mph/162.21 km/h.
2 Raymond Roche, F (Ducati); 3 Rueben McMurter, CAN (Honda); **4** Stéphane Mertens, B (Honda); **5** Steve Crevier, CAN (Yamaha); **6** Fabrizio Pirovano, I (Yamaha); **7** Jari Suhonen, SF (Yamaha); **8** Mike Baldwin, USA (Bimota); **9** Anders Andersson, S (Yamaha); **10** Tommy Douglas, CAN (Yamaha); **11** Michel Mercier, CAN (Suzuki); **12** Paul Iddon, GB (Yamaha); **13** Rene Rasmussen, DK (Suzuki); **14** Wolfgang von Muralt, CH (Honda); **15** Marino Fabbri, I (Bimota).
Fastest lap: Roche, 1m 26.901s, 101.848 mph/163.91 km/h.

Heat 2 (24 laps, 58.992 miles/94.968 km)
1 Giancarlo Falappa, I (Bimota), 34m 51.715s, 101.563 mph/163.45 km/h.
2 Rueben McMurter, CAN (Honda); **3** Fred Merkel, USA (Honda); **4** Fabrizio Pirovano, I (Yamaha); **5** Stéphane Mertens, B (Honda); **6** Mike Baldwin, USA (Bimota); **7** Baldassarre Monti, I (Ducati); **8** Terry Rymer, GB (Yamaha); **9** Jari Suhonen, SF (Yamaha); **10** Gary Goodfellow, CAN (Suzuki); **11** Anders Andersson, S (Yamaha); **12** Fabio Biliotti, I (Bimota); **13** Davide Tardozzi, I (Bimota); **14** Michel Mercier, CAN (Suzuki); **15** Rene Rasmussen, DK (Suzuki).
Fastest lap: Merkel, 1m 26.408s, 102.439 mph/164.86 km/h.
Championship points: **1** Merkel, 98; **2** Pirovano, 75; **3** Falappa, 60; **4** Rymer, 56; **5** Andersson, 52; **6** Mertens, 45.

BRAINERD INTERNATIONAL RACEWAY, Brainerd, Minnesota, USA, 11 June. 3.00-mile/4.828-km circuit. World Superbike Championship, round 4 (2 × 20 laps, 60 miles/96.56 km)

Heat 1
1 Raymond Roche, F (Ducati), 35m 08.368s, 102.44 mph/164.86 km/h.
2 Fabrizio Pirovano, I (Yamaha); **3** Stéphane Mertens, B (Honda); **4** Fred Merkel, USA (Honda) **5** Terry Rymer, GB (Yamaha); **6** Baldassarre Monti, I (Ducati); **7** Mike Baldwin, USA (Bimota); **8** Anders Andersson, S (Yamaha); **9** Tommy Douglas, CAN (Yamaha); **10** Richard Arnaiz, USA (Yamaha); **11** Rueben McMurter, CAN (Honda); **12** Fabio Biliotti, I (Bimota); **13** Gary Goodfellow, CAN (Suzuki); **14** Marino Fabbri, I (Bimota); **15** René Delaby, LUX (Honda).
Fastest lap: not available.

Heat 2
1 Raymond Roche, F (Ducati), 35m 06.251s, 102.552 mph/165.04 km/h.
2 Stéphane Mertens, B (Honda); **3** Fred Merkel, USA (Honda); **4** Fabrizio Pirovano, I (Yamaha); **5** Terry Rymer, GB (Yamaha); **6** Baldassarre Monti, I (Ducati); **7** Anders Andersson, S (Yamaha); **8** Fabio Biliotti, I (Bimota); **9** Tommy Douglas, CAN (Yamaha); **10** Gary Goodfellow, CAN (Suzuki); **11** Davide Tardozzi, I (Bimota); **12** Doug Chandler, USA (Kawasaki); **13** René Delaby, LUX (Honda); **14** Marino Fabbri, I (Bimota); **15** Wolfgang von Muralt, CH (Honda).
Fastest lap: not available.
Championship points: **1** Merkel, 126; **2** Pirovano, 105; **3** Rymer, 78; **4** Mertens, 77; **5** Roche, 74; **6** Andersson, 69.

ÖSTERREICHRING, Zeltweg, Austria, 2 July. 3.636-mile/5.853-km circuit. World Superbike Championship, round 5

Heat 1 (18 laps, 65.448 miles/105.35 km)
1 Alex Vieira, P (Honda), 34m 58.387s, 112.31 mph/180.746 km/h.
2 Raymond Roche, F (Ducati); **3** Stéphane Mertens, B (Honda); **4** Massimo Broccoli, I (Ducati); **5** Fabrizio Pirovano, I (Yamaha); **6** Baldassarre Monti, I (Ducati); **7** Malcolm Campbell, AUS (Honda); **8** Anders Andersson, S (Yamaha); **9** Terry Rymer, GB (Yamaha); **10** Jari Suhonen, SF (Yamaha); **11** Fred Merkel, USA (Honda); **12** Patrick Igoa, F (Kawasaki); **13** Giancarlo Falappa, I (Bimota); **14** Pierre Bolle, F (Kawasaki); **15** Ernst Gschwender, D (Suzuki).
Fastest lap: Monti, 1m 55.19s, 113.662 mph/182.922 km/h.

Heat 2 (15 laps, 54.54 miles/87.795 km)
1 Stéphane Mertens, B (Honda), 35m 28.937s, 92.248 mph/148.460 km/h.
2 Fabrizio Pirovano, I (Yamaha); **3** Fred Merkel, USA (Honda); **4** Massimo Broccoli, I (Ducati); **5** Patrick Igoa, F (Kawasaki); **6** Malcolm Campbell, AUS (Honda); **7** Jari Suhonen, SF (Yamaha); **8** Alex Vieira, P (Honda); **9** Anders Andersson, S (Yamaha); **10** Raymond Roche, F (Ducati); **11** Ernst Gschwender, D (Suzuki); **12** Davide Tardozzi, I (Bimota); **13** Mauro Ricci, I (Kawasaki); **14** Baldassarre Monti, I (Ducati); **15** René Delaby, LUX (Honda).
Fastest lap: Mertens, 2m 17.96s, 94.902 mph/152.731 km/h.
Championship points: **1** Merkel, 146; **2** Pirovano, 133; **3** Mertens, 112; **4** Roche, 97; **5** Rymer, 85; **6** Andersson, 84.

CIRCUIT PAUL RICARD, France, 30 July. 2.051-mile/3.3-km circuit. World Superbike Championship, round 6

Heat 1 (27 laps, 55.377 miles/89.100 km)
1 Stéphane Mertens, B (Honda), 37m 28.03s, 88.66 mph/142.685 km/h.
2 Mike Baldwin, USA (Bimota); **3** Raymond Roche, F (Ducati); **4** Terry Rymer, GB (Yamaha); **5** Giancarlo Falappa, I (Bimota); **6** Jean-Yves Mounier, F (Yamaha); **7** Baldassarre Monti, I (Ducati); **8** Fred Merkel, USA (Honda); **9** Davide Tardozzi, I (Bimota); **10** Anders Andersson, S (Yamaha); **11** Pierre Bolle, F (Kawasaki); **12** Rene Rasmussen, DK (Suzuki); **13** Jeffry de Vries, NL (Yamaha); **14** Maurice Coq, F (Yamaha); **15** Didier Handi, F (Yamaha).
Fastest lap: Baldwin, 1m 21.90s, 90.132 mph/145.055 km/h.

Heat 2 (28 laps, 57.428 miles/92.4 km)
1 Giancarlo Falappa, I (Bimota), 38m 44.40s, 88.923 mph/143.108 km/h.
2 Raymond Roche, F (Ducati); **3** Stéphane Mertens, B (Honda); **4** Fred Merkel, USA (Honda); **5** Mike Baldwin, USA (Bimota); **6** Baldassarre Monti, I (Ducati); **7** Anders Andersson, S (Yamaha); **8** Davide Tardozzi, I (Bimota); **9** Pierre Bolle, F (Kawasaki); **10** Paul Iddon, GB (Yamaha); **11** Maurice Coq, F (Yamaha); **12** Rene Rasmussen, DK (Suzuki); **13** Jean-Yves Mounier, F (Yamaha); **14** Edwin Weibel, CH (Kawasaki); **15** Eric Delcamp, F (Yamaha).
Fastest lap: Falappa, 1m 21.89s, 90.144 mph/145.073 km/h.
Championship points: **1** Merkel, 167; **2** Mertens, 147; **3** Pirovano, 133; **4** Roche, 129; **5** Andersson, 99; **6** Rymer, 98.

SUGO, Japan, 27 August. 2.335-mile/3.737-km circuit. World Superbike Championship, round 7 (2 × 25 laps, 58.375 miles/93.425 km)

Heat 1
1 Doug Polen USA (Suzuki), 47m 06.500s, 73.947 mph/119.007 km/h.
2 Michael Dowson, AUS (Yamaha); **3** Rob Phillis, AUS (Kawasaki); **4** Giancarlo Falappa, I (Bimota); **5** Tatsuro Arata, J (Yamaha); **6** Kenichiro Iwahashi, J (Honda); **7** Fabrizio Pirovano, I (Yamaha); **8** Stéphane Mertens, B (Honda); **9** Aaron Slight, NZ (Kawasaki); **10** Naoto Abe, J (Honda); **11** Shoichi Tsukamoto, J (Kawasaki); **12** Davide Tardozzi, I (Bimota); **13** Raymond Roche, F (Ducati); **14** Scott Doohan, AUS (Bimota); **15** Malcolm Campbell, AUS (Honda).
Fastest lap: Dowson, 1m 50.240s.

Heat 2
1 Michael Dowson, AUS (Yamaha), 47m 45.220s, 72.948 mph/117.399 km/h.
2 Kenichiro Iwahashi, J (Honda); **3** Giancarlo Falappa, I (Bimota); **4** Doug Polen, USA (Suzuki); **5** Takahiro Sowa, J (Kawasaki); **6** Rob Phillis, AUS (Kawasaki); **7** Aaron Slight, NZ (Kawasaki); **8** Stéphane Mertens, B (Honda); **9** Tatsuro Arata, J (Yamaha); **10** Malcolm Campbell, AUS (Honda); **11** Shoichi Tsukamoto, J (Kawasaki); **12** Fred Merkel, USA (Honda); **13** Terry Rymer, GB (Yamaha); **14** Kochichi Kobayashi, J (Honda); **15** Koh Takeuchi, J (Yamaha).
Fastest lap: Iwahashi, 1m 52.330s.
Championship points: **1** Merkel, 171; **2** Mertens, 163; **3** Pirovano, 142; **4** Roche, 132; **5** Falappa, 122; **6** Rymer, 101.

HOCKENHEIMRING, German Federal Republic, 17 September. 4.218-mile/6.789-km circuit. World Superbike Championship, round 8 (2 × 14 laps, 59.052 miles/95.046 km)

Heat 1
1 Raymond Roche, F (Ducati), 30m 30.94s, 116.104 mph/186.852 km/h.
2 Stéphane Mertens, B (Honda); **3** Alex Vieira, P (Honda); **4** Fabrizio Pirovano, I (Yamaha); **5** Anders Andersson, S (Yamaha); **6** Mike Baldwin, USA (Bimota); **7** Andreas Hofmann, CH (Honda); **8** Fred Merkel, USA (Honda); **9** Patrick Igoa, F (Kawasaki); **10** Jari Suhonen SF (Yamaha); **11** Bodo Schmidt, D (Yamaha); **12** Roger Burnett, GB (Honda); **13** Edwin Weibel, CH (Kawasaki); **14** Jean-Yves Mounier, F (Yamaha); **15** Graeme McGregor, AUS (Honda).
Fastest lap: Roche, 2m 09.37s, 117.37 mph/188.89 km/h.

Heat 2
1 Raymond Roche, F (Ducati), 30m 22.08s, 116.668 mph/187.76 km/h.
2 Giancarlo Falappa, I (Bimota); **3** Stéphane Mertens, B (Honda); **4** Fred Merkel, USA (Honda); **5** Anders Andersson, S (Yamaha); **6** Fabrizio Pirovano, I (Yamaha); **7** Mike Baldwin, USA (Bimota); **8** Alex Vieira, P (Honda); **9** Patrick Igoa, F (Kawasaki); **10** Marco Lucchinelli, I (Ducati); **11** Bodo Schmidt, D (Yamaha); **12** Andreas Hofmann, CH (Honda); **13** Udo Mark, D (Yamaha); **14** Jari Suhonen, SF (Yamaha); **15** Christophe Bouheben, F (Kawasaki).
Fastest lap: Roche, 2m 08.69s, 117.99 mph/189.888 km/h.
Championship points: **1** Mertens, 195; **2** Merkel, 192; **3** Roche, 172; **4** Pirovano, 165; **5** Falappa, 139; **6** Andersson, 121.

PERGUSA, Sicily, 24 September. 3.075-mile/4.950-km circuit. World Superbike Championship, round 9 (2 × 21 laps, 64.575 miles/103.95 km)

Heat 1
1 Stéphane Mertens, B (Honda), 36m 46.901s, 105.364 mph/169.568 km/h.
2 Fred Merkel, USA (Honda); **3** Fabrizio Pirovano, I (Yamaha); **4** Baldassarre Monti, I (Ducati); **5** Anders Andersson, S (Yamaha); **6** Jari Suhonen, SF (Yamaha); **7** Patrick Igoa, F (Kawasaki); **8** Davide Tardozzi, I (Bimota); **9** Marco Lucchinelli, I (Ducati); **10** Giorgio Bontempi, I (Honda); **11** Arnad Harmati, H (Honda); **12** Corraco Manici, I (Ducati); **13** Aldeo Presciutti, I (Honda); **14** Silvano Ricchetti, I (Honda); **15** Adriano Narducci, I (Honda).
Fastest lap: Mertens, 1m 43.632s, 106.847 mph/171.954 km/h.

Heat 2
1 Raymond Roche, F (Ducati), 36m 54.613s, 104.997 mph/168.977 km/h.
2 Fred Merkel, USA (Honda); **3** Baldassarre Monti, I (Ducati); **4** Fabrizio Pirovano, I (Yamaha); **5** Jari Suhonen, SF (Yamaha); **6** Patrick Igoa, F (Kawasaki); **7** Stéphane Mertens, B (Honda); **8** Christophe Bouheben,

F (Kawasaki); **9** Marino Fabbri, I (Bimota); **10** Marco dall'Aglio, I (Yamaha); **11** Arnad Harmati, H (Honda); **12** Giorgio Bontempi, I (Honda); **13** Aldeo Presciutti, I (Honda); **14** Corrado Manici, I (Ducati); **15** Oscar La Ferla, I (Yamaha).
Fastest lap: Roche, 1m 43.143s, 107.353 mph/172.769 km/h.

Championship points (prior to final rounds in Australia and New Zealand in November)

1	Fred Merkel, USA	226
2	Stéphane Mertens, B	224
3	Fabrizio Pirovano, I	193
4	Raymond Roche, F	192
5	Giancarlo Falappa, I	139
6	Anders Andersson, S	132

7 Terry Rymer, GB, 101; **8** Baldassarre Monti, I, 99; **9** Mike Baldwin, USA, 74; **10** Jari Suhonen, SF, 67; **11** Patrick Igoa, F, 64; **12** Alex Vieira, P, 51; **13** Davide Tardozzi, I, 39; **14** Michael Dowson, AUS and Rueben McMurter, CAN, 37.

Final results will be given in *Motocourse* 1990/91.

FIM Endurance Cup

24 HEURES DU MANS, Bugatti Circuit, Le Mans, France, 22-23 April.
FIM Endurance Cup, round 1. 731 laps of the 2.635-mile/4.24-km circuit, 1926.185 miles/3099.44 km
1 Alex Vieira/Jean-Michel Mattioli/Roger Burnett, P/F/GB (750 Honda), 23h 51m 26.83s, 84.343 mph/135.737 km/h.
2 Patrick Igoa/Pierre Bolle/Jean-Louis Battistini, F/F/F (750 Kawasaki), 721 laps; **3** Takahiro Sohwa/Kiyokazu Tada/Shouichi Tsukamoto, J/J/J (750 Kawasaki), 718; **4** Malcolm Campbell/Miguel DuHamel/Mario DuHamel, AUS/CAN/CAN (750 Honda), 717; **5** Philippe Monneret/Arnaud de Puiriet/Guy Bertin, F/F/F (750 Honda), 709; **6** Gérard Rolland-Piègue/Philippe Ronfort/Georges Furling, F/F/F (750 Suzuki), 696; **7** Richard Hubin/J. Guenette/Doug Toland, B/CAN/USA (750 Honda), 692; **8** Luc Maurel/Gérard Vallée/Yves Calatayud, F/F/F (750 Honda), 690; **9** Patrick Braud/André Gouin/Maurice Coq, F/F/F (750 Honda), 686; **10** Per Jansson/Sam Toming/Ray Moe, S/N/N (750 Honda), 685; **11** Michel Augizeau/E. Paradon/Dominique Thiault, F/F/F (750 Yamaha), 682; **12** M. Teuber/K. Gasser/M. Gopp, FL/CH/A (750 Kawasaki), 676; **13** Hazzi Maikola/Jari Kivila/Ben Nyman, SF/SF/SF (750 Kawasaki), 676; **14** Robi Schläfi/Urs Meier/Bernard Hänggeli, CH/CH/CH (750 Honda), 676; **15** Dave Railton/Tony Thompson/Richard Rose, GB/GB/GB (750 Kawasaki), 672.
Fastest lap: Campbell, 1m 48.48s, 91.348 mph/147.013 km/h.
Championship points: 1 Vieira, Mattioli and Burnett, 40; **4** Igoa, Bolle and Battistini, 34; **7** Sohwa, Tada and Tsukamoto, 30.

SUZUKA EIGHT HOURS, Suzuka International Racing Course, Japan, 30 July.
FIM Endurance Cup, round 2. 202 laps of the 3.662-mile/5.859-km circuit, 735.5 miles/1183.673 km
1 Dominique Sarron/Alex Vieira, F/P (750 Honda), 7h 58m 34.328s, 92.206 mph/148.392 km/h.
2 Shoji Miyazaki/Tadashi Ohshima, J/J (750 Honda), 201 laps; **3** Peter Goddard/Shingo Katoh, AUS/J (750 Yamaha), 198; **4** Shouichi Tsukamoto/Tadashi Maeda, J/J (750 Kawasaki), 198; **5** Yukiya Ohshima/Katsuro Takayoshi, J/J (750 Suzuki), 197; **6** Graeme Crosby/Malcolm Campbell, NZ/AUS (750 Moriwaki), 197; **7** Randy Renfrow/Dale Quarterley, USA/USA (750 Honda), 197; **8** Kevin Schwantz/Doug Polen, USA/USA (750 Suzuki), 197; **9** Hervé Moineau/Thierry Crine, F/F (750 Suzuki), 196; **10** Takumi Itoh/Shougo Kanaumi, J/J (750 Honda), 194; **11** Kenichiro Iwahashi/Hidekazu Hirai, J/J (750 Honda), 194; **12** Mat Oxley/Gilbert Roy, GB/F (750 Honda), 193; **13** Grant Hodson/Rod Cox, AUS/AUS (750 Yamaha), 192; **14** Rob Phillis/Aaron Slight, AUS/NZ (750 Kawasaki), 192; **15** Seiichi Sengoku/Shigeharu Ohtsuka, J/J (750 Yamaha), 191.
Fastest lap: Wayne Gardner/Michael Doohan, AUS/AUS (750 Honda), 2m 15.530s.
Championship points: 1 Vieira, 60; **2** Tsukamoto, 43; **3** Burnett and Mattioli, 40; **5** Campbell, 36; **6** Igoa, Bolle and Battistini, 34.

24 HEURES DE LIÈGE, Spa-Francorchamps Grand Prix Circuit, Belgium, 12-13 August.
FIM Endurance Cup, round 3. 509 laps of the 4.335-mile/6.976-km circuit, 2206.515 miles/3550.784 km
1 Alex Vieira/Stéphane Mertens/Roger Burnett, P/B/GB (750 Honda), 23h 58m 35.36s, 92.14 mph/148.285 km/h.
2 Mat Oxley/Steve Manley/Steve Chambers, GB/GB/GB (750 Honda), 506 laps; **3** Hervé Moineau/Thierry Crine/Michel Graziano, F/F/F (750 Suzuki), 503; **4** Patrick Igoa/Christophe Bouheben/Pierre Bolle, F/F/F (750 Kawasaki), 502; **5** Dirk Brand/Gerard Van Der Wal/Kees Doorakkers, NL/NL/NL (750 Yamaha), 500; **6** Robi Schläfi/Urs Meier/Christian Monsch, CH/CH/CH (750 Honda), 499; **7** Sam Toming/Ray Moe/R. Valderhaug, N/N/N (750 Honda), 491; **8** Jean-Pierre Verkenne/Claude Berger/Jean-Marc Toffolo, B/CH/B (750 Honda), 484; **9** Dave Morris/Barry Middleton/Alain Delhotellerie, GB/GB/B (750 Honda), 483; **10** Laurent Letouze/Georges Furling/Gérard Jolivet, F/F/F (750 Suzuki), 483; **11** Hanspeter Bolliger/Hermann Perren/A. Muller, CH/CH/CH (750 Kawasaki), 481; **12** Thomas Ehl/Peter Hafner/D. Karthin, D/D/D (750 Honda), 481; **13** Bruno Weynand/Christian Dupuis/Manfred Braun, B/B/B (750 Suzuki), 478; **14** Mile Crnojevic/Anton Heiler/Leonhard Schiller, D/D/D (750 Suzuki), 477; **15** Jean-Thierry Ferrer/Claude Michon/Philippe Muchery, F/F/F (750 Honda), 477.
Fastest lap: Vieira, 2m 36.16s, 100.057 mph/161.027 km/h.
Championship points: 1 Vieira, 100; **2** Burnett, 80; **3** Bolle and Igoa, 60; **5** Tsukamoto, 43; **6** Mertens and Mattioli, 40.

53e BOL D'OR, Circuit Paul Ricard, France, 9-10 September.
FIM Endurance Cup, round 4. 610 laps of the 3.610-mile/5.810-km circuit, 2202.1 miles/3544.1 km
1 Alex Vieira/Jean-Michel Mattioli/Roger Burnett, P/F/GB (750 Honda), 23h 37m 01.63s, 93.615 mph/150.659 km/h.
2 Fred Merkel/Mario DuHamel/Stéphane Mertens, USA/CAN/B (750 Honda), 609 laps; **3** Hervé Moineau/Thierry Crine/Adrien Morillas, F/F/F (750 Suzuki), 607; **4** Urs Meier/Robi Schläfi/Bernard Hänggeli, CH/CH/CH (750 Honda), 593; **5** Mat Oxley/Steve Chambers/Brian Morrison, GB/GB/GB (750 Honda), 582; **6** J.-F. Deletraz/Rémy Chaffard/Guy Meynet, F/F/F (750 Honda), 578; **7** Eric de Doncker/Yves Briguet/Marcel Kellemberger, B/CH/CH (750 Yamaha), 577; **8** Pascal Guittet/André Bouilloux/Thierry Pelletant, F/F/F (750 Honda), 576; **9** Dave Railton/Tony Thompson/Richard Rose, GB/GB/GB (750 Kawasaki), 574; **10** Michel Bobeau/Gilles Hampe/Christian Tiberio, F/F/F (750 Kawasaki), 568; **11** Patrick Braud/Maurice Coq/André Gouin, F/F/F (750 Honda), 568; **12** Doug Toland/Steve Crevier/Denis Royer, USA/CAN/CAN (750 Honda), 566; **13** Jean-Pierre Verkenne/Claude Berger/E. Bragard, B/CH/B (750 Honda), 565; **14** R. Valderhaug/Sam Toming/Ray Moe, N/N/N (750 Honda), 564; **15** Michel Simeon/Ch. Artigues/O. Roullet, B/F/F (750 Suzuki), 563.
Fastest lap: Vieira, 2m 03.62s, 105.549 mph/169.866 km/h.

Final Championship points

1	Alex Vieira, P	140
2	Roger Burnett, GB	120
3	Jean-Michel Mattioli, F	80
4	Stéphane Mertens, B	74
5=	Hervé Moineau, F	67
5=	Thierry Crine, F	67

7 Patrick Igoa, F, Pierre Bolle, F, Mario DuHamel, CAN and Mat Oxley, GB, 60; **11** Steve Chambers, GB, 56; **12** Urs Meier, CH and Robi Schläfi, CH, 50; **14** Shouichi Tsukamoto, J, 43; **15** Malcolm Campbell, AUS, 36.

World TT F1 Championship

SUGO INTERNATIONAL RACING COURSE, Japan, 14 May. 2.335-mile/3.737-km circuit.
TT F1, round 1 (50 laps, 116.75 miles/186.85 km)
1 Michael Dowson, AUS (Yamaha), 1h 21m 55.88s, 85.035 mph/136.852 km/h.
2 Yasutomo Nagai, J (Yamaha); **3** Yukiya Ohshima, J (Suzuki); **4** Rob Phillis, AUS (Kawasaki); **5** Kenichiro Iwahashi, J (Honda); **6** Doug Polen, USA (Suzuki); **7** Noboru Miura, J (Honda); **8** Mitsuo Saito, J (Yamaha); **9** Jun Maeda, J (Honda); **10** Shoji Miyazaki, J (Honda); **11** Shoichi Tsukamoto, J (Kawasaki); **12** Tadaaki Hanamura, J (Yamaha); **13** Carl Fogarty, GB (Honda); **14** Tadashi Ohshima, J (Honda); **15** Tatsuro Arata, J (Yamaha).
Fastest lap: not available.
Championship points: 1 Dowson, 20; **2** Nagai, 17; **3** Ohshima, 15; **4** Phillis, 13; **5** Iwahashi, 11; **6** Polen, 10.

ISLE OF MAN TT CIRCUIT, Great Britain, 3 June. 37.73-mile/60.72-km circuit.
TT F1, round 2 (6 laps, 226.38 miles/364.32 km)
1 Steve Hislop, GB (Honda), 1h 53m 47.4s, 119.36 mph/192.091 km/h.
2 Brian Morrison, GB (Honda); **3** Nick Jefferies, GB (Yamaha); **4** Carl Fogarty, GB (Honda); **5** Graeme McGregor, AUS (Honda); **6** James Whitham, GB (Suzuki); **7** Robert Dunlop, GB (Honda); **8** Andy McGladdery, GB (Honda); **9** Sam McClements, IRL (Honda); **10** Colin Gable, GB (Honda); **11** Charlie Corner, GB (Honda); **12** Steve Ward, GB (Honda); **13** Tony Moran, GB (Yamaha); **14** Bob Jackson, GB (Honda); **15** Phillip McCallen, GB (Honda).
Fastest lap: Hislop, 18m 39.4s, 121.34 mph/195.277 km/h.
Championship points: 1 Dowson and Hislop, 20; **3** Nagai and Morrison, 17; **4** Fogarty, 16; **5** Ohshima and Jefferies, 15.

CIRCUIT VAN DRENTHE, ASSEN, Holland, 23 June. 3.812-mile/6.134-km circuit.
TT F1, round 3 (25 laps, 95.30 miles/153.35 km)
1 Carl Fogarty, GB (Honda), 58m 06.40s, 98.391 mph/158.346 km/h.
2 Andreas Hoffman, CH (Honda); **3** Roger Burnett, GB (Honda); **4** Jari Suhonen, SF (Yamaha); **5** James Whitham, GB (Suzuki); **6** Jeffry de Vries, NL (Yamaha); **7** Brian Morrison, GB (Honda); **8** Robert Dunlop, GB (Honda); **9** Toni Rohrer, CH (Honda); **10** Trevor Nation, GB (Norton); **11** Steve Hislop, GB (Honda); **12** Peter Rubatto, D (Bimota); **13** Mario Rubatto, D (Suzuki); **14** Steve Williams, GB (Yamaha); **15** Peter Linden, S (Honda).
Fastest lap: Fogarty, 2m 17.61s, 99.711 mph/160.470 km/h.
Championship points: 1 Fogarty, 36; **2** Morrison, 26; **3** Hislop, 25; **4** Whitham, 21; **5** Dowson, 20; **6** Nagai, Dunlop and Hoffman, 17.

VILA REAL, Portugal, 2 July. 4.36-mile/7.02-km circuit.
TT F1, round 4 (25 laps, 109.00 miles/175.500 km)
1 Steve Hislop, GB (Honda), 1h 06m 59.71s, 96.343 mph/155.049 km/h.
2 Carl Fogarty, GB (Honda); **3** Brian Morrison, GB (Honda); **4** Steve Williams, GB (Yamaha); **5** Robert Dunlop, GB (Honda); **6** Dave Leach, GB (Yamaha); **7** Charlie Corner, GB (Honda); **8** Ian Jones, GB (Ducati); **9** Pedro Batista, P (Honda); **10** Russell Benney, GB (Honda).
Fastest lap: Hislop, 2m 38.08s, 97.993 mph/157.704 km/h.
Championship points: 1 Fogarty, 53; **2** Hislop, 45; **3** Morrison, 41; **4** Dunlop, 28; **5** Whitham, 21; **6** Dowson, 20.

KOUVOLA, Finland, 16 July. 1.988-mile/3.2-km circuit.
TT F1, round 5 (48 laps, 95.424 miles/153.6 km)
1 Carl Fogarty, GB (Honda), 1h 13m 25.9s.
2 Steve Hislop, GB (Honda); **3** Jari Suhonen, SF (Yamaha); **4** Robert Dunlop, GB (Honda); **5** Robert Holden, NZ (Honda); **6** Steve Williams, GB (Yamaha); **7** Mikael Lundvall, S (Kawasaki); **8** Esko Kuparinen, SF (Honda); **9** Christer Lindholm, S (Suzuki); **10** Erkki Siukola, SF (Suzuki); **11** Charlie Corner, GB (Honda); **12** Brent Gladwin, GB (Honda); **13** Göran Forsslund, S (Suzuki); **14** Peter Sköld, S (Honda); **15** Brian Morrison, GB (Honda).
Fastest lap: not available.
Championship points: 1 Fogarty, 73; **2** Hislop, 62; **3** Morrison, 42; **4** Dunlop, 41; **5** Suhonen, 28; **6** Williams, 25.

DUNDROD CIRCUIT, Northern Ireland, 12 August. 7.401-mile/11.911-km circuit.
TT F1, round 6 (13 laps, 96.214 miles/154.84 km)
1 Steve Hislop, GB (Honda), 48m 54.93s, 118.018 mph/189.931 km/h.
2 Carl Fogarty, GB (Honda); **3** Steve Cull, GB (Norton); **4** Robert Dunlop, GB (Honda); **5** Charlie Corner, GB (Honda); **6** Nick Jefferies, GB (Yamaha); **7** Dave Leach, GB (Yamaha); **8** Phillip McCallen, GB (Honda); **9** Sam McClements, IRL (Honda); **10** Dennis Ireland, NZ (Honda); **11** Eddie Laycock, IRL (Honda); **12** Woolsey Coulter, IRL (Honda); **13** Robert Holden, NZ (Honda); **14** Tony Moran, GB (Honda); **15** Steve Linsdell, GB (Yamaha).
Fastest lap: Hislop, 121.126 mph/194.933 km/h.

Final TT F1 Championship points

1	Carl Fogarty, GB	90
2	Steve Hislop, GB	82
3	Robert Dunlop, GB	54
4	Brian Morrison, GB	42
5	Charlie Corner, GB	30
6	Jari Suhonen, SF	28

7 Nick Jefferies, GB and Steve Williams, GB, 25; **9** James Whitham, GB, 21; **10** Michael Dowson, AUS, 20; **11** Dave Leach, GB, 19; **12** Yasutomo Nagai, J and Andreas Hoffman, CH, 17; **14** Yukiya Ohshima, J, Roger Burnett, GB and Steve Cull, GB, 15.

European Championship

CIRCUITO DE SINTRA, Portugal, 12 March. 2.181-mile/3.510-km circuit.
European Championship, 500 cc, round 1 (31 laps, 67.611 miles/108.81 km)
1 Peter Linden, S (Honda), 46m 36.238s, 87.047 mph/140.09 km/h.
2 Karl Truchsess, A (Honda); **3** Michele Valdo, I (Honda); **4** Rachel Nicotte, F (Honda); **5** Hansjorg Butz, D (Honda); **6** Josef Doppler, A (Honda); **7** Karl Dauer, A (Honda); **8** Romolo Balbi, I (Honda); **9** Niggi Schmassman, CH (Honda); **10** Torbjörn Bastiansen, N (Suzuki); **11** Ian Pratt, GB (Honda); **12** Hans Klingebiel, D (Honda); **13** Mark Phillips, GB (Suzuki); **14** Amedeo Perrone, I (Honda); **15** Imrich Majoros, CS (Honda).
Fastest lap: Linden, 1m 26.248s, 91.037 mph/146.51 km/h.
Championship points: 1 Linden, 20; **2** Truchsess, 17; **3** Valdo, 15; **4** Nicotte, 13; **5** Butz, 11; **6** Doppler, 10.

125 cc, round 1 (28 laps, 61.068 miles/98.28 km)
1 Gabriele Debbia, I (Aprilia), 44m 04.989s, 83.120 mph/133.768 km/h.
2 Dirk Raudies, D (Honda); **3** Rob Orme, GB (Honda); **4** Loris Capirossi, I (Honda); **5** Steve Patrickson, GB (Honda); **6** Paul Bordes, F (Honda); **7** Reinhard Strack, D (Honda); **8** Klaus Kindle, FL (Honda); **9** Alan Patterson, IRL (NN); **10** Hervé Duffard, F (Honda); **11** Jose Morillas, E (Waver); **12** Paolo Scappini, I (Honda); **13** Luigi Ancona, I (Gazzaniga); **14** Jean-Pierre Jeandat, F (Honda); **15** Arie Molenaar, NL (Honda).
Fastest lap: Patrickson, 1m 27.373s, 89.862 mph/144.62 km/h.
Championship points: 1 Debbia, 20; **2** Raudies, 17; **3** Orme, 15; **4** Capirossi, 13; **5** Patrickson, 11; **6** Bordes, 10.

80 cc, round 1 (21 laps, 45.801 miles/73.71 km)
1 Jaime Mariano, E (Casal), 35m 38.306s, 77.112 mph/124.10 km/h.
2 Jose Saez, E (Autisa); **3** Manuel Duarte, P (Zundapp); **4** Stefan Brägger, CH (Casal); **5** Stefan Kurfiss, D (Krauser); **6** Undine Kummer, D (Krauser); **7** Joaquin Gali, AND (Krauser); **8** Chris Baert, B (Casal); **9** Luis Alvaro, E (Krauser); **10** Jacques Bernard, B (Fantic); **11** Maik Stief, D (Casal).
Fastest lap: Saez, 1m 35.822s, 81.918 mph/131.87 km/h.
Championship points: 1 Mariano, 20; **2** Saez, 17; **3** Duarte, 15; **4** Brägger, 13; **5** Kurfiss, 11; **6** Kummer, 10.

Sidecars, round 1 (28 laps, 61.068 miles/98.28 km)
1 Kenny Howles/Steve Pointer, GB/GB (LCR), 46m 17.130s, 79.162 mph/127.40 km/h.
2 Michael Burcombe/John Gibbard, GB/GB (LCR-Krauser); **3** Ralph Bohnhorst/Thomas Böttcher, D/D (Schuberth-LCR); **4** Mark Reddington/Robert Parker, GB/GB (WR-Yamaha); **5** Gary Knight/Malcolm Jackson, GB/GB (Redline-Yamaha); **6** Frank Voigt/Holger Voigt, D/D (LCR); **7** Georg Neumann/Gerhard Lehmann, D/D (LCR); **8** Peter Lemstra/Edwin Nap, NL/NL (LCR-Yamaha); **9** David Lee/Richard Lee, GB/GB (Windle); **10** Niek van Bergen/Tonny van Bergen, NL/NL (Yamaha); **11** John Evans/Ian Gaunt, GB/GB (LCR); **12** Geoff Thomas/Kevin Morgan, GB/GB (Krauser).
Fastest lap: Voigt, 1m 31.930s, 85.407 mph/137.45 km/h.
Championship points: 1 Howles, 20; **2** Burcombe, 17; **3** Bohnhorst, 15; **4** Reddington, 13; **5** Knight, 11; **6** Voigt, 10.

CIRCUITO PERMANENTE DEL JARAMA, Spain, 19 March. 2.058-mile/3.312-km circuit.
European Championship, 500 cc, round 2 (28 laps, 57.624 miles/92.736 km)
1 Rachel Nicotte, F (Honda), 44m 06.981s, 78.371 mph/126.126 km/h.
2 Juan Lopez Mella, E (Honda); **3** Peter Linden, S (Honda); **4** Karl Truchsess, A (Honda); **5** Niggi Schmassman, CH (Honda); **6** Hansjorg Butz, D (Honda); **7** Michele Valdo, I (Honda); **8** Martin Trosch, D (Honda); **9** Josef Doppler, A (Honda); **10** Romolo Balbi, I (Honda); **11** Ake Dahli, S (Honda); **12** Ian Pratt, GB (Honda); **13** Alois Meyer, D (Honda); **14** Mark Phillips, GB (Suzuki); **15** Michael Kaplan, A (Honda).
Fastest lap: Nicotte, 1m 33.080s, 79.596 mph/128.098 km/h.
Championship points: 1 Linden, 35; **2** Nicotte, 33; **3** Truchsess, 30; **4** Valdo, 24; **5** Butz, 21; **6** Schmassman, 18.

250 cc, round 1 (23 laps, 47.334 miles/76.176 km)
1 Gilberto Gambelli, I (Aprilia), 35m 58.834s, 78.932 mph/127.030 km/h.
2 Engelbert Neumair, A (Aprilia); **3** Andrea Borgonovo, I (Aprilia); **4** Wilco Zeelenberg, NL (Honda); **5** Bernard Hänggeli, CH (Yamaha); **6** Josef Hutter, A (Honda); **7** Alain Kempener, B (Aprilia); **8** Mario Houssin, B (Yamaha); **9** Luis Maurel, E (Yamaha); **10** Woolsey Coulter, IRL (Aprilia); **11** Bernd Kassner, D (Yamaha); **12** Luca Pasini, I (Aprilia); **13** Yves Briguet, CH (Yamaha); **14** Hans Vontobel, CH (Yamaha); **15** Laurent Naveau, B (Yamaha).
Fastest lap: Gambelli, 1m 32.090s, 80.452 mph/129.475 km/h.
Championship points: 1 Gambelli, 20; **2** Neumair, 17; **3** Borgonovo, 15; **4** Zeelenberg, 13; **5** Hänggeli, 11; **6** Hutter, 10.

125 cc, round 2 (22 laps, 45.276 miles/72.864 km)
1 Gabriele Debbia, I (Aprilia), 36m 05.624s, 75.264 mph/121.126 km/h.
2 Manuel Hernandez, E (Honda); **3** Loris Capirossi, I (Honda); **4** Steve Patrickson, GB (Honda); **5** Jose Morillas, E (Cobas); **6** Rob Orme, GB (Honda); **7** Luis D'Antin, E (Honda); **8** Paul Bordes, F (Honda); **9** Alain Kempener, B (Honda); **10** Pietro Paolucci, I (Honda); **11** Luigi Ancona, I (Gazzaniga); **12** Paolo Scappini, I (Honda); **13** Reinhard Strack, D (Honda); **14** Manuel Gamez, E (Honda); **15** Chris Jensen, DK (Honda).
Fastest lap: Hernandez, 1m 36.793s, 76.542 mph/123.184 km/h.
Championship points: 1 Debbia, 40; **2** Capirossi, 28; **3** Orme, 25; **4** Patrickson, 24; **5** Bordes, 18; **6** Hernandez and Raudies, 17.

80 cc, round 2 (16 laps, 32.928 miles/52.992 km)
1 Jose Saez, E (Krauser), 27m 56.887s, 70.691 mph/113.766 km/h.
2 Jaime Mariano, E (Casal); **3** Roberto Sassone, I (Unimoto); **4** Jacques Bernard, B (Fantic); **5** Janos Szabo, H (Krauser); **6** Joaquin Machado, E (Bastoil); **7** Luis Alvaro, E (Krauser); **8** Antonio Sanchez, E (Cobas); **9** Joaquin Alos, E (Casal); **10** Stefan Kurfiss, D (Krauser); **11** Joaquin Gali, AND (Krauser); **12** Manuel Duarte, P (Zundapp); **13** Maik Stief, D (Casal); **14** Undine Kummer, D (Krauser); **15** Steven Lawton, GB (Lusuardi).
Fastest lap: Saez, 1m 42.483s, 72.293 mph/116.345 km/h.
Championship points: 1 Mariano and Saez, 37; **3** Bernard and Duarte, 19; **5** Kurfiss, 17; **6** Alvaro, 16.

CIRCUIT DE ZOLDER, Belgium, 2 April. 2.648-mile/4.262-km circuit.
European Championship, 250 cc, round 2 (20 laps, 52.96 miles/85.24 km)
1 Marcellino Lucchi, I (Aprilia), 35m 54.12s, 88.516 mph/142.454 km/h.
2 Andrea Borgonovo, I (Aprilia); **3** Wilco Zeelenberg, NL (Honda); **4** Steve Hislop, GB (Honda); **5** Josef Hutter, A (Honda); **6** Bruno Bonhuil, F (Yamaha); **7** Gilberto Gambelli, I (Aprilia); **8** Alain Bronec, F (Aprilia); **9** Nigel Bosworth, GB (Aprilia); **10** Yves Briguet, CH (Yamaha); **11** Leon van der Heyden, NL (Honda); **12** Bernd Kassner, D (Yamaha); **13** René Delaby, LUX (Yamaha); **14** Bernard Hänggeli, CH (Yamaha); **15** Massimo Cavina, I (Honda).
Fastest lap: Borgonovo, 1m 46.43s, 89.578 mph/144.162 km/h.
Championship points: 1 Borgonovo, 32; **2** Gambelli, 29; **3** Zeelenberg, 28; **4** Hutter, 21; **5** Lucchi, 20; **6** Neumair, 17.

125 cc, round 3 (18 laps, 47.664 miles/76.716 km)
1 Alessandro Gramigni, I (Aprilia), 34m 53.09s, 81.988 mph/131.947 km/h).
2 Gabriele Debbia, I (Aprilia); **3** Steve Patrickson, GB (Honda); **4** Jean-Claude Selini, F (Honda); **5** Dirk Raudies, D (Honda); **6** Gérard Rolland-Piègue, F (Honda); **7** Klaus Kindle, FL (Honda); **8** Luigi Ancona, I (Gazzaniga); **9** Jean-Pierre Jeandat, F (Honda); **10** Rob Orme, GB (Honda); **11** Paul Bordes, F (Honda); **12** Ralf Waldmann, D (Rotax); **13** Loris Capirossi, I (Honda); **14** Serge Julin, B (Honda); **15** Herman Scherpen, NL (Honda).
Fastest lap: Patrickson, 1m 53.74s, 83.821 mph/134.897 km/h.
Championship points: 1 Debbia, 57; **2** Patrickson, 39; **3** Capirossi and Orme, 31; **5** Raudies, 28; **6** Bordes, 23.

80 cc, round 3 (39.72 miles/63.93 km)
1 Ralf Waldmann, D (Seel), 30m 36.68s, 77.862 mph/125.307 km/h.
2 Jose Saez, E (Krauser); **3** Jaime Mariano, E (Casal); **4** Janos Szabo, H (Krauser); **5** Reiner Scheidhauer, D (Seel); **6** Antonio Sanchez, E (Cobas); **7** Stefan Kurfiss, D (Krauser); **8** Stefan Brägger, CH (Casal); **9** Jacques Bernard, B (Fantic); **10** Bernd Völkel, D (Seel); **11** Maik Stief, D (Casal); **12** Thomas Engl, D (Esch-GP); **13** Branko Rokavec, YU (Seel); **14** Undine Kummer, D (Krauser); **15** Joaquin Gali, AND (Krauser).
Fastest lap: Waldmann, 2m 01.28s, 78.61 mph/126.511 km/h.
Championship points: 1 Saez, 54; **2** Mariano, 52; **3** Bernard and Kurfiss, 26; **5** Szabo, 24; **6** Brägger, 21.

SALZBURGRING, Austria, 7 May. 2.636-mile/4.243-km circuit.
European Championship, 500 cc, round 3 (22 laps, 57.99 miles/93.35 km)
1 Simon Buckmaster, GB (Honda), 31m 33.21s, 110.293 mph/177.500 km/h.
2 Peter Linden, S (Honda); **3** Hansjorg Butz, D (Honda); **4** Josef Doppler, A (Honda); **5** Michele Valdo, I (Honda); **6** Stefan Klabacher, A (Honda); **7** Martin Trosch, D (Honda); **8** Juan Lopez Mella, E (Honda); **9** Karl Dauer, A (Honda); **10** David Crampton, GB (RGB); **11** Niggi Schmassman, CH

(Honda); 12 Romolo Balbi, I (Honda); 13 Pavol Dekanek, CS (Honda); 14 Alois Meyer, D (Honda); 15 Koos van Leyen, NL (RCB).
Fastest lap: Linden, 1m 24.64s, 112.137 mph/180.468 km/h.
Championship points: 1 Linden, 52; 2 Butz, 36; 3 Valdo, 35; 4 Nicotte, 33; 5 Doppler and Truchsess, 30.

250 cc, round 3 (18 laps, 47.448 miles/76.374 km)
1 Andrea Borgonovo, I (Aprilia), 26m 27.26s, 107.634 mph/173.221 km/h.
2 Marcellino Lucchi, I (Aprilia); 3 Josef Hutter, A (Honda); 4 Woolsey Coulter, IRL (Aprilia); 5 Engelbert Neumair, A (Aprilia); 6 Bernhard Schick, D (Yamaha); 7 Bernd Kassner, D (Yamaha); 8 Alain Kempener, B (Aprilia); 9 Nigel Bosworth, GB (Aprilia); 10 Renato Colleoni, I (Aprilia); 11 Leon van der Heyden, NL (Honda); 12 Gilberto Gambelli, I (Aprilia); 13 Yves Briguet, CH (Yamaha); 14 Mario Houssin, B (Yamaha); 15 Luca Pasini, I (Aprilia).
Fastest lap: Lucchi, 1m 26.63s, 109.561 mph/176.322 km/h.
Championship points: 1 Borgonovo, 52; 2 Lucchi, 37; 3 Hutter, 36; 4 Gambelli, 33; 5 Neumair and Zeelenberg, 28.

125 cc, round 4 (17 laps, 44.812 miles/72.131 km)
1 Gabriele Debbia, I (Aprilia), 27m 28.66s, 97.869 mph/157.505 km/h.
2 Alessandro Gramigni, I (Aprilia); 3 Loris Capirossi, I (Honda); 4 Josef Fischer, A (Rotax); 5 Dirk Raudies, D (Honda); 6 Flemming Kistrup, DK (Honda); 7 Steve Patrickson, GB (Honda); 8 Rob Orme, GB (Honda); 9 Manfred Baumann, A (Honda); 10 Reinhard Strack, D (Honda); 11 Attila Csosz, H (Honda); 12 Arie Molenaar, NL (Honda); 13 Janez Pintar, YU (Honda); 14 Wilhelm Hörhager, A (Honda); 15 Alain Kempener, B (Honda).
Fastest lap: Debbia, 1m 35.02s, 99.887 mph/160.754 km/h.
Championship points: 1 Debbia, 77; 2 Patrickson, 48; 3 Capirossi, 46; 4 Orme and Raudies, 39; 6 Gramigni, 37.

SCANDINAVIAN RACEWAY, Sweden, 21 May. 2.505-mile/4.031-km circuit.
European Championship, 500 cc, round 4 (25 laps, 62.625 miles/100.775 km)
1 Peter Linden, S (Honda), 42m 06.90s, 89.228 mph/143.6 km/h.
2 Simon Buckmaster, GB (Honda); 3 Hansjorg Butz, D (Honda); 4 Juan Lopez Mella, E (Honda); 5 Torbjörn Bastiansen, N (Suzuki); 6 Josef Doppler, A (Honda); 7 Ake Dahli, S (Honda); 8 Amedeo Perrone, I (Honda); 9 Lars Johansson, S (Honda); 10 David Larsson, S (Honda); 11 Hans Klingebiel, D (Suzuki); 12 Timo Paavilainen, SF (Suzuki); 13 Peter Graves, GB (Honda); 14 Bo Andersen, DK (Suzuki); 15 Gunnar Bruhn, S (Honda).
Fastest lap: not available.
Championship points: 1 Linden, 72; 2 Butz, 51; 3 Doppler, 40; 4 Lopez Mella, 38; 5 Buckmaster, 37; 6 Valdo, 35.

250 cc, round 4 (22 laps, 55.11 miles/88.682 km)
1 Andrea Borgonovo, I (Aprilia), 37m 19.70s, 88.545 mph/142.5 km/h.
2 Marcellino Lucchi, I (Aprilia); 3 Gilberto Gambelli, I (Aprilia); 4 Peter Linden, S (Yamaha); 5 Engelbert Neumair, A (Aprilia); 6 Alain Kempener, B (Aprilia); 7 Renato Colleoni, I (Aprilia); 8 Leon van der Heyden, NL (Honda); 9 Yves Briguet, CH (Yamaha); 10 Bernard Hänggeli, CH (Yamaha); 11 Nigel Bosworth, GB (Aprilia); 12 Hans Vontobel, CH (Yamaha); 13 Luis Maurel, E (Yamaha); 14 Luca Pasini, I (Aprilia); 15 Stefano Pennese, I (Aprilia).
Fastest lap: not available.
Championship points: 1 Borgonovo, 72; 2 Lucchi, 54; 3 Gambelli, 48; 4 Neumair, 39; 5 Hutter, 36; 6 Zeelenberg, 28.

125 cc, round 5 (20 laps, 50.1 miles/80.62 km)
1 Gabriele Debbia, I (Aprilia), 36m 15.60s, 82.89 mph/133.4 km/h.
2 Alessandro Gramigni, I (Aprilia); 3 Flemming Kistrup, DK (Honda); 4 Loris Capirossi, I (Honda); 5 Dirk Raudies, D (Honda); 6 Klaus Kindle, FL (Honda); 7 Luis D'Antin, E (Honda); 8 Håkan Olsson, S (Rotax); 9 Ian Newton, GB (Honda); 10 Alain Kempener, B (Honda); 11 Jose Morillas, E (Cobas); 12 Reijo Rosnell, SF (Rotax); 13 Arie Molenaar, NL (Honda); 14 Jukka Vanio, SF (Honda); 15 Steve Patrickson, GB (Honda).
Fastest lap: not available.
Championship points: 1 Debbia, 97; 2 Capirossi, 59; 3 Gramigni, 54; 4 Raudies, 50; 5 Patrickson, 49; 6 Orme, 39.

AUTODROM MOST, Czechoslovakia, 11 June. 2.577-mile/4.148-km circuit.
European Championship, 500 cc, round 5 (23 laps, 59.271 miles/95.404 km)
1 Peter Linden, S (Honda), 38m 34.85s, 92.192 mph/148.370 km/h.
2 Hansjorg Butz, D (Honda); 3 Rachel Nicotte, F (Honda); 4 Karl Truchsess, A (Honda); 5 Felix Beck, CH (Honda); 6 Michele Valdo, I (Honda); 7 Josef Doppler, A (Honda); 8 Romolo Balbi, I (Honda); 9 Ake Dahli, S (Honda); 10 Alois Meyer, D (Honda); 11 Georg Jung, D (Honda); 12 Martin Trosch, D (Honda); 13 Rudi Gächter, CH (Yamaha); 14 Hans Klingebiel, D (Honda); 15 Imrich Majoros, CS (Yamaha).
Fastest lap: not available.
Championship points: 1 Linden, 92; 2 Butz, 68; 3 Doppler, 49; 4 Nicotte, 48; 5 Valdo, 45; 6 Truchsess, 43.

250 cc, round 5 (22 laps, 56.694 miles/91.256 km)
1 Andrea Borgonovo, I (Aprilia), 36m 05.61s, 94.261 mph/151.699 km/h.
2 Gilberto Gambelli, I (Aprilia); 3 Marcellino Lucchi, I (Aprilia); 4 Renato Colleoni, I (Aprilia); 5 Frédéric Protat, F (Aprilia); 6 Engelbert Neumair, A (Aprilia); 7 Bernd Kassner, D (Yamaha); 8 Stefano Pennese, I (Aprilia); 9 Bernard Hänggeli, CH (Yamaha); 10 Leon van der Heyden, NL (Yamaha); 11 Siegfried Minich, B (Yamaha); 12 Marcel Kellenberger, CH (Yamaha); 13 Luca Pasini, I (Aprilia); 14 Fabrizio Furlan, I (Yamaha); 15 Harry Kallio, SF (Honda).
Fastest lap: not available.
Championship points: 1 Borgonovo, 92; 2 Lucchi, 69; 3 Gambelli, 65; 4 Neumair, 49; 5 Hutter, 36; 6 Colleoni and Zeelenberg, 28.

125 cc, round 6 (20 laps, 51.54 miles/82.96 km)
1 Loris Capirossi, I (Honda), 35m 22.68s, 87.425 mph/140.697 km/h.
2 Jean-Claude Selini, F (Honda); 3 Dirk Raudies, D (Honda); 4 Flemming Kistrup, DK (Honda); 5 Klaus Kindle, FL (Honda); 6 Jose Morillas, E (Cobas); 7 Steve Patrickson, GB (Honda); 8 Jean-Pierre Jeandat, F (Honda); 9 Gabriele Debbia, I (Aprilia); 10 Alain Kempener, B (Honda); 11 Arie Molenaar, NL (Honda); 12 Josef Amstutz, CH (Honda); 13 Alessandro Gramigni, I (Aprilia); 14 Hervé Duffard, F (Honda); 15 Marc Grau, E (Arbizu).
Fastest lap: not available.
Championship points: 1 Debbia, 104; 2 Capirossi, 79; 3 Raudies, 65; 4 Patrickson, 58; 5 Gramigni, 57; 6 Orme, 39.

80 cc, round 4 (16 laps, 41.23 miles/66.36 km)
1 Janos Szabo, H (Krauser), 30m 82.252s, 82.375 mph/132.57 km/h.
2 Stefan Kurfiss, D (Krauser); 3 Bernd Völkel, D (Seel); 4 Maik Stief, D (Casal); 5 Jacques Bernard, B (Fantic); 6 Joaquin Gali, AND (Krauser); 7 Undine Kummer, D (Krauser); 8 Jürgen Hofmann, DDR (Simson); 9 Günter Maussner, D (Krauser); 10 Claude Gourdon, F (DSM); 11 Janos Lovas, H (Honda); 12 Nicola Casadei, I (Casal); 13 Francesco Fantini, I (BBFT); 14 Luis Metello, P (Huvo); 15 Frantisek Varacha, CS (Eberhardt).
Fastest lap: Szabo, 1m 50.787s, 83.75 mph/134.789 km/h.
Championship points: 1 Saez, 54; 2 Mariano, 52; 3 Szabo, 44; 4 Kurfiss, 43; 5 Bernard, 37; 6 Stief, 26.

Sidecars, round 2 (21 laps, 54.117 miles/91.256 km)
1 Barry Smith/David Smith, GB/GB (Windle-ADM), 35m 34.215s, 91.301 mph/146.935 km/h.
2 Ralph Bohnhorst/Thomas Böttcher, D/D (Schuberth-LCR); 3 Paul Güdel/Charly Güdel, CH/CH (LCR-Yamaha); 4 Billy Gällros/Håkan Olsson, S/S (Yamaha); 5 Gary Knight/Malcolm Jackson, GB/GB (Redline-Yamaha); 6 Mark Reddington/Robert Parker, GB/GB (WR-Yamaha); 7 Frank Voigt/Holger Voigt, D/D (LCR); 8 Michael Burcombe/Phil Coombes, GB/GB (LCR-Krauser); 9 Peter Lemstra/Edwin Nap, NL/NL (LCR-Yamaha); 10 Emil Lauer/Norbert Wild, D/D (Busch-Honda); 11 Judd Drew/Bryan Houghton, GB/GB (Yamaha); 12 John Evans/Ian Gaunt, GB/GB (LCR); 13 Mordo/Berglund, S/S (JPX); 14 Geoff Thomas/Kevin Morgan, GB/GB (Windle-Yamaha); 15 Harry Smit/Ted de Rijk, NL/NL (LCR-Yamaha).
Fastest lap: Bohnhorst, 1m 40.163s, 92.637 mph/149.085 km/h.
Championship points: 1 Bohnhorst, 32; 2 Burcombe, 25; 3 Reddington, 23; 4 Knight, 22; 5 Howles and Smith, 20.

CIRCUIT VAN DRENTHE, Assen, Holland, 24 June. 3.812-mile/6.134-km circuit.
European Championship, 500 cc, round 6 (15 laps, 57.18 miles/92.01 km)
1 Simon Buckmaster, GB (Honda), 35m 03.84s, 97.93 mph/157.443 km/h.
2 Peter Linden, S (Honda); 3 Hansjorg Butz, D (Honda); 4 Rachel Nicotte, F (Honda); 5 Michele Valdo, I (Honda); 6 Karl Truchsess, A (Honda); 7 Josef Doppler, A (Honda); 8 Jeffry de Vries, NL (Honda); 9 Martin Trosch, D (Honda); 10 Niggi Schmassman, CH (Honda); 11 Felix Beck, CH (Honda); 12 Esko Kuparinen, SF (Honda); 13 Stefan Klabacher, A (Honda); 14 Pavol Dekanek, CS (Honda); 15 Alois Meyer, D (Honda).
Fastest lap: Buckmaster, 2m 18.94s, 98.757 mph/158.934 km/h.
Championship points: 1 Linden, 109; 2 Butz, 83; 3 Nicotte, 61; 4 Doppler, 58; 5 Buckmaster, 57; 6 Valdo, 56.

250 cc, round 6 (14 laps, 53.36 miles/85.87 km)
1 Wilco Zeelenberg, NL (Honda), 32m 45.44s, 97.737 mph/157.294 km/h.
2 Bernard Hänggeli, CH (Yamaha); 3 Patrick van den Goorbergh, NL (Yamaha); 4 Andrea Borgonovo, I (Aprilia); 5 Stefano Pennese, I (Aprilia); 6 Christian Boudinot, F (Yamaha); 7 Renato Colleoni, I (Aprilia); 8 Engelbert Neumair, A (Aprilia); 9 Leon van der Heyden, NL (Yamaha); 10 Steve Patrickson, GB (Yamaha); 11 Hans Vontobel, CH (Yamaha); 12 Luca Pasini, I (Aprilia); 13 Josef Hutter, A (Honda); 14 Marcel Kellenberger, CH (Yamaha); 15 Peter Linden, S (Yamaha).
Fastest lap: Marcellino Lucchi, I (Aprilia), 2m 18.46s, 99.099 mph/159.485 km/h.
Championship points: 1 Borgonovo, 105; 2 Lucchi, 69; 3 Gambelli, 65; 4 Neumair, 57; 5 Zeelenberg, 48; 6 Hänggeli, 43.

125 cc, round 7 (12 laps, 45.74 miles/73.61 km)
1 Gabriele Debbia, I (Aprilia), 30m 21.61s, 90.39 mph/145.469 km/h.
2 Thierry Feuz, CH (Honda); 3 Ralf Waldmann, D (Fotax); 4 Alessandro Gramigni, I (Aprilia); 5 Klaus Kindle, FL (Honda); 6 Jean-Claude Selini, F (Honda); 7 Arie Molenaar, NL (Honda); 8 Dirk Raudies, D (Honda); 9 Paolo Scappini, I (Honda); 10 Josef Fischer, A (Honda); 11 Adrie Nijenhuis, NL (Honda); 12 Jean-Pierre Jeandat, F (Honda); 13 Loris Capirossi, I (Honda); 14 Serge Julin, B (Honda); 15 Ian Newton, GB (Honda).
Fastest lap: Debbia, 2m 28.49s, 92.405 mph/148.713 km/h.
Championship points: 1 Debbia, 124; 2 Capirossi, 82; 3 Raudies, 73; 4 Gramigni, 70; 5 Patrickson, 58; 6 Kindle, 49.

80 cc, round 5 (9 laps, 34.30 miles/55.20 km)
1 Roberto Sassone, I (Unimoto), 24m 08.73s, 85.24 mph/137.183 km/h.
2 Jose Saez, E (Krauser); 3 Ralf Waldmann, D (Seel); 4 Janez Pintar, YU (Eberhardt); 5 Bernd Völkel, D (Seel); 6 Stefan Brägger, CH (Casal); 7 Janos Szabo, H (Krauser); 8 Jaime Mariano, E (Casal); 9 Thomas Engl, D (Esch-GP); 10 Joaquin Gali, AND (Krauser); 11 Stefan Kurfiss, D (Krauser); 12 Jacques Bernard, B (Fantic); 13 Maik Stief, D (Casal); 14 Manuel Duarte, P (Zündapp); 15 Fabrice Roy, F (Tyl).
Fastest lap: Mariano, 2m 38.74s, 86.438 mph/139.110 km/h.
Championship points: 1 Saez, 71; 2 Mariano, 60; 3 Szabo, 53; 4 Kurfiss, 48; 5 Bernard, 41; 6 Sassone and Waldmann, 35.

Sidecars, round 3 (12 laps, 45.74 miles/73.61 km)
1 René Progin/Yves Hunziker, CH/CH (LCR-Yamaha), 29m 27.37s, 93.164 mph/149.933 km/h.
2 Barry Smith/David Smith, GB/GB (Windle-ADM); 3 Ralph Bohnhorst/Thomas Böttcher, D/D (Schuberth-LCR); 4 Jos van Stekelenburg/Rinie Bettgens, NL/NL (LCR-Yamaha); 5 Paul Güdel/Charly Güdel, CH/CH (LCR-Yamaha); 6 Peter Lemstra/Edwin Nap, NL/NL (LCR-Yamaha); 7 Hans Hügli/Adolf Hänni, CH/CH (Sigwa); 8 Judd Drew/Bryan Houghton, GB/GB (LCR); 9 Gary Knight/Malcolm Jackson, GB/GB (Redline-Yamaha); 10 Raphael Clerc/Fredy Zünd, CH/CH (LCR); 11 Egon Schons/Peter Höss, D/D (BSR-Yamaha); 12 Geoff Thomas/Kevin Morgan, GB/GB (Yamaha); 13 Billy Gällros/Håkan Olsson, S/S (Yamaha); 14 Emil Lauer/Norbert Wild, D/D (Busch-Honda).
Fastest lap: Smith, 2m 25.19s, 94.51 mph/152.093 km/h.
Championship points: 1 Bohnhorst, 47; 2 Smith, 37; 3 Knight, 29; 4 Güdel, 26; 5 Burcombe and Lemstra, 25.

AUTODROMO SANTA MONICA, Misano, Italy, 9 July. 2.167-mile/3.488-km circuit.
European Championship, 500 cc, round 7 (26 laps, 56.342 miles/90.688 km)
1 Simon Buckmaster, GB (Honda), 36m 14.928s, 93.273 mph/150.109 km/h.
2 Michele Valdo, I (Honda); 3 Romolo Balbi, I (Honda); 4 Karl Truchsess, A (Honda); 5 Rachel Nicotte, F (Honda); 6 Peter Linden, S (Honda); 7 Juan Lopez Mella, E (Honda); 8 Stefan Klabacher, A (Honda); 9 Josef Doppler, A (Honda); 10 Niggi Schmassman, CH (Honda); 11 Maurizio Morselli, I (Honda); 12 Bernard Andrault, F (Honda); 13 Piero Pedone, I; 14 Leandro Becheroni, I (Suzuki); 15 Michael Kaplan, A (Honda).
Fastest lap: Valdo, 1m 22.898s, 94.12 mph/151.472 km/h.
Championship points: 1 Linden, 119; 2 Butz, 83; 3 Buckmaster, 77; 4 Valdo, 73; 5 Nicotte, 72; 6 Truchsess, 63.

250 cc, round 7 (22 laps, 47.674 miles/76.736 km)
1 Marcellino Lucchi, I (Aprilia), 30m 27.336s, 93.936 mph/151.176 km/h.
2 Stefano Pennese, I (Aprilia); 3 Andrea Borgonovo, I (Aprilia); 4 Engelbert Neumair, A (Aprilia); 5 Luca Pasini, I (Aprilia); 6 Leon van der Heyden, NL (Yamaha); 7 Bernd Kassner, D (Yamaha); 8 Siegfried Minich, B (Yamaha); 9 Hans Vontobel, CH (Yamaha); 10 Massimo Cavina, I (Honda); 11 Luca Moschini, I (Aprilia); 12 Christian Boudinot, F (Fior); 13 Luis Maurel, E (Yamaha); 14 Renato Colleoni, I (Aprilia); 15 Pietro Paolucci, I (Aprilia).
Fastest lap: Lucchi, 1m 21.932s, 95.23 mph/153.258 km/h.
Championship points: 1 Borgonovo, 120; 2 Lucchi, 89; 3 Neumair, 70; 4 Gambelli, 65; 5 Zeelenberg, 48; 6 Hänggeli, 43.

125 cc, round 8 (21 laps, 45.507 miles/73.248 km)
1 Loris Capirossi, I (Honda), 30m 54.437s, 88.355 mph/142.195 km/h.
2 Dirk Raudies, D (Honda); 3 Alessandro Gramigni, I (Aprilia); 4 Flemming Kistrup, DK (Honda); 5 Paolo Scappini, I (Honda); 6 Serafino Foti, I (Honda); 7 Arie Molenaar, NL (Honda); 8 Jean-Pierre Jeandat, F (Honda); 9 Luis D'Antin, E (Honda); 10 Gabriele Debbia, I (Aprilia); 11 Massimo Cecconi, I (Parilla); 12 Josep Volta, E (Arbizu); 13 Ian Newton, GB (Honda); 14 Gregory Gorec, YU (Honda); 15 Marc Grau, E (Arbizu).
Fastest lap: Capirossi, 1m 27.417s, 89.255 mph/143.642 km/h.
Championship points: 1 Debbia, 130; 2 Capirossi, 102; 3 Raudies, 90; 4 Gramigni, 85; 5 Patrickson, 58; 6 Kistrup, 51.

AUTODROM RIJEKA, Yugoslavia, 15 July. 2.590-mile/4.168-km circuit.
European Championship, 500 cc, round 8 (26 laps, 67.34 miles/108.368 km)
1 Rachel Nicotte, F (Honda), 42m 00.29s, 96.183 mph/154.793 km/h.
2 Karl Truchsess, A (Honda); 3 Michele Valdo, I (Honda); 4 Hansjorg Butz, D (Honda); 5 Stefan Klabacher, A (Honda); 6 Torbjörn Bastiansen, N (Suzuki); 7 Georg Jung, D (Honda); 8 Josef Doppler, A (Honda); 9 Rudolf Zeller, A (Manhattan); 10 Karl Dauer, A (Honda); 11 Timo Paavilainen, SF (Suzuki); 12 Peter Graves, GB (Honda); 13 Jim Groote, NL (Suzuki); 14 Peter Tibori, H (Yamaha); 15 Tony Carey, IRL (Honda).
Fastest lap: Truchsess, 1m 35.69s, 97.434 mph/156.806 km/h.
Championship points: see **Final points.**

250 cc, round 8 (23 laps, 59.57 miles/95.864 km)
1 Marcellino Lucchi, I (Aprilia), 36m 50.36s, 97.016 mph/156.133 km/h.
2 Bernard Hänggeli, CH (Yamaha); 3 Renato Colleoni, I (Aprilia); 4 Bernd Kassner, D (Yamaha); 5 Stefano Pennese, I (Aprilia); 6 Engelbert Neumair, A (Aprilia); 7 Luca Pasini, I (Aprilia); 8 Leon van der Heyden, NL (Yamaha); 9 Siegfried Minich, B (Yamaha); 10 Yves Briguet, CH (Yamaha); 11 Michael Schulten, A (Rotax); 12 Laurent Naveau, B (Yamaha); 13 Luis Maurel, E (Yamaha); 14 Pierre Fontannaz, CH (Yamaha); 15 Paul Streicher, D (Yamaha).
Fastest lap: Lucchi, 1m 34.77s, 98.38 mph/158.328 km/h.
Championship points: 1 Borgonovo, 120; 2 Lucchi, 109; 3 Neumair, 80; 4 Gambelli, 65; 5 Hänggeli, 60; 6 Colleoni, 54.

125 cc, round 9 (23 laps, 59.57 miles/95.864 km)
1 Dirk Raudies, D (Honda), 39m 12.03s, 91.172 mph/146.728 km/h.
2 Alessandro Gramigni, I (Aprilia); 3 Loris Capirossi, I (Honda); 4 Josep Volta, E (Arbizu); 5 Paolo Scappini, I (Honda); 6 Gabriele Debbia, I (Aprilia); 7 Klaus Kindle, FL (Honda); 8 Steve Patrickson, GB (Honda); 9 Arie Molenaar, NL (Honda); 10 Marc Grau, E (Arbizu); 11 Gregory Gorec, YU (Honda); 12 Attila Csosz, H (Honda); 13 Adrie Nijenhuis, NL (Honda); 14 Ian Newton, GB (Honda); 15 Jose Morillas, E (Cobas).
Fastest lap: Gramigni, 1m 41.14s, 92.184 mph/148.356 km/h.
Championship points: 1 Debbia, 140; 2 Capirossi, 117; 3 Raudies, 110; 4 Gramigni, 102; 5 Patrickson, 66; 6 Kindle, 58.

CIRCUIT PAUL RICARD, France, 30 July. 2.051-mile/3.3-km circuit.
European Championship, 250 cc, round 9 (24 laps, 49.224 miles/79.2 km)
1 Adrien Morillas, F (Yamaha), 33m 26.44s, 88.298 mph/142.102 km/h.
2 Stefano Fennese, I (Aprilia); 3 Renato Colleoni, I (Aprilia); 4 Luca Pasini, I (Aprilia); 5 Luis Maurel, E (Yamaha); 6 Leon van der Heyden, NL (Yamaha); 7 Frédéric Protat, F (Aprilia); 8 Woolsey Coulter, IRL (Aprilia); 9 Yves Briguet, CH (Yamaha); 10 Bernd Kassner, D (Yamaha); 11 Alain Bronec, F (Aprilia); 12 Luca Moschini, I (Aprilia); 13 Hans Vontobel, CH (Yamaha); 14 Franck Girodroux, F (Aprilia); 15 Eros Manferdini, I (Yamaha).
Fastest lap: Marcellino Lucchi, I (Aprilia), 1m 22.37s, 89.618 mph/144.227 km/h.
Championship points: 1 Borgonovo, 120; 2 Lucchi, 109; 3 Neumair, 80; 4 Colleoni, 69; 5 Gambelli and Pennese, 65

125 cc, round 10 (22 laps, 45.122 miles/72.6 km)
1 Josep Volta, E (Arbizu), 32m 29.66s, 83.297 mph/134.054 km/h.
2 Flemming Kistrup, DK (Honda); 3 Robert Duss, CH (Honda); 4 Alessandro Gramigni, I (Aprilia); 5 Dirk Raudies, D (Honda); 6 Pietro Paolucci, I (Honda); 7 Gabriele Debbia, I (Aprilia); 8 Hervé Duffard, F (Honda); 9 Steve Patrickson, GB (Honda); 10 Marc Grau, E (Arbizu); 11 Serafino Foti, I (Honda); 12 Gérard Rolland-Piègue, F (Honda); 13 Paul Bordes, F (Honda); 14 Luis D'Antin, E (Honda); 15 Luigi Ancona, I (Gazzaniga).
Fastest lap: Volta, 1m 27.50s, 84.364 mph/135.771 km/h.
Championship points: 1 Debbia, 149; 2 Raudies, 121; 3 Capirossi, 117; 4 Gramigni, 115; 5 Patrickson, 73; 6 Kistrup, 69.

Sidecars, round 4 (22 laps, 45.122 miles/72.6 km)
1 Barry Smith/David Smith, GB/GB (Windle-ADM), 31m 49.21s, 85.061 mph/136.894 km/h.
2 Paul Güdel/Charly Güdel, CH/CH (LCR-Yamaha); 3 Billy Gällros/Wolfgang Bock, S/D (LCR-Yamaha); 4 Kenny Howles/Steve Pointer, GB/GB (LCR-Krauser); 5 Gary Knight/Malcolm Jackson, GB/GB (Redline-Yamaha); 6 Ralph Bohnhorst/Thomas Böttcher, D/D (Schuberth-LCR); 7 Klaus Klaffenböck/Christian Parzer, D/D (LCR-Yamaha); 8 Mark Reddington/Robert Parker, GB/GB (WR-Yamaha); 9 C. Bay/C. Alibaux, F/F (Yamaha); 10 Jos van Stekelenburg/Rinie Bettgens, NL/NL (LCR); 11 Judd Drew/Bryan Houghton, GB/GB (LCR-Yamaha); 12 D. Lacour/P. Marais, F/F (Busch-Suzuki); 13 Jacques Heriot/Jean-Louis Heriot, F/F (JPX); 14 Frank Voigt/Holger Voigt, D/D (LCR); 15 Egon Schons/Peter Höss, D/D (BSR-Yamaha).
Fastest lap: Güdel, 1m 25.28s, 86.56 mph/139.306 km/h.
Championship points: 1 Bohnhorst and Smith, 57; 3 Güdel, 43; 4 Knight, 40; 5 Howles, 33; 6 Gällros and Reddington, 31

DONINGTON PARK CIRCUIT, Great Britain, 27 August. 2.5-mile/4.023-km circuit.
European Championship, 250 cc, round 10 (24 laps, 60 miles/96.552 km)
1 Bernard Hänggeli, CH (Yamaha), 41m 12.30s, 87.36 mph/140.59 km/h.
2 Andrea Borgonovo, I (Aprilia); 3 Kevin Mitchell, GB (Yamaha); 4 Leon van der Heyden, NL (Yamaha); 5 Renato Colleoni, I (Aprilia); 6 Gilberto Gambelli, I (Aprilia); 7 Luca Pasini, I (Aprilia); 8 Luis Maurel, E (Yamaha); 9 Bernd Kassner, D (Yamaha); 10 Martyn Jupp, GB (Yamaha); 11 Steve Patrickson, GB (Yamaha); 12 Steve Sawford, GB (Yamaha); 13 Josef Hutter, A (Honda); 14 Siegfried Minich, B (Yamaha); 15 Henri Sala, NL (Honda).
Fastest lap: Hänggeli, 1m 41.60s, 88.58 mph/142.56 km/h.
Championship points: 1 Borgonovo, 137; 2 Lucchi, 109; 3 Colleoni, Hänggeli and Neumair, 80; 6 Gambelli, 75.

125 cc, round 11 (20 laps, 50 miles/80.46 km)
1 Loris Capirossi, I (Honda), 36m 27.29s, 82.29 mph/132.43 km/h.
2 Alessandro Gramigni, I (Aprilia); 3 Steve Patrickson, GB (Honda); 4 Pietro Paolucci, I (Honda); 5 Jean-Pierre Jeandat, F (Honda); 6 Alan Patterson, IRL (Honda); 7 Ian Newton, GB (Honda); 8 Gabriele Debbia, I (Aprilia); 9 Klaus Kindle, FL (Honda); 10 Marc Grau, E (Arbizu); 11 Gérard Rolland-Piègue, F (Honda); 12 Arie Molenaar, NL (Honda); 13 Kevin Mawdsley, GB (Honda); 14 Julian Perry, GB (Honda); 15 Adrie Nijenhuis, NL (Honda).
Fastest lap: Capirossi, 1m 47.31s, 83.86 mph/134.96 km/h.
Championship points: 1 Debbia, 157; 2 Capirossi, 137; 3 Gramigni, 132; 4 Raudies, 121; 5 Patrickson, 88; 6 Kistrup, 68.

Sidecars, round 5 (20 laps, 50 miles/80.46 km)
1 Kenny Howles/Steve Pointer, GB/GB (LCR-Krauser), 35m 04.10s, 85.54 mph/137.66 km/h.
2 Paul Güdel/Charly Güdel, CH/CH (LCR-Yamaha); 3 Billy Gällros/Julian Tailford, S/GB (LCR-Yamaha); 4 Ralph Bohnhorst/Thomas Böttcher, D/D (Schuberth-LCR); 5 Barry Smith/David Smith, GB/GB (Windle-ADM); 6 Jos van Stekelenburg/Rinie Bettgens, NL/NL (LCR); 7 Michael Burcombe/Nick Roche, GB/GB (LCR-Krauser); 8 Frank Voigt/Holger Voigt, D/D (LCR); 9 John Evans/Hennigan, GB/GB (LCR); 10 Whiteside/Whiteside, GB/GB (Yamaha); 11 Niek van Bergen/van Puyve, NL/NL (Yamaha).
Fastest lap: Güdel, 1m 43.80s, 86.70 mph/139.53 km/h.
Championship points: 1 Bohnhorst, 70; 2 Smith, 68; 3 Güdel, 60; 4 Howles, 53; 5 Gällros, 46; 6 Knight, 40.

HOCKENHEIMRING, German Federal Republic, 17 September. 4.218-mile/6.789-km circuit.
European Championship, 250 cc, round 11 (12 laps, 50.616 miles/81.463 km)
1 Patrick van den Goorbergh, NL (Yamaha), 27m 11.76s, 111.665 mph/179.708 km/h.
2 Leon van der Heyden, NL (Yamaha); 3 Marcellino Lucchi, I (Aprilia); 4 Engelbert Neumair, A (Yamaha); 5 Bernd Kassner, D (Yamaha); 6 Bernard Hänggeli, CH (Yamaha); 7 Gilberto Gambelli, I (Aprilia); 8 Luca Pasini, I (Aprilia); 9 Renato Colleoni, I (Aprilia); 10 Mario Houssin, B (Yamaha); 11 J. van den Goorbergh, NL (Yamaha); 12 Frédéric Protat, F (Aprilia);

13 R. Prinz, D (Yamaha); **14** R. Brauweiler, D (Honda); **15** Luca Moschini, I (Aprilia).
Fastest lap: Hans Becker, D (Seel), 2m 14.18s, 113.164 mph/182.119 km/h.
Championship points: see **Final points.**

125 cc, round 12 (12 laps, 50.616 miles/81.463 km)
1 Dirk Raudies, D (Honda), 29m 27.22s, 103.105 mph/165.933 km/h.
2 Alessandro Gramigni, I (Aprilia); **3** Ralf Waldmann, D (Cobas); **4** Flemming Kistrup, DK (Honda); **5** Arie Molenaar, NL (Honda); **6** Gabriele Debbia, I (Aprilia); **7** Manfred Thurmayer, D (Honda); **8** Jean-Claude Selini, F (Honda); **9** O. Koch, D (Honda); **10** Jukka Vanio, SF (Honda); **11** O. Friedrich, D (Rotax); **12** Robert Duss, CH (Honda); **13** V. Heider, D (Honda); **14** W. Fritz, D (Honda); **15** Jean-Pierre Jeandat, F (Honda).
Fastest lap: Gramigni, 2m 26.22s, 103.845 mph/167.123 km/h.
Championship points: see **Final points.**

80 cc, round 6 (8 laps, 33.744 miles/54.308 km)
1 Jaime Mariano, E (Casal), 21m 10.83s, 95.586 mph/153.832 km/h.
2 Bernd Völkel, D (Seel); **3** Stefan Kurfiss, D (Krauser); **4** Henrie van Heist, D (Casal); **5** Thomas Engl, D (Esch-GP); **6** Maik Stief, D (Casal); **7** Jose Saez, E (Autisa); **8** Jacques Bernard, B (Fantic); **9** Joaquin Gali, AND (Krauser); **10** Paul Bordes, F (RB); **11** Roberto Sassone, I (Unimoto); **12** Undine Kummer, D (Krauser); **13** Jose Palencia, E (Arbizu); **14** Ettore Cezza, I (RB); **15** Stefan Brägger, CH (Casal).
Fastest lap: Kurfiss, 2m 36.16s, 97.235 mph/156.485 km/h.
Championship points: see **Final points.**

Sidecars, round 6 (11 laps, 46.398 miles/74.679 km)
1 René Progin/Yves Hunziker, CH/CH (LCR), 25m 31.16s, 109.085 mph/175.556 km/h.
2 Ralph Bohnhorst/Thomas Böttcher, D/D (Schuberth-LCR); **3** Barry Smith/David Smith, GB/GB (Windle-ADM); **4** Kenny Howles/Steve Pointer, GB/GB (LCR); **5** Jos van Stekelenburg/Rinie Bettgens, NL/NL (LCR); **6** Hans Hügli/Adolf Hänni, D/D (Sigma); **7** Mark Reddington/Robert Parker, GB/GB (WR-Yamaha); **8** Emil Lauer/Norbert Wild, D/D (Busch-Honda); **9** Michael Burcombe/Wolfgang Böck, GB/D (LCR-Krauser); **10** Gary Knight/Malcolm Jackson, GB/GB (Redline-Yamaha); **11** Peter Lemstra/Edwin Nap, NL/NL (LCR-Yamaha); **12** Paul Güdel/Charly Güdel, CH/CH (LCR-Yamaha); **13** Harry Smit/Ted de Rijk, NL/NL (LCR-Yamaha); **14** W. Eggerstorfer/M. Mayer, D/D (LCR-Yamaha); **15** G. Alati/V. Montanelli, I/I (LCR-Krauser).
Fastest lap: Smith, 2m 17.84s, 110.158 mph/177.283 km/h.
Championship points: see **Final points.**

Final Championship points (500 cc)

1	Peter Linden, S	119
2	Hansjorg Butz, D	96
3	Rachel Nicotte, F	92
4	Michele Valdo, I	88
5	Karl Truchsess, A	83
6	Simon Buckmaster, GB	77

7 Josef Doppler, A, 73; **8** Juan Lopez Mella, E, 47; **9** Romolo Balbi, I, 41; **10** Niggi Schmassman, CH, 35; **11** Stefan Klabacher, A, 32; **12** Martin Trosch, D, 28; **13** Torbjörn Bastiansen, N, 27; **14** Karl Dauer, A, 22; **15** Ake Dahli, S, 21.

Final Championship points (250 cc)

1	Andrea Borgonovo, I	137
2	Marcellino Lucchi, I	124
3	Engelbert Neumair, A	93
4	Bernard Hänggeli, CH	90
5	Leon van der Heyden, NL	89
6	Renato Colleoni, I	87

7 Gilberto Gambelli, I, 84; **8** Bernd Kassner, D, 73; **9** Stefano Pennese, I, 65; **10** Luca Pasini, I, 64; **11** Wilco Zeelenberg, NL, 48; **12** Josef Hutter, A, 42; **13** Luis Maurel, E and Patrick van den Goorbergh, NL, 35; **15** Yves Briguet, CH, 32.

Final Championship points (125 cc)

1	Gabriele Debbia, I	167
2	Alessandro Gramigni, I	149
3	Dirk Raudies, D	141
4	Loris Capirossi, I	137
5	Steve Patrickson, GB	88
6	Flemming Kistrup, DK	81

7 Klaus Kindle, FL, 65; **8** Arie Molenaar, NL, 53; **9** Jean-Claude Selini, F, 48; **10** Jean-Pierre Jeandat, F, 41; **11** Rob Orme, GB, 39; **12** Paolo Scappini, I and Josep Volta, E, 37; **14** Ralf Waldmann, D, 34; **15** Jose Morillas, E, 32.

Final Championship points (80 cc)

1	Jaime Mariano, E	80
2	Jose Saez, E	80
3	Stefan Kurfiss, D	63
4	Janos Szabo, H	53
5=	Jacques Bernard, B	49
5=	Bernd Völkel, D	49

7 Roberto Sassone, I, 40; **8** Maik Stief, D, 39; **9** Joaquin Gali, AND, 38; **10** Ralf Waldmann, D, 35; **11** Stefan Brägger, CH, 32; **12** Undine Kummer, D, 27; **13** Thomas Engl, D, 22; **14** Manuel Duarte, P, 21; **15** Antonio Sanchez, E, 18.

Final Championship points (Sidecars)

1	Ralph Bohnhorst, D	87
2	Barry Smith, GB	83
3	Kenny Howles, GB	66
4	Paul Güdel, CH	64
5=	Billy Gällros, S	46
5=	Gary Knight, GB	46

7 Michael Burcombe, GB, 41; **8** René Progin, CH, Mark Reddington, GB and Jos van Stekelenburg, NL, 40; **11** Peter Lemstra, NL, 30; **12** Frank Voigt, D, 29; **13** Hans Hügli, D, 19; **14** Judd Drew, GB, 18; **15** John Evans, GB and Emil Lauer, D, 16.

Shell Oils ACU Supercup

DONINGTON PARK CIRCUIT, 14 May. 1.96-mile/3.136-km circuit.
Shell Oils ACU Supercup, round 1 (15 laps, 29.36 miles/47.04 km)

125 cc
1 Steve Patrickson, GB (Honda), 20m 34.4s, 85.61 mph/137.75 km/h.
2 Rob Orme, GB (Honda); **3** David Lemon, GB (Honda); **4** Ian Lougher, GB (Honda); **5** Steve Lawton, GB (Honda); **6** Dave Marston, GB (Honda); **7** Stuart Nicholls, GB (Honda); **8** Alan Patterson, GB (Honda); **9** Mark Carkeek, GB (Honda); **10** Chris Palmer, GB (Honda).
Fastest lap: Patrickson, 1m 20.6s, 87.40 mph/140.66 km/h (record).

Supersport 600
1 Mike Edwards, GB (Yamaha), 19m 41.2s, 89.46 mph/143.96 km/h.
2 Rodney Knapp, NZ (Yamaha); **3** Phil Mellor, GB (Suzuki); **4** Ray Stringer, GB (Yamaha); **5** Ray Swann, GB (Kawasaki); **6** Dave Leach, GB (Yamaha); **7** Gary Weston, GB (Yamaha); **8** Howard Selby, GB (Yamaha); **9** Eric McFarlane, GB (Yamaha); **10** James Whitham, GB (Suzuki).
Fastest lap: Knapp, 1m 17.6s, 90.78 mph/146.10 km/h (record).

Superbikes
1 Roger Burnett, GB (Honda), 18m 37.1s, 94.60 mph/152.22 km/h.
2 Terry Rymer, GB (Yamaha); **3** Brian Morrison, GB (Honda); **4** Mark Phillips, GB (Yamaha); **5** Steve Hislop, GB (Honda); **6** Steve Chambers, GB (Honda); **7** Paul Iddon, GB (Yamaha); **8** Ray Stringer, GB (Yamaha); **9** Ray Swann, GB (Kawasaki); **10** Steve Williams, GB (Yamaha).
Fastest laps: Burnett and Rymer, 1m 13.5s, 95.85 mph/154.26 km/h.

250 cc
1 Steve Patrickson, GB (Yamaha), 19m 10.2s, 91.87 mph/147.84 km/h.
2 Nigel Bosworth, GB (Aprilia); **3** Ian McConnachie, GB (Yamaha); **4** Paul Lewis, AUS (Yamaha); **5** Ian Newton, GB (Honda); **6** Steve Sawford, GB (Yamaha); **7** Alan Jeffery, GB (Yamaha); **8** Rob Orme, GB (Rotax); **9** Greig Ramsay, GB (Honda); **10** Tim Couzens, GB (Rotax).
Fastest laps: Patrickson and Lewis, 1m 15.5s, 93.31 mph/150.17 km/h (record).

750 cc TT Formula 1
1 Roger Burnett, GB (Honda), 18m 36.6s, 94.64 mph/152.28 km/h.
2 Terry Rymer, GB (Yamaha); **3** Steve Spray, GB (Norton); **4** Steve Hislop, GB (Honda); **5** Phil Mellor, GB (Suzuki); **6** Steve Chambers, GB (Honda); **7** Mark Phillips, GB (Yamaha); **8** Brian Morrison, GB (Honda); **9** Paul Iddon, GB (Yamaha); **10** Ray Stringer, GB (Yamaha).
Fastest laps: Burnett and Rymer, 1m 13.6s, 95.72 mph/154.05 km/h (record).

Sidecars
1 Steve Webster/Tony Hewitt, GB/GB (LCR-Krauser), 19m 07.8s, 92.07 mph/148.14 km/h.
2 Barry Brindley/Grahame Rose, GB/GB (Fowler-Yamaha); **3** Ray Gardner/Tony Strevens, GB/GB (LCR-Krauser); **4** Mick Smith/Kevin Webster, GB/GB (Yamaha); **5** Kenny Howles/Steve Pointer, GB/GB (LCR-Krauser); **6** Mick Thompson/Ian Stapleton, GB/GB (Yamaha); **7** Robert Fisher/Trevor Crone, GB/GB (Baker Suzuki); **8** Gary Thomas/Eckhart Rösinger, GB/D (LCR-IMI); **9** Roy Lawrence/Graham Mapletoft, GB/GB (LCR-Yamaha); **10** Gary Knight/Malcolm Jackson, GB/GB (Redline Yamaha).
Fastest lap: Webster, 1m 14.5s, 94.56 mph/152.18 km/h (record).

CADWELL PARK CIRCUIT, 25 June. 2.17-mile/3.472-km circuit.
Shell Oils ACU Supercup, round 2 (15 laps, 32.55 miles/52.08 km)

125 cc
1 Steve Patrickson, GB (Honda), 25m 15.3s, 77.33 mph/124.44 km/h.
2 Rob Orme, GB (Honda); **3** Ian Newton, GB (Honda); **4** David Lemon, GB (Honda); **5** Julian Perry, GB (Honda); **6** Mark Carkeek, GB (Honda); **7** Chris Palmer, GB (Honda); **8** Graham Holland, GB (Honda); **9** Steve Sawford, GB (Honda); **10** Graham Harknett, GB (Honda).
Fastest lap: Patrickson, 1m 39.0s, 78.90 mph/126.98 km/h (record).

Supersport 600
1 Paul Brookes, GB (Honda), 24m 30.5s, 79.68 mph/128.23 km/h.
2 Brian Morrison, GB (Honda); **3** Gary Weston, GB (Yamaha); **4** James Whitham, GB (Suzuki); **5** Eric McFarlane, GB (Yamaha); **6** Steve Chambers, GB (Honda); **7** Howard Selby, GB (Yamaha); **8** Phil Borley, GB (Honda); **9** Geoff Johnson, GB (Yamaha); **10** Iain Duffus, GB.
Fastest lap: Rodney Knapp, NZ (Yamaha), 1m 36.4s, 81.03 mph/130.40 km/h (record).

Superbikes
1 Carl Fogarty, GB (Honda), 23m 33.3s, 82.91 mph/133.42 km/h.
2 Roger Burnett, GB (Honda); **3** Ray Stringer, GB (Yamaha); **4** Steve Chambers, GB (Honda); **5** Brian Morrison, GB (Honda); **6** Andy McGladdery, GB (Honda); **7** David Griffith, GB (Honda); **8** Mark Phillips, GB (Yamaha); **9** Nick Jefferies, GB (Yamaha); **10** Tim Bourne, GB (Honda).
Fastest lap: Fogarty, 1m 32.9s, 84.09 mph/135.33 km/h (record).

250 cc
1 Kevin Mitchell, GB (Yamaha), 23m 51.7s, 81.84 mph/131.70 km/h.
2 Steve Patrickson, GB (Yamaha); **3** Paul Lewis, AUS (Yamaha); **4** Woolsey Coulter, IRL (Aprilia); **5** Ian McConnachie, GB (Yamaha); **6** Matt Llewellyn, GB (Yamaha); **7** Ian Newton, GB (Honda); **8** Martyn Jupp, GB (Yamaha); **9** Mark Barker, GB (Yamaha); **10** Rob Orme, GB (Yamaha).
Fastest lap: Mitchell, 1m 33.9s, 83.19 mph/133.88 km/h (record).

750 cc TT Formula 1 (11 laps, 23.87 miles/38.192 km)
1 Carl Fogarty, GB (Honda), 17m 06.0s, 83.75 mph/134.77 km/h.
2 James Whitham, GB (Suzuki); **3** Steve Spray, GB (Norton); **4** Roger Burnett, GB (Honda); **5** Brian Morrison, GB (Honda); **6** Steve Chambers, GB (Honda); **7** Andy McGladdery, GB (Honda); **8** David Griffith, GB (Honda); **9** Ian Simpson, GB (Suzuki); **10** Nick Jefferies, GB (Yamaha).
Fastest lap: Fogarty, 1m 32.3s, 84.63 mph/136.20 km/h (record).

Sidecars
1 Eddy Wright/Ian Marchant, GB/GB (Yamaha), 24m 50.3s, 78.62 mph/126.53 km/h.
2 Robert Fisher/Trevor Crone, GB/GB (Suzuki); **3** Mick Thompson/Peacock, GB/GB (Yamaha); **4** Roy Lawrence/Graham Mapletoft, GB/GB (Yamaha); **5** Boddy/Peach, GB/GB (Yamaha); **6** Phil Balment/Craig Hallam, GB/GB (Yamaha); **7** John Cable/Tom Pettman, GB/GB (Yamaha); **8** Mick Bembridge/C. Hollis, GB/GB (Yamaha).
Fastest lap: Wright, 1m 37.5s, 80.12 mph/128.94 km/h.

THRUXTON CIRCUIT, 20 August. 2.356-mile/3.792-km circuit.
Shell Oils ACU Supercup, round 3 (15 laps, 35.34 miles/56.88 km)

125 cc
1 Alex Bedford, GB (EMC), 22m 19.4s, 94.99 mph/152.87 km/h.
2 Rob Orme, GB (Honda); **3** Ian Newton, GB (Honda); **4** Steve Patrickson, GB (Honda); **5** Julian Perry, GB (Honda); **6** Steve Lawton, GB (Honda); **7** Alan Patterson, GB (Honda); **8** Steve Sawford, GB (Honda); **9** Chris Palmer, GB (Honda); **10** M. Harrison, GB (Honda).
Fastest lap: Bedford, 1m 28.2s, 91.16 mph/146.7 km/h (record).

Supersport 600
1 Mike Edwards, GB (Yamaha), 21m 33.6s, 98.35 mph/158.278 km/h.
2 Rodney Knapp, NZ (Yamaha); **3** John Reynolds, GB (Kawasaki); **4** Brian Morrison, GB (Honda); **5** Mark Linscott, GB (Kawasaki); **6** Phil Borley, GB (Honda); **7** G. English, GB (Yamaha); **8** Dean Ashton, GB (Yamaha); **9** Ian Simpson, GB (Suzuki); **10** Steve Ives, GB (Yamaha).
Fastest laps: Edwards and Reynolds, 1m 25.1s, 99.67 mph/160.4 km/h (record).

Superbikes
1 Ray Stringer, GB (Yamaha), 20m 35s, 103.02 mph/165.79 km/h.
2 Brian Morrison, GB (Honda); **3** Steve Chambers, GB (Honda); **4** Charlie Corner, GB (Honda); **5** Steve Hislop, GB (Honda); **6** Steve Manley, GB (Yamaha); **7** David Griffith, GB (Honda); **8** Dave Redgate, GB (Yamaha); **9** Graham Thrush, GB (Honda); **10** David Crampton, GB (Yamaha).
Fastest lap: Morrison, 1m 20.9s, 104.84 mph/168.72 km/h (record).

250 cc
1 Nigel Bosworth, GB (Aprilia), 21m 6s, 100.49 mph/161.72 km/h.
2 Martyn Jupp, GB (Yamaha); **3** Kevin Mitchell, GB (Yamaha); **4** Paul Lewis, AUS (Yamaha); **5** Matt Llewellyn, GB (Yamaha); **6** Rob Orme, GB (Yamaha); **7** Steve Patrickson, GB (Yamaha); **8** Alan Jeffery, GB (Yamaha); **9** Alan Patterson, GB (Yamaha); **10** D. Wisdom, GB (Rotax).
Fastest lap: Llewellyn, 1m 23.2s, 101.94 mph/164.05 km/h (record).

750 cc TT Formula 1
1 Steve Spray, GB (Norton), 20m 31.4s, 103.32 mph/166.28 km/h.
2 Ray Stringer, GB (Yamaha); **3** Brian Morrison, GB (Honda); **4** Carl Fogarty, GB (Honda); **5** Steve Chambers, GB (Honda); **6** Trevor Nation, GB (Norton); **7** Steve Hislop, GB (Honda); **8** John Reynolds, GB (Kawasaki); **9** Steve Manley, GB (Yamaha); **10** Mark Phillips, GB (Yamaha).
Fastest lap: Spray, 1m 21.1s, 104.58 mph/168.305 km/h (record).

Sidecars
1 Steve Webster/Tony Hewitt, GB/GB (LCR-Krauser), 21m 7.9s, 100.34 mph/161.48 km/h.
2 Barry Brindley/Grahame Rose, GB/GB (Yamaha); **3** Kenny Howles/Steve Pointer, GB/GB (LCR-Krauser); **4** Mick Smith/Kevin Webster, GB/GB (Yamaha); **5** Barry Smith/David Smith, GB/GB (Yamaha); **6** Robert Fisher/Trevor Crone, GB/GB (Suzuki); **7** Mick Thompson/Ian Stapleton, GB/GB (Yamaha); **8** Roy Lawrence/Graham Mapletoft, GB/GB (Yamaha); **9** Gary Thomas/Bryan Houghton, GB/GB (Yamaha); **10** T. Rope/D. Kavanagh, GB/GB (Yamaha).
Fastest lap: Webster, 1m 22.3s, 103.06 mph/165.858 km/h (record).

MALLORY PARK CIRCUIT, 3 September. 1.370-mile/2.025-km circuit.
Shell Oils ACU Supercup, round 4 (20 laps, 27.4 miles/40.7 km)

125 cc
1 Rob Orme, GB (Honda), 18m 29.0s, 88.94 mph/143.14 km/h.
2 Steve Patrickson, GB (Honda); **3** Kevin Mawdsley, GB (Honda); **4** Alex Bedford, GB (EMC); **5** Julian Perry, GB (Honda); **6** Ian Newton, GB (Honda); **7** Steve Sawford, GB (Honda); **8** Darren Martin, GB (Honda); **9** David Lemon, GB (Honda); **10** Graham Harknett, GB (Honda).
Fastest laps: Mawdsley and Patrickson, 54.1s, 91.16 mph/146.71 km/h (record).

Supersport 600
1 Rodney Knapp, NZ (Yamaha), 17m 48.4s, 92.35 mph/148.63 km/h.
2 Mike Edwards, GB (Yamaha); **3** Howard Selby, GB (Yamaha); **4** Phil Borley, GB (Honda); **5** John Reynolds, GB (Kawasaki); **6** Gary Weston, GB (Yamaha); **7** Dean Ashton, GB (Yamaha); **8** Ray Swann, GB (Kawasaki); **9** Nick Jefferies, GB (Yamaha); **10** Geoff Johnson, GB (Yamaha).
Fastest lap: Borley, 52.5s, 93.94 mph/151.18 km/h (record).

Superbikes
1 Brian Morrison, GB (Honda), 17m 15.0s, 95.30 mph/153.37 km/h.
2 Terry Rymer, GB (Yamaha); **3** Carl Fogarty, GB (Honda); **4** Steve Chambers, GB (Honda); **5** Mark Phillips, GB (Yamaha); **6** Roger Burnett, GB (Honda); **7** Howard Selby, GB (Yamaha); **8** Geoff Johnson, GB (Yamaha); **9** Colin Gable, GB (Honda); **10** Dave Redgate, GB (Honda).
Fastest lap: Morrison, 50.9s, 96.89 mph/155.93 km/h (record).

250 cc
1 Steve Patrickson, GB (Yamaha), 17m 26.1s, 94.30 mph/151.76 km/h.
2 Kevin Mitchell, GB (Yamaha); **3** Paul Lewis, AUS (Yamaha); **4** Martyn Jupp, GB (Yamaha); **5** Woolsey Coulter, IRL (Aprilia); **6** Ian McConnachie, GB (Yamaha); **7** Rob Orme, GB (Yamaha); **8** Steve Sawford, GB (Yamaha); **9** Graeme Mitchell, GB (Yamaha); **10** Mike Otter, GB (Rotax).
Fastest lap: Patrickson, 51.3s, 96.14 mph/154.72 km/h (record).

750cc TT Formula 1
1 Terry Rymer, GB (Yamaha), 17m 09.1s, 95.85 mph/154.26 km/h.
2 Trevor Nation, GB (Norton); **3** Steve Spray, GB (Norton); **4** Carl Fogarty, GB (Honda); **5** Brian Morrison, GB (Honda); **6** Mark Phillips, GB (Yamaha); **7** Ian Simpson, GB (Suzuki); **8** Gary Weston, GB (Yamaha); **9** Roger Burnett, GB (Honda); **10** Dave Redgate, GB (Yamaha).
Fastest lap: Nation, 50.6s, 97.47 mph/156.86 km/h (record).

Sidecars
1 Steve Webster/Tony Hewitt, GB/GB (LCR-Krauser), 17m 10.7s, 95.76 mph/154.11 km/h.
2 Barry Brindley/Grahame Rose, GB/GB (Yamaha); **3** Kenny Howles/Steve Pointer, GB/GB (LCR-Krauser); **4** Robert Fisher/Trevor Crone, GB/GB (Suzuki); **5** Gary Thomas/Tony Stevens, GB/GB (LCR-IMI); **6** Eddy Wright/Ian Marchant, GB/GB (Yamaha); **7** Roy Lawrence/Keep, GB/GB (Yamaha); **8** Michael Burcombe/John Gibbard, GB/GB (LCR-Krauser); **9** Phil Balment/Craig Hallam, GB/GB (Yamaha); **10** Paul Atkinson/Tony Atkinson, GB/GB (LCR).
Fastest lap: Webster, 50.0s, 98.64 mph/158.74 km/h (record).

BRANDS HATCH INDY CIRCUIT, 17 September. 1.2036-mile/1.937-km circuit.
Shell Oils ACU Supercup, round 5 (21 laps, 25.275 miles/40.677 km)

125 cc
1 Alex Bedford, GB (EMC), 18m 16.8s, 82.96 mph/133.51 km/h.
2 Steve Patrickson, GB (Honda); **3** Robin Appleyard, GB (Honda); **4** Ian Newton, GB (Honda); **5** Rob Orme, GB (Honda); **6** Julian Perry, GB (Honda); **7** David Lemon, GB (Honda); **8** Graham Harknett, GB (Honda); **9** Ray McCombe, GB (Honda); **10** Dave Marston, GB (Honda).
Fastest lap: Bedford, 51.2s, 84.62 mph/136.182 km/h.

Supersport 600
1 John Reynolds, GB (Kawasaki), 17m 58.1s, 84.40 mph/135.828 km/h.
2 Gary Weston, GB (Yamaha); **3** Phil Borley, GB (Honda); **4** David Heal, GB (Yamaha); **5** Mark Linscott, GB (Kawasaki); **6** Ian Simpson, GB (Suzuki); **7** Ray Swann, GB (Kawasaki); **8** Rodney Knapp, NZ (Yamaha); **9** Mark Plato, GB (Yamaha); **10** Brian Nicholson, GB (Honda).
Fastest lap: Weston, 50.6s, 85.63 mph/137.81 km/h.

Superbikes
1 Terry Rymer, GB (Yamaha), 17m 09.8s, 88.35 mph/142.185 km/h.
2 Mark Phillips, GB (Yamaha); **3** Steve Chambers, GB (Honda); **4** Gary Weston, GB (Yamaha); **5** Brian Morrison, GB (Honda); **6** Dave Redgate, GB (Yamaha); **7** Colin Gable, GB (Honda); **8** Steve Hislop, GB (Honda); **9** Steve Manley, GB (Honda); **10** Ray Swann, GB (Kawasaki).
Fastest lap: Rymer, 48.4s, 89.52 mph/144.068 km/h.

250 cc
1 Kevin Mitchell, GB (Yamaha), 17m 24.7s, 87.09 mph/140.157 km/h.
2 Ian McConnachie, GB (Yamaha); **3** Nigel Bosworth, GB (Aprilia); **4** Steve Patrickson, GB (Yamaha); **5** Woolsey Coulter, IRL (Aprilia); **6** Steve Hislop, GB (Honda); **7** Rob Orme, GB (Yamaha); **8** Martyn Jupp, GB (Yamaha); **9** Steve Sawford, GB (Yamaha); **10** Matt Llewellyn, GB (Yamaha).
Fastest laps: Mitchell and Orme, 48.4s, 89.52 mph/144.068 km/h.

750 cc TT Formula 1
1 Mark Phillips, GB (Yamaha), 17m 11.6s, 88.20 mph/141.94 km/h.
2 Trevor Nation, GB (Norton); **3** Terry Rymer, GB (Yamaha); **4** Steve Spray, GB (Norton); **5** Steve Hislop, GB (Honda); **6** Steve Chambers, GB (Honda); **7** Dave Redgate, GB (Yamaha); **8** Gary Weston, GB (Yamaha); **9** Kevin Mitchell, GB (Suzuki); **10** Colin Gable, GB (Honda).
Fastest laps: Hislop and Spray, 48.6s, 90.27 mph/145.275 km/h.

Sidecars
1 Steve Webster/Tony Hewitt, GB/GB (LCR-Krauser), 17m 34.5s, 86.28 mph/138.85 km/h.
2 Barry Brindley/Grahame Rose, GB/GB (Yamaha); **3** Steve Abbott/Shaun Smith, GB/GB (Yamaha); **4** Gary Thomas/Tony Stevens, GB/GB (LCR-IMI); **5** Robert Fisher/Trevor Crone, GB/GB (Suzuki); **6** Clive Stirrat/Simon Prior, GB/GB (LCR); **7** Tony Baker/Phil

Coombes, GB/GB (Krauser); **8** Mick Thompson/Ian Stapleton, GB/GB (Yamaha); **9** Vincent Butler/Shaun Buck, GB/GB (Yamaha); **10** John Cable/Tom Pettman, GB/GB (Yamaha).
Fastest lap: Webster, 48.2s, 89.89 mph/144.66 km/h.

Final Championship points (125 cc)

1	Steve Patrickson, GB	45
2	Rob Orme, GB	43
3	Ian Newton, GB	28
4	Alex Bedford, GB	27
5	Julian Perry, GB	23

6 David Lemon, GB, 21; **7** Steve Lawton, GB, 11; **8** Steve Sawford, GB, 9; **9** Robin Appleyard, GB and Kevin Mawdsley, GB, 8.

Final Championship points (Supersport 600)

1	Rodney Knapp, NZ	31
2	Mike Edwards, GB	29
3	Gary Weston, GB	26
4	John Reynolds, GB	24
5	Phil Borley, GB	23

6 Brian Morrison, GB, 16; **7** Howard Selby, GB, 15; **8** Mark Linscott, GB, 12; **9** Paul Brookes, GB, Ray Stringer, GB and Ray Swann, GB, 11.

Final Championship points (Superbikes)

1	Brian Morrison, GB	39
2	Steve Chambers, GB	35
3	Terry Rymer, GB	28
4	Mark Phillips, GB	25
5	Roger Burnett, GB	24

6 Ray Stringer, GB, 21; **7** Carl Fogarty, GB, 18; **8** Steve Hislop, GB, 15; **9** Dave Redgate, GB, 9; **10** David Griffith, GB, 8.

Final Championship points (250 cc)

1	Steve Patrickson, GB	40
2	Kevin Mitchell, GB	37
3	Paul Lewis, AUS	30
4	Ian McConnachie, GB	28
5	Nigel Bosworth, GB	27

6 Martin Jupp, GB, 22; **7** Woolsey Coulter, IRL, 19; **8** Rob Orme, GB, 17; **9** Matt Llewellyn, GB, 12; **10** Ian Newton, GB and Steve Sawford, GB, 10.

Final Championship points (750 cc TT Formula 1)

1	Steve Spray, GB	41
2	Terry Rymer, GB	27
3	Carl Fogarty, GB	24
4=	Brian Morrison, GB	23
4=	Trevor Nation, GB	23

6 Steve Chambers, GB, 21; **7** Mark Phillips, GB, 20; **8** Roger Burnett, GB, 19; **9** Steve Hislop, GB, 17; **10** Ray Stringer, GB, 10.

Final Championship points (Sidecars)

1	Steve Webster, GB	40
2	Barry Brindley, GB	36
3	Robert Fisher, GB	31
4	Kenny Howles, GB	22
5	Mick Thompson, GB	20

6 Gary Thomas, GB, 18; **7** Roy Lawrence, GB, 16; **8** Eddy Wright, GB, 15; **9** Mick Smith, GB, 14; **10** Steve Abbott, GB and Ray Gardner, GB, 8.

Motor Cycle News/ ACU British Championships

BRANDS HATCH INDY CIRCUIT, 1 May. 1.2036-mile/1.937-km circuit.
MCN/ACU British Championships, round 1

125 cc (15 laps, 18.054 miles/29.055 km)
1 Steve Patrickson, GB (Honda), 13m 16.5s, 81.60 mph/131.32 km/h.
2 Rob Orme, GB (Honda); **3** Graham Harknett, GB (Honda); **4** Ian Lougher, GB (Honda); **5** Kevin Mawdsley, GB (Honda); **6** Alan Patterson, GB (Honda); **7** Steve Mason, GB (Honda); **8** Mark Carkeek, GB (Honda); **9** Ray McCombe, GB (Honda); **10** David Lemon, GB (Honda).
Fastest lap: Patrickson, 52.0s, 83.33 mph/134.11 km/h.

250 cc (20 laps, 24.07 miles/38.74 km)
1 Steve Patrickson, GB (Yamaha), 16m 50.5s, 85.76 mph/138.02 km/h.
2 Ian McConnachie, GB (Yamaha); **3** Greig Ramsay, GB (Honda); **4** Matt Llewellyn, GB (Yamaha); **5** Alan Jeffery, GB (Yamaha); **6** Steve Sawford, GB (Yamaha); **7** Tom Hutton, GB (Yamaha); **8** Rob Orme, GB (Spondon); **9** Jon Peerless, GB (Yamaha); **10** Terry Sanders, GB (Yamaha).
Fastest lap: Patrickson, 49.6s, 87.36 mph/140.59 km/h.

Open Sidecar (15 laps, 18.054 miles/29.055 km)
1 Barry Brindley/Grahame Rose, GB/GB, 12m 47.4s, 84.69 mph/136.295 km/h.
2 Yoshisada Kumagaya/Brian Barlow, J/GB; **3** Ray Gardner/Tony Strevens, GB/GB; **4** Clive Stirrat/Simon Prior, GB/GB; **5** Roy Lawrence/Phil Coombes, GB/GB; **6** Mark Reddington/Robert Parker, GB/GB; **7** Keith Roberts/Andrew Kennett, GB/GB; **8** Robert Fisher/Trevor Crone, GB/GB; **9** Eddy Wright/Ian Marchant, GB/GB; **10** Judd Drew/Bryan Hughton, GB/GB.
Fastest lap: Gardner, 49.07s, 87.18 mph/140.3 km/h.

MALLORY PARK CIRCUIT, 21 May. 1.37-mile/2.205-km circuit.
MCN/ACU British Championships, round 2

125 cc (12 laps, 16.44 miles/26.46 km)
1 Kris Galatowicz, GB (Honda), 11m 09.5s, 88.40 mph/142.266 km/h.
2 Rob Orme, GB (Honda); **3** Mark Carkeek, GB (Honda); **4** David Lemon, GB (Honda); **5** Graham Harknett, GB (Honda); **6** Steve Sawford, GB (Honda); **7** Steve Mason, GB (Honda); **8** Chris Palmer, GB (Honda); **9** Dave Marston, GB (Honda); **10** Ian Lougher, GB (Honda).
Fastest lap: Galatowicz, 54.9s, 89.93 mph/144.728 km/h.

250 cc (15 laps, 20.55 miles/33.075 km)
1 Ian McConnachie, GB (Yamaha), 13m 24.2s, 91.99 mph/148.04 km/h.
2 Matt Llewellyn, GB (Yamaha); **3** Steve Williams, GB (Yamaha); **4** Alan Jeffery, GB (Yamaha); **5** Rob Orme, GB (Spondon); **6** Steve Sawford, GB (Yamaha); **7** Greig Ramsay, GB (Honda); **8** Terry Sanders, GB (Yamaha); **9** Mark Barker, GB (Yamaha); **10** Martyn Jupp, GB (Yamaha).
Fastest laps: Jeffery and Llewellyn, 52.7s, 93.58 mph/150.6 km/h.

Supersport 400 (12 laps, 16.44 miles/26.46 km)
1 Ian McConnachie, GB (Kawasaki), 11m 06.8s, 88.75 mph/142.83 km/h.
2 David Heal, GB (Kawasaki); **3** John Reynolds, GB (Kawasaki); **4** Stewart Moss, GB (Suzuki); **5** Steve Carter, GB (Suzuki); **6** Graham Holland, GB (Suzuki); **7** Dave Ball, GB (Yamaha); **8** Graham Read, GB (Kawasaki); **9** Ray Wood, GB (Yamaha); **10** Darren Mitchell, GB (Yamaha).
Fastest lap: McConnachie, 54.4s, 90.66 mph/145.9 km/h.

Supersport 600 (12 laps, 16.44 miles/26.46 km)
1 Mike Edwards, GB (Yamaha), 10m 57.1s, 90.06 mph/144.94 km/h.
2 Rodney Knapp, NZ (Yamaha); **3** Gary Weston, GB (Yamaha); **4** James Whitham, GB (Suzuki); **5** John Reynolds, GB (Kawasaki); **6** Ray Swann, GB (Kawasaki); **7** Dave Leach, GB (Yamaha); **8** Phil Borley, GB (Honda); **9** Eric McFarlane, GB (Yamaha); **10** G. English, GB (Honda).
Fastest lap: Weston, 52.9s, 93.23 mph/150.04 km/h.

TT F1 (15 laps, 20.55 miles/33.075 km)
1 Steve Spray, GB (Norton), 13m 03.1s, 94.47 mph/152.03 km/h.
2 Terry Rymer, GB (Yamaha); **3** Phil Mellor, GB (Suzuki); **4** Steve Chambers, GB (Honda); **5** Carl Fogarty, GB (Honda); **6** Ray Stringer, GB (Yamaha); **7** John Reynolds, GB (Kawasaki); **8** Darren Dixon, GB (Honda); **9** Steve Williams, GB (Yamaha); **10** Gary Weston, GB (Yamaha).
Fastest lap: Rymer, 51.1s, 96.51 mph/155.32 km/h.

Production (12 laps, 16.44 miles/26.46 km)
1 James Whitham, GB (Suzuki), 10m 50.5s, 90.98 mph/146.42 km/h.
2 Dean Ashton, GB (Suzuki); **3** Howard Selby, GB (Yamaha); **4** Mark Phillips, GB (Yamaha); **5** Rodney Knapp, NZ (Yamaha); **6** Ray Stringer, GB (Suzuki); **7** Phil Mellor, GB (Suzuki); **8** Mike Edwards, GB (Yamaha); **9** John Lofthouse, GB (Honda); **10** Brendan Doyle, GB (Suzuki).
Fastest laps: Ashton and Knapp, 53.6s, 92.01 mph/148.08 km/h.

Open Sidecars (12 laps, 16.44 miles/26.46 km)
1 Barry Brindley/Grahame Rose, GB/GB (Krauser), 10m 38.5s, 92.69 mph/149.17 km/h.
2 Kenny Howles/Steve Pointer, GB/GB (LCR); **3** Vincent Butler/Shaun Buck, GB/GB (Yamaha); **4** Eddy Wright/Ian Marchant, GB/GB (Yamaha); **5** Robert Fisher/Trevor Crone, GB/GB (Suzuki); **6** Clive Stirrat/Simon Prior, GB/GB (LCR); **7** Michael Burcombe/Phil Coombes, GB/GB (LCR); **8** Barry Laidlow/Julian Tailford, GB/GB (Yamaha); **9** Steve Kirby/Len Cheeseman, GB/GB (Yamaha); **10** Phil Balment/Craig Hallam, GB/GB (Yamaha).
Fastest lap: Brindley, 52.0s, 94.84 mph/152.63 km/h.

F2 Sidecars (12 laps, 16.44 miles/26.46 km)
1 Derek Brindley/Nick Roche, GB/GB (Sabre), 11m 12.7s, 89.4 mph/143.86 km/h.
2 Richard Nelson/Mark Camp, GB/GB (Yamaha); **3** Martin Whittington/Iain Caulton, GB/GB (Yamaha); **4** Roy Hanks/Alistair Frame, GB/GB (NRTH); **5** Dave Saville/Jones, GB/GB (Sabre); **6** Boyd Hutchinson/Steve Birkett, GB/GB (Yamaha); **7** Eddy Wright/Ian Marchant, GB/GB (Yamaha); **8** Mick Haith/David Haith, GB/GB (Yamaha); **9** Joe Heys/Christian Hefti, GB/GB (Yamaha); **10** Dennis Keen/Julian Tailford, GB/GB (Yamaha).
Fastest lap: Brindley, 55.1s, 89.50 mph/144.04 km/h.

DONINGTON PARK CIRCUIT, 18 June. 1.96-mile/3.136-km circuit.
MCN/ACU British Championships, round 3

125 cc (10 laps, 19.57 miles/31.36 km)
1 Steve Mason, GB (Honda), 13m 39.6s, 85.95 mph/138.31 km/h.
2 Alan Patterson, GB (Honda); **3** Mark Carkeek, GB (Honda); **4** Ray McCombe, GB (Honda); **5** David Lemon, GB (Honda); **6** Graham Harknett, GB (Honda); **7** Chris Palmer, GB (Honda); **8** Graham Holland, GB (Honda); **9** Julian Perry, GB (Honda); **10** Doug Flather, GB (Honda).
Fastest lap: Dave Marston, GB (Honda), 1m 19.6s, 88.50 mph/142.43 km/h (record).

250 cc (12 laps, 23.48 miles/37.63 km)
1 Nigel Bosworth, GB (Yamaha), 15m 25.60s, 91.33 mph/146.97 km/h.
2 Paul Lewis, AUS (Yamaha); **3** Ian McConnachie, GB (Yamaha); **4** Martyn Jupp, GB (Yamaha); **5** Greig Ramsay, GB (Honda); **6** Matt Llewellyn, GB (Yamaha); **7** Alan Jeffery, GB (Yamaha); **8** Steve Sawford, GB (Yamaha); **9** Mark Barker, GB (Yamaha); **10** Andrew Machin, GB (Honda).
Fastest lap: Bosworth, 1m 15.30s, 93.56 mph/150.57 km/h (record).

Supersport 400 (10 laps, 19.57 miles/31.36 km)
1 Ian McConnachie, GB (Kawasaki), 13m 37.50s, 86.17 mph/138.67 km/h.
2 David Heal, GB (Kawasaki); **3** John Corrin, GB (Yamaha); **4** Ian Lougher, GB (Suzuki); **5** Graham Holland, GB (Suzuki); **6** Ian Cobby, GB (Kawasaki); **7** John Roach, GB (Kawasaki); **8** Trevor Clow, GB (Kawasaki); **9** Mark Heath, GB (Yamaha); **10** Rhys Boyd, GB (Yamaha).
Fastest lap: McConnachie, 1m 20.70s, 87.30 mph/140.50 km/h.

Supersport 600 (10 laps, 19.57 miles/31.36 km)
1 Chris White, GB (Honda), 13m 22.60s, 87.77 mph/141.24 km/h.
2 Gary Weston, GB (Yamaha); **3** Paul Brookes, GB (Yamaha); **4** Iain Duffus, GB (Yamaha); **5** Ian Simpson, GB (Suzuki); **6** Ray Swann, GB (Kawasaki); **7** Mark Farmer, GB (Kawasaki); **8** Brian Nicholson, GB (Honda); **9** Francis Williamson, GB (Yamaha); **10** David Heal, GB (Yamaha).
Fastest lap: Howard Selby, GB (Yamaha), 1m 17.70s, 90.67 mph/145.92 km/h.

TT F1 (12 laps, 23.48 miles/37.63 km)
1 Steve Spray, GB (Norton), 14m 52.50s, 94.72 mph/152.42 km/h.
2 Carl Fogarty, GB (Honda); **3** James Whitham, GB (Suzuki); **4** Trevor Nation, GB (Norton); **5** Steve Hislop, GB (Honda); **6** Steve Chambers, GB (Honda); **7** Mark Phillips, GB (Yamaha); **8** Ray Stringer, GB (Yamaha); **9** Steve Manley, GB (Yamaha); **10** David Crampton, GB (Suzuki).
Fastest lap: Spray, 1m 13.10s, 96.37 mph/155.09 km/h (record).

Production (10 laps, 19.57 miles/31.36 km)
1 James Whitham, GB (Suzuki), 13m 02.2s, 89.95 mph/144.74 km/h.
2 Howard Selby, GB (Yamaha); **3** Ray Stringer, GB (Suzuki); **4** Mike Edwards, GB (Yamaha); **5** Rodney Knapp, NZ (Yamaha); **6** Dean Ashton, GB (Suzuki); **7** Eric McFarlane, GB (Yamaha); **8** Geoff Johnson, GB (Yamaha); **9** Steve Wright, GB (Suzuki); **10** Ian Simpson, GB (Suzuki).
Fastest lap: Whitham, 1m 17.2s, 91.25 mph/146.85 km/h (record).

Open Sidecars (10 laps, 19.57 miles/31.36 km)
1 Barry Brindley/Grahame Rose, GB/GB (Yamaha), 12m 48.40s, 91.68 mph/147.53 km/h.
2 Mick Smith/Kevin Webster, GB/GB (Yamaha); **3** Robert Fisher/Trevor Crone, GB/GB (Suzuki); **4** Colin Rust/Tony Darby, GB/GB (Yamaha); **5** Vincent Butler/Shaun Buck, GB/GB (Yamaha); **6** Geoff Rushbrook/Jimmy Cochrane, GB/GB (Yamaha); **7** Roy Lawrence/Graham Mapletoft, GB/GB (LCR); **8** Eddy Wright/Ian Marchant, GB/GB (Yamaha); **9** Barry Laidlow/Andrew Hetherington, GB/GB (Yamaha); **10** Keith Roberts/Andrew Kennett, GB/GB (Yamaha).
Fastest lap: Brindley, 1m 15.40s, 93.43 mph/150.36 km/h (record).

F2 Sidecars (10 laps, 19.57 miles/31.36 km)
1 Derek Brindley/Nick Roche, GB/GB (Yamaha), 13m 49.50s, 84.93 mph/136.66 km/h.
2 Martin Whittington/Iain Caulton, GB/GB (Yamaha); **3** John Brindley/Christopher Jones, GB/GB (Yamaha); **4** Boyd Hutchinson/Steve Birkett, GB/GB (Yamaha); **5** Dave Saville/Richard Crossley, GB/GB (Sabre); **6** Eddy Wright/Ian Marchant, GB/GB (Yamaha); **7** John Coates/Gary Gibson, GB/GB (Aprilia); **8** Mick Haith/David Haith, GB/GB (Yamaha); **9** John Thompson/Peter Burton, GB/GB (Yamaha); **10** Michael Hamblin/Julian Tailford, GB/GB (Yamaha).
Fastest laps: Brindley (John) and Hutchinson, 1m 21.70s, 86.23 mph/138.77 km/h.

KNOCKHILL CIRCUIT, 9 July. 1.3-mile/2.08-km circuit.
MCN/ACU British Championships, round 4

125 cc (12 laps, 15.6 miles/24.96 km)
1 Julian Perry, GB (Honda), 12m 19.7s, 75.28 mph/121.15 km/h.
2 Steve Mason, GB (Honda); **3** Steve Lawton, GB (Honda); **4** David Lemon, GB (Honda); **5** Rob Orme, GB (Honda); **6** Steve Sawford, GB (Honda); **7** Ray McCombe, GB (Honda) **8** Ian Lougher, GB (Honda); **9** A.P. Cooper, GB (MBA) **10** Pete Banks, GB (Honda).
Fastest lap: Mason, 60.5s, 76.7 mph/123.44 km/h.

250 cc (16 laps, 20.8 miles/33.28 km)
1 Ian McConnachie, GB (Kawasaki), 15m 29.5s, 79.88 mph/128.55 km/h.
2 Martyn Jupp, GB (Yamaha); **3** Steve Sawford, GB (Yamaha); **4** Terry Sanders, GB (Yamaha); **5** Matt Llewellyn, GB (Yamaha); **6** Rob Orme, GB (Yamaha); **7** Greig Ramsay, GB (Honda); **8** Graham Taylor, GB (Aprilia); **9** Tom Hutton, GB (Yamaha); **10** Tim Couzens, GB (Rotax).
Fastest lap: McConnachie, 56.7s, 81.84 mph/131.71 km/h.

Supersport 400 (12 laps, 15.6 miles/24.96 km)
1 Ian McConnachie, GB (Kawasaki), 12m 10.5s, 76.23 mph/122.68 km/h.
2 David Heal, GB (Kawasaki); **3** John Roach, GB (Kawasaki); **4** John Corrin, GB (Yamaha); **5** Ian Lougher, GB (Suzuki); **6** Graham Holland, GB (Suzuki); **7** Ray Wood, GB (Yamaha); **8** Paul Booler, GB (Suzuki); **9** Graham Read, GB (Kawasaki); **10** Ian Hughes, GB (Suzuki).
Fastest lap: Heal, 59.8s, 77.6 mph/124.89 km/h.

Supersport 600 (12 laps, 15.6 miles/24.96 km)
1 Paul Brookes, GB (Yamaha), 11m 39.5s, 79.61 mph/128.12 km/h.
2 Rodney Knapp, NZ (Yamaha); **3** James Whitham, GB (Suzuki); **4** Gary Weston, GB (Yamaha); **5** Phil Borley, GB (Honda); **6** Howard Selby, GB (Yamaha); **7** Ian Simpson, GB (Suzuki); **8** Mike Edwards, GB (Yamaha); **9** Francis Williamson, GB (Yamaha); **10** Colin Breeze, GB (Yamaha).
Fastest lap: Brookes, 57.3s, 80.98 mph/130.32 km/h.

TT F1 (16 laps, 20.8 miles/33.28 km)
1 Terry Rymer, GB (Yamaha), 14m 49.9s, 83.43 mph/134.27 km/h.
2 James Whitham, GB (Suzuki); **3** Steve Spray, GB (Norton); **4** Mark Phillips, GB (Yamaha); **5** Nick Jefferies, GB (Yamaha); **6** Gary Thrush, GB (Honda); **7** Howard Selby, GB (Yamaha); **8** Eric McFarlane, GB (Yamaha); **9** Dale Robinson, GB (Honda); **10** Sandy Christie, GB (Yamaha).
Fastest lap: Rymer, 54.5s, 85.14 mph/137.02 km/h (outright record).

Production (12 laps, 15.6 miles/24.96 km)
1 James Whitham, GB (Suzuki), 11m 33.1s, 80.34 mph/129.29 km/h.
2 Howard Selby, GB (Yamaha); **3** Dean Ashton, GB (Yamaha); **4** Rodney Knapp, NZ (Yamaha); **5** Brendan Doyle, GB (Yamaha); **6** Mike Edwards, GB (Yamaha); **7** Steve Wright, GB (Suzuki); **8** Rory Thomson, GB (Yamaha); **9** Ray Stringer, GB (Suzuki); **10** Geoff Johnson, GB (Yamaha).
Fastest lap: Selby, 56.7s, 81.84 mph/131.71 km/h.

Open Sidecars (12 laps, 15.6 miles/24.96 km)
1 Barry Brindley/Grahame Rose, GB/GB (Yamaha), 11m 35s, 80.12 mph/128.94 km/h.
2 Robert Fisher/Trevor Crone, GB/GB (Suzuki); **3** Dennis Brown/Billy Nelson, GB/GB (Yamaha); **4** Barry Laidlow/Andrew Hetherington, GB/GB (Yamaha); **5** Martin Murphy/Jimmy Cochrane, GB/GB (LCR); **6** Gordon Shand/Phil Gravel, GB/GB (Shand); **7** Allan Budge/James Campbell, GB/GB (Suzuki); **8** Eddy Wright/Julian Tailford, GB/GB (Yamaha); **9** Ian Pugh/Bryan Garvie, GB/GB (Yamaha); **10** Michael Keenan/David Annan, GB/GB (Kawasaki).
Fastest lap: Brindley, 56.8s, 81.7 mph/131.48 km/h.

F2 Sidecars (12 laps, 15.6 miles/24.96 km)
1 Richard Nelson/Mark Camp, GB/GB (Yamaha), 12m 28.7s, 74.38 mph/119.7 km/h.
2 Derek Brindley/Nick Roche, GB/GB (Yamaha); **3** Martin Whittington/Iain Tailford, GB/GB (Yamaha); **4** John Brindley/Chris Jones, GB/GB (Yamaha); **5** Dave Saville/Richard Crossley, GB/GB (Yamaha); **6** Adrian Williams/Dave Crawford, GB/GB (Yamaha); **7** Keith Blacker/Norman Oxley, GB/GB (Yamaha); **8** Mick Haith/David Haith, GB/GB (Yamaha); **9** Mick Wright/Gary Valance, GB/GB (Yamaha); **10** Dennis Keen/Terie Salone, GB/GB (Yamaha).
Fastest lap: Nelson, 61.2s, 75.82 mph/122.02 km/h.

SNETTERTON CIRCUIT, 16 July. 1.917-mile/3.085-km circuit.
MCN/ACU British Championships, round 5

125 cc (8 laps, 15.336 miles/24.68 km)
1 Steve Mason, GB (Honda), 10m 18.8s, 89.22 mph/143.59 km/h.
2 Julian Perry, GB (Honda); **3** Ian Lougher, GB (Honda); **4** Graham Holland, GB (Honda); **5** Mark Carkeek, GB (Honda); **6** Chris Palmer, GB (Honda); **7** Doug Flather, GB (Honda); **8** Ray McCombe, GB (Honda); **9** Dave Martin, GB (Honda); **10** Patrick Corrigan, GB (Honda).
Fastest lap: Mason, 1m 15.2s, 91.77 mph/147.69 km/h.

250 cc (12 laps, 23.004 miles/37.02 km)
1 Nigel Bosworth, GB (Aprilia), 14m 14.9s, 96.87 mph/155.88 km/h.
2 Matt Llewellyn, GB (Yamaha); **3** Martyn Jupp, GB (Yamaha); **4** Ian McConnachie, GB (Yamaha); **5** Steve Sawford, GB (Yamaha); **6** Rob Orme, GB (Yamaha); **7** Paul Grubb, GB (Aprilia); **8** Terry Sanders, GB (Yamaha); **9** Graham Taylor, GB (Aprilia); **10** D. Wisdom, GB (Rotax).
Fastest laps: Bosworth and Jupp, 1m 10.4s, 98.02 mph/157.75 km/h.

Supersport 400 (8 laps, 15.336 miles/24.68 km)
1 Paul Booler, GB (Suzuki), 10m 02.3s, 91.66 mph/147.51 km/h.
2 Stewart Moss, GB (Suzuki); **3** Ian McConnachie, GB (Kawasaki); **4** David Heal, GB (Kawasaki); **5** Graham Holland, GB (Suzuki); **6** Ian Lougher, GB (Suzuki); **7** John Roach, GB (Kawasaki); **8** Ray Wood, GB (Yamaha); **9** Mark Linscott, GB (Kawasaki); **10** John Corrin, GB (Yamaha).
Fastest laps: McConnachie and John Reynolds, GB (Kawasaki), 1m 13.9s, 93.38 mph/150.28 km/h (record).

Supersport 600 (7 laps, 13.419 miles/21.595 km)
1 Rodney Knapp, NZ (Yamaha), 8m 35.2s, 93.76 mph/150.89 km/h.
2 Mike Edwards, GB (Yamaha); **3** James Whitham, GB (Suzuki); **4** Paul Brookes, GB (Yamaha); **5** G. English, GB (Yamaha); **6** John Reynolds, GB (Kawasaki); **7** Adam Lewis, GB (Yamaha); **8** Francis Williamson, GB (Yamaha); **9** Gary Weston, GB (Yamaha); **10** Adrian Squirrell, GB (Yamaha).
Fastest lap: Weston, 1m 10.7s, 97.61 mph/157.09 km/h (record).

TT F1 (12 laps, 23.004 miles/37.02 km)
1 Steve Spray, GB (Norton), 13m 34.9s, 101.62 mph/163.54 km/h.
2 Ray Stringer, GB (Norton); **3** Steve Chambers, GB (Honda); **4** James Whitham, GB (Suzuki); **5** Terry Rymer, GB (Yamaha); **6** Mark Phillips, GB (Yamaha); **7** Steve Manley, GB (Yamaha); **8** Eric McFarlane, GB (Yamaha); **9** Ray Swann, GB (Kawasaki); **10** Nick Jefferies, GB (Yamaha).
Fastest lap: Spray, 1m 06.9s, 103.15 mph/166.01 km/h (outright record).

Production (8 laps, 15.336 miles/24.68 km)
1 Rodney Knapp, NZ (Yamaha), 9m 34.3s, 96.13 mph/154.71 km/h.
2 Howard Selby, GB (Yamaha); **3** Dean Ashton, GB (Yamaha); **4** James Whitham, GB (Suzuki); **5** Steve Wright, GB (Suzuki); **6** Nick Jefferies, GB (Yamaha); **7** Eric McFarlane, GB (Yamaha); **8** Ray Stringer, GB (Suzuki); **9** Rory Thomson, GB (Yamaha); **10** Geoff Johnson, GB (Yamaha).
Fastest laps: Knapp and Stringer, 1m 10.6s, 97.75 mph/157.31 km/h (record).

F2 Sidecars (8 laps, 15.336 miles/24.68 km)
1 Derek Brindley/Nick Roche, GB/GB (Yamaha), 10m 13.2s, 90.03 mph/144.89 km/h.
2 John Brindley/Chris Jones, GB/GB (Yamaha); **3** Dave Saville/Richard Crossley, GB/GB (Yamaha); **4** John Thompson/Peter Burton, GB/GB (Yamaha); **5** Richard Nelson/Mark Camp, GB/GB (Yamaha); **6** Boyd Hutchinson/Steve Birkett, GB/GB (Yamaha); **7** Martin Whittington/Iain Caulton, GB/GB (Yamaha); **8** John Coates/Gary Gibson, GB/GB (Aprilia); **9** Mick Boddice/Robert Parker, GB/GB (Yamaha); **10** Roy Hanks/Tony Darby, GB/GB (Yamaha).
Fastest laps: Brindley (Derek) and Saville, 1m 15.1s, 91.89 mph/147.88 km/h.

MALLORY PARK CIRCUIT, 23 July. 1.370-mile/2.205-km circuit.
MCN/ACU British Championships, round 6

125 cc (12 laps, 16.44 miles/26.46 km)
1 Rob Orme, GB (Honda), 11m 16.9s, 87.43 mph/140.71 km/h.
2 Steve Mason, GB (Honda); **3** Ian Lougher, GB (Honda); **4** Mark Carkeek, GB (Honda); **5** Nigel Bosworth, GB (Honda); **6** Julian Perry, GB (Honda); **7** Steve Sawford, GB (Honda); **8** Dave Martin, GB (Honda); **9** Chris Palmer, GB (Honda); **10** Kevin Mawdsley, GB (Honda).
Fastest lap: Bosworth, 55.0s, 89.67 mph/144.3' km/h.

250 cc (15 laps, 20.55 miles/33.075 km)
1 Kevin Mitchell, GB (Yamaha), 13m 15.6s, 92.98 mph/149.64 km/h.
2 Paul Lewis, AUS (Yamaha); **3** Matt Llewellyn, GB (Yamaha); **4** Ian McConnachie, GB (Yamaha); **5** Steve Sawford, GB (Yamaha); **6** Greig Ramsay, GB (Honda); **7** Paul Grubb, GB (Aprilia); **8** Martyn Jupp, GB (Yamaha); **9** Nigel Bosworth, GB (Aprilia); **10** D. Wisdom, GB (Rotax).
Fastest lap: Mitchell, 51.8s, 95.21 mph/153.23 km/h.

Open Sidecars (12 laps, 16.44 miles/26.46 km)
1 Barry Brindley/Grahame Rose, GB/GB (Yamaha), 10m 27.3s, 94.34 mph/151.83 km/h.
2 Robert Fisher/Trevor Crone, GB/GB (Yamaha); **3** Mick Smith/Kevin Webster, GB/GB (Yamaha); **4** Colin Rust/Tony Darby, GB/GB (Yamaha); **5** Barry Laidlow/Andrew Hetherington, GB/GB (Yamaha); **6** Eddy Wright/Julian Tailford, GB/GB (Yamaha); **7** Dennis Brown/Billy Nelson, GB/GB (Yamaha); **8** M. Bembridge/C. Hollis, GB/GB (Windle); **9** Gordon Shand/Phil Gravel, GB/GB (Shand); **10** R. Tidmarsh/B. Marsden, GB/GB (Windle).
Fastest lap: Brindley, 51.3s, 96.14 mph/154.72 km/h.

F2 Sidecars (12 laps, 16.44 miles/26.46 km)
1 John Brindley/Chris Jones, GB/GB (Yamaha), 11m 09.8s, 88.36 mph/142.21 km/h.
2 Dave Saville/Richard Crossley, GB/GB (Yamaha); **3** Eddy Wright/Julian Tailford, GB/GB (Yamaha); **4** Boyd Hutchinson/Steve Birkett, GB/GB (Yamaha); **5** Keith Galtress/Neil Shelton, GB/GB (Yamaha); **6** Roy Hanks/Tom Hanks, GB/GB (Yamaha); **7** Mick Wright/Gary Valance, GB/GB (Yamaha); **8** Michael Hamblin/C. Hollis, GB/GB (Yamaha); **9** John Coates/Gary Gibson, GB/GB (Aprilia); **10** Dennis Keen/Terrie Salone, GB/GB (Yamaha).
Fastest lap: Brindley, 54.7s, 90.16 mph/145.09 km/h.

CADWELL PARK WOODLAND CIRCUIT, 30 July. 0.849-mile/1.366-km circuit. MCN/ACU British Championships, round 7

125 cc (20 laps, 16.98 miles/27.32 km)
1 Rob Orme, GB (Honda), 16m 15.80s, 62.64 mph/100.81 km/h.
2 Kevin Mawdsley, GB (Honda); **3** Steve Mason, GB (Honda); **4** Ian Lougher, GB (Honda); **5** Chris Palmer, GB (Honda); **6** Patrick Corrigan, GB (Honda); **7** Graham Harknett, GB (Honda); **8** Ray McCombe, GB (Honda); **9** Dave Moffitt, GB (Honda); **10** Martin Pollard, GB (Honda).
Fastest lap: Mason, 46.9s, 65.17 mph/104.88 km/h (record).

250 cc (25 laps, 21.225 miles/34.15 km)
1 Ian McConnachie, GB (Yamaha), 19m 18.70s, 65.94 mph/106.12 km/h.
2 Mark Barker, GB (Yamaha); **3** Rob Orme, GB (Yamaha); **4** Mick Otter, GB (Rotax); **5** Ian Taylor, GB (Yamaha); **6** Martyn Jupp, GB (Yamaha); **7** Graham Taylor, GB (Aprilia); **8** Terry Sanders, GB (Yamaha); **9** Jon Peerless, GB (Yamaha); **10** Paul Grubb, GB (Aprilia).
Fastest lap: Matt Llewellyn, GB (Yamaha), 45.10s, 67.77 mph/109.07 km/h.

Supersport 400 (20 laps, 16.98 miles/27.32 km)
1 John Reynolds, GB (Kawasaki), 16m 03.90s, 63.42 mph/102.06 km/h.
2 Ian McConnachie, GB (Kawasaki); **3** Paul Booler, GB (Suzuki); **4** John Roach, GB (Kawasaki); **5** David Heal, GB (Suzuki); **6** Graham Holland, GB (Suzuki); **7** John Corrin, GB (Yamaha); **8** Darren Powell, GB (Kawasaki); **9** David Wallis, GB (Suzuki); **10** Graham Read, GB (Kawasaki).
Fastest lap: McConnachie, 46.6s, 65.59 mph/105.56 km/h.

Supersport 600 (20 laps, 16.98 miles/27.32 km)
1 Paul Brookes, GB (Yamaha), 15m 35.30s, 65.36 mph/105.19 km/h.
2 James Whitham, GB (Suzuki); **3** Mike Edwards, GB (Yamaha); **4** Ian Simpson, GB (Suzuki); **5** Adam Lewis, GB (Yamaha); **6** Phil Borley, GB (Honda); **7** Howard Selby, GB (Yamaha); **8** Adrian Squirrell, GB (Yamaha); **9** Colin Breeze, GB (Yamaha); **10** Francis Williamson, GB (Yamaha).
Fastest lap: Brookes, 45.50s, 67.17 mph/108.09 km/h.

TT F1 (25 laps, 21.225 miles/34.15 km)
1 Steve Spray, GB (Norton), 18m 51.00s, 67.56 mph/108.73 km/h.
2 James Whitham, GB (Suzuki); **3** Gary Thrush, GB (Honda); **4** Trevor Nation, GB (Norton); **5** Steve Manley, GB (Yamaha); **6** Charlie Corner, GB (Honda); **7** Dave Redgate, GB (Yamaha); **8** Simon Watson, GB (Yamaha); **9** John Burgess, GB (Suzuki); **10** Chris Hodgson, GB (Suzuki).
Fastest lap: Spray and Nation, 44.40s, 68.84 mph/110.79 kmh/.

Production (20 laps, 16.98 miles/27.32 km)
1 Dean Ashton, GB (Yamaha), 15m 44.00s, 64.75 mph/104.21 km/h.
2 Mike Edwards, GB (Yamaha); **3** James Whitham, GB (Suzuki); **4** Rodney Knapp, NZ (Yamaha); **5** Ian Simpson, GB (Suzuki); **6** Howard Selby, GB (Yamaha); **7** Geoff Johnson, GB (Yamaha); **8** Geoff Baldock, GB (Yamaha); **9** Simon Bastow, GB (Suzuki); **10** Rory Thomson, GB (Yamaha).
Fastest lap: Edwards, 46.30s, 66.01 mph/106.23 km/h.

F2 Sidecars (20 laps, 16.98 miles/27.32 km)
1 Derek Brindley/Nick Roche, GB/GB (Yamaha), 16m 13.70s, 62.78 mph/101.03 km/h.
2 Eddy Wright/Julian Tailford, GB/GB (Yamaha); **3** Dave Saville/N. Campbell, GB/GB (Yamaha); **4** Mick Haith/David Haith, GB/GB (Yamaha); **5** Roy Hanks/Tom Hanks, GB/GB (Yamaha); **6** Martin Whittington/Iain Caulton, GB/GB (Yamaha); **7** Boyd Hutchinson/Steve Birkett, GB/GB (Yamaha); **8** John Coates/Gary Gibson, GB/GB (Aprilia); **9** Keith Galtress/Neil Shelton, GB/GB (Yamaha); **10** Adrian Williams/Dave Crawford, GB/GB (Yamaha).
Fastest lap: Brindley, 47.00s, 65.03 mph/104.66 km/h.

CADWELL PARK CIRCUIT, 24 September. 2.17-mile/3.472-km circuit. MCN/ACU British Championships, round 8

125 cc (8 laps, 17.36 miles/27.776 km)
1 Alan Patterson, GB (Honda), 13m 19.1s, 78.20 mph/125.85 km/h.
2 Steve Patrickson, GB (Honda); **3** Rob Orme, GB (Honda); **4** Ian Newton, GB (Honda); **5** Julian Perry, GB (Honda); **6** Ian Lougher, GB (Honda); **7** Steve Mason, GB (Honda); **8** Chris Palmer, GB (Honda); **9** Patrick Corrigan, GB (Honda); **10** Steve Sawford, GB (Honda).
Fastest lap: Patterson, 1m 38.0s, 79.71 mph/128.28 km/h (record).

250 cc (10 laps, 21.7 miles/34.72 km)
1 Nigel Bosworth, GB (Aprilia), 15m 34.8s, 83.56 mph/134.48 km/h.
2 Kevin Mitchell, GB (Yamaha); **3** Steve Hislop, GB (Honda); **4** Steve Patrickson, GB (Yamaha); **5** Rob Orme, GB (Yamaha); **6** Martyn Jupp, GB (Yamaha); **7** Matt Llewellyn, GB (Yamaha); **8** Mark Barker, GB (Yamaha); **9** Ian McConnachie, GB (Yamaha); **10** Tim Couzens, GB (Rotax).
Fastest lap: Bosworth, 1m 32.3s, 84.63 mph/136.20 km/h (record).

Supersport 400 (10 laps, 21.7 miles/34.72 km)
1 John Reynolds, GB (Kawasaki), 16m 48.5s, 77.46 mph/124.65 km/h.
2 David Heal, GB (Suzuki); **3** Ian McConnachie, GB (Kawasaki); **4** John Yates, GB (Kawasaki); **5** Ian Cobby, GB (Kawasaki); **6** John Corrin, GB (Yamaha); **7** Steve Ives, GB (Yamaha); **8** Graham Holland, GB (Suzuki); **9** John Roach, GB (Kawasaki); **10** Alan Cooper, GB (Kawasaki).
Fastest lap: McConnachie, 1m 38.8s, 79.06 mph/127.23 km/h (record).

Supersport 600 (10 laps, 21.7 miles/34.72 km)
1 Phil Borley, GB (Honda), 16m 18.4s, 79.84 mph/128.48 km/h.
2 Geoff Johnson, GB (Yamaha); **3** Adam Lewis, GB (Yamaha); **4** Dean Ashton, GB (Yamaha); **5** Ian Simpson, GB (Suzuki); **6** John Reynolds, GB (Kawasaki); **7** David Heal, GB (Yamaha); **8** Paul Brookes, GB (Yamaha); **9** Mark Linscott, GB (Kawasaki); **10** Gary Weston, GB (Yamaha).
Fastest lap: Johnson, 1m 36.0s, 81.37 mph/130.95 km/h (record).

TT F1 (10 laps, 21.7 miles/34.72 km)
1 Carl Fogarty, GB (Honda), 15m 29.9s, 84.00 mph/135.18 km/h.
2 Steve Spray, GB (Norton); **3** Terry Rymer, GB (Yamaha); **4** Steve Hislop, GB (Honda); **5** Steve Chambers, GB (Honda); **6** Mark Phillips, GB (Yamaha); **7** Steve Manley, GB (Honda); **8** Nick Jefferies, GB (Yamaha); **9** Phillip McCallen, GB (Honda); **10** John Reynolds, GB (Kawasaki).
Fastest lap: Fogarty, 1m 31.7s, 85.19 mph/137.10 km/h (record).

Production (10 laps, 21.7 miles/34.72 km)
1 Dean Ashton, GB (Yamaha), 16m 18.0s, 79.87 mph/128.53 km/h.
2 Rodney Knapp, NZ (Yamaha); **3** Nick Jefferies, GB (Yamaha); **4** Geoff Johnson, GB (Yamaha); **5** Howard Selby, GB (Yamaha); **6** Mike Edwards, GB (Yamaha); **7** Ian Simpson, GB (Suzuki); **8** Rory Thomson, GB (Yamaha); **9** Simon Bastow, GB (Suzuki); **10** Steve Wright, GB (Suzuki).
Fastest lap: Edwards, 1m 36.3s, 81.12 mph/130.55 km/h (record).

Open Sidecars (10 laps, 21.7 miles/34.72 km)
1 Barry Brindley/Grahame Rose, GB/GB (Yamaha), 15m 51.8s, 82.07 mph/132.07 km/h.
2 Robert Fisher/Trevor Crone, GB/GB (Suzuki); **3** Colin Rust/Tony Darby, GB/GB (Yamaha); **4** Paul Atkinson/Tony Atkinson, GB/GB (Krauser); **5** Rod Bellas/Geoff Knight, GB/GB (Yamaha); **6** Vincent Butler/Shaun Buck, GB/GB (Yamaha); **7** Barry Laidlow/Andrew Hetherington, GB/GB (Yamaha); **8** Phil Balment/Craig Hallam, GB/GB (Yamaha); **9** Gordon Shand/Sheldon, GB/GB (Shand); **10** Scarth/Scarth, GB/GB (Yamaha).
Fastest lap: Brindley, 1m 33.7s, 83.37 mph/134.17 km/h (record).

F2 Sidecars (10 laps, 21.7 miles/34.72 km)
1 Dave Saville/Richard Crossley, GB/GB (Yamaha), 16m 56.4s, 76.85 mph/123.68 km/h.
2 Mark Whittington/Iain Caulton, GB/GB (Yamaha); **3** Keith Galtress/Neil Shelton, GB/GB (Yamaha); **4** Mick Haith/David Haith, GB/GB (Yamaha); **5** Adrian Williams/Dave Crawford, GB/GB (Yamaha); **6** Boyd Hutchinson/Steve Birkett, GB/GB (Yamaha); **7** Dennis Keen/Terrie Salone, GB/GB (Yamaha); **8** C. Parkinson/G. Saville, GB/GB (Yamaha); **9** G. Dickinson/C. Attenborough, GB/GB (Yamaha); **10** T. Eade/F. McDermott, GB/GB (Yamaha).
Fastest lap: Saville, 1m 39.5s, 78.51 mph/126.35 km/h (record).

DONINGTON PARK GRAND PRIX CIRCUIT, 1 October. 2.5-mile/4.023-km circuit. MCN/ACU British Championships, round 9 (8 laps, 20 miles/32.184 km)

125 cc
1 Ian Newton, GB (Honda), 14m 45.33s, 81.32 mph/130.86 km/h.
2 Ian Lougher, GB (Honda); **3** Julian Perry, GB (Honda); **4** Robert Dunlop, GB (Honda); **5** Rob Orme, GB (Honda); **6** Steve Patrickson, GB (Honda); **7** Steve Sawford, GB (Honda); **8** Steve Lawton, GB (Honda); **9** Chris Palmer, GB (Honda); **10** Mark Carkeek, GB (Honda).
Fastest lap: Lougher, 1m 48.59s, 82.88 mph/133.38 km/h.

250 cc
1 Kevin Mitchell, GB (Yamaha), 13m 41.74s, 87.61 mph/141.00 km/h.
2 Nigel Bosworth, GB (Aprilia); **3** Paul Lewis, AUS (Yamaha); **4** Steve Patrickson, GB (Yamaha); **5** Rob Orme, GB (Yamaha); **6** Martyn Jupp, GB (Yamaha); **7** Ian McConnachie, GB (Yamaha); **8** Matt Llewellyn, GB (Yamaha); **9** Steve Sawford, GB (Yamaha); **10** Mark Barker, GB (Yamaha).
Fastest lap: Mitchell, 1m 41.04s, 89.07 mph/143.34 km/h.

Supersport 400
1 John Reynolds, GB (Kawasaki), 14m 29.96s, 82.76 mph/133.18 km/h.
2 Paul Booler, GB (Suzuki); **3** Ian Lougher, GB (Yamaha); **4** Kevin Mitchell, GB (Suzuki); **5** Ian McConnachie, GB (Kawasaki); **6** David Heal, GB (Suzuki); **7** John Yates, GB (Yamaha); **8** John Corrin, GB (Yamaha); **9** Steve Ives, GB (Yamaha); **10** Graeme McGregor, AUS (Kawasaki).
Fastest lap: Mitchell, 1m 47.27s, 83.90 mph/135.02 km/h (record).

Supersport 600
1 Paul Brookes, GB (Yamaha), 14m 08.28s, 84.87 mph/136.58 km/h.
2 Mike Edwards, GB (Yamaha); **3** Phil Borley, GB (Honda); **4** John Reynolds, GB (Kawasaki); **5** Adam Lewis, GB (Yamaha); **6** Gary Weston, GB (Yamaha); **7** David Heal, GB (Yamaha); **8** Ian Simpson, GB (Suzuki); **9** Ian Wilson, GB (Yamaha); **10** Francis Williamson, GB (Yamaha).
Fastest lap: Edwards, 1m 43.79s, 86.71 mph/139.55 km/h (record).

TT F1
1 Carl Fogarty, GB (Honda), 13m 18.57s, 90.16 mph/145.08 km/h.
2 Niall Mackenzie, GB (Yamaha); **3** Steve Spray, GB (Norton); **4** Terry Rymer, GB (Yamaha); **5** Steve Hislop, GB (Honda); **6** Roger Burnett, GB (Honda); **7** Brian Morrison, GB (Honda); **8** Steve Chambers, GB (Honda); **9** Robert Dunlop, GB (Honda); **10** Mark Phillips, GB (Yamaha).
Fastest lap: Spray, 1m 37.87s, 91.95 mph/147.98 km/h.

Production
1 Ian Simpson, GB (Suzuki), 14m 05.84s, 85.12 mph/136.97 km/h.
2 Mike Edwards, GB (Yamaha); **3** Rodney Knapp, NZ (Yamaha); **4** Dean Ashton, GB (Honda); **5** Geoff Johnson, GB (Yamaha); **6** Steve Wright, GB (Suzuki); **7** Rory Thomson, GB (Yamaha); **8** Chris White, GB (Suzuki); **9** Alex Buckingham, GB (Yamaha); **10** Geoff Baldock, GB (Yamaha).
Fastest lap: Knapp, 1m 44.21s, 86.36 mph/138.98 km/h (record).

Open Sidecars
1 Steve Webster/Tony Hewitt, GB/GB (LCR-Krauser), 13m 41.13s, 87.68 mph/141.10 km/h.
2 Barry Brindley/Grahame Rose, GB/GB (Yamaha); **3** Robert Fisher/Trevor Crone, GB/GB (Suzuki); **4** Barry Smith/David Smith, GB/GB (Windle); **5** Roy Lawrence/Keep, GB/GB (Yamaha); **6** Clive Stirrat/Simon Prior, GB/GB (LCR); **7** Colin Rust/Tony Darby, GB/GB (Yamaha); **8** Judd Drew/Bryan Houghton, GB/GB (LCR); **9** Mick Boddice/Wells, GB/GB (Yamaha); **10** Jefford/Hill, GB/GB (Yamaha).
Fastest lap: Webster, 1m 39.88s, 90.10 mph/145.00 km/h.

F2 Sidecars
1 Derek Brindley/Nick Roche, GB/GB (Yamaha), 14m 52.72s, 80.65 mph/128.78 km/h.
2 Dave Saville/Richard Crossley, GB/GB (Yamaha); **3** Richard Nelson/Mark Camp, GB/GB (Yamaha); **4** Boyd Hutchinson/Steve Birkett, GB/GB (Yamaha); **5** Mick Haith/David Haith, GB/GB (Yamaha); **6** Michael Hamblin/Bob Smith, GB/GB (Yamaha); **7** Roy Hanks/Tom Hanks, GB/GB (Yamaha); **8** G. Dickinson/C. Attenborough, GB/GB (Shelbourne); **9** Dixon/Appleby, GB/GB (Yamaha); **10** Keith Galtress/Neil Shelton, GB/GB (Yamaha).
Fastest lap: Saville, 1m 50.10s, 81.74 mph/131.55 km/h.

BRANDS HATCH INDY CIRCUIT, 15 October. 1.2036-mile/1.937-km circuit. MCN/ACU British Championships, round 10

125 cc (14 laps, 16.85 miles/27.118 km)
1 Rob Orme, GB (Honda), 12m 28.3s, 81.61 mph/131.338 km/h.
2 Julian Perry, GB (Honda); **3** Steve Sawford, GB (Honda); **4** Ian Lougher, GB (Honda); **5** Mark Carkeek, GB (Honda); **6** Graham Harknett, GB (Honda); **7** Chris Palmer, GB (Honda); **8** Mark Harrison, GB (Honda); **9** Frank Duffy, GB (Honda); **10** Patrick Corrigan, GB (Honda).
Fastest lap: Steve Patrickson, GB (Honda), 51.8s, 83.65 mph/134.621 km/h.

250 cc (17 laps, 20.46 miles/32.93 km)
1 Nigel Bosworth, GB (Aprilia), 14m 07.9s, 86.87 mph/139.8 km/h.
2 Kevin Mitchell, GB (Yamaha); **3** Steve Patrickson, GB (Yamaha); **4** Rob Orme, GB (Yamaha); **5** Mark Barker, GB (Yamaha); **6** Steve Sawford, GB (Yamaha); **7** Martyn Jupp, GB (Yamaha); **8** Matt Llewellyn, GB (Yamaha); **9** Graham Taylor, GB (Aprilia); **10** Ian McConnachie, GB (Yamaha).
Fastest laps: Patrickson and Paul Lewis, AUS (Yamaha), 48.7s, 88.97 mph/143.18 km/h.

Supersport 400 (14 laps, 16.85 miles/27.118 km)
1 John Reynolds, GB (Kawasaki), 12m 08.6s, 83.26 mph/133.99 km/h.
2 John Yates, GB (Kawasaki); **3** Rhys Boyd, GB (Kawasaki); **4** Paul Booler, GB (Suzuki); **5** Nev Potts, GB (Kawasaki); **6** Ian Cobby, GB (Kawasaki); **7** John Roach, GB (Kawasaki); **8** Mark Curtis, GB (Suzuki); **9** Adrian Butcher, GB (Yamaha); **10** Ian McConnachie, GB (Kawasaki).
Fastest lap: Reynolds, 50.8s, 85.29 mph/137.26 km/h.

Supersport 600 (14 laps, 16.85 miles/27.118 km)
1 Gary Weston, GB (Yamaha), 11m 55.4s, 84.79 mph/136.46 km/h.
2 Mike Edwards, GB (Yamaha); **3** Phil Borley, GB (Honda); **4** Geoff Johnson, GB (Yamaha); **5** Ian Wilson, GB (Yamaha); **6** Mark Plato, GB (Yamaha); **7** Adrian Squirrell, GB (Yamaha); **8** Brian Nicholson, GB (Honda); **9** Ray Swann, GB (Kawasaki); **10** Ian Simpson, GB (Suzuki).
Fastest laps: Edwards and Weston, 50.2s, 86.31 mph/138.9 km/h.

TT F1 (17 laps, 20.46 miles/32.93 km)
1 Terry Rymer, GB (Yamaha), 13m 41.0s, 89.72 mph/144.39 km/h.
2 Steve Spray, GB (Norton); **3** Gary Weston, GB (Yamaha); **4** Mark Phillips, GB (Yamaha); **5** Trevor Nation, GB (Norton); **6** Darren Dixon, GB (Yamaha); **7** Steve Hislop, GB (Honda); **8** Mark Farmer, GB (Yamaha); **9** Steve Manley, GB (Honda); **10** Dave Redgate, GB (Yamaha).
Fastest laps: Rymer and Spray, 47.6s, 91.03 mph/146.49 km/h.

Production (14 laps, 16.85 miles/27.118 km)
1 Ian Simpson, GB (Suzuki), 12m 01.0s, 84.14 mph/135.41 km/h.
2 Rodney Knapp, NZ (Yamaha); **3** Dean Ashton, GB (Yamaha); **4** Mike Edwards, GB (Yamaha); **5** Howard Selby, GB (Yamaha); **6** Roger Milne, GB (Yamaha); **7** Rory Thomson, GB (Yamaha); **8** Geoff Johnson, GB (Yamaha); **9** Steve Wright, GB (Suzuki); **10** Chris White, GB (Suzuki).
Fastest laps: Ashton, Simpson and Knapp, 50.8s, 85.29 mph/137.26 km/h.

Open Sidecars (14 laps, 16.85 miles/27.118 km)
1 Steve Webster/Tony Hewitt, GB/GB (LCR-Krauser), 11m 26.7s, 88.34 mph/142.17 km/h.
2 Barry Smith/David Smith, GB/GB (Windle ADM); **3** Clive Stirrat/Simon Prior, GB/GB (LCR-JPX); **4** Mark Reddington/Robert Parker, GB/GB (Yamaha); **5** Colin Rust/Tony Darby, GB/GB (Windle Yamaha); **6** Steve Kirby/Len Cheeseman, GB/GB (Transyam); **7** Judd Drew/Bryan Houghton, GB/GB (LCR); **8** Gary Thomas/Tony Strevens, GB/GB (LCR); **9** Brian Reeves/Dave Fordham, GB/GB (Windle Yamaha); **10** Roger Body/Andy Peach, GB/GB (LCR-Yamaha).
Fastest lap: Webster, 47.9s, 90.46 mph/145.58 km/h.

F2 Sidecars (14 laps, 16.85 miles/27.118 km)
1 Richard Nelson/Mark Camp, GB/GB (Yamaha), 12m 27.0s, 81.21 mph/130.69 km/h.
2 Dave Saville/Richard Crossley, GB/GB (Yamaha); **3** Derek Brindley/Nick Roche, GB/GB (Yamaha); **4** Mick Hamblin/Bob Smith, GB/GB (Yamaha); **5** Boyd Hutchinson/Steve Birkett, GB/GB (Yamaha); **6** Dennis Keen/Terrie Salone, GB/GB (Yamaha); **7** Gary Golder/Karl Firmin, GB/GB (Yamaha); **8** Michael Smith/Gary Smith, GB/GB (Yamaha); **9** Neville Turner/John McGregor, GB/GB (Yamaha); **10** Paul Hanson/Michael Speechley, GB/GB (Yamaha).
Fastest laps: Brindley and Nelson, 52.1s, 83.17 mph/133.85 km/h.

Final Championship points (125 cc)

1	Rob Orme, GB	91
2	Steve Mason, GB	76
3	Ian Lougher, GB	65
4	Julian Perry, GB	62
5	Mark Carkeek, GB	44

6 Steve Patrickson, GB and Alan Patterson, GB, 32; **8** Graham Harknett, GB, 30; **9** Chris Palmer, GB and Steve Sawford, GB, 29.

Final Championship points (250 cc)

1	Ian McConnachie, GB	90
2	Nigel Bosworth, GB	74
3	Matt Llewellyn, GB	63
4	Kevin Mitchell, GB	54
5	Martyn Jupp, GB	53

6 Rob Orme, GB, 49; **7** Steve Sawford, GB, 42; **8** Steve Patrickson, GB, 41; **9** Paul Lewis, AUS, 34; **10** Greig Ramsay, GB, 29.

Final Championship points (Supersport 400)

1	Ian McConnachie, GB	84
2	John Reynolds, GB	70
3	David Heal, GB	67
4	Paul Booler, GB	48

5 John Roach, GB, 32; **6** John Corrin, GB, 31; **7** Graham Holland, GB, 30; **8** Ian Lougher, GB, 29; **9** John Yates, GB, 24; **10** Stewart Moss, GB, 20.

Final Championship points (Supersport 600)

1	Paul Brookes, GB	66
2	Mike Edwards, GB	64
3	Gary Weston, GB	53
4	Phil Borley, GB	49
5	James Whitham, GB	40

6 Rodney Knapp, NZ, 39; **7** Ian Simpson, GB, 28; **8** Adam Lewis, GB, 26; **9** John Reynolds, GB, 24; **10** Geoff Johnson, GB, 20.

Final Championship points (TT F1)

1	Steve Spray, GB	104
2	Terry Rymer, GB	66
3	Carl Fogarty, GB	48
4	James Whitham, GB	42
5	Steve Chambers, GB	32

6 Mark Phillips, GB, 31; **7** Steve Hislop, GB, 24; **8** Trevor Nation, GB, 22; **9** Ray Stringer, GB, 20; **10** Steve Manley, GB, 18.

Final Championship points (Production)

1	Dean Ashton, GB	85
2	Rodney Knapp, NZ	77
3=	Howard Selby, GB	63
3=	James Whitham, GB	63
5	Mike Edwards, GB	53

6 Ian Simpson, GB, 41; **7** Geoff Johnson, GB, 26; **8** Ray Stringer, GB and Steve Wright, GB, 20; **10** Rory Thomson, GB, 17.

Final Championship points (Open Sidecars)

1	Barry Brindley, GB	102
2	Robert Fisher, GB	65
3	Colin Rust, GB	36
4	Steve Webster, GB	30
5	Clive Stirrat, GB	28

6 Barry Laidlow, GB, 23; **7** Mick Smith, GB, 22; **8** Vincent Butler, GB and Eddy Wright, GB, 21; **10** Roy Lawrence, GB, 16.

Final Championship points (F2 Sidecars)

1	Derek Brindley, GB	97
2	Dave Saville, GB	89
3	Richard Nelson, GB	58
4	Martin Whittington, GB	53

5 Boyd Hutchinson, GB, 49; **6** John Brindley, GB, 45; **7** Mick Haith, GB and Eddy Wright, GB, 31; **9** Roy Hanks, GB, 24; **10** Keith Galtress, GB, 19.